ADMINISTERING THE SCHOOL LIBRARY MEDIA CENTER

4th Edition
Revised and Expanded

Betty J. Morris

LIBRARIES
UNLIMITED

A Member of the Greenwood Publishing Group

Westport, Connecticut • London

Library of Congress Cataloging-in-Publication Data

Morris, Betty J.
    Administering the school library media center / by Betty J. Morris.—4th ed., rev.
and expanded.
       p. cm.
    Includes index.
    ISBN 0–313–32261–9 (alk. paper) — ISBN 1–59158–183–4 (pbk. : alk. paper)
     1. School libraries—Administration. 2. Instructional materials centers—
Administration. 3. Media programs (Education) I. Title.
    Z675.S3G52   2004
    025.1'978—dc22   2004041797

British Library Cataloguing in Publication Data is available.

Library of Congress Catalog Card Number: 2004041797
ISBN: 0–313–32261–9
     1–59158–183–4

First published in 2004

Libraries Unlimited, 88 Post Road West, Westport, CT 06881
Member of the Greenwood Publishing Group, Inc.
www.lu.com

Printed in the United States of America

The paper used in this book complies with the
Permanent Paper Standard issued by the National
Information Standards Organization (Z39.48-1984).

10 9 8 7 6 5 4

CONTENTS

EXHIBITS

PREFACE

The fourth edition of *Administering the School Library Media Center* brings together all aspects of administration of a school library media center in light of the qualitative standards of *Information Power: Partnerships in Learning* (American Association of School Librarians & Association for Educational Communications and Technology [AASL & AECT], 1998) and the newer technology since the last edition. The purpose of this edition is primarily the same as the 1992 edition, "to focus on practical considerations within a single school as reflected in the new developments in organizing and administering the center."

The basic philosophies reflected in this edition are: (1) the school library media center is central to the instructional program of the school; (2) the main purpose of the center is to provide service to faculty, students, and administrators in accessing, utilizing and evaluating information, developing research strategies, and utilizing technology; (3) the media center program strengthens and improves instruction in the school by developing in students lifelong learning, knowledge of information literacy skills, and a love of reading.

The general principles in *Information Power* (AASL & AECT, 1998) and computer applications are included in all appropriate chapters. All chapters from the third edition have been updated and bibliographies include current materials. Broad topics from the third edition that are still valid are retained in the new edition. Chapters 2 and 10 are contributed by Dr. Carol Truett.

The new edition contains fourteen chapters, including a totally revamped Chapter 10, written by Dr. Carol Truett. It presents a fresh new perspective on technology and its impact on school library media centers. The chapter incorporates the newer technologies that have appeared on the scene since the publication of the third edition. The virtual library begins the chapter and a technology-rich learning environment is explored specifically and throughout the chapter. Some network terminology is explained. Added features include budget planning, funding, and technology management. A discussion about ways the media specialist can keep abreast of new trends in technology is included. Topics to include and tips to use when creating a media center web page are an added feature. Web sites are provided for web creation software. Added features are technology planning and state networks. Acceptable use policies are discussed. More information about e-rate and Internet filters is included. Internet safety is discussed and ideas for using WebQuests and electronic pathfinders are explored.

Chapter 1, "The Historical Perspective," retains much of the historical perspective of school media centers from the previous edition. Updates to the chapter include information about legislative days, the first school library media White House Conference, pertinent legislation, and research on school media centers related to student achievement. Site-based management's impact on media center budgets, personnel, curriculum, and facilities is discussed. The idea that the media specialist needs to become a leader in site-based management is promoted. The chapter includes a discussion of how e-rate makes Internet access possible and how it allows schools to move toward an Internet enhanced curriculum.

Chapter 2, "Forging Partnerships Toward Information Literacy," primarily deals with forming partnerships that will result in students becoming lifelong learners through learning information literacy skills, how the school library media specialist can forge partnerships with school constituents, develop communication links within and outside the school, develop a proactive role in administering the media program, and serve as a change agent to improve instruction. Research about school library media centers and their role in student achievement is discussed. Partnerships with principals are highlighted as well as additional partnerships within the community. The role of the program administrator is presented. Web-based research is discussed and how it opens the world of information to students and teachers.

In Chapter 3, "Functions of the School Library Media Program," terminology and philosophy are updated to reflect recent trends. Activities that take place in the media center address new changes in technology and teaching of information literacy skills. Checklists are updated to include online access. A rubric is included for evaluating a school library media program; it assesses whether the services are minimum, standard, or exemplary. The concept of the virtual school library media center is introduced.

Chapter 4, "Developing a School Library Media Program," is updated to reflect trends in teaching information literacy lessons in collaboration with teachers. The instructional program includes a look at group computer instruction and e-learning. Collaborative planning templates are included as well as a checklist for planning instructional design. Two new lesson plans are provided as well as several web sites for locating them on the Internet. An added feature is a discussion about designing web pages to publicize the media program. Programming events are added as well as Internet filtering. A new chart is included that aligns information literacy skills with the subject content areas of the curriculum.

Chapter 5, "The Media Center Budget," is written by Dr. Carol Truett. The politics of budgeting is explored. Sources of funding are expanded to give a much wider perspective. Other funding sources, such as grants, are explored along with grant proposal writing. A list of web sites is provided for grant sources. A long discussion about creating a budget is a new feature of the chapter. The role of the media advisory committee in budgeting is explained.

Chapter 6, "Staff," includes updated job descriptions and levels of staffing. The technology technician is included as a member of the media center staff. State certification standards are updated and national certification standards are introduced. Recruitment issues, job search strategies, and training of staff are updated. Outsourcing of tasks is reviewed and material added.

In Chapter 7, "Facilities," essential areas of the media center facility are provided as well as web sites that can help in planning spaces for a state-of-the-art technology facility. Computer services are discussed. Web sites for floor plans are added. The thermal environment is discussed. The effect of color on student learning is an added feature of the chapter. A virtual library is described.

In Chapter 8, "Media Selection: Policies and Procedures," media selection is updated to reflect new technology such as online reviews to aid in selection. Privacy issues and confidentiality of student records is covered. Intellectual freedom issues, as they relate to censorship, are expanded.

Chapter 9, "Media Selection: Criteria and Selection Aids," includes a thorough revision of the equipment and audiovisual materials list. Web site evaluation criteria are added. Selection criteria and selection aids are revised throughout the chapter. Quantitative criteria for books, audiovisual materials and equipment are provided. Added new technology such as DVDs, video streaming, audio books, LCD projectors, white boards, MP3, and handheld computers are included.

In Chapter 11, "Acquisition and Organization," online magazines/ journals and encyclopedias are discussed and a list of online subscription databases is provided. Web sites are provided for general and specialized book jobbers as well as magazine jobbers. Ordering online is discussed. The discussion of the Library of Congress, its services and MARC records, is updated, as well as OCLC services. A listing of vendors who offer MARC records is provided. Basic cataloging texts are recommended. Two new machines are recommended for local production of materials: the poster maker machine and the art-waxing machine. Copyright information is updated to include multimedia productions and Internet information. A copyright policy is recommended.

Chapter 12, "Program Administration" provides managerial concerns consistent with *Information Power* (1998). These concerns are updated, including the one addressing program administration. A listing of frequently used automated circulation systems for K-12 schools as well as the names, addresses, and web sites of security system vendors are provided. Inventory procedures are updated to include the newest technology. New guidelines are provided for weeding the print collection and audiovisual materials. Web sites are provided that give information for repairing books.

Chapter 13, "Outside the Walls of the School Library Media Center," contains all the updated addresses for related associations and committees. New material is included about the political process. Book titles to add to the media specialist's professional collection is new as well.

Chapter 14, "Evaluation," includes updated versions of all evaluation charts and evaluation forms. One new rubric for measuring exemplary school library media programs is added.

All appendices have been updated. Three new documents have been added to Appendix IV.

This book has many web sites. Because web sites have the tendency to disappear over a period of time, there is included here a URL to the Internet Archive Wayback Machine to help retrieve information:

http://web.archive.org/web/*/http://www.archive.org/web/web.php

The author plans to update web sites periodically for the book. Check the author's web site for updated information at the following URL: http://www.drbettyjmorris.com. The web site is under construction and will be operational by October 2004.

REFERENCE

American Association of School Librarians & Association for Educational Communications and Technology. (1998). *Information power: Building partnerships for learning.* Chicago: Authors.

ACKNOWLEDGEMENTS

Many people made this fourth edition possible. Special appreciation is extended to Sharon Coatney, acquisitions editor, who was very prompt in reading the chapters and responding with excellent advice. Carol Truett did an excellent job in writing chapters 5 and 10. Her hard work is appreciated. Nancy White was invaluable as a researcher, a reader, and as my right hand in writing this book. She has my gratitude and love for always being reliable and going the extra mile. Peggy Milam was gracious in reading so many chapters and providing feedback. Her words of wisdom are greatly appreciated. Elizabeth Bennett gave great advice in the final stages of writing the book. A special thanks is extended to Barbara McKenzie for her understanding and support during the writing of this book. Mary Ann Myers and the graduate assistants at the State University of West Georgia were gracious in helping me with typing and research. I extend to them my heartfelt love and appreciation for their work.

This book is dedicated to my son, Jon Eric Morris, who is the joy of my life.

Betty J. Morris
Associate Professor
State University of West Georgia

Chapter 1

SCHOOL LIBRARY: A HISTORICAL PERSPECTIVE

INTRODUCTION

This chapter looks at the school library from the historical perspective, starting with how school libraries began in the United States, their development, and their evolution. School library standards are explored from the early Charles C. Certain Committee reports (1920, 1925) to *Information Power* (AASL & AECT, 1998). School library initiatives, such as the Knapp Project and Library Power, are discussed. The emergence of the school media center concept, legislative day, White House conferences, court cases, site-based management, and research about school library media centers are examples of other topics discussed in this chapter.

THE ERA OF THE SCHOOL DISTRICT LIBRARY

As early as 1740 Benjamin Franklin included a library in plans for his academy. However, the real beginning of the school library movement in the United States did not occur until almost a century later. New York State, under the leadership of Governor DeWitt Clinton, began the pioneer work. In 1835 the state legislature passed a law allowing school districts to use limited amounts of their tax monies to establish and maintain school libraries. When only a few districts decided to use their funds for this purpose, a second act was passed in 1839 to spur further action; it set aside a sum of $55,000 annually, to be given on a matching-fund basis, for the establishment of school district libraries. The effects were dramatic. During the school year 1841–1842, for example, more than 200,000 books were added to these collections. Several other states followed New York's leadership and passed similar legislation. In 1837, chiefly through the efforts of Horace Mann, Massachusetts enacted its first school district library law to enable school districts to raise funds for libraries. This law was liberalized in 1842 to give $15 per year from state funds to each school district that could supply a similar amount for library purposes. The Michigan law, also passed in 1837, stipulated that school districts that raised $15 maximum in taxes per year for libraries would be returned a proportion of the fines collected for breaches of the "disturbing the peace" laws! Connecticut followed with legislation in 1839, Rhode Island in 1840. By 1879, nineteen states had passed some sort of law designed to promote public school libraries.

Yet the movement to build school district libraries during this period is generally considered a failure. The collections were usually unattractive to children. They contained mainly textbooks or adult materials suitable only for a teacher's use. To capture this new book market, many unscrupulous publishers glutted the market with cheap, poorly written and produced texts, and without competently trained personnel to select library materials; many of these shoddy products found their way into collections. Facilities for housing these collections, or the requisite abilities within each school system for organizing and administering them effectively, were also insufficient. Consequently the collections often became scattered; books disappeared and frequently were incorporated into the teacher's personal library. In time disillusionment set in concerning the value of this type of library service, and in many districts the money was diverted into other channels—supplies, equipment, and even teachers' salaries. Decline of this movement is illustrated by the fact that New York State school district libraries contained twice as many books in 1853 as they did in 1890. Perhaps a more important reason for the demise of the school district library is the growth of public libraries. Legislators as well as many educators began to support the development of a more broadly based agency that would be able to supply library service to more than a small segment of the community. In Massachusetts, for example, the 1837/1842 school library law was repealed in 1850 and replaced the following year by a law providing that tax monies be used to establish and develop public libraries. In time the public library superceded the school district library.

Although the school district library movement was perhaps premature—a phenomenon far in advance of existing social conditions—it is important historically for two reasons: the principle was established that a library facility in a school could have some educational value and a precedent was created for the use of public funds to support these libraries.

THE GENESIS OF THE SCHOOL LIBRARY

The year 1876 is considered the birth date of the modern American library movement. In that year the American Library Association (ALA) was created by librarians (led by Melvil Dewey) who were attending a series of meetings on national library development during the Centennial Exhibition in Philadelphia. The first issue of *Library Journal* also appeared that year, as well as an extensive report, *Public Libraries in the United States of America: Their History, Condition and Management* (1876), issued by the United States Bureau of Education. The report's title is somewhat misleading because the publication also includes information on other types of libraries. According to the report, only 826 secondary school libraries were in existence in the United States (no elementary or grammar school libraries were reported) and their collections totaled only one million volumes.

Dismayed at the condition of school libraries in New York State and the inability of local school districts to improve these conditions, Melvil Dewey, then secretary of the Board of Regents and director of the State Library, and Andrew Draper, Superintendent of Public Instruction, drafted a bill that the legislature passed in 1892. This law, a pioneering effort, allowed for the growth of school libraries in New York State and also served as a model for library legislation in other states. As in the 1839 school district library law, the new legislation provided that a single school district could receive monies on a matching-fund basis (no more than $500 per year) for the purchase of library books. In time other schemes were used to appropriate this money, and eventually a formula based on the size of the pupil population in the district became the yardstick. Only books approved by the Department of Public Instruction could be purchased with state funds. Lists of recommended titles were issued periodically, and they consisted of reference books, supplementary reading books, books related to the curriculum, and pedagogical books for use by teachers.

To prevent a reoccurrence of the disastrous ending of the school district library, these collections were intended to remain in the school at all times, but teachers, administrators, and pupils were allowed, on occasion, to borrow a single volume at a time for a period not to exceed two weeks.

A classroom teacher was to serve as school librarian, and by annual reports to the State Superintendent of Public Instruction, these librarians were made responsible for the care and upkeep of the collection. Given these rigid regulations, it is easy to see that many schools were discouraged from applying for state funds. It soon became apparent that modifications were necessary, and in time they came. Gradually other states passed similar legislation.

In 1892 New York State also formed its School Libraries Division within the Department of Public Instruction. Annual reports from the department show an increased concern with the development of school libraries, and for the first time, in the report of 1900, a tentative standard was issued for libraries in elementary schools:

A small library is becoming indispensable to the teacher and pupils of the grammar school. In order to give definiteness to this idea of a small library, suppose it to consist of five hundred to one thousand books, containing the best classic stories, poems, biographies, histories, travels, novels, and books of science suitable for the use of children below high school. . . . It is evident that a carefully selected library of the best books of this character should be found in every grammar school. (pp. 28–29)

Other developments indicated an increasing interest in school library development. In 1896, the National Education Association (NEA) created its Library Section partly because of a petition requesting action circulated by John Cotton Dana, then president of ALA, and partly because of the impassioned speech on the importance of libraries in education delivered by Melvil Dewey at an NEA national convention in Buffalo. ALA created a committee to cooperate with NEA's Library Section. (In December 1914, ALA founded its own School Library Section.) In 1900 the first graduate of a library school in the United States, to serve as a school librarian, was employed in the Erasmus Hall High School in New York City. Several state teachers' associations began developing sections for school librarians. In 1910 New York State once more led the way, this time by creating the High School Library Section within the New York State Teachers Association. That no mention is made of elementary school librarians reflects the absence of any significant development in this area.

At this time the role of the librarian was considered primarily a clerical one, and in schools that hired professional librarians there developed a struggle for recognition of equal status in position and salary for librarians with teachers. New York was one of the first cities to recognize that librarians were essentially teachers rather than clerks. In 1914 its Board of Education adopted regulations that made salaries of qualified high school librarians comparable to those of teachers and also recommended that prospective librarians should be graduates of a one-year course in an approved library school.

Although library schools were often requested to add courses for school librarianship to their curricula, progress in this area was slow. What little professional training was available was supplied usually through courses taught in teacher training institutions and normal schools or by brief summer workshops and institutes usually sponsored by a state education department or a teachers' association.

The statistics for this period show a gradual and encouraging growth in size of school library collections. The actual sorry state of school libraries was revealed, however, in a *Library Journal* article of April 1913 entitled "Development of Secondary School Libraries" in which the author, E. D. Greenman, comments on the status of these collections:

> Most of them are small collections of reference and textbooks, poorly quartered, unclassified and neither cataloged nor readily accessible for constant use. Of the 10,000 public high school librarians in the country at the present time, not more than 250 possess collections containing 3000 volumes or over. (p. 184)

A further indication of how school libraries lagged behind development in other library areas is the national statistic, revealed by M. E. Hall (1915), that only fifty trained librarians have been appointed to schools (all secondary) between 1905 and 1915. The sad conclusion is that, although some foundation had been laid during this period for the development of school libraries, most schools had either no libraries or ones that were inadequate in size, staff, and organization.

In addition to the school library operated as an integral part of the school organization, various other structural patterns for supplying library service to children emerged during this period. These services often involved attempts to combine public and school library service. The four most important methods were: (1) In rural and remote areas without even public libraries, the state library agency provided traveling or "package" libraries to schools. (2) In urban areas, students used the public library resources exclusively, and liaison between the school and public library was maintained by such strategies as visits to the schools. (3) A branch of the public library was created in the school to supply library service for both the children and adults in the community. In 1895, for example, a public library branch was established in Cleveland's Central High School, and four years later another was set up in a high school in Newark, New Jersey. Unfortunately, these book collections were usually more suited to adults, and often this division of interests resulted in neither population being served adequately. (4) A system of joint control was established by which a public library branch to be used exclusively by students and teachers was placed in the school, but organized and administered by the staff of the public library. Once more problems arose involving the divided loyalties of the librarians and the inability of the library to respond immediately to changing curricular needs. Under this system of joint control, the library was never an integral part of the school program and was regarded as an outside agency.

Although some of these variant patterns of organizations persisted into the middle of this century, they were gradually found unsuitable, and the prevailing pattern that emerged was an independent library in individual schools under the control of a board of education. Following this development, several larger school districts formed central library agencies for supervision and guidance. In the interest of efficiency, these agencies later expanded to provide such services as centralized processing, selection centers, and district-wide circulation of special collections.

THE AGE OF DEVELOPMENT

The rapid growth of school libraries following World War I parallels a similar growth in public education. School population increased tremendously. In the thirty-year span between 1900 and 1930, the elementary school population alone rose by 50 percent, and at the secondary level the growth was even more phenomenal.

A general population increase, coupled with sustained faith in the importance of a general education, were primary factors in producing this situation: Less child labor was employed and there was a more stringent enforcement of school attendance regulations. Centralization of schools helped to promote the development of larger units that could afford the luxury of a library and the services of a qualified librarian.

Teaching systems also changed. The use of a single textbook and memorization were often supplanted by other teaching methods that stressed individualized instruction and recognition of the differences among children. New curriculum structures, such as the Winnetka Plan (1920), the Dalton (Massachusetts) Plan (1920), and the many others that grew from the influence of John Dewey and his progressive education movement, underscored the need in schools for a variety of educational materials. The logical source for the materials was a well-stocked, well-administered school library.

The beginning of the period also saw the publication of the first national school library standards. In 1915, a nationwide survey on the teaching of English was conducted by the National Council of Teachers of English. Through this report, the totally inadequate condition of school libraries in the United States came to light. This revelation prompted the NEA to appoint a committee of both librarians and educators under the chairmanship of Charles C. Certain to study secondary school libraries. The committee's final report was submitted to NEA in 1918 and was approved. ALA's Committee on Education also approved the report, and it was published by ALA in 1920. The report's official title is *Standard Library Organization and Equipment for Secondary Schools* (1920), but it is commonly known as the "Certain report."

The Certain report begins by painting a gloomy, but truthful, picture of the status of the post-World War I school library: "There are few well-planned high school libraries in the U.S. Sometimes there is a large study hall for the library—generally just one room with no workroom or conveniences of any kind for the staff" (p. 2). Specific quantitative standards are given for secondary school libraries in schools of various sizes and grade levels. Included are liberal recommendations for physical facilities (the library should accommodate five to ten percent of the school population), qualifications of librarians (an undergraduate degree, one year of library science, and a minimum of one year of library work with young adults), size of book collections (six to eight books per student), as well as details on equipment, supplies, and budget.

The standards are forward-looking and even prophetic in their espousal of the media center concept long before the term came into existence:

> The Library should serve as the center and coordinating agency for all material used in the school for visual instruction, such as stereoopticons, portable motion picture machines, stereoopticon slides, moving picture films, pictures, maps, globes, bulletin board material, museum loans, etc. Such material should be regularly accessioned and cataloged, and its movements recorded, and directed from the library. (Charles C. Certain Committee, 1920, p. 17)

The Certain high school standards (and their supplement of 1932) had a beneficial effect on school library growth. They provided the first yardstick to evaluate local libraries and also created a framework from which other accrediting agencies—library departments, regional, state, and local—could develop other sets of standards.

A second Certain report, *Elementary School Library Standards* (1925), received once more the endorsement of both NEA and ALA. In these standards the integrated media approach was restated:

> There is a need, therefore, of a new department in the school whose func-
> tion it shall be to assemble and distribute the materials of instruction.... In
> its first purpose, that of school library service, it may be thought of as the
> one agency in the school that makes possible a definite systematic manipu-
> lation and control of materials of instruction.... [The collection should
> include] moving picture films, pictures for illustrative purposes, post cards,
> stereopticon slides, stereography, victrola records. This material shall be
> recorded by the librarian and distributed from the library. (p. 5)

Once more these standards were exhaustive in the amount of specific detail given. There is also appended a list of 212 basic books for the elementary school library. Because most elementary schools had no libraries and the need for them was still generally unrecognized, the impact of these standards was not as great as that of the 1920 standards.

In 1924 the North Central Association developed the "Score Card for School Libraries," a set of standards that began concentrating attention on programs or qualitative standards rather than on quantities of materials. In 1927 this association required each member high school library to score its library.

That the Certain standards over-emphasized the quantitative aspects of school library programs was criticized in other areas as well, and when the Cooperative Study of Secondary School Standards was formed in 1933, a new study was begun. As a result, a numerical scoring technique was published to evaluate the secondary school (including the school library). Through numerous revisions, this publication evolved into the *Evaluative Criteria for the Evaluation of Secondary Schools* (1969), an instrument widely used by many accreditation associations and by schools for self-evaluation (National Study of Secondary School Evaluation, 1969).

Other documents of the period focused attention on school libraries. In 1932, a national secondary school library survey was conducted by B. Lamar Johnson as part of the National Survey of Secondary Education sponsored by the U.S. Office of Education. The resultant publication, *The Secondary School Library* (1933), supplied data on 390 libraries as well as special information on exemplary programs. Although no specific recommendations were given, indirect guidance for library program development is suggested (Johnson, 1933). The Department of Elementary

School Principals of NEA entitled its twelfth annual yearbook, *The Elementary School Library* (1933), and the second part of the forty-second yearbook of the National Society for the Study of Education was called *The Library in General Education* (Henry, 1943). Many monographs also appeared that supplied, for the first time, guidance on how to establish and maintain a school library. Lucille F. Fargo wrote an ALA publication, *The Library in the School* (1933), which had a publishing history of several editions and became the standard textbook on administering school library services. In 1951 Frances Henne wrote a detailed and sophisticated evaluation device for gathering data and measuring a school library's development entitled, *A Planning Guide for the High School Library Program*.

The second set of national school library standards, *School Libraries for Today and Tomorrow* (1945), was one of a series of documents on standards developed under the leadership of the ALA Committee on Post-War Planning. This publication represents the cooperative efforts of school library specialists then prominent in the field. The work is primarily descriptive, containing separate chapters on the purposes of school libraries and the various services offered. Quantitative standards are presented throughout the text and summarized in chart form in appendices. The standards reflect a progressive and forward-looking view concerning the role of the school library in relation to the school's objectives and the equal importance of both elementary and secondary libraries. However, these standards are less definite about the place of non-book materials in the library than were the Certain standards. For example:

> The wide use of many books, periodicals, prints, maps, recordings, films and other audio-visual aids has made it imperative that information regarding all materials in the school be available from some central source. The school library appears to be the logical place for this information even when some of the materials are housed outside the library. (p. 11)

Requirements for certification of school librarians improved and became more rigidly codified during this period. A U.S. Office of Education study conducted in 1940 showed that some provision for certifying school librarians existed in every state. Eight states provided this requirement by specific state laws, twenty-four states allowed their education departments to provide their own certification requirements, and sixteen states allowed local school boards to certify their librarians. The requirements varied considerably. For example, while one state required only two years of college and eight hours of library science, another required a bachelor's degree. For permanent certification as a school librarian, New York State required an undergraduate degree, thirty-six hours of library science (the maximum and minimum number of semester hours in each area of course work was specified), and eighteen hours in education, including student teaching. In 1925, New York State mandated the appointment of a secondary school librarian (or, when necessary, a classroom teacher to serve in this capacity) for all but very small secondary schools in the state.

Although certification requirements were written, in many states, school districts often ignored them simply by not creating positions for school librarians. In most schools the library was administered on a part-time basis by volunteers or by classroom teachers, who were given release time.

The amount of statewide supervision of school librarians increased markedly during this period. In 1939 only thirteen states employed full-time supervisors; however, by 1960 more than half the states had developed these positions. Primarily because of increased federal spending for school libraries, virtually every state had some form of statewide supervision under qualified personnel by the end of the 1960s, and many had increased the number of the supervisors to four and five times more than there had been before World War II.

The question of whether education for school librarianship should be based in library schools or in teacher training institutions continued to receive a great deal of attention. Many arguments favored the latter: Teacher training institutions were more numerous and better situated geographically; library schools were primarily public- and academic-library oriented and unwilling to give courses in time slots (summers, for example) that were convenient for school personnel who wanted to be school librarians; certification requirements were generally so minimal that teacher training institutions could easily offer these basic courses; school administrators frequently wanted to hire only part-time librarians who were also qualified as subject specialists for classroom teaching.

During the 1950s, a decided shift was noticeable from schools of education to library schools for courses in school librarianship. No single reason for this change can be given, but certain factors are apparent. Increased state standards for certification were adopted that often could be met only by attending a library school offering a complete program in library science. The proliferation of library schools, some developed from teacher training institutions, also helped. This trend tended to break the pattern of most library schools mainly being oriented toward adult services. As library schools and library school degrees became common, curricular programs expanded the number and variety of school library courses offered in library schools. Pressure also developed from within the library profession for library schools to extend into the school library area. For example, the 1951 standards for accrediting library schools stressed the importance of developing multipurpose curricula that would not be confined solely to a single area of library service. The standards permitted only five-year programs to be eligible for accreditation, which weakened the drawing power of undergraduate programs offered within teachers' colleges.

In spite of these encouraging developments, national statistics continued to show the sorry state of school libraries in the United States. The U.S. Office of Education report, *Public School Library Statistics for 1958–59* (1960), noted that about one-half of the nation's schools had no library and well over one-half did not have the services of a qualified librarian. Even in schools with libraries, collections averaged fewer than five books per student. The most seriously deprived area continued to be elementary schools, of which two-thirds were without a school library.

The decade of the 1960s is considered one of the greatest periods of school library growth. The period began with the publication of a new set of national standards, *Standards for School Library Programs* (1960), which were developed by the American Association of School Librarians (AASL) or ALA in cooperation with nineteen other professional associations. In addition to their national impact, these standards influenced development and expansion of state and local standards. Although they deal primarily with various services offered by a functioning school library and make quantitative recommendations, these standards stress the responsibility of school boards, administrators, and various kinds of supervisory personnel in developing successful school library programs. The statement concerning school libraries as instructional materials centers, adopted by AASL in 1956, is reprinted in the standards, but there is no strong recommendation that the library and audiovisual collections be combined physically. Increased cooperation is suggested, however, where these collections are administered separately. Specific quantitative standards are included for audiovisual materials and equipment.

In the early 1960s, while school librarians were trying to implement their new standards, the NEA Department of Audiovisual Instruction (DAVI) had two committees working simultaneously on developing standards for audiovisual programs. The Committee on Professional Standards was working on quantitative standards and the Consultant Service Committee on the qualitative aspects. In June 1965, the quantitative standards were approved as the official guidelines for the organization.

The greatest impetus for school library development in the 1960s came from increased financial aid from federal sources. The forerunner of this aid was the National Defense Education Act of 1958, which had as its aim the strengthening of teaching in the areas of science, foreign language, and mathematics through expenditures that could include purchases of equipment, library books, and other educational materials. Even more important was the passage of the Elementary and Secondary Education Act in 1965. Through Title II of this act, provision was made for millions of dollars to be spent developing school libraries. Other sections of the act supplied additional funds for providing library materials for disadvantaged students and for setting up model projects and demonstration libraries.

There was also an increased flow of money and support from private sources. Most notable was the Knapp School Libraries Project, which funded the establishment of several ideal school libraries across the country from 1963 through 1968. Thousands of educators visited these demonstration centers and thousands of others learned of them through written reports and other materials that were prepared to publicize the project. The Knapp Foundation later financed an intensive project to determine manpower needs in the area of school librarianship.

The effect of these new sources of support was phenomenal—hundreds of new libraries were founded, others were able to expand considerably their collections and services, and the demand for qualified librarians far exceeded the supply. Although federal support has subsequently varied greatly, the momentum for developing school libraries has also varied from time to time.

THE EMERGENCE OF THE MEDIA CENTER

The aims of American education are usually expressed in terms of a dual responsibility to society and to the individual. The societal aims involve not only the preservation of those important values accumulated through time but also provisions to ensure growth and change in society. Education also attempts to equip students with knowledge to fit into the existing society and to contribute to that society's betterment. Although different theories have evolved about how to achieve such lofty goals, basic principles involving student learning remain unchanged: (1) children learn as individuals, (2) children learn at various rates, (3) children learn according to different styles and patterns, and (4) education is a continuous process.

The attempt to translate these principles of learning into practice led educators to pursue many new teaching strategies and organizational patterns that break with traditional modes. Among them was the widespread adoption of unified media programs administered through a school library media center. Once more, professional associations helped lead the way. The first joint standards cooperatively produced by AASL and DAVI were entitled, *Standards for School Media Programs* (1969). In addition to emphasizing the positive results that unified media programs can bring and supplying detailed quantitative guidelines, the media program standards stress the necessity of fusing facilities and services to meet the challenges of education.

The 1969 *Standards* recommended that a continuous review of the national standards be undertaken to ensure proper consideration of changes and developments particularly involving educational technology and learning techniques. It was also recommended that a new set of standards be published every two years. In response to these recommendations, two task forces were jointly appointed in 1971 by AASL and the Association for Educational Communications and Technology (AECT, the new name for DAVI), one to study media service standards for the single school and the other at the district level. (Since these areas were found to be inseparable, the two reports were later merged.) The resulting document, *Media Programs: District and School* (1975), reaffirms unified approaches to centralizing media services in schools. Greater emphasis is placed on the media center's role in planning and executing the school's instructional program rather than being simply a passive support service. Emphasis on user needs and educational growth, as well as the necessity of participating in curriculum development by the library media staff, are stressed in the media programs.

In addition to furnishing specific goals and objectives for the media programs and their integration into the overall goals of the institution, these standards emphasize how sound managerial practices can help in achieving these goals.

Quantitative measurements are not ignored; for example, specific square footage is given for various physical facilities and numerical amounts for both basic and advanced collections of various kinds of materials and equipment. These measurements, however, are made somewhat flexible to accommodate the uniqueness of each library media center program. The overall recommendation is that at least ten percent of the national average per pupil operation cost (PPOC) be expended by local school boards for each student enrolled, solely for the development of materials and equipment collections within the school district.

These standards allow for more specialization and differentiation in staffing patterns within the center by distinguishing among the media specialist (a professional who has broad preparation in both education and media), the media professional (a person with extensive preparation in a specific area of educational technology such as computer science), the media technician, media aide, and support personnel.

Renewed emphasis is placed on the importance of district-wide service and developing cooperative media programs with other agencies at the regional, state and national levels. *Media Programs* (1975) and its 1969 predecessor were perhaps the most influential documents affecting the growth and development of school media programs during the 1970s and 1980s.

The concept of interdependence and the necessity of developing cooperative projects among school media centers and other information organizations received additional support beyond the 1975 standards from such agencies as the National Commission on Libraries and Information Science (NCLIS). An independent federal agency in the executive branch, NCLIS has as its major task advising the president and Congress on the status of the nation's libraries. In its initial statement of priorities and policies, *Towards a National Program of Library and Information Services: Goals for Action* (1975), it was stated that school library media centers must become part of a nationwide resource-sharing network:

> if we are to increase the opportunities for children and youth for independent study and add to their ability to become literate, well informed citizens capable of lifelong learning in a rapidly changing world. (Preface)

In January 1977, a task force consisting of representatives from existing network offices and other educational media associations as well as media personnel from local and state agencies was appointed to study the position of the library media center within the framework of a national cooperative network. The resulting document, *Report of the Task Force on the Role of the School Library Media Program in Networking* (1978), established an overriding rationale for including school media programs in a national network. The document identified five factors—psychological, political and legal, funding, communication, and planning—that inhibit cooperation. In each case immediate and mid-range recommendations are made to solve these problems. Only one long-range recommendation emerges— that within ten years "library networks in which school library media programs are full participating members be established and operating in every region, state and area in the nation" (p. 34). In 1979, NCLIS established another committee of key people in educational media, to identify priorities and to work with them to implement the report's recommendation.

Another event that focused attention on the future of all the nation's libraries, including those in schools, was the first White House Conference on Library and Information Science, held in Washington, DC, on November 15–19, 1979. The 826 delegates developed 64 recommendations that ranged from the passage of a national library act to the guarantee of adequate media services in each public school. The conference proceedings and recommendations are covered fully in its final report, *Information for the 80's* (1979).

The first meeting of the Ad Hoc Committee on Implementation of the White House Conference Resolutions met in September 1980 with the charge to establish priorities and policies concerning the implementation of the recommendations. Certainly solutions for solving the many problems facing school library media centers were identified. Unfortunately, cutbacks in government spending in the 1980s seriously delayed their implementation.

Many of education's problems in the 1980s, including those of school library media centers, involved declining financial support. Some symptoms of lack of support were seen in budget cutting, elimination of staff, increased work loads assigned to personnel, unionization, job actions within the profession, increased competition for existing funds, and rising costs of educational materials. In many areas of the country, these fiscal problems were exacerbated by declining enrollments, school closings, and "excessing" of personnel. For school media personnel, further challenges in the 1980s involved increased pressures by ultraconservatives to control collections, the emphasis from "back-to-basics" groups on the use of textbooks, and the necessity to absorb computer technology, library automation, and concepts of networking into library media center management.

A more conservative national outlook, which emerged in the 1970s, is also reflected in the growing number of censorship cases involving school library media centers in the 1980s. A landmark Supreme Court decision handed down on June 25, 1982, ended a marathon court struggle that lasted six years involving a case of book banning. The lawsuit had been bought against a suburban New York State school district (Island Trees) by five students, led by Steven Pico, who claimed that their First Amendment rights had been violated by the school board's arbitrary removal of nine books from their high school library. The titles in question had been chosen for inclusion in the school's collection by valid selection criteria, but had appeared on a list of objectionable titles circulated by a conservative parents' group.

In a five to four decision, the Supreme Court limited the power of public school officials to remove books simply because they found them objectionable, by ruling that school boards who remove books must defend their motives in court. The fact that there was such a division in the Supreme Court highlights the basic dualism involving the purposes of public education—that is, primarily to transmit the accepted values of the country or to use the classroom as a marketplace for ideas. The decision has been considered a victory for the latter concept. As Justice William Brennan stated in his opinion for the plurality: "Local school boards may not remove books from school library shelves simply because they dislike the ideas contained in those books and seek by their removal to prescribe what should be orthodox in politics, nationalism, religion or other matters of opinion" (Board of Education, 1985, p. 854).

Prior to the Pico vs. Island Trees court case, library media specialists had little recourse to deal with censorship cases; however, this case gave strength to their fight for intellectual freedom. Other documents, such as *Information Power* (AASL & AECT, 1988) emerged within the next three years, giving strength to more expanded instructional roles of the school media specialist in the schools. As a result of an alliance between AECT and AASL, the two associations jointly released *Information Power: Guidelines for School Library Programs* (1988), a document designed to promote a school library media program in which the school media specialist serves as a proactive initiator and a participative partner with other educators as a member of an instructional team. The primary focus of these guidelines is the building-level school library media specialist's responsibility to exercise leadership in establishing partnerships and initiating the planning process with teachers. *Information Power* (1988) was written as a guideline designed to foster quality school media programs:

> Promoting effective physical access to information resources and intellectual access to the content is the central unifying concept of these guidelines. Library media specialists serve as the link between students, teachers, administrators, and parents and the available information resources. The roles and services defined in this document are dynamic; they are changing and evolving in response to the societal, economic, and technological demands on education. (p. x)

Two major thrusts of the document are the definition of the roles of school media specialists and the redefinition of the mission of the school media program as it relates to physical and intellectual access to information resources utilizing the newest technologies. As defined in the document, the school media specialist performs three roles—teacher, information specialist, and instructional consultant—within the context of the educational environment, to prepare the student to think critically and to solve problems for the future. The role definitions provide the impetus to move the school media specialist into a more professional realm as an educational leader in the school.

Making the public aware of library services became an impetus for change. Many states initiated Legislative Day (1990), in which library professionals from all kinds of libraries collectively met to discuss with their governor and legislators to lobby for increased state funding. To go a step further, a nationwide lobbying effort has become an annual event in Washington, DC, where librarians from all over the country gather as a unified group to ask the members of Congress to support legislation for library funding to their respective states. National Library Legislative Day, 2002 brought approximately 450 participants from 47 states to Washington, DC, to talk to members of Congress about library issues and concerns (National Library Legislative Day, 2004). Some examples of the major legislation sought or opposed at Legislative Days over the past few years include:

1. The new Reading Excellence Act which is intended to enhance reading instruction for young children through after-school and summer reading programs.

2. Reauthorization of ESEA Title III is designed to acquire school library materials, to provide qualified school library media specialists to work with students and teachers, and to incorporate into the curriculum the new technologies for teaching, learning, and training to improve critical thinking and information literacy skills.

3. Copyright and distance education laws proposed to update the current copyright law exemptions for distance education while meeting reasonable proprietor concerns.

4. Opposition to filtering requirements that impose requirements on schools and libraries to use technology to block or filter material harmful or inappropriate for children as a condition for receiving federal funds or retaining the e-rate telecommunication discounts.

5. The Telecommunications Act of 1996 provides discounted telecommunications e-rates for libraries and schools and is responsible for increased access to the Internet in school media centers. The e-rate discounts have been instrumental in providing equitable Internet access to school libraries throughout the country (American Library Association Office of Government Relations, 2000).

The discount rate for school libraries depends on the percentage of students on school lunch programs and the location (urban/rural) of the school. Discount e-rates range from twenty percent to ninety percent for telecommunication services for those schools that qualify (Bertot, 2000).

Talking to Congressmen normally pays high dividends in library support; however, occasionally some issues go beyond Congress and are resolved by the Supreme Court. The Children's Internet Protection Act, although strongly opposed by ALA and the library community, was upheld by the Supreme Court in a June 23, 2003, decision. The bottom line implication of the decision means that school and public libraries receiving federal e-rate funding for Internet connectivity will be required to install blocking filter software on all online workstations. A media center that does not receive e-rate funding is not required by law to comply with the ruling (Goldberg, 2003).

The second White House Conference on Library and Information Services was held July 9–13, 1991, by the National Commission on Library and Information Science in Washington, DC. The themes for the conference were focused on literacy, democracy, and productivity in relation to library and information services. Delegates represented all fifty states, the District of Columbia, and six U.S. territories. Total attendance for the conference was 2,000. Ninety-seven recommendations were drafted by the delegates on such issues as funding, privacy, telecommunications, access to information, service to diverse populations, and collection development.

Preparation for the White House Conference enabled school librarians to work with other library and information science professionals to plan governors' conferences statewide as a means of drawing attention to the need for library services within the states and nationwide. Many of the governors' conferences developed the same themes as the national conference in order to provide delegate training for the state representatives who planned to attend the second White House Conference (Diehl, 1989; Donaldson, 1991; Literacy, Democracy, 1990).

Another White House Conference emphasizing school libraries held June 4, 2002, became a strongly supportive measure that fosters the idea that media centers are the cornerstones of children's education. The focus of the conference included the latest library science research as well as ideas of what makes a successful media center in schools. This conference brought together education, library, government, and philanthropic leaders to discuss the most current information about school library media centers. The proceedings of the conference documents highlight how media centers are an "indispensable element in successful school programs, enhancing learning and improving student achievement" (Institute of Museum and Library Services, 2002; Laura Bush Foundation for American Libraries, 2002).

School reform in school libraries became evident in the late 1980s and early 1990s with the nationwide Library Power Project. New York City's public elementary schools were the first to receive funding in 1988 from the DeWitt Wallace-Reader's Digest fund to improve elementary school libraries. The Fund decided to expand their investment of $45 million for a ten-year period to nineteen communities in the United States to improve teaching and learning through school library media centers. This investment was the largest private funding for school media centers since the Knapp project in the 1960s. Most of the $45 million went to each of the communities in grants of $1.2 million per site over a three-year period from 1991 through 1994.

Schools participating in the DeWitt Wallace-Reader's Digest grant agreed to employ a full-time media specialist, to provide matching funds for collection development, and to allow open access to the media center, or flexible scheduling, for students and teachers throughout the school day. Emphasis of the Library Power program was on the instructional role of the school media specialist. This focus of the grant encouraged teachers and media specialist to collaborate on the selection of materials, on planning instructional lessons, and on teaching content together. Funding was also provided for school media facility improvements to allow multiple uses of the facility and to provide an inviting atmosphere conducive to learning (Zweizig & Hopkins, 1999). Although the evaluation of the Library Power sites did not include student achievement as criteria, the reports submitted annually from Library Power directors frequently noted that student achievement had improved in the participating schools as a result of collaboration between teachers/media specialists and as a result of flexible scheduling.

The decade of the 1990s was a period of rapid technological growth for school media centers. In the early part of the decade, few school media centers had automated libraries and Internet access was almost non-existent. Over a ten-year period, the growth of technology became so rapid that by the end of the decade, the majority of school media centers were automated and Internet access was commonplace. In 2001, the average public school owned 124 computers. Internet access increased from fifty percent in 1998 to eighty-five percent in 2001 and approximately ninety-nine percent of schools had Internet access (Digest of Education Statistics, 2003).

In general, looking back from the vantage point of the 2000s, the preceding decade showed continued expansion in the school media field. The proliferation of computers in school media centers with access to the Internet, made possible by the e-rate discounts for telecommunication access, changed the way that students and faculty would do research forever. Internet access changed the ways librarians worked with students and teachers because they could instantly find information that previously required more time and effort. Never before in the history of the school media center has there been such easy access to Internet information, which is due directly to the e-rate discounts afforded school media specialists. The e-rate program allows schools to move toward an Internet-enhanced curriculum that fundamentally changes the way students learn in spite of the Children's Online Protection Act which requires schools that receive e-rate funding to install filtering and blocking software on computers to prevent student's visual access to obscenity (McDonald, 2001).

Because of the rapid technological and societal changes of the 1990s, school library media programs, in particular, made quantum-leap changes in how they approach access to information. Along with rapid technological growth, many schools became involved in site-based management, meaning educators made major decisions about how the schools would operate locally. Frequently, site-based management had an effect on school media center budgets and it became evident that school library media specialists must become leaders in their schools if they expected to receive adequate funding for their library media programs. Site-based management could influence instructional leadership for the school library media specialist in such matters as flexible scheduling and collaboration with teachers.

Site-based management involves shared decision making by all stakeholders in the school such as administrators and other teachers. It is crucial that school library media specialists be part of the site-based management team. Decisions about collaboration with teachers as partners in instruction, decisions about school library media center programs, and decisions about collection development are too important to be left to chance. Because site-based management is so important to school library media specialists, a position statement on the role of the school library media specialist in site-based management is available through the AASL web site, which takes this stand on the subject:

As a model for schools, site-based management directly impacts four major areas of decision making: personnel, curriculum, budget and facilities. All four are of vital importance in the development of library media programs, and the library media specialist should provide leadership as policies are developed in these areas. (p. 1.)

The 1990s provided evidence that school media specialists could become instructional consultants in curriculum development assuming instructional leadership roles in schools and the community. As school library media specialists became instructional leaders in the schools, their ability to assume site-based management leadership roles were enhanced. They became more articulate about their mission, more aware of public relations techniques, more knowledgeable about the newest technological advances, and better able to carry their message to the school board and beyond the library walls. A healthy attitude toward change and flexibility was demonstrated through the adoption of newer teaching strategies and collaborative ventures adopted and assimilated both within and outside the school.

The role of the school library media specialist changed dramatically over the 1980s and 1990s. No longer the keepers of the books, they became an integral part of the instructional process. They are the information literacy advocates of the school who have their own curriculum. According to Chelton (1999), they are "instructional collaborators with teachers, information-seeking process facilitators, and information literacy or problem-solving instructors in their instructional roles" (p. 275). They are computer technologists, Internet authorities, information specialists, and administrators of the biggest instructional program of the school. Although school library media specialists wear many hats, they need "supportive administrators and teachers; use of new technology, including the Internet; professional development opportunities, their own abilities and attitudes; adequate funding; and clerical support" to expand their roles (McCracken, 2001, p. 8).

Information Power (AASL & AECT, 1998) standards expanded the role of school library media specialist. They added the roles of instructional partner and program administrator to the already existing roles of teacher and information specialist. These standards emphasize flexible scheduling, collaborative planning and information literacy as major components in the school library media center's own curriculum. As *instructional partners,* school library media specialists work collaboratively with teachers, administrators and other school constituents to facilitate the students' awareness of information literacy as a lifelong learning goal. In this role, the school media specialist works collaboratively to determine links among information needs of students across curriculum content using a wide array of resources. As a *program administrator,* school library media specialists play a pivotal role in planning and designing a student-centered media program that supports ideas of collaboration, technology, and leadership. As a *teacher,* the school library media specialist collaborates with students and teachers to determine information and learning needs, to determine resources to meet needs, and to communicate content of the information found. As an *information specialist,* the school library media specialist is instrumental in modeling leadership and providing expertise in acquiring or evaluating resources in all formats. Bringing this knowledge into collaborative relationships, the school library media specialist is an advocate for the library media program and uses flexible scheduling to enhance its implementation (AASL & AECT, 1998).

Information Power (AASL & AECT, 1998) places information literacy standards as the center of focus in the guidelines, which influences how school library media specialists are perceived in their schools. The standards for student learning set the stage for flexible scheduling and collaboration, emphasizing inclusion of information literacy in the curriculum. In this time of information proliferation throughout society, it is crucial that information literacy is taught in schools if students are to live successful lives in the future. Because school library media specialists are proficient in teaching information literacy skills, they are moving to center stage as instructional leaders in the school. Their status is taking an upward turn as they are recognized as information literacy consultants.

At the same time that information literacy is magnifying the role of school library media specialists, a shortage of personnel to fill school media positions is becoming rampant because of retirements and the addition of new positions. One of the major needs of the field is currently being addressed through the appointment in 2001 of an AASL Task Force for the Recruitment of Media Specialists to the profession. The 2000s will see even more drastic changes than the 1990s because of the increased need for information specialists to decipher information on the Internet.

It is predicted that school library media centers will become more virtual reality entities where students access their resources from their computers at home. School library media specialists are becoming more valued as instructional leaders in their schools. Three events in 2002–2003 bear witness to the fact that library media centers are getting more attention and that school library media specialists make a real difference in student learning in schools: (1) the 2002 White House Conference on school libraries shows a greater awareness of the role of media centers in the instructional program of the schools, (2) the increase in research studies in a number of states showing the impact of school media centers on student achievement, and (3) the awarding of grants to over 130 school library media centers nationwide through the Laura Bush Foundation for new library materials (School libraries receive Bush Foundation grants, 2003).

Because of the research that shows the connection between student achievement and the school media center's role in improving standardized test scores, school officials are beginning to slowly acknowledge the necessity of having trained school library media specialists and well-stocked school media centers that can provide physical as well as virtual services to their students and faculty of the twenty-first century (Lance, et al., 1993; Lance, et al., 2000a; Lance, et al., 2000b; Lance, et al., 2000c).

REFERENCES

American Association of School Librarians. (1960). *Standards for school library programs.* Chicago: Author.

American Association of School Librarians. (2004, March 22). *AASL position statement on the role of the school library media specialist in site-based management.* Retrieved April 1, 2004 from the ALA web site: http://www.ala.org/ala/aasl/aaslproftools/positionstatements/aaslpositionstatementroleschool.htm

American Association of School Librarians & Association for Educational Communications and Technology. (1975). *Media programs: District and school.* Chicago: Author.

American Association of School Librarians & Association for Educational Communications and Technology. (1988). *Information power: Guidelines for school library media programs.* Chicago: Author.

American Association of School Librarians & Association for Educational Communications and Technology. (1998). *Information power: Building partnerships for learning.* Chicago: Author.

American Association of School Librarians & Department of Audiovisual Instruction. (1969). *Standards for school media programs.* Chicago: Author.

American Library Association Committee on Post-War Planning. (1945). *School libraries for today and tomorrow.* Chicago: Author.

American Library Association Office of Public Relations. (2000, May). *Key library issues & messages for Congress.* Retrieved April 1, 2004, from the ALA web site: http://archive.ala.org/washoff/keyissues05.pdf

Bertot, John C. (2000, January). Universal service in the networked environment: The education rate (e-rate) debate. *Journal of Academic Librarianship, 26*(1), 45–48.

Board of Education, Island Trees Union Free School District No. 26 et al. v. Pico et al. (1985). *U.S. Reports.* Vol. 457. Washington, DC: U.S. Government Printing Office, 853–921.

Charles C. Certain Committee. (1986). *Standard library organization and equipment for secondary schools of different sizes.* In Melvin M. Bowie (Comp.), *Historic documents of school libraries* (pp. 34–51). Littleton, CO: Hi Willow Research and Publishing. (Original work published 1920, Chicago: American Library Association)

Charles C. Certain Committee. (1986). *Elementary school library standards*. In Melvin M. Bowie (Comp.), *Historic documents of school libraries* (pp. 52–71). Littleton, CO: Hi Willow Research and Publishing. (Original work published 1925, Chicago: American Library Association)

Chelton, Mary K. (1999). Structural and theoretical constraints on reference service in a high school library media center. *Reference & User Services Quarterly, 38*(3), 275–282.

Diehl, Carol L. (1989, Fall). White House conference on library and information services. *Indiana Media Journal, 12*(1), 11.

Donaldson, Eric. (1991, August). Delegates create policy proposals for improved library and information services. *Discovery*, 1–2. (The newspaper of the 1991 White House conference on library and information science.)

Elementary school libraries, 12th yearbook. (1933, June). In *National Elementary Principal, 12*, 117–576.

Fargo, Lucille. (1933). *The library in the school* (2nd rev. ed.). Chicago: American Library Association.

Goldberg, Beverly. (2003, August). Supreme Court upholds CIPA: Libraries to revisit their bottom lines. *American Libraries, 34*(7), 12–14.

Greenman, E.D. (1913, April). The development of secondary school libraries. *Library Journal*, 38, 184.

Hall, Mary E. (1915, September). The development of the modern high school library. *Library Journal, 40*, 63.

Henne, Frances. (1951). *A planning guide for the high school library program*. Chicago: American Library Association.

Henry, N.B. (Ed.). (1943). *The library in general education*. Chicago: University of Chicago.

Institute of Museum and Library Services. (2002). White House Conference on School Libraries. Proceedings, Tuesday, June 4, 2002. Washington, DC: Author.

Johnson, B. Lamar. (1933). The secondary school library. *National Survey of Secondary Education Monograph No. 17.* Washington, DC: U.S. Office of Education.

Lance, Keith C., et al. (1993). *The impact of school library media centers on academic achievement*. Castle Rock, CO: Hi Willow Research and Publishing.

Lance, Keith C., et al. (2000a). *How school librarians help kids achieve standards: The second Colorado study*. San Jose, CA: Hi Willow Research and Publishing.

Lance, Keith C., et al. (2000b). *Information empowered: The school librarian as an agent of academic achievement in Alaska schools* (Rev. ed.). Juneau, AK: Alaska State Library.

Lance, Keith C., et al. (2000c). *Measuring up to standards: The impact of school library programs & information literacy in Pennsylvania schools*. Greensburg, PA: Pennsylvania Citizens for Better Libraries.

Laura Bush Foundation for America's Libraries. (2002, June 4). *Washington White House conference on school libraries checks out lessons for success*. Retrieved March 30, 2004, from: http://www.laurabushfoundation.org/release_060402.html

Legislative Day. (1990, April 30). *ALA Washington Newsletter, 42*,1.

Libraries and Educational Technology. (2003). In *Digest of Education Statistics 2002* (chapter 7). Retrieved March 30, 2004, from the National Center for Educational Statistics web site: http://nces.ed.gov/pubs2003/2003060g.pdf

Literacy, democracy, and productivity: Governor's 1990 conference. (1990, February). *NYLA Bulletin, 38*(2), 1.

McCracken, Anne. (2001). School library media specialists' perceptions of practice and importance of roles described in *Information Power. School Library Media Research Online,* Vol. 4. Retrieved March 30, 2004, from the ALA web site: http://www.ala.org/ala/aasl/aaslpubsandjournals/slmrb/slmrcontents/volume42001/mccracken.htm

McDonald, Dale. (2001, April/May). E-rate for everyone. *Momentum, 32*(2), 77–78.

National library legislative day 2003. (2004). Retrieved April 15, 2004 from the ALA web site: http://www.ala.org/ala/washoff/washevents/nlld/nationallibrary.htm

National Study of Secondary School Evaluation. (1969). *Evaluative criteria for the evaluation of secondary schools.* Washington, DC: American Council on Education. (ERIC Document No. ED 034 312).

New York Department of Public Instruction. (1900). *Report of committee on the relation of public libraries to public schools.* Appointed by authority of the National Council at the meeting of the National Education Association held in Washington, DC, 1898. Forty-sixth annual report of the state superintendent for the school year ending July 1, 1899. Transmitted to Legislature, April 5, 1900. Albany, NY: Author.

Report of the task force on the role of the school library media program in networking. (1978). Washington, DC: National Commission on Libraries and Information Science.

School libraries receive Bush Foundation grants. (2003, August). *American Libraries, 34*(7), 33.

Towards a national program for library and information services: Goals for action. (1975). Washington, DC: National Commission on Library and Information Science.

U.S. Bureau of Education. (1986). *Public libraries in the United States of America: Their history, condition, and management.* In Melvin M. Bowie (Comp.), *Historic documents of school libraries.* San Jose, CA: Hi Willow Research and Publishing. (Original work published 1876, Washington, DC: Government Printing Office)

U.S. Office of Education. (1960). *Public school library statistics, 1958–59.* Washington, DC: Author.

White House Conference on Library and Information Services. (1979). *Information for the 80's.* Washington, DC: National Commission on Library and Information Science.

Zweizig, Douglas L. and Hopkins, Dianne McAfee. (1999). *Lessons from Library Power: Enriching teaching and learning.* Westport, CT: Libraries Unlimited.

FURTHER READINGS

Ambrosio, John. (2004, May). No child left behind: The case of Roosevelt High School. *Phi Delta Kappan, 89*(9), 709–713.

American Association of School Librarians. (2000, September 5). *AASL position statement on flexible scheduling.* Retrieved April 4, 2004, from the ALA web site: http://www.ala.org/aasl/positions/ps_flexible.html

Benton Foundation. (2000, February). *The e-rate in America: A tale of four cities.* Retrieved April 4, 2004, from The Benton Foundation web site: http://www. benton.org/publibrary/e-rate/e-rate.4cities.pdf

Benton Foundation. (2002). *Great expectations: Leveraging America's investment in educational technology.* Retrieved April 4, 2004, from the Benton Foundation web site: http://www.benton.org/publibrary/e-rate/greatexpectations.pdf

Black, Susan. (2001, February). Today's school libraries are bustling centers of learning. [Electronic version]. *American School Board Journal.* Retrieved April 4, 2004, from the American School Board Journal web site: http://www. asbj.com/2001/02/0201research.html

Breivik, Patricia Senn & Senn, J. A. (1998). *Information literacy: Educating children for the 21st century* (2nd ed.). Washington, DC: National Education Association.

Cattagni, Anne & Westat, Elizabeth Farris. (2001, May). *Internet access in U.S. public schools and classrooms: 1994—2000.* Washington, DC: National Center for Education Statistics.

Craver, Kathleen W. (1986, Summer). The changing instructional role of the high school library media specialist: 1950–84. [Electronic version]. *School Library Media Quarterly, 14*(4), 183–191. Retrieved April 15, 2004, from the ALA web site: http://www.ala.org/cfapps/archive.cfm?path=aasl/SLMR/slmr_resources/ select_craver.html

Craver, Kathleen W. (1994). *School library media centers in the 21st Century: Changes and challenges.* Westport, CT: Greenwood Press.

DeCandido, GraceAnne Andreas. (1993, June). Library legislative day, Washington, DC. *Wilson Library Bulletin, 67,* 15.

DiMattia, Susan Smith. (1994, May 15). 500 supporters tell Congress to pass library legislation. *Library Journal, 119,* 14–15.

Doggett, Sandra. (2000). *Beyond the book: Technology integration into the secondary school library media curriculum.* Westport, CT: Libraries Unlimited.

Education & Library Networks Coalition. (1998). *Protect e-rate.* Retrieved April 15, 2004, from Education and Networks Coalition Library: http://www. edlinc.org/protect_erate.html

Farmer, Leslie. (2002, February). Harnessing the power in *Information Power. Teacher Librarian, 29*(3), 20–24.

Ferguson, Robert F. & Mehta, Jal. (2004, May). An unfinished journey: The legacy of Brown and the narrowing of the achievement gap. *Phi Delta Kappan, 85*(9), 656–669.

50 years of progress and struggle. (2004, May). *NEA Today, 22*(8), 22–23.

Flagg, Gordon. (1998 June/July). Legislative day advocates take their message to Capitol Hill. *American Libraries, 29*(6), 22.

Flagg, Gordon. (2000, June/July). 49 states represented at 26th library legislative day. *American Libraries, 31*(6), 20–22.

Gerald, Debra E. & Hussar, William J. (2001). Projections of educational statistics to 2010. [Electronic version]. *Education Statistics Quarterly.* Retrieved April 4, 2004, from the National Center for Educational Statistics web site: http://nces.ed.gov/pubs2001/quarterly/fall/feature_pes2010.html

Harada, Violet & Donham, Jean. (1998, September/October). Information power: Student achievement is the bottom line. *Teacher Librarian, 26*(1), 14–17.

Hartzell, Gary N. (1997, November). The invisible school librarian. *School Library Journal, 43*(11), 24–29.

Haycock, Ken. (1999, December). The national Library Power project. *Teacher Librarian, 27*(2), 34.

Hopkins, Dianne McAfee & Zweizig, Douglas L. (1999, May). Power to the media center. *School Library Journal, 45*(5), 24–27.

Hopkins, Dianne McAfee & Zweizig, Douglas. (1999, July). Student learning opportunities summarize *Library Power,* Parts 1 & 2. *School Libraries Worldwide, 5*(2), 97–110.

Johnson, Doug. (1997). *The indispensable librarian: Surviving (and thriving) in school media centers in the information age.* Worthington, OH: Linworth.

Johnson, Doug. (2001, March 28). *The seven most critical challenges that face our profession.* Retrieved April 4, 2004, from: http://www.doug-johnson.com/dougwri/7challenges.html

Lance, Keith C. & Loertscher, David V. (2001). *Powering achievement: School library media programs make a difference: The evidence.* San Jose, CA: Hi Willow Research and Publishing.

Latrobe, Kathy Howard. (1998). *The emerging school library media center: Historical issues and perspectives.* Westport, CT: Libraries Unlimited.

Latrobe, Kathy & Masters, Anne. (1999, December). The implementation of *Information Power. Teacher Librarian, 27*(2), 8.

Library Power executive summary: Findings from the national evaluation of the National Library Power Program. (1999, July 1). Retrieved April 15, 2004, from the Wallace Foundation web site: http://www.wallacefunds.org/research/research_detail.cfm?id_publication=750367861&id_topic=3&page=1

Loertscher, David. (2003, June). The digital school library: A world-wide development and a fascinating challenge. *Teacher Librarian, 30*(5), 14–27.

Looking ahead: School administration. (1998, January). *School Planning and Management.* Retrieved April 4, 2004, from: http://monte.k12.co.us/admin/lookahead.htm

Lowe, Carrie A. (2000). *The role of the school library media specialist in the 21st century. ERIC Digests* (ERIC Identifier ED 446 769). Retrieved April 4, 2004, from: http://www.ed.gov/databases/ERIC_Digests/ed446769.html

McCabe, Ron. (2003, August). The CIPA ruling as reality therapy. *American Libraries, 34*(7), 14–15.

McQuillan, Jeff. (1998). *The literacy crisis.* Portsmouth, NH: Heinemann.

Miller, Marilyn L. (2000, December). Media specialists are still librarians, and reading is still the key to success. *American Libraries, 31*(11), 42–43.

Miller, Marilyn L. (Ed.). (2003). *Pioneers and leaders in library services to youth: A biographical dictionary.* Westport, CT: Libraries Unlimited.

National Center for Education Statistics. *School Library Media Centers: 1993–94.* (1998). Retrieved April 4, 2004, from National Center for Education Statistics web site: http://nces.ed.gov/pubs98/98282.pdf

Oberg, Dianne, Hay, Lyn, and Henry, James. (2000). The role of the principal in an information literate school community: Cross-country comparisons from an international research project. [Electronic version]. *School Library Media Research.* Retrieved April 4, 2004, from the ALA web site: http://www.ala.org/ala/aasl/aaslpubsandjournals/slmrb/slmrcontents/volume32000/principal.htm

Olën, Sandra I.I. (1998). Information literacy and the virtual library. *Mousaion, 16*(2), 55–68.

Olsen, Renee. (2000, February.) The good fight: A band of subversives in Ohio is thwarting site-based management. *School Library Journal, 46*(2), 9.

Position Statement on the Value of Independent Reading in School Library Media Program. (1999, July). Retrieved April 4, 2004, from the ALA web site: http://www.ala.org/aasl/positions/ps_independent.html

Position Statement on the Value of Library Media Programs in Education. (2000, September). Retrieved from the ALA web site: http://www.ala.org/aasl/positions/ps_value.html

Putnam, Eleanor. (1996, Fall). The instructional consultant role of the elementary-school library media specialist and the effects of program scheduling on its practice. *School Library Media Quarterly, 25*(1), 43–49. Retrieved April 15, 2004, from the ALA web site: http://www.ala.org/ala/aasl/aaslpubsandjournals/slmrb/editorschoiceb/infopower/selectputnam.htm

Ramsey, Inez. (n.d.). *School libraries—History.* Retrieved May 6, 2004, from: http://falcon.jmu.edu/~ramseyil/libhistory.htm

Role of the school library media specialist in site-based management. (2001, April). Retrieved April 4, 2004, from the ALA web site: http://www.ala.org/aasl/positions/ps_sitemgmt.html

Schneider, Karen G. (2003, August). Let's begin the discussion: What now? *American Libraries, 34*(7), 14–15.

Shannon, Donna M. (1996). Tracking the transition to a flexible access library program in two *Library Power* elementary schools. [Electronic version]. *School Library Media Quarterly, 24*(3), 155–163. Retrieved April 15, 2004, from the ALA web site: http://www.ala.org/ala/aasl/aaslpubsandjournals/slmrb/editorschoiceb/infopower/selectshannon.htm

Simpson, Carol. (1996, November). The school librarian's role in the electronic age. *ERIC Digests* (ERIC Identifier ED 402 928). Retrieved April 4, 2004, from: http://www.ed.gov/databases/ERIC_Digests/ED402928.html

The status of library media center support of student achievement. (2000, September 1). Retrieved April 4, 2004, from the Library Research Service web site: http://www.lrs.org/documents/fastfacts/169crisis.pdf

U.S. Department of Education. National Center for Education Statistics. (1998). *School library media centers: 1993–94.* (NCES 98–282). Washington, DC: Office of Educational Research and Improvement. Retrieved from National Center for Education Statistics web site: http://nces.ed.gov/pubs98/98282.pdf

Update on e-rate funding. (2001, May 11). Government Accounting Office Report: Federal Document Clearing House, Inc. Retrieved April 4, 2004, from: http://www.gao.gov/new.items/d01672.pdf

Update on state-level funding by category of service. (2001, May 11). Government Accounting Office Report: Federal Document Clearing House, Inc. Retrieved April 4, 2004, from: http://www.gao.gov/new.items/d01673.pdf

Van Deusen, Jean Donham & Tallman, Julie I. (1994, Fall). The impact of scheduling on curriculum from consultation and information skills instruction: Part one: The 1993–94 AASL/Highsmith research award study. *School Library Media Quarterly, 23*(1), 17–25.

Wohlstetter, Priscilla & Mohrman, Susan Albers. (1994, December). *School-based management: Promise and process.* Retrieved April 4, 2004, from the U.S. Department of Education web site: http://www.ed.gov/pubs/CPRE/fb5sbm.html

Woolls, Blanche. (2004). *The school library media manager* (3rd ed.). Westport, CT: Libraries Unlimited.

Chapter 2

FORGING PARTNERSHIPS TOWARD INFORMATION LITERACY

Less than fifty years ago, the school library was simply a small classroom lined with books that was underutilized by students and faculty alike, except for occasional recreational reading. School libraries have evolved over the years in how they are used and their functions in the educational setting. At one time, they were totally book oriented, but the school library media centers of today use all types of media for instruction; they are automated and they utilize the Internet for information gathering. The school library media center program is student-centered, is integrated into the curriculum, and is a laboratory for teaching and learning.

This chapter discusses partnerships and the school library media specialist as a proactive leader, collaborating with teachers. Partnerships within and outside the school are addressed as well as communication links. A brief discussion of search engines and web-based research follows as a communication tool. The chapter concludes with a discussion of the school library media specialist as a change agent and as a program administrator.

To understand how far media centers have come, it is necessary to look backward. Only two decades ago, school library media centers were viewed as storehouses for materials by government officials and the public in general, which gave little credence to their impact on teaching and learning. The lack of understanding of the public to the impact of school library media centers to enhance learning came with the writing of *A Nation At Risk* (1983), a report of the National Commission on Excellence in Education, which made little or no reference to school libraries and their impact on education. A resounding response from librarians, *Alliance for Excellence* (1984), followed outlining recommendations for forming alliances among the school, home, and library for the attainment of educational excellence, where the library is central to the learning process. According to the report, school library media specialists hold the key to the knowledge of the future as well as the key to teaching how information can be accessed. An underlying theme of both reports is the need for lifelong learning in finding and using information effectively. These two reports placed the school library media center in a position to make an impact on information literacy implementation in schools.

Another report written by the American Library Association's Task Force on Excellence in Education, *Realities: Educational Reform in a Learning Society* (1984), summarizes the basic relationship between the goals of education and school library media centers:

> Good schools enable students to acquire and use knowledge, to experience and enjoy discovery and learning, to understand themselves and other people, to develop lifelong learning skills, and to function productively in a democratic society. Libraries are essential to each of these tasks. In libraries, students learn how to locate, organize, and use information that will expand their horizons and raise their self-expectations. Librarians are teachers, and they serve both students and teachers.
>
> As students develop library skills in finding information, they seek more information, compare and evaluate sources and opinions, and develop critical thinking. These skills, which should be a part of every school's curriculum, can be learned in school libraries.
>
> School libraries serve as learner-oriented laboratories which support, extend, and individualize the school's curriculum (p. 4).

There is still a lack of understanding by government officials and the public today regarding the role of the school media program serving as a catalyst in the educational reform movement to improve instruction. School library media centers and their role in the improvement of student achievement scores is still being overlooked, although research has shown their impact on instruction (Baughman, 2000; Baxter & Smalley, 2003; Burgin & Bracy, 2003; Gaver, 1963; Lance, et al., 1993; Lance, 1994; Lance, et al., 1999; Lance, et al., 2000a; Lance, et al., 2000b; Lance, et al., 2000c; Lance, et al., 2001; Lance, et al., 2002; Manzo, 2000; Rodney, et al., 2002; Smith, 2001).

The document, *America 2000: An Education Strategy Sourcebook* (U.S. Department of Education, 1991) was released as the result of an education summit held in February 1989 by the president and the nation's governors.

Six education goals were defined to serve as a strategy for the nation by the year 2000. Of the six National Education Goals developed at the summit, four of the goals offer a direct challenge for school media centers: (1) all students will become competent in challenging subject matter, (2) teachers will have the knowledge and skills they need, (3) every adult American will be literate, and (4) schools will promote parental involvement and participation. *America 2000* evolved into *Goals 2000* and both became the offspring of the earlier document, *A Nation At Risk* (*Goals 2000,* 1998; Ohanian, 2000).

Two additional educational summits have been held since 1989, one in 1996 and then another in 1999. Educators were excluded from participation in the first two summits as the governors, the president, and businessmen decided the future of education for the nation's children. The 1996 summit initiated the idea that all states should have standards by which to judge whether schools were doing their job as educational institutions. For the first time, educators were invited to the 1999 conference, which embraced the idea of developing state standards and national tests. According to a report, "Did You Know...," in *Gifted Child Today* (2001):

> Forty-nine states have state academic standards; 3 states have clear and specific standards in all core subjects at all grade levels. Fifty states have assessments. Ten states have aligned criterion-referenced tests in all subjects at all grade levels. Twenty-seven states have school-level ratings. Seven states have extra funding for all low performing schools. Eighteen states have exit exams that are currently required for a diploma. Nine states finance remediation for failing students. (p. 13)

Ferrandino (2000) notes three challenges identified by the 1999 summit "to improve teacher quality, help all students achieve high standards, and strengthen accountability for results" (p. 56). School media centers are not mentioned in any of the summits as a means to improving student achievement scores although research shows that schools with well-equipped school media centers with professionally trained school media specialists are more likely to have higher student achievement scores. (Baughman, 2000; Baxter & Smalley, 2003; Burgin & Bracy, 2003; Gaver, 1963; Lance, et al., 1993; Lance, 1994; Lance, et al., 1999; Lance, et al., 2000a; Lance, et al., 2000b; Lance, et al., 2000c; Lance, et al., 2001; Lance, et al., 2002; Manzo, 2000; Rodney, et al., 2002; Smith, 2001).

School media centers today operate in a society in which the proliferation of information resources is endemic and technological change occurs so rapidly that schools must struggle financially to keep abreast of the latest trends that are applicable to the learning environment. Out of this context *Information Power: Partnerships for Learning* ([AASL & AECT], 1998) was developed. The standards provide the philosophical foundation for the development of school library media programs to meet the needs of students in becoming information literate and faculty in becoming teaching partners in the learning environment. *Information Power: Guidelines for a School Media Center* (AASL & AECT, 1988) was the first set of standards to define the role of the school media specialist as an instructional consultant. However, two earlier authors, Philip Turner, *Helping Teacher Teach* (1985), and David Loertscher, *Taxonomies of the School Library Media Program* (1988) were instrumental in promoting the concept of instructional design used by school library media specialists in working with teachers. The latest standards, *Information Power: Building Partnerships for Learning* (AASL & AECT, 1998) focuses on student-centered learning where information literacy is the major focus supported through inquiry-based learning. This chapter will explore the impact of this set of qualitative guidelines on school library media centers in developing proactive leadership roles for school library media specialists, promoting collaboration between the school media specialist and teachers, fostering the formation of partnerships within the school constituency, developing links of communication within and outside the school, utilizing technology to enhance information literacy and research, and identifying the school library media specialist as a change agent and as a program administrator.

PROACTIVE LEADERSHIP ROLES OF THE SCHOOL LIBRARY MEDIA SPECIALIST

For many years, the school library media specialist was perceived as the keeper of the books, but today that stereotypical image is far from accurate. School library media specialists, as their name implies, are leaders in promoting the use of all types of media from books to CD-ROMs to computer software. The person administering the school library media program is a leader who is proactive in providing services to the school community. Being proactive means that the school media specialist anticipates a service before it is needed and is instrumental in promoting the service to library users. The school library media center, for many years static and passive, is now a dynamic, active, and aggressive program involved in the improvement of teaching and learning. The *Information Power* (AASL & AECT, 1998) guidelines provide the impetus for the school library media specialist to assume proactive, visionary leadership roles in working with other educators to provide students and faculty with the best school library media program possible. The program, designed by the school library media specialist, promotes the use of technology, determines staff development training needs, and allows active participation in staff development activities. The focal point of the school media center services is integrating the information literacy skills into all subject areas of the school curriculum. The media specialist, as a leader in school reform, becomes an instructional partner with teachers and serves as the bridge to help teachers make the connections between inquiry-based learning and information literacy skills throughout the curriculum at all grade levels.

Assertive leadership is required in working with administrators to develop school media programs that are planned to provide service that is vital, innovative, and educationally sound. In working with teachers, the school media specialist must have a clear understanding of the requirements for making the media center an integral part of the school curriculum and its potential for impact on the teaching/learning outcomes of the school. Students must recognize the expertise of the school media specialist as a credible leader who translates their educational and recreational needs into effective programs, services, and activities. The *Information Power* (AASL & AECT, 1998) guidelines identify the school media specialist as the leader who can help learners to achieve information literacy and to understand its implications.

Being a proactive leader means that the media specialist reaches out to the whole school community both within and outside the school to promote services of the library media center. Initiating programs that are needed to promote a better learning environment is one way to show proactive leadership capabilities. Leadership is needed to provide the direct teaching of information literacy skills to students, in partnership with teachers, as an important component of information services.

Information Power (AASL & AECT, 1998) fosters the emergence of the school library media specialist as an educational leader who is perceived as a viable, dynamic leader making changes in schools which are exciting, educationally sound, and stimulating. The far-reaching presence of the school media specialist is felt because of the four leadership roles introduced: the information specialist, the teacher, the instructional partner, and the program administrator. All four roles put school media specialists into the mainstream of the school's instructional program. With the appropriate leadership in implementing the roles, the school media specialist can make a tremendous difference in what students learn and how they are taught. *Information Power* (AASL & AECT, 1998) puts school media specialists in the center of what is being taught in this statement:

> As the essential link who connects students, teachers, and others with the information resources they need, the library media specialist plays a unique and pivotal role in the learning community. (p.4)

Collaboration between the school library media specialist and teachers makes a difference in how students learn and in their achievement.

Collaboration Between Library Media Specialists and Teachers

Collaboration suggests the idea that two or more people plan, teach, and evaluate instruction together. The Library Power project is an example of testing collaboration between media specialists, teachers and principals. These educators found that student achievement scores increased as the result of collaboration. It usually takes from three to five years for collaboration to become a normal part of the instructional program in a school.

The school library media specialist is knowledgeable about the current technological trends and effectively uses that knowledge to promote collaboration and partnerships with teachers. Being a technology leader in schools is an important factor for changing attitudes toward media specialists and their place on the instructional team. Their technological expertise is recognized and valued by their colleagues. For teachers, the library media specialist becomes a more visible leader who is actively involved in the research process using technology. The library media specialist anticipates research needs and provides training in technology and information literacy skills to satisfy those needs. Teaching information literacy skills becomes a joint effort with teachers when the media specialist can provide technological instruction for them and their students. The library media specialist serves as the leader to foster collaboration and build instructional teams throughout the school and into the community. Being a visible leader is crucial.

The principal is a key factor in supporting collaboration. The principal may offer substitutes for teachers to collaboratively plan with the media specialist. Evaluating teachers on their collaborative activities with the media specialist makes a tremendous difference in implementing information technology literacy within a school. The principal's expectation that collaboration will take place is what spurs collaboration in most schools.

Teachers are reluctant to collaborate, but when they see their colleagues reaping the benefits of working with the media specialist, they are willing to accept the challenge. The media specialist is commonly the one who initiates the idea of collaboration. Once collaboration becomes an established procedure in the school, teachers have a tendency to want to collaborate across grade levels and curriculum areas. Students are the benefactors of collaboration in how they are taught and what they learn.

The school library media specialist described in *Information Power* (AASL & AECT, 1998) is a leader who has the capability of uniting and forging partnerships within the entire educational community for better instruction.

PARTNERSHIPS WITHIN THE SCHOOL CONSTITUENCY

The *Information Power* (ALA & AECT, 1998) guidelines provide a plan for school media specialists to form full partnerships in the educational community. Collaboration is the keystone by which partnerships are built. Partnerships must include all stakeholders in the educational process, including principals, other administrators, teachers and students—those people directly involved in the services provided by the school media center. The idea of developing partnerships is presented in the document, *Alliance for Excellence* (1984), which was the forerunner of *Information Power* (AASL & AECT, 1988). The premise for such an alliance is that all constituents in the learning process must plan together to design and implement a school library media program that best meets the instructional needs of the school. One result of building alliances within the school constituency is the creation of open communication lines that set the stage for developing consensus regarding what is to be learned and how lessons are taught. The school library media specialist is strategically positioned to foster alliances at all levels, and one of the most important is the partnership with the principal.

Partnerships with Principals

Principals make the difference in excellent schools—a fact supported by research studies for many years. Principals are acknowledged at the 1999 educational summit as the key to successful schools. Delaware Governor Thomas Carper made this statement about principals: "I've never been in a great school where they don't have a great principal." (Olson & Hoff, 1999,

p. 1, 20). Just as the principal makes a difference in schools, the principal is also the key to the quality of the school library media programs within schools.

There are many commonalities in the jobs of the principal and the school media specialist. They are basically the only two people who have a "wide-angle view of the school's instructional program" (Pennock, 1988, p. 118). They are the only people in the school who work with both faculty and students in all curricular areas. Both of them manage a budget and they share a concern that all curricular areas are represented in their budget (Brevik & Senn, 1998, p. 26). Both of them must deal effectively with the entire faculty and staff on a daily basis. This commonality is an excellent beginning point for a productive partnership between the principal and the school library media specialist.

> Since the library media specialist is presumed an expert in the functions of the library media program and the principal is presumed expert in the organization and operation of the school's total program, sharing of professional knowledge and control seems appropriate (Naylor & Jennings, 1988, p. 239).

Both principal and school library media specialist have much to gain in a collaborative partnership. According to Haycock (1999), "both the principal and the teacher-librarian need to accept responsibility for developing teacher awareness and commitment to collaborative program planning and teaching" (p. 83). They need each other to fulfill their roles. The principal needs the school library media specialist to integrate the classroom with the school library media center by providing instructional expertise in connecting the two components. The school library media specialist needs the principal to integrate the classroom with the school media center by providing administrative support for developing an information literacy curriculum. The principal can promote the school library media specialist as a curriculum partner with teachers by expecting them both to work together on curriculum projects and to integrate information literacy across the curriculum (Kearney, 2000). By building a partnership with the principal, the school library media specialist gains support both administratively and financially for the school media program. According to Gary Hartzell (1994), the media specialist who has a strong relationship with the principal is more likely to be more visible to teachers and to be in a better position to form alliances with them. On the other hand, the principal gains a school that collaboratively functions to provide quality education for students. The school media specialist collaborates with teachers to integrate the information literacy standards into the curriculum. This collaboration places the library media center into a central role in student learning. According to *Information Power* (AASL & AECT, 1998) the principal provides administrative support by communicating to teachers and others in the community the school media program's contribution to student learning. Both partners need each other to accomplish their shared goals and to build partnerships with teachers and community leaders.

Partnerships with Teachers

Developing collegial partnerships between teachers and school library media specialist has a far-reaching impact on the instructional program of the school. One result of such partnerships is that instruction is more technologically research-oriented and less textbook-oriented. The subject content of the courses is totally integrated with the resources available in the school library media center, on the Internet, and, in some cases, with resources obtained outside the school. As teachers are required to teach the content standards, the library media specialist is in a position to connect them to the information literacy standards and to show similarities between the two standards as a collaborative planning tool.

Lessons are taught differently when the classroom teacher and the school library media specialist develop a collaborative partnership. Partnerships are formed around the teaching of information literacy skills within the curriculum where the media specialist and the teacher plan together how the content will be presented. From this perspective, the school library media specialist is a teacher, just like her colleagues, with her own goals, objectives, and curriculum. A variety of resources are used in teaching, including media in many formats. Teaching duties are shared between the teacher and the school library media specialist—it really does not matter who performs the actual teaching because they have planned the lesson together. Each partner is capable of teaching any of the lessons, however, a rule of thumb is that the partner with the most subject expertise will teach it. Students are the benefactors when they experience lessons taught by the person who has the most expertise. Instruction is improved and student learning is enhanced.

As teachers accept the school library media specialist as a member of the instructional team, they begin to see a need for more planning time to design instruction. Because of the need for planning time to develop a teaching partnership, flexible scheduling becomes more appealing. Flexible scheduling of the library media center allows collaboration to flourish because there are no time constraints to hinder the learning process.

As a member of the educational team, the school library media specialist forms a network with teachers who share the philosophy that the library media center is central to the instructional process and that information literacy is crucial to guide students to become critical thinkers and lifelong learners.

Partnerships with teachers include exploring ways to do research on how students learn and the impact of different learning strategies in terms of improved student learning. Not only can teaching strategies be studied, but the school media center's role in the instructional program can be evaluated as well to determine how students might be partners in the learning process.

Partnerships with Students

A paucity of information is provided in library literature about students and school media specialists working together to form partnerships. Nevertheless, the impact of *Information Power* (AASL & AECT, 1998) is evident when students are involved in planning for school library media activities. Partnerships with students are formed when they serve as part of an advisory committee to plan, evaluate, and promote school library media services. Asking students for input in the selection and evaluation of materials is another way to develop partnerships. Students can be encouraged to serve as advisors in the development of school library media center policies and in the creation of new learning activities, such as maintenance of the media center's homepage on the web. When students are directly involved in planning activities that affect them, they are more supportive of the school library media program, and their use of the media center increases. Students who feel ownership in the school media program and its instructional program have a better attitude about learning as well as a better attitude about the policies and the services of the center. Keeping communication lines open for their input is essential for a sound program because they are the primary targets of instruction. Forging partnerships with other agencies and community leaders can benefit the school.

Partnerships with Others in the Community

Forming partnerships with people and agencies in the community can be as large as the imagination of the school library media specialist and the teacher partners. Strong parental and community involvement is recommended as partnerships are forged. School library media centers that create links between their programs and their communities are not the exception to the rule. Within this context of connection to the community, Maxwell (1999) forged a variety of partnerships to gain support for the school library media center program at Hamilton Elementary School in Nashville, Tennessee. He suggested that possible partnerships might include:

- *Public library partnerships* are forged to gain access to resources in a bookmobile and to participate in reading programs as well as other activities of the public library.
- *University partnerships* are formed where faculty from elementary or secondary schools serve as adjunct faculty at the local university bringing their perspective of collaboration to potential teachers.
- *News/Electronic media partnerships* are established to provide a connection to the news media by promoting the school library media center through announcing uplifting news about its programs.
- *Professional partnerships* are formed by offering technology workshops or classes to professional teaching staff, or to librarians in other schools.
- *Business partnerships* are built with bookstores, media groups, foundations, technology corporations and any number of other businesses where the school library media center is the recipient of gifts of books, software and computers, donation of volunteer time, and food for special events. Businesses and schools frequently share training of personnel and participate in cooperatively planned projects. Some businesses share school facilities, such as gyms, auditoriums, or media centers for group meetings.
- *Educational partnerships* are created for parents who want to learn to use computers through instruction offered by the school library media specialist.
- *School partnerships* are formed with other schools in the community through cooperative projects such as providing food, clothing, and other resources for needy students or by donating magazines for a remedial reading assistance class.
- *Non-profit organization partnerships* are established with senior citizen organizations that provide the media center with support volunteer services.
- *In-house partnerships* are shaped to connect paraprofessionals in the school with school library media programs to provide educational services, such as training of student assistants.
- *Stakeholders partnerships* are designed to utilize parents, grandparents, and legal guardians as classroom assistants or as library assistants.

School library media specialists who want to bring about effective school change must take on additional roles as facilitators, community leaders, school reform advocates, instructional leaders, curriculum consultants, mentors, and lobbyists. Partnerships throughout the community are necessary if they are to better serve their students, parents, teachers and their communities. Proactive leadership is the key to developing community partnerships where the school library media center is a viable information literacy service center. Developing partnerships within and outside schools means building communication links to support the school media center program.

LINKS OF COMMUNICATION WITHIN AND OUTSIDE THE SCHOOL

Information Power (AASL & AECT, 1998) draws attention to the importance of communication links between members of the school constituency and agencies outside the school as a real force for achieving educational excellence and as a way to develop community partnerships. Communication is essential at all levels both within and outside the school if the school library media center is to function properly.

The school library media specialist must be the primary link between the principal, the teachers, the students, the neighboring libraries, and the professional associations. Developing links in the chain of communication within the school has a great impact on the media center program because all constituencies are working together toward a common goal—the improvement of learning. *Information Power* (AASL & AECT, 1998) identifies communication as a crucial tool in the development of exemplary school media programs. The school library media center is placed at the center of the instructional program because it is an integral part of the curriculum. Communication within the school is the first step toward that goal.

Communication Within the School

Communication with the principal is crucial if the school library media program is to flourish. Rather than taking a passive role, the school library media specialist is proactive and takes the initiative to communicate to the principal plans for the school library media program. For example, the school media specialist develops a budget for the school media center based on needs for developing an excellent instructional program that serves the entire school constituency. Frequently, principals give school library media specialists a lump sum budget based on funds available rather than what is needed for an exemplary program. Being able to communicate effectively regarding budget needs or any other program needs is an example of being a proactive initiator.

All phases of the school library media program need to be communicated to the principal, including present and future plans. Keeping the principal informed of how the library media center program is progressing and how well it is functioning is one of the most effective tools for insuring good communication. Formal written reports, such as monthly and annual reports, are normally delivered in person. When delivering the reports, it is a good time to talk to the principal about goals and objectives for the coming year and for three years in the future. The annual report can be used to promote the school library media center in the following ways: as a public relations tool to sell the library services to the school constituency, as a means to educate the public about school library media services, and as an evaluation tool.

Communicating with the faculty about their instructional needs and working with them to assure that students develop information literacy skills provides the basis for creative use of resources and a common ground for working together to achieve mutual goals. *Information Power* (ALA & AECT, 1998) identifies communication as the link between the classroom teacher and the media specialist needing to be nurtured. When there is a good working relationship between school library media specialists and teachers, the curriculum is taught not only for content, but also with the idea of developing in students critical thinking skills, visual and auditory skills, and information literacy skills simultaneously.

Students who communicate with the school library media specialist and their teachers about their instructional needs have learned that they are indeed the masters of their own fate regarding the resources and technology they need for research. The school library media specialist who develops a communication link with students, inviting their participation in policy development, materials selection, and activity planning for the school library media center is aware of the payoffs from such a partnership. When students are an integral part of the planning process for library media center activities, they are more likely to make the media center a part of their daily lives.

A major emphasis of *Information Power* (AASL & AECT, 1998) is the advocacy of communication within the school between students, principals, teachers, and school media specialists. The result of such communication is a school that meets the instructional needs of all students through collaborative planning by all school constituents. The key person in developing communication within and outside the school is the school library media specialist, who serves as a proactive initiator to start the chain of communication rolling.

Communication Outside the School

As vital as in-school communication is, it is equally important for the school library media specialist to develop networks with people outside the school. Given the financial constraints of schools, school library media specialists are compelled to go beyond the school to build networks with people that allow the exchange of ideas, technology, and resources. The result may include access to information through the Internet, online catalogs developed cooperatively with other libraries, interlibrary loans, or formal networks. Technology links students in the learning community to the outside world around the globe through electronic mail, listservs, and newsgroups. Connections between the school library media program and families of students are easily done through technology. Community resources, such as museums, public and university libraries, and other public agencies, are easily accessible through the Internet. Distance learning is becoming more widespread in the K–12 community as cooperative arrangements are made with schools and universities across district and regional boundaries. Internet links offer a broadening array of information to enhance student learning. Students have abundant information at hand to do web-based research because of the vast amount of data made available through search engines.

Web-Based Research and Search Engines

Communicating through the Internet brings the outside world into the school. Web-based research opens the world of information to both students and teachers. School library media specialists serve as the leaders in schools to teach collaboratively with teachers the information literacy skills using web-based research. Teachers, in the beginning, were technologically challenged; however, school media specialists took the initiative to train them in utilizing the Internet and search engines to find information for research. The Internet serves as the teaching ground for information literacy skills, and the search engines are the tools. Crucial to using the Internet is the ability to locate the information needed. According to Butler (2000), many educators, government officials, and parents see the Internet as a prerequisite to developing information literacy. Just having access to the Internet is not sufficient. Finding information on the Internet is difficult whether one is a novice or an experienced Internet user. Web-based research requires training of both students and teachers in how to access pertinent materials that are relevant to the research topic. Search engines serve as a tool to pull together from many sources, the research topic at hand. Because of its vastness of information, the Internet is typically searched using a search engine such as Alta Vista (http://www. altavista.com) or Google (http://www.google.com). A search engine serves as an interface to launch a software program to find information in a database. As web sites are added to the database, robots-software is used to search for new web sites by following links already in the database—or by someone submitting a valuable link (Lawrence and Giles, 1999). A search engine can only index a fraction of information on the Internet, which explains how a search done on several search engines yields different hit results. Using search engines to search the Internet has totally changed the way that research is done. Although print materials are still used in writing research papers, web-based research is becoming more prevalent. It makes research fun and exciting because of the vastness of information available on the Internet.

As the leader in developing communication links on the Internet as well as with people, the school library media specialist is the change agent responsible for improving how the school constituency works together and for increasing access to quality resources whether they are print, non-print or Internet information.

SCHOOL LIBRARY MEDIA SPECIALIST AS A CHANGE AGENT AND PROGRAM ADMINISTRATOR

As the twenty-first century is characterized by rapid refinements in technology, the need for developing new skills and new ways for accessing and using information is evolving. In *Information Power* (AASL & AECT, 1998), the school library media specialist is challenged to prepare students for the future by acting as the change agent in schools.

Change Agent

The role as change agent necessitates the library media specialist to become a proactive initiator to develop library programs that match the instructional needs of the school. As a change agent, the school library media specialist must articulate the goals of the school library media program, communicate with all constituencies within the school, develop networks outside the school, and evaluate progress toward set goals. Being a proactive initiator means that the library media specialist must look at programs with a new perspective and be willing to act as a change agent to design new ones that match the instructional needs of the school. School library media specialists accept themselves as instructional partners because they are experts in designing instructional strategies. They do, indeed, have something to offer the teacher as a full partner of the educational team. Because of their role as program administrator, they are in a position to make changes happen in the school.

Program Administrator

Information Power (AASL & AECT, 1998) for the first time identifies the role of the school library media specialist as a program administrator. Proficient as a manager, the media specialist is responsible for the total school media program including all administrative tasks associated with the center. Responsibilities include working collaboratively with members of the school community to define policies and direct activities associated with the media center. As a program administrator, the school library media specialist acts as an advocate for the school library media program and serves as a leader with the knowledge and vision to move strategically ahead in fulfilling information literacy goals in the school. In the program administrator role, the media specialist plans, manages, and evaluates the program for quality in meeting instructional goals of the school. (AASL & AECT, 1998).

The guidelines in *Information Power* (AASL & AECT, 1998) have brought the school library media specialist into the limelight to be a vital influence as an instructional team player in the schools because of the partnerships forged both inside and outside the school.

REFERENCES

Alliance for excellence: Librarians respond to a nation at risk. (1984). Washington, DC: U.S. Government Printing Office.

American Association of School Libraries & Association for Educational Communication and Technology. (1988). *Information power: Guidelines for school library media programs.* Chicago: American Library Association.

American Association of School Libraries & Association for Educational Communication and Technology. (1998). *Information power: Partnerships for learning.* Chicago: American Library Association.

American Library Association. Task Force on Excellence in Education. (1984). *Realities: Educational reform in a learning society.* Chicago: American Library Association.

Baughman, James C. (2000, October 26). *School libraries and MCAS scores.* Retrieved March 30, 2004, from: http://web.simmons.edu/~baughman/mcas-school-libraries/Baughman%20Paper.pdf

Baxter, Susan J. & Smalley, Ann Walker. (2003). *Check it out: The results of the school library media program census. Final Report.* St. Paul, MN: Metronet. Retrieved April 4, 2004, from: http://www.metronet.lib.mn.us/survey/exsummary.pdf

Brevik, Patricia Senn & Senn, J. A. (1998). *Information literacy: Educating children for the 21st century* (2nd ed.). Washington, DC: National Education Association.

Burgin, Robert & Bracy, Pauletta Brown. (2003). *An essential connection: How quality school library media programs improve student achievement in North Carolina.* Retrieved April 4, 2004, from: http://www.rburgin.com/NCschools 2003/NCSchoolStudy.pdf

Butler, Declan. (2000). Souped-up search engines. *Nature, 405,* 112–115.

Did you know... (2001, Spring) *Gifted Child Today, 24*(2), 13.

Ferrandino, Vince. (2000, January). Reaching the summit. *Principal, 79*(3), 56.

Gaver, Mary V. (1963). *Effectiveness of centralized library services in elementary schools* (2nd ed.). New Brunswick, NJ: Rutgers University Press.

Goals 2000: Flexible funding supports state and local education reform. (1998, November 16). Washington, DC: U.S. General Accounting Office. Retrieved April 4, 2004, from the U.S. General Accounting Office: http://www.gao.gov/archive/1999/he99010.pdf

Hartzell, Gary N. (2003). *Building influence for the school librarian: Tenets, targets, tactics* (2nd ed.). Worthington, OH: Linworth.

Haycock, Ken. (1999, March). Fostering collaboration, leadership and information literacy: Common behaviors of uncommon principals and faculties. *NASSP Bulletin, 83*(605), 82–87.

Kearney, Carol A. (2000). *Curriculum partner: Redefining the role of the library media specialist.* Westport, CT: Greenwood Press.

Lance, Keith C. (1994, Spring). The impact of school library media centers on academic achievement. [Electronic version]. *School Library Media Quarterly, 22*(3). Retrieved April 4, 2004, from: http://www.ala.org/aasl/SLMR/slmr_resources/select_lance.html

Lance, Keith C., et al. (1993). *The impact of school library media centers on academic achievement.* Castle Rock, CO: Hi Willow Research and Publishing.

Lance, Keith C., et al. (2000a). *How school librarians help kids achieve standards: The second Colorado study.* San Jose, CA: Hi Willow Research and Publishing. Retrieved April 4, 2004, from: http://www.lrs.org/documents/lmcstudies/CO/execsumm.pdf

Lance, Keith C., et al. (2000b). *Information empowered: The school librarian as an agent of academic achievement in Alaska schools* (Rev. ed.). Juneau, AK: Alaska

State Library. Retrieved April 15, 2004, from Alaska State Library web site: http://www.library.state.ak.us/dev/infoemxs.pdf

Lance, Keith C., et al. (2000c). *Measuring up to standards: The impact of school library programs & information literacy in Pennsylvania schools*. Greensburg, PA: Pennsylvania Citizens for Better Libraries. Retrieved April 4, 2004, from the Pennsylvania State Library web site: http://www.statelibrary.state.pa.us/ libraries/lib/libraries/measuringup.pdf

Lance, Keith C., et al. (2001). *Good schools have school librarians: Oregon school librarians collaborate to improve academic achievement*. Salem, OR: Educational Media Association. Retrieved April 4, 2004, from: http://www.oema.net/ Oregon_Study/OR_Study_exec.pdf

Lance, Keith C., et al. (2002). *How school libraries improve outcomes for children: The New Mexico study*. Santa Fe, NM: New Mexico State Library.

Lawrence, Steve & Giles, Lee. (1999). Accessibility of information on the web. *Nature, 400,* 107–109. Retrieved March 30, 2004, from: http://www.net.cs.pku. edu.cn/~webg/html/summary_ADIW.htm

Loertscher, David. (1988). *Taxonomies of the school media program*. Westport, CT: Libraries Unlimited.

Manzo, Kathleen Kennedy. (2000, March 22). Study shows rise in test scores tied to school library resources. [Electronic version]. *Education Week, 19*(28), 27. Retrieved April 4, 2004, from Education Week On the Web: http://www. edweek.org/ew/ewstory.cfm?slug=28libe.h19&keywords=test%20scores%20ti ed%20to%20school%library

Maxwell, D. Jackson. (1999, Fall). Forging partnerships: Schools, school libraries, and communities. *Teacher Education Quarterly, 26*(4), 99–110.

A nation at risk: The imperative for educational reform. (1983). Washington, DC: U.S. Department of Education.

Naylor, Alice Phoebe & Jennings, Kenneth D. (1988, Summer). An investigation of principals' perceptions of library media specialists' performance evaluation terminology. *School Library Media Quarterly, 16*(4), 234–239.

Ohanian, Susan. (2000, January). Goals 2000: What's in a name? *Phi Delta Kappa 81*(5), 344.

Olson, Lynn & Hoff, David J. (1999, October 6). Teaching tops agenda at summit. [Electronic version]. *Education Week 19*(6), 1, 20. Retrieved March 30, 2004, from: http://www.edweek.org/ew/ewstory.cfm?slug=06summit.h19

Pennock, Robin. (1988, September). Trading places: A librarian's route to the principal's office. *School Library Journal, 35*(1), 117–119.

Rodney, Marcia, et al. (2002). *Make the connection: Quality school library media programs impact academic achievement in Iowa*. Bettendorf, IA: Mississippi Bend Area Education Agency.

Smith, Ester. (2001). *Texas school libraries: Standards, resources, services, and students' performance*. Austin, TX: EGS Research & Consulting. Retrieved April 4, 2004, from the Texas State Library web site: http://www.tsl.state.tx.us/ ld/pubs/schlibsurvey/survey.pdf

Turner, Philip M. (1985). *Helping teachers teach.* Westport, CT: Libraries Unlimited.

U.S. Department of Education. (1991). *America 2000: An education strategy sourcebook.* Washington, DC: Author.

FURTHER READINGS

American Association of School Librarians. (2004, March 22). *Information literacy: A position paper on information problem solving.* Retrieved April 15, 2004, from American Association of School Librarians web site: http://www. ala.org/aasl/positions/ps_infolit.html

American Library Association. (2003). *School library media centers/School library media specialists.* Retrieved April 15, 2004, from the ALA web site: http://www.ala.org/ala/pio/factsheets/schoollibrarymedia.htm

Barker, Joe. (2000, September 7). *Things to know before you begin searching.* Retrieved April 4, 2004, from UC Berkeley Library web site: http://www.lib.berkeley.edu/ TeachingLib/Guides/Internet/ThingsToKnow.html

Barton, Paul E. (2001, March). *Raising achievement and reducing achievement.* Retrieved April 4, 2004, from National Education Goals Panel web site: http://www.negp.gov/issues/publication/negpdocs/negprep/rpt_barton/barton_ paper.pdf

Bennett, Blythe A. (2000). Internet resources for library media specialists and children's librarians. *ERIC Digests* (ERIC Identifier ED 448 783). Retrieved April 4, 2004, from: http://www.ed.gov/databases/ERIC_Digests/ed448783. html

Berkowitz, Robert & Eisenberg, Michael B. (2003). *Curriculum roles and responsibilities of library media specialists.* Retrieved April 15, 2004, from: http://www.libraryinstruction.com/curriculum-roles.html

Blank, Warren. (2001). *The 108 skills of natural born leaders.* New York: American Management Association.

Bradburn, Frances. (1999, November). Crunch time. *School Library Journal, 45*(11), 43–47.

Bull, Glenn, et al. (2001, April). Evaluating & using web-based resources. *Learning and Leading with Technology, 28*(7), 50–55.

Bush, Gail. (2002). *The school buddy system: The practice of collaboration.* Chicago: American Library Association.

Buzzeo, Toni. (2002). *Collaborating to meet standards: Teacher/librarian partnerships for K–6.* Worthington, OH: Linworth.

Buzzeo, Toni. (2002). *Collaborating to meet standards: Teacher/librarian partnerships for 7–12.* Worthington, OH: Linworth.

Church, Audrey P. (2003). *Leverage your libraries to raise test scores: A guide for library media specialists, principals, teachers, and parents.* Worthington, OH: Linworth.

Clyde, Anne (2000). Internet search tools for kids. *Teacher Librarian, 27*(3), 57–58.

Collaborative planning: Resources for teacher/librarian collaboration. (2000, July 13). Retrieved April 4, 2004, from: http://es.houstonisd.org/ScrogginsES/information/library/collabor.htm

Colorado Library Research Service. (2001, July 1). *Librarians, teachers & principals agree: "Power Libraries" lead to higher student test scores.* Retrieved April 4, 2004, from the Colorado State Library web site: http://www.lrs.org/documents/fastfacts/178powerlibs.pdf

Craver, Kathleen W. (1986, Summer). The changing instructional role of the high school library media specialist: 1950–84. [Electronic version]. *School Library Media Quarterly, 14*(4), 183–191. Retrieved April 15, 2004, from the ALA web site: http://www.ala.org/cfapps/archive.cfm?path=aasl/SLMR/slmr_resources/select_craver.html

Donham, Jean. (1999, March). Collaboration in the media center: Building partnerships for learning. *NASSP Bulletin, 83*(605), 20–26.

Donham, Jean, et al. (2001). *Inquiry-based learning: Lessons from Library Power.* Worthington, OH: Linworth.

Ensor, Pat. (2001, June 14). *Toolkit for the expert web searcher.* Retrieved April 4, 2004, from the Library and Information Technology Association web site: http://www.lita.org/committe/toptech/toolkit.htm

Essential learnings and school libraries: Building bridges by linking. (1996, September). Retrieved April 4, 2004, from: http://www.learningspace.org/instruct/literacy/ESLSLIBS.HTM#role

Farmer, Lesley S. J. (1999). *Partnerships for lifelong learning* (2nd ed.). Worthington, OH: Linworth.

Farmer, Lesley S. J. (1994). *Leadership within the school and beyond.* Worthington, OH: Linworth.

Fulton, Kathleen. (2001, March/April). From promise to practice: Enhancing student Internet learning. *Multimedia Schools, 8.* Retrieved April 4, 2004, from: http://www.onlineinc.com/MMSchools/mar01/fulton.htm

Getting America's students ready for the 21st century: Meeting the technology literacy challenge: A report to the nation on technology and education. (1996, June 29). Retrieved April 15, 2004, from the U.S. Department of Education web site: http://www.ed.gov/about/offices/list/os/technology/plan/national/index.html

Goals 2000: Flexible funding supports state and local education reform. (1998, November 16). Washington, DC: General Accounting Office, Report B-278982. Retrieved April 4, 2004, from General Accounting Office web site: http://www.gao.gov/archive/1999/he99010.pdf

Harada, Violet & Donham, Jean. (1998, October). Information power: Student achievement is the bottom line. *Teacher Librarian, 26*(1), 14–17.

Harada, Violet & Yoshina, Joan M. (2004). *Inquiry learning through teacher-librarianships.* Worthington, OH: Linworth.

Hartzell, Gary N. (1997, November). The invisible school librarian: Why other educators are blind to your value (part 1). Retrieved April 16, 2004, from the

School Library Journal web site: http://www.schoollibraryjournal.com/index.asp?layout=articlePrint&articleID=CA152978

Hartzell, Gary N. (2001). The implications of selected school reform approaches for school library media services. Retrieved April 4, 2004 from the ALA web site: http://www.ala.org/Content/NavigationMenu/AASL/Publications_and_Journals/School_Library_Media_Research/Contents1/Volume_4_(2001)/Hartzell.htm

Haycock, Ken. (1999, October). What works: Collaborative programme planning and teaching. *Teacher Librarian, 27*(1), 38. Retrieved April 21, 2004, from the *Teacher Librarian* web site: http://www.teacherlibrarian.com/tltoolkit/what_works/works_v27_1.html

Iowa Educational Media Association. (n.d.). *School library media studies on achievement.* Retrieved April 4, 2004, from the Iowa Educational Media Association web site: http://www.iema-ia.org/IEMA119.html

Johnson, Doug. (1997). *The indispensable librarian: Surviving (and thriving) in school media centers in the information age.* Worthington, OH: Linworth.

Johnson, Doug. (1999, April 1). *A curriculum built not to last.* Retrieved April 4, 2004, from: http://www.doug-johnson.com/dougwri/curriculum.html

Krashen, Stephen D. (2004). *The power of reading: Insights from the research* (2nd ed.). Westport, CT: Libraries Unlimited.

Kuntz, Jerry. (2001, May 1). Teach and they shall find. Retrieved April 4, 2004, from *School Library Journal* archives: http://slj.reviewsnews.com/index.asp?layout=articleArchive&articleid=CA73642

Lance, Keith Curry. (2004, Winter). *Libraries and student achievement: The importance of school libraries for improving student test scores.* Retrieved April 21, 2004, from the *Ciconline* web site: http://www.ciconline.com/NR/rdonlyres/etngoe4tkwbjrltxbuefu5qcpnjjdlo6lahqvx465ptmezoesuiv3azlnasiiyrcnqcio24i3umcjv6pruhewdlwiyg/WO4-librariesachievement.pdf

Loertscher, David V. (2000). *Taxonomies of the school library media program* (2nd ed.). San Jose, CA: Hi Willow Research and Publishing.

Loertscher, David V. (2003, June 19). *School library media centers and academic achievement: A bibliography and availability list.* Retrieved from: http://www.lmcsource.com/tech/ResearchStudies.html

Loertscher, David V. & Achterman, Douglas. (2002). *Increasing academic achievement through the library media center: A guide for teachers.* Castle Rock, CO: Hi Willow Research and Publishing.

McKenzie, Jamie. (2001). *Planning good change with technology and literacy.* Worthington, OH: Linworth.

McQuillan, Jeff. (1998). *The literary crisis.* Portsmouth, NH: Heinemann.

Nebraska Educational Media Association. (n.d.). *Collaborative planning: Partnerships between teachers and library media specialists.* Retrieved April 4, 2004, from Nebraska Educational Media web site: http://nema.k12.ne.us/CheckIt/coplan.html

Pitcher, Sharon M. & Mackey, Bonnie. (2004). *Collaborating for real literacy: Librarian, teacher, and principal.* Worthington, OH: Linworth.

Putnam, Eleanor. (1996, Fall). The instructional consultant role of the elementary-school library media specialist and the effects of program scheduling on its practice. *School Library Media Quarterly, 25*(1), 43–49.

Ready to read, ready to learn: First Lady Laura Bush's education initiatives. (2001, February 26). Retrieved April 26, 2004, from: http://web.archive.org/web/2003707234331/http://www.readingrockets.org/article.php?ID=266

Rhode Island Educational Media Association. (2003, January). Collaboration and leadership. *Making It Happen, 1.* Retrieved April 4, 2004, from the Rhode Island Educational Media Association web site: http://www.ri.net/RIEMA/MIHjan03.html

Russell, Shayne. (2000). Teachers and librarians: Collaborative relationships. *ERIC Digests* (ERIC Identifier ED 444 605). Retrieved April 4, 2004, from http://www.ericfacility.net/ericdigests/ed444605.html

School library media standards handbook. (2000, April). Retrieved April 4, 2004, from Missouri Department of Elementary and Secondary Education web site: http://www.dese.state.mo.us/divimprove/curriculum/library/

Scordato, Julie. (2004, April/May). A tale of two libraries: School and public libraries working together. *Library Media Connection, 229*(7), 32–33.

Starr, Linda. (2000). *Strong libraries improve student achievement.* Retrieved April 4, 2004, from Education World web site: http://www.educationworld.com/a_admin/admin178.shtml

Stephens, Diane & Boldt, Gail. (2004, May). School/university partnerships: Rhetoric, reality, and intimacy. *Phi Delta Kappan, 85*(9), 703–707.

Stripling, Barbara K. (Summer 1997). Library Power: A model for school change. *School Library Media Quarterly, 25*(4), 201–202.

Stripling, Barbara K. (1999). *Learning and libraries in an information age.* Westport, CT: Libraries Unlimited.

Tyner, Ross. (2001, Spring). *Sink or swim: Internet search tools and techniques* (v. 5.0). Retrieved April 4, 2004, from Okanagan University College Library web site: http://www.sci.ouc.bc.ca/libr/connect96/search.htm

U.S. Department of Education's 2000 performance report and 2002 program annual plan (2001, June). Retrieved April 4, 2004, from the U.S. Department of Education web site: http://www.ed.gov/pubs/AnnualPlan2002/

Weisman, Shirley. (2002). *Windows into instructional collaboration: Information Power in the real world.* San Jose, CA: Hi Willow Research and Publishing.

Chapter 3

FUNCTIONS OF THE SCHOOL LIBRARY MEDIA CENTER

Emphasis on the individual nature of learning continues to lead educators to question the methods that promote only teaching facts and rote learning, curricula that departmentalize knowledge into unrelated units, and organizational structures that produce artificial grade levels and perpetuate unrealistic expectations and rigid standards. Many organizational patterns have been developed: individualized instruction, team teaching, flexible and modular scheduling, large group/small group instruction, independent study programs, interdisciplinary studies, non-graded or multi-grades classrooms, contract teaching, extra-school internships, tutorial or directed study programs and the whole language approach to the teaching of reading.

According to *Information Power* ([AASL & AECT], 1998) the roles of the school library media specialist today are defined as a teacher, an information specialist, an instructional partner and a program administrator. The school library media center staff functions in a more people-oriented environment that supports the idea of establishing partnerships with teachers, parents, students, administrators, community leaders, and other librarians in the community. A variety of media at many levels of comprehension, easy accessibility, and a range of services and activities that involves the learner are the main components of the program. The school library is the center of information sources and is the learning laboratory for developing critical thinking and promoting information literacy. The school media specialist today, instead of reacting to requests for services, takes the initiative to anticipate needed services and to plan for their implementation. Being proactive, the library media specialist initiates ideas for instructional activities and plans ahead for units of study with teachers that support the curriculum. A variety of media at many levels of comprehension and interest, organized for easy accessibility is the foundation of the media center program. The range of services and activities that involve the learner can be as diverse as Internet online searching to interlibrary loans, to the production of audiovisual materials for classroom use, to using the computer for remedial work or for learning content. The need for unification of media and services to promote learning through carefully planned programs in which all members of the educational community are involved leads to the development of the school library media center as the heart of the instructional program of the school.

This chapter on functions has a threefold aim: (1) to express briefly the nature of school library media programs by describing the services/functions of the media center at all levels; (2) to define and describe these functions as services and activities and to define resources as well as guidelines that are helpful in planning, establishing, and maintaining these collections; (3) to formulate a plan for inaugurating or strengthening a school library media center in an individual school; and (4) to determine the direction that school library media programs may head in the future.

SERVICES

The school library media center's program provides a range of learning opportunities for both large and small groups and for individuals. The focus is on facilities and improving the learning process, with emphasis on intellectual content, information literacy, inquiry, and the learner. Because people do not react in the same way to the same medium, learners are encouraged to read, view, listen, construct, and create to learn in their own way. The media center program is a collaborative venture in which school library media specialists, teachers, and administrators work together to provide opportunities for the social, cultural, and educational growth of students. It is a coordinated effort in which activities take place in the school library media center, the laboratory classroom, and throughout the school.

Marilyn Miller (2000) conducted a national research study that included one section comparing sixteen library media center program services by region. The services provided are shown in Exhibit 3.1. By looking at the functions by region, it is easy to see that some regions put more

Exhibit 3.1.
Comparison of Library Media Center Program Services by Region.

Service	Northeast	South	North Central	West
Provides reference assistance to students and teachers.	95%	97%	96%	97%
Informally instructs students in the use of resources.	95%	94%	92%	89%
Provides teachers with information about new resources.	83%	84%	84%	85%
Provides reading/listening/ viewing guidance for students.	89%	86%	74%	79%
Collaborates with teachers.	76%	79%	81%	81%
Helps students and teachers use resources outside the school.	81%	67%	74%	59%
Provides interlibrary loan service for students and teachers.	75%	47%	62%	46%
Offers a program of curriculum-integrated skills instruction.	61%	61%	66%	54%
Helps teachers develop, implement, and evaluate instruction.	55%	62%	58%	59%
Helps parents realize importance of lifelong learning.	58%	53%	48%	48%
Assists school curriculum committee with recommendations.	48%	52%	49%	46%
Coordinates cable TV and related activities.	28%	62%	35%	31%
Conducts workshops for teachers.	31%	36%	33%	26%
Coordinates in-school production of materials.	24%	34%	33%	32%
Coordinates video production activities.	22%	32%	28%	18%
Coordinates computer networks.	21%	34%	29%	19%

Printed with permission. Source: Miller, Marilyn L. & Shontz, Marilyn L. (2000, November). Location is Everything. [Electronic version]. *School Library Journal,* *46*(11), 50. Retrieved April 4, 2004, from: http://www. findarticles.com/cf_0/m1299/11_46/67328855/p1/article.jhtml emphasis on some services while other regions place their emphasis on something entirely different.

Another study conducted by Marilyn L. Miller and Marilyn Shontz (1998) gives a comparison of twenty-two services offered by library media center programs, which they identify as high service and non-high service. Exhibit 3.2 follows with the comparison. Some of the staff functions that are basic to providing minimal services in any school library media center are:

1. Budgeting a balanced media program.
2. Selecting materials and equipment.
3. Acquiring and processing (where not centrally done) all media and equipment.
4. Organizing collections of media (including online resources) and equipment for easy access.
5. Circulating media and equipment.
6. Arranging flexible schedules that provide accessibility.
7. Handling repair procedures.
8. Preparing procedural manuals for the center.
9. Promoting the center within and outside the school.
10. Instructing in the location and use of media and equipment both print and online.
11. Offering reading, viewing, and listening guidance.
12. Providing access to the Internet and other databases.
13. Training students and teachers in the use of the Internet.
14. Training student assistants and staff in the operations of the center.
15. Collaborating with teachers, administrators, and students.
16. Troubleshooting technology problems.
17. Providing links to Internet web sites.

Another way to describe the school library media center program is through activities that take place in the center and in the school as a result of the services. Activities among centers vary by type and also by combination. Nevertheless, some of the same activities or services appear in all dynamic centers: students or teachers (individually or in groups) make PowerPoint presentations and other visuals, view videos, produce multimedia presentations, or use computers for searching the Internet for information or projects. Programs across the country reveal numerous activities and the underlying functions that support them. A collection of these

Exhibit 3.2.
Comparison of Twenty-two Services Offered by Library Media Programs.

LMC Service	High Service LMCs	Non-High Service LMCs
Offers curriculum integrated skills instruction.	92%	54%
Informally instructs students in the use of resources.	100%	93%
Conducts workshops for teachers.	65%	19%
Assists curriculum committee with recommendations.	85%	39%
Collaborates with teachers.	97%	81%
Helps teachers develop/implement/ evaluate learning.	92%	54%
Gives teachers information about new resources.	99%	86%
Provides reference assistance to students, teachers.	100%	99%
Helps students, teachers use resources outside the school.	98%	73%
Provides interlibrary loan for students and teachers.	83%	53%
Provides reading/listening/viewing guidance.	96%	90%
Helps parents realize importance of lifelong learning.	63%	50%
Coordinates in-school production of materials.	77%	19%
Coordinates video production activities.	70%	18%
Coordinates cable TV and related activities.	85%	36%
Coordinates computer networks.	60%	17%
Provides access to CD ROM searching	83%	52%
Provides online catalog and circulation systems.	99%	79%
Provides access to Internet, e-mail.	84%	56%
Provides flexible LMC schedule.	66%	30%
Communicates proactively with principal.	70%	34%
Plans instruction with teachers 2+ hours a week.	79%	40%

Printed with permission.
Source: Miller, Marilyn & Shontz, Marilyn. (1998, May). More services, more staff, more money: A portrait of a high-service library media center. [Electronic version]. *School Library Journal, 44*(5), 28-33. Retrieved April 4, 2004, from: http://slj.reviewsnews.com/index.asp?layout=article& articleid=CA152993&publication=slj

activities is presented in the following section. With a little imagination, the majority of these activities can be redesigned for use in other school library media centers.

Although the examples described below can apply in many instances to any of the three major audiences of a school library media program—students, teachers, and administrators, plus the community—they are grouped under the audiences with which they will be used most often. By comparing a function or service and the resulting activity, it becomes obvious that measurement of the objectives as they result in audience activity will give a more accurate evaluation of educational progress than will the work measures of staff.

FUNCTIONS RELATED TO USER ACTIVITIES

All the examples are arranged to show the relationship between staff function and the activities of school library media center user. The school library media center staff functions so that students, teachers, administrators, or community members can participate in an activity resulting in a learning experience.

Services to Students

Reading, Viewing, and Listening

- Organize media and equipment; preview, evaluate, and weed→Participate as members of a review committee to evaluate media.
- Compile "mediagraphies," or "webliographies"→Learn to use an annotated list that includes books, URLs, cassettes, videos, computer software, and games about a theme or topic.
- Provide for reading guidance→Give book talks to motivate students to read. Give individual reading guidance to students.
- Give multimedia presentations using school library media→Learn importance of using a variety of media, for example, books, realia, computers, maps, videos and programs such as PowerPoint and Hyperstudio to illustrate a discussion of "courage."
- Assist in developing school library media presentation skills→Present programs to groups of friends or to younger students. An eleventh-grade varsity ballplayer could highlight a talk on sports novels for eighth-graders by using PowerPoint to illustrate game techniques; an older student might help a younger one by using touch board technology to illustrate a story.
- Provide for local production of media→ Use locally produced media in a variety of ways, for example, preparing a PowerPoint presentation to sum-

marize research findings, laminating art pictures, and videotaping school reports.

Reference Work

• Provide accessible online and printed reference materials →Locate a variety of media by using mediagraphies or webliographies to establish a school library media reference collection for a third-grade unit on nature (including a provision for CD-ROM and Internet searches).

• Use of school library media to develop information literacy skills (A video unit on this part of reference work might be shown to individuals and to classes)→Recognize the need to compare and evaluate sources.

• Correlate collections or subject area use→Learn to use information on the Internet for an individualized American studies project and an art class.

• Establish liaison with public, university, and special libraries→Use interlibrary loans, for example, a student might request a scientific monograph from a cooperating research library for an advanced placement chemistry class.

Instruction

• Teach faculty how Internet filters work→Demonstrate online searching strategies that yield appropriate web sites for students.

• Teach information literacy skills and equipment use→Learn the skills for competent school library media and equipment use so a third-grade class can practice alphabetizing by working with the online public access catalog (OPAC), or a seventh-grade English class can undertake a television production of excerpts from *The Giver.*

• Give orientation tours and workshops→Learn the organization and administration of a library, for example, each grade level might participate in a series of workshops.

• Teach use of special reference materials→Students learn to use essential reference materials, for example, fifth-graders choose a suitable encyclopedia and atlas, either online or print, to complete a video report on a country. This project is collaboratively planned with the teacher.

• Help develop and teach a standard bibliographic format, including all types of media and web sites on the Internet→Students learn the school's bibliographic rules by using a computer program developed collaboratively with teachers.

• Develop ideas for teaching critical thinking skills→Compare historical accounts in fiction books with history books to determine accuracy of facts on a particular event.

Clubs, Social and Vocational Programs

- Develop assistantship programs→Learn school library media center work as a student volunteer, as a part-time paid employee, or as part of course work in a vocational course.
- Assist in extra curricular activities→Participate in social and educational activities such as trips to local libraries, theaters, and museums; plan a school library media club trip to a museum film festival or to a local book jobber.
- Sponsor paperback book fairs, film festivals, and art exhibits→Learn to share the experience and work of sponsoring exhibits. Examples: fourth-to-sixth-grade students help to run a paperback book fair; seventh-to-ninth-grade students assist in planning a film festival of novels that have been made into feature or television films; an elementary school cooperatively participates in painting scenes around the theme of wild animals and the school media center coordinates an art exhibit to display student work.
- Plan school library media center publicity→Help to promote school library media center resources and services, for example, high school journalism classes and radio clubs prepare and disseminate publicity.
- Suggest school library media use ideas for assemblies, Parent-Teacher Association programs, classroom projects, and plays→Assist in recording school meetings, speeches, and special programs, for example, prepare videos for special school programs for community use.

Services to Teachers and Administrators

Curriculum Development

- Teach use of school library media through the role model of teacher-librarian→Develop a collaboratively planned unit to be taught by a school library media specialist and teacher team, for example, a unit on myths for the fifth or sixth grade.
- Attend grade-level or subject-area departmental meetings→Participate in designing courses incorporating new uses of media, for example, a ninth-grade survey of careers that use resource people, videos, government pamphlets, and information from the Internet.
- Help to design instructional systems→Study existing curriculum to develop new instructional approaches; school library media specialist can recommend appropriate resources for a second-grade reading program using trade books, readers, enrichment videos, interactive computers, and online resources.
- Learn teachers' instructional methods and school library media needs through individual conferences→Plan collaboratively with teachers the

teaching of information literacy skills as they relate to standards in their curriculum content areas. For example, plan to teach an interdisciplinary unit on whales with the science, language arts, social studies, and art and math teachers through the study of fiction and nonfiction books. Skills gained from the lesson are improved reading, listening, storytelling, and critical thinking skills.

- Plan school library media programs for teachers' professional and recreational needs→Attend exhibits of new professional materials, screenings of noteworthy videos, and demonstrations and displays of the newest equipment and software.

Assisting in the Use of Materials

- Help teachers become familiar with the school library media center→Participate in videotaping a school library media center orientation program to use throughout the school.
- Teach use of a school library media center for research→Develop a local-history project with the classroom teacher that can be used as a demonstration of how to use the school library media center's research resources online.
- Organize routines for convenient use of materials and equipment; make self-instruction programs available→Develop simple programmed-instruction booklets or computer programs to teach youngsters some fundamental information literacy skills such as classification.
- Encourage local production of materials→Teachers and administrators can develop their own "tailor-made" materials or presentations.
- Establish departmental or auxiliary resource centers→Develop cooperatively a place for storing equipment and specialized materials within floor levels, grade levels, or departments so that they receive maximum use.

Services to the Community

- Plan programs to involve parents and community groups→Parents are invited for an evening parent/child reading program coordinated by the school media staff; take home selection lists of read-aloud books are provided for the parents.
- Observe national media-related events→Participate in special programs to highlight the National Book Awards, the American Film Festival, National Library Week, School Media Day, and so forth.
- Publicize school library media center activities→Local radio or television might produce spot announcements with school library media staff help;

newspapers may run information about school library media center programs or events.

- Engage community business and professional persons to speak to school and school library media center groups→Local persons serve as resource specialists, for example, a fireman might participate in a school library media center program on safety.

CONVERTING A SCHOOL LIBRARY MEDIA CENTER INTO A VIRTUAL LIBRARY

Many things should be explored before the task of converting a school library media center into a virtual center is begun. Perhaps the most important concern should be whether the person who is to run the center fully accepts the concept of virtual media centers and the various dissemination points for ideas and information. To embrace this concept requires acceptance of the equipment, tools and software required for the transmission of ideas or information. Once a wholehearted commitment to this philosophy is made, the specialist is ready to take some immediate steps toward developing some of the concepts associated with virtual school library media centers and to plan for some long-range steps. The process should be planned gradually and over a period of time so that support within the school is there before any major steps are taken.

The school library media specialist should assume proactive leadership throughout the entire conversion process. This leadership is vital and one of the key factors for the eventual success of such a program. But a word of caution is necessary. Experience has shown that when presenting a new program, it is best not to attempt to introduce a great number of new services in the initial stages, but to concentrate on developing a total program by adding a few services to those that have proved successful. By no means should one try to build a virtual school library media center solely by adding new or different media or computers; this approach is a denial of the basic philosophy of such a center. Instead, integrate all kinds of media and technology into the grade-level unit or course of study that is widely used in the school. Working with the faculty to develop long-range plans for the virtual school library media center is an effective way to foster support for gradually moving toward the kind of center desired. Teachers seem to be more interested when they can derive personal benefit from the program. Something as simple as providing at-home Internet access for them is a good beginning. To accomplish home Internet access for teachers and students, the library media specialist must foster support from the principal and school board. They must be key players in wanting to move in the direction of the virtual school library media center. The media specialist's expertise is crucial to the development and operation of the program.

Immediate Steps

1. Identify a curriculum or recreational area around which to build the virtual school library media concept.

2. Contact one or two teachers who are interested in working collaboratively to build a balanced media collection in one area or to develop webliographies for teaching content found on the Internet.

3. Encourage students to use a variety of media formats in developing a collection of resources for individual satisfaction as well as for classroom work. Simple production of PowerPoints, videos, and the use of computers for research are three examples.

4. As soon as a program that is collaboratively planned with teachers is completed, evaluate the services according to the educational objectives and student responses. These evaluations can serve as a basis for making future changes.

5. Encourage teachers and students to participate in the media program to the extent that staff and funds are available. Solicit the help of teachers in requesting funds from the principal for the purchase of a variety of media, and newer information technologies to support the concept of the virtual school library media center.

6. Enlist the support of the principal and administration for increasing the role of providing materials through the Internet and other available technology.

Long-Range Steps

1. Use the educational philosophy of the district and individual school together with the specific objectives for each area in the overall curricula to formulate a philosophy, a mission statement, and goals and objectives for the virtual school library media program.

2. Seek a consultant's help if possible; visit other centers that have already moved in the direction of virtual media centers.

3. Evaluate present services, resources, facilities, and so forth and see how they can be utilized effectively as the move is made in the direction of the virtual school library media center.

4. Determine technology needs that will support the program.

5. Focus on a total school library media center program that is uniquely suited to the school and set the priorities within multiyear phases (from one to three years) in which the services, newer resources, services, and remodeled facilities will be inaugurated.

6. Establish effective communication with the principal by building on the successful operation of past program services.

7. Ensure a clear organizational pattern as well as acceptance that only one person will head the school library media center operation in the school.

8. Continue to enlist the support of teachers and students by providing services they need, but of which they may be unaware.

9. Revise plans as necessary, guided by the evaluation of the program against the evaluation criteria set up in the first of the long-range conversion steps.

10. Explore the possibility of developing a unified virtual school library media program on a district level if one does not exist. A long-range plan for staffing virtual school library media centers needs to be established from the district level to ensure that all centers, regardless of size, are adequately staffed. As the move is made toward offering virtual services, it is crucial that support staff is available in the centers to ensure that collaboration between teachers and the school library media specialist is a top priority.

It is a good idea to look at the media center program and to evaluate current services offered to determine the feasibility of moving in the direction of the virtual school library media center. A set of rubrics for the Minnesota School Library Media Program Standards, based on *Information Power* (ASSL & AECT, 1998), show the different levels of school media programs. The rubric is a useful tool to determine the development of school media programs in existence as well as those programs that are being developed for the first time. The rubrics in Exhibit 3.3 can be shared with the principal and all school constituents in order to look at the existing library media center program and to develop a planning strategy for moving forward toward the virtual school library media center.

FUTURE SCHOOL LIBRARY MEDIA PROGRAMS

Technology is changing rapidly and with those changes, school library media programs are in a state of evolution. A school library media center is beginning to be referred to as a cybrary and the virtual school library media center is already emerging as a reality. Because of the nature of technology and the desire to deliver instant service, the idea of the cybrary and

Exhibit 3.3.
Minnesota Standards for Effective School Library Media Programs.

Part One, Learning and Teaching	Minimum	Standard	Exemplary
1. Is the program essential and fully integrated?	☐ 25%-50% of classes use the media program's materials and services the equivalent of at least once each semester	☐ 50%-100% of classes use the media program's materials and services the equivalent of at last once each semester. ☐ The media specialist is a regular member of curriculum teams. ☐ All media skills are taught through content-based projects.	☐ 50%-100% of classes use the media program's materials and services the equivalent of at least twice each semester. ☐ Information literacy skills are an articulated component of a majority of content area curricula.
2. Are the information literacy standards integral to the curriculum?	☐ Students complete at least two resource-based projects each year that require research skills.	☐ Students complete all resource-based projects required by the Graduation Rule's High Standards. ☐ There are a clear set of media and technology benchmarks for each grade level.	☐ All classroom projects have both content and information literacy outcomes.
3. Does the media program model and promote collaborative planning and teaching?	☐ The media specialist has a schedule that allows meeting with teachers prior to each research unit. ☐ The media center contains a professional collection.	☐ The media specialist has a schedule that allows meeting with teachers on a regular basis to plan resource-based projects. ☐ The media specialist is a member of grade level or team planning groups. ☐ The media specialist has defined responsibilities for teaching skills in each project.	☐ The media specialist participates in the assessment and grading of student projects with all staff. ☐ The media specialist is viewed as a resource for authentic assessment and project-based learning.

Exhibit 3.3. (continued)

Part One, Learning and Teaching	Minimum	Standard	Exemplary
4. Is there access to a full range of information resources and services?	☐ The media specialist is knowledgeable about and acquires some resources in print and non-print formats. ☐ The media specialist assists students and staff in gathering data from electronic resources.	☐ The media specialist evaluates, acquires, and promotes resources in print and non-print formats. ☐ The media specialist helps staff and students access other community resources.	☐ The media specialist participates in resource and service sharing with other community agencies.
5. Does the media program encourage reading, viewing, and listening?	☐ The media center contains current materials of student interest in print format. ☐ The media specialist promotes materials on a regular basis.	☐ The media center contains current materials of high student interest in a variety of formats. ☐ A formal program to encourage student reading, viewing, and listening is in place.	☐ The media program conducts events and activities that encourage independent reading. ☐ A computerized book-tracking system is available. ☐ Activities that promote media literacy are held.
6. Does the media program support diverse learning needs, abilities, and styles?	☐ Research projects are individualized. ☐ Multiple formats of information are recognized as valid.	☐ Research units have a variety of final project formats including those using graphics, sound, video or oral presentations.	☐ Students have an individualized plan for information literacy projects. ☐ A variety of multimedia projects and presentations are the outcome of research.

Exhibit 3.3. (continued)

Part One, Learning and Teaching	Minimum	Standard	Exemplary
7.Does the program foster individual and collaborative inquiry?	☐ Both individual and group research projects are assigned.	☐ Formal planning of group roles and individual tasks is a part of each project.	☐ Research projects use and foster individual interests to spur life-long learning behaviors. ☐ Teachers and media specialists articulate personal learning goals.
8.Does the program integrate the use of technology?	☐ Research is done with aid of an automated library catalog and stand-alone CD-ROM databases. ☐ Projects are word-processed	☐ On-line information sources are available and used. ☐ Students use desktop publishing, multimedia construction programs, drawing, and graphing programs to complete projects. ☐ The media center has a telephone and fax machine for professional and supervised student use.	☐ A wide variety of on-line information sources, including email and Web, are available and used. ☐ Students use digital photography and video editing to create projects. ☐ The media program teaches discriminate use of technology for effective research and communication.
9.Does the program provide a link to the larger community?	☐ The school media program encourages the use of external resources in research projects. ☐The availability and use of public and academic libraries are part of the information literacy curriculum. ☐ The media specialist assists	☐ The availability and use of a variety of community and web-based resources are a part of the information literacy curriculum. ☐ The media specialist works with classroom teachers to make them aware of resources outside	☐ The school library is a member of the regional multitype system and participates in its activities. ☐ The media program helps facilitate school to work initiatives and other community-based learning programs.

Exhibit 3.3. (continued)

	students and staff in acquiring materials through interlibrary loan.	the school of value to students.	
Part One, Learning and Teaching	**Minimum**	**Standard**	**Exemplary**
10. Does the program provide intellectual access to information and ideas for learning?	☐ The media specialist helps students and staff with basic reference and location questions.	☐ The media specialist helps students and staff with research questions using specialized tools both inside and outside the media center. ☐ The media specialist creates subject bibliographies for staff.	☐ The media specialist helps students and staff become critical users of information.
11. Does the program provide physical access to information and resources for learning?	☐ The library media center is a physical space within the school with student seating and shelving for materials. ☐ The materials in the media center are cataloged and circulated according to specified criteria.	☐ The media center has a variety of workspaces and tools for at least 3 classes to work researching and producing projects. ☐ The media center has spaces that support students working individually, in small groups and in classes. ☐ The collection and circulation systems are automated and current.	☐ The media specialist actively participates in building and remodeling committees. ☐ The facility is climate controlled and has an outside entrance for after hours use. ☐ The school's records are part of a larger, regional union catalog.

Exhibit 3.3. (continued)

Part One, Learning and Teaching	Minimum	Standard	Exemplary
12. Does the program provide a climate that is conducive to learning?	☐ The media center is a safe environment with adequate lighting, ventilation and heat. ☐ The furniture is appropriate for the age of the student being served. ☐ The media specialist is enthusiastic and encourages student use of the media center and its resources.	☐ The media center has an inviting appearance with student created works, instructional displays and informational posters. ☐ The furniture and shelving are matched and in good condition. ☐ The media center is easily accessible from all classrooms, and contains a computer lab, multi-media workstations, and a TV production facility. ☐ The media specialist conducts promotional activities to encourage student and staff use of the media center.	☐ The media center has a variety of informal and formal student areas. ☐ The media specialist plans with teachers special displays. ☐ The media center is air-conditioned for year-round use. ☐ The media center has adequate wiring and network drops, static free carpeting, and a ceiling with noise-abating tiles. ☐ The staff workroom, administrative offices, and distance-learning classroom are adjacent to the media center. ☐ The media center serves as the hub of all school information networks.
13.Does the program provide flexible and equitable access to learning resources?	☐ The media center is open, staffed and available to students during all school hours, all school days. ☐ Parents and community members may use the collection before and after school. ☐ The media center and its	☐ The media program is flexibly scheduled so the professional services of the media specialist are available when needed by students and staff. ☐ Teacher prep time and study halls are NOT provided in the	☐ The media center is open and staffed extended hours evening and weekends for community use. ☐ A policy for resource use by the community is in place. ☐ The public is informed of the availability of the media center.

Exhibit 3.3. (continued)

	resources are handicap accessible.	media center. □ The media specialist encourages the use of the media center by the public.	
Part One, Learning and Teaching	**Minimum**	**Standard**	**Exemplary**
14.Do the collections and resources support the school curriculum?	□ Materials are professionally selected using recognized review tools. □ There is a current* print collection of at least 10-15 print items per student, a selection of periodicals, and electronic research terminals for at least 25% of the largest class. □ Students have access to: . a computerized periodical index . electronic encyclopedias . a wide variety of computerized productivity programs like word processors, spreadsheets, and databases. *Current is defined as the collection having an average age of not greater than 10 years, acknowledging that some areas will need more current materials and some	□ There is a current print collection of at least 15-20 print items per student, electronic research terminals for at least 25%-50% of the largest class. □ Students have access to: . a computerized card catalog of local materials . on-line full text periodical databases . a wide variety of computerized reference tools like electronic atlases, concordances, dictionaries, thesauruses, reader's, advisors and almanacs . content area specific reference materials . videodiscs and players . full on-line access to the Internet . educational television programming . a wide range of educational computer programs including	□ There is a current print collection of over 20 print items per student, electronic research terminals for over 50% of the largest class. □ Electronic research materials are available from all networked computers in the building. □ There is a written collection development policy that shows collaboration with other libraries and outside information agencies. □ Students have access to: . a computerized union catalog of district holdings as well as access to the catalogs of public, academic, and special libraries such as MnLink from which interlibrary loans can be made . a collection of materials to support local history studies . access to

Exhibit 3.3. (continued)

	areas will have older materials.	practices, simulations and tutorials ☐ Resources are specifically chosen to support curricular needs.	desktop video conferencing stations or an interactive television classroom . emerging technologies as needed to support the curriculum
Part One, Learning and Teaching	**Minimum**	**Standard**	**Exemplary**
15. Does the program show a commitment to the right of intellectual freedom?	☐ There is a broad-adopted selection/ reconsideration policy. ☐ Circulation policies are consistent with the tenets of intellectual freedom and school policies. ☐ Internet access is unfiltered, but acceptable use is taught and Internet terminal use is monitored.	☐ The collection has materials representing a diversity of opinions on controversial topics. ☐ The media specialist works with teachers and administrators to insure students' rights to information. ☐ Student data privacy is kept.	☐ Intellectual freedom and the right to information is taught as a part of the information literacy curriculum.
16. Do the policies, procedures and practices reflect legal guidelines and professional ethics?	☐ The school has board-adopted policies on copyright and Internet/ technology acceptable use.	☐ The information literacy curriculum teaches the concepts of plagiarism, copyright, and intellectual property.	☐ The media specialist designs and conducts workshops on ethical issues associated with information and technology use.

Exhibit 3.3. (continued)

Part Three: Program Administration	Minimum	Standard	Exemplary
17.Does the program support the mission and goals of the school?	☐ The media specialist actively participates in school evaluation/ accreditation efforts. ☐ The library media program has a written mission statement that reflects the mission of the school.	☐ The media specialist formally plans yearly goals with the principal and department heads. ☐ The library media annual goals reflect the school and district goals. ☐ The media specialist actively participates as a member of the media and technology committees.	☐ The school mission and annual goals reflect the need for students to be information literate in order to become life-long learners and recognize the media program as essential in meeting those goals.
18.Is there adequate professional staffing in each building?	☐ There is at least one fully licensed full-time media professional serving each district. ☐ There is at least one fully licensed full-time media professional serving at least one half day in each school in the district. ☐ The media center is kept open with clerical help during the remainder of school hours.	☐ There is a minimum of one licensed full-time media professional in each school. ☐ The principal appraises the performance of the media specialist using tools specific to the profession. ☐ There is current job description for the media professional.	☐ There is one full-time media specialist for each 500 students in each building. ☐ The media specialist is active in professional organization activities and participates in a wide-range of school activities.
19.Is there adequate support staff for each building?	☐ The media specialist has part-time clerical and technical support.	☐ The building has sufficient clerical and technical staff to allow the professional media staff to work with teachers and students. ☐ The media	☐ When justified by school size and program, there is: . one full-time technician in each building, . a media professional who supervises media production,

Exhibit 3.3. (continued)

		professional supervises the support staff. ☐ There are current job descriptions for all support staff.	. a district-level supervisor . and support staff that assist with planning, budgeting, assessment, and materials processing.
Part Three: Program Administra-tion	**Minimum**	**Standard**	**Exemplary**
20. Does the program have on-going administrative support	☐ The principal and media specialist informally plan the media program goals and budget each year.	☐ A formal goal-setting and budgeting procedure is completed by the media specialist and building principal. ☐ The media program and media specialist are evaluated each year using the accomplishment of the goals as a criterion.	☐ An advisory committee with parents, teachers, students, and community members helps establish media center goals. ☐ A formal process is in place to report back to that group the accomplishment of those goals on a regular basis.
21. Is there a long-range, strategic plan for the program?	☐ The media specialist, principal, and department chairs collaboratively create and update long-range development plans for the media program. ☐ The district's strategic plan reflects the mission and role of the library media program.	☐ An advisory committee with parents, teachers, students, and community members helps create long-range media plans.	☐ Long-range media plans are shared with the community through public relation channels.

Exhibit 3.3. (continued)

Part Three: Program Administration	Minimum	Standard	Exemplary
22. Is there an on-going assessment of the program in place?	☐ The media specialist collects and reports basic circulation, collection size and age data.	☐ There is a means of assessing the adequacy of the program and collection through surveys done at the completion of each research unit. ☐ Annual goals and long-range plans are based on collected data. ☐ All new initiatives involving media and technology have an evaluation component.	☐ There is an effort to analyze the contributions of the media program to overall student performance in the school. ☐ Reporting of students meeting standards on identified information literacy and technology benchmarks are reported to parents and the community. ☐ The media specialist and school participate in formal studies conducted by state and academic researchers.
23. Does the program have adequate funding?	☐ The program has a written budget sufficient to keep the media program at a minimal level of service.	☐ The media specialist yearly submits a budget itemizing suggested levels of spending for collection maintenance and growth, subscription fees, supplies and other resources. ☐ The media specialist keeps detailed records of how funds were spent each year.	☐ The media specialist actively participates in school budget decision-making committees. ☐ The media specialist uses a variety of methods for obtaining resources, including cooperative purchasing, grant writing, and partnering.

Exhibit 3.3. (continued)

Part Three: Program Administration	Minimum	Standard	Exemplary
24. Do the media specialist and support staff receive adequate staff development opportunities	☐ The media specialist and support staff will receive training on resources and materials purchased for the media program. ☐ The media specialist offers classes to the staff on information resources and skills and technology integration.	☐ The media specialist attends conferences and workshops on new resources, state graduation rule updates, and information literacy curricula. ☐ There is a budget for staff development for the media specialist.	☐ The media specialist is a leader on the staff development committee and assists in planning and implementing staff development opportunities for all school staff.
25. Are the mission, goals, functions, and impact of the library program clearly communicated?	☐ The media specialist reports annually to the principal on the library media program.	☐ The media specialist communicates on a regular basis with school staff at meetings, through newsletters, and through programs in the media center.	☐ The media specialist communicates regularly with parents and the community through newsletters, web pages, parent-teacher organization presentations, service organization presentations, and notification of the local media of special events.
26. Are the human, financial, and physical resources of the program effectively managed?	☐ The media specialist oversees all aspects of the daily operation of the media center including scheduling classes, inventorying materials, and maintaining budgets.	☐ The media specialist supervises support staff and works with custodial staff on maintenance issues. ☐ The media specialist participates in the evaluation of support staff.	☐ The school media specialist actively participates on the building management team.

Printed with permission. Source: Minnesota Educational Media Association. (2002). *Minnesota standards for effective school library media programs: Checklist for assessment, planning, implementation and evaluation.* Retrieved April 4, 2004, from http://www.memoweb.org/links/standardsintro.pdf

the virtual school library media center will become commonplace as we move into the future. It is an exciting time to be a school media specialist or cybrarian. Many changes are in store for the profession.

REFERENCES

American Association of School Libraries & Association for Educational Communication and Technology. (1998). *Information power: Building partnerships for learning.* Chicago: American Library Association.

Miller, Marilyn. (2000, November). Location is everything. [Electronic version]. *School Library Journal, 46*(11), 50. Retrieved April 4, 2004, from: http://www. findarticles.com/cf_0/m1299/11_46/67328855/p1/article.jhtml

Miller, Marilyn & Shontz, Marilyn. (1998, May 1). More services, more staff, more money: A portrait of a high-service library media center. Retrieved April 4, 2004, from *School Library Journal Online:* http://slj.reviewsnews.com/ index.asp?layout=article&articleid=CA152993&publication=slj

Minnesota standards for effective school library media programs: Checklist for assessment, planning, implementation and evaluation. (2000). Retrieved April 4, 2004, from: http://www.memoweb.org/links/standardschecklist.pdf

FURTHER READINGS

Alabama Department of Education. (1999). *Literacy partners: A principal's guide to an effective library media program for the 21st century.* Montgomery, AL: Author. Retrieved April 4, 2004, from the Alabama State Department of Education web site: http://www.alsde.edu/general/LiteracyPartners.pdf

Beyond proficiency: Achieving a distinguished library media program. (2003, May). Retrieved April 4, 2004, from the Kentucky Department of Education web site: http://www.kde.state.ky.us/NR/rdonlyres/e6fusqvaxv4qioser3ewdfuds22dgh6 33h2q3ylnns7ttm5gp7ysrheqevzumavl5fc7wldtowp6dq4ehgku3t2xxhc/beyond proficiency.pdf

Ekhaml, Leticia. (2003, December). Look it up! Web reference service. *School Library Media Activities Monthly, 20*(4), 30–31.

Fisher, Julieta Dias & Hill, Ann. (2002). *Tooting your own horn: Web-based public relations for the 21st century librarian.* Worthington, OH: Linworth.

Fitzpatrick, K. A. (1998). *Program evaluation: Library media services.* Schaumberg, IL: National Study of School Evaluation.

Gonzalez, Brenda S. (1996). *Virtual school libraries: A dream or reality.* Retrieved April 4, 2004, from *Information Today* web site: http://www.infotoday.com/ MMSchools/MarMMS/gonzalez3.html

Gunn, Holly. (2002, July). Virtual libraries supporting student learning. *School Libraries Worldwide, 8*(2). Retrieved April 4, 2004, from *School Libraries Online* web site: http://www.iasl-slo.org/slwjuly02.html

Haycock, Ken. (1999). *Foundations for effective school library media programs.* Westport, CT: Libraries Unlimited.

Illinois School Library Media Association. (1999). *Linking for learning: Illinois school library media program guidelines.* Canton, IL: Author.

Lanning, Scott & Bryner, John. (2004). *Essential reference services for today's school media specialists.* Westport, CT: Libraries Unlimited.

Loertscher, David V. (2000). *Taxonomies of the school library media program.* 2nd ed. Worthington, OH: Linworth.

Loertscher, David V. & Woolls, Blanche. (2002). *Information literacy: A review of research: A guide for practitioners and researchers.* San Jose, CA: Hi Willow Research & Publishing.

McElmeel, Sharron L. (Ed.). (2000). *Shoptalk: Ideas for elementary school librarians & technology specialists* (2nd ed.). Worthington, OH: Linworth.

McElmeel, Sharron L. (Ed.). (2000). *Tips: Ideas for secondary school librarians and technology specialists* (2nd ed.). Worthington, OH : Linworth.

Manzo, Kathleen Kennedy. (1997, April 23). Libraries seeking updated role as learning center. Retrieved April 4, 2004, from *Education Week on the Web:* http://www.edweek.org/ew/vol-16/30libe.h16

Massachusetts school library media program standards for 21st century learning. (2003, November 9). Retrieved April 9, 2004, from the Massachusetts School Library Media Association web site: http://www.mslma.org/whoweare/standards/stndardsrev.pdf

Michigan Association for Media in Education. (n.d.). *Library media standards/curriculum.* Retrieved April 9, 2004, from the MAME web site: http://www.mame.gen.mi.us/resourc/standardslib.html

Minkel, Walter. (2002, October). Pew study: students prefer "virtual library"; new research report says schools not using the Internet effectively. *School Library Journal, 48*(10), 28–30.

Murray, Janet. (2000, March/April). Librarians evolving into cybrarians. *Multimedia Schools, 7*(2), 26–29.

Pearson, Tamara. (2000, November/December). Lights, camera, action: Student movies in 3 Days. *MultiMedia Schools, 7*(6), 42–45. Retrieved April 4, 2004, from: http://www.infotoday.com/MMSchools/nov00/pearson.htm

Resources for school libraries. (n.d.). Retrieved April 4, 2004, from: http://www.sldirectory.com/libsf/resf/computers.html

Riedling, Ann Marlow. (2003). *Reference skills for the library media specialist: Tools and tips.* Worthington, OH: Linworth.

School library and information literacy framework. (2000, June 8). Retrieved April 4, 2004, from Rhode Island Department of Education web site: http://www.ri.net/RIEMA/infolit.html

School library media curriculum template. (2000). Retrieved April 4, 2004, from Educational Media Association of New Jersey web site: http://www.emanj.org/documents/Template.pdf

School library standards: Library learning environment. Retrieved April 4, 2004, from Texas Education Agency web site: http://www.tea.state.tx.us/technology/libraries/lib_standards_library_env.html

Schrock, Kathleen. (Ed.). (2000). *The technology connection: Building a successful school library media program.* Worthington, OH: Linworth.

Schubert, Leda. (1999, December). School library media evaluation. Retrieved April 4, 2004, from University of Georgia web site: http://www.arches. uga.edu/~dowdyl/libraryevaluation.doc

Stripling, Barbara K. (Ed.). (1999). *Learning and libraries in an information age: Principles and practice.* Westport, CT: Libraries Unlimited.

Thompson, Helen & Henley, Susan A. (2002). *Fostering information literacy: Connecting national standards, goals 2000, and the SCANS report.* Westport, CT: Libraries Unlimited.

U.S. Department of Education. (1998). *Literature review: Assessment of the role of school and public libraries in support of the National education goals.* Rockville, MD: Westat, Inc.

Wasman, Ann M. (1998). *New steps to service: Common-sense advice for the school library media specialist.* Chicago: American Library Association.

Zilonis, Mary Frances, et al. (2002). *Strategic planning for school library media centers.* Lanham, MD: Scarecrow Press.

Chapter 4

DEVELOPING A SCHOOL LIBRARY MEDIA CENTER PROGRAM

This chapter discusses the four functions that can help the school library media specialist to make a school library media program more effective: (1) conducting the instructional program, (2) utilizing instructional components related to the media center, (3) promoting public relations methods to acquaint the school community with the center's resources and services, and (4) looking at the hours of service, attendance, and use of the online public access catalog (OPAC). Sample lesson plans are provided to show how information literacy can be integrated within the curriculum content areas and how standards can be met. Web sites for additional lesson plans are provided. Also covered in the chapter are: the importance of the school media curriculum; developing instructional objectives; group computer instruction; reading, viewing, and listening guidance; displays; media center web pages; in-service programs; Internet filtering; OPACS; and cooperation with the public library and other libraries in the community.

THE SCHOOL LIBRARY MEDIA SPECIALIST AND THE CURRICULUM

The school library media center's program for helping students and staff in the use of materials depends largely on the curriculum. It is the school media specialist's responsibility to provide the expertise and leadership necessary to ensure that the school media program is an integral part of the instructional program. It is through the school media specialist's four roles as teacher, information specialist, instructional partner, and program administrator that the information resources and services of the school media program are meshed with the individual interests and information needs of the students and staff of the school community. As an instructional partner, the school media specialist initiates planning for teaching information literacy skills with the teacher within the content area of the curriculum. The emphasis on any of the four roles of the school media specialist may vary at different schools depending on the resources, goals and objectives, and the priorities set for the instructional program (AASL & AECT, 1998). A document from the Massachusetts Department of Education (2001) delineates the four functions of the school library media specialist in Exhibit 4.1.

Regardless of the particular school, the school media specialist has the unique vantage point from which to observe, assist, and evaluate student competence in utilizing research and information literacy skills. When the media specialist works with teachers to plan instruction and the media specialist teaches the research skills in conjunction with classroom activities, the student is more likely to learn and retain the skills necessary to access, evaluate, and use information. The teaching role of the school media specialist is crucial to a good school media program. Careful planning is a fundamental factor in the success of a program in which individualized learning or independent inquiry takes place. This principle is vital to the development of any successful school library media program of instruction. It involves the curriculum, both instructional and recreational, or the curricula of the school community in its entirety. Because of the importance of the teaching role, some states require that a school media specialist be certified as a teacher. Understanding current and future teaching methods is important for each professional person on the staff; experience adds another dimension. Some states require actual years of teaching experience and certification at the level of library work practiced.

School library media programs of instruction are fundamental in a modern, growing curriculum. These programs flow directly from the classroom. Two results of such programs are increased student competence and student gratification in satisfying their emerging interests. There is a trend for state departments of education to produce curriculum guides for school library media centers for the teaching of information literacy skills based on the standards set forth in *Information Power* (AASL & AECT, 1998). Awareness of new sources of information and various formats mandates that more will be done. The curriculum will continue to be the basis for

Exhibit 4.1.
Four Functions of the School Library Media Specialist.

1. As *teacher* the LMS teaches:

   - research and information access skills;

   - media production, uses, interpretation and appreciation;

   - children and young adult literature appreciation

   - information literacy skills;

   - critical thinking, and problem solving skills pertinent to information literacy curriculum.

2. As information specialist the LMS:

   - provides access systems for print, media and technology collections, including books and periodicals, audio visual hardware and software collections, CD-ROM, and computer databases;

   - provides reference services to faculty and students;

   - informs faculty of new developments in educational resources and technology.

3. As instructional partner the LMS:

   - provides, during curriculum planning phases, appropriate information regarding resources for developing curriculum;

   - integrates information literacy objectives, units, and lesson plans into new and developing curriculum;

   - provides training and support to faculty and students when new technology is acquired;

   - maintains currency in the collections as new print and non-print resources pertinent to the program of studies are published, as the budget allows.

Exhibit 4.1. (continued)

---

4. As program administrator the LMS:

- manages scheduling, maintenance, and repair of hardware collections;

- plans and administers the school library media program;

- develops budgets;

- selects, trains and supervises school library support staff;

- manages the utilization of library facilities;

- devises public relations programs for students, faculty, parents, school committee, and community.

Printed with permission.
Source: Massachusetts School Library Media Association.
(2001, August 14) *Rationale for Today's School Library Media Center*. Retrieved April 5, 2004 from: http://www.mslma.org/whoweare/standards.html#Rationale

developing students' information literacy skills and improving technology use via the Internet for lifelong learning.

THE INSTRUCTIONAL PROGRAM

Opinions differ as to the amount of teaching of information literacy skills that should take place in the media center. Proponents of an extensive teaching program maintain that mastery of skills is necessary to produce independent, resourceful users of information and media. Opponents argue that although learning about information and its use may be necessary, too much valuable time is spent on details such as explaining the OPAC or the Dewey decimal system when the most important aspect of reference and research work is actually using the information effectively. Whatever policies are adopted, the instructional program should not be conducted in a vacuum unrelated to students' actual needs. Teaching of information literacy skills should be functional and should be integrated with the students' other educational activities in the classroom.

Students should be offered reading guidance as part of the instructional program to foster a love of reading for pleasure. Reading guidance requires the school library media specialist to determine student interests and to satisfy needs as they arise individually or in groups. Frequently, classroom teachers look for ways to monitor reading other than the student book report by having students produce videos, HyperStudio, or PowerPoint presentations. Several methods are effective to motivate students to read and to report on their reading. For example, a third-grade class might dress up as book characters and dramatize a scene from a book to present in an assembly or a classroom. A fifth-grade class could select their favorite book titles and share their selections on a bulletin board. Students might generate a bibliography of their favorite titles on the computer to be shared with the entire class. Some schools use silent reading for thirty minutes a day as a way to motivate students, faculty, and staff to read for pleasure. The school library media specialist provides reading guidance for everyone in the school.

Besides locating information in the library or on the Internet, students need to be taught how to think critically in using information. By carefully planning, the teacher and the school media specialist can determine strategies to teach units within the subject content areas that incorporate both information literacy and critical thinking skills as part of the instructional activities. The instructional program is conducted on two levels: informal and formal.

Informal Instruction

The teaching that takes place spontaneously when answering an individual student's request is an example of informal instruction. This teaching might include demonstrating how to do a search on a search engine or giving a brief, impromptu book talk to answer the question: "Could you recommend a good book to read?"

Informal instruction is certainly valuable because it directly satisfies a student's individual needs. The obvious drawbacks are that it is time-consuming and repetitious for the staff and that it depends on student willingness or ability to ask questions. To help match instruction to immediate needs, some school library media centers produce short teaching cassette tapes. Each tape deals concisely with a particular topic, for example, the arrangement of the material on shelves, instructions for operating a particular piece of equipment, or the use of the OPAC. The cassette equipment is placed close to the material or equipment described on the tape. Some centers use computer programs to acquaint students with the media center's resources and to introduce them to the Internet.

Formal Instruction

The presentation of a preplanned lesson before a group of students is an example of formal instruction. The lesson plans should adhere to established guidelines of teaching that include a statement of goals expressed in concrete behavioral terms, an introduction that catches students' attention and explains the purpose of the lesson, an effective presentation of the material to be learned, standards to be addressed, and an opportunity for feedback and evaluation. The activities of the lesson allow for the interaction between the use of materials in the school media center or information on the Internet and the learning outcomes planned by the teacher and media specialist. The lessons are usually scheduled in school library media center classrooms, or regular classrooms, where materials or Internet access is available, but where disruptions can be avoided. Many commercially prepared materials for teaching information literacy skills are available; however, it is best to ascertain that they serve the goals of the lesson planned by the teacher and the school library media specialist.

Group Computer Instruction

Over the last decade, computer technology and the Internet have influenced drastic changes in the way instruction is delivered. Group computer instruction is leading to innovative changes and improvement in content delivery. Because technology evolves so rapidly, it is advantageous to students to receive group computer instruction allowing them to learn to use, access, and evaluate information on the Internet as quickly as possible. Most group instruction takes place in labs or in school media centers where computers are more readily available. Hands-on instruction is crucial to the process. Instead of blackboards and overhead projectors being the most common instructional tools, as it was for many years, teachers are now using group computer instruction because it is more dynamic and adds a new dimension to their lessons. They enjoy making their lessons come alive for large student groups with PowerPoint and HyperStudio presentations as well as lessons using information from the Internet. Instruction is improving and students are more motivated to learn. Technology has opened up other avenues of learning, one such avenue is e-learning or distance instruction.

E-Learning or Distance Instruction

Internet technology enables students and teachers to learn anytime and anywhere through e-learning or distance learning. This method of learning utilizes a network, basically the Internet, to deliver and facilitate life-long learning. It can be offered to a group of learners simultaneously or it can be individualized and self-paced, where the learner has more control over what is learned. Advantages of implementing e-learning into the curriculum include:

> Content access to information enabling real-time, real world exploration; global learning through the use of email or live interactive online discussions; individual learning with tailored content and instruction to the unique learning interests, needs, and style of students; and improved communications that facilitate teacher to student and parent interactions. (E-Learning, 2001, p. 4)

There is still much to be learned about e-learning and its many applications in the educational environment. As different applications are explored, there may be some scheduling implications as well.

Flexible Scheduling and Instruction

The practice of using flexible scheduling of groups or classes into the media center on an informal, as-need-demands basis is becoming more accepted but not widely practiced. Not only does this promote collaborative planning between teachers and the media specialist, but it also helps achieve the goal of making school library media center instruction an integrated, cohesive part of the school curriculum. Unfortunately, there are still some schools where rigid scheduling of classes into the school library media center is still practiced. The reason for adhering to this outmoded procedure is more administrative than educational and often is in the interest of freeing teachers for planning periods. Fixed scheduling can throw both content and timing of lessons off balance, harming the entire instructional program.

One fear sometimes expressed about flexible scheduling is that, depending on the teacher, some classes will not visit the school library media center often enough or that certain information literacy skills will not be taught. In practice this fear has proved groundless. Any such danger can be avoided in a well-run program where there is constant communication with teachers and where realistic, flexible instructional programs have been adopted.

Flexible scheduling does not mean that teaching information literacy skills should be placed on a catch-as-catch-can, unstructured basis. Every school district should adopt a sequential instructional plan that delineates the skills to be mastered at each grade level. However, apart from a basic orientation to the school library media center, the teaching of these information literacy skills are integrated with subject content courses and student activities.

Collaborative Instruction

When teachers and school media specialists collaboratively plan the teaching of units in the subject content courses in conjunction with the information literacy skills, a partnership develops which integrates the classroom learning experience with the school library media center activities. Student learning is enhanced when instruction is connected to other knowledge and experience. When these connections are made explicit, the transfer of learning between media center and classroom is facilitated. Most often, the school library media specialist must initiate planning with teachers because they are sometimes unaware of the services available and the rewards of working as partners in the instructional process. Once teachers understand the concept of forming a partnership to enhance the learning experience, they are more likely to be amiable to collaborative planning, but first teachers must be aware that both parties contribute their expertise to this planning process. School media specialists who are beginning the collaboration process for the first might use Exhibit 4.2, Checklist for Instructional Design of Collaboratively Planned Unit, to aid them in planning collaboratively with teachers for instruction. This checklist reflects current trends in instructional design.

In designing lesson plans that utilize the school media specialist partnership, a collaborative planning template can be used by the media specialist to serve as a guideline for the planning process. Such a template is displayed below in Exhibits 4.3 and 4.4, which was developed by Mary Johnson (2003) to aid the process for the school media specialist and the teacher. Exhibit 4.3 shows a blank template ready to be used. Exhibit 4.4 shows the same template completed as planned by the teacher, media specialist, and the technology specialist.

Exhibit 4.2.
Checklist for Instructional Design of Collaboratively Planned Unit.

SLMS=School library media specialist; T=Teacher;
J=Joint responsibility

Instructional Design Components	Mark X when completed
Initial Contact	
Initiates contact with teacher (SLMS)	
Sets initial planning time (J)	
Initial Planning Session	
Needs assessment of topic to be taught (T)	
Determines gaps in student knowledge (T)	
Sets timeline for unit (T)	
Identifies subject of unit (T)	
Selects topics to be taught (J)	
Identifies grade level for unit (J)	
Creates criteria for judging unit effectiveness (J)	
Learner Analysis	
Selects learner analysis instrument (J)	
Determines gaps in student knowledge (T)	
Determines gaps in prerequisite skills (T)	
Determines learning preferences of students (J)	
Identifies prerequisite skills needed by students to process and access information (J)	
Identifies skills mastered by students (T)	
Decides skills to be developed by students (T/J)	
Identifies reading abilities of students (T)	
Goals and Objectives	
Writes behavioral educational goal (J)	
Writes behavior objectives to meet goal (J)	
Establish information literacy skill objectives.(J)	
Content Analysis	
Breaks content into small segments to be taught (J)	
Determines prerequisite skills needed (J)	
Determines concepts to be taught (J)	
Determines principles and rules to be taught (J)	
Determines models to be taught (J)	
Identify standards to support unit (J)	
Assessment	
Administers pretest to determine student knowledge (J)	
Designs formative evaluation strategies that are ongoing throughout unit (J)	
Observes student progress during instruction (J)	
Designs summative evaluation checklists & rubrics (J)	
Teaching Strategies & Activities	
Selects teaching strategies tied to objectives (J)	
Determines strategies for multiple intelligences (J)	
Proposes grouping for teaching information literacy skills (J)	
Identifies minimum expectations of student learning (J)	
Designs assignment check points to determine student learning (J)	
Allows for a variety of ability levels of students by differentiating assignments (J)	

Exhibit 4.2. (continued)

Materials Selection	
Selects materials for concepts to be taught (J)	
Selects materials in different formats to fit student learning styles (J)	
Selects materials to fit reading levels of students (J)	
Identifies materials to be produced (J)	
Selects web sites that support the unit. (J)	
Identifies materials to be borrowed from other libraries (J)	
Identifies materials that match student skill levels (J)	
Role Definitions	
Plans collaboratively the content to be taught and by whom (J)	
Plans to teach information literacy skills together (J)	
Plans location for instruction of both teacher and media specialist (J)	
Implementation	
Designs lesson plans (J)	
Establishes time segments for teaching the unit (J)	
Determines student groupings for instructional segments (J)	
Product Evaluation	
Designs rubrics for evaluating products, such as video, exam, multimedia presentation, research paper (J)	
Designs checklist and rubric for students to evaluate own progress (J)	
Unit Evaluation	
Evaluates unit effectiveness according to set criteria (J)	
Sets a time for evaluating unit of study (J)	
Evaluates teacher/school media specialist collaboration (J)	
Records suggested revisions of the unit based on perceived weaknesses and strengths (J)	
Revises unit and retains for future use.	

SLMS=School library media specialist; T=Teacher;
J=Joint responsibility

Exhibit 4.3.
Collaborative Planning Template.

Dates:				Teacher:		
Times:				Content Area:		
	Blocked	Unblocked		Assignment Name:		

OVERVIEW OF LESSON

STUDENT TASKS

FINAL PRODUCT/ASSESSMENT

RESOURCES/TRAINING REQUIRED

NOTES

CLASSROOM TEACHER	TECHNOLOGY STAFF	LIBRARY STAFF

Printed with permission. Source: Johnson, Mary. (2003). *Collaborative Planning Template*. Unpublished manuscript, Glenview Middle School, Colorado Springs, CO.

Exhibit 4.4.
Completed Collaborative Planning Template.

Dates:	Dec. 3/4, 2001		Teacher:	Debbie Strehlow			
Times:	8:30-10:15;12:20-2:45		Content Area:	7th Grade Science			
	Blocked	Unblocked X	Assignment Name:	Bacterial and Viral Diseases			

OVERVIEW OF LESSON

Students will research viruses and bacteria in pairs, write a 2-page paper, and prepare an in-class presentation.

STUDENT TASKS

1. Students (working in pairs) will use two days of library time to research an assigned viral or bacterial disease. 2. Students will reference a minimum of one GALE Health database article, 1 other electronic source, and 1 book source. 3. Students will cite their research in proper MLA bibliographic format. 4. Students will write one 2-page paper and present their findings on their topic to the class.

FINAL PRODUCT/ASSESSMENT

One 2-page paper and a class presentation to be assessed with a rubric developed by the teacher.

RESOURCES/TRAINING REQUIRED

The librarian will: 1. Introduce GALE Health Resources database (how to access from school and home computers, how to search, strengths and weaknesses of various sources, etc.). 2. Introduce pre-selected web sites posted on the Teams/Homework page. 3. Show two reference sets, Diseases and Sick!, as well as other non-fiction titles. 4. Demonstrate proper bibliographic format for GALE, a web page, and a reference volume. Show where sample bibliographic formats can be found on the library web pages.

NOTES

Check with Janet Meadows for bib formats and what bibliographic citation training the students have already received in Language Arts classes. Also, what is the status of student Internet approval forms and stickers in student planners?

CLASSROOM TEACHER	TECHNOLOGY STAFF	LIBRARY STAFF
1. Give the library staff a copy of the assignment. 2. Develop a rubric that includes group contribution using the Colorado Model Information Literacy Guidelines for "Student as Group Contributor." 3. Consult with the librarian as the assignment progresses.	1. Set up projection system for introductory demonstration. 2. Post the web sites for viral and bacterial diseases on the 7 Silver team page. 3. Print any missing Internet agreement stickers and place in planners.	1. Compile a list of viral and bacterial diseases and give to teacher. 2. Locate the latest videos in the collection on bacteria and viruses and check out to teacher. 3. Work with teacher on any necessary training for citing sources, particularly electronic sources. 4. Identify relevant disease web sites and annotate them for posting to team page. 5. Give teacher a copy of Colorado Model Information Literacy Guidelines.

Printed with permission. Source: Johnson, Mary. (2003). *Completed Collaborative Planning Template*. Unpublished manuscript, Glenview Middle School, Colorado Springs, CO.

INSTRUCTIONAL COMPONENTS

Several components of instruction need to be addressed as they relate to the media center. Media specialists need to plan lessons that integrate information literacy skills into the content areas of the curriculum. From those skills, the media center derives its own curriculum in the school. Both the media specialist and teachers have their own curriculum to teach. When they collaborate in teaching units, they satisfy both their curriculum needs. They must develop goals and objectives they both consider to be important to student learning. The lesson plans they design must show collaboration of both partners in the instructional process. Sometimes they search the Internet for lesson plans and adapt them to meet their own instructional goals.

Integration of Information Literacy Skills into Content Areas

The information literacy skills curriculum should be a collaboratively planned effort between the school media specialist and the classroom teacher. Some suggestions are provided for integrating the information literacy skills with the content areas in Exhibit 4.5 below.

School library media professionals and teachers collaboratively teach appropriate skills at each grade level and in each subject content area classroom. The integration of the media information literacy skills curriculum into the subject content areas is crucial for students if they are to develop the necessary skills to deal with information in the twenty-first century and if they are to become lifelong learners in a rapidly changing society. Information literacy standards from *Information Power* (AASL & AECT, 1998) provide guidelines for accessing, evaluating, and using information critically. Indicators of attaining the skills are measurable objectives by which to judge student progress and performance. The nine Information Literacy Standards for Student Learning and their indicators can be found in *Information Power: Building Partnerships for Learning* (AASL & AECT, 1998). Media specialists working with teachers will want to be knowledgeable about the subject content standards so they can be integrated with the information literacy standards as they collaborate on teaching content to students. Both the information literacy standards and the content standards web sites are provided on page 95.

Exhibit 4.5.
Integrating Information Literacy Skills Into Content Areas.

Art	
Unit:	The Nature of Art
Skills:	Location of art prints
	Use of Internet
	Use of key words
Unit:	Van Gogh, the Man and His Art
Skills:	Use of reference books
	Use of biographical sources
	Use of slides as a reference source.
English	
Unit:	Who Wrote Shakespeare's Plays
Skills:	Use of online database to find sources
	Use of reference books
	Use of index
	Use of handbooks
	Use of *British Authors*
Unit:	Write Your Own Fiction Book
Skills:	Parts of a book
	Use of Illustrations
	What is a fiction book?
Foreign Language	
Unit:	Current events on a foreign country
Skills:	Use of search engines
Unit:	Travel tips
Skills:	Prepare a bibliography
	Location of books
	Use of reference materials
Health	
Unit:	AIDS
Skills:	Use of a variety of media, such as videos, PowerPoint presentation
	Use of science periodicals
	Use of science encyclopedias
	Use of Internet
Unit:	Cure and Prevention of Common Diseases
Skills:	Location of science books
	Use of general encyclopedias
	Use of Internet
Unit:	Diseases
Skills:	Use of reference books
	Use of indexes in books
	Use of Internet

Exhibit 4.5. (continued)

Home Economics/Family and Consumer Science		
Unit:	Costumes	
Skills:	Use of reference books	
	Use of online searching	
Unit:	Foods from Other Countries	
Skills:	Location of materials	
	Classify food groups	
	Use of search engines	
Unit:	Furnishing a home	
Skills:	Use of *Consumer Reports*	
	Use of picture file	
	Use of community resource file	
Language Arts		
Unit:	Poetry	
Skills:	Use a word processor to write a poem	
	Develop an anthology of poetry.	
Unit:	Authors	
Skills:	Use of search engines	
	Develop a PowerPoint about an author	
	Use graphic organizers	
Marketing		
Unit:	Advertising	
Skills:	Synthesize information from various sources	
	Classification skills	
	Compare and contrast types of advertising	
	Use of *Consumer Reports*	
Math and Science		
Unit:	Graphing Animal Sizes	
Skills:	Use of Science encyclopedias	
	Use of general encyclopedias	
Music		
Unit:	American Composers	
Skills:	Use of music reference books	
	Use of biographical books	
	Use of *Current Biography*	
Physical Education		
Unit:	Exercise For Good Health	
Skills:	Production of a video	
	Use of Internet	
Unit:	Women & Men in Sports	
Skills:	Location of biography books	
	Use of *Current Biography*	
	Location of collective biography	
	Use of biographical dictionaries	

Exhibit 4.5. (continued)

Reading
    Unit: Caldecott Award Books
    Skills: What is a Caldecott Award?
              Location of Caldecott Award Books
              Definition of an illustrator
    Unit: Why Read for Pleasure?
    Skills: Use of graphic novels
              What is plot, theme, setting?
              Character development

Science
    Unit: Weather
    Skills: Use of weather maps
              Develop chart showing similarities in certain
              types of weather
              Use dictionary for spelling and definitions

Social Studies
    Unit: The Constitution
    Skills: What is a primary source?
              Develop a chronology
              Use of primary sources on the Internet
    Unit: Europe, Then and Now
    Skills: Map skills
              Use of the almanac
              Apply research skills through historical
              materials
    Unit: It Happened This Week
    Skills: Use of Internet
              Use of periodical databases

Information Literacy Standards Web Site:

http://www.ala.org/aasl/ip_nine.html

This site contains the nine AASL information literacy standards for student learning. To locate the indicators, one will need to consult *Information Power* (AASL & AECT, 1998).

Content Standards Web Site:

http://www.mcrel.org/compendium/browse.asp

This site contains subject content standards for K–12, including technology. Information literacy standards are not included.

Standards by State and Subject Areas Web Site:

http://edstandards.org/standards.html

This site contains K–12 standards by subject areas as well as standards by state, including AASL standards and others related to the school library media area.

The Maryland State Department of Education (2000) web site contains a draft of library media learning outcomes to be attained. Another part of the web site contains very detailed outcomes and indicators for other content areas of the curriculum (K–8), including science, social studies, mathematics, and language arts. This information can be found at the following web site: http://www.mdk12.org/mspp/mspap/whats-tested/learneroutcomes/index.html. Exhibit 4.6 provides the information about library media learning outcomes.

Eugene Hainer (1997), from the Colorado State Library, developed some examples of how to align information literacy standards with classroom content standards developed and disseminated by the Colorado Department of Education (1995–1997). Exhibits 4.7–4.15 are included below, which provide guidance in how to align both contents.

Exhibit 4.6.
Library Media Learning Outcomes. Maryland State
Department of Education.

Outcome #1
**Students will demonstrate the ability to locate and use
information resources, equipment and other technologies
effectively and efficiently.**
Outcome 1 focuses on the location and use of print,
electronic and multimedia resources. To use information
effectively and efficiently, students must formulate
compelling questions, develop information-seeking strategies,
read, comprehend and synthesize information in order to
communicate new meaning and deeper knowledge.

Indicators

- Describe the physical arrangement of the media center.
- Define the need for personal or curricular information.
- Form questions based on identified information needs.
- Use a wide range of information sources.
- Apply information-seeking strategies.
- Acquire information from varied sources through reading,
  listening, and viewing.

Outcome #2
**Students will demonstrate the ability to review, evaluate,
and select media.**
Outcome 2 focuses on the effective review, evaluation, and
selection of information resources for an identified
information need. Through examination of established
criteria, the most appropriate resources can be obtained.

Indicators

- Develop criteria for the evaluation of information
  sources.
- Determine accuracy, relevance and comprehensiveness.
- Distinguish among fact, point of view, and opinion.
- Identify inaccurate and misleading information.
- Select information appropriate to the identified
  problem.
- Assess the quality of the process and products of
  personal information seeking.
- Devise strategies for revising, improving, and updating
  self-generated knowledge.

Exhibit 4.6. (continued)

Outcome #3
Students will demonstrate the ability to learn and apply reading, research and critical thinking skills to organize, and synthesize information in order to communicate new understanding.
Outcome 3 focuses on the effective use of reading, research and critical thinking skills in order to organize information to solve problems. Library media specialists and classroom teachers collaborate in the design of authentic research tasks.

Indicators

- Integrate new information into one's own knowledge.
- Apply information in critical thinking and problem solving.
- Apply an information problem solving process model to structure effective research.

Outcome #4
Students will demonstrate the ability to comprehend content in various types of media.
Outcome 4 establishes the purpose for reading, listening, and viewing: to read for information, to perform a task, and to engage in a literary experience.

Indicators

- Seeks information from diverse sources, contexts, disciplines, and cultures.
- Derives meaning from information presented creatively in a variety of formats.
- Processes and evaluates content from a variety of sources by applying comprehension skills.

Outcome #5
Students will demonstrate the ability to retrieve and manage information.
Outcome 5 focuses on the use of technology in the school library media center and other libraries. Information may be accessed readily through electronic sources. Appropriate skills are vital if the information accessed is to serve the intended purpose.

Exhibit 4.6. (continued)

Indicators

- Use appropriate strategies to retrieve information from a variety of electronic sources.
- Devise strategies for recording information.
- Select appropriate technology tools and applications to retrieve and manage information.
- Organize information for practical application.

Outcome #6
Students will demonstrate an appreciation of literature and other creative expressions as sources of information and recreation.
Outcome 6 focuses on the appreciation of literature as a reflection of, and an influence on human experience; the pursuit of reading for pleasure and enrichment; and, the value of books and other media as sources of information and recreation.

Indicators

- Recognize authors, illustrators, publishers, and producers of literature as reflectors of the human experience.
- Recognize that literature reflects, examines, and influences the human experience.
- Develop time to read a variety of materials on a regular basis.
- Select from a variety of literary forms, genres,and themes.
- Seek information related to various dimensions of personal well-being, such as career interests, community involvement, health matters, and recreational pursuits.
- Obtain books and media for personal use.
- Use library media centers, public, and other libraries regularly for reading materials.
- Share and promote books and media as sources of information and recreation.

Outcome #7
Students will demonstrate the ability to create materials in various formats.
Outcome 7 focuses on the production of media. The processes used to produce different media are explored and criteria are developed to determine the appropriate medium for a particular purpose.

Exhibit 4.6. (continued)

Indicators

- Demonstrate knowledge of the process used in developing various type of media.
- Discriminate among the various type of media to produce the appropriate medium for a particular purpose.
- Design, develop, and evaluate information products and solutions.
- Produce and communicate information and ideas in appropriate formats.
- Share knowledge and information with others.

Outcome #8
Students will demonstrate the ability to apply ethical behavior to the use of information.
Outcome 8 focuses on responsibilities related to the fair and equitable use of information in a democratic society, such as observance of copyright law and the promotion of intellectual freedom.

Indicators

- Demonstrate the appropriate care and handling of materials.
- Demonstrate safe operation and care of equipment.
- Follow the policies of the school library media center.
- Use information technology responsibly.
- Respect the principle of equitable access to information.
- Respect others' ideas and backgrounds and acknowledge their contributions.
- Respect the principles of intellectual freedom.
- Respect the intellectual property rights.

Aligning Information Literacy with Classroom Content Standards

Exhibit 4.7.
Information Literacy and History Standards.

	HISTORY
1. Constructs meaning from information. 2. Creates a quality product. 3. Learns independently. 4. Participates effectively as a group member. 5. Uses information and information technologies responsibly and ethically.	
LMC Activities that support one or more Content Standard History: Grades 9-12 Information Literacy Standards 1, 2, 3, 5 History Standards 1, 3, 4, 6 Each student will be assigned one country to research, using library resources, that is prominent in the news today: Iraq, Russia, or Iran. Students will construct a timeline of events that helped shape United States policy towards that country. Based on the research and information, students will prepare to debate in class whether the U.S. policy toward the country should be continued or changed.	1. Students understand the chronological organization of history and know how to organize events and people into major eras to identify and explain historical relationships. 2. Students know how to use the processes and resources of historical inquiry. 3. Students understand that societies are diverse and have changed over time. 4. Students understand how science, technology, and economic activity have developed, changed, and affected societies throughout history. 5. Students understand political institutions and theories that have developed and changed over time. 6. Students know that religious and philosophical ideas have been powerful forces throughout history.

Printed with permission. Source: Hainer, Eugene. (1997). Colorado State Library, Denver, CO.

Exhibit 4.8.
Information Literacy and Reading & Writing Standards.

	READING AND WRITING
1. Constructs meaning from information. 2. Creates a quality product. 3. Learns independently. 4. Participates effectively as a group member. 5. Uses information and information technologies responsibly and ethically.	
LMC Activities that support one or more Content Standard Reading & Writing: Grades 6-8 Information Literacy Standards 1,2,4 Reading & Writing Standards 1,2,4,6 A group of three students will read a historic fiction novel and prepare a reader's theater script using one scene they feel is representative of the time period, struggle, and tone of the novel. The presentation should be 3-5 minutes and will be evaluated using a rubric by the library media specialist, classroom teacher, and students.	1. Students read and understand a variety of materials. 2. Students write and speak for a variety of purposes and audiences. 3. Students write and speak using conventional grammar, usage, sentence structure, punctuation, capitalization, and spelling. 4. Students apply thinking skills to their reading, writing, speaking, listening, and viewing. 5. Students read to locate, select, and make use of relevant information from a variety of media, reference, and technological sources. 6. Students read and recognize literature as a record of human experience.

Printed with permission. Source: Hainer, Eugene. (1997).
Colorado State Library, Denver, CO.

Exhibit 4.9.
Information Literacy and Geography Standards.

1. Constructs meaning from information. 2. Creates a quality product. 3. Learns independently. 4. Participates effectively as a group member. 5. Uses information and information technologies responsibly and ethically.	**GEOGRAPHY**
LMC Activities that support one or more Content Standard Geography: Grades 6-7 Information Literacy Standards 2, 3, 5 Geography Standards 1, 2, 6 Students will use library resources to research a South American country in preparation for creating a travel brochure on that country using Desktop Publisher. The brochure must contain information about the weather patterns, a map depicting weather information drawn by the student, and should include at least 3 destinations of cultural importance in the country.	1. Students know how to use and construct maps, globes, and other geographic tools to locate and derive information about people, places, and environments. 2. Students know the physical and human characteristics of places, and use this knowledge to define and study regions and their patterns of change. 3. Students understand how physical processes shape Earth's surface patterns and systems. 4. Students understand how economic, political, cultural, and social processes interact to shape patterns of human populations, interdependence, cooperation, and conflict. 5. Students understand the effects of interactions between human and physical systems and the changes in meaning, use, distribution, and importance of resources. 6. Students apply knowledge of people, places, and environments to understand the past and present and to plan for the future.

Printed with permission. Source: Hainer, Eugene. (1997). Colorado State Library, Denver, CO.

Exhibit 4.10.

Information Literacy and Mathematics Standards.

1. Constructs meaning from information. 2. Creates a quality product. 3. Learns independently. 4. Participates effectively as a group member. 5. Uses information and information technologies responsibly and ethically.	**MATHEMATICS**
LMC Activities that support one or more Content Standard Mathematics: Grades 4-6 Information Literacy Standards 4,5 Mathematics Standards 1,3 Students will work in small groups to plan a method for determining the number of books on the library shelves. They will be given one class period to execute their plan, and will use Excel spreadsheets to display their data.	1. Students develop number sense and use numbers and number relationships in problem-solving situations and communicate the reasoning used in solving these problems. 2. Students use algebraic methods to explore, model, and describe patterns and functions involving numbers, shapes, data, and graphs in problem-solving situations and communicate the reasoning used in solving these problems. 3. Students use data collection and analysis, statistics, and probability in problem-solving situations and communicate the reasoning used in solving these problems. 4. Students use geometric concepts, properties, and relationships in problem-solving situations and communicate the reasoning used in solving these problems. 5. Students use a variety of tools and techniques to measure, apply the results in problem-solving situations, and communicate the reasoning used in solving these problems. 6. Students link concepts and procedures as they develop and use computational techniques, including estimation, mental arithmetic, paper-and-pencil, calculators, and computers, in problem-solving situations and communicate the reasoning used in solving these problems.

Printed with permission. Source: Hainer, Eugene. (1997). Colorado State Library, Denver, CO.

Exhibit 4.11.
Information Literacy and Science Standards.

1. Constructs meaning from information. 2. Creates a quality product. 3. Learns independently. 4. Participates effectively as a group member. 5. Uses information and information technologies responsibly and ethically.	**SCIENCE**
LMC Activities that support one or more Content Standards. Science: Grades 7-10 Information Literacy Standards 1, 2, 3, 5 Science Standards 3, 5 Students will conduct research on one endangered animal. They will determine the food chain for this animal, the possible causes for the endangered status, and possible effects of this animal becoming extinct. They will have at least one source from each of the following: book, electronic database, and a Web site. They will present their findings using PowerPoint, with a minimum of 6 slides and a maximum of 10 slides, which will include one slide for MLA bibliographic citations.	1. Students understand the processes of scientific investigation and design, conduct, communicate about, and evaluate such investigations. 2. Physical Science: Students know and understand common properties, forms, and changes in matter and energy. 3. Life Science: Students know and understand the characteristics and structure of living things, the processes of life, and how living things interact with each other and their environment. 4. Earth and Space Science: Students know and understand the processes and interactions of Earth's systems and the structure and dynamics of Earth and other objects in space. 5. Students know and understand interrelationships among science, technology, and human activity and how they can affect the world. 6. Students understand that science involves a particular way of knowing and understanding common connections among scientific disciplines.

Printed with permission. Source: Hainer, Eugene. (1997). Colorado State Library, Denver, CO.

Exhibit 4.12.
Information Literacy and Foreign Language Standards.

	FOREIGN LANGUAGE
1. Constructs meaning from information.	
2. Creates a quality product.	
3. Learns independently.	
4. Participates effectively as a group member.	
5. Uses information and information technologies responsibly and ethically.	1. Students communicate in a foreign language while demonstrating literacy in all four essential skills: listening, speaking, reading, and writing.
LMC Activities that support one or more Content Standard.	
Foreign Language: Grades 6-8	
Information Literacy Standards 2, 3, 5 Foreign Language Standard 1, 2	2. Students acquire and use knowledge of other cultures while developing foreign language skills.
Students will use library resources to research one country where their foreign language is spoken. They will prepare a travelogue in that language based on their research. The travelogue should contain entries for a 4-7 day trip with descriptions of at least three popular tourist destinations. This travelogue will be presented orally to the class.	

Printed with permission. Source: Hainer, Eugene. (1997).
Colorado State Library, Denver, CO.

Exhibit 4.13.
Information Literacy and Music Standards.

	MUSIC
1. Constructs meaning from information. 2. Creates a quality product. 3. Learns independently. 4. Participates effectively as a group member. 5. Uses information and information technologies responsibly and ethically.	
LMC Activities that support one or more Content Standard. Music Grades 4-6 Information Literacy Standards 1, 4, 5 Music Standard 4 The library media specialist will read the biography, *Wolfgang Amadeus Mozart,* by Mike Venezia. Based on the historical information offered in this book, students will work in groups to find books related to Mozart's historic time period. Each group must locate three facts about that time period, and write the fact on a large chart. The following week, the library media specialist will read the biography, *George Gershwin,* by Mike Venezia. Students will follow the same procedure they did for Mozart. The third week, the students will compare and contrast the information gathered on the two composers. They will use this information to make inferences about how the cultural views of each time period affected the work of the composer and the style of the music.	1. Students sing or play on instruments a varied repertoire of music, alone or with others. 2. Students will read and notate music. 3. Students will create music. Students will listen to, analyze, evaluate, and describe music. 4. Students will relate music to various historical and cultural traditions.

Printed with permission. Source: Hainer, Eugene. (1997). Colorado State Library, Denver, CO.

Exhibit 4.14.

Information Literacy and Physical Education Standards.

1. Constructs meaning from information. 2. Creates a quality product. 3. Learns independently. 4. Participates effectively as a group member. 5. Uses information and information technologies responsibly and ethically.	**PHYSICAL EDUCATION**
LMC Activities that support one or more Content Standard. Physical Education: Grades 6-8 Information Literacy Standards 1, 2 Physical Education Standard 3 Students will use library resources to research a particular sport and produce a report on the physical requirements required to excel in the sport. They will research the effect of chemicals such as alcohol and nicotine on body functions, and determine how these chemicals might be detrimental to a person involved in the sport.	1. Students demonstrate competent skills in a variety of physical activities and sports. 2. Students demonstrate competency in physical fitness. 3. Students demonstrate the knowledge of factors important to participation in physical activity.

Printed with permission. Source: Hainer, Eugene. (1997). Colorado State Library, Denver, CO.

Exhibit 4.15.
Information Literacy and Visual Arts Standards.

1. Constructs meaning from information. 2. Creates a quality product. 3. Learns independently. 4. Participates effectively as a group member. 5. Uses information and information technologies responsibly and ethically.	**VISUAL ARTS**
LMC Activities that support one or more Content Standard.	
	1. Students recognize and use the visual arts as a form of communication.
Visual Arts: Grades 2-3	2. Students know and apply elements of art, principles of design, and sensory and expressive features of visual arts.
Information Literacy Standards 1, 2, 5 Visual Arts Standards 1, 5	
	3. Students know and apply visual arts materials, tools, techniques, and processes.
Students will view famous paintings by various artists on the Internet from a Web site selected by the library media specialist. They will list adjectives to describe the paintings in terms of appearance, color, and mood. They will select 5 of the adjectives from their list to write a poem about the painting or the artist.	4. Students relate the visual arts to various historical and cultural traditions. 5. Students analyze and evaluate the characteristics, merits, and meaning of works of art.

Printed with permission. Source: Hainer, Eugene. (1997). Colorado State Library, Denver, CO.

Developing Instructional Objectives

Educational goals are usually stated in general terms, for example, to become a better citizen or to understand the beauty of language. Worthy as such aims may be, they remain abstract and difficult, if not impossible, to measure. Student behavior is most easily cast in behavioral or instructional objectives, such as, "a pupil will be able to locate the word *dinosaur* in a dictionary in three minutes." However, since learning is based on a multitude of fundamental previous knowledge (the alphabet, in the above example), it is not a good idea to start with such a basic exercise either. The important thing is not to confine objective writing to the lowest level of cognitive, affective, or psychomotor learning. The guidelines in Exhibit 4.16 will help the school library media specialist to write objectives more skillfully.

Four specific points should be used in formulating instructional objectives. This is normally called the ABCD method for writing instructional objectives: audience, behavior, condition, and degree. Suggestions for writing instructional objectives follow:

1. Identify the audience who will receive instruction. For example, Mrs. Jones' eighth grade math class will be able to...(Audience)

2. Identify by name the behavior you expect. Specify the kind of behavior that will be accepted as evidence that the learner has achieved the objective. Ask: What should the pupil be able to do at the end of the activity that he or she cannot do now? (Behavior)

3. Define the desired behavior further by describing the conditions under which the behavior will be expected to occur. Ask: Under what limitations of time, place, and so forth will the student be expected to show the desired outcome? (Condition)

4. Specify the criteria of acceptable performance by describing how well the student must perform. Ask: Exactly how well must the student perform to be acceptable? Identify a suitable measure by which to judge the relative degree of success or failure of the activity. Ask: How can the teacher measure what the student can do? (Degree)

Following are general principles to use when formulating objectives: (1) use an active verb that describes a visible activity or one that can be measured or tested in some way; (2) leave only one interpretation possible—if the behavior is inconclusive, the testing will be also; (3) as a final check to test the validity of the objectives, ask the following four questions: What do I want the student to do? Under what conditions do I expect the student to do it? How will the student do it? How will I know when the student has done it?

Putting all these elements together in a hypothetical educational objective frame in behavioral terms, the following might result: Within twenty minutes, the sixth-grader will list on paper the location, author, and title of five media-including book and non-book materials-about computers (or any appropriate subject) with all the above information exactly as it is displayed on the terminal of the online public access catalog (OPAC). The form shown in Exhibit 4.16 will be useful in preparing instructional objectives.

Lesson plans may be written in numerous ways. Exhibit 4.17 shows lesson plans written to show the standards for reading and writing, history, and information literacy standards. Exhibit 4.18 shows a very detailed lesson plan that suggests how it may be used in various content areas but does not explicitly name the standards of those content areas. More school systems are requiring the standards to be included in lesson plans.

Exhibit 4.16.
Writing Instructional Objectives.

Item	Plan
Behavioral task: (What do you want the student to do?)	
Curriculum area	
Estimated timeline	
What intellectual process is involved? The student will:	
Learn definitions	
Apply principles	
Apply concepts	
Follow rules	
Change or paraphrase information from one form into another	
Look for relationships between ideas	
Apply principles, rules, or information to unfamiliar problems or situations	
Analyze something by breaking it down into its parts	
Produce original solutions	
Evaluating information, object, or solutions against specific criteria	
What will you provide for the student?	
Information	
Print and non-print materials	
Graphic organizers	
Equipment	
Internet web sites	
Internet access	
Others	
How will the student be observed performing the task?	
Alone	
Speaking	
In groups	
Reading	
Writing	
Listening	
Online searching	
Other	
How will you judge the success of the performance?_____	
Exam	
Observation	
Product produced	
Other	

Exhibit 4.17.
Lesson Plan, Grade 6: Pyramids.

Students are expected to research Egyptian pyramids on the Internet using a variety of search techniques. They must locate answers to specific questions. After copying and pasting that information to a Word document, they will write a paragraph summarizing the questions' answers, using their own words. Final steps are to document the source, using appropriate citation format, and save.

Standards/Benchmarks

Standard: *Reading and Writing*
  5.1   Students can follow directions and locate relevant information.
  5.2   Students can use available technology to research and produce end-product that is accurately documented.
  5.3   Students can summarize factual content.

Standard: *History*
  3   Students understand societies are diverse and have changed over time.
  3.1.3 Students describe history, contributions that make up major regions of the world.

Standard: *Information Literacy*
  2.   Students analyze information to see if useful.
  8.3   Students draw conclusions and state in own words.
  8.4   Students give credit to source using appropriate format.

Standards Activities	Literacy Activities	Technology Activities
Highlight answers about pyramids	Scan for relevant information	Demonstrate, practice five ways to search on Internet
Develop topic sentence	Recognize web site's available bibliographic information	Open new document; save in class folder and on disk
Combine notes & write paragraph		
	Put bibliographic info into MLA format	Use word processing basics
Paraphrase: use own words		

Teacher Tasks	Media Specialist Tasks
Organize students in teams of two	Prepare student worksheet
Provide computer disks	Set up class folders on computer network
Monitor students locating relevant information	Set up screen and LCD
	Present Internet strategies
Monitor students' paragraphs for topic sentences and paraphrasing	Monitor students' bibliographic citations
	Monitor if work saved appropriately

Exhibit 4.17. (continued)

Student Worksheet
PYRAMIDS—THE INSIDE STORY
Mysteries of the Nile

1. Did you know there are at least five ways to search on the Internet? What are the advantages of each? The disadvantages?
   a. A specific web address: http://www.pbs.org
   b. Keyword search: pyramids + Egypt
   c. Directory Search: social studies>cultures>ancient.....
   d. MSN search: pyramids + ?
   e. Bookmarked web site

2. Can you locate the <u>available</u> bibliographic information?
   a. URL (web address)
   b. Author or group responsible
   c. Title of web page
   d. Date of web page

3. When you locate the appropriate screen for the PBS web site, find answers to the following questions.
   a. Who do historians think built the pyramids?
   b. Why did the average Egyptian work so hard on the pyramids?
   c. Why must you be careful about believing everything Herodotus, the historian, wrote about the pyramids?

4. Open a new document in Word.
   a. Enter a heading for your document.
   b. Copy and paste answers to the three questions. <u>Copy only the necessary words, not an entire sentence</u>.
   c. Copy and paste bibliographic information from the web site. Put into correct format.
   d. Write a paragraph summarizing your notes. Use your own words. Don't forget an effective topic sentence.
   e. Save document in class folder on network and also on a disk.

Printed with permission. Source: Tate, Jeanie. (2003). *The pyramids: A lesson plan.* Unpublished manuscript, Woodland Park, CO.

Exhibit 4.18.
Lesson Plan, Grades 2-4: Fall Harvest, Social Studies.

Library Media Skills Objectives:
The student will find information about the seasons on a farm
and the activities of each season.

The student will identify in information sources (print, non-
print, and human) the equipment and tools that are used for
the activities that occur during each season on a farm.

Curriculum (subject area) Objectives:
This activity may be incorporated in a unit on farm life or
the seasons.

Grade Levels: 2-4

Resources:
Library media center collection of farms, farming, seasons,
and tools.
Access to images of farms from the Internet.
Magazines or catalogs for pictures of farm equipment.
Large sheets of mural paper.
Paint, scissors, and paste.

Instructional Roles:
This project requires collaboration of instruction and
research between the teacher and the library media
specialist. While the teacher concentrates on the seasons
and life during each season in specific geographic areas, the
library media specialist helps with the location of images of
tools and equipment that are used. The teacher and library
media specialist may wish to concentrate on the seasons in
the region or the lesson may be more generic.

Activity and Procedures for Completion:
Begin the activity by singing songs about farmers. Include
such numbers as:
"Down on the Farm" (Greg and Steve. *We All Live Together.*
Vol. 5. Youngheart Records, 1994.)
"Hard Scrabble Harvest" (Priscilla Herdman. *Daydreamers.*
Music for Little People, 1993.)
"Lotta Seeds Grow" (Mary Miche. *Earthy Tunes.* Song Trek
Music, 1987.)
"Oats, Beans and Barley" (Raffi. *Baby Beluga.* MCA Records,
1977.)
"The Planting Song" (Janice Buckner. *Little Friends for
Little Folks.* A Gentle Wind, 1986.

Exhibit 4.18. (continued)

Enjoy making movements to accompany the songs. After this, open a discussion about what farmers do. Are there farms in the area?

What is grown? If possible, invite a farmer to the school or arrange a field trip. Supplement with videotapes.

Explain to the students that they will have a chance to learn about the seasons on a farm. Identify the seasons and then allow time for students to select a season group in which they would like to work. Each group of four or five students will consider the season and the place. They will use resources to collect information on the weather and the activities that might be occurring at that particular time. (Farm murals will vary depending on whether the farm is in northeast, south and so forth. Farms may include orchards and even fish farms if the children are creative.)

The library media specialist works with the small groups to review what might be going on during a season and help in searching for pictures that show the tools involved. The library media specialist will provide books, brochures, and non-print materials, as well as the names of people who might be helpful. If possible, provide students with telephone access to farmers who have agreed to answer children's questions about what they do at each season and what tools they use.

The group uses the information collected to decide on a scene that would show a typical activity and the tools used. Students may combine painting with cut-outs of equipment. The library media specialist may assist in searching the Internet to find appropriate pictures of such equipment. (Equipment may range from large mechanical pickers to simple trowels and gloves.) Students may keep a list of what the farmer needs during the season that is represented.

Murals may be displayed prominently with the names of the artists and the sources used. Take pictures of the students with their murals.

Evaluation:
The student will use resources (print, non-print, and human) to find information about the seasons on a farm, the activities of each season, and the tools and equipment used. They will complete an illustrated mural that incorporates the information located.

Exhibit 4.18. (continued)

Follow-Up:
Students may branch off and investigate other career fields
in terms of the differences in the seasons and the tools
used.

Students may select a particular tool and find the history of
how the tool or piece of equipment was developed or how it
has changed over time.

Printed with permission. Social Studies: Fall Harvest.
(2001, October). *School Library Media Activities Monthly,*
18(2), 19-20.

Lesson Plan Web Sites

Information Literacy Web Sites

Baltimore County Public Schools:

http://www.bcpl.net/~sullivan/modules/

From Baltimore County Public schools, several lesson plans are offered that
incorporate content and information literacy standards.

Big 6 Lesson Plans:

The Big 6: http://www.big6.com/resources.htm

There are several lesson plan ideas on this web site posted by Big 6 authors,
Michael Eisenberg and Robert E. Berkowitz. Additional links are available.

Boston Public Schools:

http://boston.k12.ma.us/teach/library/default.asp

Boston Public Schools Information Literacy Curriculum from 2000
includes specific lesson plans for grades K–8.

Integrating Internet Resources into the Curriculum: Lesson Plans:

http://www.libsci.sc.edu/miller/Older.htm

This site contains lesson plans selected by Elizabeth Miller, University of
South Carolina.

Learn North Carolina:

http://www.learnnc.org/

A database of lesson plans is available at this site. Enter "information skills"
in the lesson plan search and you will have 250 plans to browse through!

Michigan Educator's Library:

http://mtn.merit.edu/resources/media/information_literacy.html

Lesson plans involving research skills are furnished by the Michigan Educator's Library.

SBC Pacific Blue Bell Web'n Learning Sites Library:

http://www.kn.pacbell.com/wired/bluewebn/#table

Blue Web'n provides a huge collection of lesson plans and other resources. Search by content, subject, or grade for a specific type of resource.

Thematic Units for Primary Grades:

http://www.libsci.sc.edu/miller/Unitlink.htm

Library science students at the University of South Carolina provide these lesson plans for primary grades.

WebQuests by Bernie Dodge:

http://edweb.sdsu.edu/webquest/webquest.html

A WebQuest is an excellent way to combine a teacher's subject area knowledge and a media specialist's research expertise to create a meaningful collaborative project that requires critical thinking and active learning on the part of students. This page offers an overview of the WebQuest strategy as well as collections of sample WebQuests created by teachers, media specialists, and student teachers.

General Content Lesson Plans

AOL Lesson Plans:

http://school.aol.com/teachers/lesson_plans.adp

AOL offers a database of lesson plans that can be searched by state standard, keyword, grade level, subject or topic.

Blue Web'N Lesson Plans:

http://www.kn.pacbell.com/wired/bluewebn/

This site is a searchable library of 1,800+ outstanding Internet learning sites categorized by subject area, grade level, and format. It includes lessons, activities, projects, resources, references, and tools. Only the most useful sites are included on this site, especially online activities targeted at learners. Searchers can be made by grade level, broad subject area, or specific subcategories. Each week five new sites are added.

Colorado State Department of Education Lesson Plans:

http://www.cde.state.co.us/action/curric/info/middle.htm

Various projects/lessons are included that incorporate curricular and information literacy standards.

Core Knowledge Lesson Plans:

http://www.coreknowledge.org/CKproto2/resrcs/

This collection contains units and lesson plans developed by teachers in Core Knowledge® schools.

Gateway Lesson Plans:

http://www.thegateway.org

This site contains many high-quality lesson plans, curriculum units, and other educational resources.

Georgia Teacher Resource Bank Lessons Plans:

http://www.teacherresourcebank.com

This site is especially designed for Georgia educators. It includes K–12 lesson plans for all content subject areas. Virtual reality views of Mars are available. Teachers may use free lesson plans and they can obtain membership to share information and participate in discussions with other educators. There are discussion groups for both preservice and inservice teachers.

Lesson Plan Library from DiscoverySchool.Com

http://school.discovery.com/lessonplans/

DiscoverySchool.com has a database of lesson plans that can be searched by grade or topic. Information literacy skills may not be addressed in all cases.

LessonPlansPage.com:

http://www.lessonplanspage.com/

This site is a searchable database of lesson plans by subject first, then by grade level. Many of the multi-disciplinary lesson plans contain content standards and information literacy standards.

MarcoPolo Lesson Plans: Internet Content for the Classroom:

http://marcopolo.worldcom.com

Professionally developed lesson plans can be found at this site. Standards-based Internet content is provided for K–12 classrooms.

Microsoft Lesson Plans:

http://k12.msn.com/LessonConnection/Teacher.asp

Microsoft Lesson Connection provides ready-to-use lesson plans available through searching by subject, grade level, and keyword.

New York Times Learning Network Lesson Plans:

http://www.nytimes.com/learning/teachers/lessons/archive.html

The New York Times has a database of lesson plans that incorporate articles from their online newspaper. State content standards are included.

PBS TeacherSource Lesson Plans:

http://www.pbs.org/teachersource/search.htm

Search the PBS TeacherSource database of more than 2,500 lesson plans
and activities correlated to more than 230 sets of state and national curriculum standards. Choose to search by keyword, grade level, subject or
topic. (Note: information literacy is not one of the standards available on
this site.)

Scholastic Lesson Plans:

http://teacher.scholastic.com/lessonrepro/index.asp

Scholastic offers this searchable database of lesson plans. This web site is
especially useful for media specialists.

Yahoo Lesson Plans:

http://dir.yahoo.com/Education/K_12/Teaching/Lesson_Plans/

Yahoo offers a comprehensive directory of lesson plans. School library
media specialists working with teachers will want to check web sites for
standards in the content areas.

PUBLICIZING THE SCHOOL LIBRARY MEDIA CENTER

Publicizing the school library media center is crucial to the success of
the school library media program. Three methods are discussed in this section that impact how the media center is perceived: (1) through library
promotions, (2) through the friendly atmosphere of the center, and
(3) through the people served by the media center or its constituents.

Public Relations through Library Promotions

Although formal and informal instruction are the principal ways of
informing students about the resources of the school library media center,
there are other approaches as well. Keeping the school community
informed of the services offered in the media center needs to be a top priority with the media specialist in charge of the center. Being an advocate
for the center includes making the media center activities an important
component of the school priorities. It means being visible in print as well
as the media specialist being visible in person. Three methods to be visible
in print include use of student handbooks, managing a school media center web site, and being a regular contributor to the school newspaper.

Student Handbooks

Some media centers prepare and distribute student handbooks to publicize its service. These publications vary considerably in size and depth of coverage. A handbook should provide the following basic information: (1) a floor plan of the center; (2) general information on the size and nature of the collection; (3) a list of center personnel and the services available to students; (4) a brief description of major locating devices used in the center (OPAC or online catalog, CD-ROM database, Dewey decimal classification, periodical indexes); (5) statements on the center's policies regarding hours of service, collection, and attendance; and (6) special services such as interlibrary loans, computer database searches, and periodicals. More elaborate handbooks also include annotations for major reference sources, longer descriptions of locating devices, and instructions on how to use various items of equipment. To decide how extensive the handbook should be, the school library media specialist should measure its projected value and expected use against the time and money that must be spent for production.

Media Center Web Sites

An excellent way to publicize the school library media center is through a media center web site. Usually this web site will be part of the school web page, but it is an excellent tool for publicizing the many offerings of the media center. Frequently school library media specialists are instrumental in developing school web sites. There are three excellent books that can assist media specialists in planning and implementing web sites as well as publicizing the services of the media center: Debra Kay Logan's and Cynthia Lee Beuselinck's *K–12 Web Pages: Planning and Publishing Excellent School Web Sites* (2001) is geared toward planning school web sites, but is equally applicable to media center web sites. Another book, by Julieta Fisher and Ann Hill, entitled *Tooting Your Own Horn: Web-Based Public Relations for the 21st Century Librarian* (2002), gives some excellent ideas for publicizing the media center.

School Newspapers

Using the school newspaper to publicize the media center is an excellent source for keeping the media center program visible in the school. Highlighting programs or fun activities in the newspaper keeps students coming to the media center to participate. Practically all students and faculty in the school normally read the school newspaper. Using it as a communication tool is an excellent way to put the school library media center at the forefront of school activities. Some suggestions for advocating the center through the newspaper might be to include book reviews by students, to spotlight new material arrivals, to provide interesting web sites, and to feature student assistants who work on special projects. Trivia quizzes where students have to do research to solve them are always a fun activity for students.

Orientation

Other ways to keep the media center visible are through new student and faculty orientation. New faculty are the most receptive to media center services when they first arrive at the school because they are looking for ways to get their classes organized and functioning. It is an opportunity to do groundwork for collaborative partners in the future. Part of the orientation program for new teachers includes a tour of the media center conducted by the staff, supplying a general introduction to the collection and the services available to the faculty. Some centers also prepare a special handbook for teachers, or a section in the general faculty handbook used in the school.

Students who receive orientation seem to have a better attitude about visiting the media center and they normally use it more frequently. A place on the media center web site may be devoted to the orientation of new students and faculty members. Orientation periods and close supervision during initial work training sessions are two useful methods of introducing new members of the center's clerical staff, student assistants, or volunteer workers to the procedures and routines of the school library media center. Staff manuals are helpful procedural training tools.

In-Service

The school library media center staff needs to be actively involved in developing in-service training for the faculty. The training can be informal: during joint planning sessions with teachers, classroom visits, or at grade level or departmental meetings. More structured presentations can be conducted at faculty meetings or during workshop sessions. Because of rapid changes in technology, the school library media specialist continually trains faculty in its use.

Before the beginning of the school year, some school districts conduct special in-service courses of one or two weeks' duration for new clerical assistants or student assistants. Basic topics that should be covered in these sessions are:

1. **General orientation**
   a. Recent developments in education and their relation to the school library media center concept.
   b. The program of the school library media center in individual schools.
   c. Media center services available outside the school (district-wide centralized services, services supplied by other libraries and information agencies).
   d. The administrative structure of the school district.
   e. The role of the clerical assistant or student assistant.
   f. Access to Internet services and procedures for use.

2. **Ordering and receiving procedures**
   a. Forms used in the district.
   b. Ordering procedures for books, texts, other instructional materials, bindery items, equipment, furniture, professional materials, supplies, and rentals.
   c. Accounting and business practices.

3. **Processing of material (If there is a centralized processing agency, coverage of this topic will be brief.)**

4. **Arrangement of material**
   a. Dewey decimal classification system.
   b. Use of the online public access catalog (OPAC).
   c. Arrangement of entries in OPAC catalog.

5. **Operation and maintenance of equipment**
   a. Demonstration and practice with various types of equipment.
   b. Simple repairs required on equipment.

6. **Local production of materials**
   a. Demonstration and practice, for example, in duplicating materials and in making videos.
   b. Techniques used, for example, in mounting materials.

7. **Care of materials**
   a. Instruction and practice in performing simple repairs on printed materials.
   b. Care and repair of non-print materials.

8. **Policies and procedures for the operation of media center**
   a. Internet Acceptable Use.
   b. Copyright.

    c. Circulation.

    d. Borrowing.

    e. Processing Materials.

In-service courses are usually supplemented in two ways: (1) with district-wide sessions during the school year to update personnel on new developments or to serve as refresher courses, and (2) at the local level, with additional in-service work to acquaint new personnel with the routines and procedures peculiar to the individual school. School media specialists usually take the initiative to provide in-service training to teachers in the use of computers, database searching, or any other procedures that will enhance the total educational program.

Public Relations Through the Media Center Environment

Good public relations requires conscious and continuous effort; such a program cannot be turned on or off at will. Every time a patron has any contact with the school library media center—directly or indirectly—an impression is created that will either enhance or damage the center's image. Every aspect of the center and its program affects public relations and vice versa.

Atmosphere

Of initial importance in public relations concerning the school library media center is the atmosphere. The center should be a friendly, cheerful place. The physical surroundings should be inviting, pleasant, convey warmth, and a feeling of hospitality. Center personnel should constantly reassess the facilities from the standpoint of users who are entering for the first time. Is the general impression favorable? Is the furniture comfortable? Is it attractively arranged? Are browsing and lounge areas conducive to relaxation and enjoyment? Are all the various parts of the collection clearly marked for easy identification? Are all display areas utilized? Are the books and materials attractive? Are there any special displays of student art, projects or collections?

Displays

Bulletin boards and display cases attract potential users to the school library media center, publicize its services, and familiarize students with the collection. Although displays are important inside the center, display facilities in corridors and classrooms should also advertise and promote it. Displays can be fitted into a number of places. Conventional bulletin boards and table- or window-type display cases are most frequently used, but any unused wall space can accommodate a corkboard or pegboard hooked onto the space, suspended by wires from the ceiling, or displayed on a simple easel set up on the floor. Easels can also be used for direct display of posters or other informational resources. Bare walls can serve as a display area for continuous multimedia shows, and corners of a school library media center area can be used to exhibit life-size displays of resources and activities.

Following are some steps for preparing a display:

1. Decide on the subject; a specific, concrete subject is usually better than a general one.

2. Select a caption; make it short, interest-catching, and large enough to be seen at a distance. Where appropriate, present it with a light touch—perhaps with a play on words or some similar device (e.g., "Take me to your reader").

3. Make a rough sketch showing both placement and color of material and backdrop; arrange the parts so that they have a logical form and the eye travels naturally and easily from one section to another. One of the most common devices is to arrange the parts so that they lead the eye to the center of the display.

4. Produce an interesting balance and keep the display uncluttered.

5. Keep it neat. Lettering is not everyone's forte; if this is the case, use commercially manufactured letters.

6. Maintain a file of materials and display ideas.

Materials for displays can be easily improvised. Attractive backgrounds can be created with wallpaper, poster paper, burlap, metallic paper, or foil. A variety of simple materials can be used for a three-dimensional effect. Mailing tubes can become large pencils or rocket ships; paper plates can become frames; and cotton batting or steel wool can serve as clouds or hair. Coat hangers make an excellent framework for mobiles.

Some other pointers include changing the display often so as not to run the risk of losing the audience and combining student projects and community resources with the school library media center's materials. If there is an art department in the school, the best pieces of student work may be obtained and become a part of the permanent art collection housed in the school media center.

Copies of the material on display should be available for circulation in the center. Using articles for which there are duplicate copies in the center or using dust jackets from books add a new dimension to displays. Color photocopiers make it easy to photocopy book jackets. With a bit of imagination and ingenuity, the center staff can easily produce attractive, eye-catching displays, but if ideas are slow in coming or time is too tight to allow for original planning, consult the many bulletin board books on the market and articles written about producing displays.

Service to Patrons

The well being of patrons is a responsibility of every worker in the center—from student assistants and parent volunteers to the school library media center's full-time staff. It is important that each person be given instructions on how to act toward patrons and how to give proper assistance. Does the staff give the patron the message "I'm happy to help you"? In some cases, simply referring the patron to a professional staff member might fulfill the person's responsibility. This simple operation, as all others, should be handled with tact and concern for the patron. All helpers should be aware not only of the established regulations governing the center's program, but also of the reasons why these regulations have been adopted. In this way, simple explanations can be given to patrons when particular policies are questioned. The center staff should also periodically review policies to determine whether they actually promote and facilitate the program or simply act as roadblocks between the patron and the services needed. The key idea behind service is doing what is necessary to make the patron feel welcome and going the extra mile to satisfy their needs.

Visibility of the Center

The media specialist should take every opportunity to be visible throughout the school and in the community. Publicizing the library can be done by giving book talks in the classrooms, providing Internet and other technology workshops for parents, inviting authors to visit the school, performing in storytelling sessions, sponsoring book fairs and by celebrating special event library days such as National Library Week, School Media Day, and so forth. Contests are effective in creating interest in the school media center, such as Write Your Own Book and The Battle of the Books. Keeping a visible profile and maintaining a friendly environment in the media center are crucial to publicizing the school media center program.

Public Relations Through the School Constituents

In wholesome public relations activities promoting school library media center services, center personnel will work with several different groups inside the school—students, teachers, administrators, and in the community—parents, community groups, local news media, and public and other library agencies. Successful communication with one group certainly affects and influences others. Developing good relationships with all groups is essential for a viable program.

Students

There are many ways to promote the school library media center and its services with students. The staff can relate the general activities of the school and the current interests and experiences of the students to the center. For example, a student play or assembly program, or an important sport event can form the basis of a display, mediography, or some special library program. Popular television programs, current movies, community activities, world events, or social issues can also become part of promotions.

All available channels of information can be used to disseminate news about the school library media center. The public address system is one such channel of information. Some centers publish their own bulletins containing such items as new acquisitions; student reviews; lists of titles that reflect reading, listening, and viewing preferences of different classes or teachers; news on school library media center events; Internet web sites of interest to particular classrooms, and mediographies of current popular subjects. In addition to the book talks and story hours offered in the center, visits can be arranged to classrooms or to club meetings to introduce appropriate material to students and teachers.

Reading, Viewing and Listening Guidance. Student reading, listening, and viewing experiences can help to promote the school library media center. Informal sharing periods are popular with students, during which they talk about titles they have enjoyed, or they give book talks to other students, or they give a HyperStudio presentation about a book they read. A separate file drawer of cards or a computer program of titles recommended by students (and arranged by students' last names) is often used. Bulletin board displays or printed booklets containing brief reviews written by students can also draw attention to student preferences. Students also enjoy dressing as book characters and having their classmates guess who they are. Any activity that promotes reading or creates an interest in books is encouraged.

Programming Events. The promotion of such special events as National Book Week and Children's Book Week, as well as media center-sponsored assembly programs, book fairs, and bookstores, not only furnish valuable services but also help publicize and promote the total program. Many school library media centers sponsor group activities, such as creative writing or reading clubs, play-reading groups, career programs, or discussion groups on topics of interest to students. Some school media centers plan a student/parent read-in night where the parents are invited to bring a book to read with their child. The event is usually planned to take place in a gym or an auditorium to allow for school-wide participation. Parents and students sit on cushions on the floor and read together for a period of time. A storytelling session where the school media specialist, the principal, or the superintendent participate by telling stories to the group is a way to show the support of administrators in the importance of reading for pleasure to the community and to publicize the services of the school media center.

Some school media centers sponsor a "Battle of the Books" program in which all students read works of fiction, following which questions regarding plot, characters, authors, and so forth are used in class competitions. Finalists from these contests comprise two panels for the Battle of the Books competition, which is held as part of an assembly program in which all students participate. Students in the audience may win points if the panelists are unable to answer a question.

Organizers of group activities who schedule meetings on a regular basis and allow sufficient time before each event to publicize it thoroughly are the most successful. It is advisable to form a planning group or club council composed chiefly of students to assure potential interest in the program. An agenda should be drawn up before each meeting. Resource persons and materials for programs can often be found within the community and backup material from the school library media center can be utilized. When appropriate, during the meeting, mention may be made of other media center material related to the topic under discussion. Specially prepared mediographies might be distributed to teachers.

Teachers

Many of the public relations techniques used with students also work with teachers. For example, using school library media center materials in joint displays in the classroom and the center are excellent ways to gain the support of teachers and at the same time promote the center's collection. Some school library media centers, particularly in very large schools where direct communication between the center and its users is difficult, have organized advisory committees composed of teachers, students, and representatives from both the central administration and the media center staff. These committees gather information on user needs, supply advice on policymaking, and, in turn, publicize and interpret those policies to the general public.

The development of special services involving the professional collection is another useful technique. These services could include routing pertinent articles from professional journals, announcing the arrival of new material, and preparing bibliographies on educational topics of current interest to the faculty. The active participation of the school library media center's staff on teacher committees and in professional organizations and the use of the staff as resource personnel for these groups will help build a liaison between the media center and the faculty.

Perhaps the best way to reach teachers is to give them the personalized attention and professional concern that will aid them in preparing, organizing, and presenting instructional programs—in short, providing the collaborative support that will help them to become better teachers. School library media center specialists sometimes assign individual staff members to act as advisers to specific grade levels, academic departments, or teaching teams. Staff time is often set aside for collaborative planning with teachers in the center. Other specialists arrange discussions with teachers in the classroom setting. In any case, faculty members should be encouraged to collaboratively plan with the media specialist, preferably in the school library media center, and become acquainted with the center's resources that are appropriate to their classroom needs. Teachers are encouraged to participate in all activities in the school media center whether informal or formal. When formal lessons are planned, the faculty member and the school media specialist work collaboratively to implement the instructional objectives.

Administrators

One of the key players in the success of the school library media program is the principal. They can either make or break the program, depending on the support they offer. It is the media specialist's responsibility to get them involved in the media center programs. Most administrators are open to attending planning sessions with teachers and the media specialist, especially if they know it will impact student achievement. The media specialist needs to work very closely with the principal as an instructional partner to make certain that student achievement is enhanced. Most principals are unaware of the latest research studies that show the media center's impact on student achievement; therefore, the media specialist needs to educate them on the findings so the two of them might work closer together. There are numerous ways the media specialist can get the principal to be a real media center advocate. Always invite them to participate in the media center programs, whether it is dressing up as a book character or reading aloud to students in a classroom. Get them involved in instructional units. Have them participate in living history portrayals and book promotions. Ask them to be a co-presenter at a conference. Most principals find these programs both exciting and enjoyable. Always remember they hold the key to the success of the media center program and they need to be an active participant themselves.

The same techniques used with students and teachers (displays, newsletters, and the like) will help make the administration aware of the various facets of the school library media center's resources and programs. The main component to remember is to get them involved in the program itself. The school administration always needs to be consulted in developing media center policies and invited to participate in any special events held in the center.

The resources of the school library media center should be made available for those activities that grow out of the administrative function. For example, the media center staff might prepare visuals to aid in a budget presentation or to illustrate and interpret a new teaching program before a parent group. The staff should also be available to provide any backup reference service required by the administration—for example, supplying specific information such as web sites, locating material, preparing mediographies, or routing professional materials. Specifically, the center staff should keep the administration abreast of the latest developments in media and school library media centers. In addition to furnishing material on these subjects, center personnel should be encouraged to invite administrators to local conferences, in-service programs, workshops, or exhibits where educational media and their utilization are demonstrated.

The school media specialist should communicate in every way possible to keep the principal informed of the center's activities. Some examples of effective communication might be: writing memorandums about the program of the school media center; writing monthly and annual reports to show advancement toward the goals of the school media program as they relate to the school and the curriculum, and discussing the reports to publicize the successes of the program and to gain principal support for the future. Building good public relations with the principal is an essential component for developing a school media program that is proactive in its approach to service.

Community

Although one of the most important elements in a good public relations program is informing the community about the services of the school library media center; this area is probably given the least attention. Getting the community involved is critical to the success of the media program. Many parents and school board officials are still not aware of the concept of the school library media center, let alone the specific activities and programs connected with it. Yet the support that the center receives from a community helps to determine its success. This support may be directly related to school budgets, or providing Internet access, or indirectly related to forwarding the school's philosophy. It is therefore essential that the media center's professional staff members devote some of their time to explaining and interpreting their program to persons who may not use their services, but who nevertheless sustain the program through financial and moral support. Several ways to get the community involved in the media center program is by forming a media center friends group who assist the media specialist with planning and implementing center events. Finding event chairpersons to assist the media specialist brings attention to the media center from an important segment of the community, such as parents, retired individuals, and community agencies. Parent volunteers are valuable assets to the media center program. Their support can provide an added dimension to services offered to the school.

Reaching Hidden Publics. Finding people in the community who may be school media center supporters requires that the media specialist get involved in the community. The media center can also offer opportunities for people in the community. Their involvement makes for a stronger program. Below are a few techniques to help reach this "hidden" public:

1. Prepare a simple PowerPoint presentation that illustrates the services given to students by the school library media center and present it (followed by a discussion period) to parent and community groups.
2. Utilize local news media to publicize the activities of the center.
3. Schedule a once-a-year School Library Media Night for parent groups to acquaint themselves with the latest programs at the center.
4. Plan special programs for those occasions—Back-to-School Night, for example—when parents visit the school.
5. Encourage parents, school board members, and community leaders to visit the center while school is in session.
6. Utilize community resources for displays and speaking engagements.
7. Make school library media center resources available for use by school-based parent groups.
8. Attend and participate in community functions.
9. Utilize parents' help for such special functions as book fairs.
10. Prepare and distribute to parents mediographies, recommended reading lists, Internet URLs, and guides to reference books and information sources.
11. Host workshops for parents who want to learn about the Internet, or newer technological developments.

Serving community needs is one way to practice valuable public relations. The community that feels ownership in the school media program will support it. Sometimes the community looks to the media center to protect their children from inappropriate use of the Internet.

Internet Filtering. Because the school serves the local community, sometimes pressure is applied to influence school library media centers to use Internet filters because parents and other community leaders see the media center and school as serving in "loco parentis" or protecting students from harmful content. Protecting students from pornography, bad language, obscenity, alternative life styles, drugs, illegal activities, hate crimes, violence, and other harmful content found on the Internet becomes a concern voiced in many communities. Even the federal government has supported the idea of filtering Internet content to the extent that some federal funds are not available to schools that do not use Internet filters. Proponents of Internet filtering see the protection of children as the major goal. They support the idea that filtering comes out of the desire to protect the emotional and physical well being of students. Opponents to filtering argue that students can access the Internet from home or anywhere and can find inappropriate material on their own. They see filtering as a device that keeps students from living in the real world.

It is difficult for media specialists and teachers to monitor student online activity; however, through their guidance they can teach students to search the Internet using appropriate searching strategies to find suitable materials. When funding issues are attached to filtering, there are few alternatives for media specialists to consider because their decision has already been made by others. For example, Children's Internet Protection Act (CIPA), compels schools to use filters if they are linked to e-rate and they receive government funding such as Elementary and Secondary Education Act (ESEA) funds and Institute of Museum and Library Act (IMLA) grants. That stipulation means that many library media centers will not be allowed to use funds to purchase new software and other computer-related items unless a filtering program is in place when they apply for funding (Chapin, 1999; Dyrli, 2001; Filtering Out the Rhetoric, 2001; Wolinsky, 2001).

Although using filters may satisfy the demands of many in the local community, it is the cooperation with agencies in the community that can provide good public relations for the school library media center.

Cooperation with Agencies. Building good relations between the school library media center and other library agencies in the community not only helps to promote and publicize the center's program but also, and more importantly, can result in better service and more effective use of material by students. An initial step is for the library staffs to become acquainted with each other and to become familiar with the resources and regulations of each other's services. In many school districts, an interlibrary council has been established to discuss mutual problems in order to develop procedures for handling them. The school library media center staff can also serve as a clearinghouse of information about other libraries by publicizing their programs, having their colleagues—especially public librarians—visit the school to talk before students and teachers, and arranging class visits to other libraries.

The school library media center staff should keep in touch with other libraries on a regular basis and notify them of school assignments, recent curriculum changes, new acquisitions, and other developments within the school that might affect the students' use of a given library's collection. This line of communication should be maintained particularly with the public library, and in turn the public library can promote special events and services offered by the school library media center. To avoid duplication and wasted time and effort, some activities, such as summer reading programs, might be jointly planned and sponsored by several media centers, together with the public library. Public libraries and school libraries can jointly select materials, develop union lists of serials and reference collections, and loan materials to one another. The more cooperation that exists with outside agencies the better service that is available to the school clientele.

It is necessary for the school library media center's staff to look outside the center and reach all groups affected by it. Each situation is unique in some respects and, therefore, will require distinct programs. For example, college and university libraries in the community might be used for high school student research. The school media center staff should make the initial contact with the academic library staff and make arrangements for the students to do research in the college library and, of course, to inform them of assignments as far in advance as possible. Some media centers and college libraries cooperate by allowing the school media specialist in the high school to issue information passes to students which will allow them to check out materials on a specific subject and so forth. This kind of arrangement is practiced between the two high school library media centers in Decatur, Alabama, and the community college library as well as the public library. Should any problems arise regarding the return of materials, the school media specialist takes care of the problem.

HOURS OF SERVICE, ATTENDANCE, AND USE OF THE OPAC

Hours of Service

School library media centers usually open for service at the time the first students and teachers arrive (about half an hour before classes begin), are open during the entire school day, and remain open for an hour or an hour and a half after the school day ends, or as long as students are present in sufficient numbers to warrant keeping the center open. The number of after school hours depends on several factors: transportation available to students who remain after school hours, other library resources available in the district and their accessibility, the number of after school activities that make use of the collection, and the flexibility of the center's circulation policies. Some school library media centers have experienced varying degrees of success with extending hours into the evenings and weekends, thus supplying students, parents, and other members of the community additional opportunities to use the collection. Special summer school library media programs are also held where there are both need and funds.

Attendance in the Media Center

The objective of attendance policies in school library media centers is to get as many students into the center as often as they want to be there. Therefore, any student who wishes to use the center should have free and open access to it. In schools with flexible schedules, students are given some choice concerning where they will spend their free time—the school library media center is a place they often choose. In more rigidly structured settings, students often must obtain passes before they are allowed to go to the media center from classrooms.

Restrictive policies sometimes have to be adopted to prevent overcrowding in the school library medial center. They can also be used to keep account of students during the school day. Since each school situation is unique to some degree, the merits and deficiencies of various plans should be studied to find the one that best promotes good use of the school library media center and at the same time allows students suitable access to the collection.

Whenever possible, teachers and the media specialist need to collaboratively plan to schedule classes or small groups into the school library media center at least a few days in advance of the visit. In this way, the school library media specialist can allocate time and material, and plan with the teacher on such preparations before the class is due. Most media centers maintain "sign-up sheets" that give the time and purpose of student visits. On a daily or weekly basis, a master schedule is distributed to teachers and administrators to inform them when the staff is free for conferences, collaborative planning, or last minute scheduling.

It is natural and normal for students to talk quietly in the school library media center; the staff should not try to prevent a healthy level of conversation. Students become accustomed to background noise and seem to be able to ignore it. Certain areas in the school library media center may be designated for quiet conversation. Spaces around the periodical collection, lounge areas, and specified tables set aside for small-group work are suitable for this purpose. On the other hand, some sections of the center, such as areas where there are individual study carrels, should be designated for quiet study where there are no distracting interruptions.

Of course, the center staff will have to cope with discipline problems at times. A staff member should try to deal with the individual responsible for the disruption in a personal conference rather than before the group. It is important for the staff to know students individually and be aware of any underlying problems in order to deal with the cause of the behavior rather than a symptom, although the episode must be handled immediately. Perhaps the best advice for school library media specialists in these situations is not to interpret such occurrences as personal affronts but to maintain a balanced view and a sense of humor. The main point to remember is that students need to feel welcome in the center. Sometimes the use of the public access catalogs (OPACS) can result in student behavior problems; however, if procedures or policies are in place dealing with potential problems, then they should lessen.

Use of the Online Public Access Catalog (OPAC)

Online public access catalogs (OPACs) are commonplace in school media centers today, replacing card catalogs. Access to materials is easier and faster. When OPACs first came into existence, they were primarily housed in stand-alone computers. Today students are able to search for library materials and to search for web resources at the same terminal as well as search other libraries in the school district, public libraries, college and university libraries within the local geographic area, or look for holdings anywhere in the world. Resource sharing is made possible because school districts have developed union databases for all of their schools' holdings in the district. Most automated systems include circulation, media and equipment booking, cataloging, patron information, and holds on materials and equipment as well as web resources access.

Because web access is part of the public access catalog, the media center should have in place acceptable use policies and other policies to insure good student behavior in the media center. Automation of media centers is a major factor in easy access to information that, in turn, promotes good public relations (Hart, 2001).

Many of the suggestions in this chapter might not be applicable or feasible in each situation, others might have to be modified, and in some cases totally new approaches may have to be devised. Professionalism, imagination, and an honest desire to provide maximum service with the materials and access available are key to the utilization and promotion of the resources of the school library media center and those beyond its walls.

REFERENCES

American Association of School Librarians & Association for Educational Communications and Technology. (1998). *Information power: Partnerships for learning*. Chicago: American Library Association.

Chapin, Rich. (1999, September). Content management, filtering and the World Wide Web. [Electronic version]. *T.H.E. Journal, 27*(2), 44. Retrieved April 5, 2004, from: http://www.thejournal.com/magazine/vault/A2221.cfm

Dyrli, Odvard Egil. (2001, April). Internet filters: Good or bad, now necessary. *Curriculum Administrator, 37*(4), 33.

E-learning. (2001, October). *Classroom Connect,* 8(2), 4–7.

Filtering out the rhetoric. (2001, Summer). *Independent School, 60*(4), 50–56.

Fisher, Julieta & Hill, Ann. (2002). *Tooting your own horn: Web-based public relations for 21st century school librarians*. Worthington, OH: Linworth.

Hainer, Eugene. (1997). *Aligning information literacy with state standards*. Denver: Colorado State Library.

Hart, Amy. (2001, May/June). Integrated library systems for school libraries— The next generation. *Book Report, 20*(1), 45–49.

Johnson, Mary. (2003). *Collaborative planning template*. Unpublished manuscript, Glenview Middle School, Colorado Springs, CO.

Johnson, Mary. (2003). *Completed collaborative planning template*. .Unpublished manuscript, Glenview Elementary School, Colorado Springs, CO.

Logan, Debra Kay & Beuselinck, Cynthia Lee. (2001). *K-12 web pages: Planning and publishing excellent school web sites*. Worthington, OH: Linworth.

Maryland State Department of Education. (2000). *Library media learning outcomes*. Retrieved April 5, 2004, from School Improvement in Maryland web site: http://www.mdk12.org/mspp/mspap/whats-tested/learneroutcomes/library_media/k-8/outcomes.html or http://www.bcpl.net/~dcurtis/ml0

Massachusetts School Library Media Association. (2001, August 14). *Rationale for today's school library media center*. Retrieved April 5, 2004, from Massachusetts School Library Media Association web site: http://www.mslma.org/whoweare/standards.html#Rationale

Social Studies: Fall Harvest. (2001, October). *School Library Media Activities Monthly, 18*(2), 19–20.

Tate, Jeanie. (2003). *The pyramids: A lesson plan*. Unpublished manuscript, Woodland Park, CO.

Wolinsky, Art. (2001, May/June). Filter gate. *Multimedia Schools, 8*(3), 22–26.

FURTHER READING

Allen, Christine & Anderson, Mary Alice. (1999). *Skills for life: Information literacy for grades K–6* (2nd ed.). Worthington, OH: Linworth.

Allen, Christine & Anderson, Mary Alice. (1999). *Skills for life: Information literacy for grades 7–12* (2nd ed.). Worthington, OH: Linworth.

Anderson, Mary Alice. (2001, September). So much information. *Multimedia Schools, 8*(4), 22–24.

Ayers, Linda. (2003). *Read it again! Standards-based literature lessons for young children.* Worthington, OH: Linworth.

Barnhart, Shari. (1999, May 12). *Collaborative planning checklist.* Retrieved April 21, 2004, from: http://www.rainbowtech.org/workshops/Unit_of_Practice/Planning/Planning.html

Barton, Holly. (2001). *Information literacy: Learning how to learn.* Retrieved April 5, 2004, from Rhode Island Network for Educational Technology web site: http://www.ri.net/RITTI_Fellows/Barton/infolit.html

Baule, Steven M. & Bertani, Laura Blair. (2000, November/December). How to gain support from your board and administration: Marketing 101 for your library media program. [Electronic version]. *The Book Report, 19*(3), 47–49. Retrieved April 5, 2004, from: http://www.linworth.com/current_article/index.html?a72

Breivik, Patricia Senn & Senn, J.A. (1998). *Information literacy: Educating children for the 21st century* (2nd ed.). Washington, DC: National Education Association.

Bush, Gail. (2003). *The school buddy system: The practice of collaboration.* Chicago: American Library Association.

Bush, Gail. (2003, September/October). Walking the collaborative talk: Creating inquiry groups. *Knowledge Quest, 32*(1), 52.

Canadian Library Association. (1997, November). *Students' information literacy needs in the 21st Century: Competencies for teacher-librarians.* Retrieved April 5, 2004, from the Canadian Library Association web site: http://www.cla.ca/divisions/csla/pub_2.htm

Capra, Steph & Ryan, Jenny. (Eds.). (2002). *Problems are the solution: Keys to lifelong learning.* Worthington, OH: Linworth.

Church, Audrey P. (2003). *Leverage your libraries to raise test scores: A guide for library media specialists, principals, teachers and parents.* Worthington, OH: Linworth.

Colorado Library Research Service. (2002, September 1). The status of media center support of student achievement. *Fast facts: Recent statistics from the library research service.* Colorado State Library, ED3 110.10(169). Retrieved April 15, 2004, from the Colorado Library Research Service web site: http://www.lrs.org/documents/fastfacts/169crisis.pdf

Donham, Jean. (1998). *Enhancing teaching and learning: A leadership guide for school library specialists.* New York: Neal-Schuman.

Ellis, Kathleen V. (2001, Summer). Libraries and Information literacy survey analysis. *Independent School, 60*(4), 14–15.

Ercegovac, Zorana. (2003, February). Bringing the library into the lab: How information literacy skills make better students. *School Library Journal, 49*(2), 52–55.

Essential skills for information literacy. (1996). Retrieved April 16, 2004, from Washington Library Media Association web site: http://www.learningspace.org/instruct/literacy/ESLINTRO.htm

Farmer, Lesley S.J. (2000, May/June). Tech-savvy public relations. *Book Report, 19*(1), 6–8.

Farmer, Lesley S.J. (2002, February). Harnessing the power in Information Power. *Teacher Librarian, 29*(3), 20–24.

Farmer, Lesley S.J. (2003). *Student success and library media programs: A systems approach to research and best practice.* Westport, CT: Libraries Unlimited.

Fitzgerald, Marianne. (2002, December). The lonely librarian. *Book Report, 21*(3), 33.

Foggett, Tracy. (2003, February). Information literacy at the primary school level? *The Australian Library Journal, 52*(1), 55–63.

Gale, Gloria. (1999, Spring). The library media specialist as leader in change. *Media Spectrum, 26*(2), 6–8.

Glick, Andrea. (2001, April). ALA filtering suit excludes schools. *School Library Journal, 47*(4), 19–20.

Hartzell, Gary. (2002, November). Why should principals support school libraries? *ERIC Digest* (ERIC Identifier EDO-IR-2002–06). Retrieved April 16, 2004, from the *ERIC Digest* web site: http://web.archive.org/web/20030622061032/http://www.ericit.org/digests/EDO-IR-2002-06.shtml

Hartzell, Gary N. (2003). *Building influence for the school librarian: Tenets, targets, tactics* (2nd ed.). Worthington, OH: Linworth.

Haycock, Ken. (2003, September/October). Collaboration: Because student achievement is the bottom line. *Knowledge Quest, 32*(1), 54.

Internet filtering software, information and demos. (2000). Retrieved April 5, 2004, from the Los Angeles County Office of Education: http://teams.lacoe.edu/documentation/internet/security/software.html

Johnson, Doug. (1999). *A 13-point library/media program checklist for building administrators.* Retrieved April 16, 2004, from: http://www.doug-johnson.com/dougwri/checklist.html

Johnson, Doug. (1999). *The new and improved school library.* Retrieved April 5, 2004, from: http://www.doug-johnson.com/handouts/new.pdf

Library media frameworks. (2000, February 14). Retrieved April 5, 2004, from Bellingham, Washington Public Schools web site: http://www.bham.wednet.edu/departments/libmedtech/libmedframeworks.htm

Loertscher, David V. & Woolls, Blanche. (1997, June 26). *The information literacy movement of the school library media field: A preliminary summary of the research.* Retrieved April 5, 2004, from CSU School of Library and Information Science: http://witloof.sjsu.edu/courses/250.loertscher/modelloer.html

Loertscher, David V. & Woolls, Blanche. (2002). *Information literacy: A review of the research, a guide for practitioners and researchers* (2nd ed.). San Jose, CA: Hi Willow Research and Publishing.

Logan, Debra Kay. (2001, September/October). Integrating the ISTE national education standards. *Book Report, 20*(2), 6–8.

Lovse, Denise. (2001, Spring). Leadership through collaboration. *Media Spectrum, 28*(2), 25–27.

Lowe, Karen. (2003, September/October). Providing curriculum support in the school library media center: Resource alignment, or how to eat an elephant. *Knowledge Quest, 32*(1), 46.

McElmeel, Sharron L. (2000, May/June). Making PR an outreach activity. *Book Report, 19*(1), 10–11.

Makemson, Carroll & Early, Sharon. (2003, September/October). Flexible scheduling: Why and how. *Knowledge Quest, 32*(1), 55.

Massachusetts School Library Media Association. (2003). *Massachusetts school library media program standards for the 21st century.* Three Rivers, MA: Author.

Milam, Peggy. (2002). *InfoQuest: A new twist on information literacy.* Worthington, OH: Linworth.

Miller, Marilyn L. (2000, December). "Media specialists" are still librarians, and reading is still the key to success. *American Libraries, 31*(11), 42–43.

Nashville, Tennessee Public Schools. (2002). *Teaching information processing skills: Collaborative unit planning sheets.* Retrieved April 5, 2004, from Metropolitan Nashville Public Schools web site: http://www.nashville.k12.tn.us/TIPSmanual/PlanningSheets.html

National forum on information literacy. (2003, August). Retrieved April 5, 2004, from: http://www.infolit.org/index.html

Needham, Joyce. (2003, June). From fixed to flexible: Making the journey. *Teacher Librarian, 30*(5), 8–13.

Neuman, Delia. (2003, Spring). Research in school library media for the next decade: Polishing the diamond. *Library Trends, 51*(4), 503–524.

North Carolina Department of Public Instruction. (1999). *Information skills curriculum.* Retrieved April 5, 2004, from North Carolina Public Schools web site: http://www.ncpublicschools.org/curriculum/information/index.html

Plotnick, Eric. (1999). *Information literacy. ERIC Digests* (ERIC Identifier ED 427 777). Retrieved April 5, 2004, from: http://www.ed.gov/databases/ERIC_Digests/ed427777.html

Prestebak, Jane. (2001, October). Standards: Recipes for serving student achievement. *Multimedia Schools 8*(5), 32–38.

Reilly, Rob. (2001, September). Filtering, protecting children, and shark repellant. *Multimedia Schools. 8*(4), 68–72.

Russell, Shayne. (2000, August). Teachers and librarians: Collaborative relationships. *ERIC Digests* (ERIC Identifier ED 444 605). Retrieved April 5, 2004, from the *ERIC Digest* web site: http://www.ericfacility.net/ericdigests/ed444605.html

Schneider, Karen G. (1997). *A practical guide to Internet filters.* New York: Neal-Schuman.

Seamon, Mary Ploski & Levitt, Eric J. (2001). *Web-based learning: A practical guide.* Worthington, OH: Linworth.

Serim, Ferdi & Murray, Janet. (2003, May/June). Literacy in (and for) our time: A conversation. *Multimedia Schools, 10*(3), 6–8.

Small, Ruth V. (2001). Developing a collaborative culture. [Electronic version]. *School Library Media Research.* Retrieved April 5, 2004, from the ALA web site: http://www.ala.org/Content/NavigationMenu/AASL/Publications_and_

Journals/School_Library_Media_Research/Editors_Choice_Resources/Best_
    of_ERIC/Best_of_ERIC.htm

Sortore, Sam M. (2001, July 15). Filtering: A piece of the puzzle. *NetConnect,
    School Library Journal* (Suppl.), 20–21. Retrieved April 3, 2004, from *Library
    Journal* online: http://www.libraryjournal.com/article/CA106233

Thomas, Nancy Pickering. (1999). *Information literacy and information skills
    instruction: Applying research to practice in the school library media center.* West-
    port, CT: Libraries Unlimited.

Todd, Ross J. (2003, April). Irrefutable evidence. *School Library Journal, 49*(4),
    52–54.

Troutner, Joanne. (2002, June). Information literacy activities and skills. *Teacher
    Librarian, 29*(5), 28–29.

Valenza, Joyce Kasman. (2003, September/October). Spreading the gospel of infor-
    mation literacy: A schoolwide initiative, year two. *Knowledge Quest, 32*(1), 49.

Washington Library Media Association. *Implementing Information Power in Wash-
    ington.* (2002). Retrieved April 16, 2004, from Washington Library Media Asso-
    ciation web site: http://www.wlma.org/Professional/Information_Power.htm

Wilson, Patricia Potter & Leslie, Roger. (2001). Igniting the spark: Library pro-
    grams that inspire high school patrons. Westport, CT: Libraries Unlimited.

Wilson, Patricia Potter & Leslie, Roger. (2001). Premiere events: Library pro-
    grams that inspire elementary school patrons. Westport, CT: Libraries Unlim-
    ited.

Wilson, Patricia Potter & Leslie, Roger. (2002). *Center Stage: Library programs
    that inspire middle school patrons.* Westport, CT: Libraries Unlimited.

Wilson, Patricia Potter & Lyders, Josette Anne. (2001). *Leadership for today's school
    library.* Westport, CT: Greenwood Press.

Witse, Ric. (2002, Spring). Media specialists are leaders. *Media Spectrum, 29*(2),
    11–13.

Yesner, Bruce & Hilda Jay. (1998). *Operating and evaluating school library media
    programs: A handbook for administrators and librarians.* New York: Neal-
    Schuman.

Yucht, Alice H. (2000, September). Strategy: Flip it! For collaborative planning
    strategies. *Teacher Librarian, 28*(1), 48–50.

Chapter 5

THE MEDIA CENTER BUDGET

by Carol Truett

INTRODUCTION

No element of today's school library media center, with the exception of the staff and the school library media program itself, is more important than the media center's budget. Indeed, it could probably be said that these three factors are the most elementary components for excellence in any school library. The facility, while significant and helpful in promoting and delivering a high level of services, by itself can never ensure excellence. Many beautiful and wonderfully designed facilities are only being used to deliver minimal or even poor services. But it would be extremely difficult even with the two other elements firmly in place (staff and program) to do the best job possible without an adequate budget. It should be developed in recognition of the role the modern and technology-rich school library media center can play in promoting a high level of student achievement while teaching the skills needed for the development of information literate and technology savvy, lifelong learners, be they students, faculty, or other school staff.

Today's school library media center budget has become an increasingly complicated entity to manage, due in large part to the use of technology in the library media center as well as throughout the modern school. The contemporary school library has become much more than a self-contained and autonomous media center; it has become a virtual library—connected to the whole school and its many classrooms as well as to the entire outside world via the Internet and the World Wide Web. A virtual library is, by definition, a local library providing books and other resources, such as CD-ROM encyclopedias, almanacs, dictionaries, and so forth, used frequently on site, while at the same time it is networked to virtually the entire outside world of information, including databases and other online libraries through modern telecommunications technology. The four or more walls encompassing the physical library media center in the school today no longer limit access to information; students and staff are not bound by time or geography as they explore the entire online universe of facts, opinions, sounds, music, images and other multimedia and telecommunications options available at the click of a mouse or the touch of a keyboard. Limitations are self-imposed in the form of computer software filters, which most school systems feel obligated to install even if they are not receiving federal funds, although most do.

Technology has improved the services available to the school library media center's patrons by installing automated, integrated library systems while increasing expectations for additional technology-related services, such as the provision of library workstations for Internet searching. Cost of this new technology is a drain on the often-dwindling local school library budgets. When an automated library system is purchased or upgraded, the media center itself frequently must bear this cost directly. School library media centers no longer receive specifically allocated funding of the 1960s and 1970s that went directly to build school library collections and could not be diverted for other purposes. Millions of dollars were channeled directly into school library book collections through the former Title II and Title IV Elementary and Secondary Education Act (ESEA) funding programs, no longer readily available for this purpose today. In order to receive current ESEA funding, reauthorized by the January 2001 passage of the No Child Left Behind Act, a school media center needs to be treated as part of one of the act's major components, such as the Reading First initiative or the Improving Literacy Through School Libraries section. This new funding is discussed in more detail later in this chapter.

The Politics of Budgeting

One of the major factors in school library media center budgeting frequently ignored by school library media specialists is the politics of education. Doug Johnson (1997) in his book, *The Indispensable Librarian*, includes an entire chapter devoted to the school library budget and he begins by discussing "budgeting for lean mean times" (Johnson, 1997, p. 93). He strongly urges librarians to "work with other groups" and "participate in local politics" in an article found on his web site (Johnson, 1999, p. 4). This suggestion means being political at the district level or at the individual school level, or both. Of course to say that budget politics does not exist at higher levels of government—city, county, state and national—is to profess an embarrassing ignorance of the realities of a fully functional democratic society; however, the major levels where media specialists can be reasonably influential are the district and school building levels. But no matter where the locus of budget power lies, it behooves the school library media specialist to become totally budget savvy and to ascertain those in the district and building who control the budget purse strings. Schools, as they have always been, remain a microcosm of society, and in our democratic society, power and politics will always be a major factor within these structures. To avoid or ignore the political aspects of budgeting is to deprive the school library media center, and by extension the entire educational program of the school, of a fair portion of the school's total financial resources. No school library media specialist should ever consider a budget request to be a selfish, self-serving action, if it clearly helps build the media center's resources in order to better serve the instructional and informational needs of the whole school. Resources of the school library media center potentially benefit *all* students and teachers, as well as other support staff. Indeed, Johnson (1999) exhorts school library media specialists to actually take it [money] away from somebody else! "If you believe in what you are doing, you have an obligation to try this," and he goes on to say that in order to do this, you must have "a thick skin and a deep-felt mission" (Johnson, 1999, p. 5). Without this approach, he cautions, you will get eaten alive.

Budget Ignorance is Never Bliss

Ignorance is *not* bliss when it comes to the school library media center budget. Many currently employed school library media specialists either have no budget and/or have no information at all about the district budget process, their own school's monetary resources, or what their "fair share" of the school budget should be. Notions that it is somehow inappropriate, indelicate, or in poor taste to ask for budget information or to request monies for the media center have no place in the thinking of today's school library media specialist. School library media specialists should be aware of the studies showing a correlation between a well-funded, professionally managed, and generously supplied school library media center and student achievement. The second Colorado study (Lance, et al., 2000) is a good starting point. The mission of every public school is to promote and foster student achievement. Current research increasingly documents the role a well-funded school library media center plays in promoting student learning.

An understanding of budgetary practice and record keeping is essential for all media specialists and becomes even more important as monies become more difficult to obtain. The school library media specialist is responsible for providing leadership in good budgetary practices and record keeping routines. Accountability is not new to education. Ever since the first sign-in sheet appeared in the principal's office, school personnel have been held accountable for the hours they work. The emphasis on program accountability has increased as available funds have decreased. Traditionally the budget has been a device for financial accounting; however, the emphasis has shifted to include accountability for program results as well. The complexities of accountability sense require an increased understanding of the budgeting process. In a broad sense, a budget is a chart for a future course of action. It records the outcome of an essentially political process in which alternative plans are examined, preferences are indicated, and decisions are made. In its final form, the budget is a statement of policy—and often even a public relations tool—on which expenditures are based. The budget represents priorities in the school that are the outcome of bargaining over conflicting goals.

A school library media center budget is only one, and all too often small, part of a school district's total executive budget, which includes the operating budget for each school. The media center portion of an overall school budget is frequently given only minor consideration due to the lack of recognition of the importance of media in instruction and the absence of a well-developed budget prepared by a knowledgeable and assertive media specialist. Too many people think of a budget as simply what they have to spend, but the budget reflects the values placed on the various functions and components of the entire school. A school library media center with no budget is seen by someone within that school (e.g., the principal, the site-based management team, or maybe even the secretary who does the school's bookkeeping and actually controls the purse strings) as having no value or role in making any significant contribution to the school's educational goals. The school library media center budget is essentially the philosophy of the center stated in quantitative terms, in the same way that a school district or school building level budget expresses the educational philosophy of its community.

The aims of the rest of this chapter are to: (1) describe the sources and levels of funding, (2) present various types of budget systems in common use in school library media centers, (3) discuss approaches to budgeting and the data and processes needed to develop the budget, and (4) illustrate examples of record keeping practices.

SOURCES OF FUNDING

Knowledge of the sources of funding is required before a school library media specialist can begin to understand the budgeting process. Some funding sources require that monies must be spent for certain items; for example, gift monies or grants are generally always designated for particular purposes, the latter often in memory of someone. The same holds true for federal monies; they frequently must be spent for specific programs. Given today's tight budget purse strings, it behooves every school library media specialist to be aware of *all possible* sources of available funding that may be tapped in developing the total school library budget as well as what constitutes the media center's fair share. Many funding sources, such as grants or large donations, only become part of the library budget through proactive efforts by the school library media specialist.

There are essentially four funding sources for a school library media center budget: (1) local school district funds (e.g., from local property taxes and other county or city sources of revenue), (2) state funds (such as from state sales tax, state income tax, state lotteries, and so forth), (3) federal monies such as those from the No Child Left Behind Act or the Library Services and Technology Act described later, and finally (4) local school level fund-raising efforts. Book fairs, parent-teacher organizations' (PTOs) donations, and grants are all examples of locally generated funding sources that fit into this last category. The second and fourth categories are becoming more important to school library media centers as federal funding shrinks for libraries, and local property taxes reach the limits taxpayers will tolerate without open rebellions such as Proposition 13, which occurred in California in 1978 or Massachusetts's Proposition 2 1/2 in 1980. The California Proposition, passed by almost a two-thirds majority of the voters, rolled back property taxes to their 1975 level and limited annual assessment increases to no more than two percent per year (Galles & Sexton, 1998). Some critics have credited the limitation on local property taxes with destroying the development of school libraries in California during the past two decades and past statistics show that California did indeed have one of the highest student to school library media specialist ratios in the country. Sources of funds such as gifts or donations are normally too sporadic or small in size to be considered a regular part of any school library budget.

Local Funding

Monies for education come mainly from local and state taxes. Historically local property taxes have been the major source of funds for public schools. Because the wealth of a community is directly tied to the wealth of its school system, great inequities in school funding result from this funding pattern. Legal cases filed in many states during the 1970s and 1980s challenged the equity of this system which resulted in poor schools and rich schools in districts, depending upon the economic conditions of their local community. Some states were asked to step in and attempt to eradicate these inequities by leveling this budgetary playing field. School funding sources and patterns still vary widely from state to state; however, there is a definite trend toward more state funding and more state control over public education (EdSource Online, 2003). These tax funds—local and state—are often the only ones that can be relied upon for budgetary purposes, and sometimes even these sources are not reliable. Nevertheless, the possibility of receiving funds from sources outside the city, district, and/or county and state needs to be thoroughly investigated.

The primary local source of funding for schools is local property taxation on real estate, both residential and commercial/industrial. The fact that these taxes are based on assessed values, which many states try to reassess periodically, at least ensures that most school districts can count on funding received in previous years. As property values go up, school districts can count on modest increases in the tax base each year. Taxpayer revolts, such as those mentioned in California and Massachusetts, hold these funding source levels steady in some cases; however, overall they continue to rise. Where there are limitations, local jurisdictions have sought new sources of revenue, such as rapidly growing, nontax fees and charges that are less visible to voters than taxes, but nonetheless continue to generate healthy local revenues (Galles & Sexton, 1998). Since the assessment and disbursement of local property taxes varies from state to state, the school library media specialist needs to explore the local school district's funding pattern and determine how the district goes about receiving these funds from the local taxing authority, city, and/or county.

As Exhibit 5.1, Local, State and Federal Funding for Selected U.S. States, clearly shows, local funds as a source of educational revenue vary widely from state to state. In many states they constitute half or more of

Exhibit 5.1.
Local, State, and Federal Funding for Selected U.S. States.

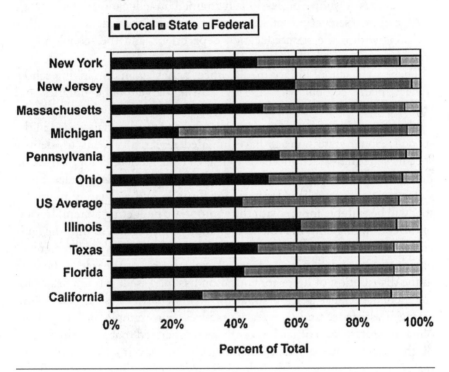

Unlike most states, California and Michigan are funded primarily through State, rather than Local, sources of revenue

■ Local ▯ State ▯ Federal

Printed with permission. Source: EdSource Online. (2003). *School finance overview. Where the money comes from.* Retrieved April 4, 2004, from the EdSource web site: http://www.edsource.org/edu_fin.cfm.

education funding, for example, New Jersey sixty percent, Illinois a little more than sixty percent. In Michigan local funds account for only a little more than twenty percent of the state's education revenues. These monies come primarily from local property taxes, but they also include such local funds as community contributions, interest income, and other local fees and taxes (EdSource Online, 2002). Local funds typically come directly from a local administrative fiscal agency, which must approve allocation of funds.

State Funds

Within each state department of education, it is common to find the responsibility of school library media programs, with the exception of such highly specialized activities as instructional television, rests in a library bureau or department devoted to instructional services. Each office generally includes a staff—professionally trained in educational technology and/or library science—that serves as liaison with the federal level, other divisions within the state education department, and the schools in the state.

These state school library media offices act as agents in linking school library media centers with already existing large public libraries and regional resource or service centers in order to form statewide media networks. The ultimate goal is to provide access to any material needed in the schools. Some state bureaus have initiated research projects to identify specific staff and student needs as well as to issue guidelines for instruction in information literacy skills—particularly in the elementary grades. Some states have also established criteria for forming and evaluating programs that will be suitable for use with the appropriate budgeting system. In view of the continuing emphasis on accountability for program results, the budgeting system suggested by the state generally includes a statement of descriptive justification for each coded expenditure. As the role of the state in the distribution of funds for education has increased, it is important for the media specialist to learn about the state department's suggestions for financial assistance and budgetary practices. For example, in North Carolina some state level officials recently recommended that a certain portion of the ADM (average daily membership or enrollment) instructional materials allocation go to the school library budget. This suggested figure resulted in about $29 per student (based on an instructional materials allocation per pupil of $48.30 times 60 percent), going to the library budget for media center purchases. Media specialists are encouraged to get in touch with their state school library media office to obtain information regarding school library budgets if such information is not available at the district level. The appropriate state education department addresses are listed in Appendix 1.

State funds are becoming more important as an income source to schools. For one thing, there is simply a national trend toward more state level control. Another reason for state funds being so important is the economic inequities between school districts and the state's role in attempting to alleviate the situation. State revenue for education varies widely as seen

Exhibit 5.2.
Funding Sources for California Public Schools,
2002–2003.

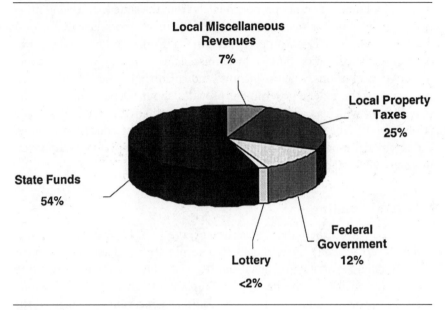

**Local Miscellaneous
Revenues
7%**

**Local Property
Taxes
25%**

**State Funds
54%**

**Federal
Government
12%**

**Lottery
<2%**

Printed with permission. Source: EdSource Online. (2002,
November) K-12 education funding comes from several sources.
Retrieved April 4, 2004, from the EdSource web site:
http://www.edsource.org/sch_fund0203.cfm

in Exhibit 5.1 from as little as around thirty-three percent (Illinois) to
around seventy percent (Michigan) of the state's education budget.

In the case of California see the above Exhibit 5.2, Funding Sources for
California Public Schools 2002–2003.

These state revenues, which comprise fifty-five percent of total education
funding, are generated mostly from state retail sales and income taxes. The
chart shows the estimated K–12 funding sources or revenues for the State of
California for the year 2002–2003 totaling $56 billion. Some states, such as
Florida and Tennessee, do not have state income taxes. It is interesting to
note in Exhibit 5.2 how small a percentage of the state's education income—
less than two percent—came from the California lottery, since so many
states without a lottery have tried to get taxpayers to approve one by claim-
ing the profits would basically all go to education. Georgia is an example of

one state that makes a truly concerted effort to put lottery money into the education budget, and, in particular, into educational technology. It should also be noted from Exhibit 5.2 that California is somewhat atypical in that more school funding comes proportionately from the state (i.e., around fifty-five percent), whereas many states are funded much more heavily by local funds for education. Local property taxes in California comprise twenty-five percent of the education budget, local miscellaneous revenues such as community contributions, interest income, and so forth, combined total seven percent, and the federal government provides about twelve percent for the year shown, which is about two percent more than the national average (EdSource Online, 2002). State funding, as a source of education income, varies widely from state to state, and even varies by school district; however, it is generally a stable and continuing source of revenue.

Federal Funding

Located within the federal government, the U S. Department of Education (DOE) is the official agency that administers and coordinates most of the federal assistance to education. It assists the president in executing education policies for the nation and implements laws enacted by Congress that provide funding for states and other education aid, such as student loan programs. The Department's overall mission is twofold: (1) to ensure that all of America's students have equal access to education, and (2) to promote excellence in our nation's schools (No child left behind—Summary of key provisions, 2002).

Brief History of the DOE

Although new as a cabinet-level agency, the DOE's history dates back to 1867, when President Andrew Jackson signed legislation creating the first education department. The main purpose of this department was to collect statistics about the nation's schools. Fears that this department would exercise too much control over local schools, and demands to abolish it, resulted in its demotion to an Office of Education in 1868. Until fairly recently, this office remained relatively small, operating under varying names and being housed in various government agencies—including the former U.S. Department of Health, Education, and Welfare (What is the U.S. Department of Education?, 2002).

Due to a variety of political and social changes beginning in the 1950s, including Russia's launching of Sputnik in 1957 and President Johnson's

"War on Poverty," federal funding to education greatly increased during the next several decades. The United States was, quite simply, embarrassed that the Russians beat our country into outer space exploration. Additionally, the civil rights movement revealed discrimination and great social as well as economic inequities within our country. As a result of these events, the federal government began to provide supplementary education monies through the National Defense Education Act (NDEA) and later the Elementary and Secondary Education Act (ESEA). Because a large part of these funds was categorical, that is, specifically designated to be spent for the purchase of books to be placed in school library media center collections, the period of the 1960s and the 1970s saw a tremendous growth in book collections in the nation's public schools.

Unfortunately, categorical funding for school library collections was discontinued in the 1980s and up until recently, federal funds were only available as part of block grant funding (most recently through Title V) and the school library had to apply, along with all other areas and departments within the individual schools, in order to receive these monies. A huge decrease in federal book expenditures for school media center collections began in the 1980s and continued into the 1990s. As a result, school library media center collections throughout the nation's public schools are outdated with copyrights averaging in the 1960s and 1970s; the sciences, the social sciences, and contemporary history and geography are especially outdated.

Congress created the present U.S. DOE when it passed Public Law 96-88 in 1979. In addition to its previous overall stated mission, this law's purpose includes supplementing efforts of state and local school systems; encouraging increased public (such as parental) involvement in federal education programs; promoting improvements in the quality and usefulness of education through federally supported research, evaluation, and sharing of information; attempting to improve the coordination of federal education programs; improving the management and efficiency of federal education activities, especially with respect to the process, procedures, and administrative structures for the dispersal of federal funds; and increasing accountability of federal education programs. The Office of Education had 2,113 employees and a budget of $1.5 billion by 1965. By early 2002, the DOE had a budget of $54.5 billion and around 4,800 people worked there (What is...?, 2002).

The latest federal funding program for public schools, Public Law 107-110, was signed into law on January 8, 2002, and reauthorized the Elementary and Secondary Education Act (ESEA). It has been called by some sources "the largest [ever] overhaul of the federal role in education" (No

Child Left Behind..., 2002; North Carolina Public Schools, 2004) and has been accompanied by the largest increase in federal school funding yet. Popularly known as the No Child Left Behind Act and called by some people the Title I law (because it focuses on children who live at the poverty level), this new legislation promotes greater accountability and testing, more flexibility in terms of transferring federal funds among and between accounts, and reporting of test results. Briefly, its key provisions include: (1) testing of reading, mathematics, and science abilities; (2) demonstrated student proficiency (up to the 100 percent level); (3) the flexibility to transfer up to 50 percent of federal funds received; (4) quality staff licensure requirements for both teachers and paraprofessionals; (5) English language proficiency testing for ESL (English as a Second Language) students; and (6) consolidation of several technology programs to ensure that more of the technology monies actually go to schools (No Child Left Behind..., 2002).

To implement this Act, Congress authorized $26.5 billion for education programs, including $22 billion for 2002. One state alone, North Carolina, received approximately $1 billion in 2002 to implement the Act's provisions. It is easy to see that federal dollars for public education in general have not dried up by any means. To monitor the status of federal level funds for education, the best source is DOE's own web site: http://www.ed.gov.

Unfortunately this federal largesse does not necessarily mean that school media centers will benefit from this money. The only way a center can directly benefit from these new federal dollars is if they are designated as part of a school district or local school's grant request for the funding, although it is aimed primarily at Title I schools. Title I means the school or district must show entitlement due to a certain poverty level within the community or district. Schools are *told* if they can apply based on the poverty criteria set forth in the legislation. However, three school districts, two in North Carolina and one in Virginia, recently received a grant for $250,000 through the Improving Literacy Through School Libraries section of the No Child Left Behind funding. School media specialists and district media supervisors are encouraged to explore this potential funding source. Nationally, federal funding for public school education comprises less than ten percent of state education budgets and has the added disadvantage that most of it goes for specific programs, such as special education, Title I students, and other similarly restricted categories.

Local Fund Raising

Book fairs, scheduled once or twice a year, have for a long time been a staple fund raising activity for school library media centers. In some cases, the PTA or PTO organization runs the fair; in this case the media center may only receive a portion of the total profits. When the book fair is run solely by the library media center and its volunteers, *all* of this money goes into the center's coffers. In the past, book fairs were considered to be public relations events, but today, given the very commercial nature of these activities (such as those sponsored by Scholastic Book Fairs, Bedford Falls Bookfairs, Usborne Books, or BookServe) one should simply accept them for what they are—fund raisers. If they are combined with a comprehensive all-school reading motivation event or program, such as an author visit or National Book Week activities, then one might reasonably call book fairs PR events. Otherwise, they are simply moneymaking events. The sad thing about this source of funding, which should never be considered anything more than a supplement to the library's regular budget, is that many school library media specialists report this as their *only* source of money for books and all other library materials and supplies.

Some book fair vendors provide virtually all the necessary flyers, posters, sample letters to parents and teachers, volunteer sign-up sheets, and similar materials needed to conduct the fair, and these vendors send the allotted number of books in boxes pre-inventoried for the librarian's convenience. Some even include books with cassette tapes, coloring books, and adult fare such as cookbooks or seasonal items. Scheduling the book fair close to holidays, such as before Christmas, often boosts sales by providing gift ideas. Most vendors also send the paperwork for accounting and a great deal of other promotional or commercial material including: videos, pens, pencils, computer software, popular youth posters, and so forth, to sell. For example, Harry Potter books and novelties have been extremely popular book fair fare as have the "Chicken Soup for the Soul" series. The authors of *Power Up Your Library* admonish media specialists: "Don't buy junk or sell junk [at your book fair]!" (Salmon, et al., 1996, p. 222).

District Media Services and the School Library Budget

According to the AASL Position Statement on Appropriate Staffing for School Library Media Centers (1991):

All school systems must employ a district library media director to provide leadership and direction to the overall library media program. The district director is a member of the administrative staff and serves on committees that determine the criteria and policies for the district's curriculum and instructional programs. The director communicates the goals and needs of both the school and district library media programs to the superintendent, board of education, other district-level personnel, and the community. In this advocacy role, the district library media director advances the concept of the school library media specialist as a partner with teachers and promotes a staffing level that allows the partnership to flourish. (ALA, 1991, p. 1). Reprinted with permission.

Unfortunately, Miller and Shontz (2001), in their biennial survey of school libraries and their expenditures note that the number of full-time district media coordinators has decreased during the past few years—more than half of the districts surveyed did not have one. When someone at the district office is designated the responsibility for school media centers, they are often required to perform many other unrelated duties (e.g., school nurses, testing), diverting their energies from school media center matters.

A school library media center program at the district level functions both as a centralized resource for the district and as support for the program in individual schools. The resources and services that form a base of operations at the district level can provide the services needed by many of the schools. Each school can retain its individuality by its own selection and use of resources as well as by its unique use of the district services.

The district school library media program includes many internal district responsibilities, several of them related to fiscal operations: (1) preparation of annual budgets; (2) interpretation of the total media program (central office and individual schools) to the public, the board of education, and the staff; (3) applications for funds from federal, state, and foundation sources; (4) administration of the funds for special projects; and (5) formulation of reports (to the district board of education, the state department of education, foundations, and so on). A recent example of a funding source, which the district coordinator might apply for, is the e-rate funds available to schools for Internet access. Two North Carolina school districts recently received well in excess of $100,000 from this source.

Two of the major tasks of the school district media program are planning and evaluating the system and providing individual school-building levels of service. Planning is generally based on a knowledge of: (1) the educational philosophy of the school system and the objectives of the instructional program, (2) staffing patterns, (3) curricula, (4) various methods of instruction, (5) availability and utilization of technology, and (6) awareness of new technology. Both of these processes are helpful in the planning and developing of new budgets, both at the district and individual school levels, as they indicate where resources are needed and/or falling short of those required to provide maximum (or even minimum) support services.

On the district level, media services under the direction of a coordinator who is knowledgeable both in the library field and in educational technology and who exhibits leadership capabilities should ensure greater development of media programs at the school-building level. This person can, for example, suggest to district principals what percentage of their school budget should be allocated for school library resources. Unfortunately, this person often does not possess all of these skills and competencies and today is quite likely to only have expertise in technology. To provide these services on a system level requires appropriate staffing, funding, and facilities. Seven percent of the school district's instructional budget is recommended to support a district media program.

Other Funding Sources—Grants, Local and State

In some states special-purpose grants are funding sources that may be tapped by school library media centers. Each state department of education continues to use federal and state funds in its own unique way to develop and strengthen both programs in school library media centers in individual schools and in county and regional agencies that help to support the development of school programs. School library media specialists should become familiar with the components of grant proposals, sources of grants for which they might apply, and the basics of grant writing. Grants are likely to become a larger source of income for school media centers in the future. A good starting point for the media specialist who wants to start writing grants would be to read a book such as *Grantsmanship for Small Libraries and School Library Media Centers* (Hall-Ellis, et al., 1999). *School and Public Libraries: Developing the Natural Alliance* (Ziarnik, 2003) contains a section on grants, and it should be mentioned that collaborative grant proposals are often solicited by funding agencies and/or given a higher priority for actual funding.

The Basic Components of a Grant Proposal

There are eight basic components which should comprise a solid proposal package: (1) the proposal summary, (2) introduction to the organization, (3) the problem statement (or needs assessment), (4) project objectives, (5) project methods or design, (6) project evaluation, (7) future funding, and (8) the project budget (The Catalog of Federal Domestic Assistance, 2003, p. 3). The following site provides an overview of these components as well as guidelines for writing proposals: http://www.cfda.gov/public/cat-writing.htm.

Sources of Grant Information

There are many other sources of information available for writing and finding grants for the school library media center. The "bible" of federal grant programs is the *Catalog of Federal Domestic Assistance Programs*, which "is a government-wide compendium of all 1,499 Federal programs, projects, services, and activities that provide assistance or benefits to the American public" (Catalog of Federal Domestic Assistance, 2002, p. 1). It may be found online at: http://aspe.os.dhhs.gov/cfda/index.htm. The following are additional sources of grants for which school media specialists can apply:

Internet School Library Media Center (ISLMC)

http://falcon.jmu.edu/~ramseyil/libraries.htm#L. More than a dozen sources of grants are listed under the Grants & Awards section.

School Grants Web Site

http://www.schoolgrants.org/. This site is aimed at the PK–12 audience in general, but could be used for collaborative grant writing and includes tips, samples and more (e.g., a listserv for grants).

Purdue University Site—Grant Writing Tutorial

http://www.epa.gov/seahome/grants/src/msieopen.htm. This site is jointly sponsored by the United States Environmental Protection Agency and Purdue University, and features such sections as enhancing a proposal, completing forms, a mock grant writing activity, three sample grant proposals, federal and state grant sources, and a glossary. Emphasis is on environmental grants and one of the samples included is environmental education.

Grant-Finder.net

http://www.grant-finder.net/. This site reviews five grant sites and evaluates their usefulness on a scale from one to ten.

Grants for School Media Centers

LSTA Funds

One funding source that has been extremely helpful in rebuilding out-dated school media center collections, as well as in implementing new community technology outreach services in recent years, has been the Library Services and Technology Act (LSTA). This act was passed by the U.S. Congress in the fall of 1996, and replaced the several decades old Library Services and Construction Act (LSCA). The major difference between the two acts was that the new LSTA included school libraries, as well as other types (i.e., academic, special, and so forth), while the former was limited only to public libraries. The LSTA, a section of the more comprehensive Museum and Library Services Act, "promotes access to learning and information resources [for] all types of libraries for individuals of all ages" (Heiser, 2003, p. 1). Funds are channeled to state library agencies using a population-based formula. These agencies use the funds to support statewide initiatives and services or they may distribute the funds through competitive sub-grant competitions or cooperative agreements to public, academic, research, school, or special libraries in their state.

Each state has to develop its own five-year plan for allocating these funds to libraries, and to determine its priorities for funding. Since 1997, Congress has appropriated funding for this act in all fifty states.

In North Carolina, LSTA funds were recently allocated to school library media centers through the state library using a competitive bid process, which had to document evaluation of the current media center collection and determine an established need. A collection development plan was submitted by the school media center showing how the funds would to be used. An additional requirement was that for every dollar received from the LSTA funds, the school had to match funds dollar for dollar. In other words, if the school media specialist asked for $5,000 in LSTA monies, the school had to provide another $5,000, for a total amount of $10,000. These requirements not only made the schools and the school districts aware of the outdated collections that were in their media centers, but they made the schools jointly responsible for updating these collections.

Currently North Carolina, through the State Library, has four categories of grants available for public schools for the 2004–2005 funding year (State Library of North Carolina, 2003). Two of these grants require that letters of intent be sent prior to applying: (1) Grants for Community-Centered Outreach Services (Unserved/Underserved), and (2) Powerful Partners Collaboration Grants. The maximum funding for these grants is

$50,000. The other two grants do not require a letter of intent, and, in fact, are called EZ Grants. These grants include the continuation of the School Library Collection Development Grants, previously described in detail, and the Grants for Planning LSTA Projects. The former grant maximum amount that may be requested is $10,000 and now only requires fifty percent matching funds from the school district, and the latter will fund up to $15,000. These grants are examples of how one state has chosen to disburse its LSTA funds from the federal government. Each state library has developed its own plan for channeling these funds to the local level.

Technology Literacy Challenge Fund

Another good example of federal funding for media centers were the High Tech Library grants received by thirteen Indiana school corporations for up to $75,000 each (Bear & Huffman, 2001). These grants were aimed at developing and improving library technology and media information programs in middle and high schools in the state. The federal government's Technology Literacy Challenge Fund funded the grants.

All public schools in Indiana were invited to submit proposals for these grants, and winning proposals "showed a well-developed plan for using school library technology, and demonstrated a commitment to working in partnership with other schools, community groups, government agencies, and business leaders..." (Bear & Huffman, 2001, p. 1). Dr. Suellen Reed, Indiana Superintendent of Public Instruction, expressed her commitment to funding technology in school library media centers by stating: "Libraries remain central to our schools and the learning process" (Bear & Huffman, 2001, p. 1), while recognizing that many school media centers are simply short of funds to support this needed technology.

Laura Bush Foundation for America's Libraries

The Laura Bush Foundation was established June 4, 2002, as a result of the White House Conference on School Libraries. The President's wife, a former school librarian, realized the importance of a well-stocked school library in ensuring that all children learn to read. Nearly $640,000 in grants was awarded to 132 school library media centers throughout the country according to an announcement in *School Library Journal* in June of 2003 (Whelan, 2003). There were more than 6,000 applications from 40 states. Funds are to be used to create or improve and expand book collections in media centers. According to Whelan, "Most of the schools receiving grants have book collections that average 15 years and some books have been on the shelves for five decades. About 93 percent of the schools awarded have students eligible for free or reduced lunch and don't have enough funds to buy one book per student per year..." (p. 1).

School Library Enrichment Grants, Governor's Book Fund, California State Library (CSL) Foundation

For several years, the California State Library Foundation has awarded grants of around $5,000 to schools for the enhancement of K–12 school library collections (Governor's Book Fund, 2003). Interestingly, all funds are raised through private donations and there is no government funding involved. The grants are competitive and schools must meet certain criteria to be eligible including showing a need based on the ratio of students to books in the existing media center. In the year 2000, forty-seven California school library media centers received these grants.

Other Grant and Funding Sources

Local financial support beyond the tax levies for educational purposes in the form of grants is encouraged, and it may be more readily available than is commonly realized. Increasing reliance on this type of local funding for media center special projects is likely. School representatives who are willing to do the necessary public relations and grant writing work may find community groups and businesses willing to donate money. In addition, special grants are available from professional organizations and foundations, for example, the American Association of School Librarians/ American Library Association, state media organizations (such as the North Carolina School Library Media Association), and comparable groups in other states. In North Carolina the Blue Ridge Electric Cooperative gives Bright Ideas grants and the Watauga Education Foundation gives awards like one recently granted for the annual Battle of the Books contest, which is frequently coordinated by the school library media specialist. Meantime, both local and state funding sources should provide the bedrock on which to build a strong school library program.

REGIONAL BUDGET ASSISTANCE

Regional networks or service centers may have implications for budgets that impact school library media specialists. They often provide a level of media services similar in many ways to that available to school library media specialists only in the largest school districts.

In North Carolina, for example, those regional service centers still in existence after the budget cuts of the 1990s provide consultation and in-service or staff development for many school library media specialists who otherwise might have no such opportunities available to them. These centers were generally established in the past with seed money from federal funds. Although school library media centers have often not been able to initiate school network systems comparable to those of public libraries (primarily because of restrictions on local funding), such services should be investigated as potential funding sources. Regional networks (whether for instructional television, videos, cataloging, computerized information sources or expensive and infrequently used materials) have proven most valuable when the contract services supply resources that are too costly for small school districts.

Networks are being used for access to electronic databases, union catalogs and Internet resources through such networks as Access Pennsylvania (http://205.247.101.10/), which pioneered the implementation and dissemination of a CD-ROM union catalog of all school and public library resources in that state, and, more recently, NC WiseOwl (http://www. ncwiseowl.org), a network of K–12 reference databases, teaching lessons, and other electronic resources available to North Carolina public schools. Because these types of networks make expensive online reference resources available free of charge to school library media centers, their existence needs to be thoroughly explored by school library media specialists because of the collection development and corresponding budgetary implications of such valuable resources. Inquiries to the existing state or regional networks are the place to start (see Chapter 10 for further information on networks).

BUDGET LEVELS OF FUNDING

Given the current state of the national (and many state) economies, it is realistic to look at different possible levels of funding that one may have to deal with in constructing a school library budget today. One is also urged to look at the following discussion on types of budget systems and specifically the concept of zero-based budgeting; however, before exploring these budget types, it is useful to make a preliminary determination as to the level on which the budget is to be constructed. Johnson (1997) quotes David Lewis in an article from *Library Journal* that maintains we are at "a zero sum game" (p. 96) in regard to public library budgets—that is the limit that the public is willing to provide in funding—and the same can probably be said for school libraries. There simply is no more money available.

Maintenance or Continuity Budget

The simplest level of budgeting and the easiest to work with is commonly called the *maintenance* or *continuity budget*. If a program is well established and productive, if the educational goals remain essentially the same, and if no unusual expansion is planned, the same level of expenditures will be maintained and the program will continue as before. Of course the budget should provide for small increases or decreases in student or faculty numbers as well as replacement and inflationary costs for goods and labor. Maintenance-level budgeting is common in an established school library media center; however, it can, lead to complacency if the person planning neither recognizes nor cares about strengthening programs or reflecting changes. Continuity or maintenance budgeting is not appropriate if the collection alignment and evaluation process reveal glaring deficiencies in the book collection in particular, nor does it necessarily take into account the budgetary demands that today's technology and the concept of the virtual library places upon the media center.

Incremental Budgeting

If there are external and internal changes, such as large increases or decreases in the number of students and staff, a desire to improve or bring a basic program up to standard goals, or, if as mentioned previously, the collection has not been kept up to date, these factors may be reflected in an *incremental budget*. It is common in incremental-level budgeting for the cost of the larger increases to be distributed throughout a three-to-five year period. This plan is especially appropriate in bringing a neglected book collection up to par.

Incremental budgeting only pertains to whether the present staff, materials, facilities, equipment and supplies are available in adequate numbers to meet program demands. One way to deal with adequacy is to apply external standards such as those found in national or state standards or guidelines. If a program does not meet the applicable standards or is found to be deficient in aligning with the established curriculum, an incremental budget may be required to correct deficiencies in small increments during a period of time. Incremental budgeting usually means giving a certain percentage increase to the amount of a previous budget. Advantages to this type of budget are: (1) the ease with which the budget is determined, (2) the small amount of paperwork required, (3) the small amount of overall work required, and (4) the lack of hard judgments on particular matters.

Expansion Budget

Finally, if major reorganization or important developments are anticipated in the immediate future, or the collection (or even the library technology) is so out-dated that only drastic measures can bring it up to an acceptable level, a third type of budget, the *expansion budget,* is preferred. For example, creative budgeting of this type would be used for initiating major new programs and in the initial planning for the opening of a new school library media center. It would also possibly involve expending capital outlay funds or other special funding. Because capital outlay money represents reserve funds, as opposed to general operating funds, from which interest revenue may be anticipated, it is generally tapped with understandable reluctance. Therefore, extensive preparation must go into expansion-level budgeting. Needs must be clearly identified and directly related to the additional funds being sought. This type of budgeting may be required as a result of technological or social change or of administrative decisions to reorganize, (such as, perhaps, district reorganization of individual schools and their boundaries) enlarge, or improve existing programs.

A realistic rule of thumb for a school library media specialist is to determine how much spending is likely to be acceptable to the administration and community and then to frame the budget to reflect that expectation. The most important factor, however, is obtaining and maintaining the support and confidence of the media center audience: students, teachers, staff, administrators, and the local community.

BUDGETING SYSTEMS

One of the most important pointers to remember about different types of budgets is that the types, as we shall see, are not necessarily mutually exclusive. For example, a formula such as "X" number of dollars per student may determine the amounts that are then placed into different lines on a line item budget.

Line Item and Object of Expenditure Budget Systems

Probably the most common types of budget systems, which actually translate into accounting codes, are the line item and object of expenditure. These are discussed together because when a line item is placed in a budget, the accounting system then used is normally called an object of expenditure code or system. Most states use some type of line item and/or object of expenditure budget. Woolls (1994) describes a line item budget in this way:

> This means that each item of the budget is placed on a line next to the account number and description of that item. Usually the budget begins with the revenues accruing to the school district.... (p. 153)

The account numbers are where these line items are placed as well as where the revenues appear. They typically come from the object of expenditure codes used by the school district, generally from a state-adopted accounting system. Originally the federal government developed a suggested model for all state local education agencies (LEAs) to use, the first of which appeared in 1957. Their purpose in doing this was to standardize school accounting procedures so that statistics collected by the federal government's education office, and now, the National Center for Education Statistics, would be comparable. A later version, called *Financial Accounting...for Local and State School Systems* (Roberts & Lichtenberger, 1973) recommends each LEA use a minimum of the first seven dimensions for its financial transactions. These include: (1) fund, (2) object, (3) function, (4) operational unit, (5) program, (6) source of funds, and (7) fiscal year. The federal government's current version of this system (Fowler, 1995) may be found online at: http://nces.ed.gov/pubs97/97096R.pdf. Each dimension has an alphanumeric code that varies state by state.

Many of the current state and local guides for school districts are based on the federal handbook. North Carolina's school accounting system may be found online at: http://www.ncpublicschools.org/fbs/coa/toc.html. The manual at this location is called the *North Carolina Public Schools Uniform Chart of Accounts* (2003). The North Carolina accounting code must be used by all local schools in the state; the manual outlines the minimum requirements consisting of these four dimensions: (1) fund, (2) function, (3) program report code, and (4) object. An example of a fund is State Public School Fund. The function is the purpose for which the activity exists or the type of balance sheet account. Four examples of these types of codes are: Accounts Receivable (Asset Codes), Accounts Payable (Liabilities, Reserves and Fund Balance Codes), Textbooks (Revenue Codes), and Regular Instructional Programs (Purpose Codes). All of these have corresponding number codes that are unique to the accounting system used in North Carolina.

The third dimension, program report code, "describes a plan of activity or a funding for a particular activity" (North Carolina Public Schools 2004, April 16, p. I-A). An example of a plan is Non-Instructional Support, which is code 003. And lastly, object code is the fourth dimension which is defined as "the service or commodity obtained as the result of a specific expenditure" (North Carolina Public Schools2004, April 16, p. I-A). North Carolina's system has seven major object category codes: 100 is Salaries; 200 is Employee benefits; 300 is Purchased services; 400 is Supplies and materials; 500 is Capital outlay; 600 is Other objects; and 700 is Transfers. Specific object code examples are 121 for Teacher's Salary and 411 for Instructional Supplies.

Exhibit 5.3, Account Codes Related to School Library Media Centers in North Carolina, lists account codes relevant to the school library budget; these codes are taken from North Carolina's account coding system and show specifically the 061 categories for Classroom Materials/Instructional Supplies and Equipment. Some of these codes of particular relevance to the school library media center budget are listed here. For example, within the 400s or Supplies one can find: 412 Supplies and materials (noninstructional), 418 Computer software and supplies, 430 Library/audiovisual services, 431 Library books (regular and replacement), 432 Periodicals (including newspapers), 433 Audiovisual supplies and materials, 434 Processing and cataloging (in a school library), and 435 Online materials/subscriptions. Whether or not there is actually money placed in these accounts, of course, remains to be seen.

All states are likely to have similar lines in their accounting systems, and it behooves the school library media specialist to check these codes out and see where possible library funding might, or should be, found. Exhibit 5.4, Sample Object of Expenditure Budget, 2001–2002, is excerpted from a real budget for an actual school library media center.

Each state has the right and privilege to adapt the federal model to conform to its plans and needs. Therefore, it is advisable that media specialists obtain and digest the appropriate alphanumeric codes and their descriptions provided by their state department of education.

Lump-sum Budget

The lump-sum type of budget exists where the principal or some other individual or group such as a school improvement team or budget committee decides that different programs, grade levels, the school library media center or departments (e.g., third grade or ninth grade, history,

Exhibit 5.3.
Account Codes Related to School Library Media Centers in North Carolina.

ACCOUNT CODE	OBJECT CODE DESCRIPTION
5100-061-542	Purchase of Computer Hardware
5200-061-411	Instructional Supplies and Materials
5200-061-418	Computer Software and Supplies
5200-061-422	Textbooks - Other
5200-061-431	Library Books
5200-061-432	Periodicals
5200-061-435	On-line Materials/Subscriptions
5200-061-461	Lease/Purchase of Non-Capitalized Equipment
5200-061-462	Lease/Purchase of Non-Capitalized Computer Hardware
5200-061-541	Purchase of Equipment
5200-061-542	Purchase of Computer Hardware
5990-061-696	Sales and Use of Tax Expense
6620-061-199	Salary - Other Assignments
6620-061-311	Contracted Services
6620-061-326	Contracted Repairs and Maintenance - Equipment
6620-061-327	Rentals/Leases (Storage Space)
6620-061-412	Supplies and Materials
6620-061-418	Computer Software and Supplies

Printed with permission. Source: Councill, Leta, Finance Officer. Watauga County Board of Education Finance Office. (2002, September) *Account codes related to school library media centers in North Carolina.* Boone, NC: Watauga County Board of Education.

English, athletics, etc.) will get a set number of dollars (i.e., a lump-sum) for a predetermined expenditure such as classroom materials, library expenses, or new textbooks. These lump sums, by the way, generally are placed into line items on a school budget. While some consider the lump-sum budget an inferior type of budget system, which implies that the

Exhibit 5.4.
Sample Object of Expenditure Budget Year 2001-2002.

Date	P. O. #	Vendor	Department	Amount	Budget Code	Description
8/6/2001	108601	Winston-Salam	Media	$141.60	1.5100.061.432	Subscription
8/6/2001	108602	Charlotte OBS	Media	$124.00	1.5100.061.432	Subscription
8/6/2001	108602	Charlotte OBS	Media	$84.00	1.5100.061.432	Subscription
8/6/2001	108603	Watauga Democ	Media	$92.00	1.5100.061.432	Subscription
8/6/2001	108604	Sirs Inc.	Media	$1,144.80	1.5100.061.431	Subscription
8/6/2001	108605	EBSCO	Media	$1,989.06	1.5100.061.431	Books
8/8/2001	108608	The Gale Group	Media	$1,272.00	1.5100.061.418	Dis. Collection
8/13/2001	108610	National Geog	Media	$19.95	1.5100.061.433	VHS
8/13/2001	108610	National Geog	Media	$8.00	1.5100.061.433	Shipping
8/13/2001	108610	NC Dept of Re	Media	$1.20	1.5100.061.433	Sales Tax
8/13/2001	108611	Wall Street J	Media	$175.00	1.5100.061.432	1 Yr. Sub.
8/15/2001	108612	WGBH	Media	$23.90	1.5100.061.433	VHS
9/20/2001	108612	NC Dept of Re	Media	$1.20	1.5100.061.433	Sales Tax
8/16/2001	108615	Gaylord	Media	$425.20	1.5100.061.461	Equipment
8/22/2001	108618	Schlessinger	Media	$45.45	1.5100.061.433	Am. Rev.
10/4/2001	108618	NC Dept of Re	Media	$2.40	1.5100.061.433	Sales Tax
8/23/2001	108619	Social Studies	Media	$485.99	1.5100.061.431	Amer. Gov.
10/4/2001	108619	NC Dept of Re	Media	$27.00	1.5100.061.431	Sales Tax
8/26/2001	108621	Young Adult R	Media	$1,232.85	1.5100.061.431	Books
8/28/2001	108623	Best Books Co	Media	$1,356.61	1.5100.061.431	Books
8/31/2001	108624	Rapesafe	Media	$35.85	1.5100.061.433	Video
10/19/2001	108624	NC Dept of Re	Media	$1.80	1.5100.061.433	Sales Tax
8/31/2001	108625	Cambridge Ed.	Media	$24.95	1.5100.061.433	Video
8/31/2001	108625	NC Dept of Re	Media	$1.28	1.5100.061.433	Sales Tax
9/4/2001	108626	Corwin Press	Media	$93.35	1.5100.061.432	Books
9/4/2001	108626	NC Dept of Re	Media	$5.71	1.5100.061.432	Sales Tax
9/7/2001	108627	West Circle B	Media	$95.21	1.5100.061.422	Books
9/7/2001	108627	West Circle B	Media	$695.49	1.5100.061.422	Books
9/7/2001	108627	West Circle B	Media	$311.60	1.5100.061.422	Books
9/7/2001	108627	NC Dept of Re	Media	$39.39	1.5100.061.422	Sales Tax
9/7/2001	108627	NC Dept of Re	Media	$19.12	1.5100.061.422	Sales Tax
9/7/2001	108627	NC Dept of Re	Media	$5.84	1.5100.061.422	Sales Tax
9/7/2001	108627	NC Dept of Re	Media	$18.12	1.5100.061.422	Sales Tax
9/7/2001	108628	Young Adult R	Media	$906.65	1.5100.061.431	Books
10/4/2001	108628	NC Dept of Re	Media	$49.68	1.5100.061.431	Sales Tax
9/10/2001	108629	ASCD	Media	$56.95	1.5100.061.418	CD-ROM
11/20/2001	108629	NC Dept of Re	Media	$3.00	1.5100.061.418	Sales Tax
9/12/2001	108630	Garrett Ed. C	Media	$2,465.13	1.5100.061.431	Books
9/12/2001	108631	Gale Group	Media	$274.24	1.5100.061.431	Books
9/12/2001	108631	Gale Group	Media	$139.53	1.5100.061.431	Books
9/18/2001	108633	Grolier Ed.	Media	$1,759.14	1.5100.061.431	Books

Printed with permission. Source: Hartley, Audrey, Media
Coordinator. Watauga High School. Watauga County Schools.
(2002, February). *Sample object of expenditure budget year
2001-2002.* Boone, NC: Watauga County Board of Education.

school library media center has little relevance in delivering the school's educational program, it is a commonly used method of allocating money in many schools today. Some defensible uses of lump-sum budgeting are to obtain emergency funds and/or to estimate initial costs. This budget method is often used when costs are not clearly known ahead of time. Of course, it is also used to limit what any one person or department can spend. It indicates a certain confidence on the part of those allocating the sums that the budget authority receiving the funds (department chair, librarian, classroom teacher, and so forth) will spend the money in a responsible manner.

Formula Budgeting

Formula budgeting takes various demographic and dollar facts and figures and converts them into proposed budgetary amounts such as how much money a given library should get for books, magazines, supplies, technology, and so forth. One well-known formula for school libraries is adapted from the Wisconsin Department of Public Instruction (Hopkins, et al., 1987). It includes the following components: current year budget figure, variation in student population, attrition by weeding, attrition by date, attrition by loss, and inflation rate. When amounts have been input for all of these factors, the result is a figure for the proposed materials budget for the upcoming year. Several parts of the formula require that table factors be added, and it is unclear how these tables were derived as well as exactly how the original formula was created. This same formula appears at the end of the first edition of *Information Power* (American Association of School Librarians & Association for Educational Communication and Technology [AASL & AECT], 1988) and may be studied there. It is not being included here because of the uncertainty of the rationale behind its original development, besides the fact that there are simpler ways to calculate or project budget needs.

North Carolina, for example, uses a simple formula based on enrollment figures called ADM (average daily membership), which uses the highest average attendance figures taken on the twentieth day of classes for two months each previous school year. Once the ADM figure is determined, the state allocates a certain amount of money per student to school districts based on these ADM figures. Within that amount, certain dollar figures and/or percentages are recommended (although a district may not necessarily spend as per this recommendation) for particular budget expenses. For example, in one recent year about $48 per student was allocated for instructional materials in North Carolina, which includes such items as library books. This amount could, but usually doesn't, go directly to the school library media center.

A simpler formula budget aimed at keeping resources up-to-date is given in Doug Johnson's book (1997, p. 99) on library management. The basic formula is: Maintenance budget = replacement rate X total number of items X average cost. The replacement rate is 100 percent divided by the life span of whatever item is being replaced. For computers it could be five years, or twenty percent; for books it could be twenty years if hardcover, or five percent. It can be used for any type of resources including computers, book volumes, VCRs, overheads, and so forth, and is extremely simple to understand even for the novice budget maker.

Formula budgeting has several advantages. Once the basic formula and figures have been determined, all one has to do is calculate totals to determine the relevant amounts. There is little or no thinking or rationalization of the budget figures involved once the basic formula has been created. Also, it gives a sense of fairness to the allocation process because proportionately all budget units (schools, libraries, and so forth) are treated equally. In fact, formula budgeting is a common way to disburse federal funds from the state to local school districts.

However, there are some serious deficiencies with formula budgets of which one should be cognizant. If a complex budget formula is being used, it may have been created with little or no regard for real world needs in any given school or library, and the very premise or rationalization behind the formula may be faulty. Also, in general, formula budgeting does not take into account unusual or unique circumstances such as age of a school library media center or its collection, a change in curriculum necessitating the development of whole new collection areas, nor even such major changes as a new teaching philosophy within a school, as, for example the use of whole language methods for reading. Formula budgeting may or may not take into account such factors as new electronic databases that may be available online, inflation, or even recessions in the economy— national, state, or local.

One school library authority feels that there is a distinct trend toward lump-sum budgeting and away from formula budgeting (at least at the local level) (Woolls, 1994), and this view is shared by others in the field. Given the widespread use of site-based management in many states and school improvement teams (often with budgetary decision making authority) it is not surprising if lump-sum budgeting is indeed becoming a national trend.

Zero-based Budgeting

Many school library media specialists in the past could count on at least a minimal budget allocation to the school library. Today, given some of the budget trends previously discussed and a move toward local, shared decision making at least in some schools, (e.g., North Carolina schools have had a mandate to implement some form of site-based management for some time now) all school library media specialists should at least be aware that a system called zero-based budgeting exists.

Zero-based budgeting requires that all possible programs or services be costed out into what are called decision packages and then ranked according to priorities by the librarian. It would be possible, for example, for a public library children's services department to determine costs for the following decision package programs: children's materials circulation, lapsit (parent/child) preschool program, nursery school or daycare outreach, children's video program series, and summer reading program. Each of these separate programs would be priced out into a decision unit (labor, materials, and so forth) and then ranked from most to least important by the staff. The children's services director or higher administrator could then decide at which point services might be cut (given a lower budget than the year before or even a midyear budget crisis resulting in cutbacks).

The flaw in using this type of budget system in a school library is that typically you have only the one program in place; it simply does not work where you have a one-person staff and a single program. But...the concept of zero-based budgeting, i.e., giving the library zero funding for a particular year, could easily be applied by a school-wide budget committee that places little or no value on the library's program. In fact, many school library media specialists have reported that the concept of zero-based budgeting for library funding has been used in their school.

Performance and PPBS Budget Systems

Performance and PPBS (Planning, Programming, Budgeting System) budgets do not appear to be relevant to, nor used often in, school library media centers today; therefore they will not be discussed here at length. They are not appropriate for many of the same reasons that zero-based budgeting is undesirable in a school library; namely, their complexity does not justify their use in such a small-scale operation as a school library media center. Indeed it is doubtful that many large organizations still use these types of budget systems, which are related.

Performance budgeting groups library activities such as cataloging, preparation of materials, and information services into activities called functions, and then they are further broken down into basic units of work so that a unit cost or work measurement can be applied to the total number of units needed for each activity. Unit costs can then be determined (e.g., the cost of doing original cataloging for one book or answering a single reference question). The overlapping nature of duties in a school media center makes the compilation of unit costs difficult at best. PPBS is a complex and detailed refinement of the performance-budgeting concept but with the emphasis on human change rather than on the materials and costs needed to bring about the change. Anyone wishing to further explore these budget systems is urged to consult earlier editions of this work. Neither system has been widely utilized, if at all, in school library media centers.

Program Budgeting

The major use for a program budget within a school library media center is for grants for which the library might apply. An excellent example of a program budget appears in *Power Up Your Library* (Salmon, et al., 1996, p. 215). It outlines the budget for an After-School Reading Buddies Program funded through a small grant and shows the projected total expenditures of $7,000. It has direct costs such as salaries, including those for volunteers, postage, printing and materials and allocations for indirect costs such as electricity and even equipment wear. Most grant budgets will be as specific as this example, but will be few in number in the school library media center. While most media specialists will not be overly concerned with program budgeting they should at least be familiar with the concepts involved. Also, greater reliance on grants in the future for school media center funding will most certainly increase their significance to media center budgets.

CREATING THE SCHOOL MEDIA CENTER BUDGET

Collecting Background Information

Preliminary to actual budget preparation is the collecting of background information in several important areas: all possible sources of funding, standards in the field—especially state guidelines, an inventory of existing collections, curricula in the school, a thorough examination of existing data or history of the school media center's last three-to-five years' budgets, and the budget system and accounting code in use in a particular district. No school library media specialist should make major expenditure decisions alone without regard to past budget history; however, even with such information available, the school library media specialist may be in for a rude awakening. Library resources may be considered adequate; therefore, budget resources will be diverted to other areas, such as schoolwide technology or major new curriculum changes, where funds are perceived to be in greater need. While some of the topics listed previously are discussed in relation to the media selection process in Chapter 8, in this chapter they are explained specifically as they relate to the budget.

Besides determining all possible sources of funding (a process discussed earlier in this chapter) there are several other steps that need to be taken before the school library media specialist begins to construct a working budget for the current or upcoming year. One step is a complete inventory of all existing materials, equipment and books in the library collection.

Collection Evaluation

One absolutely crucial step is to do a complete collection evaluation combined with vigorous weeding of the book and AV/software collection, and develop a five-year plan to rebuild the collection if this has not been done recently. We say five-year plan because with many collections that have not been weeded recently and have not been maintained by the annual expenditure of generous funds for collection development, one will most likely need far more money expended than can reasonably be expected to come to the library in any one year. The book collection, incidentally, needs to be evaluated by using a process called *curriculum alignment*. An invaluable aid in this process is a book entitled, *Resource Alignment: Providing Curriculum Support in the School Library Media Center* (2001), by Karen Lowe, which thoroughly documents the steps in this process and includes a software program to assist. When a curriculum alignment and evaluation of the collection is performed, and a number of large Dewey classification areas are found in need of updating (such as perhaps the social sciences [300s], the pure and applied sciences [the 500s and the 600s] and perhaps the history section [900s]); this process may span a three-to-five year time frame. No matter where the needs lie, it will be obvious upon completion of this process where, in the various parts of the book collection, the attention must be focused.

Technology Considerations

One consideration that is crucial to the budgeting process is technology needs, such as computer software, printing supplies, repairs to the equipment, security issues and upgrades. Schools vary in how technology is purchased and maintained. Some school districts require the technology budget to be separate from the media center budget, whereas other school districts require it to be an integral part of the center's budget. The media specialist needs to become familiar with the requirements in the school district and that knowledge will help one decide what needs to be included in the library media center budget.

Should the district require that technology items for the media center be included as a part of the media center budget, one would want to look at computer software that is needed to connect the media center to classrooms as well as online subscriptions. Peripherals, such as digital cameras and scanners, would need to be considered as part of the media center budget. Another consideration would be an amount for computer hardware repairs if that service is not provided by the district service center. If computers and printers are handled through the media center budget, then a technology plan needs to be in place which outlines how upgrades to computer hardware and software is to be handled. The media center budget will reflect the plan for upgrades each year. Supplies for technology, such as paper and ink cartridges, disks, and so forth, need to be reflected in the overall supplies needed for the center. If the media center is required to purchase security devices for hardware, the budget should reflect an amount for security devices. Keep in mind that budget increases dramatically occur when technology is a major component of the media center.

If a school-wide budget is used to purchase technology for the school, the media center will have more money to spend on media center needs, such as the collection and other essential items. Sometimes, media center technology suffers when a school-wide technology budget is used. The media specialist must be a leader in the school to assure that the budget is adequate to run a dynamic media program.

Media specialists are frequently torn between spending money for print collections versus technology. It's crucial that the media center have a budget that includes both. It always depends on the priorities set for the media center by the media specialist and the media advisory committee. Good communication with the principal and the media advisory committee normally makes a difference in budgetary amounts that can be requested. Always justify every item on the budget as a need for the instructional program (see "Justification of the Budget" later in the chapter). Principals are open to supporting the instructional program and this approach can yield more money for the media center budget. Remember the budget affects the whole school program and that's a pretty strong argument for getting the funding needed. The best rule of thumb is to keep informed and make the system in place work to the center's advantage.

Standards in the Field

After all possible sources of extra revenue have been explored, goals for the school library media center should be established. It is important to realize that national standards are ultimate goals for the majority of schools in the nation—the pinnacle toward which schools should strive. There is an increasing tendency to stress the service goals of the school library media center over any sort of quantitative goals (such as size of the book collection, number of VCRs, or even the number of computers housed in the library) and this tendency is especially evident in the most recent second edition of *Information Power* (AASL & AECT, 1998), the national school library standards published by the American Association of School Librarians, which focuses on student information literacy.

Many states have also issued suggested standards or guidelines. Usually these standards are less ambitious than the national ones because the state hopes the schools will achieve them sooner. A state's suggested standards should always be considered along with those of the national professional organizations. It should be noted that many states now have their standards posted on the Internet. For example, *Impact: Guidelines for Media and Technology Programs* (North Carolina Department of Public Instruction, 2002). North Carolina's state guidelines may be found at: http://www.ncwiseowl.org/impact.htm. While the guidelines do not have specific suggested dollar figures for budgets, it does have a great deal of practical advice for creating them, including: tips for developing an effective school library media budget, basic components of a budget proposal and what the budget should reflect, and a list of sources of funding—both primary and secondary. They also stress that the budget cycle never stops and suggest the following steps in the process:

1. Establish the plan, expressed as goals and objectives.
2. Determine specifics of how much money is needed and how it will be spent.

3. Identify sources of revenue.
4. Assess if allocated funds meet goals and objectives.
5. Revise plans or develop a new plan on assessment.

Many school officials are likely to be influenced in their decisions about media programs and funding by local standards, that is, how the schools in the local area compare. Therefore, a survey of a few neighboring school districts (or even simply nearby school surveys taken by the media specialist) or a recent survey issued to members by a regional professional library association may become a basic consideration in budgeting. A national survey of school library media expenditures is conducted by Marilyn Miller and Marilyn Shontz (2003) on a biennial basis and appears in *School Library Journal* on a regular basis. The most current report of these surveys appeared in *SLJ's* October 2003 issue.

It is helpful in creating a media center budget to study a list of possible items that might be found in one. Some of these items are listed here:

books—hardcover
paperbacks
maps and globes
newspapers
recordings—cassettes, CD audio
magazines
library supplies
equipment
furniture
professional dues
travel
substitute pay
wiring/networking costs*
computers*
software leases or purchases (including videos)*
library management system annual support
online subscriptions
photocopying*
printer supplies
equipment repairs and servicing*

cataloging services and/or supplies

*Will probably be part of an all school technology plan and/or budget.

Currently practicing librarians may, of course, have their own list of items to be included in the proposed budget.

Justification of the Budget

It is crucial that the budget is justified for all items included. As stated earlier in the chapter, principals are much more open to supporting the instructional program, and when the media center budget shows that kind of approach when writing justifications it is more likely to be better funded. Keep the principal informed of rising costs and other needs of the media center that need to be included in the budget. Some examples are provided in Exhibits 5.5–5.11.

Principals really appreciate justified budgets and will often fund everything requested because they want to be accountable for the budget, too. There are instances where a media specialist receives a small media center budget for years, but when the principal is given a justified budget all requests are honored. This approach really works well for getting better funding for the media center.

Exhibit 5.5.
School District Budget Requisition Code 5200 (Computer Hardware).

Code	Quantity	Description	Current Inventory	Budgeted Last Year	Proposed Budget	Total
061-542	2	Pentium IV WIN XP Computer	22	$1,200	$2,400	**$2,400**

Justification:

Our goal is to replace computers on a five-year schedule as they become less reliable and unable to run the latest software and Internet products. Next year, we will need to replace two aging library computers.

Printed with permission. Created by Nancy White (2004), Academy School District Twenty, Colorado Springs, CO.

Exhibit 5.6.
School District Budget Requisition Code 5200 (Equipment).

Code	Quantity	Description	Current Inventory	Budgeted Last Year	Proposed Budget	Total
061-541	1	Multimedia Cart	1	$ 250	$ 250	
061-541	1	Software Display Shelving	0		$ 400	
061-541	1	DVD Player	2	$ 500	$1,000	
061-541	1	Multimedia Projector	1		$2,500	
061-541	2	Screens 70 x 70	6		$ 300	
061-541		Audiovisual Equipment		$2,500	$8,000	$13,560

Justification:

Multimedia Cart: This is to hold the new multimedia projector purchased this year for use in classrooms in addition to the library.

Software Display Shelving: We will change our library policy next year to allow students to check out software. We need a display unit that can be located near the circulation desk for security, but one that will allow student browsing.

DVD Player: We purchased one player last year to test the usefulness of this media in classroom teaching, and we purchased several digital video disks to complement the curriculum. The popularity of this flexible teaching tool has been overwhelming. We would like to expand this offering by adding two more DVD players to the inventory.

Multimedia Projector: The one multimedia projector at our school has been in use every day of the school year. It is used in teaching students how to use library research projects such as our online databases, for projecting web activities such as WebQuests, and for student project presentations using PowerPoint. Another projector would double the availability of this teaching and presentation tool.

Screens: The section of the library used for classroom instruction would benefit from a permanent screen mounted for the increased teaching of information literacy skills in which the multimedia projector is employed to demonstrate online searching using the Internet and online databases. An additional screen is needed to replace one that was broken during the last school year.

AV Equipment: This is a huge area of concern. As our equipment is aging, we need to implement a plan to replace items such as camcorders, overhead projectors, VCRs, and TVs before we have a reduced inventory due to irreparable items. We are requesting funding for ten new TV/VCRs and carts for permanent placement in classrooms.

Printed with permission. Created by Nancy White (2004), Academy School District Twenty, Colorado Springs, CO.

Exhibit 5.7.
School District Budget Requisition Code 6620-061-412 (Supplies).

Code	Quantity	Description	Current Inventory	Budgeted Last Year	Proposed Budget	Total
061-412		Library Supplies		$ 800	$ 900	
061-412		Library Books		$11,000	$13,000	
061-412		Magazine Subscriptions		$ 1,000	$ 500	
061-412		Audiovisual Supplies		$ 850	$ 1,110	$15,510

Justification:

Supplies: An extra ten percent is requested to cover the increased cost of purchasing library supplies such as book jacket covers, spine labels, book mending materials, print cartridges, barcodes, and computer supplies.

Library Books: We will be weeding out dated and damaged library books in preparation for migrating to a new library automation system being purchased by the school district. Once that system is in place, we will need to purchase updated country, general science, and technology books. Additionally, in keeping with our school goal to promote reading, we will increase the fiction collection by 200 books to add more titles to the Accelerated Reader program. Funding is requested for a total of 1,000 new books. After weeding, this will maintain our collection size of approximately 12,000 books.

Magazine Subscriptions: We are decreasing the number of magazine subscriptions due to lack of use. Students prefer to use the online databases to research, therefore, we will only require funding for those magazines we will keep for recreational reading.

AV supply items: These include overhead projector bulbs, blank videocassette tapes for dubbing educational programs, labels, cables, and replacement bulbs for the multimedia projector.

Printed with permission. Created by Nancy White (2004), Academy School District Twenty, Colorado Springs, CO.

Exhibit 5.8.
School District Budget Requisition Code 5200 (Online Materials/Subscriptions).

Code	Quantity	Description	Current Inventory	Budgeted Last Year	Proposed Budget	Total
061-435	1	SIRS Researcher	1	$1,800	$2,100	
061-435	1	World Book Online	1	$ 550	$ 650	**$2,750**

Justification:

Electronic Media and Online Subscriptions: The cost of our online encyclopedia *(World Book Online)* and magazine/newspaper database (SIRS Researcher) is expected to increase due to our projected school enrollment and annual increases from the online providers.

Exhibit 5.9.
School District Budget Requisition Code 6620 (Salary—Other Assignments).

Code	Quantity	Description	Current Inventory	Budgeted Last Year	Proposed Budget	Total
061-199		Librarian – extended after school hours 4 hours x 40 weeks x $35		$5,600	$5,600	**$5,600**

Justification:

A librarian is needed to provide research and computer assistance to students after school closes two days a week during After School Student Help sessions. This has been a successful program in the school for the past five years.

Exhibit 5.10.
School District Budget Requisition Code 5200/6620
(Lease/Purchase and Purchased Services).

Code	Quantity	Description	Current Inventory	Budgeted Last Year	Proposed Budget	Total
5200-061-199		Conference & Travel		$ 400	$ 600	
6620-061-461		Copy Machine		$1,100	$1,100	$1,700

Justification:

Conference & Travel: The Library Media Specialist will attend the state Educational Media Association Conference. This year, one staff member will also be invited to attend the workshops set up at the conference for library paraprofessionals. The Library Media Specialist and the library staff will attend the Technology in Education Conference.

Copy Machine: This is year five of a seven-year rental contract for the copy machine. We pay $77 per month for twelve months, and $.08 per copy. Maintenance and toner are included in the price of the rental.

Exhibit 5.11. School District Budget Requisition Code 6620 (Contracted Repairs).

Code	Quantity	Description	Current Inventory	Budgeted Last Year	Proposed Budget	Total
061-326		Repairs		$ 500	$ 600	
061-326		Cleaning/Maintenance VCRs and OHPs		0	$ 500	$1,100

Justification:

More equipment needed repair last year than the budgeted amount. Although we are requesting some replacement equipment this year, we have a backlog of items that are in need of repair.

Regular cleaning and maintenance of the overhead projectors and VCRs will help prolong their life. We would like to start a regular cycle of sending these items out for cleaning during the summer to help cut back on replacement costs in future years.

Always Keep a Consideration File!

An important caveat at this point is: Never be caught without a consideration file! Always, always maintain a wish list or consideration file of items the school library media center needs. At a minimum there should be separate files for books or print items for purchase, computer software (today often these are purchased in the form of licenses for use over a network), and library equipment and furnishings needed. No school library media specialist should ever be caught without a book consideration file of titles that could be turned into an order file for up to several thousand dollars of new books within an hour or so. This consideration file is important because lump sums often come from unexpected sources without any warning and frequently must be spent quickly. It is suggested that orders be typed up ready to go to certain vendors just for this kind of windfall, or orders created and on standby via CD-ROM or online vendor ordering systems such as Follett's *Titlewave* or Baker and Taylor's *School Select*. Gifts from benefactors, the PTA/PTO organization or unexpended district funds at the end of the year, are all examples of such lump sums, which may come unexpectedly to the school library media center on very short notice. To be unprepared to spend these windfall funds is to virtually admit that you really didn't need this money after all—a dangerous position budget-wise. The other major problem with being unprepared to spend money judiciously and wisely in advance is that in order to spend money quickly there is always the temptation to purchase series of mediocre or poor quality books simply because they entice one to spend large sums of money easily with little or no regard to collection weaknesses and curriculum needs.

Performing the thorough collection evaluation and curriculum alignment discussed earlier and then developing the consideration file of titles aligned to this curriculum, which is ready and waiting for purchase, alleviates this type of impulse purchasing. So, a word to the wise—always have several consideration files on your computer ready to be downloaded when the need arises. Most book vendors or jobbers today have CD-ROMs or online databases available to help create these order files. Follett's Titlewave, for example, may be viewed online at: http://www.flr.follett.com.

Budget Calendar

A common pattern for budget development is that principals turn in budget requests for the following year late during the spring school term or semester or even in early summer for the following academic year. This process for budget development takes place even as the current school budget is being expended and accounted for, and usually starts no later than January for the following school year. All school library media specialists should obtain the school budget calendar from their principal or district business manager to be sure that they are prepared to participate in this crucial process. Media specialists also need to be aware of the fiscal year used. While public school fiscal years vary according to state law, most run from July 1 to June 30 of the following year.

It is also a common practice, where a district media coordinator is employed throughout the entire calendar year, for this person to request that all school library media specialists in the district turn in book orders, for up to half or more of the anticipated or estimated book budget for the following school year, at the end of the previous spring term *before* librarians leave for the summer vacation break. Then, if it looks likely that these budget amounts will be approved, or indeed if they are approved during the summer by the local school board or other fiscal agency, the district coordinator will go ahead and place the book orders. This process frequently results in school library media specialists having large book orders waiting for them upon their return to school in the fall or shortly thereafter.

Role of the Media Advisory Committee

Every school library media center should have a media advisory committee. Additionally, many schools today have a site-based management (SBM) or school improvement team (SIT). The media advisory committee, on which the media specialist will sit, might also include: the school principal, the instructional technology facilitator, representatives from each grade level or subject area, a representative from special areas (e.g., ESL, special education), a parent, and a student representative at the middle school and high school levels. A major responsibility of this committee is to identify and recommend resources, hardware, and the infrastructure for the school's technology plan to be implemented. Because of these responsibilities, the committee will necessarily be involved with budget recommendations. In some cases, this committee will work with the SBM or SIT committee of the school. In other cases, one of these committees may take the place of the media advisory committee; therefore, it is critical that the school library media specialist have input into these other committees.

Useful Budget Data

The studies about budgets by Miller and Shontz (2001) provide national comparative data to use when preparing your own library budget. Some information from this most recent 2003 survey follows. Keep in mind that the data was gathered in the year 2001–2002. Exhibit 5.12 provides a summary chart of the mean and median expenditures for library media centers resources from all funding sources for 2001–2002.

Book expenditures in the 1999–2000 study ranged from a low of $100 for one school to a high of $98,500 for another. The authors found that median spending for all library resources per school was $13,341 in 2001–2002. This amount was down from $14,047 two years before; however, median book spending was only up slightly at $7,100 from the previous figure of $7,000. A more revealing survey finding is that median per-pupil spending on books from *local sources* was only $8.89, not enough money to purchase one new hardcover book per student (see average book prices in Exhibit 5.13), even though "book expenditures per pupil have doubled in the last 12 years" (2003, p. 1). Miller and Shontz (2001) reported in the "1999–2000 school year, media specialists spent nearly half the amount of money on CD-ROMs, software and web resources as they did on books" (p. 2). The 2003 survey shows that books comprised fifty-three percent of total media expenditures In fact, they reported that in the "1999–2000 school year, media specialists spent nearly half as much money on CD-ROMs, software, and web resources as they did on books" (p. 2). Their report brings up an important issue that all school library media specialists will be forced to consider at budget time, (i.e., how to divide their budgets between print and nonprint resources). Unfortunately there are no hard and fast rules for this division because it will depend on many factors: the total library budget, the condition of the book collection, the availability of online databases through the Internet or state or regional networks, the school level and the teaching methods being used in the school, to name a few. The only guidance that can be garnered from Miller and Shontz is that in their 2001 study few librarians were purchasing DVDs and media specialists at all grade levels found microforms useful. They found that in the 2001 survey, $2.46 per pupil was spent on online products and other web-based resources; this was down to $2.17 in 2003. AV expenditures for 2003 were $1.25 per pupil, down from $1.44 in 2001. Periodicals decreased by one penny per pupil, which in real dollars represents a small decrease. It might also reflect the fact that many periodicals are now available in full-text through state and local online databases. Bot-

Exhibit 5.12.
Mean and Median Expenditures for LMC Resources, 2001–2002.

	Number Responding	Mean	Median
Funding Total all local funds	583	$15,707	$11,236
Total all federal funds	155	$5,318	$3,000
Total all gift/fund-raising	334	$2,492	$1,161
Expenditures (all funds)			
Books	577	$9,565	$7,100
Periodicals	574	$1,423	$1,000
AV resources/ Equipment	484	$2,647	$1,531
Computer resources/ Equipment	454	$6,426	$2,800
Total Expenditures	588	$18,385	$13,341

Printed with Permission. Source: Miller, Marilyn L. & Shontz, Marilyn L. (2003, October 1). The *SLJ* spending survey. [Electronic version]. *School Library Journal, 49*(10), 52–59. Retrieved April 5, 2004 from: http://slj.reviewsnews.com/index.asp?layout=article&articleid=CA327212#table1

tom line in 2001 was that technology expenditures were up and rising all the time; however, this trend has slacked off in the past two years.

Another useful set of data, a chart of average book prices, is published in *School Library Journal* each year, and is shown in Exhibit 5.13, *School Library Journal's* Average Book Prices 2000–2002. From this exhibit, it is clear that the $8.09 per pupil expenditure is not even purchasing *one* average priced title per year per student! (St. Lifer, 2002).

And finally, it should be helpful to revisit Doug Johnson's formula (1997) discussed earlier to come up with some justifiable budget request figures. In fact, one of Johnson's specific examples deals with book vol-

Exhibit 5.13.
School Library Journal's Average Book Prices
2000-2002.

	2000	2001	2002
Hardcover (children's and YA titles)			
Average price (all titles)	$17.57	$18.58	$18.78
Preschool to grade 4	$15.55	$16.01	$16.04
Grade 5 and up (fiction)	$15.91	$16.10	$16.83
Grade 5 and up (nonfiction)	$21.26	$21.49	$21.46
PAPERBACK (children's and YA titles)			
Trade paperbacks	$8.41	$6.63*	—
HARDCOVER (adult titles)			
Fiction	$24.96	$24.85*	—
**Nonfiction	$68.57	$76.87*	—
PAPERBACK (adult titles)			
Fiction	$15.90	$16.77*	—
***Nonfiction	$33.11	$39.34*	—

*The 2001 figures are based on 2000 data, the latest available, published in the Bowker Annual 2002.
**Prices include single-volume reference titles.
***Prices include reference and related resources.

*The 2001 figures are based on 2000 data, the latest available, published in the Bowker Annual 2002.

**Prices include single-volume reference titles.

***Prices include reference and related resources.

Printed with permission. Source: St. Lifer, Evan. (2002, April). *SLJ's* average book prices: Enhancing your buying power. *School Library Journal, 48*(4), 1-3. Retrieved April 5, 2004 from: http://slj.reviewsnews.com/index.asp?layout=articleArchive&articleid=CA202828

umes, and we'll illustrate one scenario here. If you have 10,000 volumes and you figure an average cost of $18 (as per the *SLJ* figures) and a life span of 20 years per book, then the formula to simply maintain this collection—with no allowance for growth—would be:

$$5\% \times 10,000 \times \$18 = \$9,000 \text{ per year}$$

Keep in mind that the replacement rate as defined by Johnson is 100 percent divided by the life span, or in the previous case, 1.00/20 or 5 percent. This life span will vary for each format that you are replacing. For example, computers have a life span no longer than five years, and this is probably stretching it given today's rapidly changing technology. Johnson's formulas for growth are even easier to follow and may be found in his book. Here is another example using computers. If the library has twenty computers for research use and you wish to replace them during a five-year period, here is your formula: $20\% \times 20 \times \$1,000 = \$4,000$. To state this in plain English, you must replace four computers each year at an average cost of $1,000 each using Johnson's formula.

ACCOUNTING FOR THE MEDIA CENTER'S MONEY

Finally, this chapter will end by looking at how to account for the funds received in the media center. Every school has someone assigned to keep the school's financial records, commonly called the finance officer. Despite this fact though, media specialists need to always keep their own records of their media center funds, their encumbrances (i.e., money obligated to be paid for orders sent but not yet received and paid for), and their available balances. Exhibits 5.14 and 5.15 show the state funds and the instructional media supplies budgets for schools in North Carolina and Colorado, respectively, and Exhibit 5.16 shows a book budget for a middle school media center in Colorado. The media specialist compiled these budgets on spreadsheets. Notice that encumbered funds are deducted from the budget balance although they are not actually paid until orders are received and all items are accounted for.

A spreadsheet should be used for each separate account (e.g., books, supplies, equipment, and so forth). Using a spreadsheet for these types of accounts is extremely useful; spreadsheets can be quickly reproduced if discrepancies occur and one needs to compare media specialist figures with those of the school financial officer. Mistakes do occur, and sometimes

Exhibit 5.14.
State Funds Budget for WHS Media Center 2001-2002.

P. O. #	Date	Vendor	Amount	Invoiced	TOTAL
	11/1/2001		34000.00		34000.00
108601	Aug 6 01	Winston-Salem JI	-140.00	-141.60	33858.40
108602	Aug 6 01	Charlotte Observer	-176.80	-208.00	33650.40
108603	Aug 6 01	Watauga Democrat	-92.00	-92.00	33558.40
108604	Aug 6 01	SIRS	-1080.00	-1144.80	32478.40
108605	Aug 6 01	EBSCO	-1989.06	-1989.06	30489.34
108608	Aug 8 01	Gale Group	-1272.00	-1272.00	29217.34
108610	Aug 13 01	National Geographic	-29.15	-27.95	29189.39
108611	Aug 13 01	Wall Street Journal	-185.50	-175.00	29003.89
108612	Aug 15 01	WGBH	-25.10	-23.90	28979.99
108615	Aug 16 01	Gaylord	-400.89	-425.20	28554.79
108618	Aug 22 01	Schlessinger Media	-47.85	-45.45	28509.34
108619	Aug 23 01	Social Studies Service	-517.49	-485.99	28023.35
108623	Aug 28 01	Best Books Company	-1565.63	-1356.61	26666.74
108624	Aug 31 01	Rapesafe	-37.65	-35.85	26630.89
108625	Aug 31 01	Cambridge Educational	-23.14	-24.90	26605.99
108626	9/4/2001	Corwin Press	-98.62	-93.35	26512.64
108627	9/7/2001	West Circle Books	-1257.43	-1102.30	25410.34
108628	9/7/2001	Young Adult Resources	-961.04		24449.30
108629	9/10/2001	ASDD	-59.94	-56.95	24392.35
108630	9/12/2001	Garrett Educ. Corp.	-3057.48	-2465.13	21334.87
108631	9/12/2001	Gale Group	-286.73	-413.77	20921.10
108621	Aug 28 01	Young Adult Resources	-1232.85	-1232.85	19688.25
108633	Sept 18 01	Grolier Educational	-1837.40	-1759.14	17929.11
108634	Sept 19 01	Teachers Discovery	-33.60	-31.70	17897.41
108635	Sept 19 01	Teachers Video	-277.94	-275.50	17621.91
108636	Sept 24 01	Films for Humanities	-172.84	-157.94	17449.07
108638	Sept 25 01	Discovery Channel	-48.85	-46.45	17402.62
108639	Sept 26 01	Linworth Publishing	-105.25	-100.63	17301.99
108640	Sept 26 01	Linworth Publishing	-49.00	-49.00	17252.99
108643	Oct 12 01	Library Video Company	-21.34	-20.45	17232.54
108650	Oct 22 01	EBSCO	-169.50	-147.20	17085.34
108652	void	Troxell	Void	void	17085.34
108653	Nov 5 01	CNAM	-174.90	-165.00	16920.34
108654	Nov 5 01	Queen City TV	-288.32	-289.68	16630.66
108655	Nov 5 01	Queen City	-46.64	-46.86	16583.80
108656	Nov 5 01	Microwarehouse	-2444.84	-2278.53	14305.27
108657	Nov 5 01	Camera corner	-1165.52	-1161.39	13143.88
108659	Nov 7 01	SF Travel Publications	-148.00	-138.90	13004.98
108660	Nov 14 01	National Audio Visual	-276.09	-263.15	12741.83
108662	Nov 15 01	WJ Office Supply	-20.83	-20.83	12721.00
108663	Nov 15 01	Ikon Office	-213.92	-213.92	12507.08

Printed with permission. Source: Hartley, Audrey, Media
Coordinator. Watauga High School. Watauga County Schools.
(2002, February). *State funds budget for WHS: WHS media center state budget 2001-2002*. Boone, NC: Watauga County Board
of Education.

Exhibit 5.15.
Instructional Media Supplies Budget.

AV or LMC	Req. #	P. O. #	Vendor	Order Date	Received	Paid	Encumbered	Total P & E	Balance
									12,906.00
AV	19,389.00		Warehouse	26-Jun-01	18-Aug-01		307.72	307.72	12,598.28
LMC	19,375.00	20,632.00	Follett	26-Jun-01	18-Sep-01		1,324.01	1,324.01	11,274.27
LMC	19,374.00	20,630.00	Follett	26-Jun-01	12-Sep-01	321.22		321.22	10,953.05
LMC	19,373.00	20,596.00	Library Video Co.	26-Jun-01	23-Aug-01	379.27		379.27	10,573.78
LMC	19,372.00	20,624.00	Junior Library Guild	26-Jun-01	14-Aug-01	59.50		59.50	10,514.28
LMC	19,371.00	20,623.00	BCR (SIRS)	26-Jun-01	working 8/8/01	1,500.00		1,500.00	9,014.28
LMC	19,370.00	20,595.00	Zenger Media	26-Jun-01	6-Sep-01	32.96		32.96	8,981.32
LMC	19,369.00	20,594.00	Classroom Connect	26-Jun-01	23-Aug-01	173.26		173.26	8,808.06
LMC	19,368.00	20,593.00	World Almanac	26-Jun-01	30-Aug-01	288.75		288.75	8,519.31
LMC	19,367.00	20,592.00	Farrar Straus Giroux	26-Jun-01	9-Oct-01	34.60	23.00	57.60	8,461.71
LMC	19,366.00	20,589.00	Glencoe/McGraw Hill	26-Jun-01	7-Sep-01	35.16		35.16	8,426.55
LMC	19,401.00	20,633.00	BCR (EBSCO)	29-Jun-01	1-Sep-01	417.00		417.00	8,009.55
AV	200,644.00	12,585.00	Warehouse	28-Aug-01	12-Sep-01		205.57	205.57	7,803.98
AV	JE	JE	Laminating Charges	28-Aug-01	N/A	(233.35)		(233.35)	8,037.33
AV	201,010.00	21,207.00	Troxell	7-Sep-01	9-Oct-01		91.50	91.50	7,945.83
AV	201,078.00	21,457.00	Troxell	12-Sep-01	10-Oct-01		57.00	57.00	7,888.83
LMC	201,079.00	21,458.00	Follett	12-Sep-01			981.02	981.02	6,907.81
LMC	201,346.00	13,169.00	Warehouse	19-Sep-01	part 24 Sep 01		23.57	23.57	6,884.24
LMC	LOCAL	LOCAL	Gazette	15-Sep-01	N/A	49.30		49.30	6,834.94
LMC	201,502.00	21,711.00	Capstone	26-Sep-01	20-Oct-01		157.90	157.90	6,677.04
LMC	201,503.00	21,712.00	Raintree Steck-Vaughn	26-Sep-01	31-Oct-01		99.53	99.53	6,577.51
LMC	201,533.00	21,616.00	Demco	26-Sep-01	11-Oct-01		64.98	64.98	6,512.53
LMC	JE	JE	Social Studies Dept.	27-Sep-01	N/A		(39.00)	(39.00)	6,551.53
LMC	201,621.00	21,674.00	Junior Library Guild	27-Sep-01	N/A	280.80		280.80	6,270.73
LMC	JE	JE	Stapler fund for copier	2-Oct-01	N/A	100.00		100.00	6,170.73
LMC	201,743.00	21,846.00	Culturgrams	3-Oct-01	31-Oct-01		99.39	99.39	6,071.34
LMC	201,750.00	21,849.00	Delaney Educational	3-Oct-01	4-Dec-01		273.33	273.33	5,798.01
LMC	201,807.00	13,652.00	Warehouse	5-Oct-01	11-Oct-01		31.34	31.34	5,766.67
LMC	201,914.00	21,959.00	Follett	10-Oct-01	29-Nov-01		1,032.53	1,032.53	4,734.14
LMC	201,943.00	21,968.00	Marshall Cavendish	10-Oct-00	6-Nov-01		164.67	164.67	4,569.47
LMC	201,937.00	21,965.00	Gale Group	10-Oct-01	31-Oct-01		165.00	165.00	4,404.47
LMC	202,023.00	22,035.00	Children's Press	12-Oct-01	6-Nov-01		145.20	145.20	4,259.27

Exhibit 5.15. (continued)

LMC	202,024.00	22,036.00	A & E Home Video	15-Oct-01	15-Nov-01		24.90	24.90	4,234.37
LMC	202,026.00	13,965.00	Warehouse	15-Oct-01	26-Oct-01		44.64	44.64	4,189.73
LMC			JE-Lost Book (TAG)	18-Oct-01			(20.00)	(20.00)	4,209.73
AV	202,167.00		Provantage Corp.	23-Oct-01	(part) 16 Nov 01		225.13	225.13	3,984.60
LMC	202,441.00		Warehouse	5-Nov-01			24.99	24.99	3,959.61
LMC	202,520.00	22,385.00	Follett	8-Nov-01			1,390.04	1,390.04	2,569.57
LMC	202,546.00	22,422.00	Gaylord	8-Nov-01	4-Dec-01		94.02	94.02	2,475.55
LMC	JE	JE	JE - AR Tests	14-Nov-01			(200.00)	(200.00)	2,675.55
LMC	202,683.00		PBS Video	15-Nov-01			109.98	109.98	2,565.57
LMC	LOCAL	LOCAL	Denver Post	27-Nov-01		149.00		149.00	2,416.57
LMC	JE	JE	JE-Lost Book (Soc. Studies)	27-Nov-01			(8.00)	(8.00)	2,424.57
LMC	LOCAL	LOCAL	Bookstore	27-Nov-01		43.70		43.70	2,380.87
LMC	202,809.00		Library Video Co.	27-Nov-01			13.95	13.95	2,366.92
			TOTAL			3,631.17	6,907.91	10,539.08	**2,366.92**

Printed with permission. Created by Nancy White (2003), Academy School District Twenty, Colorado Springs, CO.

Exhibit 5.16.
Book Budget.

CODE	Req. #	P.O. #	VENDOR	Req. #	ORDER DATE	PAID	ENCUMBERED	TOTAL P & E	BALANCE
			BUDGETED 2000-01						$11,148.00
640			Newspaper		1-Jul-00	$70.93		$70.93	$11,077.07
640	1486,7,8,9		Follett		1-Jul-01	$1,794.55		$1,794.55	$9,282.52
640		1770	Lucent		1-Jul-00	$114.23		$114.23	$9,168.29
640		2058	Rosen		1-Jul-00	$54.85		$54.85	$9,113.44
640		1413	Gale		1-Jul-00	$71.54		$71.54	$9,041.90
640	Local		Bookstore		24-Aug-00	$4.80		$4.80	$9,037.10
640	2210		Children's Press		5-Sep-00		$177.60	$177.60	$8,859.50
640	2212		Marshall Cavendish		5-Sep-00	$285.62		$285.62	$8,573.88
640	2220	2529	Follett		7-Sep-00	$661.83		$661.83	$7,912.05
640	2493	2659	Gale		15-Sep-00	$279.93		$279.93	$7,632.12
640	2658	2492	Follett	2492	15-Sep-00	$191.85		$191.85	$7,440.27
640	2499	2662	Rosen	2499	15-Sep-00	$119.70		$119.70	$7,320.57
640	2660	2496	Developmental Studies Ctr.	2496	15-Sep-00	$19.45		$19.45	$7,301.12
640	2489	2657	Linworth	2489	15-Sep-00	$48.10		$48.10	$7,253.02
640			JE - Lost Book Found		19-Sep-00	$13.00		$13.00	$7,240.02
640	2929	2956	Territory Titles	2929	29-Sep-00	$432.00		$432.00	$6,808.02
640	3223		Culturgrams		24-Oct-00	$104.79		$104.79	$6,703.23
640			JE - Lost Book		17-Oct-00	-$11.00		-$11.00	$6,714.23
640	4060	3622	Follett	4060	10-Nov-00	$1,021.18		$1,021.18	$5,693.05
640	4505	3896	Junior Library Guild	4505	10-Nov-00	$274.80		$274.80	$5,418.25
640	4056	3621	Libraries Unlimited	4056	10-Nov-00	$43.08		$43.08	$5,375.17
640	4055	3620	Grolier Interactive	4055	10-Nov-00	$19.26		$19.26	$5,355.91
640		4504	Enslow	4504	6-Dec-00	$97.90		$97.90	$5,258.01
640	15575		Enslow		5-Feb-01	$57.62		$57.62	$5,200.39
640	16015	1801	Newspaper		28-Sep-00	$119.60		$119.60	$5,080.79
640			PTP Austin		22-Feb-01	$870.50		$870.50	$4,210.29
640	16295		Follett		7-Mar-01	$314.42		$314.42	$3,895.87
640	16428	5185	Facts on File		9-Mar-01	$58.00	$28.67	$86.67	$3,809.20
640	16427		Enslow		9-Mar-01	$60.51		$60.51	$3,748.69
640	16429		Follett	5186	9-Mar-01	$307.35		$307.35	$3,441.34
640	16430	5187	Oxford University Press	5187	12-Mar-01	$152.02		$152.02	$3,289.32
640	16432	5188	Children's Library Resources		12-Mar-01	$560.52		$560.52	$2,728.80

Exhibit 5.16. (continued)

640		N. American Book Dist.	23-Mar-01	$103.00		$103.00	$2,625.80
640		Apple Books	16-Apr-01	$191.40		$191.40	$2,434.40
640		Gale	16-Apr-01		$48.40	$48.40	$2,386.00
640		Follett	17-Apr-01		$1,140.93	$1,140.93	$1,245.07
640		National Geographic	20-Apr-01		$26.95	$26.95	$1,218.12
640		NMSA	20-Apr-01		$27.40	$27.40	$1,190.72
640		Facts on File	20-Apr-01		$178.15	$178.15	$1,012.57
640		C-Span Archives		$25.45		$25.45	$987.12
640		W.W. Norton	7-May-01		$27.50	$27.50	$959.62
		TO BALANCE		$7.68	-$17.29	-$9.61	$969.23
		TOTAL		$8,540.46	$1,638.31	$10,178.77	$969.23

Printed with permission. Created by Nancy White (2003), Academy School District Twenty, Colorado Springs, CO.

bills are erroneously charged to the wrong account, so always keep your own records! A media specialist once sent in a book order to expend the balance of her book budget only to have it bounce back from the district accounting office with the comment that no money was left in the account. Imagine her surprise when it was discovered that a desk had been charged to the book budget. When the specialist pointed out the discrepancy, it was immediately removed and the book money was put back into the account. To this day, it is uncertain if this was an "honest" mistake, or if the principal was trying to buy himself or a teacher a new desk. Two other essential tools, which Johnson (1997) claims will increase your professional budget credibility, are a word processor, used to produce a clear and readable narrative for your budget, and a presentation program such as PowerPoint to clearly illustrate the points of your budget to your committee or public. These tools are essentials in helping sell your budget to your constituency.

And, finally, it is important to maintain a file of orders for all accounts for which you are responsible. All order information (or copies) should go into this file, including such items as a catalog page copy of what was ordered, or the list of books ordered. For nonprint, catalog order information is often useful later if cataloging records cannot be purchased or obtained free with the items. Typically order files are maintained by year, subarranged by account, and all purchase orders should be filed in the proper folders as well. It is recommended that records of orders be kept for at least five years back should there be a need to check on items received in previous years for any reason, such as determining a date of when something was purchased or to check on the warranty.

CONCLUSION

Douglas Johnson (1997) has a set of questions, which he feels need to be answered by school budget committees today, and out of all of them, the most important would seem to be:

- "How might a budget decision affect the school's climate?"
- "How many teachers and students will benefit from a particular spending decision?"
- "Ask yourself, what is my budget contributing to this ultimate goal?" (p. 109).

Clearly the budget should impact the greatest number of people possible in the school. The bottom line is student achievement.

REFERENCES

American Association of School Librarians. (1991). Position statement on appropriate staffing for school library media centers. Retrieved April 5, 2004, from ALA web site: http://www.ala.org/Content/NavigationMenu/AASL/Professional_Tools10/Position_Statements/AASL_Position_Statement_on_Appropriate_Staffing_for_School_Library_Media_Centers.htm

American Association of School Librarians & Association for Educational Communication and Technology. (1988). *Information power: Guidelines for school library media programs* (1st ed.). Chicago: AASL/ALA.

American Association of School Librarians & Association for Educational Communication and Technology. (1998). *Information power: Building partnerships for learning* (2nd ed.). Chicago: AASL/ALA.

Bear, Joe & Huffman, Stu. (2001, May 10). *First-time library grants for technology awarded to 13 school corporations.* IDOE News Release, Indiana Department of Education. Retrieved April 5, 2004, from: http://ideanet.doe.state.in.us/reed/newsr/2001/05-May/HighTechLibrary.html

Catalog of Federal Domestic Assistance. (2002). *Catalog of Federal Domestic Assistance Programs—June 2002 Update.* Retrieved April 5, 2004, from: http://aspe.os.dhhs.gov/cfda/index.htm

Catalog of Federal Domestic Assistance. (2003). *Developing and writing grant proposals.* Retrieved April 5, 2004, from: http://www.cfda.gov/public/cat-writing.htm

Councill, Leta, Finance Officer. Watauga County Board of Education Finance Office. (2002, September). *Account codes related to school library media centers in North Carolina.* Boone, NC: Watauga County Board of Education.

EdSource Online. (2002, November). *K-12 education funding comes from several sources.* Retrieved April 5, 2004, from EdSource Online: http://www.edsource.org/sch_fund0203.cfm

EdSource Online. (2003). *School finance overview.* Retrieved April 5, 2004, from EdSource Online: http://www.edsource.org/edu_fin.cfm

Fowler, William J. (1995 reprint). *Financial accounting for local and state school systems, 1990.* United States Department of Education, Office of Educational Research and Improvement. Retrieved April 5, 2004, from: http://nces.ed.gov/pubs97/97096R.pdf

Galles, Gary M. & Sexton, Robert L. (1998, April). A tale of two tax jurisdictions: The surprising effects of California's Proposition 13 and Massachusetts' Proposition 2 1/2 (property tax). [Electronic version]. *The American Journal of Economics and Sociology,* 1–10. Retrieved April 5, 2004, from: http://www.findarticles.com/cf_0/m0254/n2_v57/20824078/p1/article.jhtml?term=A+tale+of+two+tax+jurisdictions%3A++The+surprising+effects+of+California%92s+Proposition+13+and+Massachusetts%92+Proposition+2+1%2F2+%28property+tax%29

Governor's Book Fund. (2003). School library enrichment grant RFP announcement. Retrieved April 16, 2004, from: http://web.archive.org/web/20030618063829/http://www.literacynet.org/govfund/rfp.html

Hall-Ellis, Sylvia D. & Jerabek, A. (2003). Grants for school libraries. Westport, CT: Libraries Unlimited.

Hartley, Audrey, Media Coordinator. Watauga High School. Watauga County Schools. (2002, February). *Sample object of expenditure budget year 2001–2002.* Boone, NC: Watauga County Board of Education.

Hartley, Audrey, Media Coordinator. Watauga High School. Watauga County Schools. (2002, February). *State funds budget for WHS: WHS media center state budget 2001–2002.* Boone, NC: Watauga County Board of Education.

Heiser, Jane C. (2003). Grants to state library agencies. Institute of Museum and Library Services. Retrieved April 5, 2004, from: http://www.imls.gov/grants/library/lib_gsla.asp

Hopkins, Dianne McAfee, et al. (1987). *School library media programs: A resource and planning guide.* Madison: Wisconsin Department of Public Instruction.

Johnson, Doug. (1997). *The indispensable librarian: Surviving (and thriving) in school media centers in the information age.* Worthington, OH: Linworth.

Johnson, Doug. (1999). Budgeting for mean, lean times. Retrieved March 15, 2003, from: http://www.doug-johnson.com

Lance, Keith Curry, et al. (2000). *How school library media specialists help kids achieve standards: The second Colorado study.* Retrieved April 5, 2004, from Colorado Library Research Service web site: http://www.lrs.org/impact.asp

Lowe, Karen R. (2001). *Resource alignment: Providing curriculum support in the school library media center.* Millers Creek, NC: Beacon Consulting.

Miller, Marilyn L. & Shontz, Marilyn L. (2001, October). New money, old books. *School Library Journal, 47*(10), 50–60.

Miller, Marilyn L. & Shontz, Marilyn L. (2003, October 1). The *SLJ* spending survey: While funding takes a hit, libraries expand services. *School Library Journal, 49*(10), 52–59. Retrieved April 5, 2004, from: http://slj.reviewsnews.com/index.asp?layout=article&articleid=CA327212#table1

No child left behind—summary of key provisions. (2002). Retrieved April 17, 2004, from North Carolina Public Schools web site: http://web.archive.org/web/20020222201951/http://www.ncpublicschools.org/esea/summary.html

North Carolina Department of Public Instruction. (2002). *Impact: Guidelines for media and technology programs.* Program administration—budgeting for the program. Retrieved April 5, 2004, from: http://www.ncwiseowl.org/impact/program.htm#BudgetingfortheProgram

North Carolina Public Schools. (2004). ABCs of public education connects with No Child Left Behind. Retrieved April 15, 2004, from the North Carolina Public Schools web site: http://www.ncpublicschools.org/nclb/index.html

North Carolina Public Schools. (2004, April 16). *Uniform chart of accounts: Fiscal year 2003–2004.* Raleigh, NC: Compliance/Audit/Policy Section, Division of

School Business, North Carolina Department of Public Instruction. Retrieved April 15, 2004, from: http://www.ncpublicschools.org/fbs/coa/toc.html

Roberts, Charles T. & Lichtenberger, A. R. (Eds.). (1973). *Financial accounting: Classifications and standard terminology for local and state school systems. Hand-Book II* (Rev. ed.). Washington, DC: U.S. Government Printing Office.

Salmon, Sheila, et al. (1996). *Power up your library: Creating the new elementary school library program.* Englewood, CO: Libraries Unlimited.

St. Lifer, Evan. (2002, April). *SLJ*'s average book prices: Enhancing your buying power. *School Library Journal,* 48(4), 1–3. Retrieved April 5, 2004, from: http://slj.reviewsnews.com/index.asp?layout=articleArchive&articleid=CA20 2828

State Library of North Carolina. (2003, September 30). Library Services and Technology Act. Grant programs available to public school libraries for 2004–2005. Handout provided at the North Carolina School Library Media Association 3rd Annual Conference, October 2, 2003. Winston-Salem, NC.

What is the U.S. Department of Education? (2002). Retrieved April 5, 2004, from: http://www.ed.gov/about/overview/focus/what_pg3.html?exp=5

Whelan, Debra Lau. (2003, June 9). Laura Bush Foundation awards school library grants. *School Library Journal, 48*(11), 21. Woolls, Blanche. (1994). *The school library media manager.* Englewood, CO: Libraries Unlimited.

Ziarnik, Natalie Reif. (2003). *School and public libraries : Developing the natural alliance.* Chicago: American Library Association.

FURTHER READINGS

American Association of School Librarians. *Role of the school library media special-ist in site-based management.* Retrieved April 5, 2004, from: http://www.ala.org/aasl/positions/ps_sitemgmt.html

American Library Association. (2002, May). How to get new school library funds under ESEA (News Fronts Washington). *American Libraries, 13*(5), 18.

Anderson, Cynthia. (2002). *Write grants, get money.* Worthington, OH: Linworth.

Andronik, Catherine M. (Ed.). (2003). *School library management* (5th ed.). Worthington, OH: Linworth.

Baltimore County Public Schools. *Department of Curriculum and Instruction Office of Library and Information Services: K–12 school guide.* Retrieved April 5, 2004, from Baltimore County Public Schools web site: http://www.bcps.org/offices/lis/office/admin/budgetplanguidek12.pdf

Bertot, John Carlo, McClure, Charles R., & Ryan, Joe. (2002, March). Study shows new funding sources crucial to technology services. *American Libraries, 33*(3), 57–59.

Brodie, Carolyn S. (2002, February). Setting goals: The road not yet taken. *School Library Media Activities Monthly, 18* (6), 35.

Brown, Larissa Golden & Brown, John Martin. (2001). *Demystifying grant seeking: What you really need to do to get grants.* San Francisco: Jossey-Bass.

Browning, Beverly A. (2001). *Grant writing for dummies.* Foster City, CA: IDG Books Worldwide.

Bush budget cuts LSTA, eliminates NCLIS. News Fronts Washington. (2001, May). *American Libraries, 32*(5), 22.

California Department of Education. *School libraries.* Retrieved April 5, 2004, from: http://www.cde.ca.gov/library/

Carlson, Mim. (2002). *Winning Grants: Step by step* (2nd ed.). San Francisco: Jossey-Bass.

Cummins, Julie. (2001, March). Dead trees and wooden nickels: *SLJ's* average book prices. *School Library Journal, 47*(3), 11.

Dickinson, Gail. (2003). *Empty pockets, full plates: Effective budget administration for library media specialists.* Worthington, OH: Linworth.

Dickinson, Gail. (2004). Budgeting: As easy as 1-2-3. *Library Media Connection, 22*(6), 18–20.

Education bill includes school library program. (2002, February). *American Libraries, 33*(2), 14.

Everhart, Nancy. (2002, June). Filling the void: Many states are taking steps to remedy the rising shortage of school librarians. *School Library Journal, 48*(6), 44–49.

Hartzell, Gary. (2002, November). Controlling your own destiny: Why vision and mission statements are indispensable (building influence). *School Library Journal, 48*(11), 37.

Hartzell, Gary. (2002, July). The whole truth: Librarians need to emphasize what they have to offer. *School Library Journal, 48*(7), 31.

Johnson, Doug. (2002, June). Challenges: The seven most critical challenges facing our profession. *Teacher Librarian, 29*(5), 21–23.

Jones, Patrick. (2001, Fall). Showing you the money: LSTA funds and fifty-two resources to find funding for youth services in libraries. *Journal of Youth Services in Libraries, 15*(1), 33–38.

Lau, Debra. (2002, May). GA slashes school library funding. *School Library Journal, 48*(5), 16.

Lau, Debra. (2002, April). Libraries feel recession's bite: Few school and public library budgets are immune to proposed cuts. *School Library Journal, 48*(4), 20–21.

Library Services & Technology Act plan for implementation in North Carolina—2003–2007. (2002, August). Raleigh, NC: The State Library of North Carolina.

LSTA: The Library Services and Technology Act. (2003). Retrieved April 5, 2004, from: http://www.ala.org/Content/NavigationMenu/Our_Association/Offices/ALA_Washington/Issues2/Federal_Library_Programs/LSTA/LSTA.htm

Manzo, Kathleen Kennedy. (1999, October 27). Library spending regains some lost ground. *Education Week, 19*(9), 3.

Miller, Marilyn L. & Shontz, Marilyn L. (1997, October). Small change: Expenditures for resources in school library media centers, FY 1995–1996. *School Library Journal, 43*(10), 28–37.

Miller, Marilyn L. & Shontz, Marilyn L. (1998, May). More services, more staff, more money: A portrait of a high-service library media center. *School Library Journal, 44*(5), 28–33.

Miller, Marilyn L. & Shontz, Marilyn L. (1999, October). How do you measure up? Expenditures for resources in school library media centers, 1997–1998. *School Library Journal, 45*(10), 50–59.

Miller, Marilyn L. & Shontz, Marilyn L. (2000, November). Location is everything: School library spending and services FY 1997–1998. *School Library Journal, 46*(11), 50–60.

North Carolina Department of Public Instruction. (2004, March 31). *No child left behind: The North Carolina perspective.* Retrieved April 17, 2004, from: http://www.dpi.state.nc.us/nclb/coalition/perspective.pdf

Oder, Norman. (2002, November). The format dilemma: Budgets and circulation rise, but libraries must stretch to meet diverse demand. (Survey: audio video 2002). *Library Journal, 127*(11), 38.

Pittaway, Kim. (2002, October). Book learnin': Our school libraries are a national disgrace. *Chatelaine, 75*(10), 44.

Reed Business Information. (2002, May). Reed Seeks $100 Million for School Libraries in 2003 (Legislative Update). *School Library Journal, 48*(5), 17.

Rhode Island Educational Media Association. (1999, May 2). *School library and information literacy framework.* Retrieved April 5, 2004 from: http://www.ri.net/RIEMA/infolit.html

Scholarships, Grants & Prizes 2004 (8th ed.). (2003). Lawrenceville, NJ: Peterson's/Thomson Learning.

School District of Philadelphia. (2001, December). *School library budget.* Retrieved April 5, 2004 from: http://www.libraries.phila.k12.pa.us/misc/budget.html

Smith, Jane. E. *LSTA grants for school library media centers.* Retrieved April 5, 2004, from: http://www.uelma.org/conven01/grants.htm

Spira, Kirsten Hicks. (2002, July). Renovating on a shoestring: How a private school revamped its library at one-third the cost. *School Library Journal, 48*(7), 35.

St. Lifer, Evan. (2002, May). The big misperception: Politicians aren't "saving" education by cutting libraries—they're killing it. *School Library Journal, 48*(5), 11.

St. Lifer, Evan. (2002, September). The seven habits....how you can "break through" to your principal. *School Library Journal, 48*(9), 11.

Whelan, Debra Lau. (2002, November). CA slashes school library funding: Library materials budget cut by 80 percent, now only $5.32 per student annually. *School Library Journal, 48*(11), 21.

White House Conference on School Libraries. (2002, October). What's it take? Getting teachers and administrators to recognize the importance of school libraries, librarians, and media centers. *Teacher Librarian, 30*(10), 81.

White House Conference on School Libraries—Transcript. (2002, October). The role of foundations and philanthropy in supporting school libraries. *Teacher Librarian, 30*(10), 93.

Chapter 6

STAFF

The staff is the foundation of a dynamic and effective school library media center and the mainstay of a school library media program. The primary responsibility of the staff is to ensure that the media program is an integral part of the instructional program of the school. The persons who create and develop the activities are directly responsible for the overall success of the program. Each staff member usually functions in a dual capacity: individually as a specialist and collaboratively as a member of the media program team. A school library media center staff should include personnel with a broad range of experience and skills. To promote good personal relationships and ensure a well-functioning program, school administrators should encourage media specialists to participate in the selection of staff.

There are common areas of concern when dealing with human beings, including self-worth, pride, and security. Any constructive criticism and positive motivation should take these fundamental factors into account; for example, the security of having job descriptions and participatory evaluations will aid each staff member and supervisor.

This chapter takes a look at some supervisory practices concerning the school library media center. Supervision is a difficult task, but good supervision ensures good staff relations, good program results, and firm educational goals. The main purpose of this chapter is to help those who have a responsibility to select staff for a school library media center in a single school building. It addresses the five major functions of good managerial principles, the primary personnel categories, the size of the staff, and representative media center tasks, including outsourcing of tasks. It includes job descriptions for staff, levels of staffing, and an overview of certification for specialists, emphasizing staff requirements and certification as well as national certification standards. It also treats other staffing concerns, for example, recruitment, selection, staff training, and supervision or evaluation, which confront the school library media specialist. An evaluation checklist is included as well as a discussion of manuals and guides and their contents. Encouraging signs for the future of school media centers and its staff ends the discussion for the chapter.

MANAGERIAL PRINCIPLES

Good management principles must be developed when working with the staff to ensure that they have direction, and that they understand their responsibilities, the tasks to be performed and the level of performance expected. The five principles to be developed are: planning, leading, directing, controlling and revising.

Planning

Planning provides the groundwork for a good school media program. How well the staff functions, as an indispensable part of the instructional program, is the key to good management. Determining how the staff is trained to perform their duties is part of the planning process. Each staff member has a function in the overall goals of the media center. Planning carefully what each staff member is going to do in relation to library goals directly impacts on the total media center program and the course of action to be initiated. Planning is the bridge between the goals and the actual work to be accomplished.

Leading

Leadership is a key function that is essential to keep the staff motivated to accomplish established goals and to carry out a plan of action for the media center program. One aspect of leadership is the ability to communicate the plan to the staff and to involve them toward its successful achievement. A staff that works well together achieves more and establishes a better rapport with the school community.

Directing

The supervision of staff is concerned with structuring the jobs to be accomplished and with directing people who work together toward making the plan of action work. The ability to delegate authority and responsibility to other staff members who can carry out task assignments is essential. Directing group activities and task assignments fosters the cooperation of the staff and coordinates the work activities to be accomplished.

Controlling

The control function is concerned with evaluation of the staff and how effectively and efficiently they have performed their duties in the overall activities of the school media center program. One important aspect of this function is that the staff has a clear understanding of its duties and knows in advance how they will be evaluated.

Revising

The revision function is concerned with determining how to improve the work output of the staff. If some aspects of the program are not functioning as planned, it may be necessary to reassign duties, redefine tasks and make modifications. There may be factors that exist among the staff that need to be corrected to ensure quality of work and cooperation among members and allow for a teamwork approach to be utilized to the best advantage (Hicks, 1981).

Effective management of the staff is crucial to the smooth operation of the school media program. School library media specialists, who apply good management principles with library personnel whether they are clerks, volunteers, student assistants, or professionals, will improve the center's services to the users of the school media center.

PERSONNEL CATEGORIES

Although there are many ways to define staff roles, studies of human resources in school library media centers indicate three broad categories under which the majority of media center personnel may be listed: professional, paraprofessional, and nonprofessional.

Professionals

Persons educated and certified as school media specialists, librarians, or audiovisual specialists by a state or other accrediting agency are considered professionals, regardless of their primary responsibility. Media center program administrators or directors, school library media specialists, and audiovisual specialists with competency in a specialty within some communication technology—for example, television and radio—generally meet these requirements. It is their responsibility to assume leadership in planning, developing, and evaluating a program that meets the needs of faculty, students, and community. They must be interested and knowledgeable in media and the components of media, instructional materials, and communications technology, including computers. Knowledge of materials in different formats, appreciation of service as resource personnel, and the ability to operate equipment and be proficient in using newer technology (including computers) and to aid in the production of materials are their primary responsibilities. Professionals should also be proficient in the principles of teaching and learning. They need to be knowledgeable about the media program of the school and the characteristics of the students with whom they work. Because the school library media program involves students, teachers, and administrators, each staff member, especially in a single-school situation, must be able to work well with people of all ages. The center is so integral a part of the total school program that it is difficult to say where the school stops and the center begins.

A school library media center is usually located in the building that houses all its potential users. The media specialist must develop a partnership, as a faculty member, with classroom teachers in helping students make full use of the media. It is the teaching role of the media specialist that can serve as the impetus to collaboratively work with faculty members to ensure that students utilize the media center as a focal point for research, Internet use, and for their own recreational reading interests. The roles of the school media specialist as a teacher, an information specialist, an instructional partner and program administrator are more proactive where services are anticipated and planned in advance of need. The media specialist continues to find the roles challenging, exciting, and intrinsically rewarding as they expand to include being initiators and change agents in the school (AASL & AECT, 1998).

Program Administrator

The school library media center program administrator or director normally has training in library and information science and demonstrates leadership qualities. Certified persons should have the primary responsibility for administrating the school library media center at both the elementary and secondary levels. When two or more professionals are employed in the same center, only one should be in charge and responsible for the program. Normally, the person in charge of the program is the program administrator (AASL & AECT, 1998). The program administrator should have professional-level competency in all media, including technology, in addition to administrative ability. The administrator of the school media program shares a common responsibility with other center staff personnel for general services, or all phases of program work. The program administrator is also in charge of developing in other staff members the necessary knowledge, skill, and competence to perform their jobs well. As the program expands, the program administrator sees to the employment of additional staff with complementary preparation, subject specialization and technology skills. In new and developing programs with a small-size staff, where the program administrator must spend much time in administration, program planning and implementation, and evaluation and media selection, some of these tasks are redistributed. It is desirable that the program administrator be considered a departmental chairperson in schools that are departmentalized.

School Library Media Specialists

Generally, the specialists have been educated in both the field of librarianship and information science with an emphasis on instructional materials and technology. However, both by interest and training, media specialists may work with the equipment, technology, or with any part of the instructional program.

The main functions of the school library media specialist cluster around services to students and teachers. Functions commonly associated with the specialist are labeled M on the list of representative tasks (see later in this chapter). Specifically these are the tasks that contribute to the center's organization and to its circulation, instruction, technology, and selection services. In addition, the specialist helps to develop the program by implementing many of the center's activities and by integrating information literacy into the curriculum. A subject or grade-level specialization, together with some facility in technology integration, is useful. If the media specialist is the only professional on the staff, he or she assumes as much of the program administrator and specialist roles as possible, assigning priority to the most important and immediate demands. The program will grow in direct ratio to the size, qualifications, and imagination of the staff.

Audiovisual Specialists/Instructional Technologists

The audiovisual specialist is normally certified as a professional in instructional or communications technology by education, by experience, or both. Some education in librarianship is a part of the audiovisual specialist's training. The positions of media specialist and audiovisual specialist overlap in many instances, the basic difference being that the media specialist generally concentrates on the materials services and the audiovisual specialist's concern is the equipment. Technology integration is a major component of all specialists' work. Audiovisual specialists are also increasingly concerned with media instructional applications. Although this has been the typical division for staff positions, particularly on larger staffs, it is the newer role where competencies exist in both materials and equipment or technology, and the person combines them into a subject or grade-level approach that permits the specialist to become part of a team of teachers. This approach increases the specialist's usefulness to both students and teachers and fits with the idea of differentiated staffing where educational personnel assume responsibilities based on carefully defined educational functions. For this arrangement to work well, the specialist must assume the broad tasks of the media and audiovisual specialists and refine them by curriculum and grade level.

In some instances, staff responsibilities may be divided between library services (which is concerned primarily with research and the use of print materials as well as Internet access) and audiovisual services (which emphasizes audiovisual non-print materials and equipment services, including technology maintenance). An arrangement in staffing which separates the two functions of the media center into two separate entities, such as library services and audiovisual services, sometimes tends to separate the services of the center. The trend today seems to be to roll the position of audiovisual specialist into both the media specialist role and the technology technician's role.

The primary responsibilities of the audiovisual specialist frequently include non-print materials and equipment services, which at their least sophisticated level are often performed by paraprofessionals or technology technicians in some school districts. Audiovisual specialists also continue to take part in the development of the program, selection of media—particularly equipment maintenance, material production—and frequently deal with television programming copyright issues as well as maintenance of computers. The role of the audiovisual specialist in a school library media program, still in a state of transition, is largely determined by the size of the staff. In a single school with only two or three staff members, one popular, economical pattern uses a professional media specialist, a technology technician, and clerical support. The duties most commonly associated with the audiovisual specialist are labeled A on the representative tasks list (see later in this chapter).

Paraprofessionals

A person qualified in a special area of media work, for example, photography, graphics, or technology, but who does not hold a bachelor's degree generally is classified as a paraprofessional. School secretaries are sometimes considered paraprofessionals, depending on their qualifications. Likewise, technology technicians are identified as paraprofessionals as well. This person is an important staff member in any large school library media center program and, given the wide range of the technology technician competencies, a worthwhile member of a small staff. They are often recruited from industry, community colleges, and the like, and their duties are mainly in production; equipment maintenance; TV programming or off-air programming; and special services to faculty and students, with whom they often work directly. Many of their tasks are related to computer technology involving maintenance and training. Some of the technology technicians' specific tasks are noted under Paraprofessional Staff in representative tasks list T (see later in this chapter). If the post of technology technician does not exist in the center program, the duties of this position are assumed by school library media specialists and supportive personnel such as clerks or technicians.

Nonprofessionals

Audiovisual technicians and clerks form the regular nonprofessional staff of the school library media center program. They may be salaried personnel or unpaid volunteer aides, and they work under the direction of a professional. Their schooling and experience may range from a grade-school diploma to training in a technical or clerical institute to graduate study. Preparation for their work in the center is acquired by specialized training or practical experience, but they are rarely certified as media specialists. In a center with only one nonprofessional, the tasks are combined with those of the professional and paraprofessional staffs.

Audiovisual Technicians

Audiovisual technicians usually are highly specialized in some aspect of the media program, with a special emphasis on the equipment and production tasks, for example, operating and distributing equipment and producing transparencies or tapes. On a large staff, specialized areas such as computer services, display techniques, and television broadcasting usually require technicians to help the professionals. Technicians are often recruited directly from high school or technical training institutions.

Clerks

Clerks usually have either clerical, secretarial, or computer training or experience that make them especially useful in carrying out the routine business operations of a school library media center program under the supervision of a professional. Their tasks fall into the areas of acquisition, organization, material preparation, and circulation of material, along with some production of materials. Skill in word processing and knowledge of spreadsheets are major requirements for a clerk.

Volunteers and Student Assistants

Volunteers can be a valuable community liaison. They are usually parents from the school community, students, or both, and are often unpaid. In some cases, student assistants receive course credit for their work in the center; the work may be associated with vocational programs for high school technical and business students. The volunteers' work should be creative and rewarding and exploitation of the volunteer aide can be avoided if the volunteer assistant program is formulated and managed with the individual's development as a primary objective. This plan can be accomplished by:

- Assigning tedious, boring tasks, such as shelving books, infrequently.
- Rotating regularly the more desirable jobs, such as circulation deskwork.
- Offering training in more complex library work, such as helping students locate materials or use the Internet.
- Establishing continued instruction and job evaluation.

- Giving appropriate incentives and rewards for successful job performance.
- Providing opportunities for social and educational activities, such as theater and museum trips.
- Offering opportunities to select web sites for classroom/media center collaborative projects.

A newer category of volunteer is the professional center retiree or other professional personnel who may offer some time to the center. Another variation, one that is controversial, is part-time staffing both by retirees and professional school library media specialists. Each situation must be judged objectively, using the purpose and goals of the center as a final arbiter.

HOW BIG A STAFF?

The size of the media staff depends on several factors: the school enrollment and the diversity of student needs, the number of grades, the nature of the program and instructional pattern, the existence of district level media services, and community support. Many sources have recommendations on staff size, among them the national and individual state standards. State departments of education frequently address the size of the school library media staff in their documents found on their web sites.

REPRESENTATIVE CENTER TASKS

Well-developed centers with adequate staff will carry out a myriad of tasks; at least one-third of the tasks are essential in the operation of even the smallest program with the least amount of staff. Some tasks are outsourced to outside companies.

A list of representative tasks is included here and is divided between the two main categories of media center personnel: professional and paraprofessional/nonprofessional. Tasks may be interchangeable among the staff, depending on the local situation. As a general rule, however, even with only two or three staff persons, all tasks will be covered, some minimally. As the staff size increases in response to an effective program, that is, when an audiovisual specialist, media specialist, technology specialist, or clerk is added, the program administrator will increasingly assume the tasks that are starred (*), the media specialist will assume those designated M, the audiovisual specialist will take on those designated A, and the professional/nonprofessional staff will be designated as T, for technology technician; AV for audiovisual technician; S for secretary or clerk; and V for volunteers or student assistants. There is no one way in which these tasks and the many other service-related functions can be specified; the pattern ultimately depends on the nature of the program and the competencies and interests of the staff. However, tasks for each category are given in the next section; each school library media center should use them as samples in constructing workable ones for the specific situation. Some of the tasks have been modified according to the responsibilities listed on the web site for the Missouri Department of Elementary and Secondary Division of School Improvement (2002) found at the following address: http://www.dese. state.mo.us/divimprove/curriculum/library/handbook/director.htm

Outsourcing of Tasks

Some tasks are outsourced to either a district level school media program or to book jobbers. The job that is most often outsourced is cataloging and processing of new materials. Some school districts provide this service for their media centers. According to Eisenberg and Repman (1997), Hawaii went one step further by outsourcing to a book jobber to select, catalog, process and distribute books to their forty-nine public school library media centers. The book jobber was paid a flat fee of $20.94 per item. The controversy surrounding the idea that the book jobber staff selects the books and builds the collection for these libraries goes against all the principles of book selection taught in library schools. The problem arises when selection outsourcing is done by a book jobber because some locally collected materials may require original cataloging. It is a common practice to modify catalog records to meet local media center needs.

A common use of outsourcing of technology aspects is through the respective conversion of a card catalog into an online pubic access catalog (OPAC) or through the use of a commercial vendor to install a Novell or an Ethernet network. Outsourcing involves using an external company to produce a product or service that is normally done within the media center. The benefits to outsourcing normally involve reducing costs and broadening services (Eisenberg & Repman, 1997).

Personnel Tasks

The asterisk and letter symbols for the professional staff in the following list indicate tasks that will be increasingly assumed by certain persons as staff size increases in response to an effective program:

* = supervisor, district level and/or program administrator, building level

M = school library media specialist

A = audiovisual specialist

T = technology technician

P = paraprofessional

S = secretary/clerk

AV = audiovisual technician

V = volunteer/student assistant

Professional Staff

*—Determine educational goals and objectives of school library media center policies.

*—Plan programs, center operations and maintenance of the school library media center.

*—Ascertain overall school library media center policies.

*—Extend library media center roles into the curriculum.

*—Develop strategy for selecting, training and supervising of support staff.

*—Work collaboratively with architects in planning and designing new and renovated school media facilities.

*—Submit appropriate reports to administrators.

*—Form a library media advisory committee consisting of parents, staff, and students to provide feedback and guidance for library policies and procedures.

*—Oversee the school library, audiovisual, and technology budgets.

*—Assess the school library media program.

*—Plan for upgrading equipment and technology.

*—Provide an accessible and current material collection.

*—Implement policies and procedures for the school library media program.

*—Establish circulation procedure policies.

*—Assume responsibility for disciplinary decisions.

*—Develop teacher and student handbooks.

*—Work collaboratively with teachers to establish procedures for group or individual assignments.

*—Provide in-service courses and workshops for faculty and notify them of upcoming courses and workshops in the district and community for earning continuing education credit.

*—Boost professional library use.

*—Plan community public relations activities.

*—Participate in professional meetings and networks.

*—Determine a material selection policy.

M/A—Schedule use of media center facilities and expertise of specialists to work collaboratively with faculty.

M/A—Prepare media center orientation and in-service activities.

M/A—Review and participate in curriculum development.

M/A—Train support staff: student aides, clerks, and volunteers.

M/A—Initiate collaborative projects and activities relating to media and Internet resources.

M/A—Provide access to resources both within and outside the school.

M/A—Work collaboratively with faculty and administration to integrate information literacy skills curriculum into instructional program.

M/A—Develop a scope and sequence of the information literacy skills curriculum.

M/A—Provide leadership in the integration of new information technologies as a tool for learning.

M/A—Plan activities that allow students to learn to identify, analyze, and synthesize information using a variety of resources and formats.

M/A—Maintain positive public relations program for media center.

M/A—Work collaboratively with teachers and students in reading, viewing, and listening activities.

M/A—Plan collaboratively with faculty members to promote effective use of materials, Internet, and media services.

M/A—Integrate classroom work with media center program.

M/A—Participate in collaborative teaching.

M/A—Enlist faculty to participate and recommend in the selection of materials.

M/A—Generate evaluation forms.

M/A—Formulate a media philosophy combined with long- and short-range goals, and implementation/evaluation procedures for their achievement.

M/A—Evaluate and select materials and equipment based on selection policy that enhances teaching and learning.

M/A—Encourage student and teacher usage of the school media center by fostering a friendly atmosphere.

M/A—Adopt a system for scheduling, circulating, and delivering resources of the media center.

M/A—Prepare an annual budget and submit to the appropriate administrators.

M/A—Perform general reference services.

M/A—Train teachers and students in the use of newer technology.

M/A—Provide flexible scheduling to allow students and teachers unlimited access to the media center resources.

M/A—Design the school media facility based on program needs.

M/A—Reserve media collections for classroom use.

M/A—Compile bibliographies.

Paraprofessional and Nonprofessional Staff

P—Develop innovative ways to use materials and equipment.

P—Assist teachers in designing innovations in instruction.

P/S—Administer interlibrary loan services.

AV—Determine space for equipment purchased.

P/S—Create program evaluation forms.

T/AV—Work with teachers to determine needed technology and equipment purchases.

AV—Adapt commercial materials and equipment to meet special needs through innovative material production.

S—Design publicity materials in a variety of media formats.

S—Produce simple display devices for instructional use.

AV—Operate and teach the use of lettering and drawing devices.

AV—Produce materials for specialized school needs (audiotapes, videos, multimedia presentations, transparencies, laminated materials).

T—Maintain Internet access.

T—Provide access to technology through maintenance of computers and networks.

AV/T—Make repairs of equipment not under service contract.

P—Assist teachers and students in locating, using, and selecting materials and equipment.

AV—Assist teachers and students with off-air video recordings utilizing fair use copyright laws.

AV/T—Instruct teachers and students in material production techniques.

P/S—Assist students and staff with basic reference needs.

P/S—Create library displays.

P/S/T—Organize media and technology open houses.

S—Develop a variety of forms for operation of the center.

S—Maintain files for library media equipment and materials.

S—Perform routine desktop publishing activities.

AV/T—Maintain the schedule to deliver audiovisual and technology equipment.

AV/T—Maintain cumulative records of condition and maintenance work on equipment.

P/T—Perform computer software installations.

T—Assist users in solving computer network problems.

T—Configure, plan and manage LANs and WANS in the school.

P/T—Install, troubleshoot and maintain computer hardware and software in the library media center.

T—Install, repair, and troubleshoot computer system in the school.

S—Determine need for, control, order, inventory, and maintain supplies.

S—Handle clerical and secretarial work of correspondence (filing, typing, mailing, and so forth).

S—Type notices, requisitions, bulletins, newsletters and bibliographies, and so forth.

S/V—Assist in sale of paperback books.

S/V—Perform messenger service.

S—Maintain selection aids for finding new materials.

S—Check OPAC inventory list and other selection aids to prepare bibliographic data for ordering and duplicating materials.

S—Transact clerical business operations: file orders and invoices; receive credit memoranda and invoices, and transmit them to appropriate office; verify total purchase costs; follow up outstanding orders.

S—Maintain library media center records and statistics.

S/V—Unpack and check new materials and equipment received, and verify invoices with shipment and order.

S—Post receipt of periodical and newspaper issues and take care of missing items.

S/V—Prepare items received for circulation, if this service is not provided by the district media center services.

S/V—Stamp ownership mark on all materials.

S—Load cataloging data into OPAC.

P/S/V—Sort and place materials on shelves or in containers and keep them in reasonable order.

S—Process records for materials and equipment withdrawn/added to the collection.

S/V—Compile and revise bibliographies as new materials arrive.

S—Compile review files for materials and equipment.

P/S—Maintain media inventory records and assist in inventory.

T/AV/V—Set up and operate audiovisual equipment, such as videos, computers, and so forth.

S/V—Inspect and make necessary repairs to print and non-print materials and equipment.

P/S—Input data in computer.

S—Maintain a spreadsheet for budget expenditures.

P/S—Assist students and faculty in locating resources within and outside the media center, including interlibrary loan services.

S—Create appropriate documents in a variety of computer applications for media center use.

P/S—Generate circulation and overdue reports.

S/P/T—Perform basic computer operations such as data input, download and upload data, format and copy disks, and maintain data back up.

P/S—Assist students and faculty in using the Internet.

P/S—Assist faculty and students in developing graphics, sound, and videos for multimedia presentations.

P/S—Perform Internet searches to assist in media center operations.

JOB DESCRIPTIONS

The sample job descriptions that follow are for positions that most often exist in the school library media center in an individual building and for the district library media supervisor. These job descriptions agree with the tasks described earlier. They also identify some of the major specific duties that are generally universal. The use of job descriptions is recommended both for the applicant or employee and the supervisor. Each job description can be designed specifically for a particular position by using these samples as guidelines. Of necessity, the job description that evolves will contain the tasks specific to the position.

Position:	**District Library Media Supervisor** (coordinator, director, and so forth)
Supervisor:	District administrative authority, usually assistant superintendent
Supervises:	District school library media center School library program administrators
Education:	Advanced course work in a specialization or a doctorate (additional competencies beyond those for a school library media head)
Nature:	Leadership in district's school library media center development
Responsibilities:	1. Develop long-range plans consistent with the district philosophy.

2. Coordinate and give guidance to building-level staff.

3. Develop district policies and procedures.

4. Implement policies and procedures and promote a high level of professional ethics.

5. Serve on curriculum-development teams.

6. Develop a district policy for collection development.

7. Encourage resource sharing and networking.

8. Encourage the use of new technology.

9. Provide district in-service opportunities for library media staff.

10. Assist with in-service opportunities for faculty.

11. Participate in professional associations and encourage participation by staff.

12. Assist departments, curriculum committees in the selection of media and equipment.

13. Coordinate the use of community resources.

14. Assist in the development of a K–12 sequence of learner outcomes for information literacy.

15. Consult with committees and architects to plan facilities.

16. Consult with principals to plan library media programs and give assistance in problem areas.

17. Evaluate library media programs using state, regional and national standards.

18. Maintain liaison with supervisory and administrative personnel within the district.

19. Interpret library media services to teachers, administrators, board of education and community.

20. Coordinate library media services with other schools and public libraries.

21. Promote the use of volunteer helpers.

22. Evaluate and share current developments and innovations in library media programs and new technology.

23. Plan for communication among the library media staff.

24. Prepare and administer the budget.

25. Assist principals in the selection, supervision and evaluation of library media personnel.

26. Provide reports and statistics as needed by district, state, and regional accrediting agencies.

27. Provide access to district-level services and resources.

28. Coordinate the acquisition, and processing of materials and equipment.

29. Monitor state and federal laws and communicate to the building-level staff and to administration.

30. Seek grants from local, state, and federal sources.

31. Evaluate the impact of library media programs.

32. Maintain a professional collection, including online information services.

33. Keep abreast of federal and state funding, e-rate information, and available grants.

34. Maintain Internet access for district media centers in cases where not handled by technology departments.

Position:	**School Library Media Program Administrator**
Supervisor:	Principal
	District school library media supervisor
Supervises:	School library media center staff (other specialists, technicians, clerks, etc.)
Education:	Additional competencies beyond those expected of a school library media specialist, for example, administration, information science

Nature: Responsibility to administer the school library media center to help accomplish the educational goals of the school district (if there is no district director, also to plan and develop cooperatively the school library media center policy)

Responsibilities: Assume the duties, as able, of the district school library media director when there is none.

1. Serve as liaison with principal and school library media district supervisor.

2. Implement media center policies.

3. Submit reports to district supervisor and principal.

4. Help to recruit and select staff.

5. Participate in preparing job descriptions.

6. Supervise staff; develop evaluation instruments.

7. Plan systems for maintenance, scheduling, and delivery of materials and equipment.

8. Enlist faculty participation in evaluating and selecting materials.

9. Serve as curriculum consultant and also review curriculum.

10. Observe classroom work to coordinate school library media center programs.

11. Prepare instructional programs collaboratively with teachers and conduct in-service courses.

12. Plan orientation programs for students, faculty, administrators, and the community.

13. Develop and implement plans for reorganization and relocation.

14. Initiate promotional work related to media, such as publications.

15. Promote use of professional collections.

16. Participate in resource sharing and networking with other libraries.

17. Explore current developments in the field.

18. Work with professional library staff, faculty, and administrators to integrate information literacy skills into the curriculum.

19. Provide technological access to information, including the Internet, e-mail, listservs, and other innovations.

20. Serve as instructional partner with teachers.

21. Administer the media center program.

Position:	**School Library Media Specialist/Audiovisual Specialist/Instructional Technologist**
Supervisor:	School library media program administrator
Supervises:	Paraprofessionals (library and audiovisual)
	Technology Technicians
	Library Secretary
	Clerks
	Volunteers
Education:	Professional degree; the first level of professional responsibility as a fully prepared specialist
Nature:	Knowledge and ability in media and related equipment; participation as a specialist in their effective use in all categories of the curriculum
Responsibilities:	1. Help to plan scheduling and material delivery systems.

2. Schedule use of facilities.

3. Participate in curriculum development committees.

4. Help to collaboratively plan classroom work with school library media programs.

5. Introduce teachers to media in their subjects or grade levels.

6. Work with students and teachers in reading, viewing, and listening.

7. Inform teachers of new services.

8. Compile bibliographies.

9. Read widely for information on selecting materials and equipment.

10. Help to evaluate and select media, web sites appropriate for classroom use.

11. Organize and reserve special collections.

12. Perform general reference services.

13. Administer interlibrary loan and reference sharing.

14. Plan and conduct programs of instruction in research techniques.

15. Conduct in-service courses.

16. Orient students to school library media center.

17. Train clerks, student assistants and volunteers.

18. Initiate collaborative projects and activities with teachers relating to media resources.

19. Originate and conduct programs for special-interest groups.

20. Outline and conduct public relations activities, for example, write articles, maintain schedules of class activities.

21. Serve as an instructional partner with classroom teachers.

22. Meet special needs.

23. Evaluate student's special school library media center projects.

24. Assist with independent study.

25. Help students and teachers in locating and selecting media.

Position:	**Technology Technician**
Supervisor:	School library media program administrator School library media specialist
Education:	Generally two years of higher education, including specialized training and/or experience
Nature:	Competency as a team member of the staff to provide technological services and specialized operations for school library media centers
Responsibilities:	1. Help to schedule use and delivery of computer technology.

2. Produce specialized materials for school needs, such as video, multimedia presentations, and so forth.

3. Provide for production of materials using computer technology.

4. Maintain computer equipment and help with programs.

5. Assist faculty and students in the effective use of Internet and other technology innovations.

6. Train teachers and students in the use of newer computer technology.

7. Assist teachers in designing innovations in instruction.

8. Work with media center staff and teachers in determining technology purchases.

9. Assist students and teachers in developing sound and digital videos for multimedia presentations.

10. Provide access to technology through maintenance of computers and networks.

11. Perform installation of computer software.

12. Solve computer network problems as they arise in the school.

13. Configure, plan, and manage LANS and WANS.

14. Install, troubleshoot, and maintain computer hardware and software.

15. Install, repair and troubleshoot computer network throughout the school.

16. Create appropriate documents in a variety of computer applications for media center use.

17. Perform Internet searches to assist in media center operations.

18. Help to develop evaluation forms for computer technology.

19. Maintain cumulative records of repair and condition of equipment, computer hardware, and software.

20. Make repairs on equipment and investigate contract method for major repairs.

Position:	**Audiovisual Technician**
Supervisor:	School library media program administrator School library media specialist
Education:	Generally two years of higher education, including specialized training and/or experience
Nature:	Competency as a team member of the staff to provide audiovisual services and specialized operations for school library media centers
Responsibilities:	1. Help to schedule use and delivery of audiovisual equipment and materials.

2. Produce specialized materials for school needs, such as video, multimedia presentations, and so forth.

3. Provide for production of materials using audiovisual equipment.

4. Make simple display devices for instruction.

5. Operate lettering and drawing devices.

6. Handle photography and video courses for recreational related work.

7. Maintain audiovisual equipment and materials.

8. Assist faculty and students in the effective use of audio-visual equipment and materials.

9. Train teachers and students in the use of audiovisual materials and equipment.

10. Assist teachers in designing innovations in instruction using audiovisual materials.

11. Work with media center staff and teachers in determining audiovisual equipment and material purchases.

12. Assist students and teachers in developing sound and digital videos for multimedia presentations.

13. Troubleshoot minor audiovisual equipment repairs and investigate contract method for major repairs.

14. Create appropriate documents for media center use.

15. Involve and help students and teachers with production techniques.

16. Help to develop evaluation forms for using audiovisual materials and equipment.

17. Maintain cumulative records of repair and condition of audiovisual equipment and materials.

Position:	**School Library Media Secretary** (assistant, clerk, aide, and so forth)
Supervisor:	School library program administrator, school library media specialist, technology technician, or other specified head
Supervises:	Student assistants/volunteers
Education:	Secretarial training/experience, including typing ability and computer skills
Nature:	Fulfill the routine operations of a school library media center, under direction of a professional
Responsibilities:	1. Transact clerical business operations.

2. Handle secretarial work of correspondence, typing of reports, and other duties.

3. Control ordering, inventory, and maintenance of supplies.

4. Input and update data for OPAC.

5. Maintain selection aids for finding new materials.

6. Compile and revise bibliographies.

7. Maintain review files for media.

8. Type notices, requisitions, bulletins, bibliographies, and so forth.

9. Post receipt of periodicals and newspapers.

10. Process records for media withdrawn/added to the collection.

11. Maintain inventory records.

12. Assist in the inventory.

13. Compile media center statistics.

14. Maintain inventory and order supplies.

15. Work at the circulation desk as needed.

16. Assist staff and students in locating and using equipment and materials.

17. Assist staff and students in Internet use.

18. Prepare materials for circulation.

19. Plan and prepare displays for public relations.

20. Perform routine and simple print shop activities.

21. Design computer spreadsheets to keep track of budget expenditures.

22. Handle interlibrary loan requests.

Position:	**Student Assistant/Volunteer**
Supervisor:	School library media program administrator, library media specialist, technology technician, media aide or secretary, or other specified authority
Education:	Training on the job, generally
Nature:	Assistance to the staff
Responsibilities:	1. Assist at the circulation desk.

2. Unpack and check new materials and equipment, and verify invoices.

3. Place ownership and identification mark on each item.

4. Ready items received for use.

5. Sort and place items in proper locations, and maintain proper order.

6. Perform messenger service.

7. Set up, operate and retrieve equipment for teachers and students.

8. Assist in public relations work, for example, bulletin boards.

9. Perform clerical tasks as needed.

Exhibit 6.1.
Exemplary Level Recommended Professional and Parapro-
fessional Staffing for School Library Media Centers
Based on Enrollment.

Program Level Enrollment	Minimum Program Level Staffing
0-350 ADA	1 Certified Librarian 1 Para-professional
351-700 ADA	1 Certified Librarian 1.5 Para-professionals
701-1050 ADA	2 Certified Librarians 2 Para-professionals
1051-1400 ADA	2 Certified Librarians 3 Para-professionals
1401-2100 ADA	3 Certified Librarians 4 Para-professionals
2101+ ADA	Add 1 additional librarian and 1.5 additional para-professional for every 700 students

Printed with permission. Texas State Library and Archives
Commission. (2001, October 17). *School library programs:
Standards and guidelines for Texas.* Austin, TX: Author.
Retrieved April 6, 2004, from: http://www.tsl.state.tx.us/
ld/schoollibs/standards.html

Some states use guidelines to determine how their media centers are
staffed. The Texas Education Agency (2000) is one state that recommends
exemplary staffing for both school library media centers as well as a plan
for district level staffing (see Exhibits 6.1 and 6.2).

CERTIFICATION

The publication *Standards for School Library Programs* (American
Library Association & National Education Association [ALA & NEA],
1969) represented the first national recognition of the need for unified

Exhibit 6.2.
Exemplary Level Recommended District Staffing Based on Number of Programs in District.

# of Programs in the District	District Level Staffing
1–5	1 All-level Director/Coordinator w/ other district duties
6–15	1 All-level Director/Coordinator
16–40	1 All-level Director/Coordinator 1 Technical Services Certified Librarian
41–81	1 Secondary-Level Director/Coordinator 1 Elementary-Level Director/Coordinator 1 Technical Services Certified Librarian
82+	1 Secondary-Level Director/Coordinator 1 Elementary-Level Director/Coordinator 1 Technical Services Director/Coordinator 2–3 Technical Services Specialists

Printed with permission. Texas State Library and Archives Commission. (2001, October 17). *School library programs: Standards and guidelines for Texas.* Austin, TX: Author. Retrieved April 6, 2004, from http://www.tsl.state.tx.us/ld/schoollibs/standards.html

media services in the school; the standards published in *Media Programs...* (AASL & AECT, 1975) confirmed it. The American Association of School Librarians (AASL), and the Association for Education Communications and Technology (AECT) in *Information Power* (1988, 1998) fosters the development of the school library media specialist as a professional with training and experience in library science and instructional technology.

The preparation of professionals in school library media work increasingly requires certification in both teaching and library science as reflected particularly in state requirements for media coordinators. For example, in Michigan, there is no school library media specialist certification, there is only a library media endorsement; in New York there is. Both states, however, require that each media specialist or person filling that position be certified as a teacher and require certification in both teaching and library science. Preparation as a classroom teacher is generally stipulated. Although previously issued certificates are honored, as they are in most states under a grandfather clause, more balanced course work appears more and more frequently in the preparation of the media specialist. Some states permit initial certification in school media librarianship; however, the majority add this certificate to a basic teaching certificate once certain requirements have been met. Thirty-five states use some method of testing connected to preparatory programs or licenses, certification, or endorsement. Of these thirty-five states, ten states use their own test, and twenty-five states administer some part of the Praxis Series, designed and administered by the Educational Testing Service. Sixteen states require the Praxis II Specialty Area Test/Library Media Specialist for school librarian certification: Arkansas, Georgia, Hawaii, Indiana, Kentucky, Louisiana, Maryland, Mississippi, Missouri, North Carolina, Ohio, Oregon, Pennsylvania, South Carolina, Tennessee, and West Virginia. Other specialty tests are required in seven states: Arizona, Colorado, Florida, Illinois, Michigan, Oklahoma, and Texas. Applicants for certification in eighteen states are required to show certain competencies: Alabama, Kansas, Kentucky, Maryland, Massachusetts, Michigan, Minnesota, New Hampshire, New Mexico, North Carolina, Oklahoma, Oregon, Utah, Vermont, Virginia, West Virginia, Wisconsin and Wyoming. Three states use the NCATE competencies as the basis for preparatory programs training media specialists: Michigan, Oklahoma, and West Virginia (Perritt, 2000).

A common pattern in certification in the increasingly complex school library media field generally includes training in five areas: administration and supervision, organization, selection and utilization, production, and communications theory and systems, plus supporting courses that increasingly include information science. Many state plans for certification on the level of administration and supervision of media favor the newer combination of fields while remaining flexible enough to permit specialization.

Shortage of school library media specialists is becoming a serious problem and is continuing to increase. According to a survey by Nancy Everhart (2002), twenty states are experiencing severe shortages as compared to twelve in 2000. Only four states are reporting no shortages for school media special- ists. Utah and Iowa credit the lack of a shortage to the absence of a mandate for a full-time school library media specialist in each school. Rhode Island, on the other hand, has a mandate but is meeting the demand because of the Uni- versity of Rhode Island's library school. Hawaii's shortage, like Rhode Island's, is lessened because of more school library media graduates from the University of Hawaii. In 2000, many shortages were confined to rural areas or inner cities, but in 2002 more affluent areas are also feeling the crunch.

Passing a test is the only certification requirement in some states, such as Arizona, Florida, Mississippi and Missouri (Everhart, 2002). For many years Texas used testing-only as a means of addressing school library media specialist shortages by allowing anyone with a teaching certificate to become a school library media specialist; however, that practice changed in 2000 when new standards required school library media specialists to par- ticipate in a formal library-training program, to get field experience in libraries, to have teaching experience, and to hold a master's degree (not specifically in library science). A test is still required to determine if school media specialists have mastered the new standards (Glick, 2000).

Emergency certification is widespread throughout the profession. Administrators hire a teacher who agrees to work as a media specialist while simultaneously completing coursework for certification. According to the Everhart study (2002), seventeen states answering the survey issued 686 emergency certificates. California employs large numbers of uncerti- fied staff. Nineteen states mandate certified school librarians be employed. In states lacking staffing mandates, clerks and aides frequently manage school library media centers and there are seldom any requirements for pursuing a degree. In some states teachers, without any library training, have replaced school library media specialists.

Audiovisual Specialist (Instructional Technologist)

Just as the traditional certification as a school librarian continues to exist in a few states, certification as an audiovisual specialist and/or instructional technologist seems to be slowly disappearing. Because of the changes and revisions in audiovisual course titles and descriptions, including name changes, it is difficult to determine the certification requirements for this traditional type of audiovisual work in schools. Nevertheless, there are a few states that still have this type of certification, for example, Indiana. Some states continue revising certification to agree with the latest trends; others have plans, some indefinite, to work on it in the future.

School Library Media Specialist

Certification for school library media specialists exists in most states. The title of the certificate varies from school media specialist, school librarian, school media librarian, library media, library media specialist, educational media specialist, school media services, media librarian, audio-visual services, library media endorsement, school library media specialist, instructional technology specialist, media coordinator, library information specialist, school library service and even learning resources specialists. This confusion in titles reflects clearly the lack of standardization among the states in terminology, grades of certificates, number of required hours, distribution of subjects, and method of certifying. Some general observations are nevertheless possible; for example, some states issue more than one grade of certificate with a different number of hours required for each. The number of hours necessary for certification varies from a range of eight to thirty-nine hours. There are only a few states in either of these extreme categories; the majority mandate eighteen, twenty-four, or thirty hours. The master's degree and teaching experience are increasingly a part of the requirements, although the undergraduate degree is also accepted by some states, for example, Florida. The conflicts among state requirements are generally related to the different grades of certificates, the variety of the certificate labels, and the diversity of course descriptions.

The distribution of course content needed by a media specialist varies among the states. Comparatively few states require a full range of production and audiovisual courses anymore, although some do require media production and technology courses. Seven courses or areas of competency are identified for certification: (1) administration of media center programs, (2) selection of media, (3) technology/audiovisuals, (4) cataloging, (5) reference, (6) literature for children or adolescents, and (7) a practicum. Some systems require one to three years of teaching experience before permanent certification is granted (Perritt, 2000).

A state board of education is the most common way of granting certification. Certification can be given directly on examination of the applicant's records or indirectly by automatic certification on completion of an ALA or state-approved (or both) library school program. The teacher certification board in a state education department evaluates an applicant's record and responds to inquiries about the state's certification requirements. School system superintendents are also able in many instances to obtain temporary certification for their employees. However, a school library media specialist who wants to work in a state other than the one in which the course work was completed needs to check into the requirements, since there is no national system of reciprocity in accreditation.

Another method of certification is currently being explored by some states. Basic endorsement is given based on an applicant's demonstrated proficiency, through taking a test, in such areas as cataloging, materials selection, utilization and production of media, and administration. Pennsylvania, for example, requires no prescribed credit hours or courses but does require the passing of the Praxis II, core battery tests, including communication skills, general knowledge, principles of learning and teaching (K–6 or 7–12), and the specialty area test/library media specialist (Perritt, 2000). Aside from this practical examination procedure, a portfolio method of examination has also been proposed. An unsettled economic climate has contributed to slow acceptance of these methods so far.

NATIONAL CERTIFICATION STANDARDS

The national certification of school library media specialists is now possible from the National Board for Professional Teaching Standards. This certification process, voluntary and open to public and private teachers, is designed for library media teachers who teach students from pre-kindergarten through grade twelve. Library media specialists who desire national certification are required to be assessed on two components: a portfolio consisting of four entries and content knowledge through six written assessment exercises. The portfolio allows library media specialists to present samples of their classroom practice in the areas of instructional collaboration, appreciation of literature, integration of instructional technology and through their contributions to student learning. The six areas of content knowledge assessed include: organizational management, ethical and legal tenets, technologies, collection development, information literacy and knowledge of literature. School media specialists taking the content knowledge tests are allowed thirty minutes to complete each of the six assessment exercises. They receive six scores, one for each individual exercise. Many states are beginning to reward school media specialists who have national certification with higher salaries (National Board for Professional Teaching Standards, 2003).

RECRUITMENT AND SELECTION

The selection of staff is a creative task that is both difficult and rewarding. The process is usually divided into recruitment and selection. Recruitment methods generally include:

1. Advertisements in appropriate media, for example, newspapers.
2. Listings with professional organizations, such as ALA, AECT, including state and local associations.
3. Notification of college and university clearinghouses.
4. Announcements to state and regional agencies.
5. Recommendations of local staff.
6. Developing web sites.

Sometimes all of these methods are used; however, the informal "word of mouth" procedure is often the most popular and influential. Nevertheless, depending on various factors, such as geographical location, each of these six methods can be effective in recruitment. It is important that the media specialist make the principal and higher administration aware of these methods. It is also advisable for the specialist to provide them with a current list of newspapers, journals/magazines, associations, web sites, and agencies that might be of help.

The selection of personnel is a complicated and demanding responsibility. It is advisable to emphasize objective factors, while recognizing that the ability of the person to get along well with the individuals already on staff is significant. Once an applicant has been identified and an application received, an interview is usually scheduled. The application should contain at least the following: (1) name, address, and phone number; (2) educational background; (3) work experience; (4) memberships and honors; (5) interests and hobbies; and (6) other, for example, status and availability. The administrator generally verifies the educational background through the transcripts that the applicant has sent and through appropriate telephone calls or letters, for example, the persons listed for recommendations, who can substantiate facts on the resume. These facts are checked either before or after the interview depending on the pattern of the administrator and the pressure of time. The administrator and the applicant can have the luxury of accomplishing these transactions during the spring if it is known that the position will be available. However, it is not uncommon for a position to be filled at the last minute in August. Since the same procedure must be followed, the pressure on both individuals is greater.

The principal or assistant superintendent usually conducts the first interview. At this time, an objective/subjective determination is made about the applicant's abilities and personality. The former determination will be checked and the latter judged by the interviewer and others who may be added to the subsequent interviews, for example, other faculty and staff. When the selection process reaches this point, a "short list" (depending on the number of applicants or predetermined number of finalists) is generally made. These applicants can be called back for another interview with a larger group or the superintendent alone. Where time is pressing, this process is condensed. Finally, a recommendation is made to the board of education. Generally approved, the applicant then receives an official letter stipulating the already expressed working dates and salary.

An increasingly prevalent practice is for the administrator doing the hiring to include the school library media specialist early in the selection process. In the past few years, it has also been the policy of administration to include more staff and school faculty in the interview process as well. This step is based on the knowledge that such participatory action promotes good human relations.

In the majority of situations, the applicant for a professional position will receive tenure in a stipulated period of time or, in rare instances, at once. This decision depends on various conditions, such as need, qualifications, and hiring policies. It is advisable for the applicant to be advised of tenure information before or during an interview. There is always the possibility, especially in times of economic hardship that economizing will be attempted by hiring and then recommending dismissal before tenure has to be granted by policy. Fortunately, such action is not prevalent. It is advisable, however, for professionals to be aware of this concern and to determine the attitude of the employer early in the selection process. If all else is well, including the evaluations that are usually required at least annually, the board of education, based on the superintendent's recommendation, votes positively on the approval for tenure.

STAFF TRAINING

The training of the staff is crucial for the smooth operation of the school library media program. There are several methods of training that are used in school media centers: procedural manuals, orientations/demonstrations, slide/sound presentations, video productions, computer programs, and PowerPoint presentations.

Procedural Manuals

Procedural manuals are probably one of the most effective methods of training the staff. The manual contains a detailed description of the tasks to be done by each staff member showing examples of work to be done, drawings and so forth. The manual should be written by the school media specialist for each type of staff member. For example, student assistants would have their own manual. The manual is written with the idea in mind that the person doing the job can refer to the manual for any task to be done in their job. If tasks are redefined for an individual staff member, a few pages can be added to their manual. A three ring binder is a good choice for a procedural manual because items can be added or deleted as needed.

Orientations/Demonstrations

Even if the staff has a procedural manual to follow, the school media specialist should take the time for orientation of the new staff member. The staff member should be given individual attention by the school media specialist to assure that the assigned tasks are understood and that the person is capable of doing the work properly. For example, if a clerk is to work at the circulation desk, the media specialist should spend time explaining the rules and regulations and the procedures of the circulation process and allow the new employee to perform with someone to give assistance. Sometimes another staff member can help in the orientation process.

Part of the orientation of the new employee should include demonstrations by either the school media specialist or a well-trained staff member in how tasks are performed.

Slide/Sound Presentations

A detailed slide/sound presentation may be prepared to show as part of the orientation program or to show details on how a particular job is performed. A procedure of this type is beneficial because the new employee can replay the slide sound presentation as many times as needed to learn the task being described or to learn the rules of the library and so forth. The use of a slide/sound presentation for training frees the school media specialist from spending long periods of time with the new employee. Time saved can be used more constructively in providing feedback in how the tasks can be done most efficiently.

Video Productions

The same principles apply in using video productions as those for slide/sound productions; however, the use of videos for training allows a more realistic presentation because the new employee can actually see the task being done rather than observing still-slide representations of the tasks to be performed. A video production is an effective medium for both orientation and demonstrations for new staff members.

Computer Programs

There are practically no computer programs that are commercially prepared that can be used to train staff members because every situation is different and requires unique training procedures. School media specialists might design a computer-training program to use with new staff members for orientation and for demonstration of tasks to be performed. The major advantage of this type of training method is that feedback can be given immediately when errors are made. The feedback from other training methods primarily comes from the school media specialist. For that reason, the computer program would be more practical.

PowerPoint Presentations

An excellent way to train students is through the use of a PowerPoint presentation, which uses beautiful color graphics to hold the trainee's attention. The major advantage of this method is its ease in making very attractive slides, especially when explaining step-by-step processes. This type of presentation might be used in place of slide-tape presentations.

A combination of several methods may be used to design an effective training program for the staff. It is the school media specialist's responsibility to develop a program that will utilize to the fullest the potential of each staff member.

SUPERVISION (STAFF EVALUATION)

One of the more significant factors in assessment is supervision or staff evaluation. Qualities of leadership and the knowledge of a few fundamental principles form the capstone of competent supervision. The following paragraphs describe some of the most important principles and practices of school library media center supervision on all levels, emphasizing the role of the school library media specialist as supervisor of the program in the individual school.

The term coordinator is used interchangeably with such other descriptive titles as supervisor, director, program administrator, consultant, or chairperson, since the goals and functions of the positions described and of the program administrator are the same. Supervision stresses leadership, coordination, cooperation, collaboration, creativity, self-direction, and effective public relations. The school library media program administrator, as one of the instructional specialists in a school system, regional board of education, or state or federal department of public instruction, shares the responsibility for the overall educational program.

The school library media program administrator should be the leader and supervisor of the program. This person should have training as a teacher and as a media specialist. Regardless of title, the position should be equal in rank and authority to that of other administrative instructional specialists in the system. This administrative unit is the keystone for well-planned, economically sound school library media service. School media supervision exists at all levels, from federal to local.

Federal Level

The U.S. Department of Education no longer includes a supervisory position to guide and improve school library media service throughout the nation. However, a program manager responsible for the Improving Literacy Through School Libraries program was appointed as part of the reauthorization of the Elementary and Secondary Act (ESEA). This manager's role is to administer the program in a manner "that meets the statutory intent of improving literacy by improving school libraries" (McNeely, pers. comm., May 28, 2002).

State Level

In many states, the state supervisor plans and administers the overall school library media services. The state supervisor provides leadership and supervisory services to local school authorities. As a part of a state's accreditation of library schools, the appropriate bureau or division fosters the concept of the library media center as a unified program throughout the school. The state bureau reinforces the federal supervisory functions by adapting them to the state level of service. In addition, the state supervisors provide services appropriate to their unique position. These services can be classified under the categories listed here:

Guidelines

- Develop all regular qualitative and quantitative standards for school library media centers.

- Appraise and plan the remodeling of and consult on library quarters in new school buildings.

Supervision

- Design a long-range plan for school library media development in the state.
- Evaluate school library media programs in the state.
- Guide the development of programs of library and information science education in the state.
- Encourage the development of demonstration school library media centers throughout the state.

Distribution of Information

- Interpret the role and importance of media to the legislature, boards of education, school personnel, and other groups.
- Advise on and interpret state and federal legislation and regulations regarding school library media centers, especially regarding funding issues.
- Supply information and publications on school library media programs to administrators, teachers, and media specialists.
- Prepare annual reports, special reports, and articles.
- Provide sources of access to the Internet.

Statistics and Research

- Collect, analyze, and disseminate statistical data on media service in schools.
- Initiate and promote research on school library media programs.
- Secure government and private grants to further the development of school library media centers within the state.

Certification

- Serve as resource centers and advisers on professional qualifications for school library media specialists.
- Aid in the recruitment of school library media specialists.

Cooperation

- Work closely with the chief state school officer.

- Coordinate the school library media program with other programs within the state education department.
- Participate in national, state, regional, and local education and library organizations.
- Serve as consultant on school library media centers and as resource person with other groups.
- Arrange cooperative/collaborative programs and projects with other professional groups.
- Cooperate with government agencies, such as state libraries and regional boards.
- Cooperate with nongovernmental organizations, such as teachers' associations, parent-teacher-student groups, and so forth.

System, City, and District Levels

While each system network or regional cooperative service has its own services and activities that are available to the school district, some basic services and activities are offered by most of them; they are as follows:

1. Establishing a union catalog based on the collections of the cooperating schools' libraries. This may be taken one step further by including the holdings from local public and academic libraries as part of the union catalog.
2. Forming depository collections to supplement the regular school collections.
3. Assigning areas of subject or media specialization to member schools.
4. Sharing operating and maintenance costs of expensive facilities, such as television studios.
5. Using computer technology for such routines as ordering, cataloging, processing, circulating, Internet access, and inventorying media.
6. Providing central facilities and consultants for large-group meetings and instruction.
7. Coordinating in-service workshops with other groups.

Many cities and districts employ school library media supervisors to utilize federal and state supervisory services and provide effective management of the local program. A school system with five or more school buildings should establish the position. The formation of school library media centers into a separate administrative unit has proven to be educationally efficient and economically sound. In addition to directing the school district's media program, the supervisor can affect economies by assigning nonprofessional library routines to paraprofessional and nonprofessional staff. Although administering these technical services is important, the primary responsibility of the school library media supervisor lies in working with media specialists, teachers, and administrators. In essence, school library media supervision involves the development and supervision of a satisfactory school system media program designed to aid teachers in solving their instructional problems, students in participating fully in learning process, and the community in supporting the program.

A city, county, or large-school media center system usually provides a majority of the following services to its individual schools, either directly or by contractual arrangement with another district or regional agency:

1. Establishing central purchasing, cataloging, and preparation of media.
2. Maintaining additional materials for smaller schools that cannot adequately meet the variety of student and teacher needs.
3. Developing an examination system for the selection of materials and equipment.
4. Producing specialized forms of materials, such as slides, CDs, videotapes, multimedia, and so forth.
5. Maintaining equipment.
6. Establishing printing services.
7. Developing in-service programs for training the entire district faculty (e.g., on the evaluation and use of newer media, such as the Internet).
8. Assisting in recruiting and selecting media staff for the district.
9. Coordinating professional collections for teachers and administrators.
10. Initiating the borrowing or renting of costly or infrequently used materials.
11. Establishing a central source for consumable supplies.
12. Developing television services for the district that may include the following types: open circuit, closed circuit, distance education, and so forth.
13. Developing computer services for technical services, information retrieval on the Internet, and instructional assistance.

Although each local district will have unique problems, the basic functions of district school library media programs supervision are similar. The major responsibilities are:

- Advising local school administrators on the role and management of school library media centers.
- Interpreting school library media functions to the board of education, legislature, parent-teacher-student organizations, citizen groups, and other public bodies.
- Working with other supervisors and department heads to improve media service.
- Implementing school library media standards and guidelines.
- Promoting a media concept in the school by incorporating media services in the center and developing mediographies.
- Assisting in selecting and organizing the media, including equipment.
- Coordinating the work of all media centers in the school system, including purchasing acquisitions and technical services.
- Providing for local production and distribution of instructional materials.
- Evaluating school library media services according to state, regional, and national standards or guidelines.
- Serving on curriculum committees and as a resource person to other specialists.
- Initiating and directing in-service programs on school library media center materials and services for faculty.
- Recruiting and directing a qualified staff.
- Preparing and administering a budget, annual and specific reports, and articles.
- Participating in professional organizations and conferences.
- Providing a center where educational media can be examined and evaluated.
- Exploring the use of new technology, such as scanners, digital cameras, multimedia projectors, and so forth.
- Fostering research and experimentation with instructional uses of media and arrangements of media services as well as applying the results of research to the program.

Supervision in the Individual School

In a school library media center that has a small staff and lacks a supervisor on the district level, the school library media specialist assumes that supervisory role and carries out as many as possible of the district-wide functions that have been enumerated. The specialists in individual schools may consult directly with state and federal school library media departments. Other agencies, such as public and university library consortia, will also give advice and aid to the school library media specialist.

In addition to the important policymaking and program-coordinating functions, another basic task for the program administrator is staff evaluation. The sample evaluation checklist that follows can be used by both the individual who is being evaluated and by the evaluator. Both parties should independently fill out the checklist and then discuss the two perceptions. The media specialist self-evaluative checklist (Exhibit 6.3) should include, in priority, the expected perceptions. Therefore, it is desirable that each evaluation form correspond closely to the pertinent lists of duties and the announced and understood expectations of the designated authority.

MANUALS

Guides and manuals are another important aspect of staff development in school library media centers. They provide the staff with the tools they need to give efficient and more consistent service. The library staff uses manuals to enable them to follow established patterns that produce beneficial results. Aside from neighboring media centers, which may have developed some manuals, and nearby library and information science colleges, which may have examples in their libraries, some state departments of education have developed procedural manuals for use in all school media centers.

Manuals provide a rationale and a handy guide to the operation of the school library media center for various groups. Some of the most common manuals are for staff, student assistants, volunteers, and the community. Although each school library media center is different and needs to develop its own personalized manual, there are a few common concerns central to them all. The first is the district educational philosophy, which is followed by the school library media center educational rationale, which flows from the district's. The harmony of these statements and the further agreement of every procedure or role that appears with this basic philosophy is vital. No loophole should exist due to lack of logic. Another consideration is the common sense principle that the manual or guide should enable its readers to accomplish the purpose for which it is composed, for example, the student assistants should be able to do the task described and the community should be able to tell at least the educational philosophy, hours, rules, services, and any special community services. The latter will, of course, be highlighted in manuals for community use.

Exhibit 6.3.
Media Specialist Self Evaluation Checklist.

(1 = Excellent; 2 = Good; 3 = Satisfactory; 4 = Poor; 5 =Inadequate)

How do you rate in:	1	2	3	4	5
Helping to plan scheduling and delivery systems?					
Do the systems agree with the district educational policy?　　　Yes__　　No__					
Are the teachers and students satisfied?					
Scheduling the use of facilities?					
Do attendance policies encourage students to come for instructional and recreational purposes?					
Do the teachers think so?					
Participation in curriculum committees?					
Do you participate in any?　　　Yes____ No____					
In how many would a school library media specialist be able to work?　　Number_____					
Integrating classroom work with media center programs?					
Do you collaboratively plan and teach content units and information literacy skills with the classroom teacher?					
Providing access to the Internet and training students and teachers in its use?					
Introducing teachers to newest technology?					
Do you use a regular system for keeping teachers aware?					
Informing teachers of new services?					
Do you use a regular system for keeping teachers aware?					
Working with students in reading, viewing, and listening?					

Exhibit 6.3. (continued)

(1 = Excellent; 2 = Good; 3 = Satisfactory; 4 = Poor;   5 =Inadequate)

Are the students aware And satisfied with your group/individual help?					
Are you satisfied too?					
Compiling media lists?					
Do you do this on a regular basis, as needed?					
Keeping abreast of selection information?					
How many reviews of media do you regularly look at specifically for selection purposes?					
Do you do this selection as part of your work or on home time? Work___Home____					
Helping to evaluate and select media?					
Do you participate in this task as much as you can? Yes____No___					
Organizing and reserving special collections?					
Do you actively encourage the development of reserve collections? Yes__ No__					
Performing general reference services?					
Are you generally able to solve most reference requests? Yes___ No___					
Administering resource sharing and interlibrary loan?					
Do you actively encourage interlibrary loans? Yes__ No__					
Instructing students in research techniques?					
Conducting in-service courses?					
Do you have a good background or desire to teach in-service courses for teachers? Yes___ No___					

Exhibit 6.3. (continued)

Orienting students?					
Do you have a plan for conducting orientation? Yes___ No___					
Is it satisfactory to the students, teachers, and you? Yes__ No__					
Training student assistants and volunteers?					
How many do you train annually? Number:_____					
Initiating projects and activities with teachers?					
Can you highlight one or more activities that you planned and implemented with teachers the past year? Yes__ No __					
Conducting programs for special interest groups?					
Can you highlight programs you originated and conducted for this purpose, as distinct from the above? Yes__ No__					
Outlining and conducting public relations?					
Within the past year, what are some things, e.g., writing articles for the school or local newspaper, for which you were responsible in public relations for the school library media center?					
Continuing growth in education?					
Have you done anything within the past year that would show this growth? Yes__ No__					
Attitude toward students?					
Do you agree with and maintain the official district policy of discipline? Yes__ No__					
Performing any administrative procedures, such as processing of materials that has not been mentioned?					

Exhibit 6.3. (continued)

(1 = Excellent; 2 = Good; 3 = Satisfactory; 4 = Poor; 5 =Inadequate)

The production of materials?					
Do you use your skill in this work for student and teacher satisfaction? Yes__ No__					
Helping to evaluate the media center programs?					
Is evaluation an automatic part of your assessment procedure for the program? Yes__ No__					
Public relations among the following:					
Students					
Media center staff					
Teachers					
Building administrators					
Other administrators					

Manuals and guides are generally of three types: policy, procedures (or a combination), and public relations. A policy manual contains a statement explaining the basic position for each category, for example, for production and for selection (see Exhibit 6.4, Sample Content for Staff Policy Manual). In a procedural operations manual, the procedure required by each task is described. One method of constructing this type of staff manual is to outline the typical work procedure for each responsibility listed on the job description (see Exhibit 6.5, Sample Staff Manual—Student Assistants). The policy and procedures manuals can be combined if desired. The manual for public relations should tell the reader, at a minimum, the location, hours, rules, public services, educational philosophy, and special community programs in clear terms. (Three sample contents for manuals are shown in Exhibits 6.4, 6.5, and 6.6.)

Exhibit 6.4.
Sample Content for Staff Policy Manual.

- o Full Identification (Address)

- o District educational philosophy

- o Media center mission statement

- o Media center philosophy statement

- o School Library Media Center rationale

- o Roles of school library media specialists (Means of reaching staff)

- o Scheduling of media center (includes video viewing room & computer lab)

- o Budget and report examples

- o The collection (Selection objectives, procedures, procedures for handling challenged materials)

- o Maintenance of collection

- o Internet access (Regulations, including eligibility and identification means)

- o Circulation

- o Media center arrangement (floor plan)

- o The learning environment

- o Local production of materials

- o Services (loan, interlibrary loan, reference, manual and online, and so forth.)

  - o Services to students

  - o Services to teachers

  - o Services to administrators

  - o Services to community

- o Days and hours of service

- o Description of major holdings

- o Date

Exhibit 6.5.
Sample Staff Manual—Student Assistants.

o Message from media specialist

o Important papers (School Library Bill of Rights,
   confidentiality of records, and so forth)

o Policies and responsibilities

o Arrangement of media center

o Dewey Decimal classification

o Circulation and other school library media center
   procedures, for example, processing)

o Internet access (regulations)

o Rules for data entry into OPAC

o Procedures for inventory

o List and location of supplies

o Displays and bulletin board procedures

o School library media clubs

o Services

o Housekeeping chores

o Date

FUTURE

Although the immediate future of the school library media center may
be threatened by the economic reality of lowered budgets, the continuing
disparate attitudes among media specialists, and the unsettled political
position in education, the history of the media center movement indicates
that there is a cyclical and developing nature to this important part of
American education. The decade of the 2000s calls for redoubled efforts
and long-range optimism for the future of school media centers. Both
budget problems and national political attitudes toward American education must continue to be addressed realistically and constructively. These

Exhibit 6.6.
Sample Public Relations Community Handbook.

---

o Identification (Address and location in building)

o Hours of service

o Regulations

o Message from media specialist

o Message from principal

o Local official names of sponsoring group (Friends of the media center, and so forth)

o Scenario of public services

o Philosophy of media center statement

o Mission of media center statement

o Community resources

o Special community programs

o The collection (selection policy, procedures for all materials, procedures for handling challenged materials.

o Reading, viewing, and listening references

o Access to the Internet (acceptable use policy)

o A note about new things in the center

o Logos

o Date

---

factors, however, should not be used as a rationale for doing less than a superlative job. The object, as always, is to have the best staff possible.

There are many encouraging signs for the future; one is the leadership shown by many states in developing information literacy skills. Another encouraging sign is the forming of an AASL Recruitment Task Force in 2001 to study the shortage of school library media specialists throughout the nation and to develop recruitment procedures for bringing more people into the profession. A consortium of library schools are discussing the sharing of courseware for teaching distance education courses for school media specialists as a solution to solving the school media specialist shortage. An equally encouraging sign for the future of the school media center's importance in schools is the research done in many states that supports the idea that school media centers with professionally staffed school media specialists affect student achievement.

REFERENCES

American Association of School Librarians & Association for Educational Communications and Technology. (1988). *Information power: Guidelines for school library media programs.* Chicago & Washington, DC: Authors.

American Association of School Librarians & Association for Educational Communications and Technology. (1998). *Information power: Building partnerships for learning.* Chicago: Authors.

American Library Association & Association for Educational Communications and Technology. (1975). *Media programs district and school.* Chicago and Washington, DC: Authors.

American Library Association & National Education Association. (1969). *Standards for school library programs.* Chicago and Washington, DC: Authors.

Eisenberg, Mike and Judi Repman. (1997, May–June). The sky is falling, the sky is falling...or is it? *Technology Connection, 4*(3), 20–21.

Everhart, Nancy. (2002, June). Filling the void: Many states are taking steps to remedy the rising shortage of school librarians. *School Library Journal, 48*(6), 44–49. Retrieved April 6, 2004, from: http://slj.reviewsnews.com/index.asp?layout=articlePrint&articleID=CA219977 and http://slj.reviewsnews.com/index.asp?layout=articlePrint&articleID=CA218584

Glick, Andrea. (2000, November). Raising the bar: School librarianship requirements in Texas. *School Library Journal, 46*(11), 17.

Hicks, Warren B. (1981). *Managing the building-level school library media program.* Chicago: AASL & ALA, pp. 14–20.

McNeely, Margaret (2004, May 28). School library media supervisory position at the U.S. Department of Education, personal communication. May 28, 2002.

Missouri Department of Elementary and Secondary Education Division of School Improvement—Curriculum Services. (2002, February 7). *The school library media standards handbook, chapter 4: Personnel.* Retrieved April 6, 2004, from Missouri Department of Elementary and Secondary Education web site: http://www.dese.state.mo.us/divimprove/curriculum/library/Chapter_4.pdf

National Board for Professional Teaching Standards. (2003, October 17). *Early childhood through young adulthood/library media.* Retrieved April 8, 2004, from: http://www.nbpts.org/candidates/guide/whichcert/24EarlyChildYoungLibMedia2004.html

Perritt, Patsy H. (2000, June). Getting certified in 50 states: The latest requirements for school librarians. *School Library Journal, 46*(6), 50–73.

Texas Education Agency. (2000, October 9). *Texas school libraries: Standards, resources, services and students' performance.* Retrieved April 6, 2004, from: http://www.tsl.state.tx.us/ld/pubs/schlibsurvey/index.html

Texas State Library and Archives Commission. (2001, October 17). *School library programs: Standards and guidelines for Texas.* Retrieved April 6, 2004, from the Texas State Library & Archives Commission web site: http://www.tsl.state. tx.us/ld/schoollibs/standards.html

FURTHER READINGS

American Library Association. (2002). *ALCTS task force on meeting the continuing needs of paraprofessionals report.* Retrieved April 17, 2004, from the ALA web site: http://web.archive.org/web/20020220052332/http://www.ala.org/alcts/ publications/educ/paraprof.html

American Library Association. (2003). *ALA education and careers.* Retrieved April 6, 2004, from the ALA web site: http://www.ala.org/education/

American Library Association. (2003, April 28). *Position statement on the school library media supervisor.* Retrieved April 6, 2004, from the ALA web site: http://www.ala.org/Content/NavigationMenu/AASL/Professional_Tools10/ Position_Statements/AASL_Position_Statement_on_the_School_Library_ Media_Supervisor

American Library Association. (2004). Committee on Education. *Task force for review of the criteria for programs to prepare library technical assistants.* Retrieved April 17, 2004, from ALA web site: http://www.ala.org/ala/hrdrbucket/ 3rdcongressonpro/criteriaprograms.htm#TOP

American Library Association. (2004). Library employment resources. Retrieved April 6, 2004, from the ALA web site: http://www.ala.org/ala/hrdr/ libraryempresources/libraryemployment.htm

Bard, Therese B. (1999). *Student assistants in the school library media center.* Westport, CT: Libraries Unlimited.

Baule, Steven M. (2001). Appendix F: Sample Information Technology Job Descriptions. In *Technology planning for effective teaching and learning* (pp. 130–135). Worthington, OH: Linworth.

Broida, Bethany. (2000, December). School enrollment: The echo goes to high school. *School Planning and Management, 39*(12), 27. Retrieved from Gale Student Resource Center Gold Database.

Council on Library/Media Technicians. (2000). *U.S. library technician programs.* Retrieved April 17, 2004, from the Library of the University of California, Riverside web site: http://web.archive.org/web/2003041202473/http://colt. ucr.edu/ltprograms.html

Directory of institutions offering accredited master's programs in library and informa-
tion studies. (2003). Retrieved April 6, 2004, from the ALA web site: http://
www.ala.org/alaorg/oa/lisdir.html

Farmer, Lesley S.J. (1997). *Training student library staff.* Worthington, OH: Linworth.

Georgetown Independent School District. (n.d.). *Library services: Library proce-*
dures manual. Retrieved April 8, 2004, from Georgetown Independent School
District web site: http://web.archive.org/web/20021223222706/http://www.
georgetown.txed.net/curriculum/libraries/manual2.htm

Glick, Andrea. (2000, November). Raising the bar: Texas does away with an easy
route to school librarianship. *School Library Journal, 46*(11), 17.

Halifax Regional School Board. (2002). *Human resources: Library assistant/techni-*
cian (schools): Job description. Retrieved April 17, 2004, from the Halifax
Regional School Board web site: http://web.archive.org/web/2021215064030/
http://jobs.hrsb.ns.ca/job-postings/descriptions/Library_Asst-Tech_Final.html

How to update or write job descriptions. (1998). Retrieved April 6, 2004, from the
University of Maryland web site: http://www.personnel.umd.edu/OrgDev/
PrdWebPage/how_to_update_or_write_job_description.htm

How to write a mission statement. (2002). Retrieved April 6, 2004, from the Grantsmanship Center web site: http://www.tgci.com/magazine/98fall/mission.asp

Hutchinson, Carol-Anne. (2002, February). The patchwork quilt that is staffing.
Teacher Librarian, 29(3), 60–61.

Johnson, Doug. (1997). *The indispensable librarian: Surviving (and thriving) in*
school media centers in the information age. Worthington, OH: Linworth.

Kentucky Department of Education. (2001, August). *Beyond proficiency: Achieving*
a distinguished library media program. Retrieved April 6, 2004, from the Kentucky Department of Education web site: http://www.kentuckyschools.net/
NR/rdonlyres/e6fusqvaxv4qioser3ewdfuds22dgh633h2q3ylnns7ttm5gp7ysrh
eqevzumavl5fc7wldtowp6dq4ehgku3t2xxhc/beyondproficiency.pdf

Lau, Debra. (2002, September). What does your boss think about you? *School*
Library Journal, 48(9), 52–55. Retrieved April 17, 2004, from: http://web.
archive.org/web/20040417164132/http://slj.reviewsnews.com/index.asp?layout
=articlePrint&articleID=CA240049&publication=slj

Library service in the new century: Final report of the regents commission on library
services. (2000, July 14). Retrieved April 6, 2004, from the University of the
State of New York web site: http://www.nysl.nysed.gov/rcols/finalrpt.htm

Lowe, Carrie. (2001, October). The role of the school library media specialist in
the 21st century. *Teacher Librarian, 29*(1), 30–33.

McKenzie, Jamie. (2000, January). The new library in the wired school. [Elec-
tronic version]. *From Now On: The Educational Technology Journal, 9*(5).
Retrieved April 6, 2004, from the *From Now On* web site: http://www.
fno.org/jan2000/newlibrary.html

Meadville media center policy and procedure manual. (2002, February 5). Retrieved April 6, 2004, from Crawford Central School District web site: http://www.tnte.com/mmc/policy.html

No increase in the number of school librarians in Colorado. (2003, March 10). *Fast Facts, ED3 110.10*(190). Retrieved April 6, 2004, from the Library Research Service web site: http://www.lrs.org/documents/fastfacts/190_no_increase_school_librarians.pdf

One out of four Colorado public schools has no librarian. (2002, November 7). *Fast Facts, ED3 110.ED3, 110.10*(186). Retrieved April 6, 2004, from the Library Research Service web site: http://www.lrs.org/documents/fastfacts/186School_libns.pdf

Peto, Erica, et al. (1998). *Tech team: Student technology assistants in the elementary and middle school.* Worthington, OH: Linworth.

Riedling, Ann M. (2001, November/December). In search of who we are: The school library media specialist in the 21st century. *The Book Report, 20*(3), 28–31.

Staffing recommendations national, regional and state. (2002, March 14). *Prince William County Schools Librarian's Handbook.* Retrieved April 6, 2004, from: http://www.pwcs.edu/curriculum/stafflibrary/handbook/chapter_iv/iv.2.v.staffing.doc

Stilwell, William E. (2001, September 20). *Certification requirements for 50 states.* Retrieved April 6, 2004 from University of Kentucky web site: http://www.uky.edu/Education/TEP/usacert.html

U.S. Department of Labor Bureau of Labor Statistics. (2002). Library Technicians. *Occupational outlook handbook (2004–2005 ed.).* Retrieved April 6, 2004, from the Bureau of Labor Statistics web site: http://www.bls.gov/oco/

Washington Library Media Association. (2002). *Qualities and competencies for staffing an effective library media program.* Retrieved April 6, 2004, from the Washington Library Media Association web site: http://www.wlma.org/Professional/jobdescriptions.htm

Wisconsin Department of Public Instruction. (2002). Information and technology staffing. In *Information & technology literacy: A collaborative planning guide for library media and technology* (pp. 17–23). Madison, WI: Author.

Chapter 7

FACILITIES

School library media center facilities share a common purpose: to provide the physical surroundings in which the media needs of the school can be met to accomplish the mission, goals, and objectives of the library media program. Because schools have different goals and diverse media, each facility will vary to reflect the instructional requirements of the curriculum and the use of changing technologies. The facilities may, however, vary considerably in size, shape, design, and age of building or renovation. In a society characterized by change, the maxim of an earlier and more stable era, "form follows function," is now more realistically phrased as "form permits function." A school library media program, therefore, is shaped to some extent by the design, size, shape, and age of its facilities. Well-designed spaces add an important dimension to the program and enrich the school community.

This chapter covers the major points that a school library media specialist should consider in designing or remodeling a facility. Preplanning and planning with various individuals and groups are treated first, followed by a discussion of space requirements for the six major kinds of activities that take place in a center. Annotated web sites for floor plans are included. Suggestions are given for such elements as lighting, thermal environment, electrical power, acoustics, color, and furnishings. A short list of companies widely known for their school library media furnishings is included (See Appendix 3). Also treated briefly are facilities for expensive media services, that would normally be handled through a district media facility. Although the guidelines in this chapter can be used for designing a center in a new school building, the focus is on renovating school library media quarters. Specialists are advised to consult other technical sources. Some suggestions for further reading are listed at the end of the chapter.

PLANNING

The expression "form permits function" has direct application in planning school library media centers, whether the goal is designing a new facility with an architect or initiating a simple remodeling project with the help of a principal. In either case, the chief school administrator has the prime responsibility and his or her approval is needed. To plan a functional facility, a knowledgeable school library media program administrator/ school library media specialist and consultant must work together with the school administrator and architect in carefully assessing the desired outcomes of the project. Additional information can come from studying plans of other schools and visiting successful school library media centers. Many districts have found it helpful to use special consultants to advise on various matters concerning facilities. Staff, faculty, students, and other persons who will be the primary users of the center should also be involved in the planning to determine the relationship of the library media facility to the total school instructional program. Experience has shown that it is vital to have the cooperation of all groups in the school setting, from the administrator to the community users. Designs have failed because there was little or no consultation, especially at the planning stage, with those who would be using the center facilities for work, study, or recreation.

The steps in the planning process are important. Planning for library media facilities should begin as soon as the decision is made to construct, expand, or renovate a facility. Library media specialists must assume leadership in the planning process and be actively involved in the decision-making aspects of the project.

Planning involves the following steps:

1. Evaluate the existing or proposed library media program with respect to the school's educational mission, philosophy, goals, and objectives.

2. Develop a vision statement that describes the benefactors of the school media program and its importance to the school.

3. Determine a needs assessment that looks at the media program now and compares it with where you want it to be in the future.

4. Provide a list of activities that will take place in the media center, the number of people involved, and the kinds of resources needed.

5. Consider future projections of the library media program, new technology, and potential changes in delivery of information and ideas as they relate to future instructional programs.

6. Develop a written plan that incorporates guidelines suggested by the library media profession and adheres to the school system and the state guidelines. Include a statement of the philosophy, goals and objectives of the school library media program in relation to school and district philosophy and goals.

7. Provide a detailed written statement defining all spaces within the library facility, the size of the space, its users and its function as well as the relationship of the space to other areas within the library media center and the larger context of the building. Include in the list special environmental, technological, and furnishing considerations, as well as a list of fixed and movable equipment and other pertinent information.

8. Develop a long-range plan for the media center, including how technology will be used.

9. Constant monitoring is required throughout the planning process by the building level library media specialist, the district media supervisor, and the building principal to assure that program needs are understood by the architect and builder. The library media specialist must be a part of all decisions about revisions to the facilities. All revision decisions must be approved by the board of education and district administrators.

10. Develop a furniture plan that keeps in mind acoustics, thermal considerations, color, texture, flexibility of design, traffic flow, lighting, security system, and so forth. Normally architects do not consult media specialists for this information; however, having a viable furniture plan can be helpful in getting appropriate furniture for the center (Information Power [AASL & AECT], 1988; Erikson & Markuson, 2001).

Factors to investigate in the introductory planning phase are the nature of the curriculum and the teaching methods in the school, the clientele of the center, what routines and services must be accommodated, and the type and quantity of the materials, equipment, and technology to be housed. Future projections of the number of students, new services, and the size of collections should also be considered.

Other factors that influence planning are the overall design of the school building, the accessibility of community resources, technology used throughout the school, and the number of departmental or decentralized collections available elsewhere in the school or district. The importance of this initial study by the school library media specialist cannot be stressed enough. If the program is examined carefully and written down before any blueprints are drawn, it will be possible to tell the administrator and architect exactly what is needed and why.

Each school library media program takes on the characteristics of its facility. No one design can be singled out as the best; each center has a character of its own. The design of today's school library media centers stresses openness and flexibility in dividing space and providing for individual and group use with the inclusion of areas for computing, reading, viewing, and listening.

SPACE

Space requirements of the school library media center depend on the organizational pattern of the instructional program, the commitment to media services in that program, and the funds available for either new construction or remodeling. When a new or remodeled media center is planned, the first step is usually to consider location. The facility should be centrally located and accessible to all who will participate in the instructional program. It is desirable that it be near the principal's office and near the major instructional classrooms. Avoid proximity to such noise-producing areas as bus-loading zones, cafeterias, or band practice rooms. The quarters should be placed where access to the rest of the building can be restricted if necessary. This restriction facilitates use of the center in the evenings, on Saturdays, or during the summer months when the rest of the school might be closed. Restrooms need to be in this restricted area. A facility that opens to the outside permits easy delivery of materials as well as after-hours access. It needs to be as close as possible to the teacher workroom to encourage teacher use of the center and to allow them access to resources. A computer lab needs to be inside in the media center or in close proximity. The layout of the media center should permit good supervision by the school library media specialist and should encourage efficient space usage. Noise generating activities in the media center, such as production of instructional materials and group study, need to be confined in the rear of the media center rather than in several areas throughout the center. Carpeting on the floors and sound-absorbent materials on ceilings and walls help to eliminate noise. All media centers need multiple telephone lines to encourage borrowing of resources from other libraries as well as Internet access. Intercoms connecting classrooms with the media center encourage teachers to schedule media center use in advance and to request information and materials directly. (Maine Association of School Libraries, 1999; Wisconsin Department of Public Instruction, 2002).

The first step in planning media center space is to look at possible future expansion. When the original facility is located with future remodeling in mind, it will be away from stairwells, lavatories, or expensive permanent facilities that require great structural change. It will be near relatively open spaces, such as classrooms, so that walls can be removed and extensive remodeling accomplished if necessary. Expansion is also made easier if there is as least one exterior wall that faces an unused space or an interior court.

An important second step in space planning is awareness of the needs of the physically handicapped as they relate to the school library media center. Barrier-free routes are needed, with particular attention given to book stack seating areas as well as access to the online public access catalog (OPAC) and circulation areas. In multi-level buildings, an elevator or ramp will facilitate easy access. Special accommodations that are aesthetically pleasing for use by the visually or physically handicapped should be included in all plans by designing easily accessible carrels and equipment for their use.

A third step in the allocation of space is consideration of size. The school library media center is often designed as an activity area that students, teachers, and other persons frequent not only for media but also for the experience of learning. The variety of spaces throughout the facility should accommodate all activities that assist in developing and encouraging imagination and inquisitiveness about learning among the school community. The design of the facility should be flexible enough to accommodate new technology as needed and to access a vast array of information sources. Regardless of size, the design should simplify supervision for the library staff while allowing efficient traffic flow.

A fourth step in planning space is the arrangement within the facility. Consideration should be given to how the facility is divided to create a learning environment that facilitates the use of a variety of media, enhances inquiry, and motivates students to use computers, materials, and services necessary for creative learning.

Exact figures for the recommended size of a school library media center can serve only as guidelines for individual situations. Such variables as enrollment, size and nature of collections, technology needs, anticipated population, and services to be offered are important in determining space needs. There are several sources that provide square footage figures by percentage of pupils enrolled for functional areas, which is helpful in establishing footage requirements. The following are some helpful web sites from state departments of education for footage and other facility planning information:

MAINE
http://www.maslibraries.org/about/facilities/hand-book.html
 This site is one of the best for planning media center facilities. It includes a detailed description of essential areas, a discussion of general considerations, and comparison tables of library areas for schools of different sizes. A bibliography of planning resources is available as well.

MASSACHUSETTS: FACILITIES
http://www.mslma.org/whoweare/standards/standards.pdf
 Within the document *Massachusetts School Library Media Program Standards for 21st Century Learning* (2003) is a section on school library media facilities, which includes design and fundamental issues.

TEXAS: FACILITIES
http://www.tea.state.tx.us/technology/libraries/lib_st andards_library_fac.html
 Facilities for exemplary, recognized, acceptable and below standard school media centers is described at this site.

WISCONSIN: DESIGN CONSIDERATIONS FOR SCHOOL LIBRARY MEDIA CENTERS.
http://www.dpi.state.wi.us/dpi/dltcl/imt/desgnlmc.html
 This one page document gives suggestions for planning the location and design of a school library media center. Appendix N includes facility planning.

WISCONSIN: CLASSROOMS, LIBRARY MEDIA CENTERS, AND NEW TECHNOLOGY
Accessed October 5, 2002
http://www.dpi.state.wi.us/dpi/dltcl/imt/dsgn-1pg.html
 Within this document is a section about what library media centers needs when considering their design. Pitfalls to avoid are listed.

The minimum square footage space allocations can vary depending on what state requirements are. As a general rule, square footage for the different types of media centers need to exceed the minimum requirements because most guidelines are not adequate. Some minimum standards are listed here:

5,000 sq. ft.: elementary schools

7,000 sq. ft.: middle schools

10,000 sq. ft.: high school

These spaces should accommodate about ten to fifteen percent of the entire school population at any given time, with a minimum average of 50 elementary students, 70 middle school students, and 100 high school students. Most media centers have certain spaces that are considered essential areas that need to be included in all media centers regardless of grade levels served. The Maine Association of School Librarians (1999) provides a detailed description of the essential areas of a school media center in Exhibit 7.1.

Schools that produce their own television programs and have a computer lab will also need the following: (1) soundproof 40 × 40-foot television studio and control room with 15-foot ceiling and 14 × 12-foot doors, storage space for television properties, visuals, and so on—800 square feet minimum; (2) office with work space, placed back-to-back with television studio—1,200 square feet minimum; (3) 12 × 12-foot audio studio and control space, which may be near the television studio; (4) computer lab—900 square feet minimum.

The Texas Education Agency (2001) provides some guidelines or standards for judging whether a school's facilities are exemplary, recognized, acceptable or below standard. Their guidelines are shown in Exhibit 7.2.

FACILITIES FOR MAJOR FUNCTIONS

In general, areas for five major groups of functions should be worked into a plan for any school library media center: (1) reading, listening, and viewing; (2) computing or virtual library area; (3) distributing, organizing, and storing the collection; (4) producing instructional materials; (5) maintaining, storing, and repairing equipment; (6) administering of the media center.

Reading, Listening, and Viewing Areas

To reflect the emphasis on instruction in the school, reading, listening, viewing, and computing areas should be usable by large and small groups and by individuals-teachers as well as students. To accommodate these activities, a main study/reading area and adjoining rooms of various sizes

Exhibit 7.1. Detailed Descriptions of Essential Areas of the Media Center.

Library Media Center Space	Functions/Activities/Special Considerations	Equipment /Furnishings
Entrance 200-300 Sq. ft	Area where traffic flow is heavy, flows into circulation area.	Entrance for floors, attractive, durable materials such as ceramic or quarry tile. Very little furniture required. Display cases and possibly plants.
Circulation 600-1000 Ft	Area where media and materials are checked in and out. Area for returns (book drop). Should include information desk. Usually located near the library media center's main entrance. Carpet should have extra padding.	* network access * electrical outlets * charge desk and staff work area * public access catalogs * circulation computer * shelving for reserves and special collections * book carts/trucks * security system * display * telephone / intercom * cubbies for book bags * book drop * copier
General Reading, Browsing, Listening and Viewing (Student pop x 10% x 40 sq. ft.) *This area will include:*	Central room of library media center for student and faculty use. Allows adequate space for shelves (wall and free standing). Visible supervision by library personnel is a consideration. Creative use of shelving and furniture may be used to define areas in the library, which accommodate a variety of functions and different sized groups. The areas described below need not be discrete areas, but may overlap or flow into one another.	* network access * electrical outlets * carpeting * adequate lighting (natural and artificial) * acoustical treatment * variety of seating (such as carrels, lounge chairs, standard tables and chairs) for reading, quiet study, viewing, listening and research for individuals and groups of different sizes * computer stations for information retrieval using current and emerging technologies

Exhibit 7.1. (continued)

		* individual audiovisual equipment with headphones * clock * display * photocopier
Circulating collection 1000 Sq. ft per 10,000 volumes	core collection (fiction and non-fiction)	* network access * electrical outlets * shelves (adjustable and movable, with consideration given to height of students in the building and with accommodation to ADA regulations) * public access catalog(s)
reference and electronic information	non-circulating materials used for research (e.g. encyclopedias, dictionaries, gazetteers, atlases) and to include Internet and telecommunications access, CD-ROM and emerging technologies	* network access * electrical outlets * shelves (adjustable) * atlas and dictionary stands * computer stations for information retrieval using current and emerging technologies * storage space * printers
periodicals	print, microform and on-line issues of serial publications (e.g. magazines, newspapers, journals)	* electrical outlets * display rack for current periodicals * newspaper rack * microfiche / microfilm reader printer(s)
audiovisual software storage	commercially and locally produced software for student and teacher use (e.g. videotapes, laser disks, CD-ROMs, CDs, audio cassettes)	* adjustable shelving (open and closed) * storage cabinets
vertical file	an organized collection of materials such as newspaper clippings, maps, pamphlets, brochures, pictures	* file cabinet with hanging folders.
general storage	back issues of periodicals, media and seldom used materials	* adjustable shelving * cabinets

Exhibit 7.1. (continued)

Group Instruction Room 800 – 1000 Sq. ft	area for direct instruction, reading aloud, storytelling, book talks, puppet shows, video conferencing, meeting space	* network access * electrical outlets * lightening and darkening capabilities * carpeted risers or stairs * flat area with chairs and tables * whiteboard * bulletin board * flannel board * magnetic board * podium or lectern * provision for audio / video recording * projection capabilities for computer images, VCR, overhead and other resources * projection screen * computer with appropriate interface * television monitor (27" minimum)
Electronic Multimedia Production Area 800-1000 Sq. ft	area for school community to design, develop, and produce multimedia products; may include sound controlled space for audio-video recording; should be accessible by groups without disrupting activities in other areas of the library.	*acoustical vinyl or tile floors * network access * electrical plug mold around the perimeter of the room * multimedia computers with sufficient RAM capacity and hard drive capacity as required by memory intensive graphics applications; with 17" monitors. * television monitor (32" minimum) for final products * color printer * additional electrical outlets in central work areas * audio and video recording equipment * assorted software and equipment for graphics production * color copier * editing / viewing equipment

Exhibit 7.1. (continued)

		* scanner * video camera * digital camera * work tables * S video capacity * storage capacity
Electronic Control Area 550-700 Sq. ft	tile floored, secure area housing centralized electronic equipment, heavy duty capacity wiring on an independent circuit; located in a climate controlled space	* network access * electrical outlets * server(s) * CD-ROM tower(s) * media retrieval units * video distribution equipment * cable drops * wiring closet * emerging technologies * smart uninterrupted power supply for network / server shutdown
Workroom 600-800 Sq. ft	technical services area for minor repairs, materials processing, sorting, cataloging; may also include area for equipment storage and distribution and/or media production	*acoustical vinyl or tile floors * network access * electrical outlet(s) * paper cutter(s) * repair equipment and supplies * typewriter * shelving * Locking cupboards and/or cabinets * countertops with electrical plug mold and floor covering built to withstand heavy use. * sink with hot and cold water * tacking irons(s) * lamination equipment * computer station * telephone jack
Office for Media Center Administration	separate room for administration tasks, storage of administrative records and files, meetings and	* network access * cordless telephone * fax machine

Exhibit 7.1. (continued)

600-800 Sq. ft. If 2 libraries then add twice the space or 2 offices	conferences which allows an open view of the media center	* electrical outlets * intercom access * desk(s) * chair(s) * computer / printer * filing cabinet * shelving
Equipment Room 600-1000 Sq. ft	a secure room accessible to hallway, preferably adjacent to the workroom for storage, distribution, maintenance, and repair of hardware and software	*vinyl or tile floors for ease of movement of equipment same as wash room * network access * electrical outlets * work bench with electrical plug mold * cable TV outlet * telephone jack * storage racks / bins * storage for spare parts, accessories and general supplies * equipment service and repair tools * file cabinet(s) * pegboard(s) * shelves * computer station
	Recommended Additions	
Video Studio 800-1000 Sq. ft	secure and sound proof area for production and distribution of video programs; accessible without disrupting activities in other areas of the library; may also serve as ATM site for interactive distance learning and video conferencing (equipment - see ATM specifications; specialists lists in appendix); consider benefits of digital versus analog equipment.	*one wall painted blue for filming backdrop lined with sound absorbing material *vinyl or tile floor * network access * electrical outlets * built-in cabinets with locks * television cameras * tripods, dollies * video decks * mixers * microphones * lighting, track and movable * audio recording equipment * editing equipment * head end equipment

Exhibit 7.1. (continued)

		* amplifiers * table * chairs * counter work surfaces

Printed with permission. Maine Association of School Libraries Facilities Committee. (1999). *Maine School Libraries Facilities Handbook*. Retrieved April 8, 2004, from: http://www.maslibraries.org/about/facilities/detailed.html

are necessary. The combined area should be large enough to seat at least fifteen to thirty percent of the school population. An important consideration is visible control.

In the main area, approximately ten to thirty square feet is generally recommended as comfortable space for each user; it provides adequate room for furniture, aisles, and so on. Not more than 80–100 seats should be located in any one area, with experience suggesting the lesser figure as the maximum. If the reading area is to have larger seating capacity, it should be arranged in a variety of combinations of space within space; students and teachers often dislike one big room because it tends to be too noisy and too open. Flexibility for individual as well as group needs can be accommodated in the space-within-space design concept, which utilizes shelving to define areas for groups and individuals. Separate instructional rooms that are soundproof allow for better noise control in the center.

In school library media center planning, and especially in flexibly designed centers, the entire area should be visualized in sound zones in order to separate somewhat noisy group activities from quiet individual ones. For example, flexible-folding walls can create an area for large-group viewing; a furniture arrangement or shelving can build a "quiet corner" for persons who need to concentrate. Informal seating areas with comfortable chairs may be placed in the area where periodicals are accessible for perusing.

Computing or Virtual Library Area

Some school library media centers provide a full range of computer services for both administration and teaching or learning applications. The

Exhibit 7.2. Facilities Standards

Goal: To provide design guidelines for facilities to allow for manipulation, production, and communication of information by all members of the learning community.			
Level of Support of Student Achievement			
Exemplary Program Development	Recognized Program Development	Acceptable Program Development	Below Standard Program Development
Principal 1. The design of the school library is aligned with the educational objectives of the learning community. The library environment is designed for flexible access and supports all educational objectives of the Library program...			
The Librarian:			
A. Seeks input from teachers, other school campus staff, district program staff, students, and parents regarding functionality of the library. In the event of renovation or design of new facilities, the Librarian works with a design professional or consultant to develop written specifications.	A. Seeks input from teachers, other school campus staff, district program staff, student, and parents regarding functionality of the library. In the event of renovation or design of new facilities, the Librarian works with a design professional or consultant to develop written specifications.	A. Works with a design professional or consultant to gather input from teachers, other school campus staff, and district program staff regarding functionality of the library. In the event of renovation or design of new facilities, the Librarian works with and provides input in developing written specifications.	A. Does not work with a design professional or consultant to gather input from teachers, other school campus staff, and district program staff regarding functionality of the library and does not provide written specifications.
B. Networks with (including site visits) local, regional, state, and national librarians to acquire trends in design and specifications and to develop an idea portfolio for future construction or renovation.	B. Networks with (including site visits) local and state librarians to acquire trends in design and specifications and to develop an idea portfolio for future construction or renovation.	B. Networks with local librarians to acquire trends in design and specifications.	B. Does not network with local, regional, state, and national librarians to acquire trends in design and specifications or develop an idea portfolio for future construction or renovation.

Exhibit 7.2. (continued)

Library Space Allocations

Exemplary Level	Recognized Level	Acceptable Level	Below Standard
Total Square Feet			
<100 Students			
At least 6400 square feet	At least 3900 square feet	At least 1400 square feet	Less than 1400 square feet
101-500 Students			
At least 6400 square feet plus an additional 4.0 square feet for each student in excess of 100	At least 3900 square feet plus an additional 4.0 square feet for each student in excess of 100.	At least 1400 square feet plus an additional 4.0 square feet for each student in excess of 100.	Less than 1400 square feet plus an additional 4.0 square feet for each student in excess of 100.
501-2000 Students			
At least 8000 square feet plus 3.0 square feet for each student in excess of 500.	At least 5500 square feet plus 3.0 square feet for each student in excess of 500.	At least 3000 square feet plus 3.0 square feet for each student in excess of 500.	Less than 3000 square feet plus 3.0 square feet for each student in excess of 500.
2001+ Students			
At least 12,500 square feet plus an additional 2.0 square feet for each student in excess of 2000.	At least 10,000 square feet plus an additional 2.0 square feet for each student in excess of 2000.	At least 7500 square feet plus an additional 2.0 square feet for each student in excess of 2000.	Less than 7500 square feet plus an additional 2.0 square feet for each student in excess of 2000.

Computer/On-line Reference Area. Libraries with more than 12 student computers shall add 25 square feet of space for each additional computer anticipated.

Reading/Instructional Area and Reference/Independent Study Area shall be 30% of library space.

Stack Area, Circulation Desk Area, and Computer/Online Reference Areas shall be 45% of library space.

Necessary Ancillary Areas and Staff Area shall be 25% of library space.

Windows shall be placed so that adequate wall and floor space remains to accommodate the shelving necessary for the library collection size established by the School Library Standards and Guidelines.

Benefits for Students

Students:

- Access state of the art technology and resources in an ergonomically suitable environment.
- Communicate through local and wide area networks.
- Have space within the library to create a variety of projects including production and communication in a variety of formats.

Exhibit 7.2. (continued)

Principal 2. The library is designed to serve as a flexible, functional, and barrier-free simultaneous-use facility for individuals, small groups, and classes as described by state and federal guidelines. The library is also designed to maximize the use of available space to permit displays of student, faculty, and community-produced materials, and collections. The facility provides all members of the learning community opportunities to explore and meet their information and recreational needs during and beyond the school day. The library provides an exemplary level of safety, security, and an age-appropriate facility for all individuals, small groups, and classes.

Specifications for Library Facilities and Strategies for Librarians

In developing written specifications for library renovation and design of new facilities, the following should be considered.

A. The Library is a welcoming and appealing environment with displays and décor contributed by students and staff as reported in student and staff surveys at a satisfaction level of at least 90%.	A. The Library is a welcoming and appealing environment with displays and décor contributed by students and staff as reported in student and staff surveys at a satisfaction level of at least 80%.	A. The Library is a welcoming and appealing environment with displays and décor contributed by students and staff as reported in student and staff surveys at a satisfaction level of at least 55%.	A. The Library is a welcoming and appealing environment with displays and décor contributed by students and staff as reported in student and staff surveys at a satisfaction level of less than 55%.
B. At least 90% of Library shelving is adjustable with recommended standardized width of 36" and depth of 12", and located primarily on the perimeter of the library.	B. At least 80% of Library shelving is adjustable with recommended standardized width of 36" and depth of 12", and located primarily on the perimeter of the library.	B. At least 55% of Library shelving is adjustable with recommended standardized width of 36" and depth of 12", and located primarily on the perimeter of the library.	B. Less than 55% of Library shelving is adjustable with recommended standardized width of 36" and depth of 12", and located primarily on the perimeter of the library.
C. Shelving accommodates all shelved material with at least 25% extra shelf space for growth.	C. Shelving accommodates all shelved material with at least 10% extra shelf space for growth.	C. Shelving accommodates all material without extra shelf space for growth.	C. Shelving does not accommodate all shelved materials.
D. The library is designed to provide display space for community and student work on top of the shelves,	D. The library is designed to provide display space for community and student work on top of the shelves.	D. The library provides display space for community and student work on top of the shelves.	D. The library provides little or no display space for community and student work.

Exhibit 7.2. (continued)

on walls, and at special display areas.	and on walls.		
E. At least 90% of the Library furnishings and equipment is comfortable, age-appropriate, and ergonomic.	E. At least 80% of the Library furnishings and equipment is comfortable, age-appropriate, and ergonomic.	E. At least 55% of the Library furnishings and equipment is comfortable, age-appropriate, and ergonomic.	E. Less than 55% of the Library furnishings and equipment is comfortable, age-appropriate, and ergonomic.
F. The Library provides access to 100% of the special needs learners by complying with Americans with Disabilities Act (ADA) standards.	F. The Library provides access to 100% of the special needs learners by complying with Americans with Disabilities Act (ADA) standards.	F. The Library provides access to 100% of the special needs learners by complying with Americans with Disabilities Act (ADA) standards.	F. The Library provides access to less than 100% of the special needs learners and does not comply with Americans with Disabilities Act (ADA) standards.
G. Construction quality is in compliance with relevant local, state, and federal laws.	G. Construction quality is in compliance with relevant local, state, and federal laws.	G. Construction quality is in compliance with relevant local, state, and federal laws.	G. Construction quality is not in compliance with relevant local, state, and federal laws.
H. The physical design of the learning community convenient access and use for at least 15 hours per week beyond the instructional day.	H. The physical design of the learning community convenient access and use for at least 10 hours per week beyond the instructional day.	H. The physical design of the learning community convenient access and use for at least 5 hours per week beyond the instructional day.	H. The physical design of the Library does not allow the learning community convenient access and use beyond the instructional day.
I. The Library is ergonomically designed to be free of columns or other visual barriers to facilitate unobstructed view of the entire area to ensure adequate supervision of the site and the safety of learners.	I. The Library is ergonomically designed to be free of columns or other visual barriers to facilitate unobstructed view of at least 85% of the area to ensure adequate supervision of the site and the safety of learners.	I. The Library is ergonomically designed to be free of columns or other visual barriers to facilitate unobstructed view of at least 70% of the area to ensure adequate supervision of the site and the safety of learners.	I. The Library is not ergonomically designed to be free of columns or other visual barriers. The view of less than 70% of the area is obstructed and does not ensure adequate supervision of the site or the safety of learners.

Exhibit 7.2. (continued)

The Librarian:

J. Maintains sound collection management practices, assesses materials and resources inventory, and conducts a cost benefit analysis to determine if a security system is required. If justified, librarian advocates for the purchase of a security system to be installed at the library entrance.	J. Assesses materials and analyzes data to determine if a security system is required. If justified, librarian advocates for the purchase of a security system to be installed at the library entrance.	J. Does not track or report losses to the administration.
K. Is knowledgeable about professional standards such as the architectural and engineering standards published by the Illuminating Engineering Society (IES), for artificial and natural direct and indirect lighting. Librarian assesses library to determine if it is up to standard and advocates for needed improvements. When renovating an existing facility or designing a new facility, the librarian plans with the architect to design a library that	K. Is aware of professional standards such as the architectural and engineering standards published by the Illuminating Engineering Society (IES). When renovating an existing facility or designing a new facility, the librarian plans with the architect.	K. Is unaware of professional standards such as the architectural and engineering standards published by the Illuminating Engineering Society (IES).
	K. Uses professional librarian resources to recommend design or improvements when renovating an existing facility or designing a new facility, the librarian plans with the architect.	

Exhibit 7.2. (continued)

includes appropriate full spectrum lighting for each area of the library individually as well as for the overall facility at all times of the day; lighting controls for each area that are conveniently placed near the main entrance to the library and are individually controlled; and uniform illumination of all shelves.			L. Is unaware of conditions in the Library that optimally support the resources, technology, and facilities. Heating, ventilating, air conditioning, and climate control (HVAC) are not maintained as required in each of the environmental regions of the State.
L. Knows and advocates for conditions in the Library that optimally support the resources, technology, and facilities. Heating, ventilating, air conditioning, and climate control (HVAC) are maintained throughout the year as required in each of the environmental regions of the State. HVAC for the Library is separate from the rest of the school and controls are in the Library.	L. Is aware of conditions in the Library that support the resources, technology, and facilities. Librarian informs administration of the requirements for heating, ventilating, air conditioning, and climate control (HVAC) required to support the Library.	L. Is aware of conditions in the Library that support the resources, technology, and facilities. Heating, ventilating, air conditioning, and climate control (HVAC) are maintained when the school is in use.	
M. Arranges Library furniture, equipment and materials ergonomically to foster flexible, efficient and effective traffic flow and use of space and items.	M. Arranges Library furniture, equipment and materials to maximize space for flexible use. Arranges Library shelving and furniture in accordance with ADA.	M. Arranges Library furniture, equipment and materials in accordance with ADA.	M. Does not arrange Library furniture, equipment ergonomically or in compliance with ADA.

Exhibit 7.2. (continued)

Arranges Library shelving and furniture in accordance with ADA.			
N. Uses at least 90% of available display space on top of shelves, on walls, and in special areas to display student and community work.	N. Uses at least 80% of available display space on top of shelves, on walls, and in special areas to display student and community work.	N. Uses at least 55% of available display space on top of shelves, on walls, and in special areas to display student and community work.	N. Uses less than 55% of available display space on top of shelves, on walls, and in special areas to display student and community work.
Benefits for Students			
Students:			

- Access a Library that is a sanctuary that provides a non-threatening environment in which they pursue their individual interests, study independently, study with friends and groups, and attend meetings of student organizations.
- Utilize a Library that is designed and arranged to enhance its appeal and their ability to study.
- Students who are physically challenged utilize adaptive devices and furnishings to support their independent and barrier-free access to the Library.
- Display work and products in the Library.
- Utilize the Library to complete assignments during and beyond the instructional day.

amount of space allocated for computer services is determined by the nature of computer use and its relationship to the total instructional program of the school. At least three considerations should be included when deciding computer services:

1. The computer facilities throughout the school and their use.
2. The flexibility required for services such as an OPAC, Internet access, networking, and teleconferencing.
3. The library media center's relationship to other learning areas, such as distance learning labs, classroom computers, and so forth.

The computer areas may be located in a separate area within the media center; however, OPAC computers need to be located near the circulation desk and the reference desk. Classroom computers connected to the OPAC can facilitate the teaching of information literacy skills. Separate computer stations for Internet access or CD-ROMs need to be included in the computer area of the media center to allow for ease of access to information sources. Space for the following activities should be allowed: database searching, use of the OPAC or computer workstations, Internet online searching, and distance learning.

Schools moving toward a virtual library media center will need to allocate more space for computers with *Internet connectivity* through networks either within the school or outside. If an appropriate long-range technology plan is in place, it will allow the purchase of the necessary equipment and software in increments during a period of time. Planning ahead can eliminate many problems for the future. For a more detailed discussion of the virtual school library media center, networks, and Internet access see Chapter 10.

Telephone lines serve a valuable purpose in the media center. They allow access to the wealth of information outside the center found through the Internet, other libraries, and information agencies. A telephone or intercom system connecting the classrooms with the library media center encourages teachers to schedule classes in advance and to make requests for materials directly (Wisconsin Department of Public Instruction, n.d.). Group instruction rooms are essential for many school activities, including both large- and small-group work for discussing and working on projects, and previewing audiovisual or computer programs. If separate rooms are used, these should be next to or at least near the main reading room and should be soundproof. Flexibility in accommodating groups of varying sizes in a main area is one of the elements of good planning and design. In this type of arrangement, modular lighting and ventilation units are a necessity. Ideally, each separate room should be soundproof and contain darkening facilities. Sufficient electrical outlets are absolutely essential. They may be distributed on the walls, floors, tables, counters, and carrels to meet the needs of the instructional program. Even as wireless connections are more readily available, it is still a good idea to have plenty of electrical outlets in the media center. Furnishings may include retractable ceiling or wall screens, tables and chairs, shelving, and display stands. A soundproof computer lab inside the media center is desirable. In elementary school library media centers, a storytelling area equipped for electronic presentations and dramatizations is desirable to enhance the learning environment.

A large multipurpose area is frequently planned near the main area of the media center, which serves as a lecture hall, an audiovisual viewing room, a classroom, or a meeting area. Here, instruction may be given to an entire class, reference work supervised, or other activities supervised. A presentation or lecture area for the room includes a multimedia station connected to the Internet as well as a projection system (Farmer, 2002). Furniture may include student and teacher desks, tables, computer stations, carrels, bulletin boards, permanent screen, book trucks, shelving, and any furnishings appropriate to the many purposes of the room. Darkening facilities and numerous electrical outlets are also necessary. Chairs need to be easily movable (stacked, folded, and so forth) to allow for more flexibility of the space. Because of the multipurpose uses of the area, a control room that allows for special sound and lighting facilities is necessary. The room should be designed to accommodate all kinds of media and possibly teleconferences. Numerous electrical outlets are needed in the area. Floor coverings appropriate to multipurpose activities are essential. A storage area for audiovisual equipment should adjoin the multipurpose room to allow for convenient access (AASL & AECT, 1988).

A teachers' lounge/workroom is often provided for classroom preparation and professional work as well as for teachers' meetings. This area is generally combined with or placed next to the school library media center facility to allow the teacher and the school media specialist to collaboratively plan for instructional activities and engage in curriculum development. The room should be equipped with previewing equipment, laminating and photocopying machines, computers, and supplies needed for the production of materials. A nearby conference room allows for teacher/school library media specialist conferences as well as small group student activities.

If the school media center has a separate production area in which the school media staff produces materials for the faculty, the area should be adjacent to the teachers' lounge/workroom to allow faculty members easy access to the facility to monitor the progress of their requests and provide additional information as needed. This area should include several multimedia computers and other peripherals such as a scanner, printer, camcorder or digital camera (Farmer, 2002).

Distributing, Organizing, Accessing, and Storing Collections

Space—for distributing, organizing, accessing, and storing collections—is usually provided in several places: the main area, workroom, office, and storage sites. Schools with access to OPACs or other resources outside the school media center require an allocation of space for computer terminals throughout the school. In the main reading and browsing area, the circulation desk should be large enough to handle all distribution procedures for the media collections. This desk requires special attention and is one of the most important furnishings for the media center. A slot and depressible bin for the return of materials are worthwhile additions to a functional circulation desk. Desensitizing equipment needs to be under the desk and out of sight. Monitors on the desk should be able to swivel. Electrical power strips secured to the desk allows for other equipment to be used. The height of the desk needs to be convenient for the staff to look ahead or look down at computer monitors. At least one OPAC needs to be located near the circulation and reference area. One OPAC station needs to be thirty-four inches to allow for wheelchair access. If possible, shelving for temporary housing of materials should be provided in or close to the main desk. The OPAC and other indexes, in CD-ROM, on-line, or printed format, should be located near the circulation desk. A security system needs to be near the circulation desk at the school media center exit, at least eight feet from the computer system. A photocopy machine should be in this area where monitoring can be easily handled and where in-house use of restricted circulation materials is facilitated.

A computer terminal should be located at the reference desk to allow for fast information retrieval as well as guidance in using the OPAC. The back of terminals that face the wall protect against radiation emissions. Terminals need to be placed in a position that allows good traffic flow and access to shelving (Farmer, 2002).

The nature and quantity of materials housed in the main area depend on the amount of storage space available elsewhere. Extremely bulky and infrequently used materials are often housed nearby, but outside the main area. The main collections of media and the current issues of periodicals and newspapers are generally kept in the main area. Space should also be provided for display and promotional materials.

Workroom areas for many support functions should be provided, including places for material production and processing. Space is needed for verifying receipt of newly purchased items as well as providing technical services that are unavailable centrally or commercially. Sometimes these two areas are combined. Workroom access to the library and to an outside corridor is important for receipt of materials and equipment, so adequate entrances should be provided. Workroom size will vary with each school, but 600–800 square feet is suggested. Counter space with sink and running water should be included, with storage cabinets, shelving, worktables, chairs, computers, and several strategically placed electrical outlets. The workroom should be adjacent to the entrance, circulation, and media center office.

The school library media specialist will, of course, spend the major portion of the workday involved with the center's audiences in various activities. Nevertheless, an office for the specialist, separate from the workroom areas, is essential. Here, the specialist may conduct private conferences with teachers and students and deal with the administrative details of the center. The office should be 600–800 square feet in size and convenient to both the workrooms and the main area. The office needs to be surrounded with enough glass for the specialist to supervise the entire media center. Its equipment should include a desk and several chairs, computer, at least three legal-size file cabinets, shelving, a telephone for outside school communication, and sufficient electrical outlets. If two media specialists work in the same media center, then separate offices are required.

Storage areas should also be included in the plan. Three different types of media are sometimes stored close to but outside the main area: (1) print material, (2) non-print materials, and (3) instructional equipment. Laptops need to remain near the circulation desk to allow for close supervision. The environment of storage areas needs special consideration because heat sources, such as heating ducts or furnaces, can destroy some materials during a period of time (Farmer, 2002). Back issues of periodicals (although increasingly this material is handled through online databases or Internet access), supplementary library books, and sets of additional texts are common examples of print materials that are often stored. The storage area should contain an adequate amount of shelving as well as a working surface, chair or stools, and machine or equipment stands.

The types of non-print materials in storage areas will depend on what is housed in the main area. No absolute rules are possible; each media specialist will make these decisions based on variable criteria, with accessibility the final criterion. Storage space for bulky non-print materials, such as videos, models, large poster, and maps, is sometimes provided outside the main area.

Because instructional equipment tends to be cumbersome and is often mounted on rolling carts, the storage area for such equipment must be large with convenient access to the hallway or elevator. Much of the equipment for classroom use may be successfully decentralized throughout the school by department or floor level. The storage areas must be made secure by having special keys and locks made with no duplicates. Special storage bins can also be constructed in the central area to hold additional overhead projectors, screens, television sets, computer display terminals and keyboards, and LCD projectors for ready accessibility and use in the center.

Producing Instructional Materials

The size of the area for producing noncommercial materials and modifying commercial products for local curriculum use will depend on the nature of the school's program. A basic list of activities includes: (1) preparation of graphics, posters, transparencies, charts; (2) duplication of materials for teacher and student use; (3) photography; (4) producing videos; (5) audio production; and (6) PowerPoint presentations. Equipment includes duplicating machines, computers and printers, photocopiers, dry mount press, video cameras, worktables and chairs, paper cutter, and suitable supplies. Cabinets with locks provide work surface space and storage for supplies. Some centers extend the capabilities of the production area to include photographic darkrooms as well as video and recording studios. Because of the use of digital cameras, darkrooms are not deemed quite as necessary as they once were. Students are increasingly involved in the production processes through recreational as well as curricular interests. This area should be visibly accessible by library media personnel.

In addition to the workroom areas, the center often provides a separate teachers' lounge/workroom where the professional library can be housed and teachers can pursue individual projects and hold small-group meetings. Having the teacher workroom in the school library media center encourages teachers to use the center in addition to putting materials and equipment within easy reach (Wisconsin Department of Public Instruction, n.d.). Equipping the room with appropriate shelving and comfortable seating similar to that in the main area encourages teacher use. An area for previewing and evaluating print and non-print materials and equipment allows the faculty to assist in material and equipment selection. Sometimes the larger production area is set up to accommodate teachers' needs for space to accomplish their varied instruction-related activities.

Maintaining and Repairing Equipment

An area that can be used for the repair and maintenance of instructional equipment is frequently provided, especially if a technician is on the staff or available in the school. A workbench and chairs plus adequate outlets and tools should be available. In small schools, media specialists frequently rely on a contract with an audiovisual repair service to keep the equipment in good operating condition. If a work area for equipment maintenance is not required, repair space may be combined with the production work-room area or equipment storage areas. In larger school districts, the repair and maintenance of instructional equipment are part of the district-level services.

As trends in constructing and remodeling school library media centers continue to develop, the process of using space for changing needs becomes more effective. The main problem in modernizing school library media center facilities is basically one of improving the use of existing space in order to take care of variable groupings of persons pursuing different learning experiences. *Flexibility* is the word most commonly used to describe the overall attempt to solve this problem, and open planning is one of the newer approaches. In this concept, the degree and variety of flexibility as well as its purposes have to be clearly stated in planning the facilities. Flexibility can be incorporated in a design in a permanent way with additions, structural changes, and spaces for different-size groups; it can be accomplished in a temporary way with movable partitions, shelving, or furnishings that can be arranged as spaces within space. Program planning must precede any creative designing of the facility in order to integrate center activities with the total educational program in the school.

Looking at floor plans can be helpful when renovating or building a new facility. Web sites for an elementary, middle school and high school are provided with brief annotations. Some of the sites only have one floor plan, while others include several. The Judy Hauser (2001) article *Help! For library media center design, construction and renovation: A guide for consulting* contains several floor plans but the others are limited to only one floor plan for each type of media center.

Floor Plan Web Sites

Hauser, Judy. (2001). *Help! For library media center design, construction and renovation: A guide for consulting.* Retrieved April 8, 2004, from Oakland Schools web site: http://www.oakland.k12.mi.us/resources/media/01 infocenterhelpguide.pdf

Judy Hauser, Information Consultant for Oakland Schools New Media Information Center, provides an excellent resource for library media specialists who are remodeling or participating in the design of a library media center. In the appendix of this booklet you can find twenty-four floor plans for elementary, middle, and high school libraries.

High School Library Media Centers

Bartlesville High School, Oklahoma

http://www.bartlesville.k12.ok.us/bhs_construction/drawings/library.gif

This site features the architect's rendering of the library media center design. The floor plan includes a separate technology area, archives room, and a professional resources room.

Dixie High School, St. George, Utah

http://www.dixiehigh.org/MediaCenter/checkitout.shtml

This floor plan features a writing laboratory, a TV video/editing room, and an art show area. This site includes a media center tour in photographs.

Hickory High School, Hermitage, Pennsylvania

http://loretta.jonesdirect.com/Hickory/images/libdraw.jpg

This state-of-the-art facility contains a conference room, a cyber-bridge of multiple computer terminals, and a distance learning room. Photographs of the media center are available.

Leslie High School, Leslie, Michigan

http://leslie.k12.mi.us/~lhs/

This floor plan shows a separate video lab, computer lab, and small study nooks in the rounded front area.

Riverside University High School, Milwaukee, Wisconsin

http://www.ruhs.uwm.edu/departments/library/library.htm

This site shows the floor plan and photographs of the media center including computer workstations for the OPAC, which are networked with the electronic catalog and five electronic databases. Word processing and other activities are offered on thirty other computers. Photographs and a detailed description can be found at this URL.

Southwest High School, Minneapolis, Minnesota

http://web.archive.org/web/20021104104806/http://www.mpls.k12.mn.us /southwest/media/mcfloor.html

This library has two adjacent computer labs, an editing room, and a conference room.

St. Peter High School, Mankato, Minnesota

http://www.doug-johnson.com/images/stpeterfloorplan.gif

Scroll to the bottom of the web page to find the two floor plans. Although the plans are a little hard to see and read, the high school floor plan shows computing areas, a television production area, and conference rooms. The second floor plan is a school floor plan and does not highlight the media center.

Middle School Library Media Centers

Bailey Middle School, Escambia County, Florida

http://www.escambia.k12.fl.us/schscnts/baie/mediaflr.html

This library claims to be a state of the art library media center. Their library has a closed-circuit television studio, production room, conference room, group projection room, and many computers for student research.

East Middle School, Farmington, Michigan

http://www.farmington.k12.mi.us/ems/Media2.html

This unusual floor plan shows a computer lab and a classroom on each side of the media center. Computers are placed in the center to allow easy access to information.

Elementary School Library Media Centers

George F. Johnson Elementary School, Endicott, New York

http://www.uetigers.stier.org/library/ghn/floo.pdf

This floor plan features large round tables for the OPAC computers, an adjacent computer lab, and "story steps."

Nursery Road Elementary School, Columbia, South Carolina

http://www.lex5.k12.sc.us/nres/Media/Summer%20School/Whacked%20
sites/floorpla.html

The media center is sunken in this floor plan. Ramps on each side of the
center allow wheelchair accessibility. Lounging areas are on each side of
the circulation desk.

ENVIRONMENTAL ELEMENTS

Although the possibility of future changes is vital in dynamic remodeling and designing, some environmental elements are basic. They are lighting, thermal environment, electrical power, acoustics, and color.

Lighting

A functional school library media center environment requires optimal
lighting conditions for the eye comfort of its users, an adequate level of
lighting for the whole area, and local lighting for particular activities. Lighting should be glare-free and tailored to the specific need in each space and
even for task areas within the space. Energy conservation and the physio-
logical requirements of human beings live in a delicate balance. Although
extensive use of natural light is generally not recommended because of the
difficulty in controlling both brightness and heat, some degree of natural
light relieves the uniformity of artificial light, makes an interior appear live-
lier, and enriches the environment. An opportunity to glance at a distant
view through a window is a refresher for tired eyes.

Light sources, especially for independent study areas, should exhibit
some imaginative possibilities while adhering to the following general
principles of lighting:

1. The angle at which the light strikes the work surface is probably more
   important than the amount of light.
2. The height of lighting levels should depend on the age group served.
3. The type of light source should be adapted to the purpose for the space.
4. The type of light fixture should reflect area and height needs.
5. There should be capability for dimming and darkening lights.

It is advisable to avoid highly polished surfaces in a school library media
center. Warm white fluorescent lamps with diffusers is a suggested light

source. Grid fixtures that move horizontally or vertically along poles or beams, fixtures attached to permanent strips, and portable floor or desk fixtures can be used creatively to suit area and height needs. Certainly important in a school library media center is some provision for darkening areas for projection, with some means of retaining a minimum illumination in case of equipment failure and other problems. Light switches need to be located in a convenient centralized place (Maine Association of School Libraries, 1999).

Thermal Environment

Heating, cooling, and ventilating are three interdependent major considerations when deciding on the media center's thermal environment. Techniques for controlling these elements are, of course, available to planners. An independent system for heating and cooling is desirable because it allows the media center to be restricted from the rest of the school. Solutions should take into consideration such external factors as the outside climate and yearly use of the facility and such internal factors as the location of the center's main area, such as proximity to a boiler room. An independent heating and cooling system allows the media center to be restricted from the rest of the school when it is used after hours or during the summer. Computers require air conditioning in the summer months.

No one thermal factor can be evaluated separately or judged without reference to all others. A comfortable thermal environment is a matter of deciding on a proper balance. Appropriate heating, cooling, and ventilating techniques can then be used. Consideration should be given to the thermal requirements of such items as computer hardware, software, and other audiovisual materials that require the maintenance of a certain level of temperature control.

Minimum standards for thermal requirements are generally written into official building codes. In almost all cases, however, school library media specialists must see that the requirements are not only reached but exceeded, because any extreme temperature or inadequate air exchange will generally impair both physical and mental efficiency. Air conditioning is the best solution to the ventilation problem in a facility where people work in a warm, humid climate. There is need for heat control in cold climates. However, in many of the less extreme weather belts, a media specialist may have to emphasize the need for a balance of heating, cooling, and ventilation, especially with energy conservation such an important consideration.

There are several points to be considered in overseeing a thermal environment. Windows, as well as ventilation and heating outlets, should be located where they will not reduce shelf space or interfere with furniture arrangements. Opening of windows should not require unlocking gadgets or the use of step stools. The rooms that house mechanical equipment and compressors should be isolated from the center so that any noise or vibration will not intrude.

The use of outside glass will affect the thermal environment and is recommended because of energy conservation needs. Sufficient insulation should be used to ensure that the appropriate environment is maintained. A form of ventilation should be installed that will keep a temperature range between seventy and seventy-five degrees and a humidity reading of approximately sixty percent (Maine Association of School Libraries, 1999). Air conditioning is apparently the most efficient and, in the long run, most economical method of ventilation. As with lighting, temperature control facilities should allow for flexibility in space division.

Electrical Power

With the increasing use of computers, DVD players, LCD projectors, recorders, and other types of electrically operated teaching and learning equipment, electrical outlets must be provided in sufficient number and in a variety of locations to allow flexibility in use. Electrical outlets should be in abundance and placed where they will best serve the center's future as well as immediate needs, on the floor, ceiling, walls, or all three surface areas. Consideration should be given to the placement of outlets in areas where the OPAC, the security system and other computer workstations might be located in the future. Even more outlets will be needed and should be installed if there are future plans for the virtual school library media center. High voltage outlets need to be specified for workrooms where laminators will be used.

A most important factor in dealing with electrical power is safety, especially when students and volunteers use electrically operated equipment. Attention should be given to surge protection and backup power supply needs of the center. Close attention should be given to the number of outlets and their location in the following areas: circulation desk, wet carrel areas, equipment usage areas, storage areas, work space areas and technology areas where computer workstations are used. The rule of thumb is that it is better to install more outlets than presently needed to allow for future needs. The circulation desk requires an electrical strip be installed on the wall behind it or underneath the desk. When worktables are against the wall, it is a good idea to also install an electrical strip. In areas where equipment or computer workstations are used, outlets need to be installed flush with the floor (Maine Association of School Libraries, 1999).

The following steps can help to evaluate present and future electrical power requirements for the school library media center:

1. Try to determine your school's needs in relation to such activities as television, distance learning, the virtual library media center, and telecommunications that may be carried out in the center at some future time.
2. Draw up a present and future plan for needed electrical power based on step 1.

Because the costs of rewiring are prohibitive, media specialists should assume that centers in the future will utilize more electrical equipment than is presently needed.

Acoustics

Any library media center that is a focal point for learning activities in a school must deal effectively with problems of sound. Controlling the sounds make by people and machines is an important part of designing or remodeling centers. With the emergence of flexibly designed centers, an attitude toward acceptance of background noise is required as well as a better understanding of the noise that is naturally produced by young people at different ages.

Sound is highly directional; unrelated sounds of different types and intensities combine to make noise. It requires more energy for a listener or speaker to hear or be heard under poor sound conditions; therefore, a good environment controls both the sounds that originate within an area and the distracting sounds from outside that combine to produce intolerable noise levels.

There are many ways to deal with the problems of sound, such as room shape, use of acoustical materials and sound systems, and improved space dividers. Research suggests that an equal proportion of depth and width in a room provides the best sound environment. Another way to reduce sound that reflects from barriers, especially hard surfaces, is to set the walls and ceilings on slightly irregular planes, rather than in the traditional parallel pattern.

Materials to be used for sound conditioning should be tested under in-use conditions similar to those being planned. Any soft, absorbent material, such as heat insulation fibers, will muffle sound, but will allow it to be transmitted in some form to adjacent areas. Materials that impede the transmission of sound should have a high density. Baffles placed in air ventilation ducts will also retard the transmission of sound from one area to another.

As noted in the section on thermal environment, the location of the school library media center is important. Vibrations from heavy school equipment, such as printing presses in a vocational education department or natural but distracting sounds from a cafeteria or gymnasium, for example, can rarely be overcome and are best avoided.

Electronic amplification systems are used in many school library media centers, and the sounds they produce, in both speaking and hearing with the aid of this equipment, must be considered. Also, the trend toward flexibly designed centers makes the construction and design of space dividers an important consideration. For example, folding partitions easily change the area arrangement, but they generally permit an unwanted level of seepage noise. Research suggests that woven fabrics with appropriate density and decreased porosity due to the use of special materials and weaving techniques may be one answer to noise problems in an area.

In some media center areas, such as conference rooms, a certain level of sound from conversation is expected. However, in a main study area, noise and motion can be kept to a minimum in two ways: (1) by using sound-reducing materials in construction and (2) by the arrangement of the facilities. An acoustically treated ceiling will help reduce sound, as will carpeting on the floor and on wall surfaces. Studies indicate that excessive use of acoustical-tile ceilings is unnecessary, however, and may even add sound problems. For best results, at least one-third of the area to be covered should be given acoustical treatment. Noise-generating activities, such as production of instructional materials, group study and photocopying, need to be confined to one area of the media center rather than throughout.

Before deciding on the proper acoustical treatment for a floor surface, the underlying floor construction, the heating system, and the scope of activities intended for the facility must be determined. The floor should be draft-free and warm enough in winter. If the audience for the center is from pre-kindergarten children to ninth-graders, the floor plan and construction should provide for both play and work activities. Acoustic flooring may be satisfactory for specific purposes in some areas. Although higher in initial cost, carpeting equals out in cost to other flooring material over a period of time, chiefly because of savings on maintenance. Carpeting, such as that used in offices and restaurants, may be satisfactory. It is attractive, comfortable, and generally longwearing.

In planning the facilities, one should break up large areas by furnishings or shelving to avoid an uninterrupted traveling path for sound. Noise-producing activities should be isolated from sections where quiet is needed. Shelving should be located away from study areas, as should the circulation desk, entrances, and exits. Avoid arrangements that force students to walk though the main area to get to the shelves or the OPAC. A preliminary study of traffic patterns will help determine the appropriate placement of areas and furnishings to control sound.

Color

A color scheme that provides both variety and harmony can help to make the school library media center a pleasant place to work and visit. Planning for color in the environment is important because people are negatively or positively influenced by color. There is color in everything in a school library media center environment: in structural materials, walls, woodwork, furnishings, materials, equipment, and in the views outside. Care should be taken to coordinate this variety of visual experiences into a cohesive, if continuously varying, and harmonious environment.

Two general rules on color can aid the school library media specialist who must operate without the benefit of a color consultant:

1. Study scientific recommendations on the use of color as it relates to reflectivity and contrast, such as the fact that white enamel surfaces reflect light so effectively that they appear much larger in size than a similar object painted a dull black, which absorbs light. Each color shade and tone obeys similar rules of reflectivity and contrast and has a complicated relationship of harmony value to the shade and tone of other colors.

2. Use these recommendations cautiously, knowing that the students who are surrounded by color will be affected differently depending on age. Young children benefit from the stimulation of cheerful, bright areas of color; students in the middle grades or junior high school need less color stimulation and require decorative treatments that reinforce studious-ness; a more sophisticated blend of color is appropriate in the high school (Scargall, 1999).

Color and texture should add to the warm and fuzzy feeling when entering the media center, preferably reflecting the mood of the users. Bright, light warm colors are known to initiate activities and action whereas softer colors foster withdrawal. A red background generates ideas and action. Green is conducive to meditation and performing tasks. For primary grades, tints of red, blue and yellow are appropriate colors as well as peach and pink. In contrast, secondary classes performing close, visual work need tints of blue, green, gray or beige. Interestingly, subdued colors tend to limit students desire for checking out materials (Scargall, 1999).

Oversaturation—too many colors or color clashes—can be disturbing to many users and overly stimulating. Remember that the materials, equipment, and people in a school library media center generally provide much color and a plain background color scheme is often needed in contrast. Students who feel comfortable in their surroundings will learn and function better. Carpeting or flooring should be in a plain, unbroken pattern, and preferably a light color. Furniture and walls may vary from pastels to subdued shades of some of the stronger colors, depending on the age of the patrons.

With imaginative use of good design, attractive furniture, and inviting colors, the center can be an interesting, aesthetically appealing area in which to work and study.

FURNISHINGS

The traditional furnishings in schools and library media centers are being replaced today by modular, easy-to-move, compact, multipurpose furniture that answers the need for flexibility that is brought about by changing instructional techniques and various sizes of instructional groups. The trend in furniture, shelving, display cases, wall hangings, and floor coverings continues to be toward comfort and toward the aesthetic appeal that can be found by an imaginative combination of standard and eclectic designs. Minimum seating in the media center should accommodate:

Elementary: one full class
Middle School: two full classes
High School: three full classes or more

Regardless of the type of furniture in the center, some specific selection criteria should apply. The school library media specialist should try to see that all furnishings are (1) simple and safe, (2) rugged and durable, (3) useful and comfortable, (4) eye-pleasing and compact. Not every piece of furnishing can fit all these criteria, but each piece should at least be safe and comfortable.

Carrels, Tables, and Chairs

Students like movable, versatile furniture with a potential for privacy. According to Myerberg, (2002):

> Children learn best by talking to colleagues and sharing ideas...Study carrels are out; four-person tables that can be ganged together for seminars and conferences are in...The twenty-first century library will be a flexible work and social setting for multiple activities, like modern workplaces or chain bookstores. (pp. 2–3)

Students prefer table surfaces to desks in a group situation and carrels to tables for individual study. Carrels, both wet and dry, provide private places where students may work undisturbed by others or by program activities going on in the center. There are no hard-and-fast rules for locating and placing carrels. Generally, only a few should be distributed among the collections and the rest placed as spatial dividers, singly or in small groups. Large groupings give less privacy to the student and add an institutional appearance to any area.

Along with carrels, some tables and chairs should be in each area. Two important considerations for choosing the correct mix of carrels and tables are the nature and size of the instructional groups in the school, and an appropriate mixture of different seating and working arrangements. A combination of round, octagonal, rectangular, and trapezoidal tables presents an attractive variety in a large main area.

Tables and chairs, like carrels, should not be placed in regimented ways. They should be distributed judiciously within areas to help provide an atmosphere that is conducive to study. Sturdy chairs should be comfortable and attractive. It is suggested that they have legs that extend at an angle from under the seat. A beneficial extra is the convenient shelf underneath for student books and papers.

Some comfortable casual chairs and low tables are also recommended in the center. A large variety of items that can be used for sitting should be investigated. The age of the student and the purpose of the seating should be important considerations. The furniture selected must be the right size and height for the student population. Special pieces of furniture should be purchased for students who are handicapped or who have special needs.

Bricks or concrete blocks and boards can make inexpensive and attractive low tables or benches. Inflatable cushions can also be used. Informal lounge furniture is often placed close to magazine and newspaper racks to encourage recreational and informational reading.

Other standard furniture items include a circulation desk, computer stations for OPACs and Internet access, filing cabinets, book trucks and equipment carts. The circulation desk should be large enough to handle the flow of multimedia and small equipment. The OPAC computer stations should be arranged to provide easy access to materials and the Internet. The filing cabinets, some of which should accommodate legal or larger size materials, are important for pamphlets, transparencies, clippings, and small pictures. Filing cabinets are available with three or four drawers or open-faced to be used with hanging file folders. A large blueprint cabinet or bin may also be needed for large pictures and maps. Mobile book trucks and equipment carts are available from commercial suppliers (see Appendix 3). The prime requisites are ease of movement, which is determined by the size of the wheels, and sturdiness. Computer tables on wheels that hold the terminal, keyboard, mouse, printer, and paper allow for flexibility in use because of their mobility.

Shelving

Books and other materials are generally made accessible to the user on standard adjustable library shelves. There are various types of shelving: steel bracket, moving shelves; wood cases with metal strips and clips for supporting shelves; and sloping wood or metal shelves. Most shelves come in three-foot unit lengths with end panels. The use of freestanding double-faced shelving is preferable to wall shelving. The stacks should be close to the circulation area for ease of use and supervision. When arranged, the shelves should not be longer than five-foot clearance between the shelves and adjacent furniture.

From five to six shelves per section are useful in high school, but fewer fit the elementary school needs better. One good use for counter-height shelving is to define areas within a room. Rows of shelves grouped in blocks facilitate accessibility. Generally, the greater percentage of the shelves should be eight inches wide, the remainder ten to fourteen inches wide, for oversize material. Reference books and non-print items may require different types of shelving. Shelving to house a minimum of fifteen items (books, videos, computer software, and other materials) per student is the rule in planning for shelving needs.

Other Storage and Display Furnishings

Special shelving is required for big books used in elementary schools. These big book storage cabinets are frequently on rollers to allow for more flexibility of use. Movable dividers in the cabinets can be changed to allow the books to stand either vertically or horizontally.

Other types of furniture in the center should include racks to display current magazines and newspapers, paperback racks, and cabinets for videos/DVDs if these are not inter-shelved. Special multimedia shelving to interfile print and non-print materials in the same way they appear in a catalog has found an audience among some school library media specialists and is worth investigating. This type of accessibility can be explored initially by using specially constructed or locally produced multimedia shelving for a curriculum unit within one area of the Dewey decimal classification system. Legal-size filing cabinets for the vertical file can be provided for difficult-to-shelve pamphlets, pictures, and clippings. Rolling trucks for print and non-print and combination or separate atlas/dictionary stands are also useful.

Display shelving for magazines, with sloping shelves that are generally thirty-six inches wide and sixteen inches deep, lends itself to the use of imaginative as well as standard ideas. The primary purpose of any magazine display is to make the front cover as visible as possible. This method can be achieved by the creative use of a clothesline or metal rod strung across one or more areas with colorful clothespins or magnetic clamps to secure the magazines.

Other display facilities, such as bulletin boards and pegboards, exhibit cases, and various display stands, should be available and used in the main study area as well as directly outside the main entrance. Live plants add a sense of home to the center.

FACILITIES FOR SPECIAL MEDIA SERVICES

District library media facilities are designed to support the district educational goals and to enhance the library media program in the schools. Space for the facility should give priority to (1) administration of the school media programs of the district, (2) conference areas, (3) the selection and evaluation of library media, and (4) the professional materials collection. Several functions of the district media facility include technical processing of all materials, printing and graphics services, equipment repair and maintenance, video/DVD library collection, television distribution, distance learning facilities, media production, and facilities for the selection and examination of materials, including computer software.

Facilities and Functions

According to *Information Power* (AASL & AECT, 1988), requirements for the district media facility should include the following:

- An area for planning and administration of the district library media program, including necessary office space, close to curriculum specialists.
- Conference rooms, meeting rooms, and demonstration areas as needed to facilitate staff development and to provide consultative services in curriculum development and instructional design.
- A professional library and teacher center where all types of professional materials and equipment can be housed to accommodate reading, study, listening, viewing and computing of those materials by faculty and staff.
- A separate area for the selection and evaluation of library media materials and equipment, both for individual and group viewing.
- Space to house a collection of district materials that supplements the building collections. This area may be part of the professional library or may be located adjacent to the processing center. A video/DVD collection may be part of the district professional library offerings.
- An equipment services area, large enough to provide for selection, evaluation, inspection, repair, maintenance, distribution, and storage equipment, with adequate space for efficient workflow for technicians and clerical workers.
- A processing center where materials, equipment, and supplies can be received, processed, cataloged, and distributed. This area requires space for office workers, arrangement for efficient workflow, and provision for adequate storage. Easy access to outside entry and an elevator for shipping and receiving are essential.
- Careful consideration must be given to the impact of new and emerging technologies and the demand they may have on facilities. Also to be considered are computers and Internet access.
- Production areas, including multimedia, as required by the instructional program of the district and as needed to supplement the building level programs. Sufficient space must be provided in each to carry out the required functions while providing space for production specialists to plan and work. Provision must be made for areas where production specialists can confer with instructional and curriculum specialists. Production spaces include the following:

1. Graphics, photography, and printing, which require consideration of space for production of artwork and printed materials, production and reproduction equipment, printers, paper storage located near machines, refrigeration for photographic and other supplies, and an air conditioned darkroom with light locks and warning system. With the advent of digital cameras, darkrooms appear to be fading in popularity.

2. Audiotape production, which requires space for recorders, duplicators and control of sound reverberation. Combining this area with a video studio control room may be feasible.

3. Television production, which requires consideration of the extent to which television production facilities are used at individual school building sites, the contracting of television production, the use of programming by other existing agencies, the use of portable studios and portable video units, the district's involvement in two-way television, distance learning, and the emergence of interactive video technology.

4. Multimedia production, which requires computers, digital cameras, and Internet access.

Distance education requires special facilities and is an emerging technology throughout the country. The use of distance education continues to grow in many different directions and is a viable instructional tool. Only the larger school systems or the more forward-looking smaller ones have tried to incorporate this medium and they have generally done so from a district or regional level.

Existing facilities may serve as a constraint for developing a school library media program; however, plans for better facilities should be shared with the administrators. New or renovated facilities will become necessary as learning resources and technological changes become more evident in school media centers. Planning for future technology is essential. The most important consideration to remember is that the ultimate design reflects the goals and objectives of the media center and the total instructional program of the school for the present and the future.

REFERENCES

American Association of School Librarians & Association for Educational Communications and Technology. (1988). *Information power: Guidelines for school library media programs.* Chicago: Authors.

Bailey Middle School, Escambia County, Florida school library media center floor plan. (n.d.). Retrieved April 8, 2004, from: http://www.escambia.k12.fl.us/schscnts/baie/mediaflr.html

Bartlesville High School, Oklahoma school library media center floor plan. (n.d.). Retrieved April 8, 2004, from: http://www.bartlesville.k12.ok.us/bhs_construction/drawings/library.gif

Dixie High School, St. George, Utah school library media center floor plan. (n.d.). Retrieved April 8, 2004, from: http://www.dixiehigh.org/MediaCenter/check-itout.shtml

East Middle School Media Center, Farmington, Michigan. (n.d.). Retrieved April 17, 2004, from: http://www.farmington.k12.mi.us/ems/Media2.html

Erikson, Rolf & Markuson, Carolyn. (2001). *Designing a school library media center for the future.* Chicago: American Library Association.

Farmer, Lesley S.J. (2002, April/May). Facilities: The tech edge. *Book Report, 20*(5), 26–28.

George F. Johnson Elementary School Library, Endicott, New York school library media center floor plan. (n.d.).Retrieved April 8, 2004, from: http://www.uetigers.stier.org/library/ghn/floo.pdf

Hauser, Judy. (2001). *Help! For library media center design, construction and renovation: A guide for consulting.* Retrieved April 8, 2004, from Oakland Schools web site:
http://www.oakland.k12.mi.us/resources/media/01infocenterhelpguide.pdf

Jones Library, Hickory High School, Hermitage, Pennsylvania school library media center floor plan. (n.d.). Retrieved April 8, 2004, from: http://loretta.jonesdirect.com/Hickory/images/libdraw.jpg

Leslie High School, Leslie, Missouri school library media center floor plan. (1997, January 26). Retrieved April 8, 2004, from: http://leslie.k12.mi.us/~lhs/

Maine Association of School Libraries. (1999). *Maine school libraries facilities handbook.* Retrieved April 8, 2004, from the Maine Association of School Libraries web site: http://www.maslibraries.org/about/facilities/handbook.html

Massachusetts school library media program standards for 21st century learning. (2003). Retrieved April 17, 2004, from the Massachusetts School Library Media Association web site: http://www.mslma.org/whoweare/standards/standardsrev.pdf

Myerberg, Henry. (2002, September/October). School libraries: A design recipe for the future. *Knowledge Quest, 31*(1), 11–13. Retrieved April 17, 2004, from *Knowledge Quest on the Web:* http://www.ala.org/ala/aasl/aaslpubsandjournals/kqweb/kqarchives/volume31/311myerberg.htm

Nursery Road Elementary School Media Center, Columbia, South Carolina. (n.d.). Retrieved April 17, 2004, from: http://www.lex5.k12.sc.us/nres/Media/Summer%20School/Whacked%20sites/floorpla.html

Riverside University High School LMC Floor Plan, Milwaukee, Wisconsin. (n.d.). Retrieved April 8, 2004, from: http://www.ruhs.uwm.edu/departments/library/library.htm

Scargall, Hollie. (1999, November/December). Color: An unsuspected influence. *Library Talk, 12*(5), 11–12.

Southwest High School, Minneapolis, Minnesota school library media center floor plan. (n.d.). Retrieved April 17, 2004, from: http://web.archive.org/web/20021104104806/http://www.mpls.k12.mn.us/southwest/media/mcfloor.html

St. Peter High School, Mankato, Minnesota school library media center floor plan. (2002, February 20). Retrieved April 8, 2004, from: http://www.doug-johnson.com/dougwri/buildingquestions.html

Texas Education Agency. (2001, November 5). *Facilities standards.* Retrieved April 8, 2004, from the Texas Education Agency web site: http://www.tea.state.tx.us/technology/libraries/lib_standards_library_fac.html

Wisconsin Department of Public Instruction. (n.d.). *Design considerations for school media centers.* Retrieved April 8, 2004, from the Wisconsin Department of Public Instruction web site: http://www.dpi.state.wi.us/dpi/dltcl/imt/desgnlmc.html

Wisconsin Department of Public Instruction. (2002, March 2). *School library media design and technology considerations.* Retrieved April 8, 2004, from the State of Wisconsin Department of Public Instruction web site: http://www.dpi.state.wi.us/dpi/dltcl/imt/design.html

FURTHER READINGS

Anderson, Mary Alice. (2001, May, June). Fighting the good fight: Designing a library media center. *The Book Report, 20*(1), 6–9.

Barrett, Bets, et al. (1999, March). Media central: The high school library goes high tech. *Electronic School.* Retrieved April 8, 2004, from: http://www.electronic-school.com/199903/0399f3.html

Barron, Daniel D. (2001, September). School library media facilities planning: Physical and philosophical considerations. *School Library Media Activities Monthly 18*(1), 48–50.

Baule, Steven M. (1998, May/June). Remodeling the media center. *Book Report, 17*(1), 24–25.

Baule, Steven M. (1999). *Facilities planning for school library media and technology centers.* Worthington, OH: Linworth.

Baule, Steven M. (1999, November/December). First steps in planning for facilities renovation. *Library Talk, 12*(5), 6–7.

Baule, Steven M. (2001). *Technology planning for effective teaching and learning.* Worthington, OH: Linworth.

Baule, Steven M. (2002, September/October). Developing bid specifications for facilities projects. *Knowledge Quest, 31*(1), 14–17.

Blodgett, Teresa & Repman, Judi. (1995, January, February). The electronic school library resource center: Facilities planning for the new information age. *Emergency Librarian, 22*(3), 26–30.

Brown, Carol R. (1995). *Planning library interiors. The selection of furnishings for the 21st century.* Phoenix, AZ: Oryx Press.

Brown, Robert A. (1992, February). Students as partners in library design. *School Library Journal, 38*(2), 31–34.

Clyde, Laurel A. (2000). *Managing infotech in school library media centers.* Westport, CT: Libraries Unlimited.

Cochran, Sally & Gisolfi, Peter. (1997, February). Renovate it and they will come: Designing a popular high school library. *School Library Journal, 43*(2), 25–29.

Codell, Cindy Darling. (1995, February). Brick by brick: Building a school library from the ground up. *School Library Journal, 41*(2), 20–23.

Cohen, Elaine. (1994, Winter/Spring). The architectural and interior design planning process. *Library Trends, 42*(3), 547–563.

Conklin, Nancy. (1998, September/October). New technologies, new considerations. *Knowledge Quest, 27*(1), 31–32.

Cramer, Marianne. (2002, May/June). Rebuilding and renovating the school library. *Media and Methods, 38*(6), 6.

Day, C. William. (2001, December). Untangling the maze: Planning for technology cable management now can save headaches in the future. *American School and University, 74*(4), 43–45.

Dewe, Michael. (1995). *Planning and designing libraries for children and young people.* Lanham, MD: Bernan Associates.

Doll, Carol A. (1992, Summer). School library media centers: The human environment. *School Library Media Quarterly, 20*(4), 225–229.

Dotten, Rose. (n.d.). *Library alive: A new look for the future.* Retrieved April 8, 2004, from the California Library Association web site: http://cla.ca/slip/library-alive.pdf

Farmer, Lesley S.J. (1996, June). Making your library technology-friendly. *Technology Connection, 3*(4), 20–22.

Feinberg, Sandra, et al. (1998). *Learning environments for young children: Rethinking library spaces and services.* Chicago: American Library Association.

Fenton, Serena. (1999, February). Architectural follies. *School Library Journal, 45*(2), 26.

Focke, John. (1998, May/June). Beyond books: The expanding role of the media center. *The High School Magazine for Principals, Assistant Principals, and All High School Leaders, 5*(5), 36–41.

Grundborg, Mary Ann. (1999, March). Planning libraries for the 21st century. *Catholic Library World, 69*(3), 23–25.

Harrington, Drew. (2001, December). Six trends in library design. *Library Journal Buyer's Guide,* 12–14.

Holt, Raymond M. (1989*). Planning library buildings and facilities: From concept to completion.* Lanham, MD: Scarecrow Press.

Horner, Kirk C. (2000, February). Today's media centers/libraries: Changing roles, changing spaces. *School Planning and Management, 39*(2), 48–49.

Illinois School Library Media Association. (1999). *Linking for learning: The Illinois school library media program guidelines.* Canton, IL: Author.

Information access and delivery. (2002, 7 August). Retrieved April 8, 2004, from the North Carolina Department of Public Instruction web site: http://www.ncwiseowl.org/Impact/Information.htm#Specifications%202

Jadwin, Peggy. (1996, June). Three media solutions. *School Planning and Management, 35*(6), C1–C4.

Johnson, Doug. (1997). *Indispensable librarian: Surviving (thriving) in school media centers in the information age.* Worthington, OH: Linworth.

Johnson, Doug. (2000, May/June). Building digital libraries for analog people: Ten common design pitfalls and how to avoid them. [Electronic version]. *Knowledge Quest, 28*(5), 10–15. Retrieved April 8, 2004, from: http://www.doug-johnson.com/dougwri/diglib.html

Johnson, Doug. (2002, February). Some design considerations when building or remodeling a media center (ERIC Document No. ED 425 609). Retrieved April 8, 2004, from: http://www.doug-johnson.com/dougwri/buildingquestions.html

Kirby, Lynn. (1995, February). Door to door: How to get your library moving...painlessly. *School Library Journal, 41*(2), 26–27.

Klasing, Jane. (1991). *Designing and renovating school library media centers.* Chicago: American Library Association.

Klasing, Jane & Callison, Daniel. (1992, Summer). Planning learning environments for library media programs: An introduction. *School Library Media Quarterly, 20*(4), 204.

Lankford, Mary D. (1994, February). Design for change: How to plan the school library you really need. *School Library Journal 40*(2), 20–24.

Lau, Debra. (2002, March). The shape of tomorrow. *School Library Journal, 48*(3), 57–60. Retrieved from Ebsco database.

Lenk, Mary Anne. (2002, October/November). FAQs about facilities: Practical tips for planning renovations and new school library media centers. *Knowledge Quest, 31*(1), 27–31.

McCarthy, Richard. (2000). *Designing better libraries: Selecting and working with building professionals.* (2nd ed.). Fort Atkinson, WI: Highsmith.

McDermott, Irene E. (1998, January). Solitaire confinement: The impact of the physical environment on computer training. *Computers in Libraries, 18*(1), 22, 24–27.

Maryland State Department of Education. (1998). *Facilities guidelines for library media programs* Baltimore, MD: Author. (ERIC Document No. ED 419 375)

Meyer, Randy. (1995, February). A roundup of eye-catching new libraries. *School Library Journal, 41*(2), 24–25.

Mikovsky, Edward. (1997, September/October). Techniques for distance learning instruction. *Media & Methods, 34*(1), 24.

Millen, Jean & Millen, George. (1999, January/February). Fulfilling a ten-year dream: Building a school library media center. *Knowledge Quest, 27*(3), 18–20.

Minkel, Walter. (2001, October). Small town, amazing library. *School Library Journal, 47*(10), 17.

Missouri Department of Elementary and Secondary Education Division of School Improvement—Curriculum Services. (2002, February 7). Facilities and equipment. In *The school library media standards handbook* (chapter 8). Retrieved April 8, 2004, from Missouri Department of Elementary and Secondary Education web site: http://www.dese.state.mo.us/divimprove/curriculum/library/Chapter_8.pdf

Morgan, Alex. (2003, May/June). R. Morgan and his class reflect on the new school library. *Knowledge Quest, 31*(5), 32–34.

Moyer, Mary & Baker, Rosalie M. (2004, April/May). Re-designing a school library media center for the 21st century. *Library Media Connections, 22*(7), 24–25.

Musgrove, Penny. (1997, May/June). Re-create your media center and program. *Multimedia Schools, 4*(3), 16–20.

Pantano, Phil. (1999, January). Flexible spaces that work: Renovating today for tomorrow's needs. *School Planning and Management, 38*(1), 74–75.

Perry, Karen. (1997, Summer). Form follows function: Redesigning the school library media center. *North Carolina Libraries, 55*(2), 72–74.

Planning for school library resource centers. (1998). Arlington, VA: Educational Research Service. (ERS Info-File #N2–32)

Rawlings, Mildred S. (2003, May/June). Transformations in the secondary school library: Morphing to meet the challenges of the twenty-first century. *Knowledge Quest, 31*(5), 42–45.

Sannwald, William. (2001). *Checklist of library building design considerations* (4th ed.). Chicago: American Library Association.

Sapp, Michael J. (2001, July). Public/private libraries. *School Planning and Management 40*(7), 40–41.

Scherer, Jeffrey. (1999). Light and libraries. *Library Hi Tech, 17*(4), 358–371.

Simpson, Carol. (2002, September/October). Information technology planning: Computers in the school library—How many are enough? *Knowledge Quest, 31*(1), 23–26.

Spira, Kirsten Hicks. (2002, July). Renovating on a shoestring. *School Library Journal, 48*(7), 35.

Sutton, Rodney K. (1996, June). New world forces libraries to adapt. *School Planning and Management, 35*(6), C1–C4.

Taney, Kimberly Bolaw. (2002). *Teen spaces: The step-by-step library makeover.* Chicago: American Library Association.

Texas State Library and Archives Commission. (1997, May 19). *School library programs: Facilities.* Austin, TX: Author.

Truett, Carol. (1994, Winter). A survey of school and public children's library facilities: What librarians like, dislike, and most want to change about their libraries. *School Library Media Quarterly, 22*(2), 91–97.

Usalis, Marion D. (1998, February). The power of paint: Refurbishing school libraries on a budget. *School Library Journal, 44*(2), 28–33.

Valenza, Joyce Kasman. (1996, November/December). Library as multimedia studio. *Electronic Learning, 16*(3), 56–57.

Van Dam, Janet M. (1994, January). Redesigning schools for 21st century technologies: A middle school with the power to improve. *Technology and Learning, 14*(4), 54–61.

Washington Library Media Association. *Library facilities.* Retrieved April 8, 2004, from: http://www.wlma.org/Professional/libraryfacilities.htm

Weinberg, Frederick. (1992). *School library facilities design.* Augusta, ME. Maine Educational Media Association.

Wrightson, Denelle & Wrightson, John M. (1999). Acoustical considerations in planning and design of library facilities. *Library Hi Tech, 17*(4), 349–357.

Chapter 8

MEDIA SELECTION: POLICIES AND PROCEDURES

The library media center collection is in many ways like a living organism—it grows and develops; it is dynamic and ever-changing, expanding in some areas while contracting in others. To supervise this growth and to regulate these changes is exciting, taxing, and ultimately one of the most professional tasks performed by the library media specialist.

To build a collection wisely and well, the school library media specialist should develop judgment and good taste along with a thorough knowledge of all the variables that influence selection, like the needs of the community and the nature of the curriculum. The library media specialist must be alert to changes and trends; show impartiality and objectivity; be imaginative, curious, and resourceful; and be dedicated to the public and the schools being served.

This chapter discusses the background body of knowledge necessary for the creation of the selection process as well as information on how to organize it. Other areas treated are the development of a selection policy, selection aids, and practical points on selection. Web sites are included for selection/collection development policies. How to handle censorship complaints are also discussed.

Media selection must be considered an ongoing process; although orders for media are placed only a few times each year, selection occurs daily. The machinery of selection should swing into action each time a reference question raised at the center cannot be answered with the available material on a subject—for example, when a hitherto ignored part of the world suddenly becomes newsworthy or a different fad hits a school population. The arrival of a new issue of a reviewing periodical should also signal the selection process to start.

No two library media centers contain—or should contain—the same collection. Each center's collection should reflect the specific needs of the school it serves. Yet while each media center is thus unique, all centers share three basic aims: (1) to help satisfy the needs of students for curriculum-related materials, (2) to fulfill students' wishes concerning materials for recreational purposes, and (3) to provide teachers with professional information. In good school programs, as in good educational materials, the first two aims often become intermingled and indistinguishable.

BACKGROUND KNOWLEDGE

Before beginning the selection process, the school library media specialist must learn something about the community; the students, faculty, and curriculum; media; bibliographic and reviewing tools; the existing collection; and budgeting.

Knowledge of the Community

Every community has many aspects that must be considered by the library media specialist. To learn the characteristics of the population, the specialist must investigate inhabitants' ethnic and religious backgrounds, age groupings, occupations, general economic status, cultural and recreational interests, and educational levels. Each of these factors will be reflected in the young people attending the schools. The nature of residential buildings, the kinds of businesses, and even transportation routes provide clues helpful in understanding the community. The media specialist should also become familiar with the community's other libraries and cultural resources as well as its recreational resources. Does the average child come from a home where there is at least a basic reference collection? How numerous and accessible are other public and private collections of educational materials? How adequate are these collections? Are there art galleries or other cultural institutions nearby? What provisions are there for recreational facilities, athletic fields, meeting rooms for clubs and hobby groups? One device to use in studying a community is to draw a simple map of the community and locate on it the various community resources and the school and public bus routes as well as other modes of transportation.

Knowledge of Students

In addition to knowing the general age and grade levels in the school, the media specialist should probe deeper into the activities and interests of the students. It is essential to determine the range of abilities and the degree of concentration of these abilities at various levels—for the whole school as well as for each class. Reading ability must be determined and test scores used to help verify range and concentration. Becoming familiar with the interests and activities of each age group—their hobbies, favorite sports and social interests, popular TV shows, part-time jobs, and size of allowances—will provide the specialist with valuable insights. What are the general social and emotional maturity levels of the students? How sophisticated, independent, and experienced are they at handling social adjustments, emotional problems, concerns about physical growth and maturation, relations with other members of the family, school assignments, and contemporary affairs? Both general and specific reading interests must be analyzed. General reading interests are the common interests of a specific age group. For example, junior high school boys generally enjoy science fiction and stories of true adventure. However, within these general-interest categories, and in addition to them, there are subtleties of taste that are characteristic of the individual school. A study of circulation records and comparisons with the experience of others working with the same age group will help bring some of these differences into focus. Although it may seem an impossible task, in order to know more than just names and faces the school library media specialist should try to collect this mass of information not only for the student body as a whole but also for each actual and potential user of the center. One important consideration is how knowledgeable students are of the Internet and new technological advances. The media specialist must be aware that the students of today will need both the skills in using materials and information as well as technological skills that will prepare them for lifelong learning as they move through the twenty-first century.

Knowledge of the Faculty

The interests, backgrounds, strengths, and weaknesses of the faculty are reflected in their teaching assignments, their classroom use of media, their use of technology, and the ways in which they and their students use the media center. The media specialist should be aware of the teaching methods employed, the nature of media center use by specific departments and at various grade levels, and areas where in-service work in media use seems needed. Frequently, technology is the area where teachers need the most in-service training. Each term the media specialist should find out the courses being taken by teachers for continuing education so that additions may be made to the professional collection to assist them.

Knowledge of the Curriculum

Knowing about the school's curriculum involves more than just knowledge of what subjects are taught and when. It also means knowing the missions, goals, and objectives of the school and how the library media center relates to them. Knowledge of curriculum and technology integration is necessary. It involves attending curriculum meetings, collaborating with teachers about lessons to be taught, becoming thoroughly familiar with the classroom textbooks used, and appropriate Internet web sites for lessons. Media specialists need to work with teachers in presenting collaborative lessons that include information literacy skills and instructing in the use of media and technology skills.

Knowledge of Media

The media specialist must become familiar with the various forms of educational materials, their characteristics, strengths, and limitations, and their potential for use in various situations. A thorough knowledge of technology is crucial. Information about the newest technological equipment and training faculty and students in its use is a top priority for a media specialist. There is no substitute for firsthand knowledge. Library media specialists, at every opportunity, should be reading books, viewing videos or DVDs, learning to use new equipment, experimenting with the newest technology, and engaging in other activities that will continually augment their knowledge of media centers and their contents. This body of knowledge should be applied when considering future acquisitions.

Knowledge of Bibliographic and Reviewing Tools

Not all material can or should be appraised locally. Opinions of experts outside the immediate school district should be consulted. There are literally hundreds of bibliographies, media lists, and reviewing journals that can help the media specialist in selection, both in print sources and on the Internet. These selection aids are issued by professional associations, commercial publishers of reviewing media, government library agencies (federal, state, and local), producers and publishers of educational media, and many library systems. Details on the types of selection aids and criteria for their evaluation are given in Chapter 9.

Knowledge of the Existing Collection

If a library media center has been in existence for some time, the media specialist must determine the size, nature, strengths and weaknesses, age and general physical condition, and basic usefulness of its contents before undertaking new selection. Several methods can be used to gain this knowledge. First, the computer shelf list and equipment inventory may be examined to determine which areas have been stressed or slighted, the amount of duplication, and the age of titles and equipment. Another method is to "read" the shelves, glancing particularly at unfamiliar titles. Another method is to check the collection against standard bibliographies to determine what proportion of these basic titles is present. The media specialist needs to become acquainted with web sites that can fill the gap in the collection when searching for recent information. The school library media specialist can also become acquainted with the media center's holdings by repeated use of the online public access catalog (OPAC). In evaluating an existing collection it is important to check outside the media center to find out what the school's holdings are, for example, in textbooks, classroom collections, study centers, and departmental libraries as well as on the Internet. Collections available at other libraries in the community need to be evaluated as to their ease of access for students and faculty. If local schools are connected through wide area networks (WAN), the collections in those schools may have an impact on media selection in the center. Library consortiums that share resources are another resource to consider.

Knowledge of the Budget

Before beginning to select media, the library media specialist should have at hand the budget allotments for the current year and, if at all possible, for the coming year or years. The selector of media must inquire about the share of additional funds that might be available through federal, state, or local funding programs over the next five years. Long-range planning, particularly for expensive books sets, online encyclopedias and other reference works, video/DVD materials, Internet access, and audiovisual equipment, is necessary. Unfortunately, less expensive substitutes will sometimes have to be found or the purchase of a desired item postponed to ensure balance and equity in distribution of budgetary funds.

Knowledge of Research Databases and Other Research Sources

School library media specialists must be knowledgeable about research databases that will fulfill the needs of the school media program. Subscriptions to full-text periodical databases, such as ProQuest or Ebsco, are necessary for student research projects. Both of these products are collections of databases and they include professional materials used primarily by faculty and students for research. Additionally, media specialists need to be knowledgeable about site licenses for online products such as encyclopedias and other reference materials.

ORGANIZING THE MEDIA SELECTION PROGRAM

The number and extent of selection services provided by the single school will depend largely on how many related services are available at the district level. The keynote is the development of a systematic process in which each supplements the other without unnecessary duplication of effort. Certain services, such as maintaining a book examination center or exhibiting samples of media center furniture, are best handled in a centralized, district-wide agency, but routing of bibliographies to individual faculty members, for example, should logically be administered at the individual-school level. Patterns of organization will therefore differ considerably from one situation to another, depending on local conditions. Some school districts provide a separate space at the district level media facility for the selection and evaluation of library media materials and equipment before purchases are made; however, this trend is slowly disappearing. Although a first-hand evaluation is not feasible for all media purchases, it is still the most preferable method to assure that the media suits the needs of the school community. The reviewing sources that are available for many materials (for example, library books) are of sufficient quantity and quality that to ignore these sources in favor of local reviewing not only wastes time and duplicates effort but also fails to utilize the expertise of the knowledgeable critics and subject specialists who review in these publications.

In areas where the reviewing media are inadequate or where the items under consideration are either very costly or highly specialized, some form of local reviewing is preferable. The cost of an initial investment, for example, the purchase price of videos or DVDs, will often mandate previewing sessions for evaluation if large quantities are being considered. In individual schools, committees may be organized according to academic departments or specific grade levels to review materials being considered for purchase. The committee normally uses some type of form to report local evaluations of materials. A rating scale is often used for each criterion on the form—this could be a numerical scale ranging from 5 for excellent to 1 for poor. Spaces are supplied for the name of the person requesting a review, dates of the request and of the review, kind of material and its subject area and general grade level, an overall priority rating (basic or supplementary), and a space for the evaluator's comments. Other items generally covered in these forms include: (1) bibliographic information, for example, title, author, producer, vendor, publisher; (2) format or technical aspects, for example, quality of sound, color, picture, binding; (3) content, for example, scope of work, limitations of coverage, up-to-date coverage, and objectivity; (4) organization and presentation, for example, suitability of length, logic, clarity of presentation, interest, pacing, amount of review, and repetition; (5) suitability, for example, appropriateness to the medium as well as to subject and grade levels, and special uses; (6) teachers' aids, for example, manuals, workbooks, and other correlated materials. Similar forms may be devised for equipment evaluation. The evaluative criteria found in Chapter 9 may also be used.

As stated earlier, responsibilities for selection are assigned in various patterns at the district and single-school levels. The single school will share some of the duties with the district center, for example, workshops on media evaluation. However, the following selection-related activities should be initiated at the single-school level:

1. Organize and administer the reviewing procedures within the school.
2. Obtain, either through the school library media center or the district office, previous copies of material requested by teachers.
3. Maintain liaison with the central selection agency and jointly coordinate activities.
4. Involve as many people in the school as possible in the selection process.
5. Route bibliographies and other selection aids, asking for purchase suggestions.

6. Attend faculty meetings as well as departmental or grade-level meetings to become acquainted with curriculum changes and to discuss future acquisition plans.

7. Conduct interest inventories with students to determine what topics interest them most and least. These inventories may be arranged alphabetically in checklist form—from "airplanes" to "zoos."

8. Maintain a file of locally reviewed educational materials and basic commercially produced selection aids.

The following list gives some selection activities that seem best suited to be performed at the district level; some might be shared with individual schools or where centralized selection services are nonexistent, initiated with the schools:

1. Organize and administer a district-wide reviewing network for materials for which standard reviewing sources are inadequate or that need supplementary local appraisal.

2. Print, disseminate, and maintain a permanent file of reviews of the locally reviewed items.

3. Schedule and make provisions for individual and group faculty visits to the examination center on a regular basis.

4. Arrange for preview privileges for material when examination copies are unavailable for extended loan.

5. Maintain liaison with other central administrative and curricular agencies or departments to ensure coordination of efforts.

6. Establish and develop cooperative acquisition projects between individual schools in the district and with other libraries in the area—public, academic, and special.

7. Act as liaison between public schools and manufacturers' representatives; maintain a file of current commercial catalogs of materials and equipment.

8. Maintain a cataloged permanent collection of basic titles that can be used as a guide in establishing new collections or reevaluating established collections.

9. Provide an exhibit collection of current books and other print and nonprint media representing at least the current and immediate past publishing seasons. Photocopy reviews from standard selection aids and insert them in the material on exhibit.

10. Organize a sample collection of audiovisual and technology equipment as well as center furniture.

11. Work closely with media specialists in the district in determining full-text databases to be used for research in individual media centers and on the wide area network (WAN) for the district.

12. Assemble special multimedia displays or media fairs on specific subjects, and when possible, route these to individual schools.

13. Be a clearinghouse for new bibliographies and selection aids that should be brought to the attention of other media personnel and a dissemination point for the lists produced in individual schools.

14. Purchase and make available expensive or specialized reviewing sources that normally would not be purchased or made available by individual schools.

15. Conduct workshops for teachers and media specialists on the evaluation of media.

16. Coordinate an exhibit and offer a workshop on the newest technology available.

17. Evaluate research databases and give advice to media specialists about the ones that best serve the school's needs.

Whatever administrative patterns evolve in the selection process, two considerations are paramount: organization and participation. If these selection processes can be achieved within a congenial atmosphere conducive to free expression and the development of professional attitudes, a successful program should result.

WRITING A MEDIA SELECTION POLICY

Considering the amount of published material on the necessity for a written media selection policy, it is amazing how many school districts have not adopted such a document. Yet in reality it should be the cornerstone of a media program, giving both shape and direction to the development of that program. A written selection policy can serve several purposes. It can supply a blueprint for future growth and refinement and prevent haphazard collection development. It can also help prevent extended and unnecessary disputes involving controversial material. Besides supplying criteria and selection procedures for the center's staff, it can help clarify these matters for the rest of the school personnel and the community.

Before developing a policy statement, the media specialist should become familiar with the basic documents concerning intellectual freedom. The American Library Association's (ALA) "Freedom to Read Statement" and

"The School Library Bill of Rights" from the American Association of School Librarians are two such documents (see Appendix IV, Key Documents). One or more of these documents is often incorporated into the selection policy. Additional policies and hints on developing them may be found in the books listed in the bibliography at the end of this chapter. Other useful material, including the *Newsletter on Intellectual Freedom,* is available from ALA's Office of Intellectual Freedom. This is a bimonthly newsletter published by the Intellectual Freedom Committee. It includes articles and reviews of recent books on censorship, a state-by-state survey of censorship challenges as well as important developments in federal and state laws.

The selection policy should not be constructed in a vacuum. It certainly should include broad universal principles, but as well must reflect local conditions. All groups affected by the policy should participate in its formation. This group includes representatives from the library media center staff, faculty, administration, students, and the community. The policy should be officially accepted by all of these groups, including the district school board. After adoption, it should be disseminated widely. No policy statement, however, should be considered permanent; instead it should reflect a dynamic stage of growth and be capable of easy amendment or revision when conditions warrant a change. It should also be broad enough to cover many contingencies, but precise enough to prevent ambiguity. Material selection policies often contain the following elements:

1. A mission statement of the school district and individual school philosophy, particularly in relation to educational materials and intellectual freedom.

2. A similar statement summarizing the goals and objectives of the library media center in relation to this overall school philosophy as well as selection objectives.

3. A list of those who participate in selection and of the specific objectives of the selection function.

4. An indication of delegated as well as final responsibility for selection including a definition of the media center personnel in this operation.

5. A list of the types of media found in the center and of the criteria applied to the selection of each.

6. An enumeration of the selection aids most frequently consulted.

7. A description of the procedures, forms, and practices used in selection.

8. An indication of areas of the collection that will be either stressed or de-emphasized.

9. A statement on how materials will be weeded and their disposal.

10. Additional or modifying criteria for the various clientele served. For example, a different set of standards might apply when buying professional materials for teachers than for purchasing high-interest material for slow or reluctant readers.

11. Statements concerning the media center's policies toward gifts, sponsored material, weeding, duplication, and replacement.

12. Information concerning any cooperative acquisition projects in which the center is involved with other schools and libraries.

13. Information on how research databases will be selected in the media center taking into account any databases available through districtwide area networks.

14. A position statement on intellectual freedom and the importance of access to information.

15. A statement about controversial subjects and reviewing as well as selection aids used to support the collection of those materials.

16. A description of the procedures for handling complaints and a copy of any forms used when a request is made to reevaluate a particular piece of material.

17. A statement on how the Internet will be used and how web sites will be selected for classroom research.

Other Policies Related to the Selection Process

Collection Development Policy

Selecting materials is only one part of policies and procedures related to the collection. Material selection policies are frequently the only policies written for many schools, leaving how the collection will be developed to chance. It is desirable that an overall collection development policy be written to tie all aspects of collection management together. The main focus of the collection development policy is to identify the plan to be used in building a media center collection. This chapter will not delve into coverage of collection development; however, Van Orden and Bishop (2001) define the components of a collection development policy providing an excellent source for material in taking the selection process beyond the scope of this chapter. Following are several web sites of collection development/material selection policies:

- Baltimore County Public Schools Selection Criteria for School Library Media Center Collections

  http://www.bcps.org/offices/lis/office/admin/selection.html

- Bentley School Material Selection Policy
  http://www.bentleyschool.net/intranet/library/ls_mspolicy.html
- Groton, Connecticut Materials Selection Policy
  http://www.groton.k12.ct.us/mts/matselect.htm
- Hickory Public Schools, North Carolina instructional resource selection policy
  http://www.hickory.k12.nc.us/Technology/State_Tech_Plan/Policies/Instructional_Materials_Selection.htm
- Rogers Public School System, Arkansas District Instructional Materials Selection Policy
  http://www.rogers.k12.ar.us/users/mcook/selection.html
- Philadelphia Selection Policy for School Library Materials
  http://www.libraries.phila.k12.pa.us/misc/selection-policy.html
- Washington Library Media Association. (2002). *Policies and procedures impacting school library media centers*
  http://www.wlma.org/WaLibraries/policyconcepts.htm
- Washington Library Media Association. (2002). *Statutes and policies for school libraries*
  http://www.wlma.org/WaLibraries/policies.htm
- Wilmington, Vermont collection development policy
  http://www.dves.k12.vt.us/html/libpol.html

Web Site Selection Criteria

Because of the widespread use of web sites for research purposes, selection criteria for web sites is necessary in a policy for school media centers. Please note that the Bentley School Material Selection Policy above contains web site selection criteria established by the Association of Library Services to Children, which is a good beginning for writing web site selection policies.

STANDARDS

A variety of published standards specify norms for the quantities of materials in a school library media center collection and, in some cases, the quality of the center's collection. The historical background on these standards is discussed in Chapter 1.

Standards can fulfill several beneficial functions. They can become a blueprint for future growth for both new and established media centers and serve as a method of evaluating existing collections. They should be seen primarily as a method that can help schools to implement their educational goals. It is often very difficult to state objective standards in certain areas, particularly where the quality of a program is to be measured. Even when quantities of material are specified, standards are hard to formulate because of frequent changes in education techniques and teaching practices. For these reasons, standards should be under constant review and revised when needed.

In applying standards it is necessary to relate each recommendation to the whole set of standards. A single standard regarding recommended numbers of particular media should be related to other parts of the existing collection; and, on a larger scale, the size of the entire collection, actual or recommended, should be seen in terms of the school's educational philosophy and objectives. It must also be noted that quantities of materials do not in themselves indicate a quality program—they merely supply one of the conditions on which a fine program can be built.

Standards are of two types, *comparative* and *projective*. Comparative standards are usually short range and are based on existing, not optimum, conditions. For example, a school district with a superior materials collection in one school might attempt to bring the collections in other schools up to this level by using the size of the single collection as a standard for the other schools. Projective standards are long range and deal more abstractly with ultimate goals. Most published well-developed standards are projective. Often these standards are stated in terms of phases that represent various stages of growth. Many state departments of education provide standards for collections. There are usually three phases: *basic* (or minimum), *good*, and *advanced* (or excellent). This breakdown can be utilized as a rating scale and can serve also as a guideline for developing short-term or immediate goals.

Several agencies have issued standards. The principal ones are at the federal and state levels, although school districts, too, often develop and adopt local standards. The district standards are usually closely associated with short-term goals and are often comparative in nature and based on an exemplary program either within the district or in a neighboring district. The district standards are easily modified or enlarged to meet changing local conditions. Flexibility is one of the chief advantages of this type of goal.

The school library media specialist should become familiar with as many as possible of the various sets of standards, particularly those at the national, state, and local levels that impact directly on the school's media program. It is also the responsibility of the media center staff to make other interested groups—administrators, faculties, parents, and school boards—aware of these standards and their implications for expansion of existing facilities and programs.

SELECTION AIDS

Like the serious researcher, the media specialist in the process of selection has available both primary and secondary sources. Primary source means that the material or equipment is itself examined before purchase. Media specialists have many opportunities to do this. Visiting exhibits at professional conventions is an excellent way. Opportunities to see demonstrations of equipment and materials and make on-the-spot comparisons and evaluations are possible at these conferences as well as chances to browse through a publisher's stock of new books. At the local level, previewing prints or on-approval copies can often be secured. Many jobbers and wholesalers allow media personnel to visit and preview the stock. There are, of course, many functioning media examination centers scattered about the country, some operating at the school district or citywide level, others at the multi-district or state level. Many public library systems also have examination centers. There is also a very accessible resource that media personnel apparently seldom use—the collections of their colleagues in other media centers and libraries.

With the explosion of information in all media and with the age of specialization upon us, however, prior examination of all material is neither possible nor practical. Media personnel must depend on the opinions and advice of professional specialists, which are often found in various reviewing media. Commonly called selection aids, these are bibliographies, catalogs, indexes, review periodicals, and "basic" or "best" lists. The proper interpretation, evaluation, and understanding of these aids is one of the essentials of effective selection.

The two major kinds of selection aids are the *retrospective* and the *current*. Retrospective aids list materials that are time-tested and generally recommended for specific needs. They are helpful in building the initial collection and can be used with existing collections to indicate material has been missed but is still useful and important. Examples of retrospective aids are *Senior High School Library Catalog* (New York: H. W. Wilson) and *The Elementary School Library Collection* (Williamsport, PA: Brodart).

Current aids, such as *Booklist* (ALA) or *School Library Journal* (Reid Elsevier, Inc.), are primarily intended to report on new material. See also Chapter 9 for selection aids. Many current selection aids must be used to obtain a range of critical opinion. Selecting material on the basis of its recommendation in only one source is extremely unwise. Because less than fifty percent of all material that might be useful in the school is reviewed in the standard tools of the trade, the librarian must also consult reviews in such specialized professional journals as *English Journal* (from National Council of Teachers of English). Selection aids are further subdivided according to the type of media reviewed: general or special subject, single format or multimedia, and so on. Regardless of how the aid is classified, the would-be user must explore it thoroughly and become familiar with its contents before it can be utilized effectively. There are many bibliographies that list recommended selection aids. Some examples are:

AASL resource guides for school library media program development. (2004, May 6). Retrieved May 7, 2004, from the ALA web site: http://www.ala.org/aasl/ resources/collection.html

Collection development and weeding resources. (n.d.). Retrieved April 10, 2004, from: http://www.bccls.org/youth_services/collectiondev.htm

Gillespie, John T. & Folcarelli, Ralph J. (1998). *Guides to Collection Development for Children and Young Adult.* Westport, CT: Libraries Unlimited.

Curtis, Della. (2002, April 5). *Media selection.* Retrieved April 10, 2004, from: http://www.bcps.org/offices/lis/office/admin/mediaselection/indexmedia.html

Van Orden, Phyllis J. & Bishop, Kay. (2001). *The collection program in schools: Appendix B.* Englewood, CO: Libraries Unlimited.

Ward E. Barnes Library. University of Missouri. (2002, October 23). *Children and young adult literature resource guide.* Retrieved April 10, 2004, from Ward E. Barnes Library web site: http://www.umsl.edu/services/scampus/ERSubGkittdlit.html

Individual selection aids are listed in Chapter 9 following the criteria for selecting educational material or equipment.

Criteria for Choosing Selection Aids

The media selector should be aware of the strengths and weaknesses of a bibliography before using it for selection purposes. When there is an understanding of the general nature as well as the specific limitations, the possibility of using each wisely and effectively increases. The criteria for selecting media, equipment, and Internet resources (presented in Chapter 9) should be applied, after which the following specific questions should be asked to make certain that all pertinent information has been collected.

Authority

- Who are the reviewers and editors and what are their qualifications?
- Do the reviewers represent a particular point of view?
- Are the reviews signed?

Scope

- Is this a selective (such as the "best of" type) or an all-inclusive bibliography?
- What types of material are listed? Are there limitations on inclusion, including format (classes of material), subject, time period, age group, language, and place of origin?
- Are adequate directions on how to use the aid provided?
- What is the intended audience?
- How often does the bibliography appear?
- How up-to-date are the reviews?
- In general, how much bibliographic data is included?

Arrangement

- Is it arranged alphabetically, by classification, or subject, chronologically, by format, or by a combination of these?
- Is there an index?
- Is the index cumulated? How often?

Annotations or Reviews

- What is their average length?
- Are they descriptive, critical or both?
- Is each piece of material reviewed separately?
- Does the review include comparisons with other similar material, or with the producer or author's other works?

- Is there some indication, perhaps through a coding system, as to whether the material is basic or supplemental?
- Are the reviews generally consistent in length, point of view, scope, and treatment?
- Do the reviews indicate comprehension, suitability, and interest levels and make suggestions for possible use?
- Has the reviewer objectively tested the accuracy, reliability, and currency of the material?

Special Features

- Does the aid include any special material, such as directories of publishers, professional organizations, manufacturers, distributors, selection centers, rental libraries, or depositories?
- Are the reviews indexed or excerpted in another publication, such as the print version of *Book Review Digest* or *Book Review Digest Plus*, the online version.

PRACTICAL POINTS TO AID SELECTION

Following is a list of practical hints and guidelines that should be followed to ensure the development of useful, well-rounded collections. Some are offshoots and extensions of the general principles stated earlier in the chapter; others introduce new factors into the selection process.

Participation in the Selection Process

As many of the school's population as possible should be involved in selecting materials for the media center. Reviewing periodicals and preview copies of materials may be routed to the faculty for comments and suggestions. School personnel should be invited to special previewing sessions. Students should also become involved. Involving others in the selection process not only adds new dimensions to the collection but also provides better insight into users' tastes and interests, and new avenues of communication are opened between the center and its patrons. Media specialists also find that participation of this sort results in increased interest in the general welfare of the center. Keeping everyone involved in the selection process is an excellent public relations tool.

Diversity in Material

Although satisfying the needs of the center's patrons is the major guiding principle behind selection, when building the basic or core collection, the maxim should be: "Get something on everything." This statement means that the center's collection should contain information in each of the important divisions of human knowledge. In a high school, for example, Greek philosophy may not be a topic of great popularity, yet most certainly the library media center should have some material on it.

Diversity in Students

Within classes in any heterogeneously organized classroom there are three basic achievement levels of students: above average, average, and below average. Translated specifically into terms of reading ability, there will be those reading above grade level, those reading at the expected level, and those reading below it. When buying material on a given topic, the media specialist must, therefore, bear in mind the various ability levels of the students who will be investigating this topic and try to obtain a sufficiently wide range of materials at each of these levels.

The student population is very culturally diverse in most schools in this country. Students from other cultures need to find materials that interest them in the media center. Books that accurately depict the cultures found in the school are essential in the media center collection.

Purchasing for Non-users

One selection trap that must be avoided is purchasing solely for the teachers and students in the school who use the library media center regularly. If the taste and interests of the non-users are not represented in the collection, appropriate material is not at hand when the opportunity occurs to convert them into center users. Thus a second maxim might be: "There should be something for everybody."

Input from the School Library Media Specialist

Throughout this chapter stress has been placed on the involvement of a number of people in the selection process. This does not in any way mean that the media specialist abdicates responsibility in this area. Unlike many college libraries that buy material only on specific request from faculty members, library media specialists initiate some orders, act as representatives for those who are not involved in selection, and have the final word in approving items for purchase.

Selection, Not Censorship

Selection is a positive process. In evaluating the contents of materials, remember that the purpose is neither to shock nor to protect. Overprotection can be as harmful as overexposure. Certain guidelines and limitations are adopted for purchasing media center material solely because of the maturity of the center's audience, but emphasis must not be on what shouldn't be purchased but what should be. Young people are much more knowledgeable today—about social issues and once taboo subjects—than their counterparts a generation ago.

In trying to avoid controversial subjects or shunning basic realities, the media center collection can become so safe that it is deadly dull and out of touch with the students. Where an item is purchased that is a particularly potent target for the censor, a special file should be kept noting reviews or discussions involving it in other censorship battles. The ALA's *Newsletter on Intellectual Freedom* is a good source of information for this file.

Subjectivity versus Objectivity

The temptation is always present to buy from the standpoint of one's own interests. If, for example, a burning interest in Greek drama is not shared by members of the faculty and student body, or is not part of the curriculum, purchases in this area will be minimal. On the other hand, the subject of automobiles may appear to be quite dull, but it is usually one of the primary interests of teenage boys. Purchases should be made from the user's point of view—not only what the student *should* be reading or using but also what students want, need, and are capable of using.

Media and Messages

When selecting materials, match the message with appropriate media. The question that should be asked is: Is this medium the most appropriate and best suited to convey the contents of the material? As an example, a video/DVD that shows how seeds travel would probably be a good choice for purchase because the idea of movement is such an integral part of this medium.

Duplication

User demand is the yardstick that determines the extent to which duplication of materials takes place. Yet some library media specialists associate duplication of titles with wastefulness; they think that buying a second copy uses funds that could be spent on a different title, thus increasing the general scope of the collection. Obviously, however, it is better to have five copies of a book that is constantly in circulation than five different titles, four of which stay unread on the shelves. With books, paperbacks afford an easy and inexpensive way to supply additional copies of a popular title.

Selection and Space Limitations

If space limitations are interfering with new purchases, explore more efficient storage systems so new material can still be added to the collection. Two obvious ways are to retire infrequently used items to other parts of the school and to rotate collections of recreational reading materials to various classrooms.

Technical Services and Selection

Library media centers that are responsible for some of their own processing should try to prepare an item for circulation as quickly as possible. This idea applies particularly to materials that have been specifically requested. If rapid processing is not possible, the material should be allowed to circulate for a time uncataloged. The rapidity with which users' requests are answered will be directly reflected in their interest in future acquisitions.

Use of Multiple Selection Aids

Using only one or two selection aids is restrictive; using many aids will help assure wiser decisions in purchasing materials that add greater depth and more points of view to the collection. See Chapter 9 for a bibliography of selection aids.

Review of Selection Aids

Tastes and needs are constantly changing; a book considered unsuitable one school year might be useful the following year. Therefore, a system of continuous review of selection aids should be organized. The basic retrospective aid needs to be checked at least once a year to determine if it still meets the media center's needs.

Cooperative Acquisitions

There are many cooperative acquisition projects presently operating at the university and public library levels. One of the earliest was the Farmington Plan, involving purchase of foreign-language materials. Schools within a particular area can also band together to form mini-Farmington Plans, whereby each school at a particular level is assigned a particular subject specialty or area of concentration (these could be determined by thorough examination of curriculum requirements). This method could also be used to ensure that at least one cooperating school has a copy of expensive items like a multi-volume reference work.

Out-of-Print Materials

An out-of-print notice from a jobber, publisher, or producer should not be interpreted as meaning complete unavailability. With print materials, if their acquisition is extremely important, check with out-of-print dealers, catalogs of facsimile-edition companies, or the book production services of University Microfilms in Ann Arbor, Michigan, as well as out-of-print Internet web sites. These routes are particularly valuable in building up local history collections.

Publishers' and Manufacturers' Catalogs

Extreme care must be exercised in using publishers' or manufacturers' catalogs in the selection process. They should be considered only as descriptive announcements of what is available, not an indication of quality. Buying on the basis of the blurbs found in these catalogs is dangerous. Quotes from dependable reviewing sources published in these annotations are often misleading; excerpting can turn a panning into what appears to be a rave. An exception should be pointed out: Several jobbers and wholesalers have hired reputable media personnel to compile lists of recommended materials, basic book lists, and the like. If the authority that compiled the work is noncommercial and reliable, the list may be considered a valid selection aid.

Series, Comics, and Graphic Novels

Even the most prestigious of series may vary in quality from one title to the next, and regardless of the standards of quality within a series, in all likelihood not all titles will be suitable for a collection. Each item should be treated as an individual entity that must be evaluated on its own merits. Educators in general are scornful of such "pulp" series as the Hardy Boys and Nancy Drew. Certainly the literary quality of these books is practically nonexistent. But if this is the only level on which students are reading, inclusion of some of these series books and similar titles should be seriously considered. Here, at least, is a beginning on which the media center staff can perhaps build through proper reading guidance.

The same policy should apply to comics and graphic novels. Here the question of quality is not quite as important because there are a number of comics of acceptable quality now in paperback format that could easily be included in a school library media center collection. Some examples are *Peanuts, Mad,* and *Ripley's Believe It or Not.* Graphic novels are becoming a popular entity in school media centers and need to be treated pretty much the same way as comics.

Book Clubs

Through use of petty cash or similar contingency funds, many library media centers join book clubs. They are generally of two main types: those that distribute hardcover editions (for example, the Junior Library Guild, for ages three to sixteen, and the adult clubs, Book-of-the-Month and Literary Guild of America) and the clubs designed for children (for example, the various Scholastic Book Services clubs), and the paperback clubs, Quality Paperback Book Club. While both types of clubs offer carefully selected, appealing titles, the hardcover clubs give subscribers the advantage of getting new books quickly and at a fair discount as opposed to publishers' prices (although sometimes not as much as a book jobber might give) and paperback clubs offer very inexpensive reprints of well-received hardcover editions and in some cases original titles that are available only through the clubs. The following is a list of some of the major book clubs:

- Junior Library Guild, Editorial Offices, 29 John Street, Suite 1602, New York, NY 10038; http://www.juniorlibraryguild.com
- Children's Book-of-the Month Club, P. O. Box 6432, Indianapolis, IN 46206-6432; http://www.cbomc.com

These two book clubs above are primarily for younger children; however, the Junior Literary Guild includes books for the teenage reader.

- Book-of-the-Month Club, Member Service Center, 6550 East 30th Street, P.O. Box 6300, Indianapolis, IN 42606-6300; http://www.bomc.com
- Literary Guild of America, 6550 East 30th Street, P.O. Box 6300, Indianapolis, IN 42606-6300; E-mail: service@literaryguild.com
- Doubleday Book Club, 6550 East 30th Street, P.O. Box 6325, Indianapolis, IN 46206-6325; http://www.DoubledayBookClub.com

These three book clubs above provide fiction and non-fiction books for adults.

- Scholastic Book Services, 557 Broadway, New York, NY 10012, 212-343-6100; http://www.scholastic.com/

Numerous books clubs are provided through Scholastic, mostly for younger children.

- Doubleday Large Print Book Club, 6550 East 30th Street, P.O. Box 6309, Indianapolis, IN 46206-6309; http://www.JoinDLP.com

This book club provides large print books for those who are visually disabled or who prefer to read large print.

Jobber for Book Clubs on the Internet

- BOOKSPAN, 1271 Avenue of the Americas, Time and Life Building, 3rd Floor, New York, NY 10020, 212-522-4200; http://www.bookspan.com

This web site offers a number of book clubs in one location for both adult and children.

Gifts and Free Materials

Media centers should welcome gifts as possible additions to the collection. In developing a policy for receiving gifts two points should be stressed: (1) only items appropriate to the collection will be kept, and (2) the center may dispose of the remaining material any way it wishes.

A wealth of free material commonly referred to as "sponsored material" is available from various industries, manufacturers, transportation companies, and so on. Before accepting items of sponsored material for the collection, check to see if there is excessive advertising or proselytizing, distortion of facts to promote products or points of view, or material about one company's wares stated in a way that would prejudice the reader or viewer against a competitor's products. Some school districts have adopted specific regulations concerning the presence of advertising in the schools. Inquiries should be made on the matter before final selections are made.

The Professional Library

Faculty members should have available to them a collection of up-to-date, well-selected professional literature. At the single-school level, the size and nature of this collection will depend on budgetary limitations and the resources available at the district level or from other agencies. Because the faculty should be largely responsible for selecting the contents of this special collection, a committee made up of teachers and a representative from the media center should be charged with developing acquisition and administrative procedures.

In addition to basic and current books, periodicals, and pamphlets on education, the professional library should contain such items as sample textbooks, workbooks, curriculum guides, indexes to periodicals, media catalogs, and local, state, and federal documents related to education. Professional research databases such as ERIC, Dissertation Abstracts, and other educational databases need to be a part of the professional collection. The media specialist needs to develop a source file for web sites of lesson plans for teachers to access when planning their lessons. Books on technology and using the Internet should be a part of the professional collection. To ensure access to other collections of related materials, the media specialists will have to organize or become part of a network that facilitates borrowing from the district library, other school systems, neighboring colleges and universities, or perhaps the state's central library agency.

Local-History Collections

Each school library media center should build up a collection on local history and community affairs, whether or not these topics are considered a formal part of the curriculum. The material can be used in a variety of ways: at election time, for background information on community projects, for debating clubs, when classroom discussions turn to topics on public affairs with local implications. In addition to regular printed and pictorial sources, including pertinent community directories, a special file should be maintained of clippings from local newspapers and available material on community industries, clubs, churches, and professional organizations. An entry in the OPAC can provide information on local resources—field trips, speakers, collections of materials, and so on—that are available to the school. Many schools have instituted photography projects and have supplemented the media center collections on local topics with photographs of key installations, historical landmarks, and persons of local importance. Others have developed oral history collections by taping interviews with prominent residents and storing the tapes in the media center. Particularly important interviews may be transcribed and used in print form.

Reevaluation of the Collection

Collections often just grow. Media selectors should bear in mind that with each new addition or deletion new balances and relationships are created. Continuous reevaluation of the collection is necessary to determine what areas are showing greatest growth, whether the greatest-growth areas are commensurate with users' needs, and that all types of media are being added in proper balance. This kind of watchdog activity can keep the collection balanced, vital, and in line with the school's needs.

Long-Range Planning

To ensure continuity, perspective, and orderly progression in collection development, the library media specialist needs to look at future goals and the steps by which they will be reached. Planning can be carefully outlined by the media specialist in collaboration with faculty and administration. Priorities must be stated and timetables organized that specify the sequential stages for achieving desired growth. This kind of planning is particularly important in respect to major expenditures, such as investing in new equipment. If possible, a one-to-three year plan should be developed. Because of rapid changing technology, a shorter long-range plan is more appropriate than a three-to-five year plan; however, in some cases the longer plan would still work. To ensure the long-range plan's flexibility and use under various circumstances, it should state for each year alternative courses of action that take various levels of funding into consideration.

Other aspects of the interrelationship between the selection process and the school library media center budget are discussed in Chapter 5.

Internet Resource Materials

School library media specialists need to make decisions as early as possible about Internet resources and how they will be used in the media center as well as potential uses in the classrooms. The selection policy should reflect how web sites will be selected and an explanation given for those web sites that will be omitted from the collection. If the web sites are going to be part of the OPAC materials list, a description needs to be in the selection policy stating how they will be provided. The following web site is a resource developed by Kathleen Craver (n.d.) that can assist in determining selection criteria and subject scope guidelines for an Internet collection:

- Internet collection development policy & procedures. http://207.238. 25.30/library/libraryinfo/InternetCollection.htm

CENSORSHIP AND THE SCHOOL LIBRARY MEDIA CENTER

Complaints concerning the appropriateness of some of the materials housed in the school library media center fall into two categories. The first could be considered the routine, often in-house request to reevaluate specific material, perhaps because it is now out of date or is no longer suited to the curriculum. These are usually generated by teachers within the school and are often settled quickly and without rancor. The second, arising from citizens' complaints, are usually more complex and less easily solved. The subject areas in which most challenges occur are sex, race, religion, profanity, drugs, and sex-role stereotypes. Unfortunately, some people tend to evaluate books and other educational materials not on intrinsic merits but on sets of personal values and prejudices; however, as stated in the "Students' Right to Read Statement": "Censorship leaves students with an inadequate and distorted picture of the ideals, values, and problems of their culture" (National Council of Teachers of English web page: http://www.ncte.org/positions/right-to-read.shtml). There is increased activity in book banning in schools recently and in spite of the Island Trees decision (see Chapter 1), schools need to make advance preparation.

A preliminary step to prevent or forestall censorship of educational materials in a community has already been mentioned: the preparation and adoption of a sound, detailed selection policy. As well, the community should be informed of this policy and have an opportunity to discuss it; it can be reaffirmed by various interest community groups including the local Parent-Teacher Association (PTA). Some superintendents of school districts also ask the PTA to form a committee specifically charged to hear such complaints. One such committee in existence consists of one teacher, one library media specialist, one central administrator, five members of the community, and when the material questioned is at the junior high school level or above, three high school students. In the case of highly controversial subjects, permission from parents is sought before eliciting responses from students. In other districts these committees are composed entirely of educational personnel and are appointed in an ad hoc fashion to hear a particular case. One such committee consists of a library media specialist, a classroom teacher, a subject specialist, and a principal. If possible, members of the committee should not be staff members of the school where the complaint originated.

In addition to setting up the mechanics to handle complaints, the school district should adopt or develop a Citizen's Request Form for Reevaluation of Learning Resource Center Materials (see Appendix IV, Key Documents, for a sample). These forms should identify the complainant, any group or organization that he or she represents, the particular work in question, and the strengths and weaknesses of this work. Further information sought includes the suitability level, the statement that the complainant has read or seen the entire work, a determination that critical reviews of the item have been consulted, and a recommendation concerning the eventual disposition of this material (for example, restrict its use or eliminate it entirely). Each form should also be signed by the complainant.

After these advance preparations, the steps used in complaint handling are as follows. When the presence of a particular piece of material in the library media center has been challenged on unsound grounds, an explanation should be given to the complainant of the selection procedures or policies in effect (perhaps even supplying a copy of the selection policy will help), the criteria used, and the qualifications of the selector. The library media specialist should make certain all the salient facts about the complaint have been made known. An offer to supply the complainant with suitable documentary evidence (such as reviews and recommendations) could also be made if necessary.

If the principal and/or the library media specialist are not able to convince the complainant of the necessity of retaining the material, the complainant should file the full complaint form. The material in question should not be removed from the shelves during the reevaluation process, as this will be interpreted as an admission of error.

Several organizations can offer assistance when dealing with censorship problems. The following is a list of organizations to assist when censorship issues arise.

ALA/Office for Intellectual Freedom
50 E. Huron Street
Chicago, IL 60611
1-800-545-2433
Fax 312-280-4227

People for the American Way
2000 M Street, NW Suite 400
Washington, DC 20036
1-800-326-7329
E-mail: pfaw@pfaw.org

National Coalition Against Censorship
275 Seventh Avenue
New York, NY 10001
212-807-6222
E-mail: ncac@ncac.org

The next step is to refer the matter to the reevaluation committee along with copies of the material in question and pertinent data, including reviews. Usually the date of the first committee meeting is made public so that anyone in the district may have the opportunity to submit evidence. The decision of the committee is often sent to the superintendent for review. It is eventually given to the complainant. Some sort of regulation should be enforced that prohibits a further reevaluation of that material for a given period, usually three years. Although this process will usually end with the superintendent's notification, some of these complaints will eventually be decided in court. Certainly, two elements are necessary if the library is to prevail in these cases: (1) a detailed, explicit, and widely distributed set of policies and procedures, and (2) the support and loyalty of the school board and administrators at all levels. Unfortunately, censors are rarely convinced that their causes are not just and proper and in spite of a defeat will often seek out new materials to challenge. For more information on censorship and the Internet see Chapter 10.

REFERENCES

Baltimore county public schools selection criteria for school library media center collections. (n.d.). Retrieved April 10, 2004, from the Baltimore County Public Schools web site: http://www.bcps.org/offices/lis/office/admin/selection.html

Bentley school material selection policy. (2003). Retrieved April 10, 2004, from the Bentley School web site: http://www.bentleyschool.net/intranet/library/ls_mspolicy.html

Brown, David K. (2001). *The children's literature web guide.* Retrieved April 10, 2004, from: http://www.ucalgary.ca/~dkbrown/

AASL resource guides for school library media program development. (2004, May 6). Retrieved May 7, 2004, from the ALA web site: http://www.ala.org/aasl/resources/collection.html

Collection development and weeding resources. (n.d.). Retrieved April 10, 2004, from: http://www.bccls.org/youth_services/collectiondev.htm

Craver, Kathleen. (n.d.). *Internet collection development policies and procedures.* Retrieved May 6, 2004, from: http://207.238.25.30/library/libraryinfo/Internet Collection.htm

Curtis, Della. (2002, April 5). *Media selection.* Retrieved April 10, 2004, from: http://www.bcps.org/offices/lis/office/admin/mediaselection/indexmedia.html

Gillespie, John T. & Folcarelli, Ralph J. (1998). *Guides to collection development for children and young adults.* Westport, CT: Libraries Unlimited.

Groton, Connecticut materials selection policy. (2003). Retrieved April 10, 2004, from: http://www.groton.k12.ct.us/mts/matselect.htm

Hickory Public Schools, North Carolina instructional resource selection policy. (n.d.). Retrieved April 10, 2004, from: http://www.hickory.k12.nc.us/Technology/State_Tech_Plan/Policies/Instructional_Materials_Selection.htm

National Council of Teachers of English. (1998–2004). *The students' right to read.* Urbana, IL: Author. Retrieved May 6, 2004, from the NCTE web page: http://www.ncte.org/about/over/positions/category/cens/107616.htm

Philadelphia selection policy for school library materials. (2002, February 5). Retrieved April 10, 2004, from: http://www.libraries.phila.k12.pa.us/misc/selection-policy.html

Rogers Public School System. (n.d.). *Arkansas district instructional materials selection policy.* Retrieved May 12, 2004, from: http://web.archive.org/web/2030416125129/http://www.rogers.k12.ar.us/users/mcook/selection.html

Van Orden, Phyllis J. & Bishop, Kay. (2001). *The collection program in schools: Appendix B.* Westport, CT: Libraries Unlimited.

Ward E. Barnes Library. (2002, Fall). *Children and young adult literature resource guide.* Retrieved April 10, 2004, from: http://www.umsl.edu/services/scampus/ERSubGkittdlit.html

Washington Library Media Association. (2002). *Policies and procedures impacting school library media centers.* Retrieved April 10, 2004, from the Washington

Library Media Association web site: http://www.wlma.org/WaLibraries/
policyconcepts.htm

Washington Library Media Association. (2002). *Statutes and policies for school
libraries*. Retrieved April 10, 2004, from the Washington Library Media Association web site: http://www.wlma.org/WaLibraries/policies.htm

Wilmington, Vermont collection development policy. (n.d.). Retrieved April 10, 2004,
from: http://www.dves.k12.vt.us/html/libpol.html

FURTHER READINGS

*Access to resources and services in the school library media program: An interpretation of
the library bill of rights*. (2000, July 12). Retrieved April 10, 2004, from the
ALA web site: http://www.ala.org/aasl/positions/ps_billofrights.html

Albanese, Andrew, et al. (2003, March). Amend Patriot Act I (intellectual freedom). *Library Journal, 128*(4), 17–18.

Alpine school district. (1983, November 8). *Media Selection Policy*. Retrieved April
10, 2004, from: http://www.alpine.k12.ut.us/depts/media/guidelines/dist
selectionpol.html

Alpine school district. (1999, January). *Media center guidelines for collection management: Weeding books*. Retrieved April 10, 2004, from: http://www.alpine.
k12.ut.us/depts/media/guidelines/weedingbks.html

American Association of School Librarians. (2002, December 18). AASL
resource guides for school library media program development. Retrieved
April 10, 2004, from the ALA web site: http://www.ala.org/aasl/resources/

American Library Association. (1998, October). *Workbook for selection policy writing*. Retrieved April 10, 2004, from the ALA web site: http://www.ala.
org/Template.cfm?Section=Dealing_with_Challenges&Template=/Content
Management/ContentDisplay.cfm&ContentID=11173

American Library Association: Office for Intellectual Freedom. (2002, June).
Libraries & the Internet toolkit. *Teacher Librarian, 29*(5), 58–60.

Anderson, Joanne S. (Ed.). (1996). *Guide for written collection policy statements*.
Chicago: ALA.

Bertland, Linda. (2003, August 5). *Collection development*. Retrieved April 10,
2004, from: http://www.sldirectory.com/libsf/resf/coldev2.html

Bielefield, Arlene & Cheeseman, Lawrence. (1994). *Maintaining the privacy of
library records*. New York: Neal-Schuman.

Bielefield, Arlene & Cheeseman, Lawrence. (1999). *Technology and copyright law:
A guidebook for the library, research, and teaching professions*. New York: Neal-
Schuman.

Block, Marylaine. (1998, September/October). Creating an Internet collection
development policy: Principles of selection. *Knowledge Quest, 27*(1), 46–47.

Bruwelheide, Janis H. (1997). *The copyright primer for librarians and educators* (2nd
ed.). Chicago: ALA.

Cassell, Kay Ann. (1999). *Developing reference collections and services in an electronic age.* New York: Neal-Schuman.

Chapin, Rich. (1999, September). *Content management, filtering and the World Wide Web.* [Electronic version]. *THE Journal, 27*(2), 44. Retrieved April 10, 2004, from: http://www.thejournal.com/magazine/vault/A2221.cfm

Chenoweth, Karin. (2001, September). Keeping score. *School Library Journal, 47*(9), 48–51.

Crews, Kenneth D. (2000). *Copyright essentials for librarians and educators* (2nd ed.). Chicago: ALA.

Curtis, Donnelyn, et al. (2000). *Developing and managing e-journal collections.* New York: Neal-Schuman.

Davis, Trisha L. (1997, Winter). Evolution of selection activities for electronic resources. *Library Trends, 45*(3), 391–403.

Deegan, Marilyn & Tanner, Simon. (2002). *Digital futures: Strategies for the information age.* New York: Neal-Schuman.

Doll, Carol & Barron, Pamela. (2002). *Managing and analyzing your collection: A practical guide for small libraries and school library media centers.* Chicago: ALA.

Evans, G. Edward. (2000). *Developing library and information center collections* (4th ed.). Westport, CT: Libraries Unlimited.

Gregory, Vicki L. (2000). *Selecting and managing electronic resources.* New York: Neal-Schuman.

Hoffman, Gretchen McCord. (2001). *Copyright in cyberspace: Questions & answers for librarians.* New York: Neal-Shuman.

Hutchinson, Carol-Anne. (2002, June). Collection development: Bordering on dysfunction. *Teacher Librarian, 29*(5), 54–56.

Jones, Patrick. (2003, March). To the teen core: A librarian advocates building collections that serve YA readers. *School Library Journal, 49*(3), 48–50.

Kachel, Debra E. (1997). *Management for school libraries: Preparing for cooperative collection development.* Westport, CT: Greenwood Publishing.

Kibirige, Harry M. (1996). *Foundations of full-text electronic information delivery systems.* New York: Neal-Schuman.

Kluegel, Kathleen. (1997, Spring). Redesigning our future. *RQ, 36*(3), 330–334.

Kovacs, Diane. (1999). *Building electronic library collections: The essential guide to selection criteria and core subject collection.* New York: Neal-Schuman.

Lee, Stuart D. (2002). *Electronic collection development: A practical guide.* New York: Neal-Schuman.

Lukenbill, W. Bernard. (2002). *Collection development for a new century in the school library media center.* Westport, CT: Libraries Unlimited.

McDonald, Frances B. (1993). *Censorship and intellectual freedom: A survey of school librarians' attitudes and moral reasoning.* Lanham, MD: Scarecrow Press.

McGregor, Joy, et al. (Eds.). (2003). *Collection management for school libraries.* Lanham, MD: Scarecrow Press.

Massachusetts School Library Media Association. (n.d.). *MA school library media program standards: Resources standard specifications.* Retrieved April 10, 2004, from the Massachusetts School Library Media Association web site: http://www.mslma.org/whoweare/standards/specs2.pdf

Mason-Robinson, Sally. (1996). *Developing and managing video collections in libraries.* New York: Neal-Schuman.

Methuen Public Schools. (n.d.). *Massachusetts selection policy.* Retrieved May 6, 2004, from: http://www.methuen.k12.ma.us/media/Selection%20Policy%20 rev2.htm

Minkel, Walter. (2001, March). Policy discussion. *School Library Journal, 47*(3), 41.

Missouri Department of Elementary and Secondary Education. (2002). *Standards for Missouri school library media centers.* Retrieved April 10, 2004, from: http://www.dese.state.mo.us/divimprove/curriculum/standards/lmcstand.htm

Montana State Library. (n.d.). *Collection development policy guidelines for school library media programs.* Retrieved April 10, 2004, from: http://www.msl. state.mt.us/slr/cmpolsch.html

Munroe, Mary H, et al. (Eds.). (2001). *Guide to collection development and management: Administration, organization, and staffing.* Lanham, MD: Scarecrow Press.

Office of Intellectual Freedom. *Intellectual freedom manual* (6th ed.). Chicago: ALA.

Pastine, Maureen. (Ed.). (1998). *Collection development: Access in the virtual library.* Binghamton, NY: Haworth Press.

Pearlmutter, Jane. (1999, June). Which online resources are right for your collection? (Creating collection policies for online resources). *School Library Journal, 45*(6), 27–30.

Policies and procedures in ISB libraries. (n.d.). Retrieved April 10, 2004, from the International School Bangkok web site: http://www.isb.ac.th/Content/Detail. asp?ID=519

Ramsey, Inez L. (1999, September 13). *Intellectual freedom.* Retrieved April 10, 2004, from: http://falcon.jmu.edu/~ramseyil/free.htm

Renaissance Learning. (2002). *National reading studies validate accelerated reader, reading renaissance.* Retrieved April 10, 2004, from the Renaissance Learning web site: http://research.renlearn.com/research/pdfs/140.pdf

Reichman, Henry. (2001). *Censorship and selection: Issues and answers for schools.* Chicago: ALA.

Simpson, Carol. (2000). *Copyright for schools: A practical guide.* (3rd ed.). Worthington, OH: Linworth.

Smith, Abby. (2002, Winter). Strategies for building digitized collections. *Microform & Imaging Review, 31*(1), 7–30.

Smith, Mark. (1999). *Neal-Schuman Internet policy handbook for libraries.* New York: Neal-Schuman.

Snyder, Becky A. (2001, January). Seeking value on the Internet. *THE Journal, 28*(6), 66. Retrieved April 10, 2004, from: http://www.thejournal.com/magazine/ vault/A3272.cfm

St. Lifer, Evan. (2002, August). Graphic novels, seriously: Why this emerging genre belongs in both public and school libraries. *School Library Journal, 48*(8), 9.

Symons, Ann K. & Harmon, Charles. (1995). *Protecting the right to read.* New York: Neal-Schuman.

Talab, R. S. (1999). *Commonsense copyright.* Jefferson, NC: McFarland.

Thomsen, Elizabeth. (1996). *Reference and collection development on the Internet.* New York: Neal-Schuman.

University of Wisconsin-Madison School of Education. (2003, September 3). *Cooperative children's book center.* Retrieved April 10, 2004, from: http://www.soemadison.wisc.edu/ccbc/index.htm

Van Orden, Phyllis. (2000). *Selecting books for the elementary school library media center.* New York: Neal-Schuman.

Van Orden, Phyllis R. & Bishop, Kay. (2001). *The collection program in schools: Concepts, practices, and information sources* (3rd ed.). Westport, CT: Libraries Unlimited.

Washington Library Media Association. (2002). *Issues for school libraries.* Retrieved April 10, 2004, from: http://www.wlma.org/Professional/issues.htm

Washington Library Media Association. (2002). *Policies and procedures impacting school library media centers.* Retrieved April 10, 2004, from WLMA web site: http://www.wlma.org/WaLibraries/policyconcepts.htm

Wood, Richard J. (2003). *Library collection development policies: A reference and writer's handbook.* Lanham, MD: Scarecrow Press.

Chapter 9

MEDIA SELECTION: CRITERIA AND SELECTION AIDS

In selecting materials and equipment, the use of criteria helps to make objective an otherwise subjective operation. Quantitative criteria establish the need for materials and equipment. Two levels of selection criteria are necessary: criteria that apply to all materials, and more specific criteria that apply only to a particular genre such as videos, books, or online databases. This same distinction applies to criteria for purchasing equipment. In this chapter, general and specific criteria are given for educational materials, online resources, and equipment selection, followed by a list of appropriate selection aids. It also includes specific criteria for selecting materials for reluctant readers.

QUANTITATIVE CRITERIA FOR EDUCATIONAL MATERIALS AND EQUIPMENT

The school media center provides in each building a collection of materials, and the equipment needed to use it, that fits in variety and scope both the curricula of the school and the interests and abilities of the users. In determining all possible resources, the collection should include, besides the items housed in the school, those materials that can be borrowed through interlibrary loan as well as those accessed electronically through the Internet.

Collection Size and Variety

The range of the collection can be broad, from books and games or videos/DVDs to community resource files and computer software or compact discs. The collection should include some material in every available medium including visual, audio, print, and electronic resources.

Basic initial collections should be available in every school. Each school, regardless of enrollment, should have a fully cataloged and processed print, non-print, and online collection, which insures access by all users. The quantity of material in a basic collection will depend on enrollment, range of grades, variety of subjects taught, and special needs of the school population. The funds needed for initial collections should be included in capital-outlay budgets. The acquisition and technical processing must be done before the collection is ready and the school library media program can be initiated. The building of a collection ideally should begin when a new or remodeled school library media center is first planned. Some duplication should be anticipated if decentralized resource centers by subject area or grade level are to be housed in the same building.

The size of the collection in a school library media center can be established based on enrollment for different levels of schools. This approach to collection building reinforces the unified concept of a school library media center.

Many state education departments also issue recommendations, sometimes in phases or developmental stages that can be used by the media specialist. (See Appendix 1 for the appropriate state address.) Depending on the particular state and the structure in the education department, either the department that handles the combined school library media business or the departments that treat the school library and media concerns should be contracted. Following are guidelines for quantities of items for collection development based on the State of New Mexico's (New Mexico Task Force for School Libraries, 2001) recommendations to carry on a basic media program and to meet minimum standards for collections. The guidelines have been divided into minimum, average, and exemplary standards. The quantities for elementary and secondary print and non-print materials should be combined in schools where the library media center serves K–12. The basic collection should include both print and non-print items—twenty per student for both elementary and secondary schools in exemplary programs. A variety of media closely linked to the school curriculum should be represented in the media collection. Formats of media include but are not limited to videos/DVDs, transparencies, compact discs, computer software, realia, kits, models, photographs, study prints, charts, maps, globes and games.

No one way of assigning print, non-print, and electronic resources according to a predetermined percentage scale is necessarily the best for each school. Instead a primary consideration should be that the subject matter—instructional and recreational—is represented in as many formats and to the same degree that is needed by the faculty and students of the school. The charts below from the State of New Mexico (New Mexico Task Force for School Libraries, 2001) provide standards for collection currency, collection size, periodicals, and audio visual material.

Equipment

Recommendations for quantities of equipment follow the same pattern as those for the collection because the equipment is so closely tied to the material with which it is used. There is no maximum or minimum quantity; the amount depends on the school's program. However, careful con-

Exhibit 9.1.
Standards for Collection Currency

Currency Standard	Minimum	Average	Exemplary
70% of the collection area is current, i.e. publication date is no older than 12 years from the current date	Time-Sensitive Sections: Social Sciences (Call # 300-389) Science (Call # 500-599) Technology (Call # 600-699) Geography, travel, biography, modern history (Call # 900-999) Reference (Call # R)	Nonfiction collection (Call # 001-999)	Total collection Fiction and Nonfiction

Exhibit 9.2.
Standards for Collection Size: Numbers of Titles.

School Size Number of students	Minimum	Average	Exemplary
Fewer than 300	3000 titles	4500 titles	6000 titles
301-600	6000	9000	12,000
601-1000	10,000	15,000	20,000
1001+	12,500 or 12 titles per student, whichever is greater.	15 titles per student	20 titles per student

Periodicals—Every school library should have at least one (1) or more online Internet periodical database that provides extended access to full-text articles in a wide range of journals suitable to the school's grade levels. For staff professional use and for student patrons' recreational and literacy development reading needs, the following standards for hard copy periodicals pertain.

Printed with permission. New Mexico Task Force for School Libraries. (2001, January). *Standards for New Mexico school libraries: Collections.* Retrieved May 8, 2004, from the New Mexico Library Association web site:
http://www.rluds.com/upload/files/LSNMstandards.pdf

sideration must be given to equipment purchasing because obsolescence is an integral part of technology. This fact should not, however, prevent the school library media specialist from incorporating into the program new developments in equipment. It should caution the media specialist that complete information about each type of equipment should be gathered and attention given to current technological developments. Attention to compatibility of equipment hardware and software needs to be the guiding principle by which purchases are made.

Ideally a plan for using the equipment throughout the school, as well as in the media center itself, is appropriate. The list of equipment shown in Exhibits 9.5 and 9.6 suggests quantities for the three phase levels in elementary schools and secondary schools of minimum, average, and exemplary collections.

Exhibit 9.3.
Standards for Periodicals.

Standard by School Size and Level	Minimum	Average	Exemplary
Elementary School Fewer than 300 students	8 magazine titles; 1 newspaper title	12 magazine titles; 2 newspaper titles	16 magazine titles; 4 newspaper titles
Elementary School 301-600	10 magazine titles; 1 newspaper title	14 magazine titles; 2 newspaper titles	18 magazine titles; 4 newspaper titles
Elementary School 601+	12 magazine titles; 1 newspaper title	16 magazine titles; 2 newspaper titles	20 magazine titles; 4 newspaper titles
Middle/Jr High School	16 magazine titles; 2 newspaper titles	24 magazine titles; 4 newspaper titles	32+ magazine titles; 5 newspaper titles
High School	25 magazine titles; 2 newspaper titles	35 magazine titles; 3 newspaper titles	45+ magazine titles; 5 newspaper titles

Languages: It is expected that schools serving students with first languages other than English will have those languages represented by library materials throughout the collection.

Non-print materials (including videocassette titles, CD-ROM titles, computer software titles and other non-print media) should equal at least one (1) percent of the total print collection.

Printed with permission. New Mexico Task Force for School Libraries. (2001, January). *Standards for New Mexico school libraries: Collections*. Retrieved May 8, 2004, from the New Mexico Library Association web site: http://www.rluds.com/upload/files/LSNMstandards.pdf

Quality of the Program

The quality of the program cannot be measured solely by the size of the collection. However, when only a minimal quantity of media is provided, educational opportunities for students are limited. Although it is difficult to prove that a given quantity of materials, online resources, and equipment will ensure that a child will learn, the knowledge gathered from

Exhibit 9.4.
Audio Visual Material Collections.

Enrollments	Minimum	Average	Exemplary
Fewer than 300	300	450	600
301-600	600	900	1,200
601-1,000	1,000	1,500	2,000
1,001+	1,250 or 12 titles per student, whichever is greater	15 titles per student	20 titles per student

experience and research is that young people are more likely to show educational gains within an environment that includes a variety of media.

National standards and state and local organization recommendations,
when available, can serve as guidelines in the development of collections
for both materials and equipment. Many national associations provide
helpful guides that school library media specialists can use. One of the
more important documents for many years was *Media Programs: District
and School* published in 1975 for quantitative standards. *Information Power*
published in both 1988 and 1998 are not quantitative standards but rather
qualitative.

In addition, state organizations that represent the school library media
field may issue guidelines, for example, the New York Library Association.
Regional or local organizations in the field sometimes recommend guidelines, for example, the Long Island School Media Association (LISMA),
which combines the former School Library and Educational Technology
organization for Long Island, New York. Other organizations are listed in
Appendix II.

GENERAL CRITERIA FOR SELECTING
EDUCATIONAL MATERIALS

Authority

The term *authority* refers to the qualifications of the people responsible
for creating the material (the author, the producer or publisher) and how

Exhibit 9.5.
Equipment Collections for a Basic Media Program.

Equipment	Minimum	Average	Exemplary
Alpha smart-type portable keyboards	1 class set per 6 elementary teachers	1 class set per four elementary teachers	1 class set per elementary classroom
Audiocassette recorder	1 per 6 teachers	1 per 4 teachers	1 per classroom
Cassette players/recorders	1 per 6 teachers	1 per 4 teachers	1 per classroom
CD players	1 per 6 teachers	1 per 4 teachers	1 per classroom
Closed circuit television	All schools should consider	All schools should consider	All schools should consider
Computers	4 per media center	10 per media center	20-30 per media center
Camera, digital	1 per school	3 per school	6 per school
Camera, digital video	1 per school	3 per school	6 per school
Camera, 35mm	As needed	As needed	As needed
DVD player	1 per school	1 per grade level/department	1 per classroom
Laptop computers	1 classroom set	4 classroom sets	1 classroom set per grade level/department
Laser disk player	1 per school	1 per grade level/department	1 per classroom
Laser printer	As needed	As needed	As needed
LCD projector	1 per school	1 per grade level/department	1 per classroom
Maps and globes	1 set per grade level/department	1 set per grade level/department	1 set per classroom
Opaque projector	1 per school	1 per school	1 per school
Overhead projector	1 per 6 teachers	1 per four teachers	1 per classroom
Palm computers (PDA)	1 classroom set	4 classroom sets	1 classroom set per grade level/department
Paper cutter	1 per media center	2 per media center	3 per media center
Photocopying machine	1 per media center, coin operated	2 per media center, coin operated	3 per media center, coin operated
Portable screen	1 per 10 teachers	1 per 6 teachers	1 per 4 teachers

Exhibit 9.5. (continued)

Equipment	Minimum	Average	Exemplary
Printers	As needed for computers	As needed for computers	As needed for computers
Projection cart	1 per piece of portable equipment	1 per piece of portable equipment	1 per piece of portable equipment
Projection screen, large	4 per school	1 per grade level/department	1 per classroom
Realia	As needed	As needed	As needed
Scanner	1 per media center	2 per media center	3 per media center
Slide projector	1 per 10 teachers	1 per 8 teachers	1 per grade level/department
Smart board	4 per school	1 per grade level/department	1 per classroom
Television, large screen digital	1 per school	4 per school	1 per grade level/Department
Tripod	As needed	As needed	As needed
Video editing equipment	1 per school	1 per school	2 per school

capable and prepared they are to have undertaken the project in question. Information on their background, education, experience, reputation, and previous works will supply useful clues. Also, a determination of the nature and reputation of research sources used is useful. If the item under consideration is an adaptation or revision of another work, the extent and nature of the differences should be determined; often these are so slight that a media center that owns the old work may not wish to purchase the revision.

Scope

Essentially, scope refers to the overall purpose and coverage of the material. When the breadth and limitation of scope are determined, the work should be compared with others on the same subject to see if it presents a fresh viewpoint or if it displaces, amplifies, or simply repeats existing material in the collection.

Format and Technical Quality

The physical makeup of the material should be appropriate to its content. It should meet acceptable production standards and be of sufficient quality to help promote use. Each form of educational material has distinctive physical characteristics.

Exhibit 9.6.
Miscellaneous Equipment to be Purchased As Needed.

Equipment	Minimum	Average	Exemplary
Cassette duplicator	As needed	As needed	As needed
Copy stand	As needed	As needed	As needed
Equipment repair tools	1 per media center	1 per media center	1 per media specialist
Fax machine	1 per media center	1 per media center	1 per media center
Instant print camera	1 per media center	1 per media center	1 per media specialist
Large paper cutter	1 per media center	1 per media center	1 large and one small
Laminator	1 per media center	1 per media center	1 large and one small
Manual lettering device	1 per media center	1 per media center	1 per media center
Mechanical lettering device	1 per media center	1 per media center	1 per media center
Portable bulletin boards	As needed	As needed	As needed
Portable PA system	1 per media center	1 per media center	1 per media center
Splicer, cassette tape	1 per media center	1 per media center	1 per media center
Splicer, video cassette	1 per media center	1 per media center	1 per media center
Telephone	1 per media center	1 per media center	1 per media specialist and staff members
35mm slide viewer	1 per media center	1 per media center	1 per media center
Transparency production kits	1 per media center	1 per media center	1 per media center
Video cassette rewind	1 per media center	1 per media center	1 per media center

These pieces of equipment are recommended as minimum, average, and exemplary according to needs of the media center program.

Authenticity

The contents should be checked for validity, reliability, and completeness, as well as for the degree of bias or objectivity. Recency is also important. The copyright date and imprint date should relate favorably; sometimes they are valid guides to the currency of the material. However, the contents will usually have to be examined to make a final and accurate determination.

Treatment and Arrangement

The material should be clearly presented in a well-organized fashion. This particular criteria involves a logical development; the sequence of the content should flow naturally and easily from one section into another. The material should be well balanced and place emphasis on the elements of greatest importance. The arrangement should bear a direct relationship to use of the material and be judged by the degree to which it facilitates that use. The style of presentation, the general comprehension level, and the nature of the concepts being developed must be appropriate, both to the intended audience and to the nature and depth of coverage intended. The material should be developed in light of sound educational principles and make provision for such elements as review and reinforcement. Finally, the work should catch and hold the user's interest and provide stimulation for further learning.

Aesthetic Considerations

The item must be acceptable artistically, with separate elements combining to form an aesthetically pleasing whole. The material should appeal to the imagination, to the senses, and to the intellect, so that the user's taste and sense of artistic appreciation will be developed.

Price

The acquisition of any piece of material, and particularly expensive items, must be seen in relation to existing budget limitations. It might be necessary to find out if a satisfactory substitute at a lower price is available. Certainly the initial cost will be weighed against the amount of intended use.

Special Features

The media specialist should try to ascertain the characteristics, if any, that make the item under consideration distinctive among others of the same type and on the same subject. These might be, for example, an unusual approach to a subject matter, the presence of usage guides, sets of questions and answers, or a list of suggested follow-up activities.

General Suitability

Having evaluated the material in the preceding general terms, the media specialist now must view the material in light of the school's existing collection. The appropriateness of the material to the school's educational objectives and curriculum is an important factor. Other questions to ask might include: Is there sufficient need for the item? How many will use it? Is it suited to the particular needs and abilities of those who will use it?

SELECTION CRITERIA FOR SLOW OR RELUCTANT LEARNERS

A special set of criteria needs to be applied when selecting materials for slow or reluctant learners. Students with learning disabilities frequently have a short attention span and are unable to retain facts for long time periods.

In selecting materials for reluctant readers or those with learning disabilities, several criteria should be considered: Repetition, reinforcement, segmented learning, and visual impact.

Repetition

Repeating main points help to reinforce the learning of content. Repeating points, in summary, is an effective method for the learning disabled student to learn content. For example, a video might discuss the different kinds of machines. Examples of each kind of machine might be given and a summary at the end would go over the main points again.

Reinforcement

Students who are slow learners need to have correct answers reinforced in the learning process and incorrect answers replaced with correct answers. For example, students might be shown the pictures of each kind of machine and then asked to name it. Correct responses allow the student to go to the next machine. Incorrect responses require the student to remediate and try again.

Segmented Learning

Students who are slow learners need to learn content or concepts in small segments. Small amounts of content can be learned at one time;

therefore, materials must be designed in a format that keeps the number of concepts to a minimum. For example, the student would learn about the wheel and axle before attempting to learn about the pulley.

Visual Impact

Students that are slow learners retain information for longer periods of time when simple pictorial examples accompany the text. The relationship between the text and the illustrations is crucial.

SPECIFIC CRITERIA FOR SELECTING EDUCATIONAL MATERIALS

Books

Regardless of how varied the materials are in the school's media center, books will remain one of the mainstays of the collection. Each center will strike different balances concerning the number of titles found in various subject areas; such factors as differences in curricula and student abilities mandate that such variations in collections should exist from school to school. Exhibit 9.7 gives a general indication of the average size of various parts of book collections; however, these figures will and should vary from one media center to another. The figures are arranged, as are the collections they represent, by Dewey decimal numbers.

In addition to the general criteria for selection, criteria related to format are also important. The book's size should be appropriate to its audience. The paper should be of good quality and sufficiently opaque to prevent seeing through to the next page. Besides being clear and easy to read, the typeface should be suitable for the intended user. Adequate spacing between words and the leading between lines are important. The binding must show the necessary durability and strength related to the type of use the book will receive. Interesting page layouts, pleasing use of color, and an eye-catching cover help make the book physically attractive. Hardcover books should lie flat when open.

Furthermore, specific types of books, such as fiction, require specific criteria.

Fiction

Whenever possible fiction titles should reach acceptable literary standards, although in providing stories for reluctant and slow readers, these standards might have to be modified or altered in some way. Good fiction generally has the characteristics described here:

Exhibit 9.7.
General Guidelines for Distribution of the Collection.

Dewey Classification	Subject	Percentage of Collection	
		K-6	7-12
000-099	General Works & Reference (R)	2-5%	6-8%
100-199	Philosophy, Psychology	.5%	1-2%
200-299	Religion & Mythology	1-2%	1-2%
300-399	Social Sciences, Folklore	5-10%	10-15%
400-499	Language	.5%	2-5%
500-599	Pure Science	10%	5-10%
600-699	Applied Science	10%	5-10%
700-799	Fine Arts, Recreation	5%	5-10%
800-899	Literature	5%	5-10%
900-999	History, Geography, Biography	20%	20%
F	Fiction	20%	20-25%
E	Easy books, Picture books	20-25%	

Characterization. The characters should be believable and constant. Changes in character should arise naturally and convincingly from the plot. Stereotypes should be avoided. The author should use imaginative but suitable ways to reveal characterization through combinations of direct exposition, dialogue, thought, and action.

Plot. This is probably the most important element for young readers. It should be logical and well constructed, move at an active rate, and appropriately reflect the central theme or purpose of the novel. The story should advance in a continuous, well-balanced flow.

Setting and atmosphere. The setting and concomitant creation of atmosphere should be appropriate to the author's purpose and should be emphasized or de-emphasized depending on the nature of the novel.

Style. An author's writing style may vary from the objectivity of writers like Hemingway to the subjectivity of Proust or Joyce. Regardless of its nature, the style should suit the material and theme, be smooth and dynamic, and not be so self-conscious that it intrudes on and detracts from the reader's enjoyment of the work.

Theme. Any theme is valid if the author is able to combine the above elements to make the central idea valid, believable, and important. The nature, complexity, and subtlety of themes should vary with the author's purpose and be appropriate for the intended audience.

Picture Books

In picture books and other books that rely heavily on illustrations to convey messages, the pictures should be clear, simple, and of suitable size, and they should interpret the story truthfully and be unified with the text. The medium used in the pictures (water colors, pen-and-ink drawings, line blocks) should be appropriate to the setting and the atmosphere created in the story.

Graphic Novels

Graphic novels, comics in book format, attract reluctant readers. The same criteria for selecting any work of fiction still apply. The illustrations should interpret the story truthfully and sequentially. The graphic novel is an excellent device for initial teaching about plot, characterization, setting, style, and theme. For older reluctant readers, the comic format is more appealing. Bindings are frequently fragile for this medium and attention needs to be paid to reinforce the bindings, such as clear book tape. Some jobbers offer reinforced bindings for graphic novels at a higher cost.

E-Books

E-books are traditional print books in an electronic format. They can be downloaded to and read on a handheld computer, a personal computer, or a smartphone using an e-book reader. Various search and navigation, bookmarking, cross-referencing, and annotation facilities can be used when using e-books (AskOxford, 2002). They are easily obtainable and some vendors offer what they call "Webscriptions" where it is possible to download a number of books for a small fee per month.

E-books have many advantages. (1) They can be quickly downloaded, making them instantly available. (2) No shipping charges or waiting are involved. (3) A user has direct access to technical information for a computer. (4) They are never out of print. (5) Page images can be magnified. (6) They are less expensive than printed books. (7) A number of books can be stored on a PC, handheld computer, or smartphone, making them very portable. (8) Information on e-books can be easily updated. (9) Sections can be sold separately when needed. (10) They are lighter to transport than printed books. (11) They can include multimedia activities, such as video, sound, and games. (12) E-books have search engine and electronic navigation capabilities. (13) Clicking is easier than page turning (Advantages of an e-book over a printed book, n.d.; Advantages of e-books, n.d.; Johnson, 2002; Publidisa Publicaciones Digiatales, n.d.; Webman Studios, 2002).

E-books also have some disadvantages. (1) They can only be accessed from within the old Adobe E-Book Reader or the new Adobe Reader 6.0. (2) An e-book file cannot be modified or edited in any way. (3) It cannot be accessed from more than one computer. (4) Libraries need to load titles on reading devices. (5) Archival potential is still unknown. (6) Reading devices are changing rapidly, without upgrade options. (7) The price of reading devices is high. (8) Libraries don't get discounts as they do with books. (9) Screen resolution is below that of printed paper. (10) Titles are seldom reviewed by respected reviewing sources. (11) Copyright and lending issues need to clarified and simplified (Johnson, 2002; Macatea Productions, 2001–2003).

Nonfiction Books

Most nonfiction titles are correlated to the curriculum of the school with emphasis on a diversity of reading and maturity levels to meet student needs. Student and faculty interests should be addressed in selecting nonfiction titles. In selecting nonfiction books, the following characteristics should be evaluated, in addition to the general criteria:

Accuracy: Current factual information is provided to answer questions raised in the curriculum and to provide background material on a subject. All facts must be accurate, up-to-date and impartially presented. Distinctions between opinions and facts should be evident.

Divergent Viewpoints: For controversial issues, all divergent points of view should be represented in the collection in several different formats. For example, students might need reference books, videos/DVDs, pamphlets, periodicals, books, and audiovisual materials expressing the various viewpoints.

Illustrative Materials: Illustrations, graphs, charts and photographs should enhance the content and be located in close proximity to the text descriptions.

Availability: The criteria of availability may be crucial for selecting materials in particular subjects such as current events, biographical accounts of famous people as high interest-low vocabulary materials.

Ease of Use: Special features should be considered that make the book easy to use. For example, does the book contain a glossary or index, key words or other devices to enhance its use?

Other Considerations: Series. Series items must be judged independently. Different authors may write books in a series and all may not write equally well. An author that writes all books in a series may not be an authority on all subjects.

Reference Books

Reference books and many other books of general nonfiction can be used effectively and efficiently if they contain the following: running heads (as in dictionaries), thumb indexing, extensive illustrations placed close to the related text, thorough indexes, cross-references, and pronunciations of difficult words. For multi-volume sets, such as encyclopedias, the media specialist should also explore the revision policy as well as the nature and quality of supplements or yearbooks.

Textbooks

For many years the textbook was the main teaching tool. It still supplies a common body of knowledge for all students and in many ways can help to organize and facilitate instruction. Critics maintain, however, that the single-textbook concept stifles inquiry and critical thinking, deals with events superficially, does not allow for the individual student's needs and interests, and tends to lock the curriculum into a fixed sequence, and that the text is often poorly written. For these reasons the single text is increasingly being abandoned in favor of resource-based instruction that uses a variety of educational materials.

Textbooks are usually chosen by a selection committee. The committee should include at least one representative from the media center, and each of the basic criteria involving authority, scope, treatment, authenticity, and suitability must be vigorously applied. In addition, the following questions should be asked when a text is being considered:

1. Does the content of the textbook relate well to the syllabus of the course?
2. Are the reading and interest levels within the text suited to the students who will use it?
3. Is the material presented in a way to encourage further study and critical thinking?
4. Is the material interestingly presented?
5. Are illustrations used often and effectively?
6. Does the author present the material in a fair, unbiased manner?
7. If differing opinions exist, are all sides of a controversial question presented objectively?
8. In the area of social studies, is proper balance shown to the contributions of various racial, ethnic, and religious groups?
9. Are supplementary teaching aids available?
10. Are extensive bibliographies provided for further study?
11. Are such learning aids as a glossary, index, extensive table of contents, pronunciations, summaries, and lists of supplementary activities present?
12. Can the material be easily reorganized to accommodate the different needs of various teaching situations?
13. In what way, if any, can the material be updated?
14. Does the text suggest possible age-appropriate web sites and other online resources to be used?

Paperbacks

Many studies show how effective paperbacks can be for individualizing and enriching instruction in the schools. These studies indicate that young people usually prefer a paperback to its hardcover counterpart. Although the distinction between categories in paperbacks is now frequently blurred, paperbacks are usually classified as *mass market* or *quality,* the differences usually being price, format, and distribution patterns. Mass-market paperbacks are generally less expensive and are presented in substantially different formats than the original hardcover editions. Quality paperbacks tend to be a little higher in price, but they are often superior in format. They are available directly from publishers as well as from hardcover and paperback book jobbers.

Some basic uses of paperbacks include: (1) to explore new areas of reader interest, (2) to supply a variety of material to special students, (3) to provide multiple copies, (4) to make available more books for the reluctant or slow reader, (5) to provide ephemeral material that has high but short-term appeal, (6) to supply material that may rapidly become outdated, (7) to supply material unavailable in any other format, (8) to supply collections of books through paperback book fairs, (9) to extend the curriculum, and (10) to provide individualized instruction.

Magazines and Newspapers

The habit of reading magazines grows during childhood, and by adolescence, magazines are usually preferred more than all other kinds of reading. Many reasons have been suggested for this: Magazines are easily accessible; their contents cater to a wide variety of interests; the use of color and illustrations makes them attractive (they are, in a sense, the adolescent version of the picture book); and their articles are short, usually in easy-to-read language, and do not demand a great time commitment. Perhaps the most important reason, however, is that they deal with current information and today's events, tastes, and interests. In short, they are up-to-date and help keep their readers that way.

Newspaper reading also increases during the school years. In childhood, first the comic-strip pages and next the sports sections are usually important. As the child matures, the quality and quantity of newspaper reading expands. An increased emphasis in the curriculum on current affairs and problems has added even greater importance to the presence of extensive, well-rounded collections of newspapers and magazines in the media center.

Magazines and newspapers purchased by schools should comply with the standards of quality required of other media. The same criteria apply to online magazines and newspapers. The selections should supply a variety of points of view and cater to the students' varied interests. The newspapers in the collection and online should jointly reflect local, state, and national coverage. Remember, also, that magazines and newspapers are excellent bait for catching the attention of reluctant readers and attracting them to the media center. Some schools use newspapers to teach reading skills to reluctant readers in high schools because the articles are short, easy to read, and no stigma is attached to reading this type of media.

Whether a magazine or newspaper is indexed by one of the standard services, for example, *Reader's Guide to Periodical Literature*, or provides its own cumulative index, as does the *New York Times*, a selection criterion for magazines or newspapers is that they are to be used primarily for research. Many of the magazines popular for recreational reading are not found in the standard indexes. Availability in online databases or CD-ROM research databases needs to be considered before purchase. In any case, subscription lists should be reviewed thoroughly every year, and each title reevaluated at that time as to availability of printed and online resources. Magazine jobbers can be consulted to allow titles to be ordered from one source. See Chapter 11 for specific jobbers.

Online Magazine/Newspaper Databases

Electronic access to magazines and newspapers is provided through online databases. Most of these databases are full-text magazine or newspaper articles, which allow students to do research on current topics. Criteria for selecting online databases includes:

1. How well is the indexing done?
2. Does it use Boolean searching?
3. Is the database updated regularly?
4. Are the magazines and newspapers appropriate for the curriculum? Does the database cover an appropriate number of years to be worth its cost?
5. Does the vendor offer training or other services?
6. Does the online version of the magazine or newspaper allow faster access to the information than the printed version?
7. Are the magazines or newspapers on the database ones that would normally be purchased as print versions?
8. What is the cost?
9. What licensing agreements are required and what are their restrictions?

Web Sites

The World Wide Web, often referred to simply as the web, is one of the most widely used services on the Internet. For students doing research, the Internet provides a wealth of information, however, it is crucial that students learn how to evaluate appropriate web sites. Because of the vast number of inappropriate web sites for students, school library media specialists serve as leaders in teaching students those deemed appropriate and in selecting web sites for classroom instruction.

When evaluating web sites, the following criteria should be used:

1. Is the author listed with appropriate credentials?
2. Is the site bias-free?
3. Does the site have support from a reputable institution?
4. What is the purpose of the web page?
5. Does the web page meet curriculum objectives?
6. Is there limited advertising?
7. Do the links work?
8. Is the site well organized and easy to use?
9. Are the web pages written at an age appropriate reading and knowledge level?
10. Are updates current?
11. Is the web site visually pleasing to students?
12. Will the web site challenge learners to use critical thinking?
13. Does the web site relate to learning objectives? (Shelly, et al., 2002).

Pamphlets and Clippings

The vertical file in a library is the depository for pamphlets, clippings, pictures, student reports, and other ephemeral material. When well organized and kept current, it can be a valuable adjunct to the regular collection. Because of the vast amounts of current information available on the Internet, the vertical file is becoming of lesser importance in keeping the collection current. As a collection of current local materials, it continues to be valuable to the collection. When developing a vertical file, keep in mind that items that cannot be easily found elsewhere are those that are needed. Some purposes it can serve are:

- To update the regular collection. Pamphlets and clippings often contain much more current information than do other media. It provides fast and easy access to hard-to-find information.
- To supplement and extend material in the existing collection. A pamphlet might, for example, serve as a source of information on a specific subject for which the media center would not purchase more expensive sources.
- To supply information and illustration on subjects not covered elsewhere or not treated elsewhere in similar depth.
- To furnish a variety of points of view on a subject. This is of particular value with material on controversial subjects. Whereas a book usually reflects a single attitude, a series of clippings may reveal a great difference and range of opinion on the same subject.

Much of the material that is placed in the vertical file is either free or inexpensive. The major sources for clippings are magazines and newspapers, as well as discarded books where the information is still current. Pamphlets are available from a variety of sources, for example, current magazines and government sources. Media specialists should familiarize themselves with the many bibliographies of these free and inexpensive materials and collect materials to supplement information on hard-to-locate topics.

Two points to consider in pamphlet selection are: (1) because much of this material is free, it needs to be checked thoroughly for excessive or misleading advertising and for evidence of propaganda; (2) the vertical file needs to be thoroughly and frequently weeded to dispose of materials that have outlived their usefulness.

Government Documents

Media centers often tend to overlook the wide and rich storehouse of materials available from the various government agencies at local, state, national, and international levels. The materials these sources issue are rather misleadingly called government documents. One tends to think of a government document solely as a published treaty, law, or the like. Instead, the scope of government documents is as wide as the interests and concerns of today's governments. The Government Printing Office in Washington, DC, for example, is now officially known as the world's largest publisher. The pamphlets, books, maps, and CD-ROMS, and subscriptions available from that office alone deal with such diverse subjects as childcare, farming, Civil War battles, cooking, crime, and the national parks. Media centers should avail themselves of this large wealth of materials—much of it is free or inexpensive.

Motion Pictures

Videos, DVDs, Laser Discs, and Video Streaming

The characteristics of motion present in so-called motion pictures is actually an optical illusion that exploits the eye's inability to distinguish adequately between images that are shown in quick succession. Because the eye retains an image for a fraction of a second after it is shown, this "retention of vision" causes a blending with the next image. If the images are closely related in sequence, the effect is one of movement.

The most popular format today for viewing films is the video; however, DVD and video streaming are fast becoming alternative formats. Both the video and DVD project images through a videocassette recorder or a DVD player to a television screen.

Videocassettes (Videos)

The use of videos has grown in popularity for several years because students like the medium of television and are naturally motivated to view films via this format. Also, the cost of the medium is economical. In the early stages of development, videos were viewed on regular television screens, which made large group viewing prohibitive; however, with the advent of the wide television screen and the projected video image on regular classroom projection screens, the medium has become more adaptable to large group viewing and thus its popularity for classroom use has soared.

A videocassette recorder (VCR) is used to play videos. The videotape is enclosed in a cartridge for recording sound and visual elements. The videocassette (VHS) format is virtually the most popular format used for this medium; however, as more DVD titles are added for viewing, that could change. The video is played back in conventional television sets via a videocassette player/recorder. The videocassette may contain a commercially produced program or be blank for off-the-air taping. Off-air taping regulations are discussed in Chapter 11.

Videos may be classified by content. Traditionally they have, like books, been considered either educational (curriculum oriented) or recreational (entertainment oriented). Videos can and should instruct and entertain at the same time. Classification by subject area—for example, science, history, and geography—is often used. Other terms used in classifying videos are animations, travelogs, agency-sponsored, training videos, documentaries, and dramas.

Because young people spend such a great deal of time before television, a movement to produce greater visual/media literacy among the young has grown in American education. People who use videos with students should familiarize themselves with the techniques and capabilities of the medium and convey these to their students. When one is able to "think" with the eyes, the more one is able to appreciate the alternatives available to a director in filming a scene, the variety of effects produced by different types of film shots, the techniques and considerations used for cutting from one sequence to another, and other relationships that exist among the camera, the subject, and the viewer.

Perhaps better than any other medium, video motion pictures convey the greatest sense of reality to an audience. The attention of the viewer is easily attained and identification possibilities are numerous. Through the medium of the realistic film, the audience can easily be taken to a distant country to study a foreign culture or transported back in time to witness important events of the past. In addition, film is also capable of conveying "unrealistic" motion. By filming at a very fast rate and then projecting at normal speeds, the effect of slow motion is produced and details perhaps otherwise undetectable become visible. On the other hand, through time-lapse photography—shooting pictures at a slower rate than usual, but projecting them at the normal speed—phenomena that ordinarily might take hours or days to take place can be shown in a matter of seconds. In the variation of time-lapse photography called the stop-motion effect, the cameraman shoots only a single picture at a time and the objects photographed are changed slightly for each picture so that an illusion of motion is produced in the final product.

Besides the advantages of wide range and of types of images that can be carried using video, DVD, or video streaming, there are other more basic reasons for using it. Tests have shown repeatedly that material, particularly of a factual nature, presented through the motion picture medium is learned faster and retained longer than material presented through a more traditional medium. The skills necessary to absorb information from videos are minimal—poor readers can grasp material presented in film far more readily than they can material in a printed format. Other assets of film are: new formats and equipment now make it possible for children to operate the machines and to allow for a greater range in the size of the group viewing the video and details are easily presented on film. Local production of videos is fairly simple and not too costly. A wide variety of videos at various levels and in various formats is available for purchase or rental.

There are some advantages to the medium of video. They have steadily decreased in price, making them more affordable for most school libraries. Potential purchasers should bear in mind that a video's time of usefulness will be limited (1) by the degree of recency in its content and (2) by the rate of its physical deterioration. When a videocassette is damaged and repaired, it usually loses sound quality. The number of video titles available continues to grow.

A limitation placed on the use of videos is that some teachers still consider them a form of entertainment—to be used as a reward for their students—rather than an important instructional aid. As a result, there has been more misuse of this medium in the classroom than of any other non-print material. Videos are easy to load and most teachers are familiar with them. A darkened room is not required to view a video, which allows opportunities for note taking and decreases the possibility of behavioral problems.

Many schools do their own video productions. Those productions may be newscasts provided daily to the school population.

DVDs (Digital Versatile Discs)

DVDs bring the advantage of digital to the viewing of motion pictures. It adds outstanding picture and sound to movies, like CDs do for music. A DVD is very similar to a CD except it holds about seven times more data. For example, it can hold approximately eight hours of CD-quality music per side.

There are many advantages of DVDs. (1) They are easy to use and set up. (2) They provide superior picture and sound quality. (3) There is no degrading of picture quality over time; it is an indestructible format. (4) Freeze framing allows more intense study of selected areas of interest. (5) Sound or picture quality is not affected with each playback. (6) It is easy to search for scenes. (6) The compact size takes less space for storage than videos. (7) Portable players are available. (8) DVD video players allow CDs and CD-ROMs to be played in them.

DVDs have some disadvantages as well. (1) There is not as much material available in this format—it will take many years for DVDs to become as widely available as videos. (2) There is some incompatibility among players and discs. (3) Copy protection is built-in. (4) If the disc is poorly compressed, it may be fuzzy, vague, or blurry. (5) Few players can play in reverse at normal speeds. (6) Televisions need adjustment for handling DVDs for clarity of picture and sound. (7) DVDs are basically available for home entertainment, and educational materials lag far behind in development.

In selecting DVDs, it is especially important to make certain that the disc and the equipment are compatible. The DVD should be judged with the same criteria for content as other audiovisual materials. Attention needs to be paid to the quality of the digital compression of the disc and to buy only those discs that have clarity of sound and picture. Normally, that would mean buying only from reputable dealers who guarantee their products.

Laser Discs

One of the main questions that most consumers want to know is which format is better, the laser disc or the DVD. They both have their advantages and disadvantages. The main problem with laser discs is that they are more expensive than DVDs. Because of the price, some manufacturers make laser disc titles available only as box set editions, which often include such items as books, posters, and other items that may not be wanted or needed by the consumer. The laser disc is larger (twelve inches) than DVDs, heavy and fragile, which makes it not as appealing for school use. It requires that great care be taken in storage to prevent warping and deterioration of the discs aluminum coating. Poorly manufactured discs may lose their aluminum reflective qualities over time, resulting in video noise. One of the main advantages of laser discs is that one purchased anywhere in the world can be played on any standard laser disc player. Laser discs are not compressed as DVDs and do not have the content copy guarded. Laser discs are not the most popular medium for use in schools because of their cost and their deterioration over time; however, some schools still use them.

Video Streaming

One of the latest innovations for viewing movies is called video streaming or video-on-demand. Schools in Georgia are using video streaming as a way to distribute instructional television programming. Video streaming basically involves watching a video on a computer screen accessed through the Internet from the server to a client. Video streaming normally involves a client request for a web page or server directory containing embedded video. It is as simple as clicking on a hyperlink, which tells the computer to begin playing the video on the desktop. The client plays the incoming video as it is being received. Initially, the video image received on the computer was about the size of a postage stamp but now it can be played full screen and can even be projected for an entire classroom.

A Realtime server is usually dedicated to streaming movies where they can be uploaded or downloaded to the server for later viewing by a group of people or an individual. Movies that are used on streaming video must be in digital format. If movies are in an analog format, they must be converted to digital. Once the movies are digital, they can be saved to the hard drive of a computer. The movie can be edited, and such things as sound, titles, and graphics can be added, and uploaded to the web so the movie can be streamed. Prior to uploading a movie to the Real streaming server, a free software called RealPlayer or QuickTime can save and/or compress the movie in different formats. The software allows the movie to run once the file or hyperlink is opened. Once on a streaming server, it takes only a few seconds to start the video while the computer caches or downloads the remaining segments to be played as the movie runs.

There are many commercial streaming video products available, and research is being conducted to look at the limitations to this medium. Some companies allow downloads of videos to local computers or Intranets so they can be used in multimedia projects in classrooms. In some instances, schools are using this technology as a training device for faculty and students. Few companies have comprehensive video libraries large enough to offer a curriculum video-on-demand service; however, AIMS Multimedia DigitalCurriculum.com stands out as the pioneer in the area.

Some schools in Georgia are beginning to offer video streaming as a part of the instructional program. Video streaming in media centers is currently not being practiced that much; however, it has great potential for school media centers. The potential for media specialists to use this medium for in-service training of faculty is tremendous. Teaching students how to do research or providing library orientation are just two applications that would be beneficial in a library media center. It is as simple as the media specialist using a digital video camera to design video presentations that could be video streamed to instruct faculty or students. The main requirements needed are access to a computer, a digital camcorder, and downloading the free RealPlayer or Quicktime software.

One of the major advantages of streaming video is that the classroom setting is no longer the place where instruction must take place. The beauty of this medium is that large numbers of people can view a video anyplace or anytime they choose. Streaming video is an excellent training vehicle for teachers and students.

Some disadvantages to streaming video are: (1) to create streaming video for training, one has to learn to create digital movies and have access to a computer with the necessary software and peripherals and (2) to view the video, one must have Internet access with broadband connections such as a cable modem or a DSL connection.

Private companies currently provide video streaming services for clients for a fee. Most of the providers use either QuickTime or RealPlayer software to facilitate the use of video streaming, with RealPlayer being the most commonly used. RealPlayer allows the viewer to enjoy streaming video on both an Intranet and the Internet. It is also capable of providing more than 2,000 Internet based radio station broadcasts. Most Internet sites utilize RealPlayer for their video streaming primarily because of the file size and popularity of Windows machines versus the QuickTime (Adam, 2002).

The general criteria for evaluating educational materials may be used with videos, DVDs, laser discs, and video streaming. Specific points to remember when selecting them are: (1) the content should be more effectively presented via this medium than is possible in another format; (2) if being considered for purchase, the cost must be weighed heavily against the number of subject areas in which it may be used, the length of time it will have value in the curriculum, and the number of showings anticipated per school year; and (3) the quality of the acting, the scenario, and the presentation techniques, as well as the nature of the photography, sound, and color, should be of acceptable standards or better. Current reviews for videos are featured in such standard reviewing media as *School Library Journal* (Reed Elselvier) and *Booklist* (ALA).

Projected Still Pictures

Slides and Microslides

Slides used in media centers today are basically of two types: (1) the two-by-two-inch slides used with carousel slide projectors with trays, on slide sorters or in individual viewers; and (2) microslides. PowerPoint presentations decrease the use of slides considerably because they are much easier to design and there is no need to go through the time consuming process of developing and processing film and making a sound tape to use with the slide presentation.

Microslides, or microscope slides, may be produced locally, but more frequently commercially prepared slides are purchased. Microslides can be projected by a microprojector so that a large group may see together what otherwise could only be seen by one person using a microscope. The advantages of microprojectors are many: The need for each student to have a microscope is eliminated; the teacher can point out the important aspects of each slide to an entire class at once; time spent in instruction on the use of the microscope, focusing techniques, and such, is reduced or perhaps eliminated. Even slides showing living organisms can be projected in this way, but close care must be taken not to let heat generated from the light of the microprojector damage the slide material.

There are several advantages of using slides. They can be arranged in any sequence that will best suit the presentation; carousel trays make sequencing and projection simple. Slides may be produced locally and presentation may be varied to meet local and individual class needs. In many cases, such as recording a field trip, this simply means taking photographs in the usual way. For photographing diagrams, flat pictures, or parts of a book, a copy stand must be used, but this is a relatively simple procedure. Duplication of locally produced slides is possible through the use of the negatives, or of commercially produced slides (within copyright restrictions) through special equipment.

There are some disadvantages of using slides. First, because each is a separate, small entity, sets of them can easily be disarranged. Second, most slides do not have captions, so an accompanying manual, taped commentary, or teacher's remarks is often needed to interpret each slide. Third, it is difficult to access them in rapid succession. Last, producing and processing slides is time consuming.

Selection criteria for slides: How durable is the mounting? What is the quality of the color? Does the continuity of the slides seem appropriate for the subject content? Is the length of the presentation appropriate for the intended audience? Is the organization within the set logical?

Transparencies

Transparencies are a single sheet or continuous roll of clear acetate containing images that are enlarged through viewing with an overhead projector. The images may be those that are computer generated or those that are written by hand. Of all audiovisual innovations introduced into the school, certainly the overhead is one that has received the widest adoption for the longest period of time. Perhaps this is because it combines the advantages of an old and trusted teaching tool, the chalkboard, with the capability to project pictures. Transparencies may either be purchased commercially or prepared within the school. The simplest of the latter type is produced by writing on the acetate with a marking pen or grease pencil. Using computers to prepare transparencies is a simple process as well. Most single-sheet transparencies are eight and a half inches by eleven inches when mounted, but this size has been far from universally adopted. The illuminated surface or size of the overhead projector is approximately ten inches by ten inches, and the actual size of the aperture in the transparency mounting is about seven inches by nine inches. Transparencies can be quite elaborate; a number of additional sheets, called overlays, can be placed on top of the original transparency to show complex relationships or progressive stages of development. The overlays are usually hinged to the mounting of the basic transparency and are used to instruct about multiple relationships, such as the parts of the human body. Many commercially produced transparencies come in sets, while others are sequenced and placed in binders.

Computer-generated transparencies are easy to make which means that an instructor can easily produce their own designed for their own teaching specifications. Because of PowerPoint presentations, commercial transparencies are not used as often in schools; however, those made using the computer continue to be utilized.

Transparencies have many other advantages. The overhead is mechanically easy to handle and operate and supplies a large, clear image in a normally illuminated room—which allows note taking in comfort if desired. The overhead can be placed at the front of a class so that the user can face the audience, control attention, and observe student reactions. The transparency is always visible to the teacher, who is free to change it at will. The instructor maintains control over the pacing and sequencing of the presentation. Particularly through the use of overlays, complex subjects may be gradually and logically introduced. The use of the overhead is suited particularly to medium-size groups. Transparencies may be produced locally, which is the greatest advantage. The simplest method, as noted above, is produced by handwriting or by using the computer, and this is less time-consuming than writing on the chalkboard. Computers allow fonts to be enlarged and to produce writing that can be easily read by viewers. (See also Transparency Making in Chapter 11.)

The disadvantages of transparencies are few, but should be enumerated. First, their use is awkward, although certainly not impossible, for an individual viewer. A final disadvantage, of the professionally produced transparency, is lack of standardization in both size and packaging.

Commercially available transparencies are listed in dealers' catalogs and multimedia catalogs. Many manufacturers allow previewing privileges on sets of transparencies. Specific criteria in choosing commercially produced transparencies include quality of mounting, clarity and sharpness of picture, suitable definition of detail, use of color, omission of irrelevant material, ease of transparency identification by labeling and other devices, logical sequencing and organization if they are in sets, and durability of packaging.

Audio Materials

Audio learning materials make available a great variety of experiences through sound—drama, music, lectures, foreign languages, readings, actual occurrences, and recreations of events. They have been found to be particularly effective in curricular areas involving speech, language, and music. Programs to develop reading skills have also used with success such audio techniques as allowing children to follow the text of the book while listening to a recording of it.

Specific listening skills are needed to make maximum use of the medium. It is easy for a student to "tune out," or generally fail to pay attention while supposedly listening to a presentation. It is often impossible to detect when this inattention sets in. The distraction level is also much higher for audio experiences than for those that involve both sight and sound. Sudden movements or extraneous noises can easily distract the listener. The material that can be presented solely through sound is also limited. For example, the text of a poem or the pronunciation of a foreign phrase are easily conveyed by this medium, but a description of a complex scientific process is not. However, because it lacks the specificity that visual materials present, audio experience often stimulate the imagination by allowing students to supply their own visual dimensions.

Three types of audio materials are generally used in media centers: (1) compact discs, (2) cassette tapes, and (3) audio books. Not included in this list are microcassettes and mini-compact disks because they are not normally items that circulate freely in media centers. Phonograph records have become obsolete in media centers and have been replaced by cassettes or compact discs.

Compact Discs

Compact discs (CDs) are primarily the sound recording medium used most often. The CD player uses a small optical laser that never touches the surface of the disc to "read" audio information digitally encoded on the surface of the disc. These discs are 4.75 inches in diameter and carry up to seventy-four minutes of recorded information.

Compact discs have several advantages over cassette recordings: (1) the capability of the compact disc to play a selection in any desired sequence; (2) to repeat selections as needed; (3) better fidelity is possible because the range of intensity is more discriminating in providing a greater sound quality; (4) sound quality is not lost with frequent playing; (5) signals are digital and are not as prone to wear; (6) they do not damage easily, making them ideal for school use; (7) they are inexpensive and easy to use and their players as well. The disadvantages are: (1) when using with large groups, amplifiers are needed; (2) they can be easily stolen; (3) there are not a variety of materials available on CDs suited for educational purposes, other than music.

With a computer and a CD-R drive, compact discs can be easily created by anyone who desires. There are several formats of compact discs: CD-ROMs, CD-Rs, CD-RWs, and DVD-ROMs.

- **CD-ROMs (Compact Disc Read-Only Memory).** This format of compact discs uses basically the same laser technology as audio CDs except that it can contain graphics, text, video, animation as well as sound. A CD-ROM holds about 650 MB of data or 450 times more information than a high-density 3.5 inch floppy disk.
- **CD-Rs and CD-RWs.** Most computers on the market contain either a CD-R or CD-RW drive as standard equipment. A compact disc-recordable (CD-R) is a compact disc that allows recording of textual, graphic, or audio information. Although one might write on one part of the disc at one time and then another part of the disc at another time, once the information is written it cannot be erased. On the other hand, a compact disc-rewritable (CD-RW), is an erasable disk that allows writing to be done multiple times.
- **DVD-ROMs.** A digital videodisc read-only memory (DVD-ROM) stores much more information than a CD-ROM. It not only surpasses the storage capacity of a CD-ROM but the quality as well. A DVD-R (recordable) and a DVD-RW (rewritable) are available, which work much like the CD-R and the CD-RW.

Cassette Tapes

Basically, cassette tapes use a magnetic tape, the non-shiny side, which is capable of carrying recorded sound. The cassette tape is used as both a recording and listening medium; however, CDs are the most popular source of sound recordings. Cassettes are 1/8-inch thick, enclosed in a container, and played at 1 7/8 ips. They are easily snapped into place in the player without threading. Cassettes vary in the amount of tape they contain. They are classified, therefore, by the amount of playing time each contains—from 30 to 120 minutes.

Like compact discs, cassettes can serve as both a listening and recording medium. The element of participation has produced a variety of uses for cassettes, particularly in language study. They are also less prone to damage and may be erased and used again and/or played back many times without changing the quality of the sound. One of the major disadvantages of cassettes is related to making repairs should a tape break. It is extremely difficult to pry open the container and make the necessary repairs. In spite of fast-forward and rewind controls, a major drawback in cassette use continues to be the difficulty of locating specific material recorded on the tapes.

Audio Books

Audio books are fast becoming a popular medium for listening to books and other recorded information. They are normally recorded on cassettes, CDs, and MP3 CDs. The Internet has numerous sites where one can join an audio book club, or download an audio book to a computer. It allows one to listen to a newspaper, a public radio program or a favorite book. Some sites will give a member an MP3 recorder for recording and playing the audio books. These recorders store approximately seventeen hours of audio. The same criteria for selecting books would apply to audio books. MP3 recorders/players would require the same general criteria as cassettes or CDs. (For more information on MP3 technology, please see Chapter 10.) Examples of web sites where audio books can be obtained are listed here:

http://www.audible.com

http://www.audiobooks.com

http://www.audiobookclub.com

The general criteria for evaluating educational media apply to audio materials, but because distractions are often encountered in a listening situation, the selector must be especially aware of the quality of the performance as well as the quality of the recorded sound. The material must be appropriate, of suitable length, effectively presented, interesting, and, if possible, appealing to both the emotions and the intellect. Be sure to determine whether the content is best suited to a recorded form. For example, a cassette recording of a play rehearsal has some distinct uses, but videotaping the same rehearsal might be more effective. In evaluating the technical quality, clear, distortion-free sound is important. Cassettes and CDs should be made of durable material and clearly labeled to indicate titles, performers, times, and playback speed.

Television

Television is the most powerful communication medium yet invented. Virtually no aspect of American life has remained unchanged since the use of television became widespread. The field of education has conducted so many research studies with television that the conclusion is now obvious: Children learn through television as much as, if not more than, by conventional classroom presentations. Because of television's great potential as a teaching tool, most classrooms contain them and use them primarily for viewing broadcast educational programs, or for viewing videos owned by the media center.

Because of the popular use of television in the classroom, most schools have access to digital cable or satellite dishes to allow for a large selection of channels to view. Television can do a great deal for education. It can bring the whole world, together with its best teachers and educational materials, into the classroom. Because it is such a high-intensity medium, it can shape attitudes as well as convey factual information. New courses can be offered and existing ones enriched. With the development of video-cassettes and camcorders and the possibility of instant playback, students and teachers have opportunities otherwise unavailable for self-evaluation because of the recording capabilities.

Television supplies a combination of visual and verbal stimuli. In addition it has several distinct advantages. It can reach a number of audiences simultaneously, and it can be both broadcast and received at the same time. Furthermore, no additional equipment, such as screens or separate speakers, are required, nor are special viewing conditions like darkened rooms necessary. It is also capable of supplying eyewitness news items. However, television programs are not able to provide for the great range of student differences; allow for audience reaction, or feedback; or check to see if the material is being understood.

There are several web sites that provide television educational programming information. Below are several sites that provide this information:

Web Sites for Information on Television Educational Programming

A & E Classroom

http://www.aetv.com/class/

This award-winning site provides outstanding educational materials to assist students in their reading, writing, and critical thinking skills.

Bravo TV in the Classroom

http://www.bravotv.com/

This free site combines arts programming and resource materials to enhance arts and humanities studies at the secondary level. It is provided to schools by a local cable company.

Cable in the Classroom Online
http://www.ciconline.org/default.htm

This site provides a vast array of experiences including video voyages, earthquake simulations, and the elements to produce original multimedia lesson plans. The online resources include tools and content that can be used "to engage children in learning, to enrich the professional lives of teachers, and to reinforce learning at home."

CNN Student News
http://learning.turner.com/newsroom/

This free web site is a ready-to-use, integrated broadcast program created for students and teachers.

C-SPAN in the Classroom
www.c-span.org/classroom

This free membership service offers information and resources to assist educators in their use of C-SPAN television and web resources as they teach their classes. Although membership is not mandatory, there are a variety of benefits to get one started and to provide ideas, activities, and classroom tools for tapping into C-SPAN's primary source, public affairs video.

Discovery Channel
http://school.discovery.com/

This site is dedicated to making teaching and learning an exciting, rewarding adventure for students, teachers, and parents. Innovative teaching materials are included as well as resources for students.

History Channel Classroom
http://www.historychannel.com/

This site offers The History Channel Classroom Calendar, which features programming information that allows teachers the time to think and create innovative lessons around programs. Information is presented as a service for teachers, commercial-free, five days a week. Taping is encouraged at this site.

Nickelodeon

http://teachers.nick.com/

This site provides teachers with classroom resources that complement Nickelodeon programming. Nickelodeon airs both preschool and educational programming for use in the classroom. Elementary programs include *Nick News with Linda Ellerbee* and special Nickelodeon program initiatives such as *The Big Help* and *Kids Pick the President* It also offers programming for such shows as *Bill Nye the Science Guy, 3–2–1 Contact, Ghostwriter,* and, *A Walk In Your Shoes.* It also offers preschool programming such as *Blue's Clues, Little Bill, Maisy Bear,* and *Little Bear.* Programs air commercial-free.

PBS Teacher Source

http://www.pbs.org/teachersource/tvteachers.htm

This site offers resources by curricular subject, topic and grade level and standards. In-depth professional development services like PBS Mathline and Scienceline are offered. Details on PBS station outreach activities in the community are available as well as tips on how to effectively teach with technology; PBS television programs with extended taping rights for educators and access to convenient online shopping for PBS videos. Best practices information from other teachers is provided as well as recommended books and web sites. This site offers interdisciplinary teaching suggestions, free weekly electronic newsletter highlighting new TV and online programming from PBS, and more.

In addition, consult local affiliates about upcoming, locally produced programs; local cable and digital dish companies for their programming schedules as well as *TV Guide* for any supplemental listings. Library media specialists may also purchase or rent videos or films of television specials for a nominal fee from many distributors. Sources for free video rental and also rentals for a nominal fee can be found on the Internet. Two examples of web sites are listed below for free video rental.

Sources for Free Video Rentals

FreeMedia.Org

http://www.freemedia.org/welcome.html

This site offers free video rentals to teachers. One of the outstanding features of this site is that it provides teacher and student reactions to the videos.

Video Placement Worldwide
http://www.vpw.com/

This site offers free educational videos and teaching materials. The materials can only be shipped to a school address. Videos are categorized by appropriate grade levels and subject areas with a complete description of the program. The videos are provided on permanent loan which means they may be kept as long and be shown as often as needed. The only requirement to obtain the videos is to answer a survey that is included with each program. The videos are sponsored by commercial vendors, which means that care should be taken in ordering.

Criteria for television programs are as follows. (1) The program should show adequate planning and effective presentation. (2) Each program should attempt to use the potential of the medium and not be simply a filmed lecture. (3) The picture should be clear and undistorted, with details easily discernible, and when possible, it should be employed to clarify and add emphasis.

Used with care and with wisdom, television supplies a fascinating avenue to knowledge. Television is also a viable tool for distance education.

Digital Television (DTV)

A new world of television viewing is available with digital. It offers improved quality in resolution of the picture and in audio quality. Digital television will gradually replace analog television; the scheduled date is through 2006, because existing analog television broadcasts will cease. This change may result in replacing all analog televisions; however, there are data converters available that transforms old analogs to digital. Digital television (DTV) is expensive and may result in financial problems in schools that replace their classroom analog televisions. Like analog televisions, DTVs will eventually decrease in price over time. Some questions to ask before purchasing a DTV include:

1. Do all jacks and other connecting devices match current VCR, DVD, and cable box connectors? Or will new ones have to be purchased?
2. Does the DTV have capabilities to be upgraded to use newer devices of the future?
3. Is a new cable box required to receive local DTV broadcasts?

4. What kind of high definition programming will be available from the satellite TV provider?

5. What kind of local technical assistance is available?

Visual Materials

Art Reproductions

Like many public libraries, school media centers are now collecting mounted and framed art reproductions for home circulation to both faculty and students. Conventional collections continue to contain unmounted prints either singly or in portfolios. When purchasing art reproductions, check, if possible, the fidelity of the copy in terms of color and detail. The degree of size reduction, if any, will depend on intended use. The quality and durability of the frame and mounting are also important considerations.

Graphic Materials

The word *graphics* is a broad term that refers to a whole group of materials with one characteristic in common—each visualizes information through combinations of words and drawings. Computer graphics have added a new dimension when producing graphic materials. Usually the data are presented in a summary or otherwise condensed form. Web-based graphics allow illustrations, logos, and other images to be included on web pages.

Graphics include (1) graphs; (2) charts, tables, and diagrams; (3) cartoons; and (4) posters. Regardless of type, graphics share basic criteria for quality. The material should be presented clearly and simply—in an uncluttered way and with non-relevant elements either de-emphasized or omitted. The graphic should show that attention has been paid to such basic artistic principles as balance and harmony in spatial relationships and an overall unity of presentation. Lettering should be clear and legible and color, if used, should fulfill more than a decorative purpose. The graphic should have impact and demand attention. Last, it should not be awkward or unmanageable in size but it should be large enough for its intended use.

Graphs

A graph is a pictorial device used to present numerical data and their relationships. Statistics can suddenly become meaningful when presented in graph form. The material should be clear, interestingly organized, and capable of revealing comparisons easily. There are four major types of graphs. The *line* graph, the simplest and most popular type, presents data in a simple continuous line in relation to a horizontal and vertical grid. The *bar* graph is easiest to read; it represents relationships by the length of the bars. The *circle* or *pie* graph is used to show the relation of the parts to the whole. The *pictograph* or *picture* graph uses symbols rather than lines or bars to present the material. The pictograph, which has gained in popularity in recent times, had its origins in the way in which primitive tribes kept their records.

Charts, Tables, Diagrams

These terms are often used interchangeably, but charts and tables are, generally speaking, drawings that classify or otherwise analyze data. Some examples of charts are business charts, weather charts, and mariner's charts. Youngsters can draw their own charts to organize their schoolwork or to trace progress in a particular school subject. Tables are used to list or tabulate data, usually figures. Common examples are airline and bus schedules and railroad timetables. Diagrams are graphics that show relationships, as in a process or device. They do not necessarily have to be realistic in representation. Diagrams include flow sheets or flow charts, used to represent a sequence of operations; time lines, to plot relationships in time and events; family trees, or genealogical diagrams; and flip charts that show sequences or steps on a series of sheets rather than in a single diagram.

Cartoons

A cartoon is a drawing or series of drawings that tells a story quickly. Cartoons may be used either to instruct or to entertain. Generally, they are so small that some sort of projection device, an opaque projector, for example, must be used for group viewing. Political and satirical cartoons rely heavily on symbols, which often must be explained to students before a cartoon can be understood.

Posters

Posters also tell short stories. Good posters relay a single specific message in a clear, dynamic manner. They have instant appeal and clarity of design and are large enough to be seen at a distance. Some sources of free or inexpensive posters are travel agencies, museums, art galleries, government offices, and industrial concerns.

Multimedia Kits

Many manufacturers package together different types of media dealing with the same subject. For example, a kit on a foreign country might contain items of realia, a portfolio of pictures, a video, slides, and perhaps a book. Many schools have assembled their own kits, particularly in areas of local history, industry, and social conditions. Individual components of a kit or multimedia device should be evaluated separately as well as in relation to the rest of the material. This medium seems to be disappearing from media centers.

Educational Games and Toys

Educational games and toys attempt to involve the learner in an educational situation while at the same time providing interest and amusement. Most games try to simulate a real-life situation. Thus, through projection and role-playing, the student undergoes experiences very similar to reality. Games have been developed around historical events, social problems, family situations, and political and economic questions. An imaginatively structured game that is accurate in detail can be an exciting way to produce active participation in the learning process.

Computer Software

Commercially produced computer software is available in almost all curriculum areas. The programs are designed to motivate students to learn subject content. Software is available for all ability levels; however, it is especially useful for slow learners who are lacking basic competency skills.

Because computer software involved in instruction is essentially an automated form of programmed instructional material, basically the same evaluative criteria, such as logical construction, thorough instruction, adequate reinforcement, apply to both. The expression "user friendly" is a criterion for computer software, which means that a program stimulates users and guides them comfortably and with imagination from one step to the next.

It should be pointed out, however, that software is not interchangeable from one platform to another in most cases; however, great strides are being made in that direction. Programs are often available in a series of formats. Because of the high cost of programs, it is advisable, whenever possible, to schedule teacher previews of each program before purchase and to maintain files of these evaluations. Unfortunately, some manufacturers and distributors of software packages are reluctant to supply preview copies, primarily for fear of copyright infringements, but increasingly more are granting this privilege.

For software packages involving instruction, that is, essentially information handling, the following additional criteria should be used:

- Clarity of instruction and ease of use. The program should either be specifically formulated to clearly display user choices (menu method).
- Storage capacity appropriate for amount of data to be handled.
- Provision made for data security and privacy of records.
- Fast input and retrieval time.
- Various appropriate data handling formats available, for example, editing and sorting.
- Word processing capabilities present.
- Child tested to determine if it motivates learning.

Several questions should be kept in mind before choosing computer software:

1. Does the program contain the information needed and is the approach used compatible to teaching goals and objectives?
2. How well does the program suit the developmental needs and skills of students?
3. Is the information in the program logically and interestingly presented without being boring?
4. Is the content valid, accurate, factual and free of errors?
5. Does the content meet state standards?
6. Is the content free of stereotypes and racial bias?
7. Is the length of the material suitable and age appropriate?
8. Is the program user-friendly and interesting?
9. Is the software reliable and free of system errors?
10. Can students exit the program at any time and then restart the program again where they stopped?
11. Will the program hold student attention while accommodating their skill and ability levels?
12. How is feedback provided in the program to allow a variety of student responses?

13. Are prompts and incorrect answers handled properly for student feedback?
14. Can the teacher set the user level and does it automatically advance?
15. Is a variety of ability/skill levels covered?
16. Is sound easily controlled?
17. What is the quality of graphics and animation?
18. Is the program child tested and appropriate for those who will use it?
19. Is the program amply field-tested to assure its quality?
20. What computer hardware is available to use with the program?
21. Is the software compatible with the platform being used?
22. Does the hardware have the memory capacity to run the software?
23. Is the hardware equipped with the appropriate disc size (three and a half inch floppy, zip drive, or CD)?
24. Is other equipment required for the program to run?
25. What platform does the program require?
26. What kind of vendor support is available for the program?
27. Is documentation easy to use and understand?
28. Is an 800 or 888 support number available?
29. Is on-screen assistance provided for the program without referring to the documentation?
30. Does the program load easily?
31. Can the program be upgraded?
32. What kind of licensing does the program require?
33. Once the program is purchased, how many stations are allowed to use software?
34. Does the vendor provide a preview copy of the program before purchase?
35. Does the program offer tutorial help that is clear and easy to use?
36. Can a replacement of the program be easily obtained if it is damaged during use? (Doll, 1987; Doll, 1988; Shelley, 2002)

It is important to try computer programs with students to evaluate their effectiveness before purchasing when possible. Prearrange with the publisher the return or exchange of programs that do not meet the instructional needs of the school. The purchase of software should be a thirty-day approval arrangement allowing enough time to know the program, how it works, what it teaches, and how students interact with it.

Maps and Globes

Maps and globes are to-scale representations of a geographical area or areas. Both media involve sophisticated abstractions and their use, therefore, requires of students special skills related to the students' comprehension levels and ability to deal with symbols.

Maps and globes may sometimes be used together, but they differ basically in two qualities: dimension and accuracy. Whereas a globe is a three-dimensional model, usually of the world, most maps are flat or two-dimensional. No map can be considered as accurate as a globe. Even raised-surface topographical relief maps cannot usually convey the rounded quality of the total earth's surface, while flat maps of the earth may in fact distort the true nature of the earth's surface (this distortion varies from one projection to another). On the other hand, detail is difficult to portray on a globe, and only one-half of a globe can be seen at one time.

Globes can portray a variety of conditions—geographical, political, economic, or social—but if more than two relationships are shown on a single globe, there is a danger of confusion. Globes come in many sizes. A sixteen-inch diameter is usually the smallest suitable for group viewing. Larger globes are expensive and take up greater amounts of space. Many have raised surfaces to indicate physical features. Others, usually called slated globes, are constructed of materials that can be written on, but easily erased. Globes should be constructed of a durable material and, except in unusual cases, come in a flexible mounting—that is, one that allows the globe to be easily attached or detached. A popular form of mounting is the cradle mount with a gyro or horizon ring that allows for simulation of the earth's spinning.

Maps, like globes, can also portray a variety of relationships and, in comparison with globes, are much more flexible, versatile, and capable of conveying a greater variety of facts. Again, there is always the danger of overcrowding, of trying to convey too much material on a single map. In their zeal to provide accurate and complete information, cartographers can obscure the essentials through excess detail. This is particularly true on many historical maps that attempt in-depth coverage of great periods of time.

Maps vary in size according to the use for which they are intended. In addition to a degree of simplicity relative to use, a map's symbols should be easy to read, its scales and area markers should be plainly visible, and its colors and type size should be suitable to the contents. Additional considerations for maps are: (1) nature of the projection and its suitability to the material; (2) method of indicating the projection; (3) presence of an index;

(4) up-to-date or, with historical maps, a cross-reference from old place names to those currently in use; (5) number of inserts and their value; (6) inclusion of parallels of latitude and meridians of longitude and their frequency; (7) accuracy of directions, boundaries, and areas; (8) storage facilities necessary (some maps can be folded, others must be stored flat); and (9) construction strength and glare-proof qualities. Maps and globes are available from a variety of sources. In addition to commercial outlets, travel agencies, and transportation and petroleum companies, the U.S. government, as well as newspapers and periodicals, are fine sources that may be tapped.

Models, Dioramas, Mockups

A *model* is a recognizable, three-dimensional representation of an object that often involves a change in size relationship with the real thing. Through the use of models an object can be brought into a classroom in replica form that in real life would be too large or too small for convenient viewing. Also, cutaway models can show the inside of an object, for example, the interior of an internal-combustion engine or of human anatomy.

A *diorama* depicts a scene by using realistic replicas of objects in the foreground and a painted curved backdrop that gives the impression of depth. Thus the illusion of reality is created. Dioramas are often used to portray historical events or distant places.

A *mock-up* differs from an ordinary model in two ways: (1) it usually has moving parts, and (2) it is more abstract and less realistic than the model. Unnecessary details are either eliminated or abridged, and important elements are stressed.

In evaluating models, dioramas, and mock-ups, make sure that size relationships are made clear, that parts are suitably labeled, and that colors and composition of the materials help stress important features. The size of the model in relation to the nature of the group using it is also important, and finally, if the model can be taken apart, it should be easy to reassemble.

Opaque Pictures and Objects

Opaque projection is one of the oldest and simplest methods of showing materials to a group. It allows projection of still pictures of unique material. Its chief asset is its versatility. Materials that may be projected include almost all kinds of printed matter—book pages, pictures, clippings, maps, and students' papers—as well as a wide variety of specimens and objects such as leaves, rocks, coins, stamps, seashells, and fabrics. Time to prepare materials for projection is almost nil, and the enlarged projections can be easily traced onto a newspaper print or poster board for further classroom use. An additional advantage of the opaque projector is its ease of operation. Many teachers and media specialists use the opaque projector for projecting drawings that can be enlarged and traced for bulletin board displays.

On the deficit side are several limitations. First, because this mode of projection relies on reflecting, or bouncing light off an object rather than having light pass through it, the source of light must be very strong and, more importantly, the room kept in total darkness. Second, for best results the projector is usually placed in front of the group; thus the teacher's back is to the audience, the view for students directly behind the projector may be restricted, and opening and closing some projectors results in sudden and distracting periods of intense glare for those close to the machine. Last, opaque projectors are often more bulky and cumbersome than other kinds of projection equipment. Some companies are providing smaller opaque projectors, which allows for more mobility.

Realia

Realia are authentic materials or real objects and include such diverse articles as a leaf, a piece of cloth, an Indian arrowhead, or a frog preserved in formaldehyde. Bringing real objects into the educational process allows students direct, firsthand experiences. They are able, if necessary, to touch, smell, handle, taste, or manipulate the object. There is no language barrier to overcome, and the essential qualities of the material are conveyed much more accurately and clearly than through any type of reproduction.

The need for realia varies with the students' experiential level, availability of objects, and feasibility of incorporating the realia into a media center collection. Many real objects are too large, for example, or too expensive for inclusion. The media center staff should work with faculty, parents, and students to build a collection of objects particularly those found in the everyday environment. Some examples: stamps; coins; butterflies, leaves, and other examples of flora and fauna; election posters, buttons, and related materials; fabrics; raw materials; and utensils.

Certain problems are inherent in the use of realia. Many objects are too small to be seen by a large group at once, others are too fragile or costly to be handled by students, and still others might create safety problems if not used with care. Nevertheless, the use of realia helps to bridge the gap between classroom teaching and real life and is also an excellent way to attract and hold the attention of students.

GENERAL CRITERIA FOR SELECTING AUDIOVISUAL EQUIPMENT

Criteria for selecting audiovisual equipment vary considerably depending on the type of items being selected and the specific use for which each is intended. Some general criteria—that may be applied regardless of the nature of the equipment under consideration—follow. Specific lists on individual items (projectors, tape recorders) are given in the next section.

Safety

This consideration is of particular importance if the equipment is to be used by children. Make sure that there are no rough protruding edges, that the equipment is well balanced and does not topple easily, that dangerous moving parts (such as fan blades) are not exposed, and that electrical connections are suitably covered and grounded. Where applicable, simple and direct instructions for use should be included, preferably printed on the machine. It is also important to determine that no further hazards are produced during use—for example, a machine that generates excessive heat during operation can be a potential source of danger for youngsters.

Ease of Use

One frequent stumbling block to the use of audiovisual equipment is the complexity of the procedures necessary for its operation. Factors to be considered in determining ease of use are the number of steps necessary for operation, number of controls (switches, plugs) to be activated, accessibility and ease of use of these controls and any directions for their operation, and the manual dexterity needed. The length and nature of the formal instruction for successfully operating the machine are also important.

Performance

The piece of equipment must operate efficiently and consistently at a high level of performance. Depending on the type of equipment, this high standard involves such factors as the nature of the picture or image, fidelity of sound reproduction, presence of speed controls, amount of distracting noise or light produced, and quality of mechanical construction.

Size, Weight, Design

The physical properties of a piece of equipment often predetermine use levels. For example, lightness of weight and carrying ease are two essential characteristics of equipment intended for home circulation. Great bulk inhibits use; so do poor or inadequate cases or carrying devices. Not only should the design and exterior be attractive; it should also be capable of withstanding hard use.

Maintenance and Service

Equipment should be built sturdily enough to hold up under the tough wear of a school situation. Strongly built equipment requires fewer repairs, but if minor ones become necessary, these machines should be constructed so that the repairs can be made quickly and easily. Replacement parts should be available, and suitable warranties or guarantees should be issued at the time of purchase. Two additional items for consideration are (1) the amount of on-the-spot repair service available from the manufacturer or distributor as opposed to the time-consuming, costly process of sending an item back to the factory, and (2) the availability from the manufacturer of personnel to give in-service training in the operation of the equipment.

Compatibility

Each new piece of equipment under consideration must be seen in relation to the school's entire media inventory to determine whether the acquisition of this new equipment will provide a logical extension of the existing collection. Often only special materials can be used with a particular machine, making the dual investment in both equipment and materials prohibitive. If a new item does essentially the same job as a model already in the collection, perhaps a duplication of existing equipment might be advised over buying the new material and expending valuable in-service-training time in acquainting patrons or student assistants with its operation. The specifications of each new piece of equipment should be checked to see if spare parts and repair operations are similar to those used with equipment already in the collection.

Versatility

The number and variety of uses that can be made of a piece of equipment should strongly influence selection, particularly when funds are limited. Often the same machine can be used effectively in a variety of teaching situations—for large-group and small-group instruction, at home and in the classroom, or with primary children and high school students.

Availability of Software

There are incidences of manufacturers marketing equipment for which there is not a sufficient amount of compatible educational material issued to justify the initial equipment purchase. The media selector should determine the nature and extent of the materials available that are suitable for the equipment under consideration.

Cost

The price of each prospective purchase must be evaluated in terms of the school's total equipment budget. Sometimes the purchase of expensive items will have to be postponed, or less expensive ones substituted, because of budgetary limitations. However, in the selection process the quality of the product should always be emphasized. Price lists can be consulted to find out costs of comparable equipment from other companies, but it should be stressed that when an item is priced higher than that of a competitor, superior performance standards could be the reason.

Need

Finally, all the above factors must be weighed against the answers to questions that probe the long-range usefulness of the acquisition: Is the purpose for which this equipment is being purchased worthy of the expense? What will be the consequences if the equipment is not acquired? Will the equipment be used often enough and by enough people to warrant purchase now?

SPECIFIC CRITERIA FOR SELECTING AUDIOVISUAL EQUIPMENT

Audio Equipment

Cassette Recorders/Players

Cassette recorders are easily loaded and often inexpensive. The speed with which tape passes through the machine is measured in inches per second (ips), and 1 7/8 ips is the standard for cassettes. The quality of sound is an important evaluative criterion and depends primarily on the uses to be made of the machine. For voice reproduction only, inexpensive recorders/players will usually suffice. Sound quality can be tested simply by recording and playing slow music through the machine. Other criteria include convenience and speed of rewinding, erasing or dubbing mechanisms, ease of operating, type of microphone supplied (most are unidirectional, some are bidirectional or omnidirectional), presence of an automatic level control that adjusts the sound level being recorded, and the nature of the power source (AC current, battery, or both). Both volume and tone controls should be present. Optional accessories are often earphones, a microphone stand, and in some cases, a carrying case.

Compact disc players

In purchasing a compact disc player, there are several points to consider. First, the use of the player will determine whether you want to purchase a single or multiple disc player. For playing music selections, most schools would use a single disc player because the class periods would limit the amount of playing time. For use as a research tool or an on-line catalog, the multiple disc player might be more appropriate depending on the amount of data to be stored and accrued. Second, a look at the programming capabilities is needed. For example, does the programming allow back tracking and replays as needed? Does it allow the use of a remote control? The major disadvantage of compact disc players is the inability to record; however, the fact that the CD-R and CD-RW technology allows recording to be made using computers makes this disadvantage less important. Another problem with compact disc players is the unavailability of proper repair service. As the compact disc becomes more popular in schools and for home use, the problem of repair service will improve.

MP3

One popular device for storing and listening to music is the MP3. Some students utilize MP3 technology at home; others might try to download MP3 music files onto the media center computers. The MP3 compresses sound files, usually music, into small convenient packages. Because MP3 is a file format, rather than a physical medium such as a tape or CD, music is played directly from the memory area holding it. For example, songs play from the hard drive on PCs. On portable MP3s, music is played from built-in memory chips (A little revolution is good for the soul, 1999). Controversy about MP3s and copyright infringement keeps appearing in the limelight due to the ease that music can be transferred across the Internet. Numerous web sites keep popping up all over the Internet that are designed specifically to share music files. One of the most infamous being Napster, which resulted in a legal battle over copyright infringement. The major outcome from this case was the principle of time-shifting (listening to a tape at a more convenient time than the broadcast time) which became a part of fair use (Kolln, 2001).

MP3 has many advantages. (1) Some music web sites provide downloads to MP3 files free of charge. (2) MP3 allows fast downloading of music files. (3) All that is needed to play an MP3 file is a media player that supports the MP3 format. (4) It allows the sharing of files easily. (5) Custom CDs can be easily made. (6) Transferring of files over the Internet is easy.

MP3 has some disadvantages. (1) It offers lower music quality than CDs. (2) MP3s can be difficult and time consuming to convert to player format. (3) MP3s can only record from the computer. (4) Storage capacity is limited (Arnolda, 2002; *Minidisc the clear portable solution over* MP3, 2000).

Still Picture Projectors

Opaque Projectors

Size, weight, and overall bulk have always been important evaluation points for opaque projectors. The size of the aperture and the maximum thickness of objects that can be projected should also be determined. The necessary amount of light should be produced without excessive heat or undue glare when the aperture is opened during operation. Some opaque projectors come equipped with built-in pointers to indicate particular parts of a picture as well as with additional lenses. Opaque projectors are valuable for media specialists and teachers who want to project enlarged pictures and other objects for making bulletin boards. The enlarged image can be projected, traced on a piece of cardboard or poster board, cut out, and then placed on the bulletin board or display surface. This method of making bulletin boards is fast and economical.

Overhead Projectors

The overhead projector is, for reasons chiefly involving ease of use and versatility, one of the most frequently found pieces of AV equipment in today's schools. Before choosing an overhead, apply the general equipment criteria as well as the following points: The projection stage or aperture should be able to accommodate various sizes of transparent material for both vertical and horizontal projection (the standard stage size is ten inches by ten inches, and commercially produced transparencies are usually seven and a half inches by nine and a half inches). Some heat buildup in the stage is inevitable, but check, by operating the machine for about thirty minutes, to see if this buildup is so excessive that it melts grease markings or makes the stage difficult to touch.

The projector should be easily focused. For example, close-up projection on a small screen requires that the lens must be moved away from the transparency; this adjustment, as well as those necessary for tilting the head (preferable to tilting the entire machine) should be easily accomplished. Note that if a line drawn from the lens of the projector to the center of the screen does not form a right angle, a keystone or wedge-shaped image will be projected. This distortion is particularly noticeable if the projector is placed below and close to the screen. To minimize this effect, the top of the projection screen should be tilted toward the overhead projector. On some models additional lenses are available, such as wide lenses for use close to the screen and long lenses for auditoriums.

The image should be bright and consistently sharp and clear at both the center and the edges. Absence of glare and extraneous light is desirable—some models are equipped with glare shields. Most overheads are cooled by a blower controlled by some variation on a thermostatic control. The blower should be quiet and vibration-free. The machine should have an attachment to enable the use of blank rolls of transparent material, such as acetate. The low maintenance cost is an established asset for the overhead. Few moving parts and simplicity of operation help reduce this cost. Related to overall ease of operation is the ease of changing the projection lamp; some machines offer, as an option, replacement attachments that involve only switching a knob or pressing a lever to make a change when a lamp burns out. Other maintenance features include convenience of fuse replacement, ease of cleaning, and simplicity of control switches. The outlet cord should be attached to the machine to prevent its loss. The standard length of the cord is approximately fifteen feet. On portable machines a storage space should be provided for the cord.

Many models have unusual features and accessories. For example, some machines are turned on or off simply by placing a transparency on the stage. One useful model is a portable folding compact projector that is easily transported. Transparencies used on these machines are generally smaller than those used on conventional models.

LCD Projectors

LCD projectors are used to project displays from the computer screen onto a larger classroom screen where an image can be seen in greater detail. The projector attaches to the computer and uses its own light source to display the image on the computer screen. They use liquid crystal technology and range in size from those that are mounted on walls to those that are portable. Some schools use LCD projection panels, also a liquid crystal display technology, which is designed to be placed on top of an overhead projector and projected onto a classroom screen.

Television Receivers and Recorders

For use with groups, a television receiver should have a minimum screen size of forty inches, but the larger the screen the better the view. The newer VCRs and DVD players allow projection on a regular classroom projection screen, which is an improvement over the small screen televisions. Some schools have purchased large screen televisions to use in a central location where videos can be viewed by large groups. DVD players allow the viewer to experience clearer and brighter images than those on VCRs. Controls for brightness, contrast, and vertical and horizontal hold should be easily operated. The presence of jacks for a cassette recorder, a videocassette recorder, and/or headphones increases the versatility of the receiver. Other criteria concern loudspeaker size and quality of sound and whether the set may be easily adjusted for closed-circuit television. Criteria for videocassette recorders (VCR), DVD players, and video streaming are discussed earlier in this chapter. When purchasing camcorders, the same general criteria are applicable; however, the light weight is a factor to be considered in selection as well as the ability to record in low lighting.

Computer Equipment

A number of factors should be considered when selecting computer equipment. They include:

1. **Availability of software.** In the long run probably the major investment will not be in the equipment but in the software it can accept. Basically this software can be of two kinds: systems software that performs internal housekeeping chores and applications software that actually performs the task. The availability of all kinds of software to satisfy these needs is of paramount importance in selecting a system.

2. **Memory.** Not only should one check the size of the central processor memory but also the size to which it can be expanded and at what cost.

3. **Storage options.** In computers this can be done on floppy discs, zip discs or CDs. Options for various kinds of disc storage must be considered, plus the limitations on how much disc storage can be added at what cost.

4. **Speed.** With all computers, the time necessary to run programs can be an important factor. The speed required for different applications needs to be considered. For example, less speed is required for surfing the Internet, word processing, and sending email than the speed needed when doing graphics or video editing.

5. **Interfaces.** In the computer, the interface involves the potential to extend basic functions by attaching such peripherals as printers or hard drives using the input/output ports on the machine. The more ports available, the greater the flexibility and opportunity for expansion. The limits of the power supply in individual models may also in turn limit the number of accessories possible. The total number of terminals that can be connected is important as well as limitations on remote location of these additional terminals. The number and quality of accessories that can be added to a computer are varied and impressive. A few are light pens and joysticks (particularly important for learning-disabled students who cannot type), delays, music synthesizers, speech synthesizers, and speech recognition boards, robots, and graphic capabilities, as well as multimedia components.

6. **Display.** Deciding on the size of monitor to use depends on the intended users. A larger monitor allows the display of more information at once, but is usually more expensive. Clarity of resolution is determined by the number of pixels (an abbreviation of picture elements) the display has. The more pixels, the clearer the image. Certainly color and graphic capabilities are to be considered. Larger display monitors allow students in classrooms to view images and multimedia more easily.

7. **Keyboard.** A suitable keyboard is essential. This input device allows one to enter data, programs, commands and user responses into the computer by pressing keys on the keyboard. A cordless or wireless keyboard is popular in classrooms because it can be passed easily from student to student while they work on projects.

8. **Printers.** Availability and quality of suitable printers are important criteria to be considered. Although the smaller inkjet printers might be adequate for internal use, however, laser printers are necessary where large amounts of printing occurs, for example, near research databases or where Internet access is available. Media specialists need their own laptops with software for PowerPoint and HyperStudio presentations as well as palm computers. Print speed and print density (number of characters per inch) are additional factors to be considered.

9. **Compatibility and flexibility.** This involves the degree to which the equipment can be networked to additional terminals, disc drives, and other peripherals, and, indeed, to remote terminals and other computer systems.

10. **Service and maintenance.** A prospective buyer will want to determine the quality and speed of the repair and maintenance services available, as well as the nature and cost of service contracts.

11. **Documentation.** Guide manuals and other instructional devices supplied with the machine or software that explains how to use it is called the documentation. Their thoroughness and clarity of presentation can help considerably in facilitating use. Many companies and dealers supply free training and instruction to groups to familiarize users with their products.

12. **Peripherals.** External devices that attach to the computer are called peripherals. Examples of peripherals are scanners, digital cameras, and printers. When selecting these devices, it is wise to make certain that they are compatible to the computer being used.

13. **Security devices.** Keeping computers secure is necessary in media centers. Devices that lock down computers are called security devices.

14. **Interactive whiteboards.** This teaching tool allows an image to be projected onto a large screen with a touch-sensitive surface. It serves as an interactive presentation system that turns a computer and an LCD projector into a powerful teaching tool. One can write notes or highlight important information with the whiteboard pens or one can simply touch the screen to move a slide in a PowerPoint presentation.

15. **Other considerations.** Several more general criteria that could apply to other types of educational equipment, such as portability and weight, need to be considered.

Some media centers circulate a mobile set of laptop computers for classroom use. Handheld computers (Personal Digital Assistants) are smaller and can also be circulated easily. Usually the laptops or the PDAs will be stored on a mobile unit that can be locked for security. Wireless technology makes this kind of set up easier to use; however, it is not always possible to have a wireless unit in some situations.

Handheld computers

Advantages of handheld computers are (1) their size—they can be carried in the pocket; (2) they weigh between five and seven ounces; (3) battery life is good; (4) ease of use is a major consideration; (5) synchronization allows easy data transfer between a handheld and a desktop computer; (6) speed, memory, and portability make handhelds a versatile tool.

The disadvantages of handheld computers are: (1) there is little standardization or compatibility among handhelds, and one must stick with one platform once a purchase is made; (2) very little software is available other than the standard programs; and (3) the more memory in a hand-held, the more expensive it becomes.

Handheld computers are useful in media centers and in classrooms. They can be used to give PowerPoint presentations, send e-mails, browse the web, work collaboratively in the classroom, tap into wireless technology, to name a few applications. Peripherals available for handhelds include keyboards, modems, digital cameras, and extra memory (O'Donovan, 2000).

Cameras

Media centers use cameras to record happenings in the media center and to allow production of instructional materials. Digital cameras are fast becoming first choice when selecting cameras for media centers.

Digital Cameras.

The beauty of using digital cameras is that the user can take pictures and store the photographed images digitally rather than on traditional film. Once pictures are taken, they are downloaded to the computer where they can be edited with photo-editing software, viewed, printed, posted on a web site, or included in a PowerPoint presentation. Digital camcorders use the same kind of technology with the added feature of motion. The major advantages of digital cameras are that film is no longer required and that instant pictures are possible. Digital cameras offer unlimited opportunities for production of instructional materials. The major disadvantage is their high cost; however digital disposable cameras are definitely going to change the cost factor.

SELECTION AIDS FOR EDUCATIONAL MATERIALS

Selection Tools

Retrospective-General

American Library Association. (2003). *ALA's guide to best reading in 2003.* Chicago: American Library Association.

Anderson, Vicki. (1998). *Fiction sequels for readers 10 to 16: An annotated bibliography of books in succession* (2nd ed.). Jefferson, NC: McFarland.

Anderson, Vicki. (1998). *Sequels in children's literature: An annotated bibliography of books in succession or with shared themes and characters, K–6.* Jefferson, NC: McFarland.

Ansell, Janis. (2001). *What do children read next? A reader's guide to fiction for children.* Farmington Hills, MI: Gale Group.

Association of Library Service to Children. (2001). *The Newberry and Caldecott Medal Books, 1986–2000: A comprehensive guide to the winners.* Chicago: American Library Association.

Association of Library Service to Children. (2004). *The Newberry and Caldecott Awards: A guide to the medal and honor books.* Chicago: American Library Association.

Barr, Catherine. (Ed.). (1998). *From biography to history: Best books for children's entertainment.* Westport, CT: Libraries Unlimited.

Barr, Catherine. (Ed.). (1999). *Reading in series: A selection guide to books for children.* Westport, CT: Libraries Unlimited.

Bauermeister, Erica & Smith, Holly. (1997). *Let's hear it for the girls: 375 great books for readers 2–14.* New York: Penguin Publishers.

Becker, Beverley C. & Stan, Susan M. (2002). *Hit list for children 2: Frequently challenged books.* Chicago: American Library Association.

Beers, Kylene & Lesesne, Teri. (Eds.). (2001). *Books for you: An annotated booklist for senior high* (14th ed.). Urbana, IL: National Council of Teachers of English.

Berman, Matt. (1999). *Children's book awards annual, 1999.* Westport, CT: Libraries Unlimited.

Berman, Matt & Dupuy, Marigny J. (1998). *Children's book awards annual, 1998.* Westport, CT: Libraries Unlimited.

Book Review Digest. Bronx, NY: H.W. Wilson. Print and electronic. (Monthly except for February and July.)

Books for the teen age. New York: The New York Public Library. (Annual.)

Books in print. New Providence, NJ: R.R. Bowker. (Annual, nonevaluative.)

Brown, David K. (1999, March 4). *Best books of the year: A roundup of annual book lists published on the Web.* Retrieved April 10, 2004, from: http://www.ucalgary.ca/~dkbrown/bestbooks.html.

Canadian books in print: Author and title index. (1975–). Toronto: University of Toronto Press.

Carter, Betty B., et al. (2002). *Best books for young adults* (2nd ed.). Chicago: American Library Association.

Children's books. Washington, DC: Library of Congress. (Annual.)

Children's books 2002: One hundred titles for reading and sharing. (2002). New York: The New York Public Library.

Children's books in print. New Providence, NJ: R.R. Bowker. (Annual, nonevaluative.)

Children's books of the year. Child Study Children's Book Committee, Bank Street College of Education. (Annual.)

Children's book review index. (2003). Farmington Hills, MI: Gale Group. (Annual cumulation.)

Children's literature review. Farmington Hills, MI: Gale Group. (Annual.)

Davis, Robin Works. (1999). *Big books for little readers.* Lanham, MD: Scarecrow Press.

Deeds, Sharon & Chastain, Catherine. (2001). *New books kids like.* Chicago: American Library Association.

DeLong, Janice A. & Schwedt, Rachel E. (1997). *Core collection for small libraries: An annotated bibliography of books for children and young adults.* Lanham, MD: Scarecrow Press.

Denman-West, Margaret W. (1998). *Children's literature: A guide to information sources.* Westport, CT: Libraries Unlimited.

Dillon, Martin & Hysell, Shannon Graff. (Eds.). (2004). *ARBA in-depth: Children and young adult titles.* Westport, CT: Libraries Unlimited.

Fiction catalog (14th ed.). (2001). Bronx, NY: H. W. Wilson. Print and electronic.

Forthcoming books. New Providence, NJ: R.R. Bowker. (Bimonthly.)

Gillespie, John T. (2000). *Best books for young teen readers. Grades 7–10.* Westport, CT: Libraries Unlimited.

Gillespie, John T. (2001). *Best books for children: Preschool through grade 6* (7th ed.). Westport, CT: Libraries Unlimited.

Gillespie, John T. & Barr, Catherine. (2004). *Best books for children* (7th ed.). Westport, CT: Libraries Unlimited.

Gillespie, John T. & Barr, Catherine. (2004). *Best books for middle school and junior high readers.* Westport, CT: Libraries Unlimited.

Gillespie, John T. & Barr, Catherine. (2004). *Best books for high school readers.* Westport, CT: Libraries Unlimited.

Gunning, Thomas G. (1998). *Best books for beginning readers.* Boston: Allyn and Bacon.

Homa, Linda L., et al. (1998). *Elementary school library collection: A guide to books and other media phases 1- 2–3* [CD-ROM version]. Williamsport, PA: Brodart.

Horn Book & Association for Library Service to Children. (2001). *Newbery and Caldecott medal books: 1986–2000: A comprehensive guide to the winners.* Chicago: American Library Association.

Horn book guide. Westport, CT: Greenwood Publishing Group. (Biannual.)

Hunt, Peter. (2001). *Children's literature.* Oxford, UK: Blackwell Publishers.

Jones, Delores Blythe. (1998). *Building a special collection of children's literature in your library: Identifying, maintaining, and sharing rare and collectible items.* Chicago: American Library Association.

Jones, Patrick, et al. (2003). *A core collection for young adults.* New York: Neal-Schuman Publishers.

Lee, Laura K. (Ed.). (2000). *The elementary school library collection: A guide to books and other media, phases 1-2–3, 2000* (22nd ed.). Williamsport, PA: Brodart.

Lewis, Valerie V. and Mayes, Walter M. (1998). *Valerie & Walter's best Books for children: A lively, opinionated guide.* New York: Avon Books.

LiBretto, Ellen V. & Barr, Catherine. (2002). *High/low handbook: Best books and websites for reluctant teen readers* (4th ed.). Westport, CT: Libraries Unlimited.

Lindskoog, Kathryn Ann. (1999). *How to grow a young reader: Books from every age for readers of every age.* Wheaton, IL: Harold Shaw Publishers.

Lipson, Eden Ross. (2000). *The New York Times parent's guide to the best books for children* (3rd ed.). New York: Crown Publishing Group.

Lynch-Brown, Carol & Tomlinson, Carl M. (1998). *Essentials of children's literature* (3rd ed.). Boston: Allyn & Bacon.

McClure, Amy A. & Kristo, Janice V. (Eds.). (2002). *Adventuring with books: A booklist for pre-K–grade 6.* Urbana, IL: National Council of Teachers of English.

McElmeel, Sharron L. (1998). *100 most popular children's authors: biographical sketches and bibliographies.* Westport, CT: Libraries Unlimited.

Matthew, Kathryn I. & Lowe, Joy L. (2002). *Neal-Schuman guide to recommended children's books and media for use with every elementary subject.* New York: Neal-Schuman Publishers.

Middle & junior high school library catalog (8th ed.). (2000). Bronx, NY: H.W. Wilson. Print and electronic.

Norton, Donna E. (1999). *Through the eyes of a child: An introduction to children's literature.* Upper Saddle River, NJ: Prentice-Hall.

O'Dell, Katie. (2002). *Library materials and services for teen girls.* Westport, CT: Libraries Unlimited.

Office of Children's Services. *Children's books.* New York: New York Public Library. (Annual.)

Pearl, Nancy. (1999). *Now read this. A guide to mainstream fiction, 1978–1998.* Westport, CT: Libraries Unlimited.

Pearl, Nancy. (2002). *Now read this II. A guide to mainstream fiction, 1990–2001.* Westport, CT: Libraries Unlimited.

Pierce, Kathryn Mitchell. (Ed.). (2000). *Adventuring with books: A booklist for pre-K–grade 6.* (12th ed.). Urbana, IL: National Council of Teachers of English.

Post, Arden Ruth. (2000). *Celebrating children's choices: 25 years of children's favorite books.* Newark, DE: International Reading Association.

Price, Anne & Yaakov, Juliette. (Eds.). (2001). *Children's catalog* (18th ed.). Bronx, NY: H.W. Wilson. Print and electronic.

Senior high school library catalog (15th ed.). (2002). Bronx, NY: H.W. Wilson. Print and electronic.

Shearer, Kenneth D. & Burgin, Robert. (2002). *The readers' advisor's companion.* Westport, CT: Libraries Unlimited.

Simkin, John. (Ed.). (1999). *The whole story: 3000 years of sequels & sequences* (2nd ed.). Westport, CT: Libraries Unlimited.

Smith, Henrietta M. (Ed.). (1999). *Coretta Scott King awards books: 1970–1999.* Chicago: American Library Association.

Spencer, Pam. (1999). *What do young adults read next?: A reader's guide to fiction for young adults* (Vol. 3). Farmington Hills, MI: Gale Group.

Stephens, Claire G. (2000). *Coretta Scott King Award Books: Using great literature with children and young adults.* Westport, CT: Libraries Unlimited.

Stover, Lois T. & Zenker, Stephanie F. (Eds.). (1997) *Books for you: An annotated list from 1994–96 for senior high students* (13th ed.). Urbana, IL: National Council of Teachers of English.

Tomlinson, Carl M. (Ed.). (1998). *Children's books from other countries.* Lanham, MD: Scarecrow Press.

Trelease, Jim. (2001). *The read-aloud handbook* (5th ed.). New York: Penguin Books.

University press books selection for public and secondary school libraries. Association of American University Presses. (Annual.)

What do I read next? (1999). Farmington Hills, MI: Gale Group.

Wyatt, Flora R., et al. (1998). *Popular nonfiction authors for children: A biographical thematic guide.* Westport, CT: Libraries Unlimited.

Young Adult Library Services Association (ALSA): Quick picks for reluctant young adult readers. Westport, CT: Libraries Unlimited. Retrieved from the ALA web site: http://www.ala.org/yalsa/booklists/quickpicks.

Young Adult Services Division. *Best books for young adults.* Chicago: American Library Association. (Annual.)

Zarnowski, Myra, et al. (Eds.). (2001). *The best in children's nonfiction: Reading, writing and teaching Orbis Pictus award books.* Urbana, IL: National Council of Teachers of English.

Retrospective—Subject Specific

Adamson, Lynda G. (1998). *American historical fiction: An annotated guide to novels for adults and young adults.* Westport, CT: Oryx Press.

Adamson, Lynda G. (1998). *Literature connections to American history K–6 and 7–12: Resources to enhance and entice.* Westport, CT: Libraries Unlimited.

Adamson, Lynda G. (1998). *Literature connections to world history, K–16 and 7–12: Resources to enhance and entice.* Westport, CT: Libraries Unlimited.

Ammon, Bette D. & Sherman, Gale W. (1998). *More rip-roaring reads for reluctant teen readers.* Westport, CT: Libraries Unlimited.

Barr, Catherine. (Ed.). (1998). *From biography to history: Best books for children's entertainment and education.* Westport, CT: Libraries Unlimited.

Barrera, Rosalinda B., et al. (Eds.). (1997). *Kaleidoscope: A multicultural booklist for grades K–8* (2nd ed.). Urbana, IL: National Council of Teachers of English.

Baxter, Kathleen A. & Kochel, Marcia Agness. (2002). *Gotcha! Nonfiction booktalks to get kids excited about reading.* Westport, CT: Libraries Unlimited.

Baxter, Kathleen A. & Kochel, Marcia Agness. (2002). *Gotcha again! More nonfiction booktalks to get kids excited about reading.* Westport, CT: Libraries Unlimited.

Black experience in children's books. (1999). New York: The New York Public Library.

Blass, Rosanne J. (2002). *Booktalks, bookwalks, and read-alouds: Promoting the best children's literature across the elementary curriculum.* Westport, CT: Libraries Unlimited.

Blazek, Ron. (2000). *The humanities: A selective guide to information sources.* Westport, CT: Libraries Unlimited.

Bleiler, Richard. (1999). *Reference guide to mystery and detective fiction.* Westport, CT: Libraries Unlimited.

Bodart, Joni Richards. (1998). *Booktalking the award winners 4.* Bronx, NY: H.W. Wilson.

Bodart, Joni Richards. (2000). *The world's best thin books: What to read when your book report is due tomorrow* (Rev. ed.). Lanham, MD: Scarecrow Press.

Bouricius, Ann. (2000). *The romance readers' advisory: The librarian's guide to love in the stacks.* Chicago: American Library Association.

Braille book review. Washington, DC: National Library Service for the Blind and Physically Handicapped. (Annual.)

Buker, Derek M. (2002). *The science fiction and fantasy reader's advisory: The librarian's guide to cyborgs, aliens, and sorcerers.* Chicago: American Library Association.

Butzow, Carol M. & Butzow, John W. (2000). *Science through children's literature: An integrated approach.* Westport, CT: Libraries Unlimited.

Campbell, Laura Ann. (1999). *Storybooks for tough times.* Golden, CO: Fulcrum Resources.

Carpan, Carolyn. (2004). *Rocked by romance: A guide to teen romance fiction.* Westport, CT: Libraries Unlimited.

Cecil, Nancy Lee & Roberts, Patricia L. (1998). *Families in children's literature: A resource guide, grades 4–8.* Westport, CT: Libraries Unlimited.

Charles, John, et al. (2002). *The mystery readers' advisory: The librarian's clues to murder and mayhem.* Chicago: American Library Association.

Complete directory of large print books and serials 2003. (2003). New Providence, NJ: R. R. Bowker.

Dodson, Shirleen. (1998). *100 books for girls to grow on.* New York: Harper.

Dole, Patricia Pearl. (1999). *Children's books about religion.* Westport, CT: Libraries Unlimited.

Evans, Caroline W., et al. (2001). *Math links: Teaching the NCTM 2000 standards through children's literature.* Westport, CT: Libraries Unlimited.

Fast and easy books for teenagers. New York: New York Public Library. (Annual.)

Flanagan, Alice K. (1999). *Career exploration through children's literature: A 6–8 correlation to the National Career Development guidelines.* Chicago: Ferguson Publishing.

Flanagan, Alice K. (1999). *Elementary career awareness through children's literature: A K–2 correlation to the national career development guidelines.* Chicago: Ferguson Publishing.

Fonseca, Anthony J. & Pulliam, June Michele. (2002). *Hooked on horror: A guide to reading interests in horror fiction.* Westport, CT: Libraries Unlimited.

For younger readers: Braille and talking books. (1997–). Washington, DC: National Library Service for the Blind and Physically Handicapped, Library of Congress.

Forgan, James W. (2003). *Teaching problem solving through children's literature.* Westport, CT: Teacher Ideas Press.

Fredericks, Anthony D. (1998). *The integrated curriculum: Books for reluctant readers, grades 2–5.* Westport, CT: Libraries Unlimited.

Fredericks, Anthony D. (2001). *Investigating natural disasters through children's literature: An integrated approach.* Westport, CT: Libraries Unlimited.

Fuhler, Carol J. (1998). *Discovering geography of North America with books kids love.* Golden, CO: Fulcrum Resources.

Gannon, Michael B. (2004). *Blood, bedlam, bullets, and bad guys: A reader's guide to adventure/suspense fiction.* Westport, CT: Libraries Unlimited.

Gillespie, John T. & Naden, Corinne J. (2001). *The Newbery companion: Booktalk and related materials for Newbery medal and honor books.* Westport, CT: Libraries Unlimited.

Givens, Archie. (Ed.). (1997). *Spirited minds: African American books for our sons and our brothers.* New York: W. W. Norton.

Global beat. (1998). New York: The New York Public Library.

Hardy, Lyda Mary. (2000). *Women in U.S. history: A resource guide.* Westport, CT: Libraries Unlimited.

Helbig, Alethea. (2001). *Many peoples, one land: A guide to new multicultural literature for children and young adults.* Westport, CT: Greenwood Press.

Herald, Diana Tixier. (1999). *Fluent in fantasy: A guide to reading interests.* Westport, CT: Libraries Unlimited.

Herald, Diana Tixier. (2000). *Genreflecting: A guide to reading interests in genre fiction* (5th ed.). Westport, CT: Libraries Unlimited.

Herald, Diana Tixier. (2003). *Teen genreflecting: A guide to reading interests* (2nd ed.). Westport, CT: Libraries Unlimited.

Herald, Diana Tixier & Kunzel, Bonnie. (2002). *Strictly science fiction: A guide to reading interests.* Westport, CT: Libraries Unlimited.

Hooper, Brad. (2000). *The short story readers' advisory: A guide to the best.* Chicago: American Library Association.

Hurt, C. D. (1998). *Information sources in science and technology* (3rd ed.). Westport, CT: Libraries Unlimited.

Index to poetry for children and young people, 1993–1997. (1998). Bronx, NY: H. W. Wilson.

Jacob, Merle L. & Apple, Hope. (2000). *To be continued: An annotated guide to sequels* (2nd ed.). Westport, CT: Oryx Press.

Jweid, Rosann. (2001). *Building character through literature: A guide for middle school readers.* Lanham, MD: Scarecrow Press.

Keane, Nancy J. (2002). *Booktalking across the curriculum, middle years.* Westport, CT: Libraries Unlimited.

Kuharets, Olga R. (2001). *Venture into cultures: A resource book of multicultural materials and programs* (2nd ed.). Chicago: American Library Association.

Lesesne, Terri S. & Chance, Rosemary. (2002). *Hit list for young adults 2: frequently challenged books.* Chicago: American Library Association.

McArthur, Janice & McGuire, Barbara E. (1998). *Books on wheels: Cooperative learning through thematic units.* Westport, CT: Libraries Unlimited.

McCaffery, Laura Hibbets. (1998). *Building an ESL collection for young adults: A bibliography of recommended fiction and nonfiction for schools and public libraries.* Westport, CT: Greenwood Press.

MacDonald, Margaret Read. (2001). *The storyteller's sourcebook: A subject, title, and motif index to folklore collections for children.* Farmington Hills, MI: Gale Group.

Mediavilla, Cindy. (1999). *Arthurian fiction: An annotated bibliography.* Lanham, MD: Scarecrow Press.

Mort, John. (2002). *Christian fiction: A guide to the genre.* Westport, CT: Libraries Unlimited.

Multicultural review: Dedicated to a better understanding of ethnic, racial and religious diversity. (1992–). Westport, CT: Greenwood Press.

Niebuhr, Garry Warren. (2003). *Make mine a mystery. A reader's guide to mystery and detective fiction.* Westport, CT: Libraries Unlimited.

Norton, Donna E. (2001). *Multicultural children's literature: Through the eyes of many children.* Upper Saddle River, NJ: Prentice-Hall.

Norton, Donna E. & Norton, Saundra E. (1998). *Through the eyes of a child: An introduction to children's literature* (5th ed.). Upper Saddle River, NJ: Prentice-Hall.

Pearl, Nancy. (1999). *Now read this: A guide to mainstream fiction, 1978–1998.* Westport, CT: Libraries Unlimited.

Perry, Phyllis J. (1999). *Exploring our country's history: Linking fiction to nonfiction.* Westport, CT: Libraries Unlimited.

Ramsdell, Kristin. (1999). *Romance fiction: A guide to the genre.* Westport, CT: Libraries Unlimited.

Reese, Jean. (1999). *Internet books for educators, parents, and students.* Westport, CT: Libraries Unlimited.

Richards, Phillip M. & Schlager, Neil. (2000). *Best literature by and about blacks.* Farmington Hills, MI: Gale Group.

Roberts, Jerry. (1999). *Rain forest bibliography: An annotated guide to over 1600 nonfiction books about Central and South American jungles.* Jefferson, NC: McFarland.

Roberts, Patricia. (1998). *Language arts and environmental awareness: 100+ integrated books and activities for children.* New Haven, CT: Linnet Professional Publications.

Roberts, Patricia. (2000). *Family values through children's literature.* Lanham, MD: Scarecrow Press.

Robertson, Judith P. (Ed.). (1999). *Teaching for a tolerant world, grades K–6: Essays and resources.* Urbana, IL: National Council of Teachers of English.

Sands, Karen. (1999). *Back in the spaceship again: Juvenile science fiction series since 1945.* Westport, CT: Greenwood Press.

Saricks, Joyce G. (2001). *The readers' advisory guide to genre fiction.* Chicago: American Library Association.

Schall, Lucy. (2001). *Booktalks plus: Motivating teens to read.* Westport, CT: Libraries Unlimited.

Schon, Isabel. (2000). *Recommended books in Spanish for children and young adults, 1996 through 1999.* Lanham, MD: Scarecrow Press.

Sherman, Gale W. & Ammon, Bette D. (1998). *More rip-roaring reads for reluctant teen readers.* Westport, CT: Libraries Unlimited.

Smith, Henrietta M. (Ed.). (2004) *Coretta Scott King Awards: 1970–2004.* Chicago: American Library Association.

Sosa, Maria & Gath, Tracy. (Eds.). (2000). *Exploring science in the library: Resources and activities for young people.* Chicago: American Library Association.

Stephens, Claire Gatrell. (2000). *Coretta Scott King award books: Using great literature with children and young adults.* Westport, CT: Libraries Unlimited.

Stephens, Elaine C. (1998). *Learning about the civil war: Literature and other resources for young people.* New Haven, CT: Linnet Professional Publications.

Stern, David. (2000). *Guide to information sources in the physical sciences.* Westport, CT: Libraries Unlimited.

Subject guide to books in print 2003–2004. New Providence, NJ: R.R. Bowker. (Annual.)

Subject guide to children's books in print. New Providence, NJ: R.R. Bowker. (Annual.)

Sullivan, Edward T. (1999). *The holocaust in literature for youth: A guide and resource book.* Lanham, MD: Scarecrow Press.

Susag, Dorothea M. (1998). *Roots and branches: A resource of Native American literature: Themes, lessons, and bibliographies.* Urbana, IL: National Council of Teachers of English.

Sweeney, Wilma K. (1998). *The special-needs reading list: An annotated guide to the best publications for parents and professionals.* Bethesda, MD: Woodbine House.

Thomas, Cathlyn & Littlejohn, Carol. (2003). *Still talking that book: Booktalks to promote reading, grades 3–12* (Vol. 4). Worthington, OH: Linworth.

Toussaint, Pamela. (1999). *Great books for African-American children.* New York: Dutton/Plume.

Volz, Bridget Dealy, et al. (2000). *Junior genreflecting: A guide to good reads and series fiction for children.* Westport, CT: Libraries Unlimited.

Walker, Barbara J. (1998). *Developing Christian fiction collections for children and adults.* New York: Neal-Shuman Publishers.

What fantastic fiction do I read next? (1999). Farmington Hills, MI: Gale Group.

What inspirational literature do I read next? (2000). Farmington Hills, MI: Gale Group.

What mystery do I read next? (1999). Farmington Hills, MI: Gale Group.

What romance do I read next? (1999). Farmington Hills, MI: Gale Group.

What western do I read next? (1999). Farmington Hills, MI: Gale Group.

Wilson, Patricia Potter. (1996). *The professional collection for elementary educators.* Bronx, NY: H.W. Wilson.

Wright, Cora M. (1998). *Hot links: Literature links for the middle school curriculum.* Westport, CT: Libraries Unlimited.

Wright, Cora M. (2002). *More hot links: Linking literature with the middle school curriculum.* Westport, CT: Libraries Unlimited.

Yokota, Junko. (Ed.). (2001). *Kaleidoscope: A multicultural booklist for grades K–8* (3rd ed.). Urbana, IL: National Council of Teachers of English.

York, Sherry. (2003). *Children and young adult literature by Native Americans: A guide for librarians, teachers, parents and students.* Worthington, OH; Linworth.

Current—General

Book links: Connecting books, libraries and classrooms. Chicago: American Library Association. (Bimonthly.)

Bookbird: A journal of international children's literature. Ontario, Canada: International Board on Books for Young People. (Quarterly.)

Booklist. Chicago: American Library Association. (22 issues.)

Book review index. Farmington Hills, MI: Gale Group. Print and electronic. (3 annual issues.)

Bulletin of the center for children's books. Urbana–Champaign, IL: Publications Office, Graduate School of Library & Information Science. (Monthly except August.)

Choice. Chicago: American Library Association. (Monthly except July/August issue.)

Choices. Newark, DE: International Reading Association. Available at http://www.reading.org/choices. (Annual.)

CM: Canadian review of materials. Winnipeg, MB Canada: The Manitoba Library Association. (Biweekly.) Electronic reviewing journal.

Horn book magazine. Boston, MA: Horn Book, Inc. (Monthly.)

Kirkus reviews. New York: Kirkus Services. (Semimonthly.)

Library journal. New York: R.R. Bowker. (Monthly, September–May.)

Library media connection. Worthington, OH: Linworth. (7 issues.)

Media & methods. Philadelphia, PA: American Society of Educators. (7 issues/ year.)

Reviewing librarian. Toronto: Ontario School Library Association. (Quarterly.)

School library journal & school library journal online. New Providence, NJ: Reed Business Information. Available at http://slj.reviewsnews.com. (Monthly.)

School library media research. Chicago: American Association of School Librarians. Retrieved April 10, 2004, from the American Library Association web site: http://www.ala.org/aaslslmrTemplate.cfm?section=slmrb

Teacher librarian: The journal for school library professionals. Vancouver, BC: Dyad Services. (Bimonthly except August.)

VOYA: Voice of youth advocates. Lanham, MD: Scarecrow Press. (Bimonthly.)

Current—Subject Specific

ALAN review. Athens, GA: Assembly on Literature for Adolescents, National Council of Teachers of English. (3 issues/year.)

American biology teacher. Reston, VA: National Association of Biology Teachers. (9 issues.)

American music teacher. Cincinnati, OH: Music Teachers National Association. (Bimonthly.)

Appraisal: Science books for young people. Boston: Northeastern University. (Quarterly.)

Arithmetic teacher. Reston, VA: National Council of Teachers of Mathematics. (Monthly.)

Curriculum review. Little Falls, NJ: PaperClip Communications. (9 issues/year, September–May.)

Educational leadership. Alexandria, VA: Association for Supervision and Curriculum Development. (8 issues/year.)

English journal. Urbana, IL: National Council of Teachers of English. (Bimonthly.)

History teacher. Long Beach, CA: Society for the History of Education. (Quarterly.)

Interracial books for children's bulletin. New York: Council on Interracial Books for Children. (8 issues/year.)

Journal of geography. Macomb, IL: National Council for Geographic Education. (Bimonthly.)

Journal of learning disabilities. New York: Professional Press. (10 issues/year.)

Language arts. Urbana, IL: National Council of Teachers of English. (Monthly, September–May.)

Mathematics teacher. Reston, VA: National Council of Teachers of Mathematics. (Monthly, except June–September.)

Multicultural review. Westport, CT: Greenwood Publishing Group. (Quarterly.)

Multimedia schools: A practical journal of technology for education, including multimedia, CD-ROM, online, Internet and hardware in K-12. Medford, NY: Information Today. Available at http://www.infotoday.com/MMSchools/default.shtml. (Bimonthly.)

Online: The magazine of online information systems. (1970–). Wilton, CT: Online, Inc.

Reading Teacher. Newark, DE: International Reading Association. (8 issues/year.)

Science and children. Washington, DC: National Science Teachers Association. (8 issues/year, September–May.)

Science books and films. Washington, DC: American Association for the Advancement of Science. (9 issues/year.)

Science teacher. Washington, DC: National Science Teachers Associations. (Monthly, September–May.)

Social education. Arlington, VA: National Council for the Social Studies. (7 issues/year.)

Talking book topics. Washington, DC: Library of Congress, National Library Service for the Blind and Physically Handicapped. (Bimonthly.)

Picture Books

Axel-Lute, Melanie. (2003). *Numbers! colors! alphabets!: A concept guide to children's picture books.* Worthington, OH: Linworth.

Cianciolo, Patricia J. (2000). *Informational picture books for children.* Chicago: American Library Association.

Hall, Susan. (2000). *Using picture storybooks to teach character education.* Westport, CT: Oryx Press.

Hall, Susan. (2001). *Using picture storybooks to teach literary devices: Recommended books for children* (Vol. 3). Westport, CT: Libraries Unlimited.

Kriesberg, Daniel A. (1999). *A sense of place: Teaching children about the environment with picture books.* Westport, CT: Teacher Ideas Press.

Lima, Carolyn W. & Lima, John A. (2001). *A to zoo: Subject access to children's picture books* (6th ed.). Westport, CT: Libraries Unlimited.

McElmeel, Sharron L. (2000). *100 most popular picture book authors and illustrators: Biographical sketches and bibliographies.* Westport, CT: Libraries Unlimited.

Nespeca, Sue McCleaf & Reeve, Joan B. (2002). *Picture books plus: 100 extension activities in art, drama, music, math, and science.* Chicago: American Library Association.

Polette, Nancy & Ebbesmeyer, Joan. (2002). *Literature lures: Using picture books and novels to motivate middle school readers.* Westport, CT: Teacher Ideas Press.

Reference Books

American book publishing record. New Providence, NJ: R. R. Bowker. (Annual.)

American reference books annual. Westport, CT: Libraries Unlimited. (Annual.)

Bleiler, Richard J. (1999). *Reference guide to mystery and detective fiction.* Westport, CT: Libraries Unlimited.

Bowker annual library and book trade almanac. New York: R. R. Bowker. (Annual.)

Dillon, Martin & Hysell, Shannon Graff. (Eds.). (2004). *Recommended reference books for small and medium-sized libraries and media centers.* Westport, CT: Libraries Unlimited.

Kennedy, Scott E. (1999). *Reference sources for small and medium-sized libraries* (6th ed.). Chicago: American Library Association.

Lang, Jovian P. & O'Gorman, Jack. (2000). *Recommended reference books in paperback* (3rd ed.). Westport, CT: Libraries Unlimited.

Lewis, Valerie V. (1998). *Madame Audrey's guide to mostly cheap but good reference books for small rural libraries.* Chicago: American Library Association.

Mirwis, Allan N. (1999). *Subject encyclopedias: User guide, review citations, and keyword index* (2 vols.). Westport, CT: Oryx Press.

O'Brien, Nancy P. (2000). *Education: A guide to reference and information sources.* Westport, CT: Libraries Unlimited.

Quinn, Mary Ellen. (2002). *Reference books bulletin, 1999–2000.* Chicago: American Library Association.

Reference and subscription books review column in *Booklist.*

Safford, Barbara Ripp. (1998). *Guide to Reference materials for school library media centers* (5th ed.). Westport, CT: Libraries Unlimited.

Skreslet, Paula Youngman. (2000). *Northern Africa: A guide to reference and information Sources.* Westport, CT: Libraries Unlimited.

Government Publications

Hajnal, Peter I. (Ed.). (2001). *International information: Documents, publications, and electronic information of international government organizations* (2nd ed., Vol. 2). Westport, CT: Libraries Unlimited.

Hoffmann, Frank W. & Wood, Richard J. (1998). *Guide to popular U.S. government publications, 1995–1996* (5th ed.). Westport, CT: Libraries Unlimited.

Monthly catalog of United States government publications. (1895–). Washington, DC: U.S. Government Printing Office.

Morehead, Joe. (1999). *Introduction to United States government information sources* (6th ed.). Westport, CT: Libraries Unlimited.

Pearson, Joyce A. McCray & Tull, Pamela M. (1998). *U.S. government directories, 1982–1995.* Westport, CT: Libraries Unlimited.

Robinson, Judith Schiek. (1998). *Tapping the government grapevine: The user-friendly guide to U.S. government information sources.* Westport, CT: Oryx Press.

U.S. government books. (1982–). Washington, DC: U.S. Government Printing Office.

Magazines, Newspapers, Textbooks

Children's magazine guide. (1948–). New York: R. R. Bowker. (9 issues, Annual cumulation.)

El-Hi textbooks and serials in print. New Providence, NJ: R. R. Bowker. (Annual.)

Google directory. Retrieved April 10, 2004, from: http://directory.google.com/Top/Kids_and_Teens/News/Magazines_and_E-zines/

Katz, Bill & Katz, Linda Sternberg. (2000). *Magazines for libraries* (10th ed.). New Providence, NJ: R. R. Bowker.

Kids and teen magazines (Gifted). Retrieved April 10, 2004, from: http://www. hoagiesgifted.org/magazines.htm

LaGuardia, Cheryl. (Ed.). (2002). *Magazines for libraries* (11th ed.). New Providence, NJ: R. R. Bowker.

Magazines for kids and teens. (2003, May 15). Retrieved May 8, 2004, from: http://web.archive.org/web/20030626085810/http://www.madisonpubliclibrary. org/youth/magazines.html

Patron, Susan. (2004, March). Miles of magazines. *School Library Journal, 50*(3), 52–57.

Selected Internet sites for publishers, books, journals and newspapers. Retrieved May 8, 2004 from: http://web.archive.org/web/20030608192904/http://web2010. brevard.cc.fl.us/library/periodical.html

Teaching tolerance magazine. Retrieved May 8, 2004, from: http://web.archive. web/20030622194149/http://www.splcenter.org/teachingtolerance/tt-mainbtm. html

Top magazine subscriptions. Retrieved April 10, 2004, from: http://www.top-magazine-subscriptions.com

Pamphlets and Free Materials

Consumer education catalog: An index of selected federal publications of consumer interest. (2003). Pueblo, CO: Consumer Information Center. (Quarterly.)

Consumer information catalog. Pueblo, CO: Consumer Information Center.

Educator's guide to free family and consumer education materials (20th ed.). (2003). Randolph, WI: Educators Progress Service, Inc.

Educator's guide to free films, filmstrips and slides (63rd ed.). (2003). Randolph, WI: Educators Progress Service, Inc.

Educator's guide to free guidance materials (42nd ed.). (2003). Randolph, WI: Educators Progress Service, Inc.

Educator's guide to free health, physical education and recreation materials (36th ed.). (2003). Randolph, WI: Educators Progress Service, Inc.

Educator's guide to free Internet resources—Elementary/middle school edition (2nd ed.). (2003). Randolph, WI: Educators Progress Service, Inc.

Educator's guide to free Internet resources—Secondary edition (21st ed.). (2003). Randolph, WI: Educators Progress Service, Inc.

Educator's guide to free multicultural materials (6th ed.). (2003). Randolph, WI: Educators Progress Service, Inc.

Educator's guide to free science materials (44th ed.). (2003). Randolph, WI: Educators Progress Service, Inc.

Educator's guide to free social studies materials (43rd ed.). (2003). Randolph, WI: Educators Progress Service, Inc.

Educator's guide to free videotapes: Elementary/middle school edition (4th ed.). (2003). Randolph, WI: Educators Progress Service, Inc.

Educator's guide to free videotapes: Secondary edition (50th ed.). (2003). Randolph, WI: Educators Progress Service, Inc.

Free materials for schools and libraries. Seattle, WA: Dept. 284, Box C34069. (5 issues/year.)

Oakes, Elizabeth H. (Ed.). (1998). *Free and inexpensive career materials: A resource directory.* Chicago: Ferguson.

Sources: A guide to print and non-print materials available from organization, industry, government agencies, and specialized publications. New York: Neal-Schuman. (3 issues/year.)

Vertical file index. New York: H. W. Wilson. (Monthly.)

Web Sites and Electronic Collections

Best books of the year: A roundup of annual book lists published on the Web. Retrieved April 10, 2004, from: http://www.ucalgary.ca/~dkbrown/bestbooks.html

Booklist online. Retrieved April 10, 2004, from the ALA web site: http://www.ala.org/Content/NavigationMenu/Products_and_Publications/Periodicals/Booklist/Booklist.htm

Booksoutofprint.com [Electronic]. New Providence, NJ: R. R. Bowker. (Annual subscription.)

Bowker on the Web: Booksinprint.com [Electronic]. New Providence, NJ: R. R. Bowker. (Annual subscription.)

Children's choices, teachers' choices and young adults' choices booklists. (2003). Retrieved April 10, 2004, from the International Reading Association web site: http://www.reading.org/choices/

Directory for Horn Book web site. (2001). Retrieved April 10, 2004, from: http://www.hbook.com/directory.shtml

E-booksinprint.com [Electronic]. New Providence, NJ: R. R. Bowker.

Gregory, Vicki L., et al. (1999). *Multicultural resources on the Internet: The United States and Canada.* Westport, CT: Libraries Unlimited.

Hernon, Peter, et al. (2001). *U.S. government on the Web: Getting the information you need.* Westport, CT: Libraries Unlimited.

Jasco, Peter. (1999, August). Database selection tools. *Dialog's Dialindex and SilverPlatter Online & CD-ROM Review, 23*(4), 227–229.

Kovacs, Diane. (1999). *Building electronic library collections: The essential guide to selection criteria and core subject collections.* New York: Neal-Schuman.

Library of Congress. (2003, August 13). *Web braille: That all may read.* Washington, DC: National Library Service for the Blind and Physically Handicapped. Retrieved April 10, 2004, from: http://www.loc.gov/nls/

Library titlewave. McHenry, IL: Follett Library Sources. Retrieved April 10, 2004, from: http://www.titlewave.com/

Literatureplaces.com: Where literacy begins with books. Retrieved April 10, 2004, from: http://literatureplace.com

Miller, Elizabeth. (2001). *The Internet resource directory for K–12 teachers and librarians.* Westport, CT: Libraries Unlimited.

Web feet K-8 online. Retrieved April 10, 2004, from: http://www.webfeetguides. com/wfk8/wfk8_online.htm

GENERAL AUDIOVISUAL SOURCES

AV market place. New Providence, NJ: R. R. Bowker. (Annual.)

AV online. Wellesley Hills, MA: Silver Platter Information Services. (Annual.)

Audio video review digest. Detroit: Gale Group. (3 issues/year, annual cumulation.)

Media review digest. (1970–). Ann Arbor, MI: Pierian Press. ✳

CD-ROMS, Discs, Databases

Books in print on disc. New Providence, NJ: R. R. Bowker. (Annual subscription.)

Books in print with book reviews on disc. New Providence, NJ: R. R. Bowker. (Annual subscription.)

Bowker's audio & video database on disc. New Providence, NJ: R. R. Bowker. (Annual subscription, updated quarterly.)

Bowker/Whitaker global books in print ON DISC™. New Providence, NJ: R. R. Bowker. (Annual subscription.)

CD-ROMs in print 2000 (18th ed.). (2003). Farmington Hills, MI: Gale Group.

Choices for young readers. Library/teacher professional edition [CD-ROM]. Evanston, IL: John Gordon Burke Publications.

Gale directory of databases (2004 ed.). (2003). Farmington Hills, MI: Gale Group. ✳

NoveList. Birmingham, AL: EBSCO Information Services. Retrieved April 10, 2004, from: http://www.epnet.com/public/novelist.asp

Videos, DVDs, Slides, and Digital Images

Albitz, Rebecca S. (2002). *Video reference tools and selection aids in video collection development in multitype libraries* (2nd ed.). Westport, CT: Greenwood Press.

Association for Library Service to Children. *Notable children's films.* Chicago: American Library Association. (Annual.)

Blenz-Clucas, Beth. (Ed.). (1990–). *Video rating guide for libraries.* Westport, CT: ABC-Clio.

Bowker's audio and video database [CD-ROM]. New Providence, NJ: R. R. Bowker. (Updated quarterly.)

Bowker's complete video directory. New Providence, NJ: R. R. Bowker. (Annual.)

Bowker's directory of videocassettes for children K–12. (1999). New Providence, NJ: R. R. Bowker.

Directory of videos, multimedia, and audio-visual products. (1996–). Fairfax, VA: International Communications Industries Association.

Handman, Gary P. (2002). *Video collection development in multi-type libraries. A handbook.* Westport, CT: Libraries Unlimited.

Landers film reviews. Escondido, CA: Landers Associates. (9 issues/year, bimonthly September–June.)

Librarian's ultimate to children's video and DVD. Westport, CT: Libraries Unlimited.

Library video company, Wynnewood, PA. Retrieved April 10, 2004, from: http://www.libraryvideo.com/

Motion picture guide annual. New York: R. R. Bowker. (Annual.)

Pittman, Randy. (1986–). *Video librarian.* Retrieved April 10, 2004, from: http://www.videolibrarian.com/index.html

Schell, Terri. (Ed.). (1979–). *Video source book* (22nd ed.). Farmington Hills, MI: Gale Research.

Sightlines. New York: Educational Film Library Association. (Bimonthly.)

Totten, Herman L., Brown, Risa W., & Garner, Carolyn. (1996). *Culturally diverse videos, audios, and CD-ROMS for children and young adults.* New York: Neal-Schuman.

Variety's video directory plus. New Providence, NJ: R. R. Bowker.

Walker, John. (Ed.). (2003). *Halliwell's film and video guide, 2003.* New York: HarperCollins.

Walker, Sandra C. & Beetham, Donald W. (Eds.). (1999). *Image buyers' guide: An international directory of sources for slides and digital images for art and architecture* (7th ed.). Westport, CT: Libraries Unlimited.

Wood, Irene. (1999). *Culturally diverse videos, audios, and CD-ROMs for children and young adults.* New York: Neal-Schuman.

Software and Audio Books

Dewey, Patrick R. (1998). *303 software programs to use in your library: Descriptions, evaluations, and practical advice.* Chicago: American Library Association.

Educational software selector. Educational Products Information Exchange Institute. (Annual.)

Guide to free computer materials. Randolph, WI: Educators Progress Service, Inc. (Annual.)

Kliatt: Reviews of selected books, educational software and audio books. (1978–). Wellesley, MA: Kliatt.

Lopez, Victor D. (2000). *Free and low cost software for the PC.* Jefferson, NC: McFarland.

Microcomputer software guide online. New Providence, NJ: R. R. Bowker. (Updated monthly.) Retrieved April 10, 2004, from R. R. Bowker web site: http://www.bowker.com/bowkerweb/catalog2001/prod00075.htm

Software encyclopedia. New Providence, NJ: R. R. Bowker. (Annual.)
Software reviews on file. (1985–). New York: Facts on File.

Recordings

Baird, Susan. (2000). *Audiobook collections and services.* Fort Atkinson, WI: Highsmith.
Bowker's directory of audiocassettes for children. (1999). New York: R. R. Bowker.
Music Library Association. (1997). *Basic music library: Essential scores and sound recording* (3rd ed.). Chicago: American Library Association.
New Schwann record and tape guide. Boston: New Schwann. (Monthly.)
On cassette: A comprehensive bibliography of spoken word audio cassettes. New York: R R. Bowker. (Annual.)
Schwann opus. (1949–). [Stereophile]. Santa Fe, NM: Schwann Publications. (Annual.)
Schwann spectrum. (1992–). [Stereophile]. Santa Fe, NM: Schwann Publications. (Annual.)
Words on cassette. New Providence, NJ: R. R. Bowker. (Annual.)

Selection Aids for Equipment

Audio visual presentations. Retrieved April 10, 2004, from: http://www.kintron ics.com/presentations.html
Epiegram: Equipment. Stony Brook, New York: Educational Products Information Exchange. (Monthly.)
Google directory. Retrieved April 10, 2004, from: http://directory.google.com
Nextag.com. Retrieved April 10, 2004, from: http://www.nextag.com/Audio_Visual~yz901037zmzjb8szhszmainz5-htm
The audio-visual equipment directory. Fairfax, VA: National Audio-Visual Association. (Annual.)
The equipment directory of audio-visual, computer and video products. (2001). Fairfax, VA: International Communications Industries Association. (Annual.)
Foreman, Gordon P. (2003). *PC buyer's handbook.* Jefferson, NC: McFarland.

REFERENCES

Adam, Jean-Robert. (2002, February). Streaming with RealPlayer. Retrieved April 10, 2004, from *Connections:* http://www.niehs.nih.gov/Connections/2002/feb/adam.htm
Advantages of an e-book over a printed book. (n.d.). Retrieved April 10, 2004, from: http://www.geocities.com/ugopublish/advantages.html
Advantages of e-books. (n.d.). Retrieved April 10, 2004, from: http://www.ukoln.ac.uk/public/present/internet/ebooks-internet/sld018.htm

Arnolda, Ewan. (2002, May 9). *MP3 advantages and disadvantages.* Retrieved April 10, 2004 from: http://www.suite101.com/article.cfm/mp3_music_net/91735

AskOxford. (2002). *The wizardry of e-books.* Retrieved April 10, 2004, from: http://www.askoxford.com/languages/culturevulture/general/ebooks/

Doll, Carol A. (1988, March/April). Software purchasing strategies. *Media and Methods, 24*(4), 19–23.

Doll, Carol A. (1987). *Evaluating educational software.* Chicago: American Library Association.

Johnson, Charlotte. (2002, February). *Ebook advantages over pbooks.* Retrieved April 10, 2004, from: http://faculty.mckendree.edu/william_harroff/ebe/ebook_advantages_over_pbooks.htm

Johnson, Charlotte. (2002, February). *Ebook disadvantages compared to pbooks.* Retrieved April 10, 2004, from: http://faculty.mckendree.edu/william_harroff/ebe/ebook_disadvantage.htm

Kolln, Lonny L., II. (2001, April 13). *MP3 technology and the evolving law around it.* Nicholas Johnson's University of Iowa Cyberspace Law Seminar Spring 2001. Retrieved April 10, 2004, from: http://www.uiowa.edu/~cyberlaw/cls01/kolln3.html

A little revolution is always good for the soul, and occasionally for the pocketbook. (1999, May). *Computer Source Magazine,* 1–7. Retrieved May 8, 2004, from: http://web.archive.org/web/20030610175906/http://archive.sourcemagazine.com/archive/599/feat5991.asp

Macatea Productions. (2001–2003). *Advantages of ebooks.* Retrieved April 10, 2004, from: http://www.macatea.com/ebook/advantages.shtml

MiniDisc the clear portable solution over MP3. (2000, June 22). Retrieved April 10, 2004, from: http://www.epinions.com/elec-review-585B-F508351-39522558-prod5

New Mexico Task Force for School Libraries. (2001, January). *Standards for New Mexico school libraries: Collections.* Retrieved April 10, 2004, from the New Mexico Library Association web site: http://www.rlusd.com/upload/files/LSNM-standards.pdf

O'Donovan, Eamonn. (2000, October). Update: Handheld devices. Small wonders. *Technology & Learning, 21*(3), 15–19.

Publidisa Publicaciones Digitales. (n.d.). *Advantages of ebooks over books in paper format.* Retrieved April 10, 2004, from: http://www.publidisa.com/serv_produccion_beneficios_ing.html

Shelly, Gary B., et al. (2002). *Integrating technology in the classroom: Teachers discovering computers* (2nd ed.). Boston, MA: Thomson Learning.

Webman Studios. (2002). *What are the advantages of e-books?* Retrieved April 10, 2004, from: http://www.webman.com.au/ebook_advantages.htm

FURTHER READINGS

Evans, G. Edward. (2000). *Developing library and information center collections* (4th ed.). Westport, CT: Libraries Unlimited.

Fullner, Sheryl Kindle. (2004, January). Perks, rewards, and glory: The care and feeding of volunteers. *Library Media Connection, 22*(4), 38–39.

Gillespie, John T. & Folcarelli, Ralph J. (1998). *Guides to collection development for children and young adults.* Westport, CT: Libraries Unlimited.

Johnson, Mary J. (2004, March). Primary sources in the library: From object to inquiry. *Library Media Connection, 22*(6), 18–20.

Kachel, Debra E. (1997). *Collection assessment and management for school libraries: Preparing for cooperative collection development.* Westport, CT: Greenwood Press.

Kan, Kat. (2003, April/May). Getting graphic at the school library. *Library Media Connection, 21*(7), 14–19.

Kovacs, Diane. (1999). *Building electronic library collections: The essential guide to selection criteria and core subject collections.* New York: Neal-Schuman.

Lukenbill, W. Bernard. (2002). *Collection development for a new century in the school library media center.* Westport, CT: Libraries Unlimited.

MacMillan, Kathleen. (2004, March). Hands-on collection building: A librarian offers tips for sign language materials selection. *School Library Journal, 50*(3), 46–47.

Selection tools: A brief exploration of websites for selecting children's literature. (2002). *School Libraries in Canada, 21*(4), 36.

Van Orden, Phyllis J. & Bishop, Kay. (2001). *Collection program in Schools: concepts, practices, and information sources. Appendix B* (3rd ed.). Westport, CT: Libraries Unlimited.

Wrenn-Estes, Beth. (2002, Spring). Online selection tools: The future for collection development in public schools. *Colorado Libraries, 28*(1), 14–15.

Chapter 10

TECHNOLOGY: THE CRUCIAL LINK

By Carol Truett

INTRODUCTION

"The ultimate impact of technology on school libraries could be compared to Gutenberg's invention of the printing press in the middle of the fifteenth century" (Morris, 1992, p. 361). The opening statement from this same chapter over a decade ago is even truer today. Technology has brought more information to the end user, be that user a student, teacher, librarian, parent, administrator or other school staff member, than any previous invention since the printing press, with the possible exception of television. Callison (2002) defines technology as: "[A]ny tool or medium that helps people accomplish tasks or produce products more efficiently, and computers are only the latest in a long line of innovations...that have changed the way humans interact with the world and with each other. Computers...are changing the balance of power in schools. Increasingly, the 'techies' rather than the educators, hold the power to make educational decisions" (p. 36).

This chapter begins with technology competencies needed by school library media specialists in the context of the new technological world. The second section looks at definitions of the virtual library, the Internet and the World Wide Web and then discusses implications for the future of the book as well as the changing role of the media specialist in the virtual library. The third section includes a discussion about technology planning, budgeting, funding, and preparing the school for technology. The fourth section looks at the status of automation in today's school media center and networks that can connect it to the outside world. Technology and student learning follows. The importance of using electronic pathfinders, directed searching, WebQuests, and student web site evaluation are also discussed. Technology management follows. Implications of new technologies related to copyright issues, wireless technology, and web page creation is presented. Standards and their relationship to technology are explored in the next section. The final section examines the Internet, acceptable use policies and Internet filters. The chapter concludes with lists of Internet sites for school media specialists and technology journals.

Technology Competencies for Today's School Library Media Specialist

Within the technology environment of the school, library media specialists need specific technology competencies to manage the media center. Current school library media management students, many of whom are already employed in school library media centers, were queried (Truett, 2002) as to what technology skills the media specialist should possess or develop in doing their jobs. Their responses include the following skills or competencies that are in no particular order. The school library media specialist should be able to: (1) use online journal sources; (2) use automated library systems; (3) use in-house video conferencing equipment (example: doing an author study with four different fourth grade classes at the same time) plus other video/TV production; (4) have knowledge of types of CD-ROMs available; (5) use and construct a WebQuest; (6) know how to work with teachers who are technophobic; (7) collaborate with teachers to integrate the subject curriculum with technology skills in a manner which fosters the development of higher order thinking skills; (8) be proactive in keeping current with technology; (9) decide what needs to be on library computers and how many workstations are needed in the media center; (10) speak knowledgeably about software and Internet copyright, as well as software licensure, and help teach about copyright, plagiarism, evaluation of web sites, citing electronic sources, and so forth; (11) advocate for a full-time technology teacher in their school; (12) conduct ongoing technology staff development training and in-service, and, in particular, training which focuses on technology the school actually has in place and available for use; (13) participate in equipment and software selection and standards; (14) consider networking options; (15) understand, model, and promote ethical issues and uses of technology; (16) use basic productivity software such as Microsoft Office, Front Page, Microsoft Works,

Power Point, HyperStudio, Kid Pix, and so forth (including such skills as use of spreadsheets, databases, word processing, desktop publishing, presentation and web page creation software, and so forth); (17) help teach basics of equipment operation to staff and students; (18) assist with basic equipment maintenance; (19) assist with design of library computer placement when possible; (20) make suggestions for the school technology plan and the school's acceptable use policy, as well as Internet safety; (21) locate sources for technology funding; (22) provide helpful hints such as quick reference sheets, beside computers, for frequently asked questions; and, (23) keep abreast of future developments in technology. Additionally, the media specialist should buy into the use of technology throughout the school and foster the development of a sense of ownership by all school personnel so that computers and all educational technology become central to the educational mission of the school.

THE VIRTUAL LIBRARY

Today the modern school library media center, thanks to computer technology, is becoming a virtual library. The concept of the virtual library is not a new one. Carol Kuhlthau's (1996) work begins with a chapter by Virgil Blake where he defines the virtual library and traces its development back to the early 1990s. While the vision of a national library network was not a new concept even then, in "1990, in the effort to obtain passage of the National Research and Education Network (NREN), the vision…reappeared in the guise of the 'virtual library' " (Blake, 1996, p. 3). The virtual library is basically synonymous with the networked library. A school media center may have a virtual library component that provides digital information to students, faculty, and administrators. Another component of the media center may also contain onsite collections of both print and electronic works that are heavily used at that site.

Several definitions are needed to clarify terminology, such as the Internet, the World Wide Web, and the virtual library. First, the *Internet* is defined by Shelley, et al. (2002) as " the world's largest network which is a collection of networks that links together millions of businesses, governments, educational institutions, and individuals using modems, telephone lines, and other communications devices and media" (p. 1.17). The same authors define the World Wide Web as a "Worldwide collection of electronic documents that have built in hyperlinks to other related documents (web pages)" (p. 1.18). Pacifici (1997) defines a *virtual library* in its broadest sense as:

a system by which users access information that resides solely in electronic format on computer networks, without respect to physical location of the location of the information. The virtual library exists independently of the amount or nature of the electronic information to which it provides access. There are no limits on the size, content or value of data in a virtual library. Its definition is shaped by individual or organizational need. (p. 1)

The Status of Virtual Libraries in Schools Today

Lowe (2001) states: "School libraries [today] have no boundaries. The 'library' is not a place; rather, library is everywhere" (p. 2). The *IFLA/UNESCO School Library Manifesto* (IFLA/UNESCO, 2000) clarifies the school library's position within the total universe of electronic information: "The school library is an essential partner in the local, regional and national library and information network" (p. 1). Blake (1996) asserts that the virtual library has appeal and relevance for the school library media center for a number of practical reasons. The high cost of books and magazine subscriptions, not to mention the costly technology itself, and the struggle to keep aging collections up to date, all require that the school library media specialist use every option to broaden the resources available to students, faculty, and staff. Many schools are beginning to add e-books to their collections as a first step toward becoming a virtual library. Another step in this direction is the trend of more media centers making online public access catalogs (OPACs) available.

In a survey by Miller and Shontz (2001), school library media specialists were asked to estimate what percent of the book collection was out of date. Almost a fourth of respondents (twenty-three percent) reported that thirty-one percent to *over seventy-one percent* of their collection was dated. Today at the mere click of a mouse and the tap of a few computer keys, the whole universe of information is available, and given the relatively recent development of the Internet, this information is often the most current. Virtually all information is being transformed into digital format, including books, movies, TV, and video, and, of course, music.

Many people predict the end of the dominance of the print format. Think for a moment of the implications this prediction has for the school library media center. No longer will ownership of materials be the crucial factor, as in, "This library has 'X' number of volumes," or "the library has 10 books per student"—an old regional accrediting agency formula—but *access* to the world of electronic information will be the most important characteristic of a school library media center. Today, the virtual school library can truly claim to be the heart and soul of meaningful, authentic learning throughout the school. Networks tie classrooms to the library's computers, its catalog, its databases, and all the resources available on the World Wide Web. The entire world of electronic information becomes a global village of learning throughout the entire school.

Is the Virtual Library the Demise of the Book?

But does this really mean the demise of the book in the school library? "Even though school libraries may offer a lot of electronic resources, they still need books" (Brown, 2000, p. 4). And Marilyn Shontz stated in this same article: "...[B]ooks are especially important in elementary school. It's tough to run an elementary school library without a good collection of children's literature....Children need to hold a book, to look at the pictures" (Brown, 2000, p. 4). Marilyn Miller (2000) sums up the discussion best with a recent statement in *American Libraries:* "Media specialists are still librarians, and reading is still the key to success" (p. 1). Books are *how* you learn to read. And today most popular books are not yet available in digitized form, the Harry Potter series being a case in point. Herring (2001) gives ten reasons why the Internet is no substitute for a library in an article by the same name, and concludes with the comment: "The Internet is ubiquitous but books are portable" (p. 78).

Books, despite the current proliferation of e-books (electronic books available on the web), will continue to exist side by side in the library with computers and other new technologies in the modern school library media center. Just as movie theater films, home videos and DVDs, and live television now coexist, and there is no substitute for viewing a large screen movie in a local theater, neither is there any substitute for curling up with a good book. And finally, Barron (2000) sums up the controversy over money for books versus technology quite succinctly: "And the answer to the question 'Do you want money for books or technology?' is very simple—more for both!" (p. 51).

Library Media Specialist's Changing Roles in the Virtual Library

Two points need to be made in regard to the virtual library concept and the school library media specialist. One point is that the school library media specialist is not seen as the owner or the keeper of the school network. The specialist, because of expertise and knowledge of the broad range of learning resources in all media formats including electronic information, is an integral member of the technology team in the school but not a technician, although knowledgeable about technology. Nor is the media specialist the network supervisor. Novell or other network certification can be earned at a two-year technical college—it does not require a four-year or advanced master of library science degree. Hopefully, there is a certified, licensed technology teacher with whom the school library media specialist works on almost a daily basis, and this partnership benefits both persons because together they know virtually all segments of the information environment. The North Carolina Department of Public Instruction (2001), in fact, in its combined guidelines *Impact for Administrators: A Resource for Evaluating Media and Technology Programs and Personnel* recommends that *both* a full-time media specialist and a full-time technology coordinator be employed by every school.

The second major point is that neither the librarian nor the technology teacher should be teaching technology in isolation. Both should team with teachers and incorporate the tools and information resources of technology into the subject curriculum of the school. Science, for example, should incorporate the state mandated science objectives into meaningful lessons which include the relevant library/information literacy skills to be taught, and use of the appropriate computer technology skills and competencies which are, after all, tools to make student learning more authentic and relevant to the real world. In too many schools today, technology becomes a subject similar to library, and students are dropped off at the door to be taught contrived lessons and skills that have little meaning to the students because they are taught in almost total isolation.

The American Association of School Librarians and the Association for Educational Communications and Technology state these two professional organizations' positions quite clearly in the following quote from *Information Power* (American Association of School Librarians & Association for Educational Communication and Technology [AASL & AECT], 1998):

> The library media specialist is a primary leader in the school's use of all kinds of technologies—both instructional and informational—to enhance learning. Acting as a technologist (rather than a technician) and as a collaborator with teachers, the library media specialist plays a critical role in designing student experiences that focus on authentic learning, information literacy, and curricular mastery—not simply on manipulating machinery. A technician works with hardware and systems software, while the school library media specialist uses technology from the perspective of the technologist, integrating people, learning, and the tools of technology. (p. 54)

Blake (1996) also reminds us that: "Downsizing may not be limited to corporate America" (p. 5). There has been a slight, but noticeable, trend lately for school principals to hire technology-trained staff who have no library media certification or licensure to work in the school library media center. Many schools use site-based management (SBM) teams to make major curriculum and budget decisions. These teams plan goals for the overall school program, with the technology plan for the entire school often being a major responsibility of this group. School improvement teams (SITS) may or may not have the library media specialist as a member. School library media specialists need to secure a place on these teams whenever possible. The media specialist needs to keep abreast of new trends in technology and work with site-based management or school improvement teams to keep them informed of the newest technological advances so informed decisions can be made.

Keeping Abreast of New Trends

School library media specialists need to develop a plan for keeping abreast of new technological trends. The first item on the plan might include attending professional conferences, such as AASL, ALA, NECC and others, and visiting vendor booths to see the newest technology available. The larger professional organizations have exhibits that allow the media specialist to talk to vendor representatives about their products as well as see demonstrations of how products work.

Secondly, reading professional journals is another way to keep abreast of newer technological developments. It is important that the media center subscribe to some professional journals that focus on technology so the media specialist can read about what is happening in technology. A listing of technology journals is provided at the end of this chapter.

A third way to keep abreast of technology is to ask vendor representatives to do an onsite demonstration at the media center when a purchase is being considered for a particular product. Normally, the representatives will discuss how their product will fit into the media center's needs. In this case, several vendors might be asked to demonstrate their products. Sometimes the demonstrations will provide helpful information for writing grant proposals.

A fourth way to keep abreast is to visit other media centers that have state-of-the-art technology. Talk to the media specialist about technology decisions made prior to purchasing new technology products. Sharing knowledge among media specialists is invaluable in keeping informed.

Finally, taking university technology courses is an excellent way to keep abreast of the newest hardware and software and how to use it effectively. The media specialist needs to continually be learning about new software that would be beneficial to the media center and the school. Not only does the media specialist need to learn about using specific software in the media center, an effort needs to be made to teach the media center staff and faculty about software that would benefit them in their daily work with students.

The idea of keeping abreast of technology innovations is crucial when the media center is moving toward becoming a virtual school library media center. The media specialist must see that the media center is fully integrated into the school's overall technology plan, playing a central role in today's networked school environment. This role can only be accomplished if the library media specialist is a key player in the school's technology planning team. Planning for technology is discussed in the following section.

TECHNOLOGY PLANNING

The Need for a Technology Plan

One cannot overemphasize the need for collaborative and ongoing technology planning that is comprehensive in nature, holistic in its approach (i.e., considers the entire school neighborhood or learning community including classrooms, computer labs, the library media center, and the administration) and focuses on integrating technology throughout the entire school curriculum, while folding computer/technology skills and information literacy skills into this plan. One of the requirements of e-rate funding (see the following discussion) from the federal government is that school districts must have a technology plan in place. Many state departments of education also have a requirement that they will not allocate state technology funds to local school districts that do not have a current and updated district technology plan on file with the state, which has been approved by the local district board of education.

Impact for Administrators (North Carolina Department of Public Instruction, 2001), a document with guidelines for both programs and personnel in media and technology, recommends both short-term and long-term planning. Short-term plans take a year or less to complete and are aimed at making minor changes, solving problems, or for covering minor expenditures. "Long-term plans, on the other hand, provide vision and direction for a two- to five-year period and for planning major changes or acquisitions that require large expenditures. Effective student-centered media and technology programs are based on careful planning by the Media and Technology Advisory Committee" (p. 13).

Budgeting for Technology

Budgets are never certain and that is especially true with technology. Technology is a large investment that keeps recurring over short periods of time because of both hardware and software upgrades. Once the initial cost for wiring is done, there is a tendency to still want to get faster access and even upgrades in wiring become an added expense. Many school systems have made their own initial investment in technology to find that three years later upgrades are needed.

Technology is always in a state of flux requiring a large budget just to keep afloat with the many changes occurring. Added to the problem of keeping afloat with technology, changes in district priorities, reduction in available funds and new personnel such as school board members, superintendents, and principals make necessary funding for technology take a back seat. It's that recurring expense, which never ends, that makes some administrators stop cold in their tracks.

Careful budgeting practices need to be in place if technology is to gain the financial resources necessary for a viable program. Technology planning that includes budget planning is an absolute necessity. Justifying all budget recommendations and relating them to district goals is a major first step. Chapter 5 discusses funding sources and grants as potential sources of revenue. Most technology funds come from sources other than media center budgets, however, there are instances where that is not true and the only source of funding available is the media center budget. Besides having a technology plan for the school, there should also be one for the media center as well. It is the media specialist's responsibility to see that the two plans mesh in the school. When deciding the budget plan, it can be a cumulative process over a period of time. For example, if the media center needs to replace five new computers each year in order to keep them current, a money source needs to be identified that will support the upgrades. Other needed items would be treated the same way by determining when replacement is needed and putting the amount needed for the replacement in the budget plan.

Technology budget plans need to be for a three-year period with a revision at the end of each year to allow for unanticipated expenditures. Within the plan should be a three-year rotating hardware or equipment replacement/upgrade plan. This plan would involve replacing some pieces of hardware or equipment every year, but the plan would specify the equipment that would be replaced over the three-year period. Although there is the three-year plan for long range planning, short-range plans can change and the three-year plan should be revised annually. Priorities should be determined as to the most urgent needs when planning the budget needs over time.

The media specialist needs to report annually to the principal how the budget plan was met and to provide a new three-year budget. Principals sometimes receive unexpected funds and if they know that a need exists in the media center, they will be more open to giving the funds where they know it will do the most good for the school.

Some media centers use their own budget to pay for network drops and peripherals, such as printers, digital cameras, scanners, and so forth. Printing supplies are normally paid from the media center budget unless the district includes these items on their supply orders. In order to budget effectively, usage statistics on printing and workstation availability need to be maintained to determine needs.

The Cost of Technology

The cost of technology is a major concern in most schools. According to the Consortium of School Networking (1999), "the annual cost of operating a computer in the school environment is about equal to the purchase price of the computer itself" (p. 10). The costs of technology change over a period of time. Most of the cost in the beginning is devoted to hardware and setting up networks. After a period of time, a greater proportion shifts to staff development, support and upgrades. Usually the line items that normally appear in the budget include hardware, software, charges for setup and upgrades, network access fees, insurance, operating costs (such as phone lines and utilities), security, personnel costs (including a coordinator, and professional development), and infrastructure improvements such as T-1 lines, network wiring, and so forth. In some cases, fees for a consultant may be part of the budget (North Central Regional Educational Laboratory, *Develop*...[n.d.]; North Central Regional Educational Laboratory, *Indicator*...[n.d.]).

Funding for Technology

School districts normally allocate technology funds from the general budget; however, that source alone is unlikely to provide enough resources for a viable technology plan. The normal sources for additional funding may come from the state, the U.S. Department of Education, or from e-rate funding. The federal government offers a vast array of federal funding of which many schools are unaware. School partnerships with businesses involved with state-of-the-art technology is also a potential source of resources. Some schools are pilot sites for major hardware vendors and as a result receive free software, hardware, and training. Other schools participate in demonstration technology projects that provide a similar reward (Southern Technology Council, 1997). Grants are a viable source for obtaining technology funds. Chapter 5 discusses grants and funding in more detail.

Planning Teams and Plan Components

How the local school goes about developing its technology plan varies from school to school. Some schools will likely have a technology planning committee while others will use a joint committee or the task may be delegated to the site-based management team or the school improvement committee. In any case, their role should be to seek maximum input from all stakeholders when developing the school technology plan. Some members who might sit on this committee include: teachers, school media specialists, technology coordinators and/or teachers, instructional technology facilitators or supervisors at the school level, administrators, students, parents, and any others whose input due to interest or expertise could be helpful in developing a comprehensive technology plan. Some topics that should be covered in a school technology plan include, but are by no means limited to, the following: (1) acceptable use and other technology policies for Internet access, lab access, and so forth; (2) computer networks, which include infrastructure and connectivity issues; (3) technology budget, including average cost of items; (4) total cost of ownership for technology (e.g., maintenance and upkeep of equipment), including necessary cycle of replacement and updating of materials and equipment; (5) staff development plan for technology training (North Carolina recommends that twenty to thirty percent of the technology budget be spent on technology staff development and training); (6) how technology and information literacy skills will be integrated into the overall curriculum; (7) media and technology facilities; (8) media and technology staffing; (9) how the plan relates to the overall mission of the school; (10) technology services which will be provided (e-mail, listservs, web pages, and so forth); (11) how the school technology plan will be evaluated, revised and updated; (12) how the school technology plan meets the requirements of the state technology plan specifications, and, finally; (13) the actual resources, hardware, software, and peripherals needed to facilitate the plan.

PREPARING THE SCHOOL FOR TECHNOLOGY

Before any technology can be implemented in the school, of course, a network must be set up. This network is dependent upon having a school building that has network wiring connected to all the classrooms, offices, media center, and other significant areas of the school.

Networks

Some network terms are defined in Exhibit 10.1 with which all school library media specialists should become familiar. These terms are LAN, WAN, and MAN. Definitions are taken from the *North Carolina School Technology Plan: Technological Recommendations and Standards* (North Carolina Department of Public Instruction, 2002, p. 6), which may be found online at: http://tps.dpi.state.nc.us/standards/.

It is these networks, of course, that make possible the virtual library. A set of hardware standards appears at this same site, but since hardware technology changes so rapidly its specifications are not included in this chapter. One is urged to check one's own state, district, or local hardware standards for updated information.

Network Cabling Choices

While network wiring and cable decisions should be left up to the experts who install computer networks, having as much information as possible can only be an advantage when school library media specialists serve on the technology planning teams that must communicate with technical personnel who design the network configurations. The following information is provided to assist with this communication process.

The basic difference between traditional network cable and fiber optics is that the former uses copper wire to transmit data while the latter utilizes light, a much faster mode of transmission to carry information over the lines. Both types are used in schools today. T-1 lines, commonly used in schools, are dedicated lines for access to the Internet at high speeds. They are a North American and Japanese standard for communicating at 1.54 million bits per second, and are considered a high-quality option for small to large networks (ACS Telebroker Services Info, 2003). There are several types of wiring that can be used for the network. (1) The unshielded

Exhibit 10.1
Networks—Some Definitions.

LAN: Local area networks link computers over a relatively small geographic area and should be part of an integrated model. Integrated models of networked schools are those designed to connect all parts of the school, so that technologies are accessible and useful wherever they are needed.

WAN: Wide-area networks enable users to connect to sites outside the school, expanding student, teacher, and administrator outreach to external resources, databases, library resources, video retrieval, and other individuals.

MAN: Metropolitan Area Networks provide regional wide area connectivity. This inter-connected data transmission system connects users and LANs in a localized geographical area. The metropolitan area network is media independent and provides high data rates [of transmission] with single mode fiber. Fiber here no doubt refers to fiber optics, which is the technology of light transmission through very fine flexible glass or plastic fibers. It is commonly used today to wire networks due to its high capacity for rapid transmission of computer data or information.

Printed with permission. Source: North Carolina Department of Public Instruction. (2002). Retrieved from the World Wide Web: http://tps.dpi.state.nc.us/standarts, p. 6.

twisted pair (UTP) wire normally used for telephone lines for voice applications also has data network applications for ultrahigh-speed data transmission, which is a category 7 wire, is one of the most common types of wiring for LANS today (see Exhibit 10.2 for other wiring categories). (2) Fiber optic cable uses light to carry data rather than electricity. (3) Coaxial cable is a well-known cable type that contains several layers of materials surrounding a common axis and this type of cable is used mostly for video distribution. (4) Wireless allows radio or microwave data transmission for networks (Northwest Regional Educational Consortium, 1998).

T-1 lines can be brought into the school on fiber optic cables to carry voice and data transmissions in digital format. Fiber optic cables are "long,

Exhibit 10.2.
Network Cable Types.

Common Network Cable Choices	
1. Category 5 (Cat5)	Unshielded Twisted Pair, most common cabling currently installed, performance is limited to 100Mbps and above.
2. Category 5e (Cat5e)	Unshielded Twisted Pair, has replaced Cat5 as the most commonly installed UTP cable, supports 1000Mbps up to 100 meters.
3. Category 6 (Cat6)	Unshielded Twisted Pair, currently proprietary by manufacturer, supports 1 Gbps speeds but can be costly to install due to complex testing procedures.
4. Category 7 (Cat7)	Shielded Twisted Pair, still in development stage, expensive.
5. 62.5/125 Multimode Fiber	Increasingly becoming the cable of choice, especially in schools, prices continue to drop, relatively easy to terminate, install and test, and it supports speeds in excess of 1Gbps. Longer drop lengths, greater pull strength, and immunity to interference and crosstalk make it appropriate for schools.

Source: Holland, Jim (2002, August). Networking issues across schools. *Media and Methods, 38*(7), 23. Reprinted with permission.

thin strands of very pure glass about the diameter of human hair. They are arranged in bundles called optical cables and used to transmit signals over long distances" (Freudenrich, 1998–2003, p. 1). Normally, the T-1 line plugs into the network router for the purpose of carrying data. It allows multiple users on a network requiring fast speed to work simultaneously; hundreds of users can comfortably share a T-1 line. It is one of the most common ways that schools connect their LAN to the rest of the world (Brain, 1998–2003). Exhibit 10.2 further defines some cable choices.

Holland (2002) provides some excellent tips regarding cable wiring. For example, he suggests pre-qualifying network installation bidders by setting conditions and standards on potential contractors, and even checking their references and financial status. And the issues of adequate power, particularly in old buildings, and cooling should be considered. Holland also suggests removing the network cabling from building construction projects if at all possible and subcontracting this out as a separate, autonomous project.

State Technical Standards for Networks

The State of North Carolina Department of Public Instruction (2002) has its *North Carolina School Technology Plan: Technological Recommendations and Standards* for schools clearly posted on its web site at: http://tps.dpi.state.nc.us/standards/. These standards cover a multitude of areas such as: collaboration, connectivity, recommendations for hardware configurations, networks, network and computer security, and definitions of terms. Included are everything from LANs to MANs, and thin clients to wireless technology requirements. The State Education Department at the University of New York has its New York State Technology Framework (State Education Department. The University of The State Of New York, 2003) for public schools posted on the web at: http://www.emsc. nysed.gov/deputy/Documents/technology/fm-2–03-draftframework.html. These are but two examples of state plans, which also include local technology plan expectations. Media specialists should check with their own state department of education for recommendations and specific elements that must be addressed in their individual school and/or district level technology plan.

State Networks—The Wave of the Future?

Many states have implemented, or are currently developing, statewide networks for school libraries. Most seem to focus on one or both of two possible areas for regional networking: (1) statewide school library union catalogs, or (2) access to electronic databases for which the state picks up the financial tab. Following are two examples of state networks. The North Carolina network provides access to electronic databases and also provides links to other resources of the World Wide Web. Florida's network, SUNLINK, began as a union catalog for media centers. The union catalog of the network is used as a cataloging resource for school library media centers. It also provides numerous web sites of interest to media specialists.

North Carolina. NCWiseOwl (located at: http://www.ncwiseowl.org) is a statewide network developed and maintained by the North Carolina Department of Public Instruction (2003). It provides reference sources such as encyclopedias; newspaper databases; full text journal articles; a junior reference center; Scribner writers reference resources; and links to professional resources at the North Carolina Department of Public Instruction such as the subject area curriculum guides, WebQuest development resources, and a broad array of other technology resource links. There are sections for students, teachers, media specialists, and parents, and the main menu is further divided by school level. NCWiseOwl is completely free to all public schools in the State of North Carolina although schools must provide their own hardware and Internet access. Funding for the network and its resources is provided by the state legislature.

Florida. A final network for discussion is Florida's SUNLINK. This union catalog database had over 1.3 million titles as of January 27, 2003, from 2,187 K-12 schools in the state of Florida and nearly 11,000 web sites. One can search for machine-readable cataloging (MARC) records of all these titles to aid in cataloging one's own collection, see who has what titles (locations are provided), or view sample school library web sites. Funded by the Florida Department of Education and supported by the University of Central Florida, SUNLINK is like "a giant card catalog or electronic catalog" (*What is SUNLINK?*, 2002, p. 1) in cyberspace from which members can borrow materials. It is available on the World Wide Web at: http://www.sunlink.ucf.edu/. The primary purpose of SUNLINK is "to promote resource sharing among Florida public schools. Schools are able to locate needed resources and borrow them by project-established interlibrary loan procedures. In the 2001–2002 school year, 71,959 resource sharing transactions were reported by SUNLINK schools to the project office" (p. 1).

What is the significance of all of these types of networks for school libraries? In the future, it is predicted that virtually all states will have school library union catalogs and networks, which will greatly enhance services to school library media centers throughout the country. The number of resource sharing transactions in one year alone by SUNLINK previously cited shows that school libraries are willing to participate actively in interlibrary loan and other resource sharing activities. The value of school library networks is summarized in the results of three studies conducted in Alaska, Pennsylvania, and Colorado by Hamilton-Pennell, et al (2000) who concluded: "There is, however, one clear and consistent finding that is supported by our research: a school library media program with a full-time library media specialist, support staff, and *a strong computer network* (one that connects the library's resources to classrooms and labs) leads to higher student achievement, regardless of social and economic factors in a community" (p. 1). Extend this network to the rest of the world via the Internet and one can only imagine the effect on student learning.

TECHNOLOGY AND STUDENT LEARNING

The biggest innovation in technology and student learning at the beginning of the twenty-first century is the almost universal use of the Internet for accessing information. In terms of impact and importance, the educational applications of technology and, in particular, the use of the Internet for research and instructional purposes is the most significant application in the school setting.

Gersh (2001) describes technology's role in creating the shared learning environment: "Library media specialists, teachers, and students are each important players in schools today to make sure that the curriculum is enhanced through technology. When these three groups work together, the environment in the school becomes a sharing community, allowing lots of people to learn from each other" (p. 49). School media specialists, according to Gersh, are key players in this shared learning environment primarily because they "have technological expertise in electronic information resources, library-management software, and electronic resources available in content areas, as well as an understanding of information literacy" (p. 51). In partnership with teachers, library media specialists can help teach what Gersh refers to as Internet basics. The skills to be taught to students include cyberspeak, browsing the net, online searching, citing Internet sources, and evaluating web sites. Students are taught the significance of acceptable use policies (AUP), and the issues concerning copyright and web.

Technology-Rich Learning Environments

Marjorie Pappas (1999) describes in great detail what she calls the "technology-rich learning environments" of today's school library media center. "It is easy," according to Pappas, "to become enamored with technology" (p. 26). Interaction with global experts, simulations, virtual field trips and museums, access to primary source documents such as historical newspapers, journal articles, old photographs, letters, ships' logs and manifests, or maps, and full-text databases, such as those for journals, are some of the many technology benefits Pappas cites as characteristics of this technology-rich environment to be found in modern schools. However, she cautions that such a "profile must be very fluid because technology changes almost as we blink" (p. 26). Pappas provides a table in her article describing the basic characteristics of the technology-rich learning environment profile:

(1) computer workstations available through-out the school, (2) individual computers for learner or teacher use, (3) flexible access to computers in labs, (4) an array of information tools and resources in all formats available which reflect curriculum needs, (5) Internet access throughout the school, (6) visual and audio hardware which enables large group use of technology throughout the school, (7) professionals who staff the library media center and computer labs who work collaboratively with learners and teachers to integrate technology across the curriculum, (8) technicians to maintain the hardware and software, (9) required individual professional technology staff development for all staff, (10) technology mini-courses offered throughout the year, (11) selection policies reflective of all curricular needs, (12) an AUP, and, (13) a technology planning process that is both ongoing and inclusive. (p. 27)

How does the technology-rich environment relate to learning? "The presence of a technology-rich learning environment and an authentic curriculum fuels a change in the roles and behaviors of both learners and teachers" (Pappas, p. 28). Callison (2002) also describes the new learning environments possible through the integration of technology into the school and media center curriculum as: multisensory, multipath in their progression, multimedia, collaborative, proactive, and authentic and real world in context. To see one particular way that technology integration can be implemented, see the discussion of electronic pathfinders, guided searching, cyber inquiries and WebQuests that follows.

Electronic Pathfinders

Electronic pathfinders, created by the school library media specialist (in collaboration with teachers), are not only a good safety measure for student searching, but in the long run they save media specialists time because they avoid the necessity of hunting for the same frequently used resources over and over again. The idea of library pathfinders is not new. They have been around for at least two or more decades, and have long been a staple library instruction tool for university and public libraries. "Created by the subject librarians, these powerful instruction tools serve as a starting point for further research and provide an introductory map to library and Web resources. Besides including useful subject headings, call number ranges, and outlines of basic search procedures, these pathfinders list relevant reference books, journals, electronic databases, and Web resources" (Allen, Bhat, & Canepi, 2001, p. 1). Other topics typically included in library pathfinders are definitions of the topic, sources for an introduction or overview of the topic (typically a general or subject encyclopedia), and

nonprint resources the library may house, such as CD-ROM or tape databases or videos. For school libraries, where pathfinders are becoming
increasingly popular, the subject headings would be Sears and the suggested classification numbers would be from the Dewey Decimal Classification System. There are numerous articles on the topic of library
pathfinders in general and electronic pathfinders in particular; however,
one by Block (2001) puts forth not just the basic idea of electronic library
pathfinders, but some additional educational and search pointers that can
be built into them to instruct students along the way. She points out: "In
an ideal world, teachers would notify librarians of their assignments in
advance, and we could build pages for those assignments. But even if they
don't, we can build Web pages for each department and build pages around
absolutely predictable assignments like Martin Luther King, Jr., Women's
History Month, science fairs, and such. We can also create Web pages on
topics that regularly arouse students' interests" (p. 2). Block mentions such
topic regulars as abortion, gun control, censorship, child labor, Internet filters, and rock music. Web pathfinders can serve as a strong collaboration
tool for school library media specialists and teachers when designing
search assignments. By creating pathfinders in school media centers, these
valuable resource tools allow the media specialist to advocate their use and
to show teachers an interest in helping their students do research. Media
specialists need to demonstrate their skills and show they *are* part of the
information age. Pathfinders can be posted prominently on the library's
web page, even on the OPAC when possible.

An excellent book resource that tells how to create electronic pathfinders and contains literally dozens of examples on all sorts of curriculum topics is *Finding the Right Path: Research Your Way to Discovery* (Sutter &
Sutter, 1999). Block (2001) suggests building pathfinders that assist students in finding answers to specific questions instead of simply leading
them to numerous web pages, and mentions X-Refer, which searches sixty
online reference books and can find specific categories of information
about well known people, such as Martin Luther King, Jr. under biography, history and quotations from his speeches. According to Block (2001),
dividing pathfinder information into categories such as megasites, support
(for), oppose (against), legislation, and so forth, is another way to teach
students, as it forces them to recognize bias, and the fact that controversial
topics have opposing viewpoints, as well as laws that frequently take one
side over another.

Block (2001) offers further advice for creating instructional pathfinders,
such as linking to both for-pay and public databases, and teaching the

value of full-text journal databases. She points out that journal articles have typically undergone at least one level of editorial review and can, therefore, be considered somewhat more reliable as sources, even if they contain mostly the author's viewpoints.

A pathfinder assists students in asking good questions (perhaps linked to an accompanying worksheet which poses or assists in asking questions about the topic), and then helps in narrowing the topic into a useful teaching search strategy. The reader is particularly urged to consider Block's discussion of wedge words, terms that can be used by searchers to narrow their topic, and to find particular aspects of interest for their research. As a final word of caution, remember that a pathfinder, print or electronic, is not meant to be an exhaustive bibliography on the topic, but a guide through the enormous variety of information that relates to a particular subject. Pathfinders should be created on popular and frequently taught subjects, not on esoteric topics that the majority of library users would never bother researching. Well designed, frequently updated (especially in terms of web sites that come and go, or change their URL [Uniform Resource Locator]) addresses, and aimed at filling a real need in the particular library media center, electronic pathfinders will save librarians time when whole classes or groups of students come to the center for research and study.

Directed Searching, CyberInquiries, and WebQuests

Pathfinders are a preliminary step, or at least one done concurrently, when creating directed searching exercises, or CyberInquiries; then they are finally developed into full-blown WebQuests. CyberInquiries are more linear than WebQuests, and they focus on individual exploration and writing. They have an overview, an introduction, an investigation, gathering and sorting, and an evaluation, and students struggle with answering an essential question while completing one. A CyberInquiry can progress into a fully developed WebQuest (Seamon & Levitt, 2001).

What then is a WebQuest? Both CyberInquiries and WebQuests are research models that focus on how students learn to use information. A WebQuest is a method of teaching that maximizes the Internet as a teaching tool and integrates technology into the school curriculum. Bernie Dodge, creator of this concept, provides a definition: "A WebQuest is an inquiry-oriented activity in which some or all of the information used by learners is drawn from the Web. WebQuests are designed to use learners' time well, to focus on using information rather than looking for it, and to support learners' thinking at the levels of analysis, synthesis and evaluation" (North Carolina Department of Public Instruction, NCWiseOwl, *WebQuest...*, 2003, p. 1).

One of the best web sites for learning more about WebQuests is the San Diego State University, Bernie Dodge web site found at: http://Webquest. sdsu.edu/ (Dodge, 1995–1997). In particular, one may wish to read Dodge's original article found there on the topic "Some Thoughts About WebQuests." WebQuests have certain distinguishing characteristics they must contain. (1) An introduction to the problem or research question. (2) The task(s) to be accomplished, which should be both "doable" and interesting. (3) The process to be followed to accomplish the task(s) and solve the problem. (4) Resources to be used (generally this is, or at least includes, the electronic pathfinder). (5) Evaluation (including any rubrics to be used) of the final product(s) which should guide the process. (6) A conclusion, or summary, of what the students have learned to bring closure to the process. Other components that could be included are curriculum educational/instructional objectives, credit page (for web sites, graphics, evaluation rubrics), and a teacher page (which might include time frame, other resources, overview, and follow-up activities). Group activities, motivational elements, and single or interdisciplinary design may also be used, according to Dodge. In addition, there are a number of possible formats that could be used in WebQuests. For example, a WebQuest could use a case study format, scientific inquiry, detective, reporter, or a simulation to engage students in the learning process. But the bottom line is the Internet and its resources must be used in order to complete the assigned tasks of the WebQuest. Following are some pages with sample WebQuests to help the reader more fully understand the concept of this learning model.

San Diego State's WebQuest Portal: Matrix of Examples:
   http://Webquest.org

Saskatoon (East) School Division No. 41 Teacher Resource Site:
   http://sesd.sk.ca/teacherresource/Webquests.htm

Spartanburg District 3 County Schools:
   http://www.spa3.k12.sc.us/WebQuests.html

Kathy Schrock's Guide to WebQuests:
   http://school.discovery.com/schrockguide/Webquest/Webquest.html

San Bernardino County (California) WebQuest Samples:
   http://www.itdc.sbcss.k12.ca.us/curriculum/Webquest.html

Hewitt's Index of Best WebQuests and Resources:
   http://web.archive.org/web/20030622105327/http://www.davison.k12.mi.us/academic/hewitt14.htm

WebQuests Written by Memphis City School Teachers:
http://www.memphis-schools.k12.tn.us/website_index/website_index_
frames.htm. Archived WebQuests from Memphis City School Teachers
can be found: http://web.archive.org/web/2002127052450/http://www.
memphis-schools.k12.tn.us/admin/tlapages/web_que.htm

Math WebQuests: http://www.wfu.edu/~mccoy/NCTM99/

EdHelper.com: http://www.edhelper.com/

Concept to Classroom:
http://www.thirteen.org/edonline/concept2class/month8/

Region 20 San Antonio, Texas WebQuests:
http://www.esc20.k12.tx.us/etprojects/

Florida State University English Education WebQuests:
http://web.archive.org/web/20030605123512/http://www.fsu.edu/~CandI/
ENGLISH/Web.htm#second

For an updated and much more comprehensive list of web sites and
resources on WebQuests, the reader is urged to search, of course, the web
itself. Google is recommended as an excellent search engine for this purpose.

Teaching Students to Evaluate Web Sites

One of the skills that should be an essential part of any information literacy skills curriculum is that of teaching students (and staff) to evaluate
the reliability and credibility of web sites. Anyone can publish on the web;
all it takes are some modest computer skills and space on a computer file-
server somewhere. So deciding what is and is not an acceptable source for
information on the web is something all students should be taught. Following are some Internet resources to teach students about evaluating web
sites.

Evaluating Web Resources
http://www2.widener.edu/Wolfgram-Memorial-
library/Webevaluation/Webeval.htm

Two librarians provide evaluation criteria for a variety of web sites such
as advocacy webs, business/marketing pages, general informational and
news web pages, as well as providing original teaching materials, including
a PowerPoint presentation and a bibliography of web evaluation articles
and books.

Kathy Schrock's Evaluation Criteria for Educators

http://school.discovery.com/schrockguide/eval.html

This site includes criteria for all three school levels, plus an evaluation survey for virtual tours. Other items included are evaluation articles and additional web sites.

Susan Beck's "Evaluation Criteria: The Good, the Bad & the Ugly"

http://lib.nmsu.edu/instruction/evalcrit.html

This site reviews five basic criteria: accuracy, authority, objectivity, currency, and coverage.

North Carolina Department of Public Instruction Criteria for Evaluating Web Sites

http://www.ncwiseowl.org/Professional/criteria.htm

This web site divides criteria into two broad categories of content and technical aspects.

ALA's Great Web Sites for Kids

http://www.ala.org/parentspage/greatsites/criteria.html

These selection criteria were established by the first ALSC Children and Technology Committee in 1997 and are used in selecting their 100+ great web sites.

Hadley Parrot Library Checklist of Website Evaluation Criteria

http://www.emh.org/hll/hpl/criteria.htm

Though this source is a health science library, it contains five basic criteria, plus other considerations such as market orientation (i.e., is it commercial to sell a product?), quality of links, instability, and so forth to evaluate sites.

In addition to the web sites previously listed to use with students, Chapter 9 provides some actual selection criteria for media specialists to use when selecting web sites as part of the collection.

Staff Development and Technology

The media specialist needs to be involved in staff development in the school, teaching teachers how to use and integrate technology into their instruction. Although teachers need to be instructed on how to use new software and to integrate it into their classrooms, they need to be involved in a seamless information literacy program that combines both technology and other media as tools to support student learning. In those schools that have technology technicians who train the staff, the media specialist needs to collaboratively work with them to make certain that both technology and media are included as part of the staff development program. Planning with the technician and collaboratively teaching the staff will pay dividends to the school media program and to student achievement as well.

TECHNOLOGY MANAGEMENT

Managing the Automation System

While managing technology has been mentioned briefly in other parts of this chapter, in this section some of the major technology-related tasks, which the school library media specialist may be asked to manage are discussed, along with some tips to assist in this process. Some media specialists are asked to manage the entire school network. It is highly recommended that a certified network administrator be responsible for this duty, not the media specialist. But the media specialist does need to supervise those parts of the school-wide network, which relate specifically to the media center and its mission, such as information access. Certainly keeping the OPAC, along with the circulation system, up and running, plus any other systems such as ordering, booking, reserves, and so on, as well as handling the cataloging component of the automation system all fall under the media specialist's purview. Young (2003) discusses the MARC record cleanup process that may be part of media center catalog maintenance. Many school library media centers automated early and quickly, and as a result their catalogs often contain brief records, or poor quality MARC records, which do not conform to today's MARC21 standard. Young provides a ten-step overview of this cleanup process and also lists questions that the media specialist should ask vendors being considered for MARC record cleanup services. While he strongly recommends hiring a vendor to do this, he also recommends software such as MARC Magician from MITINET/Marc Software to perform this task if done in-house. Bookwhere 2000 and MarciveWeb SELECT enable one to download MARC records directly from the Internet. The Library of Congress has download capabilities as well.

Another technology management task which practicing media specialists may have to deal with is what Simpson (2003b) calls migration to a new and improved automation system. It may be an upgrade, for example, to a Windows version of one's current system, or it may involve purchasing a totally new automation program. Of course, if one does this, then RFPs (Requests for Proposals) must be developed and advertised, bids accepted, opened, and compared. The process is not unlike the selection of an initial automaton system, with the most likely exception being that the collection is already represented by MARC cataloging records so that complete retrospective conversion is unlikely to have to be undertaken twice. Of course, if MARC cleanup on current records has taken place prior to switching over to the new system, so much the better. Simpson (2003a) gives important pointers for installing a new system, including, among others, that it will take longer than you originally planned, and the media specialist will have to train people (staff, teachers, and students) to use the new system.

Some media specialists will be in charge of the school's computer labs, or a computer classroom adjacent to the media center. While it is recommended that these computers be supervised by the technology facilitator or network administrator, if the school media specialist must manage these facilities, a number of tasks may be involved such as scheduling their use, troubleshooting the equipment, and servicing the printers.

Performing Weekly Maintenance and Other Tasks

Certain tasks need to be accomplished frequently to keep the library computers and workstations performing at their top notch best. Crispen (2003) discusses tasks to do weekly to maintain media center computers. These include keeping virus scanners up to date (not to mention, of course, being sure they are actually running and scanning the computers), regularly running Windows update programs, running the Microsoft ScanDisk program and the Defrag program, and, finally, backing up all data on a regular basis. ScanDisk, by the way, repairs errors on the hard drive of computers and Defrag simply reallocates the files on the hard drive in a more efficient manner which should result in increased access speed to stored data. While automation programs will vary as to when they recommend that you do a complete backup, one should at least do full backups once a week, and the day's transactions (i.e., circulations) should be backed up on a daily basis. Crispen provides an excellent technology problem report form, which includes troubleshooting questions, such as: Is the computer plugged in? Asking these questions can frequently obviate the need for expensive technical repairs when the problem is simply human error.

Starr (2002) recommends attaching laminated cards to all technology equipment (e.g., laptops) that includes the name and address of the school as well as listing all accessories in the case. She also suggests storing each lab computer's CD software in a numbered zippered bag and placing it beside each computer. Starr stresses the importance of keeping keyboards clean. It is highly recommended that all students wash their hands before going to the computer lab, those in the media center or computer class-rooms. One particularly useful recommendation is to set up teams of computer helpers. Assign each team a different room in the building and have them clean or dust the computers and monitors on a weekly basis.

Managing the Technology Peripherals

One frequently required technology management duty is keeping peripherals such as printers or photocopy machines up and running. While few school library media specialists went to library school to learn how to change toner cartridges or yank paper out of possessive printers or copiers, these duties unfortunately often come with the territory. Should the sup-plies for these machines come out of the media center budget, it is amaz-ing how quickly funds are depleted when users are allowed unlimited access to these services. Johns (2003) recommends documenting just exactly how much paper, toner, ink, and so on is being used, and even the amount of waste that results. She also recommends solutions to these management concerns such as charging for copies, or putting printers back behind the circulation desk to decrease the number of love letters or song lyrics being printed out. Of course, there are also high tech solutions to controlling printer or copier costs such as limiting copies per student per day by requiring use of copy or printer cards.

Repairing the photocopier is another job on the list of management tasks that a media specialist may be required to perform, despite the highly specialized nature of this job. Fullner (2003) explains the rationale for not undertaking true repairs, and also describes how students can be delegated the task of troubleshooting the photocopy machine if the media center is in charge of this equipment. Allowing students to maintain and manage the photocopier can often, according to Fullner, lead to creative produc-tion of audiovisuals as well as relevant lessons on copyright law, plagiarism, and conservation of natural resources.

Reading Motivation Programs and the Media Specialist

Perhaps one of the more controversial duties some media specialists are asked to assume is that of managing the computer component of the school's commercial reading incentive program. Accelerated Reader and Reading Counts are two examples of these types of programs. Students read books with certain point values and then answer computer generated test questions based on their reading. In order to count the books, the student must achieve a certain score on the test. Prizes and incentives are given for reading in these programs. The value of these reading programs is a source controversy even though they have become common in many schools throughout the country. Whether the media specialist or the teachers should be managing these computer programs is often a moot question. If the principal assigns this duty to the specialist, then that is who will manage the program.

Managing Electronic Databases and Reference Resources

If the media center subscribes to a number of online reference databases, the school media specialist must manage these services. Databases may need to be loaded onto network computers, or access software might need to be installed. The media specialist must be network literate. Miller and Shontz (2003) state that "54 percent of schools and media centers access their online resources via local area networks and 58 percent through wide area networks.... Online resources are now nearly ubiquitous at most of our nation's schools: nearly 100 percent of students have access to state-funded databases and 91 percent of school librarians say the Internet is available for teaching and learning" (p. 2). While state supported databases do not require the media specialist to individually manage them, teaching students and staff to access and successfully search them are still needed at the local media center level.

Performing Annual Inventory and Other Year End Tasks

While it is uncertain why schools perform an annual, and often very time consuming, inventory of their collection and equipment every year, this is one activity most school media specialists will be required to do at the end of each spring semester or term. Continuous inventory is recommended; however, this procedure is simply not practical for many school media centers. Basically it consists of inventorying a section or two every month as part of the monthly collection maintenance duties (e.g., all the Dewey 900s or all the fiction books). The theory behind continuous inventory is that if the book is either on the shelf, or checked out and not overdue or reported lost, then it is counted as part of the collection.

No matter the type of inventory conducted, the process is much simpler today than it was before automation and the bar code scanner or wand were used. Even so, Smallwood (2003) refers to the taking of inventory as "this dreadful task" (p. 115). All materials are normally checked in before inventory begins, although inevitably late materials are returned. A portable bar code reader can assist in reading and arranging the shelves when doing inventory. Smart readers such as the Follett Ph.D. even indicate when materials are out of order. Once all shelves are scanned and the inventory inputted into the automation system, inventory reports can be generated showing numbers of volumes in the collection, lost books, returned items (previously reported missing), lost and paid for books or other materials, and so on. Smallwood recommends storing all technology equipment in an air-conditioned room at the end of school, out of direct sunlight, and unplugging and covering all computers. Backup disks need to be made of all programs that the media center owns before the year's end.

The end of the school year is a good time to plan technology purchases for the following year because, as equipment is examined prior to storage, the condition of each item can be determined. The media specialist will often notice that certain equipment needs to be replaced before the next school year begins.

Managing Instructional Technology

When it comes to managing instructional technology, there is much advice to make this task easier for the school library media specialist. Starr (2002) offers thirty-three tips from experts to help deliver technology and instruction in the smoothest possible way. For example, typing directions for frequently used programs and/or operations and placing laminated copies beside computers avoids having to reinvent the wheel every time someone asks how to perform a common procedure. Assigning student classroom technology managers for each class that the media specialist trains is another useful tip. These tech managers can do such mundane chores as taking attendance and making sure all machines are up and running before a class begins.

Seat assignments in a computer lab make the beginning of classes go much more quickly than having everyone scramble around for a seat. Creating a Start folder with programs for students, and asking the technology coordinator to set up Internet resource folders also facilitate the delivery of technology instruction. Always remind students to save their work (staff too!), and provide disks for free or sale so that is possible. This tip is especially helpful when eager students want to dive into a project without waiting: Put PLEASE WAIT FOR INSTRUCTIONS on standard size sheets of paper, laminate them, and tape them so they hang down over the screens of the computers. Students are not to flip them back on top of the monitor until all assignment instructions are completed. Students can be rewarded with a free pencil when anyone teaches the media specialist a new technology skill.

In summary, technology applications must be managed in the school media center and the media specialist must be knowledgeable and up-to-date on the various applications used, and manage them properly if the media center is to achieve maximum effectiveness as provider and purveyor of information and resources. When the media center technology runs smoothly, no one really notices. But when something goes awry, everyone notices.

IMPLICATIONS OF THE NEW TECHNOLOGIES

Today there are so many new technology developments that have current or potential implications for the school library media center, such as wireless technology or connectivity, DVD, MP3, handheld computers, to mention but a few. To presume to know where these newer technology innovations are all going in the future would require a crystal ball. In schools, today's hot tech is tomorrow's obsolescence. Only a few years back, schools still using laser or videodiscs predicted they might replace the VHS video format. Enter the DVD, and now one can hardly find a videodisc player in a school. A few years ago, media centers were installing CD-ROM towers and setting up networks to accommodate the plethora of CD-ROM reference titles. Today these databases are being accessed via the Internet and online connections, or through regional networks. Wireless technology, copyright laws for the digital age, and Internet safety will be discussed later. For a discussion of MP3, DVD, and handheld computers, see Chapter 9.

Copyright Laws for a Digital Age

The current general copyright law is the Copyright Act of 1976, which date alone tells us something about its contents, i.e., that it predates the digital revolution of the past two decades. There are two updates to the Copyright Act: the Audio Home Recording Act of 1992 (AHRA) and the 1998 Digital Millennium Copyright Act (DMCA), both aimed at grappling with the advances of the newer technologies. The AHRA was an attempt to limit what is known as serial copying, the reproduction of large numbers of excellent copies from a single copy of digital music. That there is a large business in the selling of such pirated copies is no secret. "The rights of consumers [via AHRA] are protected by (1) allowing digital audio recording devices to be bought and sold with minimal government regulation, and (2) allowing consumers to make copies of the original recordings they have purchased for their own personal, noncommercial use (i.e., as backups). The rights of the copyright holders are protected by (1) creating a royalty fund to compensate them for anticipated copying, and (2) requiring that digital audio recording devices incorporate a serial copy management system in order to prevent consumers from using such devices to make serial copies" (Kolln, 2001, pp. 4–5).

Two of the five titles that comprise the Digital Millennium Copyright Act affect MP3 technology. Title I, section 1201 forbids circumventing technological measures that control access to copyrighted works and Title II limits copyright infringement liability for Internet service providers (Kolln, 2001). Napster relied upon the latter in defending its MP3 activities but lost its initial case against major recording companies in U.S. District Court.

On February 12, 2001, the 9th U.S. Circuit Court of Appeals ruled that users and the founder of Napster knew they were violating U.S. copyright laws. A week later Napster offered $1 billion to settle the lawsuit, an offer refused by recording industry officials (*Napster offers $1 billion...*, 2001). The company later tried to convert to a subscription service, but was finally forced to declare bankruptcy in June, 2002 (*Bankruptcy tune played for Napster,* 2002) after refusing a buyout offer by German media company Bertelsmann AG (the bankruptcy court actually refused to allow the company's sale), a company which had already loaned Napster $85 million to keep it afloat (*Napster may face liquidation,* 2002).

> Online music-swapping is still going strong, thanks to a [recent] stunning court ruling dismissing copyright infringement charges against two firms that sprang up after the demise of Napster.... The decision was a major setback to the music and entertainment industries that fought to stop unau-

thorized 'peer-to-peer' file-sharing over the Internet of copyrighted material, like music and films. (Iafrica.com, 2003, pp. 1–2)

What is the significance of the Napster case and this most recent court ruling? Basically it has changed the recording industry forever in removing the stranglehold that the large companies had on the industry. Others have moved in and set up similar music sharing services on the Internet, and the music companies themselves are setting up their own fee-based file-sharing services on the web. While the last word has not been heard from either side of this controversy, it is also certain that technology will always be one step ahead of any laws created to protect intellectual property and creative human endeavor. Media specialists need to keep abreast of copyright laws and include them in the media center copyright policy.

Wireless Technology

One of the things that annoys most computer owners is all the wires needed to hook them up, not to mention the dozens of outlets required for even a small number of workstations and printers. Anyone who has ever built a new media center, or had to rewire an existing facility for networks, knows what a challenge it is to ensure that adequate new wiring is part of this plan. While wireless networks are certainly the wave of the future, Breeding (2002) points out two major drawbacks that he says are currently keeping wireless from replacing wired networks: (1) security issues, and (2) slow speed. These networks can be up to 100 times slower than wired networks. "[W]ireless networks have serious security risks. Without adequate protection, a wireless LAN can provide a free on-ramp to the Internet or the means for hackers to invade an organization's network. Speed, while acceptable for many functions, can be slow compared with what most users expect from typical LANs" (p. 1). In order to maintain network security, Breeding says that wireless networks must be carefully and distinctly separated from the library's business network and administrative applications. In fact, breaking into wireless LANs, he states, has "grown into a hackers' sport, often called 'war driving'" (p. 1).

Despite these drawbacks, Breeding sees a future for wireless in the school library media center, and maintains that they "are part of the evolving development of Internet technology, and librarians need to remain active participants in that experimentation" (Breeding, p. 1). How does wireless work? A traditional wired computer network sends packets of information over cables that send electrical impulses over copper wires or glass (fiber) strands. Wireless networks obviously have no cables; they depend on transmission of data by radio waves over the air, not unlike cellular phones. However, unlike cellulars, they transmit this data only for short distances, perhaps around 300 feet although this varies considerably. The connecting computer must be close by its access point for the system to work. The access point, or hot spot for wireless connectivity, must itself be connected to an existing network, typically connecting to an Ethernet jack. A computer equipped with a wireless network card can then access the wireless network. Access points, according to Breeding, cost around $175 and the wireless network cards run about $80 or less, so setting this configuration up is not particularly expensive. The access point works as a transmitter and receiver, as an Ethernet hub, and as a router, and generally results in a transparent connection as far as the user is concerned.

Mobile access to the Internet remains the key feature of wireless technology as far as Breeding is concerned, and the "ability to surf the Web and grab e-mail while out and about can be considered the killer application that drives Wireless Fidelity (Wi-Fi)" (Breeding, 2002, p. 1). Many providers of fee-based services are creating wireless hotspots in airports, hotels, coffee shops, and this has certainly become a major attraction for those who want to be on the cutting edge of computer technology. Media centers, of course, can join this bandwagon, and it is certain that students will enjoy roaming the school campus with their laptops or even handheld computers accessing this Wi-Fi environment without losing access to the Internet. "If the academic or corporate campus provides wireless access to its students and faculty, then the library or information center mustn't be left out. It is important for libraries to be well integrated into the network infrastructure of its larger organization, be it wired or wireless" (p. 1).

Internet Safety

One of the best ways to protect students from inappropriate sites and their contents on the web is to use preventive measures. For example, Internet safety practices can be taught to students and the web itself is a valuable resource for information and tips in this regard. Electronic pathfinders can be developed that guide students only to recommended and approved sites, which teachers or media specialists themselves have personally visited and explored, and found to be safe. And, finally, the development of directed searching exercises, cyber inquiries, and WebQuests by teachers and media specialists can further ensure that students do not need to "surf" the web for resources in a haphazard manner which could result in their wandering into undesirable sites or even viewing ads which contain adult products.

Most school districts today do not rely solely on filters, blocking software, or simply having students sign an AUP statement. Internet safety is often an integral part of the computer curriculum taught in the schools. There are many excellent sites available to help students, parents and teachers learn about Internet safety. Some Internet safety web sites are listed here:

CyberAngels: A Program of Guardian Angels

http://www.cyberangels.org/

This site calls itself the "World's Oldest and Largest Internet Safety Organization." The main menu includes: CyberStalking, Hacking, and Virus. It was founded in 1995 as the "first cyber-neighborhood watch and is one of the oldest in online safety education...to address the concerns of...on-line abuse and cyber crime, while supporting the right of free speech." Tips for Parents, Parental Agreement, Just for Kids, and Tips for Tweens (includes safety tips) are included. The site is aimed more at older children.

FBI Publications—A Parent's Guide to Internet Safety

http://www.fbi.gov/publications/pguide/pguidee.htm

This site provides questions and answers, plus useful advice for parents who wish to avoid having their children victimized by online criminals. Advice is based on actual crimes the FBI has investigated.

GetNetWise

http://www.getnetwise.org/

According to the site information, it is a "public service brought to you by a wide range of Internet industry corporations and public interest organizations" aimed at helping Internet users "make informed decisions about their family's use of the Internet." The site appears to be aimed mainly at parents although it includes: Online Safety Guide, Tools for Families, web sites for Kids, and Reporting Trouble.

The Librarian's Guide to Cyberspace for Parents & Kids (from the American Library Association)

http://www.ala.org/parentspage/greatsites/guide.html
http://www.ala.org/parentspage/greatsites/safe.html

These two sites include what parents should know, safety tips, and help for parents. Included are more than 700 great sites "for kids and the adults who care about them."

Microsoft's Learn About Internet Safety

http://www.microsoft.com/info/safeonlinedefault.htm

The site includes a list of sites offering tips on child Internet safety divided into a side for parents and a side for educators, 30 Ways to Stay Safe Online and Microsoft's Safe Kid Site (with teacher's guide).

SafeKids.com

http://www.safekids.com/

A site where one can find "tips, advice and suggestions to make your family's online experience fun and productive!" Topics include: Child Safety on the Information Highway, What Are the Risks?, Kids' Rules for Online Safety, Privacy Issues, and Family Contract for Online Safety (to post by your computer).

SafeTeen.Com

http://www.safekids.com/safeteens/

Part of the SafeKids.Com site, this area is aimed particularly at teens: staying safe online, protecting your privacy, and knowing the rules (general safety for teenage girls from the National Center for Missing and Exploited Children).

Yahooligans! Parents' Guide

http://www.yahooligans.com/parents/

The site links to related web sites: blocking and filtering, browsers for kids, safety sites, sites about privacy. Information includes surfing as a family adventure, safe communication online, plan against inappropriate material, and savvy surfing quiz.

CREATING A SCHOOL LIBRARY MEDIA CENTER WEB PAGE

One of the more fun technology projects that a school library media specialist may decide to do is the creation of a library home page. In the discussion under educational applications and the library that follows this section, creating a library media center web page is mentioned as an excellent way to start integrating library and computer skills into the curricula subject areas because sample electronic pathfinders and WebQuests can be posted to this site. A media center web page is also an excellent public relations device to demonstrate how it is part of the cutting edge of not just technology, but the life and total learning environment of the school.

Possible topics for consideration for a web page might include the following:

1. An attractive picture of the media center, preferably featuring students and faculty actively engaged in research.

2. Library policies, hours, checkout rules, and services offered for both students and staff, as well as the types of materials found in the library media center.

3. Links to electronic pathfinders, WebQuests, and other reference resources available online, plus links to community resources such as the local town, county and/or public library home pages.

4. A title list of the magazine subscriptions in your library.

5. A library map and floor plan.

6. An online library orientation.

7. A link to your online library catalog.

8. Special library events and programs.

9. Student book reviews.

10. New materials lists and/or special bibliographies, for example, Martin Luther King Jr., Women's History Month, Mrs. Jones' English class biography titles.

11. Information and pictures of current student assistants, as well as all the library staff members. (However, be careful about putting names or other personal information on the web.)

12. Equipment and special facilities that the media center provides, for example, multimedia production lab with computer workstations, teacher workroom, laptop computers for checkout, video room, and so forth.

For more ideas about content of web pages, consult Chapter 12.

Web Creation Software

Web creation software has proliferated to the point that today there is probably some user friendly software package for just about anyone interested. Before buying *any* web creation software, it is strongly recommended that one try some of the better known programs available and have someone more experienced demonstrate their use. Most software can be downloaded in a trial version to test before actual purchase. Of course, local workshops on web page creation can also be helpful, and they will most likely be geared toward teaching the program that the local school district supports. This support system is important when the need arises to ask someone for help or when the inevitable glitches occur.

The first thing to do, however, is to contact the person in the school district who is in charge of the network, or who posts or uploads web pages, and have that person set up a site for you with an address for the media center web pages. Ask to be assigned a user ID and a password. This security measure prevents other people from changing the home pages once they have been designed and published on the web. Check the district's policy about what can and cannot be posted on local web pages. For example, many schools do not permit students' faces or names to be posted on web sites without permission (from parents as well as from the students). And some districts require that one person at the district level must approve all pages before they can be uploaded to any school system web sites.

Doing a study of sample school library media center home pages prior to building a web site is a good idea to learn about backgrounds, design features and what is attractive. Remember to observe copyright laws, and to be certain that anything used from other web sites is legal to include on the media center's web site. Hundreds of sites claim to have free graphics, backgrounds, animations, signs, symbols, sounds, and so forth for web creation. These sites may require that the source be given, which is always a good idea. When linking to other web sites, it is always imperative to get permission from the creators or web masters. There are also commercial web sites where personal web pages can be launched; however, a word of caution is required against using these so called free services. These sites generally are supported through and contain advertisements on their web pages. The advertisements are not controlled by the person who made the web page. It could be a great deal more than embarrassing to have condom ads, for example, popping up on your elementary school library home page—try explaining that to your school superintendent!

Web creation software web sites, where software can be purchased directly, generally allow free downloads for thirty or sixty days as a trial offer. Although most school personnel must order through their business office, the trial period allows the software to be used and to be judged as to its suitability for the computing levels of the media center staff and to determine if it meets the web creation needs of the media center. Following are some sites that have web creation software:

Cool Page Software: http://www.coolpage.com/cpg_nn4.html

This web page looks interesting.

Microsoft Front Page: (Part of the Microsoft Office Professional Software Suite): http://www.microsoft.com/office/

A standard part of Microsoft Office, this program is probably available in most school districts already.

Easy Web Editor: http://www.easyWebeditor.com/create_Web_page_000007.htm

Available in CD or electronic format, this software looks quite reasonable.

Sausage Software, HotDog Web Editors: http://www.sausage.com/

This site includes HotDog Professional, HotDog PageWiz, and HotDog Junior. One of the original html editors, Hot Dog is well known for its excellent online tutorials on web creation.

Jasc Software: http://www.jasc.com/support/learn/?

This site contains tutorials on web design for features such as backgrounds, buttons, animations, working with images, and so forth.

Macromedia Dreamweaver: http://www.macromedia.com

Used at the postsecondary level to develop online courses, this software is becoming increasingly popular with webmasters.

City Max Online Web Site Builder: http://www.citymax.com/

This site contains inexpensive products and claims to help one "quickly build your own professional Website, complete with email, pictures, newsletters and much, much more in just a few short minutes." It looks pretty commercial.

Simply the Best Shareware: http://simplythebest.net

If the media center has no money for software, this site provides shareware web design software programs.

A word of caution is in order here. The previous listing of the web sites and their software does not constitute a recommendation, but rather it is provided for information only. Be certain to ask for educator discounts or network licensing information when purchasing software packages for the school. Single user or commercial packages can cost considerably more than these discounted prices.

STANDARDS AND THEIR IMPACT ON TECHNOLOGY

Since the governor's summit of 1996, standards have emerged from professional organizations, state departments of education, and district school systems in an effort to determine if schools are doing their jobs. Three types of standards will be discussed: Information literacy standards for student learning (AASL & AECT), the national educational technology standards (ISTE), and state technology skills standards.

Information Literacy Standards for Student Learning

Before jumping wholeheartedly into a discussion of the Internet and the many issues involved in its use in today's schools, it is appropriate to look again at the nine information literacy standards found in *Information Power* (AASL & AECT, 1998). It can readily be seen from even a cursory study of these standards, that virtually all have implications for teaching technology competencies, and, in a sense, information literacy is synonymous with technology literacy. At the very least, the two concepts go hand in hand. For example, the first three standards require that today's student be able to access information on the Internet through effective use of technology and the implementation of search strategies to find the most accurate, up-to-date, and unbiased information available. Or, where two sides of an issue exist, the student must present both sides clearly, or present their stand in a manner that addresses the opposition's views rationally. Print sources will only furnish part of the story on any current topic. Students will generally have to access the web to get the full picture. They will need to learn to evaluate this information critically and carefully (Standard 2), as anyone with computer access and their own web site can publish their views and information on the World Wide Web today. And learning to cite web sources certainly fits into Standard 3. For all nine standards, *Information Power* provides levels of proficiency, examples of related content area standards, and indicators of proficiency. For more information see Chapter 4 and access the ALA web site at the following URL: http://www.ala.org/

aaslTemplate.cfm?Section=Information_Power&Template=/Content-Management/ContentDisplay.cfm&ContentID=19937.

ISTE National Educational Technology Standards

The International Society for Technology in Education (2000–2002), "a nonprofit professional organization with a worldwide membership of leaders and potential leaders in educational technology...dedicated to providing leadership and service to improve teaching and learning by advancing the effective use of technology in K-12 education and teacher education" (p. 1) has developed a set of six National Educational Technology Standards for Students (NETS) which they feel apply to all students. These standards may be found online at: http://cnets.iste.org/curr-stands/cstands-netss.html. ISTE claims that forty-four states reference the NETS standards in their state level curriculum documents for the teaching of computer technology skills.

State Technology Skills Standards

Virtually all states have computer skills curricula that go far beyond the mere teaching of basic Internet skills. For example, the state mandated comprehensive curriculum called the *North Carolina Standard Course of Study* (North Carolina Department of Public Instruction, 2003), may be found online at: http://www.ncpublicschools.org/curriculum/computer.skills/index.html. One for the middle school level (Baldridge, 1997) may be found at: http://www.soms.oldham.k12.ky.us/soms/compcurr.htm.

Anyone wishing to examine other samples of state computer skills should type in the words computer and/or technology skills curriculum on an Internet search engine such as Yahoo, Web Crawler, or Ask Jeeves to find many other examples. Typically these curricula are organized around such broad topical areas as societal and ethical issues, knowledge and skills in actual hands-on use of computer technology, and information accessing.

AUTOMATION AND THE INTERNET

Probably two of the most dramatic technology developments affecting education over the last decade of the twentieth century were the automation of the media center and the dissemination of the Internet. These two innovations made information readily accessible to everyone in the school.

The following research study shows that schools are fast approaching one hundred percent access to the Internet.

The Status of the Internet in Schools

In a research survey, Miller and Shontz (2001) reported that 88 percent of their school library media specialist respondents had access to the web for searching and reference. This data would appear to coincide with other figures: "According to Quality Education Data (QED), [a]nd based on plans for the 1998–99 school year, QED projects that almost 96 percent of public schools will be connected to the Internet by the end of the 1998–99 school year" (SafeKids, 2003, p. 1). This figure approaches close to 100 percent today.

The Status of Library Automation in Schools

In the same study by Miller and Shontz (2001), the results showed that an increase in automation has occurred among the school library media centers surveyed. Ninety percent of respondents had an automated circulation system and eighty-two percent had an online catalog. One could probably conclude, therefore, that library automation among school library media centers today is rapidly becoming an almost universal phenomenon.

Library Automation Information Resources on the Web

An excellent online source of information on library automation may be found at the International Association of School Librarianship's web site (2002) under the topic School Library Automation, Resources on the Internet at: http://www.iasl-slo.org/libaut.html. This site "provides links to Internet resources related to all aspects of the automation of school library functions, including cataloging, circulation, inventory, serials management, acquisitions/ordering" (p. 1) and includes general coverage of library automation, school library automation system sites, sources of MARC cataloging records, and other relevant web sites for those interested in learning more about automating their school media center. Chapter 12 provides a list of vendors of library automation systems.

Internet Use Issues

Technology in the school library media center has changed the way the media center is managed and the way teaching is done in this setting in many positive ways. But it has also brought with it a series of problems or issues for the media specialist. Some of the issues include: (1) acceptable use policies must be developed to ensure that students do not search inappropriate web sites, (2) e-rate funding legislation mandates the use of filters in school settings, and (3) copyright in the electronic environment becomes a major problem. Organizations such as the American Library Association and the American Civil Liberties Union have challenged the U.S. Government in censorship law suits, which have gone through U.S. District Courts and even as far as the Supreme Court. Copyright in the electronic age continues to be an issue, and it is predicted to continue to be a thorny problem as new digital formats develop. This section discusses and explores some of the more pressing of these issues.

Acceptable Internet Use Policies (AUPs)

Probably almost from its first introduction into school libraries and classrooms, teachers, administrators, and school media specialists have considered the use of acceptable use policies (AUPs) for the Internet as part of their selection/collection development policy within their school, although for many it is also part of their overall technology and implementation plan. The major rationale for school Internet access is the support it provides in teaching a current and relevant educational curriculum. Some educators claim that Internet access in schools for recreational purposes is a legitimate reason to use it, a precedent that has been set by books for recreational reading because a part of all media center collections contain such materials. However, responsible educators supervise students who use the Internet and provide guidance in locating appropriate materials. The vast wealth of information on the Internet, much of it in the form of primary research sources, makes it both powerful and dangerous to use in a school setting. But to not use the Internet today in schools is to deprive teachers and students, as well as other staff, of one of the largest and most valuable resources of information, opinions, and ideas ever created.

Mather (1996) defines acceptable use policies as "local documents that state a school or district's Internet usage plan. This may include instructional strategies and rationales, but an AUP needs to offer, in concise, clear language that students at all levels understand, guidelines for what is and isn't appropriate when online" (p. 3). The Virginia Department of Education (2003) defines the AUP as "a written agreement in the form of guidelines, signed by students, their parents and their teachers, outlining the terms and conditions of Internet use, rules of online behavior and access privileges" (p. 1).

The AUP also needs to clearly state the *consequences* of inappropriate use or abuse of the Internet, indicating that its use *is a privilege,* not a right, in the schools. Besides teaching students responsible use, an AUP can also protect educators and their organizations from liability attacks. Mather (1996) explains the crucial role parents need to play in creating the school's AUP, for they are the bellwether and the keeper of the community's mores, and virtually all authors agree that both students and parents, plus teachers, need to sign the AUP agreements.

Must schools implement an AUP? According to Gardner (2001/2002), two federal laws, the Children's Internet Protection Act (CIPA) and the Neighborhood Children's Internet Protection Act (NCIPA) require not just Internet filters to be installed on computers with Internet access, but that school districts receiving any federal funding must implement Internet safety policies. The NCIPA requires that local school districts allow all groups with a stake in education, such as community groups and parents, an opportunity to review and comment upon the district's Internet safety policy while it is being created (Gardner, 2001/2002). It must be publicly posted, providing time for public review and feedback.

What should a well written AUP contain? Some components that should be considered for inclusion in a thorough AUP are:

1. A statement of the district and/or school's educational philosophy and a rationale for Internet usage in the schools, along with a list of permitted educational uses, and a statement that its use in the school is a privilege.

2. A discussion on responsible use for students (as well as other school staff) with examples of acceptable and unacceptable behaviors and consequences for the latter. Points to be considered for inclusion are searching behaviors, use of CHAT rooms (or not), student use of e-mail (whether it's even allowed, and, if so, language not allowed), copyright, downloading information, computer viruses, filters, hacking, guarding personal information (name, address, and other information about students), and so forth. One section of the AUP might include an Internet code of conduct.

3. Responsibilities of all school personnel when using the Internet, including teachers, staff, students, parents, administrators.

4. A disclaimer absolving the school district or local school of responsibility when the proper procedures have been followed.

5. A statement that the school or district's AUP complies with state and national telecommunication rules and regulations.

6. A signature form for teachers, parents, and students to sign indicating they read and understand the AUP, and agree to abide by its strictures (Virginia Department of Education, 2003).

Flowers and Rakes (2000) did a content analysis of twenty-four selected AUPs and found the following components which might also be part of a well written AUP:

7. Netiquette (often defined as polite network behavior).
8. Network security statements.
9. Orientation (to the Internet) requirements.
10. A detailed list of services available, such as e-mail, information and news services, discussion groups on various issues, and connections to libraries, companies, and so forth, plus a statement that these services might not always be available.

Network security statements might include how passwords might be handled to give both patrons and staff needed access. For example, students and faculty may only have access to the OPAC and the password they use determines their access rights. Another example, media paraprofessionals or volunteers might have access to check materials in and out but might not have access to circulation records or cataloging modules of the automation system. Using this type of hierarchical password system based on what the user needs to know provides a safeguard against hacking, and its patrons' privacy is protected. A word of caution is needed about passwords. Media specialists need to establish their own passwords and not rely on default passwords that are automatically set in the software; it allows them to be vulnerable to hacking. Passwords need to be carefully chosen using both letters and numbers. Beware of using obvious passwords such as pet names, spouse name, and so forth. Media specialists need to be careful with passwords and not leave them around for others to find. According to Elizabeth Bennett (personal communication, October 10, 2003), if passwords are not protected, the media center can still be just as vulnerable as they would be without a network security system.

Some examples found by Flowers and Rakes (2000) of inappropriate behaviors include: "1) violation of copyright laws, 2) use of the system for commercial, political or religious purposes, 3) violation of the privacy rights of others, and, 4)...activity that might be pornographic, profane, sexually oriented..." (p. 5).

There are many web sites that provide guidance in writing an acceptable use policy (AUP). Dyrli (1996) urges educators to review other AUPs before writing one's own. He also recommends focusing on understandable user behaviors, avoiding the negative (one AUP had at least eight "do nots" listed), and writing in a concise manner.

Following are web sites with sample AUPs and advice in writing them.

Virginia Department of Education http://www.pen.k12.va.us/go/VDOE/Technology/AUP/home.shtml

Indiana State AUP Requirements http://www.siec.k12.in.us/aup/require.html

Houston Independent School District Acceptable Internet Use Policy http://www.rice.edu/armadillo/auppolicy.html

Eugene, Oregon AUP http://www.4j.lane.edu/4jnet/4jnetguidelines.html

The Rice School, Houston Independent School District http://outreach.rice.edu/~trsler/handbook01/forms/01policy_aup.pdf

Kings County California Acceptable Use Policy http://www.kings.k12.ca.us/AcceptableUsePolicy.htm

SEIRTEC/SREB Appropriate Use Policies From Various States from the SouthEast Initiatives for Regional Technology in Education Consortium and Southern Regional Education Board Web Site http://www.sreb.org/programs/EdTech/seritec/AppropriateUsePolicies.asp

Monroe County (Bloomington, Indiana) Community School Corporation Student Access to Networked Information Resources http://www.mccsc.edu/policy.html

New Mexico Council of Technology Education: Internet Use Policies http://sde.state.nm.us/nmcte/aup.html

Caroline County, Maryland Public Schools http://cl.k12.md.us/AUP.html

Mankato, Minnesota, Area Public Schools AUP http://www.isd77.k12.mn.us/district/isd77policies/524.pdf

Acceptable Use Policies http://www.coedu.usf.edu/internetsafety/acceptab.htm

In addition to these web sites, Reilly (2000) includes ten additional AUP resource sites with comments about each at the end of his article, "Laying down the law: Crafting acceptable use policies," in *Multimedia Schools*.

E-Rate and Internet Filters

It is virtually impossible to discuss the e-rate for schools without discussing the issue of Internet filtering software. The e-rate "provides discounts to assist most schools and libraries in the United States to obtain affordable telecommunications and Internet access. Three service categories are funded: telecommunications services, Internet access, and internal connections" (Universal Service Administrative Company, Schools and Libraries Division, 2002, p. 1). That these discounts are not insubstantial is attested to by the fact that they may "range from 20% to 90% of the costs of eligible services, depending on the level of poverty and the urban/rural status of the population served" (p. 1). The e-rate was established as part of a Congressional bill called the Consolidated Appropriations Act of 2000 (Public Law 106-554), which, while vaguely titled, had tremendous implications for schools and public libraries. These funds are collected by telecommunications companies that charge a fee on all customers' bills and then pay "contributions" to the Federal Communications Commission (FCC). And, despite what it looks like on a monthly telephone bill, the courts have ruled that this charge is not a tax. It just looks and acts like a tax since it ends up funding a major federal initiative, the e-rate program. Its funds are specifically targeted at paying telecommunications and inside wiring costs that libraries incur in hooking up to the Internet. Any additional costs must be borne by the media center or school district. Presumably this program is bridging the Digital Divide gap by providing the Internet to America's libraries and schools. The Digital Divide is defined as the wide discrepancy in Internet access between the middle class and the rich in this country and the poor, who may actually have no access to computers except in schools and public libraries, if at all (Digital Divide Network, 2004).

Two of the program's components already mentioned, the Children's Internet Protection Act (CIPA) and the Neighborhood Children's Internet Protection Act (NCIPA), affect both school districts' and public libraries' eligibility for e-rate funds (Gardner, 2001/2002). In order to be eligible for e-rate funds, which are capped at $2.25 billion for any single year, a school or public library must comply with the CIPA and NCIPA regulations. These regulations require installation of Internet filtering or blocking software on any computer available to minors (defined by the legislation as anyone under the age of seventeen), and that "appropriate" policies for Internet use are in place. The overall purpose of e-rate funding is to reduce the digital divide. The digital divide is a term that "describes the fact that the world can be divided into people who do and people who don't have access to use-modern information technology... such as the Internet" (*Digital divide—A what is question*, 2000–2003). Normally the idea suggests that Blacks and Hispanics use the Internet less than whites and Asians (*Definitions: Digital divide*, n.d.).

The Universal Service Administrative Company, Schools and Libraries Division (2002), which administers the disbursement of these monies to libraries, requires that a five step process be followed in applying for these funds. The first step is to prepare a five-point technology plan that shows how technology will improve education or library services. The plan must include: (1) clear goals and a realistic strategy to improve education or library services; (2) a professional development plan for staff training; (3) an assessment of the services, hardware, software and other services needed; (4) a sufficient budget for the non-discounted charges; and (5) an evaluation process to monitor progress. The other four steps basically involve filling out the required forms and meeting the established deadlines for submissions.

According to Schuyler (2002), problems are quite involved in complying with form requirements, documenting discounts, and frequent and arbitrary auditing procedures. "Phone calls to the help desk, for example, frequently result in SLD [Schools and Libraries Division staff] reading the answer from a web page that you have open before you already" (p. 34). School library media specialists need to be aware of this source of funding and ensure the appropriate school district personnel apply for these funds if the district deems it advisable. Media specialists are also urged to consult the original source for any updates to these forms or deadlines.

Internet Filtering: Censorship or Protection?

Perhaps the most controversial aspect of e-rate funding is the requirement to install filtering or blocking software where minors have access to the Internet in school media centers and public libraries. At least one author, Karen Schneider (2002), states that "the FCC has been interpreting CIPA and the e-rate" so that "even if you choose not to filter you can still get discounts on your data lines and your internal connections" (p. 1). Almost all schools receive some federal funding and therefore, must comply with CIPA or NCIPA. These funding sources include, besides e-rate, funds from Title III of the Elementary and Secondary Education Act (ESEA) used to purchase computers for Internet access or to pay direct costs associated with accessing the Internet, and state-administered monies from the Library Services and Technology Act (LSTA) that fund access to the Internet (Gardner, 2001/2002).

The major controversy surrounding the use of filters is the dilemma of finding filtering technology that is truly effective in keeping out undesirable content, while at the same time not blocking substantial amounts of protected First Amendment speech. To understand this dilemma, one must know something about how blocking or filtering software works.

How Software Filters Work

While the complete and specific technical details of exactly how filters work is beyond the scope of this work, there are basically four types of blocking or filtering software available. One type of software only permits sites from an approved list of Internet sites to be shown or viewed on the blocked computer. Within this type of software, there is a subcategory of filters that work in conjunction with a formal system of site labeling. The second type is keyword blocking accomplished simply by keeping out any site that contains certain phrases or images found at the site by the software. Thus, for example, an article about early detection of breast cancer might be blocked by this type of software filter because the word "breast" is on its forbidden or blocked list. The third type is a web rating system where web sites are rated in terms of levels of sex, nudity, language, and violence. The ratings can range from level 4 (the highest nudity rating), which shows provocative frontal nudity, to level 1 (the lowest nudity rating), which shows revealing attire to not rated at all. The fourth type is called a "walled garden approach or combination," which allows access to a set of approved links, something analogous to book selection (Ormes, n.d.).

According to Schneider (2000), "all of these studies [which attempt to determine how effective filters are at blocking 'porn' and other objectionable sites and sounds] are weakened by the same premise: that there is an objective, generally-agreed-on body of content that everyone feels should be blocked by Internet filters....you can't even get 40 librarians to agree on the nature of 'offensive.' Filters are simply mechanical tools wrapped around highly subjective and often idiosyncratic decisions. There is no scientific filter..." (p. 103).

The Supreme Court Rules On CIPA

On June 23, 2003, the Supreme Court of the United States ruled on the constitutionality of the Children's Internet Protection Act in *United States v. American Library Association, Inc., No. 02–361* "...[T]he Court held, 6–3, that the First Amendment does not prohibit Congress from forcing public libraries—as a condition of receiving federal funding—to use software filters to control what patrons access online via library computers" (Hilden, 2003, p. 1). Hilden considers this decision to be "a repudiation of the longstanding 'unconstitutional conditions' doctrine—which holds that Congress can't force the states to violate [citizens' civil] rights in order to get funds" (2003, p. 1).

Two constitutional issues are involved in this decision. The first, and major one, is whether filters violate library users' free speech rights guaranteed under the First Amendment. The other issue, as previously stated, is whether Congress can force states to deprive citizens of their freedom of speech rights in order to obtain federal funding.

Some libraries interpret CIPA as requiring filters or blocking software on *all* computer workstations, not just on those available to underage users such as in schools or children's departments. But the opinion of Justice Kennedy, which joined the decision of the plurality on the Supreme Court but not in the opinion, apparently sets up a contradictory position which "requires that filtering companies create filters that can be immediately and easily dismantled to meet the information needs of library users" (Clark, et al., 2003, pp. 1–2). Three district level school library media/technology supervisors recently interviewed indicated that this was not possible in their districts because the filters were controlled at the district level by a network administrator, and they were not even sure that this individual could easily turn this software off or on to permit an individual at a single school on a particular workstation to access blocked sites (Interview with Karen Kiser, Karen Lowe, and Judith Ray, 2003).

Justice Breyer, who also concurred in the plurality Supreme Court decision, but wrote his own opinion, apparently is under the impression that filters and blocked sites can be turned off or on at will by library employees. He maintains that CIPA "allows libraries to permit any adult patron access to an 'overblocked' web site; the adult patron need only ask a librarian to unblock the specific web site or, alternatively, ask the librarian, 'Please disable the entire filter' " (Chmara, 2003, p. 1). According to Hilden (2003), basically the "government promised...that the libraries could, and would, remove the filters if users asked them to do so. It also promised that users would not have to explain why they were making the request" (p. 2). This, it should be pointed out, has not been the case in the past where patrons had to explain their reasons. Justice Kennedy, according to Hilden, "suggested that if it turned out that, in practice, unblocking was slow or difficult, and impeded users' computer access, then patrons would not be prevented from suing the government, or perhaps the libraries..." (p. 3), a sobering thought to say the least. So, if libraries don't "hop to it" when asked to unblock their Internet computers, they could find themselves in court facing a First Amendment rights lawsuit.

According to Goldberg (2003b), "...Chief Justice William H. Rehnquist wrote that because CIPA allows librarians to disable a filter 'without significant delay on an adult user's request,' the goal of 'protecting young library users from material inappropriate for minors' outweighs any temporary inconvenience to adults" (p. 12). Schneider (2003) and Goldberg (2003a) both express concerns that the Supreme Court decision will open up a flurry of state legislation aimed at censorship of the Internet on public (and maybe even private) computers.

While school librarians may perhaps remove themselves from the filter controversy, after all schools weren't part of the CIPA lawsuit and school districts and school boards are unlikely to remove filters from school computers regardless of the outcome of any future court cases, there are some other thoughts to consider. Teachers today use the Internet for their own professional development, research, and knowledge acquisition, perhaps at least as much as their students do; their needs are at a mature adult level. Using filter or blocking software in schools is somewhat akin to having all library books chosen by a third party who refuses to share criteria being used for selection, and who is choosing only what is appropriate for very young children. This dilemma results in denying adults and teenagers in the schools access to much material that is perfectly appropriate for their levels of maturity and understanding. And always remember that no software filter is foolproof; students should never be allowed to surf the web without direct adult supervision, either the media specialist, a teacher, or some other responsible adult.

INTERNET SITES AND TECHNOLOGY JOURNALS FOR SCHOOL MEDIA SPECIALISTS

The media center must be central, integrated, indispensable, and highly visible in promoting the educational and administrative technologies that are driving today's schools. This chapter concludes with a selective list of some recommended Internet sites for school library media specialists and some technology journals of interest.

School Library Resource Sites on the Internet

American Association of School Librarians Home Page

http://www.ala.org/aasl

ALA's division for school librarians features announcements of the national AASL conference, National School Library Media Program of the Year Award information, association news, professional tools, education and careers, issues and advocacy, and much more.

LION (Librarians Information Online Network)
http://www.libraries.phila.k12.pa.us/lion/index.html

This site is absolutely one of the best school librarian's sites available. Examples of information to be found include: automation for school libraries, children's literature on the web, issues in school librarianship, lesson plans and teaching activities for school librarians, organizations, periodicals for school librarians and more.

International Association of School Librarians—School Libraries Online
http://www.iasl-slo.org/

This site includes research on school libraries, school library resources on the Internet, school librarianship documents, IASL Journal, annual conferences, and references to other useful sites.

School Library Journal
http://slj.reviewsnews.com/index.asp?publication=slj

Articles and news of interest to school librarians are included plus reviews of new materials, both print and nonprint.

Internet School Library Media Center (ISLMC) Children's Literature and Language Arts Resource Page
http://falcon.jmu.edu/~ramseyil/childlit.htm

This site includes book awards, book and media reviews, authors and illustrators, and much more.

School Libraries on the Web—Resources for School Librarians
http://www.sldirectory.com/libsf/reslibs.html#top

Sites are grouped under the broad headings: learning and teaching, information access, program administration, technology, education and employment, and continuing education. This site is maintained by a Philadelphia school librarian.

The Internet Public Library

http://www.ipl.org/

Though it says public library, this site contains useful information and web links of interest to school librarians, including the reference center, youth resources (KidSpace, TeenSpace), subject collections, reading room, searching tools, and special collections. It is sponsored by the School of Information, University of Michigan.

School Library Internet Resources

http://www.library.vanderbilt.edu/peabody/books/internet/ktwelve/library.html

This site includes links to major school library sites such as the American Association of School Librarians web site, LION (Librarians Information Online Network), and a directory of school libraries on the web, among many others. It originates from Peabody College Library, Vanderbilt University.

School Library Internet Research Center

http://home.tampabay.rr.com/centans/portalindex.html

The Academic Online Portal for K12 School Libraries contains research links to language arts, fine arts, science, history, geography, world cultures, government, sports, math, computers, business, and technology resource subject areas.

Grand Ledge High School Library Internet Citation Page

http://scnc.glps.k12.mi.us/~hslib/internet_citation.htm

This is a great guide to citing Internet resources, including Turabian, Chicago, APA, and MLA style manuals.

Technology Periodicals for School Librarians

Cable in the Classroom
http://www.ciconline.com/default.htm
Cable in the Classroom
1724 Massachusetts Avenue, NW
Washington, DC 20036
Phone: 202-775-1040
Fax: 202-775-1047

Computers in Libraries
http://www.infotoday.com/cilmag/default.shtml
Information Today, Inc.
143 Old Marlton Pike
Medford, NJ 08055-8750
Phone: 609-654-6266
Toll-Free: 800-300-9868
Fax: 609-654-4309
custserv@infotoday.com

Electronic School (Supplement to the *American School Board Journal***)**
http://www.electronic-school.com/
American School Board Journal
1680 Duke Street
Alexandria, VA 22314
Phone: 703-838-6722

From Now On: The Educational Technology Journal
http://www.fno.org/
Jamie McKenzie
Network 609
500 15th Street
Bellingham, WA 98225
Phone: 360-647-8759
fromnowon@earthlink.net

Learning & Leading with Technology
http://www.iste.org/LL/30/8/index.cfm
International Society for Technology in Education
480 Charnelton Street
Eugene, OR 97401-2626
Phone: 800-336-5191 (U.S. and Canada)
International: 541-302-3777
Fax: 541-302-3778
iste@iste.org

Media & Methods
http://www.media-methods.com/
Media & Methods Magazine
1429 Walnut Street,
Philadelphia, PA 19102
Phone: 800-555-5657
Fax: 215-587-9706

MultiMedia Schools Magazine
http://www.infotoday.com/MMSchools/default.shtml
Information Today, Inc.
143 Old Marlton Pike
Medford, NJ 08055-8750 USA
Phone: 800-300-9868
Fax: 609-654-4309
custserv@infotoday.com

T.H.E. Journal (**Technological Horizons in Education**)
http://www.thejournal.com/
T.H.E. Journal Subscriptions
17501 17th Street, Suite 230
Tustin, CA 92780
Phone: 714-730-4011

Technology and Learning
http://www.techlearning.com/content/about/tl_current.html
Technology & Learning
Subscription Department
PO Box 5052
Vandalia, OH 45377
Phone: 800-607-4410
Techlearning@sfsdayton.com

REFERENCES

ACS Telebroker Services Info. (2003). *The future of telecommunication management, data services-Internet T1*. Retrieved April 10, 2004, from: http://www.acstelebroker.com/www/html/services_data_T1.html

Alexander, Jan & Tate, Martha Ann. (1999). *Evaluating web resources*. Retrieved April 10, 2004: http://www2.widener.edu/Wolfgram-Memorial-Library/l webevaluation/webeval.htm

Allen, Georgia, Bhatt, Anjana & Canepi, Kitti. (2001). *Dynamic web pathfinders: Subject librarian empowerment*. Information Strategies 2001 proceedings. Ft. Myers: Florida Gulf Coast University. Retrieved April 10, 2004, from: http://library.fgcu.edu/Conferences/infostrategies01/presentations/2001/canepi.htm

American Association of School Librarians & Association for Educational Communications and Technology. (1998). *Information power: Building partnerships for learning*. Chicago and London: American Library Association.

American Library Association. (2003, March 28). *Great web sites for kids selection criteria*. Retrieved April 20, 2004, from the ALA web site: http://www.ala.org/ala/alsc/greatwebsites/greatwebsitesforkids/greatwebsites.htm

Baldridge, Kenneth. (1997, April 20). *Computer skills curriculum.* Retrieved April 10, 2004, from the South Oldham Middle School web site: http://www.soms. oldham.k12.ky.us/soms/compcurr.htm

Bankruptcy tune played for Napster. (2002, June 3). *Silicon Valley/San Jose Business Journal.* Retrieved April 18, 2004, from: http://www.bizjournals.com/sanjose/ stories/2002/06/03/daily11.html

Barron, Daniel D. (2000, June). Keeping current: Information technology: Cost considerations for school library media specialists. *School Library Media Activities Monthly, 16*(10), 48–51.

Beck, Susan. (1997). *Evaluation criteria: The good, the bad & the ugly: Or, why it's a good idea to evaluate web sources.* Retrieved April 20, 2004, from: http://lib. nmsu.edu/instruction/evalcrit.html

Blake, Virgil L. P. (1996). The virtual library impacts the school library media center: A bibliographic essay. In Carol Collier Kuhlthau (Ed.), *The virtual school library: Gateway to the information superhighway* (pp. 3–5). Westport, CT: Libraries Unlimited.

Block, Marylaine. (2001, Summer). Teaching kids indirectly [Electronic version]. *Library Journal, 126*(11), 33–34.

Brain, Marshall. (1998–2003). *How does a T1 line work?* Retrieved April 10, 2004, from: http://computer.howstuffworks.com/question372.htm/printable

Breeding, Marshall. (2002, August). A hard look at wireless networks: Marshall Breeding reviews the pros and cons of this hot new technology. *School Library Journal, 48*(8), 14–17.

Brown, Mary Daniels. (2000, August 1). Outdated school libraries: What can you do to update yours? School administrators article. [Electronic version]. *Education World,* 1–7. Retrieved April 10, 2004, from: http://www.education-world.com/a_admin/admin181.shtml

Callison, Daniel, & Abilock, Debbie. (2002, February). Key words in instruction: Technology. *School Library Media Activities Monthly, 18*(6), 36–40.

Chmara, T. (2003, June 23). *Quick summary of CIPA decision.* Retrieved April 10, 2004, from: http://www.ala.org/Content/NavigationMenu/Our_Association/ Offices/Intellectual_Freedom3/Intellectual_Freedom_Issues/Related_Links6/ Quick_Summary_of_CIPA_Decision.htm

Clark, Larra, et al. (2003, June 23). *ALA denounces Supreme Court ruling on Children's Internet Protection Act.* Retrieved April 20, 2004, from: http://www.ala. org/ala/pressreleasesbucket/pressreleases2003jun/aladenounces.htm

Consortium of School Networking. (1999, June). *Taking TKO to the classroom: A school administrator's guide to planning for the total cost of new technology.* Retrieved April 20, 2004, from: http://web.archive.org/web/20000818235317/ http://www.cosn.org/tco/tco2class.pdf

Crispen, Patrick. (2003). The weekly fab five: Things you should do every week to keep your computer running in tip-top shape. In Catherine Andronik (Ed.), *School library management* (5th ed.) (pp. 120–121). Worthington, OH: Linworth.

Definition: Digital divide. (2000–2003). Retrieved April 10, 2004, from: http://www.adversity.net/Terms_Definitions/TERMS/Digital_Divide.htm

Digital divide—A what is question. (2000–2003) Retrieved April 10, 2004, from: http://whatis.techtarget.com/definition/0,,sid9_gci214062,00.html

Digital Divide Network. (2004). *Digital divide basics.* Retrieved May 12, 2004, from: http://www.digitaldividenetwork.org/content/sections/index.cfm?key=2

Dodge, Bernie. (1995–97). *Some thoughts about WebQuests.* Retrieved April 10, 2004, from: http://edWeb.sdsu.edu/courses/edtec596/about_Webquests.html

Dyrli, Odvard Egil. (1996, January). Does your school have an acceptable use policy? *Technology & Learning, 16*(4), 2.

Flowers, Beverly F. & Rakes, Glenda C. (2000, Spring). Analyses of acceptable use policies. *Journal of Research on Computing in Education, 32*(3), 351–365.

Freudenrich, Craig C. (1998–2003). *How fiber optics work.* Retrieved April 10, 2004, from: http://electronics.howstuffworks.com/fiber-optic1.html

Fullner, Sheryl Kindle. (2003). Don't tread on me: A copier saga. In Catherine Andronik (Ed.), *School library management* (5th ed.) (pp. 125–126). Worthington, OH: Linworth.

Gardner, Carrie. (2001, December/2002 January). To government regulations be true. *Educational Leadership, 59*(4), 39–41.

Gersh, Shelia Offman. (2001, October). Technology's role in creating the shared learning environment. *Multimedia Schools, 8*(5), 48–51.

Goldberg, Beverly. (2003a, August). Libraries to revisit their bottom lines. *American Libraries, 34*(7), 13–14.

Goldberg, Beverly. (2003b, August). Supreme Court upholds CIPA. *American Libraries, 34*(7), 12–13.

Hadley Parrot Library. (1998–2003). Checklist of website evaluation criteria. Retrieved April 20, 2004, from: http://www.emh.org/hll/hpl/criteria.htm

Hamilton-Pennell, Christine, et al. (2000, April). Dick and Jane go to the head of the class. *School Library Journal, 46*(4), 44–47.

Herring Mark. Y. (2001, April). 10 reasons why the Internet is no substitute for a library. *American Libraries, 32*(4), 76–78.

Hilden, Julie. (2003. July 1) A recent Supreme Court decision allowing the government to force public libraries to filter users' Internet access is less significant than it might at first appear. *FindLaw's Writ. Legal* Supreme Court *Commentary.* Retrieved April 10, 2004, from: http://writ.news.findlaw.com/hilden/20030701.html

Holland, Jim. (2002, August). Networking issues across schools. *Media and Methods, 38*(7), 23.

Iafrica.com. (2003, April 29). *Ruling keeps web music-swapping alive.* Retrieved April 10, 2004, from: http://cooltech.iafrica.com/technews/232307.htm

IFLA/UNESCO. (2000, February 16). The school library in teaching and learning for all. *The UNESCO school library manifesto.* Retrieved April 10, 2004, from: http://www.nlc-bnc.ca/9/2/p2-9905-06-e.html

International Association of School Librarianship. (2004, February 21). School library automation and library automation systems. Retrieved April 10, 2004, from: http://www.iasl-slo.org/libaut.html

International Society for Technology in Education. (2000–2002). *Curriculum and content area standards, NETS for students.* Retrieved April 10, 2004, from: http://cnets.iste.org/currstands/cstands-netss.html

Johns, April. (2003). Out of paper… again? In Catherine Andronik (Ed.), *School library management* (5th ed.) (pp. 122–124). Worthington, OH: Linworth.

Kathy Schrock's guide for educators: Critical evaluation information. (1995–2004). Retrieved April 20, 2004, from the Discovery Channel web site: http://school.discovery.com/schrockguide/eval.html

Kolln, Lonny L., II. (2001, April 13). *MP3 technology and the evolving law around it.* Nicholas Johnson's University of Iowa Cyberspace Law Seminar Spring 2001. Retrieved April 10, 2004, from: http://www.uiowa.edu/~cyberlaw/cls01/kolln3.html

Kuhlthau, Carol Collier. (Ed.). (1996). *The virtual school library: gateway to the information superhighway.* Westport, CT: Libraries Unlimited.

Lowe, Carrie. (2001, October). The role of the school library media specialist in the 21st century. *Teacher Librarian, 29*(1), 30–33.

Mather, Mary Anne. (1996, September). Exploring the Internet safely—what schools can do. *Technology & Learning, 17*(1), 1–3.

Miller, Marilyn L. (2000, December). As school librarians race forward, it's time to dispel some myths. *American Libraries, 31*(11), 42–43.

Miller, Marilyn L. & Shontz, Marilyn L. (2001, October). New money, old books. *School Library Journal, 47*(10), 50–60.

Miller, Marilyn L. & Shontz, Marilyn L. (2003, October). The *SLJ* spending survey [Electronic version]. *School Library Journal, 49*(10), 1–3. Retrieved April 10, 2004, from: http://slj.reviewsnews.com/index.asp?layout=articlePrint&articleID=CA326338

Morris, Betty J. (1992). *Administering the school library media center* (3rd ed.). New Providence, NJ: R.R. Bowker.

Napster may face liquidation. (2002, September 3). *Business Journal.* Retrieved April 20, 2004, from: http://www.bizjournals.com/sanjose/stories/2002/09/02/daily14.html

Napster offers $1 billion to settle suit. (2001, February 21). Cable News Network. *CNN.com/LawCenter.* Retrieved April 10, 2004, from: http://www.cnn.com/2001/LAW/02/20/napster.settlement.03/

North Carolina Department of Public Instruction. (n.d.). *Criteria for evaluating web sites.* Retrieved April 10, 2004, from: http://www.ncwiseowl.org/Professional/criteria.htm

North Carolina Department of Public Instruction. (2001). *Impact for administrators: A resource for evaluating media and technology programs and personnel.* Retrieved April 10, 2004, from: http://www.ncwiseowl.org/Impact/Impact.htm

North Carolina Department of Public Instruction. (2002, March 14). *North Carolina school technology plan: Technological recommendations and standards.* School Technology Team. Office of Information Technology Services. Raleigh: North Carolina Department of Public Instruction. Retrieved April 10, 2004, from: http://tps.dpi.state.nc.us/standards/

North Carolina Department of Public Instruction. (2003). *North Carolina standard course of study.* Raleigh: North Carolina Department of Public Instruction. Retrieved April 10, 2004, from: http://www.ncpublicschools.org/curriculum/

North Carolina Department of Public Instruction. (2003). *WebQuest information: A definition.* NCWiseOwl. Retrieved April 10, 2004, from: http://www.ncwise owl.org/WebQuest/Info/Definition.htm

North Carolina Department of Public Instruction. (2003). Welcome to NCWise-Owl. Retrieved April 10, 2004, from: http://www.ncwiseowl.org

North Central Regional Educational Laboratory. (n.d.). *Develop a technology budget.* Retrieved April 10, 2004, from: http://www.ncrel.org/sdrs/areas/issues/methods/technlgy/te3lk76.htm

North Central Regional Educational Laboratory. (n.d.). *Indicator: Comprehensive, prioritized funding.* Retrieved April 10, 2004, from: http://www.ncrel.org/engauge/framewk/sys/fund/sysfunra.htm

Northwest Regional Educational Consortium. (1998, February 13). *A guide to networking for K–12 schools.* Olympia: Washington State Office of the Superintendent of Public Instruction. Retrieved April 10, 2004, from the Northwest Regional Consortium web site: http://www.netc.org/network_guide/

Ormes, Sarah. (n.d.). *Filtering—Is this the answer?* Retrieved April 10, 2004, from: www.ukoln.ac.uk/public/present/london/school1.ppt

Pacifici, Sabrina I. (1997, February 14). *Virtual libraries: Myth and reality.* Retrieved April 10, 2004, from: http://www.llrx.com/features/virtual.htm

Pappas, Marjorie L. (1999, September). Changing learning and libraries in schools. *School Library Media Activities Monthly, 16*(1), 26–32.

Reilly, Rob. (2000, October). Laying down the law: Crafting acceptable use policy. *Multimedia Schools, 7*(5), 78–80.

SafeKids Home Page, Microsoft. (2003). Retrieved April 10, 2004, from: http://www.microsoft.com/presspass/safekids/

Schneider, Karen G. (2000, September). Round up the usual suspects: Filters, COPA, and all that. *American Libraries, 31*(8), 103.

Schneider, Karen G. (2002, January). E-rate: The agony and the ecstasy. *American Libraries, 33*(1), 94.

Schneider, Karen G. (2003, August). Let's begin the discussion: What now? *American Libraries, 34*(7), 14–16.

Schuyler, Michael. (2002, May). It's not paranoia if they're really out to get you. (The view from the top left corner). *Computers in Libraries, 22*(5), 32–34.

Seamon, Mary Ploski & Levitt, Eric J. (2001). *Web-based learning: A practical guide.* Worthington, OH: Linworth.

Shelley, Gary B., et al. (2002). Integrating technology into the classroom. (2nd ed.). Boston, MA: Course Technology.

Simpson, Carol. (2003a). Migration: A moving experience. In Catherine Andronik (Ed.), *School library management* (5th ed.) (pp. 112–114). Worthington, OH: Linworth.

Simpson, Carol. (2003b). Migration: Not just for ducks. In Catherine Andronik (Ed.), *School library management* (5th ed.) (pp. 110–111). Worthington, OH: Linworth.

Smallwood, Carol. (2003). Still no magic wand for annual inventory. In Catherine Andronik (Ed.), *School library management* (5th ed.) (pp. 115–116). Worthington, OH: Linworth.

Southern Technology Council. (1997). *Making technology happen: Best practices and policies for exemplary K–12 schools.* Research Triangle Park, NC: Author.

Starr, Linda. (2002, February 6). Managing technology: Tips from the experts. [Electronic version]. *Education World.* Retrieved April 10, 2004, from Education World web site: http://www.education-world.com/a_tech/tech116.shtml

State Education Department. The University of The State Of New York. (2003, February). *Draft technology plan.* Office for Elementary, Middle, Secondary and Continuing Education. Albany, NY: State Education Department. The University of The State Of New York. Retrieved April 10, 2004, from: http://www.emsc.nysed.gov/deputy/Documents/technology/fm-2–03-draftframework.html

Sutter, Lynne & Sutter, Herman. (1999). *Finding the right path: Research your way to discovery.* Worthington, OH: Linworth.

Truett, Carol. (2002, November). *Class survey of students in LIB 5040: Management of the school library media center.* Boone, NC: Appalachian State University.

Universal Service Administrative Company, Schools and Libraries Division. (2004, March 19). *Forms-Applicant forms.* Retrieved April 19, 2004, from: http://www.sl.universalservice.org/form/

Universal Service Administrative Company, Schools and Libraries Division. (2002, July). *E-Rate discounts for schools and libraries.* Retrieved April 10, 2004, from: http://www.universalservice.org/

Virginia Department of Education, Division of Technology. (2003). *Acceptable use policies—A handbook.* Virginia Department of Education, Division of Technology. Retrieved April 10, 2004, from: http://www.pen.k12.va.us/go/VDOE/Technology/AUP/home.shtml#components

What is SUNLINK? (2002, September 3). Retrieved April 10, 2004, from: http://www.sunlink.ucf.edu/about/what.html

Young, Jr., Terence E. (2003). The weakest link: Library catalogs. In Catherine Andronik (Ed.), *School library management* (5th ed.) (pp. 105–109). Worthington, OH: Linworth.

FURTHER READINGS

AAA Bandwidth: T1, T3, frame relay. Retrieved April 10, 2004 from: http://www.aaabandwidth.com/T1lines.cfm

Barron, Ann E., Orwig, Gary W., Ivers, Karen & Lilavois, Nick. (2002). *Technologies for education: A practical guide* (4th ed.). Westport, CT: Libraries Unlimited.

Blowers, Helene & Bryan, Robin. (2004). *Weaving a library web: A guide to developing children's websites.* Chicago: American Library Association.

Boechler, Patricia M., Dawson, Michael R. & Boechler, Kelvin R. (2002). An introduction to custom web browsers for the qualitative study of hypertext navigation. *Journal of Educational Multimedia and Hypermedia, 11*(3), 221–235.

Brandt, D. Scott. (1996). *Evaluating information on the Internet.* Retrieved April 20, 2004, from the Purdue University Libraries web site: http://thorplus.lib.purdue.edu/rguides/studentinstruction/evaluation/evaluatingwebsites.html

Bristol Evening Post. (2003, January). Teach children Internet safety. *Europe Intelligence Wire.* Retrieved from Gale Group Database.

Carlson, Randy. (2002, January/February). A network primer for media specialists. *Book Report, 20*(4), 41–45.

Caywood, Carolyn. (1999, December). *Library selection criteria for WWW resources.* Retrieved April 20, 2004 from: http://web.archive.org/web/20021202071448/http://www.pilot.infi.net/~carolyn/criteria.html

Chiles, Linda, et al. (2003, October). Are you breaking the law: Copyright guidelines for video streaming and digital video in the classroom. *THE Journal, 31*(3), 36–39.

Dahl, Candice. (2001, May). Electronic pathfinders in academic libraries: An analysis of their content and form. *College and Research Libraries, 62*(3), 227–237.

Dennison, Russell F. (1999, May/June). Web searching—A group project. *The Technology Teacher, 58*(8), 6–9.

Djoudi, Mahieddine & Harous, Saad. (2001, November). Simplifying the learning process over the Internet. *THE Journal, 29*(4), 50–55.

Dorr, David L., Bray, Kaye L. & Holcomb, Terry L. (2002, July/August). Deep linking: Revisiting and updating. *Tech Trends, 46*(4), 3–7.

Everhart, Nancy. (1996). *Web page evaluation worksheet.* Retrieved April 10, 2004, from the Duke University web site: http://www.duke.edu/~de1/evaluate.html

Farmer, Lesley S. J. (2001). *Teaming with opportunity: Media programs, community constituencies, and technology.* Westport, CT: Libraries Unlimited.

Fitzgerald, Mary Ann, Orey, Michael & Branch, Robert. (Eds.). (2002). *Educational media and technology yearbook 2002* (Vol. 27). Westport, CT: Libraries Unlimited.

Gillan, Bud. (2003, November/December). Crossing the great divide with networks, teaching, interactivity. *Library Media Connections, 22*(3), 38–42.

Goldsborough, Reid. (2002, June). Making working alone work for you. *Teacher Librarian, 29*(5), 42.

Helena School District, Montana. (1999). *The secretary's conference on educational technology-1999.* Retrieved April 10, 2004, from: http://www.ed.gov/rsch stat/eval/tech/techconf99/sptlitcontcts.html

Himelstein, Linda. (2002, May 14). Napster's CEO splits on a sour note—Voice and data. *BusinessWeek Online.* Retrieved April 6, 2004, from: http://www. Businessweek.com/technology/content/may2002/tc20020514_1069.htm

Hopkins, Janet. (2004). *Assistive technology: An introductory guide for K-12 library media specialists.* Worthington, OH: Linworth.

Information Today, Inc. (2001, October). Library launches Internet safety web site. *Computers in Libraries, 21*(9), 8.

International Society for Technology in Education. (2000–2002). *About ISTE.* Retrieved April 10, 2004, from: http://www.iste.org/about/

Ito, Alexandra. (2003, October). The reality of anytime, anywhere learning. *THE Journal, 31*(3), 36–39.

Ivers, Karen S. (2003). *A teacher's guide to using technology in the classroom.* Westport, CT: Libraries Unlimited.

Ivers, Karen S. & Barron, Ann E. (2002). *Multimedia projects in education: Designing, producing, and assessing* (2nd ed.). Westport, CT: Libraries Unlimited.

Jaber, William E. & Moore, David M. (1999). A survey of factors which influence teachers' use of computer-based technology. *International Journal of Instructional Media, 26*(3), 253–266.

Janes, Joseph. (2003, September). Seething over CIPA. *American Libraries, 34*(8), 84.

Johnson, Doug. (1997). *The indispensable librarian: Surviving (and thriving) in school media centers.* Worthington, OH: Linworth.

Johnson, Doug. (2003). *Learning right from wrong in the digital age: An ethics guide for parents, teachers, librarians, and others who care about computer-using young people.* Worthington, OH: Linworth.

Junion-Metz, Gail. (2000, April). Armed against danger. *School Library Journal, 46*(4), 39.

Kent, Susan. (2002, November). Going global. *Library Journal, 127*(18), 44–47.

Lamb, Annette. (2002). *Building treehouses for learning: Technology in today's classrooms* (3rd ed.). Emporia, KS: Vision to Action.

Lathrop, Ann & Foss, Kathleen. (2000). *Student cheating and plagiarism in the Internet era: A wake-up call.* Westport, CT: Libraries Unlimited.

Loertscher, David V. (1999). *Reinvent your school's library in the age of technology: A guide for principals and superintendents.* San Jose, CA: Hi Willow Research and Publishing.

March, Tom. (2000, October). WebQuests 101. *Multimedia Schools, 7*(5), 55–58.

March, Tom. (2000, November/December). The 3 R's of WebQuests. *Multimedia Schools, 7*(6), 62–63.

Marcovitz, David M. (2004). *Powerful powerpoint for educators: Using visual basic for applications to make powerpoint interactive.* Westport, CT: Libraries Unlimited.

McCabe, Ron. (2003, August). The CIPA ruling as reality therapy. *American Libraries, 34*(7), 16.

McCorkle, Sandra K. (2003). *Web pages for your classroom: The easy way.* Westport, CT: Libraries Unlimited.

McKenzie, Jamie. (2003, November/December). The techno-savvy book-rich media center. *Library Media Connection, 22*(3), 14–18.

Mendrinos, Roxanne. (1997). *Using educational technology with at-risk students: A guide for library media specialists and teachers.* Westport, CT: Greenwood Press.

Metallica hails Napster decision as music downloads continue—Napster says it will appeal ruling. (2001, February 13). *CNN.com/LawCenter.* Retrieved April 20, 2004, from the Cable News Network web site: http://www.cnn.com/2001/LAW/02/12/napster.decision.05/index.html

Minkel, Walter. (2000, September). The e-textbooks are coming. *School Library Journal, 46*(9), 18–19.

Minkel, Walter. (2000, December). Who owns e-information. *School Library Journal, 46*(12), 43.

Minkel, Walter. (2001, December). 2002's top tech trends: What we should be watching for in libraries and schools next year. *School Library Journal, 47*(12), 25–26.

Minkel, Walter. (2002, August). Stretch your network. *School Library Journal, 48*(8), 52–53.

Minkel, Walter. (2004, March). The online engines that could. *School Library Journal, 50*(3), 36.

Mutch, Andrew, & Karen Ventura. (2002, August). Does your library need a different browser? Andrew Mutch and Karen Ventura propose that alternative web browsers can return sanity and security to public Internet computers. (Innovation Reports on Technology). *School Library Journal, 48*(8), SS22.

Napster: Stealing or sharing? Napster timeline. (2001). *CNN.com—In-Depth Special.* Retrieved April 20, 2004, from the Cable News Network web site: http://www.cnn.com/SPECIALS/2001/napster/timeline.html

Napster says it will appeal ruling. (2001, February 12). *CNN.com/LawCenter.* Retrieved April 20, 2004, from the Cable News Network web site: http://www.cnn.com/2001/LAW/02/12/napster.decision.04/

Needleman, Mark. (2000). Z39.50—A review, analysis and some thoughts on the future. [Electronic version]. *Library High Tech, 18*(2), 158–165. Retrieved April 10, 2004, from: http://dois.mimas.ac.uk/DoIS/data/Articles/julfsernry:2000:v:18:i:2:p:158–165.html

Oddie, Carolyn. (1999). Copyright protection in the digital age. *Information Management and Computer Management, 7*(5), 239–240.

Oder, Norman. (2002, July). CIPA aftermath: Part of law stays. *Library Journal, 127*(12), 16–18.

OpenNap: Open source Napster server. (2001, November 15). Retrieved April 10, 2004, from: http://opennap.sourceforge.net

Orey, Michael, et al. (2004). *Educational media and technology yearbook* (Vol. 29). Westport, CT: Libraries Unlimited.

Pappas, Marjorie. (2003, November). State virtual libraries. *School Library Media Activities Monthly, 20*(3), 27–31.

Pappas, Marjorie. (2004, January). Finding information on the state virtual libraries. *School Library Media Activities Monthly, 20*(5), 30–32.

Pemberton, Jayne A. (2000, Fall). Update: RIAA v. Diamond Multimedia Systems— Napster and MP3.com. *The Richmond Journal of Law & Technology, 7*(1), 1–13. Retrieved April 20, 2004, from: http://web.archive.org/web/20030123042024/ http://law.richmond.edu/jolt/admin/v7i1/note3.html

Rajala, Judith B. (2003, October). Wireless technology in education. *THE Journal, 31*(3), 28.

Regarding the Internet in selected K-12 schools. *Journal of Research on Computing in Education, 32*(3), 4.

Richardson, Ronny. (2003, October). Digital imaging: The wave of the future. *THE Journal, 31*(3), 48–49.

Serim, Ferdi. (2001, May/June). Child safety and the Internet—From fear to fulfillment. *Multimedia School, 8*(3), 18–21.

Smith, Alastair. (2002, December). *Evaluation of information sources.* Retrieved April 10, 2004, from: http://www2.vuw.ac.nz/staff/alastair_smith/evaln/evaln.htm

Summers, Jan. (1996). Using the Internet to enhance teaching and learning. In Carol Collier Kuhlthau (Ed.), *The virtual school library: Gateway to the information superhighway* (pp. 21–27). Westport, CT: Libraries Unlimited.

Summerville, Jennifer. (2000, March). WebQuests. *TechTrends, 44*(2), 31–35.

Talab, Rosemary Sturdevant. (2001, July/August). Permissions, "fair use," and production resources for educators and librarians. *Tech Trends, 45*(4), 4–7.

Tillman, Hope N. (2001, March). *Evaluating quality on the net.* Retrieved April 10, 2004, from: http://www.hopetillman.com/findqual.html

Valenza, Joyce. (2003, November/December). A letter to parents about the Internet. *Library Media Connection, 22*(3), 30–31.

Vesey, Ken. (2004, April/May). Building a better clicks-and-mortar library. *Library Media Connections, 22*(7), 28–29.

Wilensky, Robert. (1994, September). *Developing a more effective protocol for client/server information retrieval.* Retrieved April 10, 2004, from the University of California, Berkley web site: http://elib.cs.berkeley.edu/admin/proposal/ proj-des/node6.html

Wilkinson, Gene L. (1997, May). *Evaluating the quality of Internet information sources.* Retrieved April 10, 2004, from the University of Georgia Instructional Technology web site: http://it2.coe.uga.edu/Faculty/gwilkinson/Webeval.html

Yates, Jan M. (2003). *Interactive distance learning in PreK-12 settings: A handbook of possibilities.* Westport, CT: Libraries Unlimited.

Chapter 11

ACQUISITION AND ORGANIZATION

Staff functions and program activities depend not only on the resources of the center but also on the organizational patterns that the center adopts. The main goals of this managerial function are to acquire resources and make them available as quickly and efficiently as possible. An efficient processing system is a prerequisite for achieving these goals. Many individual school library media centers rely on commercial processing as an important adjunct to organization.

This chapter deals with the general rules that apply to acquisition in school library media centers, with emphasis on the minimally staffed center in an individual school building. The system of bidding is explained, and technical services, such as purchasing, processing, and cataloging, are covered along with local production of education materials and copyright.

When a budget is approved by a board of education, final decisions about expenditures must be made. If the funds are allocated as requested, the procedure is generally predetermined. If budget requests have been reduced, the media specialist must design a priority system for expenditures. Since reductions affect the entire instructional program, the media specialist should discuss these problems with the media advisory committee and work with them to come to some decision about how to allocate funds. Once these preliminaries are completed, the specialist is ready to proceed to the two fundamental steps in the acquisition process: bidding and purchasing.

BIDDING

The federal government as well as many state education departments and school systems require competitive formal bidding for purchase of materials, supplies, or equipment in excess of specified amounts; the amounts vary from state to state—in some, for example, the cutoff figure is $1,000. These agencies may require a less formalized bidding process for amounts that fall under a specified minimum, for example, $300. State law, city ordinance, school board resolution, or administrative order are some of the regulations that mandate competitive bidding for all types of purchases, including materials and equipment.

Most districts have a bid list, but some districts place more importance on adhering to it than others. Some districts require that the bid vendors must be consulted first before ordering. If the item can't be found from the bid vendor, an order can be made to another vendor not on the list. Other districts do not expect media specialists to look at a bid list when ordering books or audiovisual materials and equipment. The aim of bidding in expending public funds is to get the best goods and services at the lowest possible cost; the bid serves as a guard against favoritism to a vendor as well as a device for conserving public funds. The formal bid should protect the school and media center by the inclusion of penalty provisions and cancellation clauses for substandard or delinquent service on the vendor's part. It is also designed to give the supplier or vendor an opportunity to be considered by a larger buying audience, that is, an entire state. In practice, however, each media specialist with experience in competitive bidding realizes that bidding raises many problems: the negotiation of the contract through a fiscal agency (usually at the school district level, but sometimes through state or federal agencies), the possibility of poor service from the vendor, and the accuracy of the billing. Vendors, on the other hand, have encountered problems in dealing with some schools because of delayed payment, lack of partial payment on merchandise received, and seasonal ordering. Both find that unless the school media center works closely with the business office or the school purchasing agency, the lack of coordination complicates the process.

Formal Bidding

The term "formal bidding" usually refers to a system in which sealed bids from vendors for certain items advertised locally are publicly opened on a given date. Firms that meet certain qualifications and have given satisfactory service in the past are invited to enter a bid. Some nonstandard or monopoly items for which there are too few firms to compete may be exempt from the bid requirements, for example, a specialized type of equipment.

Another type of formal bidding is the state contract method by which firms negotiate a contract for a period of time with a state education department. As an alternative to local competitive bidding, school library media centers may be able to use state contracts. A list of dealers who have a contract with a state education department is generally available from the local district business office. As a typical example of a state that requires formal bidding, the New York State Education Department expects all items to be placed on bid unless they represent either or both of the following categories: (1) an annual total expenditure for one item or type of item within a school district of less than $1,000, (2) a monopoly item (that is, an item available at a fixed price from only one source).

Informal Bidding

The term, informal bidding, suggests a less formalized bidding method and usually means that the bid need not be advertised. As few as two or three firms may be asked, even by telephone, for a bid price on the item or items needed. This system is widely used when the expenditure for an item falls between the minimum and maximum figures required for informal and formal bidding, for example, $100 and $1,000.

If neither the competitive bid nor the state contract bid method is used, the school library media center and local business office should agree on a standard bidding practice and set up guidelines. Whatever the procedure, the bidding should: (1) provide satisfactory service to the media center, (2) guarantee fiscal integrity to the business office, and (3) grant realistic specifications on items for the vendors. The following guidelines should be written into the bids:

- **Specifications.** A detailed description of the item, for example, for binding, saddle-stitching might be requested.
- **Ordering frequency.** A schedule for anticipated ordering, such as large orders in the fall and spring with regular school year biweekly orders.
- **Time of delivery.** A time schedule for delivery expectations, for example, a 50 percent fulfillment of order within 60 days with a 90–120 day period for completion of order.

- **Substitutions and changes by suppliers**. A definition of what substitutions and changes will be acceptable, such as revisions of older titles or newer models of equipment, but not a different video on the same subject.

- **Quality and condition of merchandise**. A list of unacceptable conditions, such as transparencies that differ in definition or color from the samples; prints that are damaged in transit.

- *Policy on service and returns*. A two-part statement on the expectations of (1) the service desired—a first-time service visit to install and put in working condition sophisticated equipment such as smart boards, and (2) the conditions under which materials may be returned, for example, books with missing pages.

- **Invoices and packing slips**. A notice that lists the number and disposition of the shipping and billing statements, such as sending duplicate copies of invoices to the media center and guaranteeing the arrival of shipments, with enclosed slips listing the material or equipment delivered.

- **Bid security**. A statement that requires a bond or stipulates penalties in case of default of the agreement. For example, a school may ask a vendor (1) to secure a bond before the school will entertain a bid in excess of $2,000, for instance, LCD projectors, or (2) to deduct a percentage of the final payment if all material or equipment has not been received at the agreed-on delivery termination period.

- **Discounts**. A list by type of material or equipment of the acceptable range of discounts, for example, ten to twenty percent for technical or scientific print titles, thirty-three to forty percent for trade print titles, ten percent off list price for new model equipment, or larger discounts for quantity orders.

- **Full and partial payments**. An agreement to reimburse the vendor within a reasonable time period for both orders delivered in full and in partial shipments, such as guaranteed payment by school within thirty to sixty days of completion of either type of order fulfillment.

- **Exhibit and exhibition merchandise**. A written contract form that stipulates such things as the time period between receipt and return of goods; the condition of the materials; the kind and amount of materials and necessary display items; the method and length of payment if the materials are to be sold, the legal responsibility for the consignment, insurance coverage, and so forth.

- **Services of an area representative**. A statement that explains the expectation of a distant company's field representatives, such as the availability of a sales or service person from a national producer of videos or manufacturer of photocopying equipment to adjust claims or advise on use.

- **Cancellation clause**. An enforceable statement that notes the conditions under which either the vendor or school may cancel an order, for example, if the vendor is not reimbursed after a reasonable period of time, if a delivery is delayed beyond a reasonable period of time, if the titles in an order are substituted for those originally specified, and so on.

- **Consignment privileges**. A list of conditions under which materials may be delivered and sold or used under a deferred-payment agreement, such as paperbacks for sale in a media center-operated store or at a materials fair may be purchased on consignment and paid for as they are sold; book clubs often use some form of this method. Time periods and accounting methods are important in the listing of consignment privileges.

- **Conditions of warranty**. A statement that describes the circumstances under which materials or equipment may be repaired or exchanged, such as cassette player may be exchanged or a missing or malfunctioning part repaired free of charge within ninety days of purchase.

No standardized bid form that covers all these guidelines is presently in general use. The forms devised by governing bodies vary from one type for all merchandise to many different types, some of which may contain detailed specifications for a particular commodity. Some agreement among purchasing officials does exist, however, about the importance of the basis on which bids are evaluated: the least bid price in relation to the bidder's responsibility to the vendor. The lowest dollar amount bid price should not be the sole criterion, because the service and the speed with which it is given are also fundamental concerns in the acquisition of media. The responsibility of the bidder, whether manufacturer, producer, dealer, or agent, rests on many factors, including a sound financial condition, some experience in the work, and good past performance. Whenever circumstances permit, the media specialist should consult with the school business officer on these matters.

In dealing with the bidding process, the media specialist should also be aware of the following points:

1. Each item, from pamphlets to videos to newspapers, often requires a different vendor or purchasing method. For example, the materials may be produced privately or commercially, issued by governments, societies, universities, or others, or be available on exchange. These factors often serve to exempt school library media center materials from a bid requirement.

2. Some state laws and local school system regulations exempt library materials from a bid requirement.

3. The school district has certain requirements.

It is necessary to build a solid working relationship in which the school library media center's needs may be mutually understood and determined with the school district business office and in which the media specialist participates in the evaluation of the bids.

General Considerations in Relation to Vendors

Orders should be placed with reputable vendors. Some procedures that can help media specialists avoid unsatisfactory service or fraudulent business practices are:

- Examine and appraise items on deposit at education media centers prior to ordering when possible.
- Utilize lists of sources in the professional literature.
- Seek out other media specialists' recommendations.
- Get information about local firms from the Better Business Bureau.

In addition, the media specialist should expect a vendor to fulfill the following criteria:

- Maintain adequate physical facilities and a warehouse with a sizable inventory of items described in the state contract specifications or descriptions of the firm, in order to be able to fill a majority of orders from stock.
- Have assets, capital, and a credit rating sufficient to handle potential business.
- Offer a discount schedule that is competitive with other vendors' schedules, while still giving assurance of satisfactory service.
- Have the staff for production and operating routines necessary to fulfill service requirements, including prompt reporting and follow-up on shipping orders.
- Have a satisfactory record in fulfilling similar orders for others. This record should involve such considerations as accuracy of orders filled (such as specified edition or binding), percentage of orders filled (unfortunately an out-of-stock report on an order often reflects the jobber's in-house stock rather than the publisher's), length of delivery time, nature of billing procedures, and quality of service when rectifying errors that have been made.

Materials may be ordered from their originating source—a publisher, producer, or manufacturer—or from wholesalers or jobbers. Many media specialists will order items in a variety of ways, depending on how the format is traditionally distributed. Some print-oriented wholesalers stock nonprint items in an effort to simplify the media center's acquisition problems. Wholesale distributors who sell a combination of print and nonprint items to a regional area are best identified through their advertisements in school media and library periodicals, particularly in notices in professional organization bulletins and newsletters. One important source for help in identifying suppliers and vendors for specific items is the *AV Market Place* (R. R. Bowker, annual), a directory that identifies over 1,250 audiovisual products, services, and suppliers.

PURCHASING

Another part of the acquisitions process is the preparation of purchase orders, which lends itself to an organized, routine approach. A network of libraries or a school system with a central administrative unit can avail itself of the purchasing economies that result from the central coordination of orders, and the entire routine of purchasing may be handled online.

Online Ordering

Vendors use different procedures for ordering online—some will work with purchase orders, whereas, others require payment up front. The order can be placed with online order forms, or order forms can be printed and then faxed or mailed to the companies. Some purchasing can be done online where purchase orders are automatically routed to the district office and then forwarded to the vendor. Some districts will only allow online ordering for local money. The order is paid by a media center or school credit card. Overall, this procedure decreases the time to receive items. It is not normally acceptable to order online when using federal funds; they must have a written purchase order.

Online ordering not only frees the specialist from arduous clerical routines but also allows for printout reports in a variety of formats, such as by vendor, author, or purchase order. By adding additional information (subject headings, classification numbers), more uses can be made of the data, such as cataloging and the preparation of subject bibliographies, and union lists. Many districts employ a system-wide purchasing system to order all media center materials. Other districts allow the individual school library media centers to order online through a jobber, such as Follett through *Titlewave*, Bound-to-Stay-Bound, and others. Other districts allow the media specialist to have a media center credit card to pay for materials when attending professional conferences.

The major book jobbers offer a variety of services that make the acquisition process much easier. Jobbers such as Follett and Baker & Taylor have extensive online portals where you can search for titles by curricular needs, number of reviews, reading level, and more. Full-text reviews are available for many of the titles. Media specialists can create accounts at no charge to access the book lists that they create and store for future online orders. Most jobbers offer a free typing quotation service that allows selections for ordering to be submitted in a variety of formats, including handwritten notes, review sources pages, or pages from catalogs. The jobbers offer books and audiovisual materials that can be purchased in one location. Specialized jobbers that deal primarily in providing books with sturdy bindings include, for example, Bound-to Stay Bound and Perma-Bound Books. Although Amazon.com is not a book jobber specializing in library materials, it can be used for ordering those items that are needed immediately. They accept purchase orders, which has simplified the ordering process. The major jobbers that serve libraries and their web sites are listed here:

General Jobbers:

- **Baker & Taylor:** http://www.btol.com/
- **Follett** *(Titlewave):* http://www.titlewave.com/index.html or http://www.flr.follett.com/login/
- **Brodart, Inc.:** http://www.brodart.com/

Specialized jobbers:

- **Bound-to-Stay Bound Books:** http://www.btsb.com/
- **Perma-Bound Books:** http://www.perma-bound.com/

Other school systems have contracted with book jobbers to use their online acquisition system for book selection as well as the generation of purchase orders and accounting documents. In such a situation, the library media specialist selects material from the jobber's lists and encodes ordering information on special forms that can be either printed or ordered online.

Ordering from the Local School

Where the ordering is not centralized, the ordering system should be designed by the media specialist in the individual school and approved by the school business office. Two considerations are important: The procedures should eliminate unnecessary duplication and they should use simple standardized order forms. Frequency of ordering varies from school to school. To simplify bookkeeping procedures, many business offices prefer fewer and larger orders to a multitude containing only a few items each. Infrequent, once-or-twice-a-year ordering, however, can result in a lack of currency in collections and the risk of non-fulfillment of orders because an item has gone out of stock or out of print.

The school fiscal year is sometimes calculated from July 1 through June 30. In decentralized library media programs, professional personnel are not available to place or check orders during the summer months. District business offices will often not allow ordering after a specified date (sometimes March 1) to ensure delivery and confirmation of payment before the end of the school year. To make certain that all budgeted funds will be expended in a given year, library media specialists will sometimes append supplementary lists of materials (usually books) in order of purchase priority with a "do not exceed" amount. These materials can then be substituted for items not available in the jobber's warehouse until all the funds have been spent. Before leaving for summer vacation, the library media specialist usually prepares several orders to be charged to the next year's budget. This procedure allows materials to be delivered over the summer so they will be available at the beginning of the next school year. At a minimum, these are orders for magazine and newspaper subscriptions, supplies, new books, and audio-visual materials. Although it is sometimes difficult, one must exercise restraint in order to ensure adequate funding for the rest of the school year.

Material Request Records

Request cards, available commercially from library supply houses or produced locally, contain appropriate spaces for order information. The cards may also be easily adapted to supply other needed data. They may be used early in the selection process by teachers, administrators, students, and community members, as needed in the particular situation, to note their requests for materials. The library media center personnel can also use them when checking selection aids.

Items that should be included on material request cards are: (1) author (or counterpart), (2) title, (3) format, (4) publisher (or producer), (5) publication date, (6) edition, (7) number of copies wanted, (8) department making recommendation, (9) individual making recommendation, and (10) authority (review media, date, and page). Space might also be provided for the International Standard Book Number (ISBN), a numeric device that, through coding, identifies a specific book by country of origin, publisher, and title. Increasingly, book jobbers and other vendors are utilizing this code for ordering purposes and using the conventional bibliographic information for verification purposes only. The back of the card could be used for a brief content note. When the item is received and a "New Additions to the School Library Media Center" or a bibliography is being prepared, the annotation will already have been written.

If the media center has a web site, a material request form can be made available online. The form can then be submitted to the media center for ordering if funds are available. This method of requesting materials is an easy way for teachers, students, and administrators to get their requests to the media center. It would certainly encourage their participation in selection of materials.

Because acquisition is a continuous process, the center's patrons should be regularly reminded to turn in their material requests to the media center. This cumulative file, often called a *consideration file*, can be kept by subject, grade level, or larger curriculum division in order to allocate funds equitably. When the appropriate fund for purchase of the item is assigned, the request may be filed in a separate awaiting-purchase file. Usually these files serve more efficiently if they are subdivided by media format, because they are frequently sent to vendors who specialize in one type of media, for example, academic games.

Before a purchase order is made, a clerk should carefully check the OPAC against the center's holdings to determine whether the center already owns or has ordered the item. The accuracy of the basic ordering information should also be checked against indexes, reviews and catalogs, such as *Books in Print, NICEM* indexes, *Booklist, School Library Journal*, or *Hornbook*. Once the item from the consideration file has been appropriately checked in the OPAC, a multiple-copy requisition form may be typed for each item should the media center need more than one copy of the item.

It is always a good idea to have orders for certain jobbers or publishers ready for sending just in case the principal locates media center money that needs to be spent in a short period of time. Items not received after an order is completed (usually because of out-of-print status) are kept in another file known as the desiderata file, which should be checked periodically. If an item is still in demand, an alternate method of acquisition could be tried (for example, use of out-of-print dealers [print or online], purchase of a facsimile copy, or interlibrary loan).

ORDER PROCESSING

This section deals with order-processing methods and several steps of physical preparation of material (other than classification and cataloging, discussed later in this chapter) that are required to make the item usable in the school library media center.

Single-School Ordering and Processing

When the media center in the individual school is responsible for taking care of its own technical services, it must develop its own appropriate ordering and processing procedures.

Ordering

The information from the material request file that should be used to order online or to be placed as an order on a purchase order includes: author, title, publisher, date of publication, edition, price, number of copies, and ISBN when available. Additional information includes date ordered, name of vendor, and name and address of school that appears on the purchase order. If an order is too large to be written on the purchase order itself, a statement on the purchase order ("see attached list") should be used. Each school district will have a set number of copies of the purchase order that is needed and the designated places it will go. Usually a copy is needed for the following: vendor, school business office, media center, and district business office. The media center copy needs to be filed as an on-order file arranged by vendor or purchase order number while awaiting the arrival of the material. If several funds are used in the media center, the file should be with those purchase orders used for ordering from each individual fund.

The school's standard purchase order, which contains all the pertinent information, such as: vendor, address, total price (if not a bid price, the list price is usually given), and special instructions should be attached to the copies and then sent to the school business office for official authorization and mailing to the vendor. Some jobbers offer free typing of orders upon request by the school media specialist.

For efficient follow-through in the ordering procedure, the school business office should retain a copy of the purchase order for its office files. School districts should also allow the media specialist to telephone or order online for rush orders as needed on assurance to the vendor of an immediate confirmation purchase order. The media specialist should carefully check the center's expenditure records for the balances in each budget account, as well as the records that are kept in the school business office, before using this system of confirmation-purchase-order ordering. The media specialist needs to periodically reconcile purchase order amounts with the school business accountant.

Processing Preparations

When materials are received in the media center, they should be opened, checked, and prepared for processing. A clerk or student assistant may check the items and the enclosed packing slip against the purchase order. On receipt of the items, the consideration file slip, together with any processing kits (if not attached), should be put with the item as it is checked in and placed on the cataloging shelf. The status of the shipment should be noted by date on the media center's copy of the purchase order. It's a good idea to place the date of receipt of items on the purchase order. Purchase orders should be filed by vendor or purchase order number, whichever is used in the business office, to give the media specialist a quick-access file that corresponds to the accounts for the center in the school business office. Once the packing slip has been checked against the purchase order, the materials are ready for cataloging by the media specialist.

Some media centers put an accession number for materials received each year on the page behind the verso of the title page in pencil to denote when the material was received. For example, the accession number might be 03-1 (year, and order item received). Some media specialists find this information helpful when weeding the collection and when keeping records of the number of items added to the collection each year. This record allows the media specialist to have a running total of books and other materials purchased each year.

Because of the special characteristics of some of the media that are acquired by a center and the number of vendors needed for purchasing a variety of materials and equipment, the media specialist should strive for the best possible working relationship with the school and district business offices in order to streamline ordering procedures, eliminate unnecessary paperwork, and guarantee the speedy receipt of media. One of the ways to ensure the latter, as well as the goodwill of suppliers, is to arrange for prompt payment of invoices.

The media center should receive a copy of the vendor's invoice, from either the vendor or the business office, so that a running statement of the media center account funds can be kept in the center. In this way the media specialist will be able at any time to determine the encumbrances against the account balances. Once an order is complete, draw a large "C" on the purchase order to denote, at a glance, that the order is complete.

Magazine Acquisition

To secure a maximum discount for library media centers and ensure continuity of coverage, magazines are usually ordered through a magazine jobber. Some of the better known jobbers are:

W T Cox Subscriptions, 201 Village Road, Shallotte, NC 28470. Phone: 800-571-9554; Fax: 910-755-6274; E-mail: Info@wtcox.com; web site: http://www.wtcox.com

Demco, Inc., Attention: Periodicals Department, P.O. Box 7760, Madison, WI 53707-7760. Phone: 800-448-6764/608-241-1471; Fax: 888-329-4728; E-Mail: periodicals@demco.com; web site: http://www.demco.com/webprd_demco/other_objects/per_services.htm

Ebsco Information Services, P.O. Box 1943, Birmingham, AL 35201-1943. Phone: 205-991-6600; Fax: 205-995-1636; web site: http://www.ebsco.com

Ebsco Subscription Services Online, 630 Peter Jefferson Parkway, Suite 160, Charlottesville, VA 22911. Phone: 800-787-1414/434-817-1800; web site: http://magazinecity.net/?AID=1633295&PID=942610

Magazines of America, 13400 Madison Avenue, Lakewood, OH 44107. Phone 800-528-9468; web site: http://www.magazinesofamerica.com

Magazine Values, 149 Okaloosa Drive, Winter Haven, FL 33884. Phone: 863-326-1125 (no phone orders); Fax: 508-374-8599; web site: http://magazinevalues.com/

Research Periodicals & Book Services, Inc., 9207 Country Creek Drive, Suite 200, Houston, TX 77036. Phone: 800-521-0061; Fax: 713-779-2992; web site: http://www.rpbs.com

Turner Subscription Service, 1005 West Pines Road, Oregon, IL 61061. Phone: 800-847-4201; Fax: 815-732-4489

Back issues:

Alfred Jaeger, 66 Austin Blvd., P.O. Box 9009, Commack, NY 11725-9009. Phone: 800-969-JAGR/631-543-1500; web site: http://www.ajaeger.com

Periodicals Service Company, 11 Main Street, Germantown, NY 12526.
   Phone: 518-537-4700/518-537-5899; web site: http://www.periodicals.
   com

Many other reputable regional agencies could be added, and by dealing
locally, complaints or problems might be more expeditiously handled. Members of local school library media associations or personnel from the state
school library media agency will be able to help in choosing a suitable magazine jobber. These agencies will usually supply the necessary order forms. If
using your own form, be sure to include the following data: (1) name and
address of school library media center to which the magazine should be
addressed, (2) name and address to which bill should be sent, (3) name of
magazine and length of subscription (usually one year), (4) number of copies
wanted, (5) whether it is a new subscription or a renewal, (6) date of issue
that will begin the subscription, for example, "Begin all subscriptions with
the September issue unless otherwise noted." Most magazine agencies will
supply prospective customers with copies of catalogs that give recommendations of purchases for various types of libraries, indication of where the magazine is indexed, frequency of publication, and discount information. Some
magazines (free ones, for example) and most newspapers cannot be ordered
through magazine agencies but must be ordered separately. Evaluative criteria, tips on handling, and specific selection aids for magazines and other educational media are given in Chapter 9.

When magazines are received, they are checked in on a special magazine
file in which there are cards arranged in alphabetical order for all the magazines to which the center subscribes. Commercial library supply houses
can supply record cards to record daily, weekly, or monthly periodicals, as
well as index cabinets or book units to store these cards. In addition to the
name of magazine and space for checking when an issue is received, this
check-in card sometimes has entries for other kinds of information, such
as where the periodical is indexed and subscription expiration date. This
file should be accessible to all patrons, but it is also advisable to prepare
lists of the school library media center's magazine holdings that can be distributed within the school and placed close to the periodical indexes and
magazine storage facilities. Some circulation systems have a magazine
module that checks in magazines and then the titles are displayed on the
OPAC. Other media centers keep their magazine subscription information on spreadsheets where they record those received and those missing
items. After a new issue of a periodical is checked in, the double-faced
security strip is attached. The magazine is, then, stamped with the center's

ownership marks, placed in a single-issue magazine binder, and put on the magazine rack or other suitable display unit. The superseded issue is retired to storage. Current issues of magazines should be displayed in transparent protective covers on shelves or racks. A checking record for daily newspapers is usually unnecessary unless the media center's holdings are extensive. Weekly newspapers are processed like magazines.

Online Full-Text Magazine Databases

Overall, media centers want to decrease their expenditures on magazine orders and concentrate on ordering magazines for research as well as popular reading magazines for students to hold in their hand. The online magazine/newspaper databases are the easier source of current articles for research, searchable by subject, keyword and so forth. The cost for buying around thirty print magazines and the cost of an online magazine subscription that indexes hundreds of news magazines and journals, newspapers, and other reference resources is basically around the same price. For that reason, most media centers, find that they get more for their dollar when they subscribe to a online full-text magazine/newspaper database and then buy a few of the more popular magazines for students to browse in the media center. Subscribing to online databases normally gives the media center an enormous number of accessible magazines and journals as compared to the ones they could order as individual subscriptions from a jobber. There are also magazines/journals that are free online. The budget is impacted as a result of magazine/journals subscriptions obtained online because most media centers need to have some of the more popular magazines and journals to be available for in-house perusal by students and faculty as well as online subscriptions for research. Elementary teachers like to have hard copies of magazines, such as *Mailbox, School Days*, and so forth, so they can make copies from their activities. Usually the cost for having both the physical magazines/journals in the media center and also having a subscription online as well increases the annual budget considerably. One consideration for both is that research and pleasure reading are covered adequately and access is increased.

There are several sources for ordering online subscription magazines/newspaper databases—too many to include in this chapter. The following list is provided for those frequently used in school library media centers:

- **BCR,** 14394 East Evans Avenue, Aurora, CO 80014-1478. Phone: 800-397-1552/303-751-6277; Fax 303-751-9787; web site: http://www.bcr.

org. This collection offers a great list of online databases at discount prices for members. If you are a library in Colorado as well as several other states, you are automatically a member.

- **EBSCO (EBSCO Publishing World Headquarters),** 10 Estes Street, Ipswich, MA 01938. Phone: 978-356-6500/800-653-2726; Fax: 978-356-6565; web site: http://www.ebsco.com/home/. This database offers a variety of reference and literary sources, some award-winning. The combination of user-friendly interfaces and quality full-text content from popular magazines, education journals, newspapers, pamphlets, reports, primary source documents, biographies, almanacs, dictionaries, encyclopedias, photos, maps, flags, and other reference sources make this database a valuable resource in schools. Databases that are designed specifically for elementary, middle school, and high school make this one of the most valuable online database sources for K-12 schools.

- **Facts On File,** Facts On File, Inc., 132 W. 31st Street, 17th Floor, New York, NY 10001. Phone: 800-322-8755; Fax 800-678-3633; web site: http://www.factsonfile.com/. These reference databases are interdisciplinary, interactive, and cover subjects such as American history, careers, science, geography, careers and more.

- **Gale InfoTrac,** Gale Group, 27500 Drake Road, Farmington Hills, MI 48331-3535. Phone 800-877-GALE; Fax 800-414-5043; web site: http://www.galegroup.com. This collection is one of the largest containing fourteen databases covering such topics as computer technology, business, health, contemporary authors, and other disciplines. Full text of many articles is available online. The InfoTrac OneFile searches all the databases at once. Each collection includes magazine and journal articles, newspaper articles, and reference materials.

- **Grolier Online,** Scholastic Library Publishing, 555 Broadway, New York, NY 10012-3999. Phone: 800-621-1115, x 2543; web site: http://www.scholasticlibrary.com. This educational portal provides access to information from many sources, both print and electronic. It consists of seven databases, with the foundation being three of the best-known encyclopedias: *New Book of Knowledge, Grolier Multimedia Encyclopedia,* and *Encyclopedia Americana.* This collection is more than just a collection of encyclopedias and associated reference tools, it is also a source of over 100,000 full-text periodical articles, directly accessible from encyclopedia articles. The database is updated weekly, and offers periodical and primary source links, carefully monitored web links, dictionaries, educational games, and more.

- **OCLC FirstSearch,** OCLC Online Computer Library Center, Inc., 6565 Frantz Road, Dublin, OH 43017-3395. Phone: 614-764-6000/800-848-5878; Fax: 614-764-6096; web site: http://www.oclc.org/

firstsearch/. This database provides instant online access to more than seventy-two databases, including several OCLC databases: OCLC WorldCat, FirstSearch Electronic Collections Online, ArticleFirst, PAIS International, PapersFirst, ProceedingsFirst, and Union Lists of Periodicals. FirstSearch is a comprehensive reference service with a large collection of databases and with links to the World Wide Web, over 10 million online full text articles, and full-image articles from over 4,000 electronic journals. It also contains reference tools such as directories, almanacs and encyclopedias.

- **Opposing Viewpoints Resource Center,** Gale Group, P.O. Box 9187, Farmington Hills, MI 48333-9187. Phone: 800-877-GALE; web site: http://www.galeschools.com. This database offers overviews of history and the controversial issues that students research most as well as full-text articles from more than twenty-five major newspapers and periodicals. The contents of Gale's *Information Plus* series provides current statistics, government data, laws, legislation and more.

- **ProQuest,** ProQuest Company, 300 N. Zeeb Road, Ann Arbor, MI 48103. Phone: 734-761-4700; web site: http://www.umi.com/. This collection contains millions of articles originally published in some 3,000 journals, magazines, and newspapers. The newspaper collection contains full-text newspapers including *New York Times, Minneapolis Star Tribune, Wall Street Journal, Washington Post,* and *Los Angeles Times.* The psychology collection includes full-text articles of other 300 journals, magazines, and other publications in psychology, sociology, and related fields.

- **Reader's Guide Full Text,** H.W. Wilson, 950 University Avenue, Bronx, NY 10452-4297. Phone: 800-367-6770; web site: www. hwwilson.com. This database is a comprehensive index to popular literature, covering all subjects such as education, politics, history, science, sports, and more as well as current events from 1983 to present. It indexes and abstracts over 240 popular general interest periodicals. Full text is provided from over 120 of these periodicals.

- **Science Online,** American Association for the Advancement of Science (AAAS), 1200 New York Avenue NW, Washington, DC 20005. Telephone: 202-326-6400/800-322-8755; web site: http://www.scienceonline.org/. All content on this database is divided into science curriculum content established by the National Science Education Standards. It enables teachers to access diagrams, definitions, biographies, and essays in a specific subject area or science discipline. Content of the essays and diagrams is organized by the National Science Content Standards and Benchmarks for grades six through twelve. By offering hundreds of diagrams, *Science Online* allows a researcher to follow them to a definition and a related essay or biography. This database provides a comprehensive look at general science. Since science is a subject that is most difficult to keep current in media centers, this database may be the answer. This database is the winner of the "Readers' Choice Award for Digital Reference Tools, 2001."

- **SIRS,** SIRS Publishing, Inc., P.O. Box 272348, Boca Raton, FL 33427-2348. Phone: 800-232-SIRS/561-994-0079; Fax 561-994-4704; web site: http://www.sirs.com/. *SIRS Knowledge Source* is a comprehensive database portal, updated daily, which is comprised of several distinct reference databases including SIRS Researcher®, SIRS Government Reporter®, SIRS Renaissance® and SKS WebSelect™ with available links to SIRS Interactive Citizenship™, SIRS Discoverer® and Discoverer WebFind™. It provides information on social issues, science, history, government, the arts and humanities. It contains full-text articles and Internet resources from thousands of domestic and international publications and respected organizations. It includes an up-to-the-minute coverage of breaking news events. An interactive dictionary and thesaurus complete the reference package.

Online Encyclopedias and Other Reference Materials

The ordering of encyclopedias and other reference materials for the media center is an evolving process. No longer are printed sets of encyclopedias adequate for research. Most media centers need not only printed encyclopedias but also those online or on CD-ROMs as well. The printed versions are very expensive compared to those available online or on CD-ROMs. As a budget consideration, online reference materials such as dictionaries, almanacs, atlases, encyclopedias and so forth are much more affordable. Students seem to prefer online reference sources instead of printed versions. For the cost of one printed set of encyclopedias, most media centers can have an array of online encyclopedias as well as almanacs, dictionaries, thesauri, and atlases to name a few. The online versions normally connect the user to other related magazine articles. Because of tight budgets in schools, it is predicted that more media centers will rely on the online versions of reference sources because they are less expensive and easier to use than the printed versions.

Careful consideration needs to be taken when ordering online items (magazines, newspapers, encyclopedias). Although online products may be cheaper, there is always a continuing expense every year. Frequently, media center budgets fluctuate from year to year. For example, there may be money in one year's budget to buy a printed encyclopedia or to subscribe to several online. The following year, there may be no money for either. In that case, the media specialist might want to consider buying the printed copy when money is available so there will be at least one new encyclopedia in the media center for those years when money is not available.

Monopoly Items and Standing Orders

Some materials are available from only one source and cannot be ordered through a jobber. These materials are sometimes referred to as monopoly items and often include materials for which no library discount is given. If such an item is inadvertently ordered from the jobber, an "Order Directly from Publisher" report will probably appear on a future invoice.

Although library media specialists will ordinarily evaluate each item individually, occasionally, as in the case of encyclopedia yearbooks or other annuals, the center will automatically want future volumes. To save the inconvenience of constant reordering, an arrangement known as standing orders can be made whereby the jobber or publisher will automatically ship specified series or continuations to the center. This arrangement for ordering materials needs to be discussed with the school bookkeeper before making an initial order.

Pamphlet and Other Vertical File Materials

There have been recent articles about vertical files saying they are obsolete because of the Internet; however, they are useful for students doing research and should not be discarded so easily. It is true that the Internet does allow fast access to current material, but students who have access to current vertical file materials find it to be a source where information from a variety of sources can be found in one place. Students love to use the vertical file because it saves them a lot of time when doing research. Of course, everything depends on the quality of the vertical file in each media center.

Because much of the material for the vertical file is either free or inexpensive, acquisition of this material is best done at the single-school level rather than involving the business office in a multitude of small transactions. If possible, the library media center should have petty cash funds available so that checks or money orders can accompany requests. If these funds are not available through the central office, perhaps monies raised through book fairs, parent-teacher organizations or similar activities could be earmarked for this purpose. To facilitate the acquisition of pamphlets, most media centers develop a form letter or postcard requesting the material. For free materials, space should be left in the letter for the address, an indication of where the material was listed (such as Vertical File Index), title(s) or subject of the material requested, and number of copies needed. The letter should also contain the address to which the material should be sent and a sincere "thank you" for their generosity and help. Letters involving transmittal of money should also contain a statement, "Enclosed please find a check (money order) for. . . ."

When the material has been received and screened for suitability (see specific criteria and selection aids for pamphlets and clippings in Chapter 9), ownership marks and date of receipt should be stamped on the material. (This will be of value for future weeding of the file.) Because these items, usually referred to generically as *ephemeral material*, do not warrant the expenditure of time and money for cataloging, they are housed in file cabinets, usually in hanging file folders (clippings and pictures might also be placed in manila envelopes for safekeeping), and arranged alphabetically by subject. The subject lists used to organize these holdings should correspond to the one used for other materials (such as Sears List of Subject Headings or the Library of Congress Subject Headings). To direct patrons to this ephemeral material, a brief MARC record with the appropriate subject tag can be created to point them to the materials in the vertical file. Some libraries prefer to have an online document showing the vertical file subjects. An example of authors included in the vertical file can be found at the following web site: http://nutrias.org/~nopl/info/louinfo/vf/vfauth.htm

Government Documents

One of the easiest ways to stretch the center's acquisition budget is to investigate and utilize the wide variety of materials available from government agencies. Some materials are free; others are generally inexpensive when compared with their commercial counterparts. The range of subject matter is as wide as the types of formats and depth of coverage. The Government Printing Office (GPO) is the major publisher of U.S. government documents. These documents are distributed by the Superintendent of Documents, or SuDocs. The full address is Superintendent of Documents, Government Printing Office, 732 North Capitol Street NW., Washington, DC 20402-0003. Phone: 202-512-1803/866-512-1800; Fax: 202-512-1293; web address: http://www.gpo.gov.

The many bibliographies of government documents (some are described in Chapter 9) detail the instructions for ordering. The basic information needed is title, date, and stock number. Payment can be made in a variety of ways, for example, by check, money order, or use of a deposit account, or credit cards, including MasterCard, Visa, Discover, and American Express. Deposit accounts must be a minimum of $50. In addition to the mail-order service, there are approximately fifteen GPO bookstores located in major cities throughout the country, each stocking about 1,500 of the more popular titles, and offering subscriptions and electronic products. Two other important sources are The Consumer Information Center, Pueblo, CO 81009, http://www.pueblo.gsa.gov and the Library of Congress, Washington, DC 20540. To purchase government publications, contact the U.S. government online bookstore at http://bookstore.gpo.gov/ or the U.S. government subscription catalog at http://bookstore.gpo.gov/subscriptions.

Centralized Ordering and Processing

Processing at the single-school level has been unsatisfactory in several respects, mostly related to the time factor. Centralized processing or use of commercial sources relieves the individual media specialist of this responsibility. Much has been written about the advantages of central or commercial processing. In summary, the advantages are:

- Personnel in the school library media center are freed to supply increased services to patrons.
- Substantial savings in time, labor, and money are produced through larger discounts from jobbers, utilizing clerks for routine jobs, and reducing duplication of effort.
- A large-scale, systematized workflow produces greater efficiency and reduces processing time.
- There is uniformity in cataloging and classification.
- Business routines are centralized and simplified.
- Union catalogs to facilitate interlibrary loan and prevent unnecessary duplication of expensive materials can be prepared easily.

Some of the larger school systems have developed processing centers that work very well for all school library media centers in the district. Normally, there are two ways that processing is handled in a centralized system. The first way is a system by which materials are ordered and processed within a centralized unit and personnel prepare the processing and cataloging of materials. The second way is a system where a district profile is developed for all media centers in the district and vendors provide the processing and cataloging according to specifications. Finally, some media centers are on their own when it comes to cataloging and processing.

In the first system, a method for handling centralized processing may be done where materials are delivered to a central library office. At this processing center, materials arrive and personnel completely process the materials for delivery to the individual media centers. They may order the kits for processing materials from the jobbers and then use a cataloging utility to copy-catalog materials in the MARC format before delivery to the schools. When the materials arrive at the school, they are ready to be put on the shelves. Marcive has a pay-as-you-go copy cataloging system. One can search their database of records online, request items for download, and pay a fee. An extra fee is paid to retrieve records from the AV Access database for videos, DVDs, and software MARC records. These records will be formatted according to a profile submitted with Marcive in advance, so there is very little editing that needs to be done.

In the second centralized system, a MARC record profile is created for all the schools in the district so that all schools do their processing the same way. The profile is sent to the major vendors, jobbers, and publishers used by the district, that then give a price for cataloging and processing according to the school district's specifications. To make certain that the MARC records can be loaded, the vendor agrees to format the MARC disc a specific way to avoid batch errors. The vendors determine a cost for fully processed and cataloged materials to be delivered to the school district based on the MARC record profile. Vendors who agree to provide the cataloging and full book or audiovisual material processing according to the profile are then added to a preferred vendor list distributed to all the media centers in the district. The MARC disks are mailed to a central processing office in the district where the records are batch loaded into the system. Some districts use special programs that do not allow items already in the system to be loaded. If a MARC record already exists, the holding information is transferred to the existing record in the database. Once the records are loaded into the database, the individual school library media specialist can go into the database, attach any extra holding information needed, scan in a barcode number (if barcodes were not ordered with the MARC disk) and then the item is immediately available for viewing on the OPAC.

Normally, most media centers in a centralized system receive MARC records on disk for about eighty percent of the items purchased. The rest of the time, such as when media specialists can't wait to get popular titles into their media centers and they go shopping at a local bookstore, or when books are donated, or when libraries get free books as a result of a book fair, then some cataloging is done. Original cataloging may be done or cataloging that uses a MARC bibliographic utility, such as ITS.MARC from The Library Corporation. There is normally some editing that needs to be done to the MARC records received from vendors.

There are several alternative approaches to establishing a central processing center in each school district, and local conditions differ so considerably that in some cases efficiency and economy might suggest other solutions. Commercial cataloging is now available at reasonable prices through several companies. Although their major strength has been in the area of book processing, coverage for processing non-book materials is also available. A web site from the University of California, Berkeley gives a list of vendors who provide AV MARC records for libraries: http://www. lib.berkeley.edu/MRC/vrt/vrtcatvendors.htm. Regardless of the pattern adopted, media should arrive at the school ready for use.

Finally, there are individual media centers that determine their own processing requirements and contract with vendors to meet their needs. The system used by individual media centers is basically the same process as centralized processing but is done for only one school. This method is not efficient for a whole school district because each school may be doing something entirely different. Should the school district decide to have a union catalog in the future, this system will result in expenditures of time and money for data work to create uniform MARC records. Forward-thinking media specialists need to consider this possibility as they make decisions about how to handle cataloging in the district. Some media centers, because of money constraints, still do their own processing and cataloging of materials. Processing at the single-school level can be confined to those few educational materials produced within the school and those items purchased locally or those received as gifts. Novice media specialists need to know where information can be found to assist them in their daily routines, such as cataloging and processing. The Oklahoma Department of Education's web site contains some excellent information about ordering materials, shipment arrivals, processing of books and non-print materials, and more. The classifying/cataloging process is discussed including downloading MARC records. The URL for this web site is: http://title3.sde.state.ok.us/library/Procedures %20Manual%20Elite/acquisition.html.

CLASSIFICATION AND CATALOGING

In organizing a collection a media specialist should keep accessibility and user convenience uppermost in mind. Materials on the same subject should be integrated and stored together if at all possible. Where physical conditions dictate housing parts of the collection by format, the same criteria involving accessibility should apply equally to all formats. Traffic flow, economical use of space, and user safety are factors of importance in deciding organizational patterns, but these patterns should be sufficiently flexible to allow for some modification.

Classification

Classification is the systematic arrangement of materials into groups according to some predetermined list of criteria. Of the number of classification schemes in existence, the one that has been almost universally adopted in media centers is the Dewey Decimal Classification (DDC), developed by Melvil Dewey after his careful study of several systems used to classify knowledge. Dewey began work on his system in 1872 while a student library assistant at Amherst College in Massachusetts. When it was published in 1876, it was greeted unenthusiastically by many librarians, but its growth in popularity paralleled the tremendous library expansion in the twentieth century. Its major rival is the Library of Congress (LC) classification system, which was developed in 1897 specifically for the recataloging of the Library of Congress's vast collection. The LC system uses both letters and numbers as location devices, and because of the complexity and the minuteness of its breakdown of subject matter, it has been adopted only for use with large or specialized collections. For help with Dewey Classification, OCLC provides a tutorial at the following web site: http://www.oclc.org/dewey/about/tutorials.htm. DDC has many advantages for use in school media centers:

1. It brings materials on the same subject together in a logical and uniform sequence.
2. It is sufficiently simple to be understood by both staff and patrons without frequent referral to classification schedules.
3. Materials organized by this system can be found and retrieved quickly.
4. Because the system moves from large subject areas to more specialized ones through the addition of numbers, the degree of sophistication of the classification can vary with the size and nature of collections.

5. It is the system most familiar to students because it is used most often in media centers.

6. Commercial cataloging sources as well as standard bibliographies and media-reviewing tools extensively utilize this classification system.

Some media centers use DDC for the print collection but have devised other classifying arrangements for audiovisual items. The simplest and most common variation is to label the material with the type of material, such as video, and to use DDC the same way it is used with books. This method of classifying audiovisual materials allows all subject areas to be shelved together. Some media centers store materials by format, for example, all CDs are shelved together. It is recommended that DDC be used for classifying all types of media.

Cataloging

The online pubic access catalog (OPAC) is an index to the media center's collection and thus is the basic key to center resources. Its primary purpose is to indicate the materials that are in the collection and their location. It also provides bibliographic data and a description of content for each item. Because locating nonprint materials is done primarily from the subject approach, the subject field has become the largest and most-used part of the OPAC. Of the several types of entries that may be in the OPAC, the three basic types are: main entry (author, artist, composer, issuing agency), title (with many such non-book materials as transparencies, the title frequently is also the main entry), and subject. Other added entries may include (joint authors, illustrators), analytical data (specific content), and cross-references. Although some media centers still have shelf lists, it is not necessary to maintain one now that computers can keep a record of the inventory. They are no longer needed because computer printouts can provide the necessary information. Additionally, inventory is normally done with a portable barcode reader lessening the need for a shelf list. Multiple copies of materials can be determined by viewing a report of the entire collection that most automated library systems can generate.

Library of Congress MARC records

In 1911, the Library of Congress began its system of printing catalog cards and offering them to libraries at a reasonable rate. Since then many commercial sources have developed and marketed cataloging services.

Most libraries use two Library of Congress services as the basis of their catalogs. The first service is known as MARC records. In 1968, the Library of Congress began distributing their bibliographic or cataloging records on Machine-Readable Cataloging (MARC) magnetic tapes or CD-ROMs. Currently, the Library of Congress Cataloging MARC Distribution Service offers MARC 21 bibliographic, authority and classification records via Internet FTP (file transfer protocol), tape cartridge or 9-track tape reel. They provide MARC 21 records for books, maps, music, serials, and some audiovisual material such as sound recordings. Library of Congress offers MARC records that can be downloaded online. It provides cataloging for materials in hundreds of languages. A search of the Library of Congress online catalog can be done from the following web site: http://catalog.loc.gov/. A search of their authority files can be done from: http://authorities.loc.gov/.

The second service, which can also be included in the MARC database, is known as Cataloging in Publication (CIP) and was begun in 1971. Publishers submit galleys or advance publication data to the Library of Congress, whose catalogers determine the Dewey and LC classification numbers, LC card number, and basic cataloging information, including added entries and, in the case of children's books, a brief annotation. This information now appears in LC catalog card format on the verso of the title page in published books. Some libraries that do their own cataloging use these entries for preliminary cataloging before the actual cards arrive. Some commercial catalogers use CIP data to make cataloging information available on or before the actual publication date of the book.

The third service, a Retrospective Conversion Service (Select MARC) was started in 1989 to provide MARC records for books, serials, maps, and audiovisual materials for libraries that needed to convert their collections into the MARC format for use with automated online circulation systems. This service is no longer offered by the Library of Congress.

A fourth service of the Library of Congress Cataloging Distribution Service, Alert, allows the library to select specific subjects of interest for their collection. The Alert service provides current full cataloging as well as Cataloging in Publication (CIP) records. The Alert service provides up-to-date bibliographic records for books and magazines in over 2,000 subject categories before they are published, usually three to six months in advance. This is a costly service, and one that few media centers would be able to afford.

Because most libraries are automated, the MARC records continue to be a major need to provide descriptive information for library materials. Fritz and Fritz (2003) define MARC as:

a standard for entering bibliographic information into a computer record that can be used by a library automation system to provide a library catalog. (p. xiii)

Cataloging experts agree that all libraries need to follow the same rules when cataloging materials. The nationally accepted standard in this country is the Anglo-American Cataloging Rules or AACR2. The MARC format is the standard by which libraries provide information about library materials in machine-readable form suitable for online public access catalogs (OPACS). Libraries use either Library of Congress Subject Headings (LCSH) or Sears List of Subject Headings. As a general rule, Library of Congress subject headings are used most frequently when libraries want to share resources. Media centers are switching to Library of Congress subject headings in resource-sharing situations because it provides consistency across library catalogs. Most media centers use Abridged Dewey Decimal Classification rather than Library of Congress classification system to classify the materials. The main purpose of both classification systems is to put together materials of similar content. MARC allows libraries to share records and to be consistent with other library's records. MARC allows media centers to plan ahead and to be prepared for sharing their records and resources with other media centers or other types of libraries when the time comes to develop a union catalog. MARC allows media centers to share their resources through interlibrary loan with other libraries. MARC records usually contain the following information:

- **Location device**. Usually the call number, consisting of the Dewey decimal number and the first two or three letters of the main entry (in the case of biographies, the name of the person written about is used).
- **Main entry**. In book materials, the author or person chiefly responsible for the content.
- **Title (and subtitle).**
- **Medium identification**. Video, CD, transparency and so forth.
- **Additional main entry information.** Such as coauthor, illustrator, editor or narrator, for example.
- **Imprint**. Publisher, producer, manufacturer, and copyright date.
- **Collation**. Description of the physical quality of the material, for example, number of pages or volumes, frames, sound or silent, length of running time, color or black and white. When applicable, a series note is included.
- **Annotation or contents summary**. Optional.

- **Tracings.** List of headings for which additional entries have been prepared, such as subject headings, analytics and so forth.

When necessary, this MARC data can be modified to make a local OPAC as simple and efficient as possible while still supplying the necessary information and points of access the patron will need. Some possible shortcuts are to include statements on illustrators, joint authors, translators, and series only if deemed necessary; to assign subject headings only to major topics. Use analytics only when deemed necessary to provide patron access. For example, subject analytics for collective biographies or title and author analytics for story collections. Some pointers on preparing specific parts of the MARC record are:

1. **Author entry:** Use the author's name as it appears on the title page (but of the work; with nonprint media, frequently the title. Check the OPAC for possible variations). It is always a good idea to decide on the entry to be used and keep an authority file for reference. Anthologies are entered under the editor, but translations are listed under the original author. Pseudonyms should be used (as Mark Twain). Corporate entries are arranged from the highest to the lowest appropriate level of the organization (such as U.S., Department of Agriculture; ALA, Young Adult Services Division); serial publications such as almanacs and encyclopedias are entered under the title as main entry.

2. **Descriptive material.** Use the title as it appears on the title page. Always include imprint information (publisher and date) and number of pages (or other appropriate format information in the case of AV material), but the inclusion of other descriptive material should be weighed against usefulness.

3. **Classification and tracings.** After examining the dust jacket, table of contents, and preface, determine the principle subject of the work and, using Sears and Dewey, assign subject headings and classification number (check OPAC for integration with the main collection), assign additional subject headings when necessary (never more than four per title). Add additional tracings when necessary, such as an additional title entry for a volume that contains two novels. If the subject of the book is also the title, for example, Astronomy or Albert Einstein, make only a subject entry.

4. **Cross-references.** Check in Sears/LC to make certain that proper *see* and *see also* references exist in the OPAC for the subjects assigned. When the work slip has been completed, double check the OPAC to see that all entries have been properly entered.

Bibliographic Utilities

The 1970s saw the growth of a number of online bibliographic utilities. Most of these utilities focus on supplying cataloging information to member libraries. Each maintains a large bibliographic database or union catalog and also supplies, with varying degrees of access, additional services such as interlibrary loan, serials control, and acquisition subsystems. However, the supplying of cataloging information is the key service supplied by these organizations. A bibliographic utility is a vendor that provides libraries access to bibliographic and authority records, in the MARC format. Their purpose is to offer cooperative cataloging among libraries.

Many independent regional networks contract with these bibliographic utilities to supply services to their member libraries. Therefore, many local libraries utilize the services of these large utilities, but through the conduit of a regional network. These bibliographic utilities provide cooperative cataloging records, which allow resource sharing through interlibrary loan. At present, the two largest bibliographic utilities are: (1) RLIN, for Research Libraries Information Network, now owned and managed by the Research Library Group (RLG), it confines its activities to large academic libraries and (2) OCLC (Online Computer Library Center, Inc.), the largest and most used network. Bibliographic utilities are provided to smaller libraries, such as school library media centers, through CD-ROM formats or through FTP online bibliographic utilities. Rather than provide a list of bibliographic utilities vendors in this chapter, one is available from the Texas State Library and Archives Commission web site: http://www.tsl.state.tx.us/ld/pubs/bibutilvendors/. Because a large percentage of users are affiliated with OCLC, let us look more closely at how their cataloging system operates.

OCLC (Online Computer Library Center)

OCLC is a nonprofit membership organization serving 43,559 libraries in 86 countries and territories around the world. Membership in OCLC is a unique cooperative venture, giving libraries global access to all services and databases, including WorldCat. Together OCLC member libraries make up the world's largest consortium. OCLC's online database holds over 49 million cataloging records created by libraries around the world, with a new record added every fifteen seconds. The records span over 4,000 years of recorded knowledge with 400 languages represented. Through original input cataloging, users contribute most of the nonbibliographic records to the catalog; the rest comes from records generated at the national libraries (for example, Library of Congress MARC records). Users indicate that they have a ninety-four percent success rate in locating the item being searched. OCLC's FirstSearch service offers users access to seventy-two databases including familiar names from leading information providers as well as resources provided exclusively by OCLC. OCLC databases include: WorldCat, ArticleFirst, Electronic Collections Online, PAIS International, PapersFirst, ProceedingsFirst, and the OCLC Union Lists of Periodicals.

OCLC offers several services and databases, including (1) *collection management, cataloging and metadata* which allows libraries to process materials more economically, get them ready for circulation faster as well as providing more access options; (2) *reference* which provides access to abstracts, full text indexes and bibliography through online, interlibrary loan, document supplier, or library archive; (3) *resource sharing* through the OCLC interlibrary loan service (ILL); (4) *databases* such as WorldCat (the OCLC Online Union Catalog) and First Search which provide the world's largest databases of bibliographic information; and (5) *digitization and preservation resources.* OCLC also offers software (CatME for Windows) that combines interactive online searching with offline editing from the media center's computer work station. Through CatME, the media specialist can access WorldCat (OCLC's union catalog and authority file). The software allows editing of records offline without being connected to OCLC and it allows the option to work online. The address for OCLC is: Online Computer Library Center, 6565 Franz Road, Dublin, OH 43017-3395.

Commercial Sources of Cataloging

There are many sources of commercial cataloging services available. The largest distributor is still the Library of Congress Cataloging Distribution Service (CDS), but for school library media centers, LC's product does not have the customized features available through commercial outlets. CDS provides the most current cataloging, including records for books about to be published. Some companies, however, supply cataloging and processing services only when the book is also purchased from them. For example, Baker & Taylor allows registered customers to access MARC records from their web site and download them for items purchased. This system gives customers instant MARC records just by surfing the web. Other vendors supply these services with or without book orders (Brodart) while others sell cataloging services exclusively (Marcive).

Using MARC records supplemented by in-house cataloging, many commercial producers now have holdings of a vast number of titles. The following list of vendors offer MARC records. Their services may include distributing MARC 21 records, such as records for copy cataloging, records supplied with materials, records used for recon purposes, updated records, conversion services, and so forth. For more information about these vendors, please see their corresponding web sites.

- **Brodart Retrospective Conversion** http://www.brodart.com/automation/proacacus.htm
- **Follett Alliance Plus** http://www.fsc.follett.com/products/allianceplus/
- **Follett Authority Record Program** http://www.fsc.follett.com/products/authority_record/index.cfm
- **The Library Corporation's ITS.MARC™** http://www.itsmarc.com/
- **LibraryCom by CASPR** http://www.caspr.com
- **Library Technologies, Inc.** http://www.authoritycontrol.com
- **MarciveWeb SELECT** http:// www.marcive.com
- **MARC Link Retrospective Conversion** http://www.marclink.com
- **NOTEbookS MARC Import** http:// www.rasco.com
- **Sagebrush Corporation** http://www.sagebrushcorp.com/dataservices
- **SLC Library Cataloguing Services** http:// www.slc.bc.ca/

In addition to this list, Ron Sherman-Peterson (2003) provides a cataloging resource directory that can be found at this URL: http://www.bsd405.org/libraries/card.htm

For the school library media center that does not have access to a centralized processing agency, the use of commercial cataloging and processing has many advantages:

- **Time**. The chief gain is in time saved by the library media staff to free them to supply more services to their patrons.
- **Cost**. Weighing the cost of in-house cataloging and the time for inputting data in the computer against the value of purchasing MARC records on disk or buying the kits makes economical sense. Sets of processing materials or kits can be purchased for under a dollar, slightly more with full processing. It would be impossible for the single library media center or even an average-size school district to come close to this level of economy, even with the most efficient operation.

- **Flexibility**. A number of options concerning specific cataloging requirements are available. As a basic choice, most offer: (1) LC classification with LC subject headings, (2) unabridged Dewey classification with LC subject headings, and (3) abridged Dewey classification with Sears subject headings (most frequently used by school library media centers).

- **Quality**. The copy is prepared by professional catalogers and, therefore, the quality should be uniformly high, certainly greater than the caliber that could be produced locally.

The salient disadvantage in using commercial cataloging and processing is the need to adhere to cataloging decisions made outside the library media center. In some cases, for example, where subject headings are specifically modified to fit particular curriculum requirements, it is difficult to adjust to outside decisions. Therefore, when choosing a jobber that supplies commercial cataloging services, one must be particularly aware of the degree of individualization of service available. There are vendors that offer media centers the option to order MARC records and adjust the DDS numbers to fit the center's cataloging requirements. In evaluating these cataloging and processing services, the following criteria will be helpful:

1. **Types of materials cataloged:** books, paperbacks, audiovisual material, and out-of-print materials.

2. **Services offered:** full processing, partial, kits, or disks only.

3. **Options allowed in cataloging:** nature of specific requirements accommodated: classification systems, types of subject headings, flexibility in call number choice, choice of alternate symbols (such as F or Fic, R or Ref, 921 or B), ease in changing these specifications when needed, and number of options available.

4. **Consistency in cataloging**.

5. **Quality of processing:** plastic jackets, pockets, date-due slips, spine markings, bar codes, ship installation of theft-detection devices, and binding for paperback books.

6. **Clarity and readability of products.**

7. **Cost:** in line with competition.

8. **Ordering procedures:** kinds of ordering information accepted, for example ISBN, LC number, or regular bibliographic information (author, title, publisher), or ordering method, and minimum order requirements.

9. **Speed of delivery:** most suppliers guarantee that orders will be filled within one week of receiving method of shipping (ordinary mail, UPS, first class), quality of packaging.

10. **Method of payment:** billing procedures.
11. **Order fulfillment record:** percentage of orders actually received, number of MARC records received on disk, back-ordering arrangements.

Media centers catalog materials in many different ways. Original cataloging (that is, done for the first time) is still done in many media centers, especially for local materials that are not being included on bibliographic databases. Book and audiovisual material jobbers offer MARC records to be downloaded into the OPAC for each items purchased. Once the record is downloaded, editing of the records can be done to fit each individual media center's collection. Many media centers subscribe to a bibliographic database available on CD-ROM that contains MARC records for recently published titles. The initial cost for the CD-ROM and the on-line bibliographic utilities are basically the same. The advantage of the CD-ROM is that there are no online fees for use; however, most online bibliographic utilities offer offline options to correct bibliographic information. The major disadvantage of CD-ROMs is the lag time of the information from publishing to the database. Several online bibliographic utility vendors provide a CD-ROM version for cataloging purposes that allows the media center to maintain their MARC records completely in-house.

The CD-ROM database can be searched using the LC number, the ISBN (International Standard Book Number), and other bibliographic information. Once a record match is found, it can be downloaded on a disk or directly into the OPAC. Other media centers use an online bibliographic utility to download MARC records.

The way the system works is that the library that catalogs an item in MARC the first time follows standard cataloging rules; the record is then added to the union catalog where other catalogers download an exact copy of the record they want into their library automation system. This is called copy cataloging. Most catalogers who do copy cataloging do some editing of the records to fit their own library.

When doing copy cataloging, records can be retrieved through a variety of methods using various search keys: author (main or added entry), title, government document number, LC card number, ISSN, ISBN, or special OCLC numbers. When the user is satisfied that the record displayed on the computer screen is the same as the data wanted, the record is downloaded and imported into the library automation system. This sounds like a complicated process, but in reality, it is much easier than original cataloging. Most media centers are required to do some original cataloging for some materials. It is good to remember that copy cataloging is cost-effective because of the time it saves the media specialist.

Tips for the Do-It-Yourself Cataloger

When it is necessary to do original cataloging within the library media center, it should be done as simply and as quickly as possible. Here are some pointers:

1. Assemble basic tools to help you. Unless you catalog using the Library of Congress system, the four basic documents are:

Abridged Dewey decimal classification and relative index (13th ed.). (1997). Albany, NY: Forest Press.

Anglo-American cataloging rules. (2002). (2003 update.) Chicago: American Library Association.

Library of Congress subject headings (23rd ed.). (2000). Washington, DC: Library of Congress, Catalog Distribution Service.

Sears List of subject headings (17th ed.). (2000). Bronx, NY: H.W. Wilson.

Some cataloging manuals that are useful as references include:

Bowman, J. H. (2002). *Essential cataloging.* New York: Neal-Schuman.

Byrne, Deborah J. (1998). *MARC manual: Understanding and using MARC records.* Westport, CT: Libraries Unlimited.

Evans, G. Edward, et al. (2002). *Introduction to technical services* (7th ed.). Westport, CT: Libraries Unlimited.

Fritz, Deborah A. (2004). *Cataloging with AACR2 and MARC21: For books, electronic resources, sound recordings, videorecordings, and serials* (2nd ed.). Chicago: American Library Association.

Fritz, Deborah A. & Fritz, Richard J. (2003). *MARC 21 for everyone.* Chicago: American Library Association.

Intner, Sheila. (2001). *Standard cataloging for school and public libraries* (3rd ed.). Westport, CT: Libraries Unlimited.

Maxwell, Robert L. (2004). Maxwell's handbook for AACR2: Explaining and illustrating the Anglo-American cataloging rules through the 2003 update. Chicago: American Library Association.

Mortimer, Mary. (2000). *Learn descriptive cataloging.* Lanham, MD: Scarecrow Press.

Mortimer, Mary. (2000). *Learn Dewey decimal classification (edition 21).* Lanham, MD: Scarecrow Press.

Olson, Nancy B. (1998). *Cataloging of audiovisual materials and other special materials: A manual based on AACR2* (4th ed.). DeKalb, IL: Minnesota Scholarly Press; distributed by Soldier Creek Press.

Piepenburg, Scott. (2003). *Easy MARC: Incorporating format integration* (4th ed.). San Jose, CA: F&W Associates.

Taylor, Arlene G. (2002). *Wynar's introduction to cataloging and classification* (9th ed.). Westport, CT: Libraries Unlimited.

Zuiderveld, Sharon. (Ed.). (1998). *Cataloging correctly for kids: An introduction to the tools* (3rd ed.). Chicago: American Library Association.

Specifically to help with nonprint materials there is *Cataloging Nonprint and Internet Resources* (2002) by Mary Beth Weber (Neal-Schuman). Very basic material is also covered in Ann M. Wasman's (1998) *Steps to Service,* American Library Association.

2. Become familiar with these tools, particularly with the basic structure of the Dewey decimal system and the methods of subdivision. The introduction to the abridged edition is helpful, as is the prefatory material in Sears and the LC Subject headings.

3. Do not catalog in a vacuum. Use the resources within the existing collection and the OPAC to help. For example, use MARC records as examples to follow concerning format. These records are particularly helpful in cataloging AV materials. Not only will this promote consistency in format, but also it will help solve problems involving the contents of the OPAC records. In this way you will be cataloging within a fixed framework and into an existing collection. Also, frequent referral to your copy of Sears (provided it has been marked properly and kept up-to-date) will be invaluable in assigning subject headings that are consistent with those already used.

4. Know the existing policies within the library media center concerning cataloging and classification, for example, the number of letters used from author's last name in the call number, the classification of biography (B, 921, and so on), use or nonuse of Cutter book numbers, special treatment of reference works or other materials.

5. Use blank 3 × 5 inch slips or cards as workslips. These cards are convenient as data is entered into the computer.

Processing

Ownership marks should be stamped on all library materials. With books, this is usually done on the page after the title page, along the edges, and on the book pocket. If the material has not been processed commercially, a few additional steps are necessary. For example, when processing kits are not used, a book pocket and date due card, and a pressure-sensitive label with the call number on it should be prepared. Security strips should also be attached to the material being processed. The physical processing of the material can be completed manually, especially for those items that receive original cataloging. A bar code should be attached to the book or audiovisual material. Most vendors with commercial processing will attach plastic book covers and bar codes as well as security strips to the materials ordered. Plastic covers are often used over dust jackets. They are attractive and also protect the binding. It has been estimated that these covers double the shelf life of a book.

The processing of audiovisual materials is done using the same general principles as books, but because of their format, the procedures are different. Ownership tape, purchased from a supply catalog, such as Highsmith, which has customized printing of the name and address of the school media center, is attached to all materials. Some media centers prefer to use an ownership stamp with the name of the media center and address. In the case of kits including several items, such as videos, teacher's guides, maps and so forth, ownership tape is attached on each individual item. A pocket is prepared to hold the date due card and a pressure-sensitive tape with the call number is attached to a specified place on the material. If the audiovisual material is a kit, a pocket is prepared showing the contents of the kit (for inventory purposes). Separate labels will be prepared for all items in the kit. Bar codes are attached to the material for circulation.

Many of these processing procedures are routine and, providing that the steps are logically organized and flow easily, can often be handled by students or other volunteers. The organization and delegation of these routines, including acquiring and organizing library material, should not be so time-consuming that they take the professional staff away from more essential aspects of the program.

LOCAL PRODUCTION OF MATERIALS

Although the range and variety of commercially prepared educational materials are expensive and increasing at a rapid rate, there will always be a need in schools for educational materials that are useful only in a specific local situation and are, therefore, not available for purchase. The school library media center is normally the headquarters for the production of a wide variety of educational materials suitable for learning experiences unique to a particular school. This section describes the major types of local-production equipment and supplies found in many school library media centers and their major uses. Specific equipment items that accept both commercially and locally prepared materials, are described in Chapter 9, as are the general criteria for selecting equipment. These criteria may also be applied to equipment for local production. Specific emphasis, however, should be placed on versatility, for example, many laminating machines can also be used to produce color-lift transparencies, and photocopiers can be used to make transparencies.

Poster Maker Machines

With this machine, the use of posters in the media center and throughout the school takes on a new dimension. The machine uses rolls of paper similar to bulletin board paper. Huge posters can be made with this machine. Several applications for using posters might be PTA night, posters for high school sports events, a banner for a school store with items and prices listed, to name a few.

Art Waxing Machine

One of the popular machines in media centers is the art waxing machine. When making posters, the machine puts a waxy finish on posters, which makes them stiff and allows them to adhere to the wall. Posters roll through a machine that is similar to a laminator. When used along with the poster making machine, the media center has tremendous applications to try both in the media center and throughout the school.

Mounting and Laminating Equipment

A number of techniques can be used for mounting flat pictures. The conventional method using rubber cement requires no special equipment, but the process is time-consuming and the results can vary considerably in quality. A faster and more professional-looking product can be obtained by using the dry-mount technique. Dry-mount tissue is very thin paper coated on each side with adhesive that becomes sticky when heat and pressure are applied. A dry-mount press and tacking iron needs to be part of the media center's basic equipment. Large maps or charts that require rolling and folding for convenient storage may also be mounted by this process by using a special backing cloth coated with adhesive on only one side. The center's dry-mount press should be big enough to handle the largest size material that it expects to mount and laminate.

Laminating, or affixing a transparent protective film to the face of a picture, can also be done in the dry-mount press. Also available are laminating acetates that may be applied by hand or with a cold-process laminating machine. Laminating machines that use the roll process to laminate materials is one of the most efficient machines for lamination. It takes only seconds to laminate pictures, charts, and other flat materials such as posters.

Photocopying Machines

Multiple copies of printed material for use by teachers and students may be produced in a variety of ways, the simplest and most common of which is photocopying. Through their industrial arts classrooms or central printing facilities, many schools also have available to them more sophisticated equipment for producing printed materials, for example, printing machines.

Transparency-Making Equipment

Perhaps the most common locally produced transparencies are those handmade by drawing directly onto acetate sheets. Users of this technique should make sure that their drawing materials work well on acetate. Media center supplies should include a number of suitable felt pens and grease or wax pencils (with various size points), plus a supply of acetate and transparency mounts.

Laminating equipment (both hot and cold) as well as the dry-mount press can be used to transfer both black-and-white and color pictures onto transparency acetate. Regardless of the picture-transfer method used, the original must be printed on paper stock that is clay coated. It is also important to remember that the original is destroyed during the process of color lifting.

Transparencies made by computers are common in schools because they are so easy to make and require so little time. It is as simple as enlarging fonts so that the lettering on the transparency can be read easily. The principles of design need to be followed when making transparencies: not too much information on each transparency, only one concept at a time, the path the eye follows when reading an audiovisual material. Remember the most important information needs to be in the upper left hand side of the transparency because that is where the eye first focuses.

Photographic Equipment

Increasingly, both teachers and students are utilizing photographic equipment of all types to produce a variety of educational materials: from still photographs and slide presentations to videos. To accommodate these needs, the media center should have at least a basic inventory of cameras, including SLR cameras, digital cameras and digital camcorders. Copy stands with lighting attachments, light meters, and tripods are also important adjunct equipment. Digital cameras have eliminated the need for a dark room facility because of the instant access they provide. Digital cameras are now available as disposables, which makes their cost reasonable.

Because of such innovations as cartridge loading and simplified focusing devices, very young children can become expert filmmakers. The further addition of the zoom lens permits a smooth and easy transition from one field of vision to another. Basic equipment for motion picture making involves video digital camcorder, light meters, tripods, floodlights for special indoor filming. Two essential steps to take before purchasing a major piece of photographic equipment for the media center are: (1) get the advice of knowledgeable persons in the field and (2) request a demonstration at which some of the prospective users can be present.

Lettering and Display Equipment

Within the media center, there should be services to help teachers and students produce posters, charts, dioramas, and other graphic material. Providing guidance and materials for bulletin boards, exhibits, and other forms of displays are services that a media center should offer. Some of the skills involved in producing these instruction materials are specialized, but with the use of commercially produced aids and other simplifying techniques, locally produced materials can be both attractive and professional looking. There are, for example, many inexpensive ready-to-use lettering devices on the market. A few of these are three-dimensional letters (with or without pin backs), gummed punch-out letters, dry-transfer letters, rubber-stamp letters, and stencil lettering guides. A more expensive method, the Kroy Lettering Machine, prints letters on transparent tape, which can be applied to numerous items for a professional look. The media center should contain not only a generous sampling of these but also a variety of other artist's supplies, including a wide selection of drawing pens, markers, and pencils, a supply of drawing paper and an illustrating board, spray-can paints, T-squares and other simple drafting instruments, and various cutting tools. Equipment should include a drawing board and a paper cutter. The computer can be used to produce graphics, posters, and other materials for display. For example, the *Printshop* software is excellent for making banners and for making posters.

COPYRIGHT AND THE SCHOOL LIBRARY MEDIA CENTER

In recent years, producers and publishers of educational materials have become increasingly alarmed at what appears to be a flagrant disregard of existing copyright regulations as well as either vagueness or absence of statements in the law regarding the use of newer technologies, such as information copied from the Internet. After many years of hearings and debates, Congress passed the Copyright Revision Act of 1976 (P.L. 94-553). Because the implications of this act are important for all libraries, professional personnel should acquaint themselves with at least the basic responsibilities and limitations imposed by this law as it relates to education and specifically school media specialists and teachers.

Printed materials. In regard to books, periodicals, and other printed materials, the copyright guidelines state that single copies for teachers can be made of: (1) a chapter from a book; (2) an article from a newspaper or periodical; (3) a short story, essay, or short poem; or (4) a pictorial work from a book, periodical, or newspaper. It should be remembered that these regulations apply only to works currently in copyright. The regulations for multiple copies for classroom use are much more stringent: (1) copying shall be for a specific course and not exceed one copy per student in that course; (2) the time between the decision to use the material and the actual use must be insufficient to receive permission to copy (the test of spontaneity); (3) an article must be fewer than 2,500 words, book excerpts fewer than 1,000 words, and a poem or excerpt from a poem no more than 250 words (the test of brevity); (4) no more than nine such multiple copying instances are allowed per course per term and this copying shall not create or replace existing anthologies; (5) absolutely no copying is permitted from consumable works, for example, workbooks and standardized texts.

Videos and audio recordings. Media specialists need to tread cautiously when it comes to viewing a video in the media center. A classroom of students can only view a video in the library if it is done in conjunction with face-to-face teaching activities. Videos and audio recordings may be played in the classroom only when they pertain to the lesson being taught. When distance learning is used to teach classes, a video cannot be used even though it would be considered fair use if the course was face-to-face. The law is equally strict in its delineation of circumstances that allow for the reproduction of audio recordings. In general this law prohibits reproduction unless the copy is being used for archival purposes or the original is deteriorating and a replacement is not available at a fair price.

Off-air broadcast programs. There are several limitations on recording off-air broadcast programs: (1) Television broadcasts may be used in classroom instruction one time within ten days of the broadcast and a second classroom showing may be used to reinforce the first showing within the ten day period; (2) retention of the copies of the broadcast shall not exceed forty-five days after the original recording, which allows time either for purchasing a copy of the program or securing a license to retain the existing copy; (3) taping a program must be initiated by the request of a specific teacher and the program can be shown no more than two times per class by that teacher (the second showing supposedly for review or reinforcement purposes); (4) tapes for other teachers can be made provided they meet the other guidelines (such as advance request and use within ten days), and; (5) these guidelines do not apply to entertainment videos that might be taped for use at lunchtime or for assembly programs. These tapes cannot be placed in the media center catalog as a permanent circulation material. When videos are brought into the school library media center for showing by teachers, the media specialist is obligated to determine whether they are lawfully made copies and to permit only lawfully made copies to be used in its facilities.

Computer software. Some concern among educators exists concerning the copyright law and its interpretation as applied to computer software. Back up copies can be made of software, including documentation. As far as networking situations, the software must be licensed and it must not exceed license limitations.

Internet information. Once a material is put in tangible form, such as on a web site, it is protected by copyright regardless of whether the web site shows it as holding a copyright. Although many documents on the Internet show no copyright ownership, it still exists. The best policy when using Internet information is to get permission to use the information or to cite the information in a bibliography giving proper credit to the author. It is permissible to place links on web pages because links are considered to be facts and not protected by copyright. It is totally inappropriate to copy another's web page and then use it as your own.

Multimedia production materials. Only limited amounts of materials can be used in multimedia productions. It is always a good idea to get permission when using excerpts or video clips. When material is used in a PowerPoint or a Hyperstudio presentation, it is advisable to cite source materials and the copyright owner (Simpson, December 2001/January 2002).

At present these guidelines are simply a gentleman's agreement to ensure fair use and compensation for authors, producers and copyright owners. Similar to the regulations in the copyright act, they attempt to bring harmony to the often conflicting interests of proprietors and users. To achieve this balance requires the cooperation of both groups. It is always best to get permission to use educational materials. Permissions for using printed works can be obtained from the Copyright Clearance Center, 222 Rosewood Drive, Danvers, MA 01923; Phone: 978-750-8400; Fax 978-646-8600. In short, the law prohibits copying that can act as a substitute for the purchase of materials.

A copyright policy needs to be included in a policy and procedures handbook. In Georgia, media specialists are responsible for having this information in their media policies and are accountable for the faculty, students and administrators knowing the copyright laws.

REFERENCES

Fritz, Deborah A. & Fritz, Richard J. (2003). *MARC 21 for everyone.* Chicago: American Library Association.

Oklahoma State Department of Education. *Acquisition of instructional materials and audiovisual equipment.* Retrieved April 12, 2004, from the Oklahoma State Department of Education web site: http://title3.sde.state.ok.us/library/Procedures%20Manual%20Elite/acquisition.html

Sherman-Peterson, Ron. (2003, March 27). *CaRD: Cataloging resources directory.* Retrieved April 12, 2004 from: http://www.bsd405.org/libraries/card.htm

Simpson, Carol. (2001, December/2002, January). Understanding the law: Copyright 101. *Educational Leadership, 59*(4), 36–38. Retrieved May 8, 2004, from the ASCD web site: http://www.ascd.org/publications/ed_lead/200112/simpson.html

University of California, Berkeley. (2001). *AV cataloging vendors.* Retrieved April 12, 2004, from: http://www.lib.berkeley.edu/MRC/vrt/vrtcatvendors.htm

FURTHER READINGS

Canadian Library Association, et al. (2002). *Anglo-American cataloging rules* (2nd ed.). Chicago: American Library Association.

Barclay, Donald. (2000). *Managing public access computers.* New York: Neal-Schuman.

Bertland, Linda. (2003). *School libraries on the web: publishers and vendors.* Retrieved April 12, 2004, from: http://www.sldirectory.com/libsf/resf/vendor.html

Bielefield, Arlene & Cheeseman, Lawrence. (1999). *Interpreting and negotiating licensing agreements: A guidebook for the library, research, and teaching professions.* New York: Neal-Schuman.

Bielefield, Arlene & Cheeseman, Lawrence. (1999). *Technology and copyright law.* New York: Neal-Schuman.

Bowman, J. H. (2002). *Essential cataloging.* New York: Neal-Schuman.

Brown, David K. (1998, March 30). *Children's publishers on the Internet.* Retrieved April 12, 2004, from: http://www.acs.ucalgary.ca/~dkbrown/publish.html

Caplan, Priscilla. (2003). *Metadata fundamentals for all librarians.* Chicago: American Library Association.

Chan, Lois Mai. (1999). *A guide to the Library of Congress classification.* Westport, CT: Libraries Unlimited.

Copyright basics. United States Copyright Office. Retrieved April 12, 2004, from the Library of Congress web site: http://lcweb.loc.gov/copyright/circs/circ01.pdf

Copyright law of the United States, Title 17 of the United States Code. Retrieved April 12, 2004, from the Library of Congress web site: http://www.loc.gov/copyright/title17/

Crews, Kenneth D. (2000). *Copyright essentials for librarians and educators.* Chicago: American Library Association.

Curtis, Donnelyn, et al. (2000). *Developing and managing electronic journal collections.* New York: Neal-Schuman.

Day, Michael. (2003). *Metadata: An introduction and practical guide.* New York: Neal-Schuman.

Dittmann, Helena & Hardy, Jane. (2000). *Learn Library of Congress classification.* Lanham, MD: Scarecrow Press.

Eggleston, T. S. (1998). *What every webmaster needs to know about copyright.* Retrieved April 12, 2004, from: http://pw1.netcom.com/%7Enuance/crlaw.html

Evans, G. Edward, et al. (2002). *Introduction to technical services* (7th ed.). Westport, CT: Libraries Unlimited.

Field, Thomas G., Jr. (2002, December 7). *Copyright for computer authors.* Retrieved April 12, 2004, from: www.fplc.edu/tfield/cOpyNet.htm

Fountain, Joanna F. (2001). *Subject headings for school and public libraries.* Westport, CT: Libraries Unlimited.

Fritz, Deborah A. (2004). *Cataloging with AACR2 and MARC21: For books, electronic resources, sound recordings, videorecordings, and serials* (2nd ed.). Chicago: American Library Association.

Ganendran, Jacki. (2000). *Learn Library of Congress subject access.* Lanham, MD: Scarecrow Press.

Garland, Ken. *Cataloging resources for school libraries.* Retrieved April 12, 2004, from the Librarians Information Online Network: http://www.libraries.phila.k12.pa.us/lion/cataloging.html

Gillespie, Joe & Yoffa, Sarah R. (1997). *There is an attitude on the web*...Retrieved April 12, 2004, from: www.wpdfd.com/H5/997.htm

Gorman, Michael. (1998). *Technical services today and tomorrow.* Westport, CT: Libraries Unlimited.

Hagler, Ronald. (1997). *The bibliographic record and information technology* (3rd ed.). Chicago: American Library Association.

Harmon, Charles. (Ed.). *Using the Internet, online services, and CD-ROMs for writing research and term papers.* New York: Neal-Schuman.

Hoffman, Gretchen McCord. (2001). *Copyright in cyberspace: Questions and answers for librarians.* New York: Neal-Schuman.

Hoffman, Herbert. (2002). *Small library cataloging.* Lanham, MD: Scarecrow Press.

Hsieh-Yee, Ingrid. (2000). *Organizing audiovisual and electronic resources for access.* Westport, CT: Libraries Unlimited.

Intner, Sheila & Weihs, Jean. (2001). *Standard cataloging for school and public libraries* (3rd ed.). Westport, CT: Libraries Unlimited.

Jones, Wayne, et al. (2001). *Cataloging the web.* Lanham, MD: Scarecrow Press.

Kaplan, Allison G. & Riedling, Ann Marlow. (2002). *Catalog it! A guide to cataloging school library materials.* Worthington, OH: Linworth.

Kaplan, Michael. (1997). *Planning and implementing technical services workstations.* Chicago: American Library Association.

Kyker, Keith & Curchy, Christopher. (2004). *Educator's survival guide for television production and activities* (2nd ed.). Westport, CT: Libraries Unlimited.

Kyker, Keith & Curchy, Christopher. (2004). *Television production: A classroom approach* (2nd ed.). Westport, CT: Libraries Unlimited.

Library of Congress, Copyright Office. (2003, January 10). *United States copyright office: A brief history and overview.* Retrieved April 12, 2004, from the Copyright Office web site: http://www.copyright.gov/circs/circ1a.html

Library of Congress, Network Development and MARC Standards Office. *MARC standards.* Retrieved April 12, 2004, from the Library of Congress web site: http://www.loc.gov/marc/

Maxwell, Robert L. (2002). *Maxwell's guide to authority work.* Chicago: American Library Association.

Maxwell, Robert L. (2004). *Maxwell's handbook for AACR2: Explaining and illustrating the Anglo-American cataloging rules through the 2003 update.* Chicago: American Library Association.

Millsap, Larry & Ferl, Terry Ellen. (1997). *Descriptive cataloging for the AACR2R and the integrated MARC format.* New York: Neal-Schuman.

Minow, Mary & Lipinski, Tomas A. (2003). *The library's legal answer book.* Chicago: American Library Association.

Mortimer, Mary. (1999). *Learn Dewey decimal classification* (21st ed.). Lanham, MD: Scarecrow Press.

Mortimer, Mary. (2000). *Learn descriptive cataloging.* Lanham, MD: Scarecrow Press.

Olson, Hope A. & Boll, John J. (2001). *Subject analysis in online catalogs.* Westport, CT: Libraries Unlimited.

O'Mahoney, Benedict. (2002). *The copyright website!* Retrieved April 12, 2004, from: http://www.benedict.com

Piepenburg, Scott. (2000). *MARC authority records made easy: A simplified guide to creating authority records for library automation systems.* San Jose, CA: F & W Associates.

Piepenburg, Scott. (2002). *Easy MARC: Incorporating format integration* (4th ed.). San Jose, CA: F & W Associates.

Russell, Carrie. (2004). *Complete copyright: An everyday guide for librarians.* Chicago: American Library Association.

Santa Clara (CA) County Office of Library Services, Library Services. (2001). *Where do I start? A school library handbook.* Worthington, OH: Linworth.

Simpson, Carol. (1999, September/October). Managing copyright in schools. *Knowledge Quest: Journal of the American Association of School Librarians, 28*(1), 18–22.

Simpson, Carol. (2001). *Copyright for schools: A practical guide.* Worthington, OH: Linworth.

Taylor, Arlene G. (1999). *The organization of information.* Westport, CT: Libraries Unlimited.

Taylor, Arlene G. (2002). *Wynar's introduction to cataloging and classification* (9th ed.). Westport, CT: Libraries Unlimited.

Walker, Geraldene & Janes, Joseph. (1999). *Online retrieval: A dialogue of theory and practice.* Westport, CT: Libraries Unlimited.

Wasman, Ann M. (1998). *New steps to service.* Chicago: American Library Association.

Weber, Mary Beth. (2002). *Cataloging nonprint and Internet resources.* New York: Neal-Schuman.

Wherry, Timothy Lee. (2002). *The librarian's guide to intellectual property in the digital age: Copyrights, patents, and trademarks.* Chicago: American Library Association.

Chapter 12

PROGRAM ADMINISTRATION

This chapter covers some of the practical aspects of administering the school library media center, such as circulation techniques, maintaining the collection, inventory, record keeping, developing web pages, honoring privacy/confidentiality of student records, and conducting a successful book fair.

CIRCULATION PROCEDURES

The chief aim of any circulation system is to facilitate the use of materials and ensure the accessibility of these materials to the users of the media center. Major criteria in evaluating a circulation system are ease of use, absence of friction-causing elements, economy, and efficiency. Supplementary considerations involve the desirability of formalizing registration procedures and issuing borrowers' identification cards; the simplicity of charging and discharging routines; the handling of overdues; the flexibility of the system in accommodating such preferred items as reserve books, serial management, interlibrary loan, circulating vertical-file materials; and the ease of collecting circulation statistics. The majority of media centers use automated circulation systems; however, there are still some media centers that are not automated. For that reason, a discussion of manual circulation systems is briefly included in this chapter.

Manual Circulation

Most media centers use some variation of the Newark (NJ) Circulation System when using a manual procedure. The essential elements are a book card (similar cards are used for other types of materials and equipment) and a date-due slip. The routines in the Newark System are so simple and so easily learned that day-to-day operations can be handled by clerical or volunteer help. The user is asked to sign his or her name and homeroom number on the first vacant line of the book card. The due date is stamped next to the user's name on the book card and on the date-due slip. Book cards are placed in the circulation file until the material is returned and discharged. They are usually filed under due date by call number (or alphabetically by author in the case of fiction). Materials may be renewed easily by duplicating the initial procedure: the book card is retrieved from the circulation file and the borrower again signs name and homeroom number and a new due date is stamped on the card and slip.

Simple variations of this system may be used for materials that do not have book cards. For example, cards that include the title and date of publication should be made for each magazine title to be circulated. To check out a magazine, the borrower writes his or her name and homeroom number on the card. The due date is then stamped on the card. Some centers also stamp the due date on a slip pasted in the magazine or attach a date-due slip to the back cover with a paper clip. When the magazine is returned, the borrower's name is crossed off the card. Some centers use a prestamped date-due card that replaces the book card in the book pocket.

Vertical file materials may be checked out by writing the borrower's name, homeroom number, the number of items checked out and their subject headings on a book card marked "Vertical File." The material is placed in a protective envelope to which a date-due slip is attached. Some libraries place a cover sheet on an envelope that allows a borrower to sign his or her name, the homeroom teacher, the subject of the vertical file, the number of articles taken and the date due. When the articles are returned, the discharge procedure is faster because the number of borrowed articles is listed on the envelope. The discharging procedure is the same as that with magazines.

When a patron requests material that is currently in circulation, a reserve slip is made giving call number, main entry, title, and the name and homeroom number of person making the request. The circulation file is then checked, and a flagging device (usually a metal clip or a transparent, color-coded book-card cover) is placed on the card for the title desired.

When the item is returned, the reserve slip is located and placed in the material with the book card, and the prospective borrower is notified.

Automated Circulation System

In an automated circulation system, a laser light pen or scanner is used to link the borrower and the material borrowed. A bar code placed on the material (book, kit, video) serves as the unique number to identify the item. No two bar codes are alike. Another bar code is placed on the borrower's identification card. When the light pen is passed over the bar code on the material and the bar code on the patron's identification, the computer records the transaction. When the material is returned, a similar procedure occurs to record the return. Most automated systems circulate all types of materials, including magazines, vertical file materials, and audiovisual materials. These systems allow reserve materials to be automatically flagged by the computer to alert the librarian that the material has been requested. A majority of school media centers use automated circulation systems. Some attempts have been made to develop library networks among schools, such as the BOCES in New York. Some school systems have joined library networks with public, academic, and special libraries. For example, the high schools of Decatur City Schools, Decatur, Alabama have joined Library Management Network. Some of the more frequently used automated circulation systems in K-12 schools are:

Athena (Sagebrush Corporation)
3601 Minnesota Drive, Suite 550
Minneapolis, MN 55435
Phone: 800-328-2923 or 952-656-2999
Fax: 952-656-2993
Web site: http://www.sagebrushcorp.com/athena

Brodart Automation (Brodart Company)
500 Arch Street
Williamsport, PA 17701
Phone: (800) 233-8467; Fax 570-327-9237
Web site: http://www.brodart.com

Circulation Plus (Follett Software Company)
1391 Corporate Drive
McHenry, IL 60050-7041
Phone: 800-323-3397 or 815-344-8700; Fax 815-344-8774
Web site: http://www.follett.com

Dynix Horizon (Dynix)
400 West 5050 North
Provo, UT 84604
Phone: 800-288-8020 or 801-223-5200
Web site: http://www.dynix.com/solutions/school/

Mandarin (Mandarin Library Automation, Inc.)
P.O. Box 272308
Boca Raton, FL 33427-2308
Phone: 800-426-7477 or 561-995-4010
Fax: 561-995-4065.
Web site: http://www.mlasolutions.com/

Spectrum Suite (Sagebrush Corporation)
3601 Minnesota Drive, Suite 550
Minneapolis, MN 55435
Phone: 800-328-2923 or 952-656-2999
Fax: 952-656-2993
Web site: http://www.sagebrushcorp.com/tech/spectrum.cfm

Library.Solution for Schools (The Library Corporation)
Research Park
Inwood, WV 25428-9733
Phone: 800-325-7759 or 304-229-0100
Fax: 304-229-0295.
Web site: http://www.tlcdelivers.com

Loan Periods

Length of loan periods and the number of items that may be checked out by an individual borrower should be as flexible and liberal as possible. Although some curtailment might be necessary when collections are small and demand is heavy, when the collection reaches numerical adequacy, ten or more books per student, restrictive loan policies should be dropped and replaced with others that match users' needs. A few media centers have been bold enough to adopt a loan period that can be as long as the school year when the material is not wanted by another patron. In these cases, instead of the due date, the checkout date is stamped in the material. Other centers allow items in the general collection to circulate for a semester. Extended loan periods are particularly important for students engaged in long-term independent study projects. Most centers, however, use loan periods of two to four weeks. To borrowers an easy way of remembering due dates, some centers have adopted a fixed date for returning materials. For example, all materials checked out in a particular week are due on a specified Monday two or three weeks later. Thus, Monday (or the first school day after, in case of holidays or vacations) becomes the day each week on which loaned materials are due back in the center. This system could be labor intensive for staff that must shelve all returned materials on the same day. A better system is to have materials checked out for two or three weeks and to be returned all days of the week rather than one day.

Although no specific limits should be placed on the number or type of items that may be borrowed from the center, some reasonable and temporary restraints may have to be imposed, as necessitated by demand and circulation requirements. For example, when duplicate copies of heavily used reference books are not owned in the center, a system of overnight loans might have to be used. The same problem can arise with media placed on reserve by teachers, current issues of periodicals, or pieces of equipment scheduled for use during the school day. Many of these situations can be avoided through judicious duplication of titles and extensive preplanning with the faculty. In unavoidable cases, restricted loans should be applied as sparingly as possible and always with the needs of users in mind.

Overdues and Fines

Handling problems related to overdues has plagued librarians since library materials first began to circulate. Automated circulation systems have alleviated most of the headaches associated with the problem. It is an easy process to print out an overdue list. The assessment of fines for students not returning materials on time is a decision that must be addressed by the school media specialist. One recourse has been to impose fines, on the theory that students who lack feelings of obligation toward others will develop them when their (or their parents') finances are tapped. Many centers have abandoned the collection of fines, however, chiefly because they find it does not work—students are often quite willing to pay the small amount as a form of rent to keep the material they want. Perhaps more important, fines represent a negative or punitive measure that contradicts the attempt in schools to build attitudes of responsibility and citizenship. Opponents to fines in media centers point out that collecting them is very time-consuming and that excessively repressive regulations create hostility and can lead to increased theft and mutilation of material. Still other centers compromise and levy fines only on material that is placed on a highly restricted loan schedule, such as overnight books, when the absence of the material from the center can produce great inconvenience for other users. It is illegal in some states to collect library fines from students.

Regardless of whether fines are collected, other procedures are often adopted to remind students (and sometimes faculty) that the material they have on loan should be returned or renewed. The most widely accepted method is sending printed overdue notices to homerooms. In the case of interlibrary loan overdue notices produced at another library, they must be first checked against the computer to see if any materials have been returned during the lag time between the printing of the overdue notices and their arrival in the media center. In the case of material on which a reserve has been placed, the overdue notice should be sent out as soon as the item is due. If within another week (or longer, depending on center policy) and the material has still not been returned, a second notice is sent out, and so on. Other techniques are sometimes used, such as setting aside certain days during the school year to have overdue or unused materials returned (in centers where fines are collected these are sometimes called amnesty days).

When a student is directly responsible for the loss of an item or damage to it, some form of reimbursement should be made to the media center. However, because some accidents are unavoidable and some losses are not the fault of the borrower, adjustments might have to be made in order not to inflict unfair penalties. These decisions, as well as those involving delinquent borrowers, should be made only by the center's professional staff. In a few severe cases, it is necessary to take strong measures—such as sending notices to parents. However, before resorting to anything like this measure, a professional staff member should contact and inform the student personally of the items that are still overdue and the consequences that might occur should they not be returned.

Privacy and Confidentiality of Student Records

Media specialists need to honor the confidentiality of student records. Instead of giving a class list to a teacher to announce those students having overdue books, it is a better policy to give the notices individually to the students themselves. Student records are very confidential. Student records on the OPAC are also confidential and should not be discussed with anyone.

For more information about privacy and confidentiality issues, consult the following ALA web site: http://www.ala.org/Template.cfm?Section= Intellectual_Freedom_Issues&Template=/ContentManagement/Content Display.cfm&ContentID=25304.

AV Material and Equipment

If possible, it is advisable to have circulation materials such as pockets, labels, barcodes, security strips and so forth affixed to all media so that the same circulation procedures can be used as with books. With large items like videos, this is usually not a problem, but with smaller items that are not large enough for these items to be attached, it is. Having a system where all items circulate in a similar manner helps to promote less confusion for the patron and better understanding of library procedures.

It should not be too difficult in affixing a pocket to each piece of audiovisual material. This method of circulation allows all kinds of materials to be checked-out in the same way. The circulation of equipment also poses problems. If space permits, in small and medium-size schools, the delivery of equipment to the classroom should emanate from the library media center. Requests should be made on sign-up sheets in the media center at least one day in advance or on the media center's web page, although advance bookings for at least two weeks ahead should be possible. Sign-up sheets or web sign ups should include: (1) period of time material is needed, (2) teacher's name, (3) room number, (4) equipment needed, and (5) pickup time. Student AV squads or aides can be used to facilitate delivery and return. In elementary or very small schools, teachers are normally responsible for getting their own equipment. Barcodes can be placed on equipment and checked out the same way as other materials. Through in-service training, teachers as well as student helpers, should become familiar with operating basic equipment.

In larger schools, AV equipment is often assigned to a teaching station or cluster of classrooms. In these cases, it is still necessary to formulate some circulation policies to prevent conflicts or abuse of privileges. When equipment is decentralized and control is remote, it is often difficult to maintain an accurate inventory of equipment in good operating condition or to determine when booking conflicts might occur. Therefore, it is a good policy to circulate all equipment and to do all bookings from the media center.

Theft-Detection Devices

Recent sharp increases in theft of materials in many school library media centers have compelled the staff to examine the effectiveness of the security measures they have adopted to prevent these losses. Sometimes a rearrangement of the collection and facilities, like placing the charging desk close to an exit, can help. Converting two entryways into one entrance and one exit might help control security. Some centers have instituted book checks at exits and either hire additional personnel or use staff members to supervise them. Others use such methods as placing sections of the collection, particularly expensive or sought-after items, on reserve.

The theft of library materials is becoming a major problem in media centers. According to Weiser (2003), media centers lose ten percent to fifteen percent of their library collections through theft. One example of how theft has gotten totally out of hand is in Springfield, Missouri. In that school district alone, $65,000 in library books were stolen in one year and only one school had a security system (Riley, 2002). If the annual loss is so great that the center is losing thousands of dollars per year, the installation of a theft-detection system is crucial to protect the library collection. Usually security systems pay for themselves in two or three years by saving the replacement costs of materials that would potentially be lost. Most of these devices involve a system of sensitizing-desensitizing library materials by placing an adhesive or tag on the material that can be activated or deactivated by an electronic device. If the material is not desensitized through the checkout system, an alarm sounds should anyone try to remove it from the center. The names and addresses of some security system vendors used in K-12 schools are:

3M Security Systems (3M Library Systems)
3M Corporate Headquarters
3M Center
St. Paul, MN 55144-1000
Phone: 888-364-3577
Fax: 800-223-5563
Web site: http://www.3m.com/library

Checkpoint (Checkpoint Systems, Inc.)
101 Wolf Drive, P.O. Box 188
Thorofare, NJ 08086
Phone: 800-257-5540 or 609-848-1800
Fax: 609-848-0937
Web site: http://www.checkpointsystems.com

Dynatag (DynaTag, Inc.)
2425 NW 71 Place
Gainesville, FL 32653
Phone: 352-375-9903

Fax 352-375-8860
Web site: http://www.dynataginc.com

FlashScan (Phiga Corporation)
1916 Old Cuthber Road, Suite B13
Cherry Hill, NJ 08034
Phone: 800-832-7481 or 856-428-9571
Fax: 856-428-2594
Web site: http://www.flashscan.net

ID Systems (Vernon Library Supplies)
2851 Cole Court, Norcross, GA 30071
Phone: 800-878-0253 or 770-446-1128
Fax: 800-466-1165 or 770-447-0165
Web site: http://64.71.141.130/IDElectro.asp

Ketec Security Systems (Vernon Library Supplies, Inc.)
2851 Cole Court
Norcross, GA 30071
Phone: 800-878-0253 or 770-446-1128
Fax: 800-466-1165 or 770-447-0165
Web site: http://64.71.141.130/ketecs.asp

Knogo (Sentry Technology Corporation)
1881 Lakeland Ave.
Ronkonkoma, NY 11779
Phone: 631-739-2000
Web site: http://www.sentrytechnology.com/comp1.htm

Prospective buyers should be aware of the hidden costs associated with each system. Not only is there an initial cost, there are often charges involved in installation, leasing, and service contracts. As well, sensitizing each piece involves money for both materials and staff time. For example, commercial processors now charge between thirty-five and sixty-five cents per item to install theft-detection devices on items ordered and processed through them. Other considerations involve the effectiveness of the system, the false-alarm rate (with some systems, keys, jewelry, magnets, and such can activate the system), the ability to accommodate audiovisual materials, and the amount of inconvenience the system produces for both patrons and staff. One major consideration regarding the security system is the ongoing cost to the annual budget to install theft strips or tapes in all materials. If detection strips are attached to all magazines, the budget for supplies will reflect a substantial increase. For example, a box of 1,000 detection strips from 3M cost approximately $250 per box. Another consideration in selecting security systems is how well they work with automation systems. Normally, they are expected to work in tandem with each other.

INVENTORY AND WEEDING PROCEDURES

An accurate inventory will reveal an exact account of the resources at hand. It is useful for many reasons: to indicate missing or lost materials, to reveal numerical strengths and weaknesses in the collection, to identify materials in need of repair, to serve as a vital part of the process of weeding the collection.

Precautions must be taken, however, to ensure that the inventory does not unduly disrupt the center's normal services. Closing the center for inventory, as is frequently done during the last week of school, can deprive students of center use at a time they need it most. Two possible alternatives are: (1) scheduling inventory at a time school is not in session (to facilitate performing this and other housekeeping chores); many districts have placed at least part of the media center's staff on an eleven-month, rather than the conventional ten-month contract, and (2) making inventory a continuous process by drawing up a staggered schedule that covers the entire collection once per year, but in a piecemeal fashion. Now with the handheld barcode readers, taking inventory is a much easier process than doing a manual inventory. Inventory procedures are sufficiently simple. It usually can be handled by clerical personnel or well-trained student assistants.

The steps in taking inventory are:

1. Arrange the material to be inventoried in correct order. With handheld bar code readers this step is not necessary; however, it does allow the media center to be arranged properly.

2. It is a good idea to have at least two handheld barcode readers so two people can work on the inventory at one time.

3. The physical condition of the material is also checked at this time.

4. Remove from the shelf any material that needs repair.

5. Once the inventory is done, have the computer print a report of missing items.

6. Check for missing items in other sources, such as bindery records, reserve collections, materials in classrooms or in workrooms for repair, and in display cases.

7. Prepare inventory records giving a numerical count of the items in the collection and those that are missing.

8. Put a note in the OPAC record that the material is missing.

9. If the item has still not been located after a suitable waiting period (usually two years), the material should be withdrawn from the collection and OPAC records need to be updated. Later, decisions concerning replacement will have to be made.

Weeding

The term *weeding* means in library terms what it does in gardening: to eliminate the unsuitable or unwanted. Four types of material should be weeded: (1) the out-of-date and no longer authentic; this condition occurs very frequently with science material, but no single subject is immune; (2) the worn-out or badly damaged; sometimes repairs can be made—for example, books can be rebound—but costs should be weighed carefully against the price of a replacement versus adding a different title; (3) duplicate titles that are no longer of interest to students or faculty; and (4) the unpopular or unused. These titles are perhaps the most difficult to throw out because in some cases it is an admission that an inappropriate purchase has been made; in other cases, however, it simply means that tastes and interests have shifted. Nevertheless, it is useless to have collections clogged with deadwood material that no longer attracts youngsters. It is recommended that four to five percent of a collection should be weeded each year. This recommendation applies only to collections that have been in existence for a few years. The weeding process is unique to each library media center because of the differences in curricula, the student population, and the teaching methods used in the school. Weeding guidelines based on Dewey Decimal Classification are suggested in Exhibits 12.1 and 12.2 as well as those based on the kind of material.

The previous information is a compilation of several of the following web sites:

- *Weeding.* In *Library Media Center Handbook,* **Norfolk Public Schools.** http://www.nps.k12.va.us/aaa/media/manual1002/ch20_wd.pdf. Excellent guidelines are provided for weeding.

- *Weeding: Reassessment of Library Media Collections.* Maryland State Department of Education. http://www.infohio.org/demo/Documents/UC/WeedingguidelinesMaryland.doc. This site contains weeding guidelines based on the Dewey Decimal system.

Exhibit 12.1.

Weeding Guidelines Based on Dewey Decimal System.

DDS	Subject	Comments
000	Encyclopedias Bibliographies Reading	Replace one set of encyclopedias every five years, based on copyright. Circulate older sets for no more than 8 years. Move toward online subscriptions for encyclopedias and some reference items, such as almanacs, atlases, thesauri, and dictionaries. Computer materials need to be updated after 3 years; consider paperbacks. Bibliographies obsolete after 10 years.
100	Ethics	Determine by use. Unscholarly works, discard after 10 years. Look at dated pictures and concepts in self-help psychology and guidance materials. Scholarly psychology works should be replaced every 5-8 years.
200	Religion	Determine by use. Collection needs to represent all religions and sects. Remove propaganda. Try to have current material on every major religion. Review each material individually and the collection collectively.
300	Social sciences	Remove materials on customs & folklore only because of poor condition. Keep items on communication, transportation and economics from historical perspective. Collection needs to represent all sides of controversial issues. Review audiovisual materials for dated dress and mannerisms. Remove books on government after 10 years. Look for newer government materials to supercede older volumes. Currency is needed for materials on local, state and national government. Keep historical education materials; replace non-historical materials after 10 years. Remove discredited theories of education. Remove careers after 5 years.
400	Languages	Weed old grammars; examine for dated examples and illustrations. Keep basic materials. Check dictionaries for words included, especially slang words added to common usage. English as a second language and foreign language materials may need to be replaced frequently.

Exhibit 12.1. (continued)

DDS	Subject	Comments
500	Pure sciences	Most books out of date in 5 years. Botany and natural history books can be kept longer. Need to purchase new materials each year. Astronomy materials may be dated before botany. Energy materials need to be updated regularly. Some environmental materials are still relevant after 15 years while items about atoms might be inaccurate after 2 years. Discard obsolete theories.
600	Applied sciences	Keep an update collection of popular culture. Keep repair manuals for cars. Remove most subjects after five years, except for basic information on medicine, inventions, and anatomy. Remove materials on radio and television after 5 years except for volumes in demand as historical reference. Keep most cookbooks. Remove business books after 10 years. Keep useful books on crafts, toys, guns & clocks
700	Arts and Recreation Music	Keep handsomely illustrated sources of art, music and fine arts. Keep art and music histories. Some materials may be irreplaceable. Heavy use materials need to be considered for replacement or rebinding. Keep current stamp and coin catalogs. Some hobbies may need updating. Sources on sports need to be current with duplicate copies available. Remove sports and recreational materials as interests change.
800	Literature	Keep literary history and criticisms; replace with superseded more authoritative works. Keep local author's works. Look at collections versus individual works of poets, novelists, & playwrights. Weigh curriculum needs and use. Keep those titles indexed in standard reference indexes, if content is relevant.
900	History	Determine by use and community needs. Look at accuracy of information and fairness of interpretation. Examine historical materials for use patterns and bias. All historical periods should

Exhibit 12.1. (continued)

		be represented in the collection and examined for coverage. Add materials with better coverage as available. Geography and travel become dated quickly. Discard travel books after 2-5 years and replace. Keep travel books useful from historical perspective or personal accounts. Remove atlases after 5 years. Keep only outstanding materials about wars and other historical events.

- *Guidelines for Weeding Library Materials.*
  http://www.sbac.edu/%7Emedia/guid_weeding.html. This site offers helpful guidelines for weeding.

- *Weeding. Arizona State Library. Collection Development Training.*
  http://www.lib.az.us/cdt/weeding.htm. This site explains the importance of a weeding policy.

- *Weeding the Library Media Center Collection.*
  Iowa State Department of Education. http://www.iema-ia.org/IEMA209.html. A good beginning source on weeding.

- *Weeding in Libraries: A Partial Index To What's Out There.*
  http://www.havana.lib.il.us/library/weeding.html. Numerous sites are provided about weeding.

- **Sunlink Weed of the Month Club.**
  http://www.sunlink.ucf.edu/weed/. This program is designed to assist media specialists in Florida with weeding items each month.

Some special considerations are required when weeding the reference collection, especially as it relates to the electronic resources. The same criteria apply to the reference collection as well as to the circulating collection. Some reference materials are considered classics and will remain valuable. When a new revised edition of a reference work appears, it is time to remove the older edition. Dictionaries do not fit in this category, especially unabridged editions. New quotation books supplement the older edition and are not intended to replace them.

Keep and Mend. Be aware that it is impractical to keep everything. Mending an item, in some cases, makes perfect sense. If the item is expensive or difficult to replace, mending may be the answer. Decide whether to send the material away for rebinding or whether to mend it in-house.

Disposing of an Item. Once the decision is made to discard an item, another decision needs to be made about disposing of it. There are three

Exhibit 12.2.
Weeding Guidelines Based on Kind of Material.

Subject	Comments
Biography	Replace older volumes whenever better ones become available. Determine by use. Keep those outstanding in content and literary value. Keep up with personalities of both political and historical figures.
Fiction Easy Story Collections	Determine by use. Popular materials may not always be popular. Duplicates may not be needed. Rebinding out of print items is option for materials that fill a curriculum need. Remove old-fashioned dated titles that have not circulated in 3-5 years. Replace classics as newer editions become available. Young adult fiction should be less than 10 years old.
Periodicals Newspapers	Remove magazines after two years unless indexed. If indexed, keep 5 years, those needed for reference. Keep local newspapers for 1 year or clip for vertical file. Some magazines might be bound after 1 year. Discard bound volumes after 10 years. Determine by use. Place more emphasis on online magazines/periodicals.
Vertical File	Weed once a year. Keep only most current materials not found elsewhere. Date materials as added.
Government documents	Order as needed. Determine by use and requests of patrons.
Subject encyclopedias	Remove when content inaccurate.
Almanacs Yearbooks Statistical	Superseded by newer volume. Keep for teaching purposes for 3-5 years. Special articles in science yearbooks need to be considered before weeding. Replace almanacs in reference section after 2 years. Consider online almanacs for future.
Picture files	Remove unaesthetic, dated or damaged prints.
Maps Globes	Remove items that are outdated and inaccurate.

Exhibit 12.2. (continued)

Professional Collection	Remove materials after 8-10 years and also materials that no longer support curriculum.
Audiovisual Materials	Weed regularly like print materials. Do small sections at a time. Need to view or listen to each item. Issues to address: hard to borrow on interlibrary loan, format, may want to transfer format to a newer one. Check for broken cases, missing pieces, poor sound or visual quality. Replace cassettes with CDs, tapes with audiobooks and Videos with DVDs. Check videos for wear after 100-150 circulations, replace after 200-250 showings. Check CDs for chips, cracks & scratches. Check computer disks for viruses & demagnification.

options when disposing of materials: (1) sell it, if it is useable; (2) give it away to teachers, students or organizations in community; (3) destroy, as a last resort when items cannot be salvaged by selling or giving away. Many times, it is not the media specialist who makes this decision. Frequently, it is often decided by the school district and sometimes even state policy dictates how to dispose of educational materials and equipment.

Update the catalog. Make certain that all records of weeded materials have been updated in the OPAC. Customers looking in the catalog need to know materials currently available and not be concerned with items that have been weeded but not updated in the records.

MAINTAINING THE COLLECTION

Preventive maintenance can ensure longer life for library materials. Items needing repair are usually identified at the charging desk or through inventory. In any case they should be removed from the shelves as soon as damage has been detected. In some cases, such as torn pages or wobbly spines, repairs are fairly easily accomplished with the use of a suitable transparent non-brittle tape or application of glue inside the end pages. Other repairs, like tipping in pages, require more expertise. Many supply houses distribute (often free of charge) repair manuals that explain these procedures, and sometimes they will send representatives to demonstrate techniques for groups of library media specialists. Unfortunately, crayon or ballpoint pen markings are difficult to erase. In such cases, if the damage is widespread, discarding the book is probably necessary. Following are some web sites that give instructions for repairing books:

- **Book Repair:**
  http://www.mtsu.edu/~vvesper/repair.html
- **Washington University Libraries Book Repair and Conservation Treatment:**
  http://library.wustl.edu/units/preservation/publicbookrepair.html
- **A Simple Book Repair Manual:**
  http://www.dartmouth.edu/~preserve/repair/html/hingerepair.htm
- **Procedures and Treatments Used for Book Repair and Pamphlet Binding:**
  http://door.library.uiuc.edu/preserve/procedures.html

When the spine of a book is broken and signatures are loose or falling out, a decision concerning rebinding must be made. Because of the high cost of rebinding, this should be done only when the book is otherwise in excellent condition and has ample margins to accommodate re-sewing, and the cost of replacement is significantly higher than rebinding. Exceptions should be made for books that are still needed in the collection but out of print. Books are usually sent to the binder only once or twice a year, including one shipment over the summer months. Keep a list of books sent to the bindery; it can serve as a bindery record. Before choosing a bindery, be sure to check out its reliability, speed of delivery, and quality and attractiveness of the final product. Following are some book binding vendors:

- **ICI Bindery Corporation,** http://www.icibinding.com/about/bui.htm
- **Utah Bookbindery Company, Inc.** http://www.utahbookbinding.com/
- **Heckman Bindery, Inc.,** http://www.boundtoplease.com/
- **Southern Library Bindery Company,** http://www.southernlibrarybindery.com/aboutus.htm

Simple repairs to audiovisual material and equipment, like splicing tapes and changing bulbs on overhead projectors, can be done at the school level, but more serious repairs should be done either by a district center or by an outside commercial firm. Equipment should be checked regularly (ideally after each use) and there should also be a thorough annual check of each piece of equipment. The usual standard of quality (efficiency, reliability, repair time, cost) should be applied before contracting with an outside agency to do equipment repairs. Keep records of all repairs done to equipment. This information will be useful when making decisions about replacing old equipment. Keeping accurate records and making reports are crucial to the administration of the media center.

RECORDS AND REPORTS

Record keeping and preparation of school library media center reports serve several purposes. Internally, these functions reveal to the center staff otherwise hidden strengths and weaknesses in the program and thus indicate areas for possible change or improvement. Externally they can serve as a communication device to acquaint others with the scope and nature of the program, its needs and future plans, and recommendations for rectifying shortcomings.

Records

The maintenance of accurate records is an integral part of a media center's operation. It is an administrative detail that cuts across the areas of acquisition and organization. Each school media center will develop its own system, but certain records are essential. There are basically four kinds of records prepared and maintained in the media center: (1) financial, (2) organizational, (3) service, and (4) archival.

Financial Records

The originals of many school library media center financial records are kept in the school or district business office, with copies in the center. Examples of financial records are:

- Budget requests, annual and special
- Budget requests, annual and special repeat
- Budget allocations
- Current statements of expenditures
- Shipment receipts and invoices
- Requisitions and purchase orders, with notations on partial order status and final disposition
- Receipts of any monies collected or expended by the library media center outside of regular financial procedures
- Petty cash funds

Organizational Records

The organizational records usually include as priority items a computer-generated shelf list and any supplementary inventory system for nonprint materials and equipment.

The shelf list is a classified list of all the holdings of a school library media center. The list contains full bibliographic information, the number of copies, and the list price of the item. In centers that keep collections housed separately by format, an additional computer-generated printout for nonprint media arranged by format can be useful for inventory. In addition, a printout for the equipment handled by the media center is useful for both inventory and repair and maintenance records. The appropriate information about the equipment, including vendor, list price, model number, warranty conditions, date of purchase, and repairs, should be noted when the item is being repaired. A separate list should be kept of equipment out for repair. Other records for material that is out of the center for other reasons, for example, binding, should also be kept. Typical organizational records include:

A computer-generated shelf list of materials and equipment

Inventory records

Quantitative record of current holdings

Collections in other locations (duplicates to departments, grade levels, or resource areas)

Subject authority file, such as Sears or Library of Congress

Want lists or consideration file

Record of materials on order

Records of loans and gifts

Checklist of periodical holdings

Records of materials and equipment being repaired and serviced

Lesson plans, instructional programs, tests, and assignments

Files of promotional materials, for example, successful displays, exhibits, and programs

Materials describing school library media center procedures

Licenses for computer programs and online databases

Manuals

It is suggested that a single all-inclusive manual be prepared. From this, individual parts can be excerpted or adapted to prepare more specialized manuals (for example, for volunteers or student helpers) as needed. A suggested table of contents for the basic manual is:

1. Introduction, mission statement, philosophy, goals, and objectives
2. Hours of service
3. Services and activities
4. Size and nature of collection
5. Selection and acquisitions policies and procedures
6. Floor plan of center
7. Arrangement, storage, and maintenance of materials
8. Circulation and distribution practices (reserves, charging, overdues, and renewals)
9. Personnel and work responsibilities
10. Budget
11. Record keeping, reports, and evaluation
12. Public relations, publicity, and displays
13. Acceptable use policy (Internet)

More detailed information on manuals is given in Chapter 6.

Inventory Records

Another area of organizational records is the inventory. After a complete inventory is finished, fairly accurate figures should be available for the center's holdings by format (that is, books, videos, equipment, and so on). Using these figures as a base, a separate record for each medium should be kept in a loose-leaf binder or a computer-generated list to record changes caused by additions or deletions and a running tally of items in the collection. A simple four-column page could be used with these headings: (1) date, (2) number of items added, (3) number of items withdrawn, and (4) current balance. This will supply a valuable up-to-date inventory of the collection. Using these figures, monthly summary statistics should be prepared on a page listing, in a column at the left, each media type (books, transparencies, and so forth) with separate columns across the page for the numbers on hand at the beginning of each month of the school year (such as September 1 through June 1). In this way it is possible to indicate with some accuracy the actual holdings of the center at any given time during the school year. These statistics are also invaluable in preparing monthly, midyear and annual reports.

Inventory records should also be kept for audiovisual equipment. A simple list of equipment on hand can be kept on a computer. Each type of equipment (such as overhead projectors or LCD projectors) should have an inventory number. This number is one assigned by the center, usually in consecutive order by equipment type, to easily identify each piece of equipment. This number is also stamped or placed on a label on the equipment. In addition to this running inventory number, a separate record—again usually in a loose-leaf binder, or a computer-generated list—should be kept for each item of equipment indicating at the top of the page the type, manufacturer, cost, date of purchase, model and serial number, and leaving (in column style on the rest of the page) spaces for repair and inspection records.

Equipment stored in specific areas in the school can be listed to show where items may be located quickly. Some school districts require that the location for the storage of AV equipment be shown on their inventory for insurance purposes.

Service Records

Service records include chiefly statistical data on attendance, circulation, number of classes taught and so forth. Some centers also keep records on such items as number of reference questions asked and number of bibliographies prepared by the staff. To prevent statistics collecting from becoming an end in itself, it should always be determined in advance whether the data produced serve a sufficiently worthwhile purpose to warrant the expenditure of time and effort. It is also necessary to check the reports required by district centers, state departments of education, or accrediting agencies to find out the type of statistics required and the form they should take. The use of sampling techniques should be explored. They often produce similar results with greater economy of time and effort. For example, instead of counting attendance or circulation every school day, records might be kept for only a randomly selected number of school days. Computer-generated lists for both daily and monthly circulation figures should be kept, preferably in a loose-leaf binder. Some modifications might have to be made in these reports, however, if figures are to be broken down by both Dewey classification and format.

Some examples of service records are:

Job description and analysis of the library staff
Records of circulation and use of materials and equipment

Attendance records

School library media center instruction records

Procedural manual for school library media center instruction

Workshops held for teachers and students

Internet use

Instructional technology training sessions

Circulation statistics are an important part of a media center's organizational record keeping. They are usually kept on a daily basis and cumulated weekly, monthly, and annually, and provide one of the common foundations for evaluating service. Media circulation records can be used to evaluate how well the objectives of a media center are being met. For example, the material can be recorded by medium, subject class, or grade level. Finer breakdowns by curriculum or by recreation-related areas, for example, weather or science fiction, may be obtained by including extra information about coursework or interest area when the items are checked out. The need to keep service records might be waived in special instances, for example, when student participation and performance in library programs are used as a measure for accountability in place of circulation count.

Other records important to media center operation are the schedules for equipment usage, group use of facilities, and library teaching in the classroom and center. A compilation of these records will be an important part of the monthly and annual reports to the administration. They will also provide statistics for a graphic record—charts, graphs, and so on. In a small center, a large monthly wall calendar will sometimes serve well as a visual record.

Perhaps the overriding consideration for the individual school library media specialist with a small staff is to set up the simplest routines possible and to know precisely for what purpose any record is kept. A continuous reevaluation to bring each routine and its desired purpose more closely into line is vital. With a good circulation system, most of these records can all be kept, counted, and printed electronically with little work on the part of the library media specialist.

Archival Records

The archival file contains a copy of each important document related to the history of the media center. Financial records, administrative announcements, policy statements, media center publications, and statistical data are organized (usually by school year) and stored to supply a written record of the center's history. In some media centers, this activity is expanded to include such material as minutes of faculty meetings, student publications, and newspaper clippings related to the school and its programs.

Reports

Many state departments of education annually distribute to school library media centers forms for reporting the center's activities. The information requested is generally statistical in nature and includes such data as attendance figures, number of faculty members, number of classes taught, media center hours, size of collection, number of new acquisitions, number of materials withdrawn, circulation statistics, personnel figures, and budget information.

The school library media specialist or program administrator usually prepares an annual report for distribution to administrators at various levels. This information, which may be shared with the school faculty, chronicles the year's activities in narrative form but also supplies guidelines for future growth. This annual report can also be used to trace and compare developments from year to year. It should cover four areas of information: program, statistics, staff, and recommendations.

Program

The program, the most important section of the report, is a summary of the activities and accomplishments of the center during the preceding year. Information on services provided to students and teachers should be included, as well as details on such areas as the center's part in curriculum development, reading and study guidance (for example, bibliography preparation). Special projects and programs (book fairs or assembly programs) and the center's work in promotion and publicity are essential to the report. If the school library media center sponsors special clubs or a student assistant group, include material on these as well.

Statistics

The raw material for this section may be obtained from figures, already collected, related to such areas as size of collection, attendance, center hours, and circulation. When possible the data should be reduced to the most meaningful units. For example, in addition to yearly totals, daily average figures should also be expressed. In this area, charts and graphs can be used to good advantage. This part of the report contains a financial summary on appropriations and gifts as well as expenditures.

Staff

This section covers the professional activities of the staff, including activities related to the growth of staff competencies, such as participation in professional associations, courses taken, attendance at workshops and conferences, and publications.

Recommendations

This section presents a series of recommendations concerning the future of the center, based on the material in the preceding sections of the report. The recommendations should be stated in terms of achieving specific short- and long-term goals, rather than as simple statements of need. It should be indicated that action might not be possible on all of the proposals.

In addition, the center will periodically prepare other types of reports. Decision on the content and treatment of the material in these reports should bear on: (1) why the report is being prepared—its purpose, and (2) the people who will read the report—its audience. For example, a primarily selling report—one that is intended to exert influence on a decision involving the center—should be brief, to the point, without extraneous material, and should carry its message with maximum impact. The use of charts, graphs, or other visuals can help achieve the goal of this type of report. Often school library media specialists are asked to make monthly and weekly reports that can become the yearly report for the state or for the school district. It is necessary to know what is ultimately expected and keep good records. Sometimes the school reports are more instructional in nature, whereas the state and district reports are more statistical.

Web Pages

As a program administrator, it is crucial to have a school media center web page to publicize the program. Fundamental considerations are needed as one begins the process of developing web pages:

- *Copyright*—Anything chosen to put on the page needs to have permission whether it is a document or a link.

- *Accessibility*—Make certain that equipment and software is compatible to allow access by all patrons, especially those with special needs.
- *District Policies and Guidelines*—Most districts have web page guidelines. Consult and follow any guidelines provided.
- *Safety of Students*—Most district policies have guidelines about keeping students safe. Be aware of those guidelines and follow them. For example, one should not show students' pictures with their names.
- *Design*—Keep the design of the web page functional, appealing, and appropriate. Possible considerations are site structure, navigation, layout, use of graphics, fonts, and how it looks.

According to Logan and Beuselinck (2001), the web page may include the following types of information:

1. **Informative facts**—Some facts that would be beneficial might include, policies of the media center, contact information, media center program facts, mission and philosophy statements, staff information, historical facts, scheduling forms, services, volunteer information, wish lists, surveys, reading lists, and promotional materials.
2. **Curricular connections**—This part of the web page can show links to online databases, e-library information, OPAC database, WebQuests, pathfinders, assignments, worksheets, tips, teaching tools, archive of lesson plans, links to lesson plans, and student project pages.
3. **Showcase of student work**—The web page offers an excellent opportunity to display student work for the community.
4. **Revenue generation**—For those media centers that have to do fundraising to support their media centers, one can use the web page to publicize the events, such as book fairs and other fund-raising activities.

Chapter 10 contains a more detailed discussion of school library media web pages. For further information, two books that can be helpful when designing and publicizing web pages for school library media centers include: *K-12 Web Pages: Planning and Publishing Excellent School Web Sites* by Debra Logan and Cynthia Beuselinck and *Tooting Your Own Horn: Web-Based Public Relations for the 21st Century Librarian* by Julieta Fisher and Ann Hill.

Program administrators normally provide money-making fun activities in the media center, such as book fairs, that bring about good public relations. Book fairs are normally a lot of work, but they help to promote goodwill within the school and the community.

MANAGING A BOOK FAIR

Traditionally, book fairs have been held to introduce children to books, to stimulate reading, and to promote growth of home libraries. They are also a way of earning money to help some educational project in the school library media center. Because of the high cost of hardcover books, paperbacks are now almost exclusively sold at fairs. Paramount to a successful book fair is choosing a distributor that is reliable, has experience in book fairs, and has a large inventory (or will order copies especially for your fair). As part of the planning process for a book fair, the following checklist is a useful tool:

1. Is a planning kit provided by the company?
2. Are multiple copies of each book or just a single copy provided by the company?
3. Are the books provided in self-contained cases or in boxes that must be unpacked and arranged?
4. Is an inventory required before the fair?
5. Is an inventory required at the end of the fair?
6. What is the price range of the books?
7. What cash profits does the company offer?
8. Is there a combination of cash and book profits offered by the company?
9. What kind of bonuses does the company offer, such as gifts, coupons, or books?
10. Does the company provide a toll-free number?
11. Is a local company representative available for easy consultation?
12. Are selections varied enough to meet student needs and interests?
13. What kind of return policy does the company offer?
14. Is a reorder policy in place?
15. What procedures are available for students to order materials from booklists or order forms?
16. Are publicity materials provided in advance of the book fair?
17. Are there any sale items (and if so, what are they)?
18. Are taxes collected for book fair items sold?
19. What reading incentive programs are available?

There are several companies that deal in providing materials for book fairs. The following four companies provide this service:

Chinaberry, Inc. Book Fairs
2780 Via Orange Way, Suite B
Spring Valley, CA 91978
Phone: 619-670-9904
Web site: http://www.chinaberrybookfairs.com/contact.cfm

Scholastic Book Fairs
Southern Region (check web site for other regions)
3600 Cobb International Blvd., Suite 100
Kennesaw, GA 30152
Phone: 800-241-1448 or 770-425-0203
Fax: 770-425-0156
Web site: http://www.scholastic.com/bookfairs/chair/contact/offices.htm

Southwest Book Company Book Fairs
13003 H. Murphy Road
Stafford, TX 77477
Phone: 281-498-2603
Fax: 281-498-2603
Web site: http://www.txla.org/conference/exhibits/exhcompanyname.asp?
    cname=118&year=2004

There are basically two types of book fairs. In one type, a single copy of a title is displayed and the children order from this display. With this type of fair, much of the excitement of purchasing a title is lost and there is also a great deal of paperwork and accounting necessary, particularly if some of the titles later prove to be out-of-stock. However, this kind of fair requires the least supervision and space. In the other type, multiple copies of titles are supplied. Some distributors work from bookmobiles or portable cabinets. The following book fair guide is geared to the conventional in-house fair, but it can be adapted for other formats.

Planning the Book Fair

Make plans for the book fair from six to twelve months in advance. Decide the date for the event and contact the potential companies. Select a company, determine dates for the book fair and make tentative arrangements. Allow at least two months' preparation time to order books, prepare committees, and build interest. Fairs are usually held for two or three days. The length of time should be sufficient for each class to visit the fair at least once (twenty to thirty minutes per class) plus free time for those who wish to come again. The fair should stay open an hour after school to allow visitors from other schools to attend and one evening to encourage family participation.

Find a space to hold the fair where books can be displayed and central control can be exerted over entrances, exits, and traffic flow. Suggested places are an all-purpose room, auditorium stage, part of a gymnasium, corridors, or a student commons. If the school library media center is used, conventional services will have to be curtailed and the consequences should be weighed against the resultant benefits.

Publicity

Advance interest can be generated through publicity releases, display of posters, distribution of promotional pieces, and contests (for example, designing bookmarks, posters, writing limericks). When specific titles are known to be in the fair, a list of them under such headings as Scary Stories, Adventure, and so on, should be prepared and distributed. One to two weeks before the fair, put up posters around the school. Talk to the teachers about class visits and cooperatively decide a time. Send a book fair letter home to the parents and remind volunteers of the time they will be needed. When the books arrive, arrange displays or representative titles in display cases around the school.

Book Fair Volunteers

Many helpers will be needed; therefore, reliance on volunteer help, particularly parents, is essential. Some helpers can be used to set up the fair (allow at least one-half day for this). During the fair four to six adults will be needed at all times: two to handle the cash and the others to supervise displays, straighten and replenish stock, and help the professional staff give reading guidance.

Selection and Ordering of Books

There are several ways to select books for the fair. One method is to give the book jobber some basic information, number of students and range of their ages and interests, and allow the jobber to do the selecting. Several wholesalers operate solely on this principle and many have now refined their selection techniques so that a reasonably good selection is assured. Unfortunately, some tend to err on the side of safe titles like the classics and old standbys. Consequently, one whole segment of the reading public, the slow or reluctant reader, will find few appealing titles. A second method is to select only certain basic titles (for example, those you know will be used for class assignment or for which students have expressed a special interest) and allow the jobber to fill in the remaining titles. A third method is for the library media specialist to select and order all of the books, using standard selection guides. However, not all wholesalers will accept this type of order because they think that special orders on consignment are too time-consuming and unprofitable. Often a wholesaler with a large stock on hand will allow librarians to browse in the warehouse and order from the available stock. If the titles on hand are sufficiently varied and numerous, librarians using this selection method will have the satisfaction of a large variety from which to order and also the security of knowing the exact titles that will be available at the fair. Whatever selection method is used, orders should be placed well in advance. A minimum of one month is necessary; six to eight weeks is better. It may be difficult at first to estimate the number of books needed. The ability to do this comes with time and experience.

On average, one to two books are sold per student (of course, many more than this should be ordered to ensure a range in choice), but usually a wholesaler expects no more than one-third of the original order returned. In more affluent communities, and where reading is more popular, the average sold may be as high as five or six books per student.

In making selections, keep all levels of interest and ability in mind and base choices on what they will enjoy reading. Although quality literature should be presented, do not hesitate to include some popular fare—just-for-fun materials such as cartoon books, television tie-ins, and books on sports and romance. Reference books such as English-language and foreign-language dictionaries, a thesaurus, and those titles that provide guidance material and self-help tips are also popular.

Setting Up the Book Fair

When the books arrive, check the invoice to make sure you have received all the books for which you are being billed. If any books are unacceptable, remove them and place them in a separate box marked, RETURN TO THE JOBBER. Verify that all copies of a title have the same price. Designate one copy as a final copy. Place a note inside the final copy—"Last copy-do not sell," if you plan to take reorders.

Inventory control is essential. One effective method is to insert a small slip of paper with the price written on the exposed end into each book.

Sheets of these slips with various denominations are easy to photocopy and cut apart by scissors or paper cutter. These slips are then taken out of the book at the cash desk to provide a rough inventory control, as well as a count of how many books are sold on a given day or to a particular class or group.

Arrange the books in the fair to produce a natural flow of students from the entrance to the exit. One advantageous arrangement is a long row of tables in front of which students pass to make their selections and behind which are some adult helpers arranging and replenishing stock. Books should be arranged by categories similar to those used on the lists distributed earlier. Signs can be used to designate each category. The cash desk should be at the end of the line and close to the exit.

In the single-display-book type of fair, or when all copies but the last of a title have been sold, orders can be taken. The necessary order form should be photocopied in advance of the fair and contain spaces for the student's name, homeroom number, homeroom teacher, author, title, and price of paperback. Such book orders are paid for and the order slips retained at the cash desk. After the fair an order for these out-of-stock titles is placed with the jobber.

Finally, an important element to be considered in setting up the fair is the creation of a gala atmosphere. Special programs can be held before or during the book fair. Such programs could involve bringing a visiting author or illustrator to the school for a presentation, scheduling special storytelling or booktalk sessions about books in the fair, or showing one or more video based on a book or books in the fair. Contests during the fair, such as guessing the total number of books sold, are also fun.

After the Fair

Determine the value of the books ordered and paid for by students. That amount should be set aside to pay future invoices when the books arrive, or to refund the money to students if the books cannot be delivered. Sort out the unsold books by price, determine their value in each of the price categories, and subtract these totals from those on the original jobber's invoice. The difference remaining is the amount owed the jobber for copies sold; the difference between the book fair's receipts and the amount due the jobber represents the profit. Although jobbers sometimes give a twenty-five to thirty percent discount off list price for paperback fairs, the profit may be less due to losses sustained during the sale and the value of prices that have been given away.

It is always advisable to keep both financial and anecdotal records of your fair. The latter should include notes on best-selling titles and categories, detailed accounts of mistakes and pitfalls to avoid in the future, descriptions of successful procedures, and any recommended changes for subsequent fairs (Thibodeaux, personal communication, May 13, 2003).

REFERENCES

American Library Association. (2002, June 19). *Privacy and confidentiality.* Retrieved April 13, 2004, from the ALA web site: http://www.ala.org/Template.cfm?Section=Intellectual_Freedom_Issues&Template=/Content-Management/ContentDisplay.cfm&ContentID=25304

Arizona State Library, Collection Development Training. *Weeding.* Retrieved April 13, 2004, from Arizona State Library web site: http://www.lib.az.us/cdt/weeding.htm

Fisher, Julieta Dias & Hill, Ann. (2002). *Tooting your own horn: Web-based public relations for the 21st century librarian.* Worthington, OH: Linworth.

Guidelines for weeding library materials. (n.d.) Retrieved April 13, 2004, from: http://www.sbac.edu/%7Emedia/guid_weeding.html

Iowa Department of Education. (1994). *Weeding the library media center collections.* (2nd ed.). Retrieved April 13, 2004, from the Iowa Educational Media Association web site: http://www.iema-ia.org/IEMA209.html

Logan, Debra Kay & Beuselinck, Cynthia Lee. (2001). *K-12 Web Pages: Planning & Publishing Excellent School Web Sites.* Worthington, OH: Linworth.

Maryland State Department of Education. *Weeding: Reassessment of Library/Media Collections.* Retrieved April 13, 2004, from the Maryland State Department of Education web site: http://www.infohio.org/demo/Documents/UC/WeedingguidelinesMaryland.doc

Norfolk Public Schools, VA. Weeding. (2002, May). *Library media center handbook.* Retrieved April 13, 2004, from Norfolk Public Schools web site: http://www.nps.k12.va.us/aaa/media/manual1002/ch20_wd.pdf

Riley, Claudette. (2002, July 14). *Schools losing the war against book thefts: $65,000 in library books gone in Springfield alone last year; only one school has a security system.* Retrieved from: http://www.librarystuff.net/archives/2002_07_14_index.html

Thibodeaux, Annette. Bookfairs. Personal communication, May 13, 2003.

Sunlink Weed of the Month Club. (n.d.) Retrieved April 13, 2004, from the Sunlink web site: http://www.sunlink.ucf.edu/weed/

Weeding in libraries: A partial index to what's out there. Retrieved April 13, 2004, from: http://www.havana.lib.il.us/library/weeding.html

Weiser, Christine. (2003, February). Library collection security. *Media & Methods, 39*(4), 30–31.

FURTHER READING

Andronik, Catherine. (Ed.). (2003). *School library management notebook* (5th ed.). Worthington, OH: Linworth.

Baldwin, Carol. (2002). *School book fairs: A great opportunity for market research.* Retrieved May 10, 2004, from: http://www.writing-world.com/children/book fair.shtml

Barron, Ann E., et al. (2002). *Technologies for education: A practical guide* (4th ed.). Westport, CT: Libraries Unlimited.

Bilal, Dania. (2002). *Automating media centers and small libraries.* Westport, CT: Libraries Unlimited.

Billings, Harold. (2002). *Magic and hypersystems: Constructing the information sharing library.* Chicago: American Library Association.

Church, Audrey P. (2003). *Leverage your library program to raise test scores: A guide for library media specialists, principals, teachers, and parents.* Worthington, OH: Linworth.

Clyde, Laurel A. (2000). *Managing InfoTech in school library media centers.* Westport, CT: Libraries Unlimited.

Evans, G. Edward, et al. (2002). *Management basics for information professionals.* New York: Neal-Schuman.

Evans, G. Edward & Ward, Patricia Layzell. (2003). *Effective library management: A guide.* New York: Neal-Schuman.

Everhart, Nancy. (2003). *Controversial issues in school librarianship.* Worthington, OH: Linworth.

Farmer, Lesley S.J. (1995). *Leadership within the school library and beyond.* Worthington, OH: Linworth.

Foust, J'aime. (2002). *Dewey need to get organized? A time management and organization guide.* Worthington, OH: Linworth.

Giesecke, Joan. (1998). *Scenario planning for libraries.* Chicago: American Libraries Association.

Giesecke, Joan. (2001). *Practical strategies for library managers.* Chicago: American Library Association.

Hartzell, Gary N. (1994). *Building influence for the school librarian.* Worthington, OH: Linworth.

Hansel, Patsy. (1998). *Managing overdues.* New York: Neal-Schuman.

Job, Amy & Snare, Mary Kay. (1997). *The school library media specialist as manager.* Lanham, MD: Scarecrow Press.

Job, Amy & Snare, Mary Kay. (2001). *Now what do I do? Things they never taught in library school.* Lanham, MD: Scarecrow Press.

Johnson, Doug. (2003). *Learning right from wrong in the digital age: An ethics guide for parents, teachers, librarians, and others who care about computer-using young people.* Worthington, OH: Linworth.

Lavender, Kenneth. (2001). *Book repair* (2nd ed.). New York: Neal-Schuman.

Lazzaro, Joseph J. (2001). *Adaptive technologies for learning & work environments* (2nd ed.). Chicago: American Library Association.

Loertscher, David. (2000). *Taxonomies of the school library media program.* 2nd ed. Worthington, OH: Linworth.

McCain, Mary Maud & Merrill, Martha. (2001). *Dictionary for school library media specialists: A practical and comprehensive guide.* Westport, CT: Libraries

Martin, Murray S. & Park, Betsy. (1998) *Charging and collecting fees and fines: A handbook for libraries.* New York: Neal-Schuman.

Mason, Marilyn Gell. (1999). *Strategic management for today's libraries.* Chicago: American Library Association.

Melling, Maxine & Little, Joyce. (2002). *Building a successful customer service culture: A guide for library and information managers.* New York: Neal-Schuman.

Reed, Sally Gardner. (2001). *Making the case for your library.* New York: Neal-Schuman.

Reed, Sally Gardner. (2002). *Small libraries: A handbook of successful management* (2nd ed.). Jefferson, NC: McFarland.

Sager, Donald J. (2000). *Small libraries: Organization and operation* (3rd ed.). Fort Atkinson, WI: Highsmith Press.

Salmon, Sheila, et al. (1996). *Power up your library: Creating the new elementary school library program.* Westport, CT: Libraries Unlimited.

Schmidt, William D. & Rieck. Donald A. (2002). *Managing media services: Theory and practice.* Westport, CT: Libraries Unlimited.

Shuman, Bruce A. (1999). *Library security and safety handbook: Prevention, policies and procedures.* Chicago: American Library Association.

Shuman, Bruce A. (2001). *Issues for libraries and information science in the Internet age.* Westport, CT: Libraries Unlimited.

Shuman, Bruce A. (2002). *Case studies in library security.* Westport, CT: Libraries Unlimited.

Stein, Barbara L. & Brown, Risa W. (2002). *Running a school library media center* (2nd ed.). New York: Neal-Schuman.

Stueart, Robert D. & Moran, Barbara B. (2002). *Library and information center management.* Westport, CT: Libraries Unlimited.

Sykes, Judith A. (2002). *Action research: A practical guide for transforming your school library.* Westport, CT: Libraries Unlimited.

Thelan, Laurie N. (2003). *Essentials of elementary school library management.* Worthington, OH: Linworth.

Torrans, Lee. (2003). *Law for K-12 libraries and librarians.* Westport, CT: Libraries Unlimited.

Valenza, Joyce. (2004). *Power tools recharged: 125+ essential forms and presentations for your school library information program.* Chicago: American Library Association.

Wasman, Ann M. (1998). *New steps to service: Common-sense advice for the school library media specialist.* Chicago: American Library Association.

Wilson, Patricia Potter & Lyders, Josette Ann. (2001). *Leadership for today's school library: A handbook for the library media specialist and the school principal.* Westport, CT: Libraries Unlimited.

Woolls, Blanche. (2004). *The school library media manager* (3rd ed.). Westport, CT: Libraries Unlimited.

Wright, Kieth & Davie, Judith F. (1999). *Forecasting the future: School media programs in the age of change.* Lanham, MD: Scarecrow Press.

Yee, Martha & Layne, Sarah Shatford. (1998). *Improving online public access catalogs.* Chicago: American Library Association.

Yesner, Bernice L. & Jay, Hilda (1998). *Operating and evaluating school library media programs.* New York: Neal-Schuman.

Zilonis, Mary Frances, et al. (2002). *A long-range planning guide for school library media centers.* Lanham, MD: Scarecrow Press.

Chapter 13

OUTSIDE THE WALLS OF THE SCHOOL LIBRARY MEDIA CENTER

Many concerns of the school library media specialist exist beyond the daily routines of the individual center. Some with immediate and future implications, such as networking, are discussed in previous chapters. This chapter treats three important areas of immediate and future interest: associations, highlighting a few that are especially important to the school library media specialist; some government agencies of value to the specialist based on the knowledge that the political process in general and legislation in particular are vital; and a list of key publications for the media specialist.

ASSOCIATIONS

Some associations exert a strong influence on the everyday operations of a school library media center. Although they exist on different geopolitical levels, the associations should be familiar to the school library media specialist. One way to identify these associations is by subject specialty, another by geographic level. An attempt is made here to present associations that tend to integrate many of the disciplines incorporated in school library media centers.

There are some extremely active and influential associations on the international scene. One that has earned the respect of the multi-national library community is the International Federation of Library Associations (IFLA). Another, especially for school library media specialists, is the

International Association of School Librarianship (IASL), established in the late 1960s by Jean Lowrie, a former ALA president, to conduct international meetings and share in the transfer of information across continents. Also prevalent are special-interest associations, such as the International Board on Books for Young People (IBBY), which has played a significant role in its sphere since the end of World War II. The associations highlighted in this chapter, although national in scope, engage in extensive international cooperative ventures.

Three of the largest national associations, besides the American Library Association (ALA), that are vital in many ways to the development of school library media centers are the American Association of School Librarians (AASL), the American Society for Information Science and Technology (ASIST), and the Association for Educational Communications and Technology (AECT). The first and third associations deal with both library and media issues, and also with a recognition of and participation in the latest stage of technology—computerization. The second association devotes itself to school library media center concerns—computerization and information transfer. Each of these three is highlighted in the following list of associations. Both AASL and AECT have extensive state affiliations; ASIST has local college chapters for graduate student members.

A finely attuned communications procedure links the national associations and those of each state. In addition, there are at least two types of state organizations: (1) combined school library and media organizations, and (2) separate library and media organizations. The California Association of Educational Media and Technology (CAEMAT) is an example of the first. Some states follow the second example in not combining their library and media organizations. Alabama is an example of a state that has two associations, namely the Alabama Library Association and the Alabama Instructional Media Association. For school library media specialists, this means that both state associations have to be considered for membership. The Florida Association of Media Educators (FAME) includes media, school library, and education personnel, as well as others, and illustrates another type of state organization, one that centers on the school itself. All three types include the strength of affiliation throughout the state, as well as the many functions that are generally performed. These may include committee work; annual conventions; regional meetings; creation of guidelines for evaluation; discussion of current issues and recurring problems; and publications, including a regular periodical. Some of the publications currently on sale through one of the state associations, the

New York Library Association (NYLA) are: *Basic Young Adult Services Handbook; Libraries Serving Youth; Talk it Up: Book Discussion Programs for Young People; What Works: Developmentally Appropriate Library Programs for Very Young Children; Library Stories Video;* and *Libraries Search for the Future Video.*

Fortunately, there are local school library media associations for many specialists. (Local associations lend the aid and comfort of like-minded individuals who work in school library media centers and share many of the same concerns.) These associations can be small or large and still exert a strong force in the region. An example is the Long Island School Media Association (LISMA), a combined library and media organization that operates in Long Island, New York. This highly developed local group provides an annual media fair for its members and others, a regular newsletter *(LISMA INK)*, an information network of local members, an informal placement service that coordinates its efforts through a central bureau at Palmer School of Library and Information Science, C.W. Post College, Long Island University, and more. Local associations can provide support for the individual school library media specialist.

Media specialists should be aware of the many important associations that are available and, within individual constraints, each person should join and participate in as many as possible for the maximum effect, from local to state to national to international. The continuing development of school library media specialists and centers depends on the strength that individuals are willing to lend to this effort. A list of helpful associations follows, beginning with a highlight summary of three large national groups.

American Association of School Librarians (AASL), 50 East Huron Street, Chicago, IL 60611. Telephone: 800-545-2433; web site: http:// www.ala.org/aaslhomeTemplate.cfm?Section=AASL&Template=/Tagged Page/TaggedPageDisplay.cfm&TPLID=17&ContentID=23240.

AASL is a division of the American Library Association (ALA) whose primary mission is to "advocate excellence, facilitate change, and develop leaders in the school library media field" (AASL, 2003 web site, p. 1). The association strives to ensure that school library media specialists: provide leadership in the field, serve as collaborative partners in teaching/learning in schools, take steps to link learners with ideas and information, equip students to be lifelong learners/readers, informed decision makers, and users of information technology. Some other divisions of ALA of interest to a school library media specialist are:

Association for Library Service to Children (ALSC)

Association for Library Collections and Technical Services (LCTS)

Association of Specialized and Cooperative Library Agencies (ASCLA)

Library Administration and Management Association (LAMA)

Library and Information Technology Association (LITA)

Reference and User Services Association (RUSA)

Young Adult Library Services Association (YALSA)

One of the largest divisions of ALA, AASL is interested in improving and extending library media services for young people. It is also responsible for planning programs of study and service in grades K–12; evaluating, selecting, utilizing, and promoting an awareness of school library media centers; encouraging research in the field; integrating the activities of other ALA divisions that are pertinent to AASL concerns; interpreting school library media centers to other educational associations; stimulating professional growth; encouraging organizational participation among school library media specialists; conducting activities and projects; and so on. There are approximately forty committees, among them are:

AASL @ Your Library

AASL Alliance for Association Excellence

Appointments Committee

Awards

Bylaws and Organization

ICONnect: FamiliesConnect

ICONnect: Online Courses

Institute Planning

Intellectual Freedom

International Relations

Knowledge Quest Editorial Board

Leadership Forum Planning

Legislation

NCATE Coordinating

Nominating

Publications

Research and Statistics

School Library Media Research Editorial Board

Teaching and Instruction Committee

Web Advisory

There are also special committees, such as Reading for Understanding and task forces, such as Recruitment for the Profession and a strong state-affiliate assembly, which are not permanent committees. The members of the AASL affiliate assembly are generally directly involved with individual district and school library media centers, as well as with people who are interested in one of the many areas of the field. The association is actively engaged in publicizing and granting awards to exceptional school library media center programs and people across the nation. It holds an every other year national conference in addition to the one held annually in June/July by the parent organization, ALA. AASL held its eleventh annual fall conference in Kansas City, Missouri in October 2003, at which it featured the theme, Information Matters.

Publications of the AASL include *Knowledge Quest,* the official periodical for members and other interested persons both online and printed, and *School Library Media Research,* an online journal related to school library media research. ALA Editions, the book-publishing imprint for ALA offers many publications applicable for school library media centers. Publications available from the ALA Bookstore include: *Designing a School Library Media Center for the Future* (2001); *Managing and Analyzing Your Collection: A Practical Guide for Small Libraries and School Media Centers* (2002); *Best Books for Young Adults,* 2nd ed. (2000); *Censorship and Selection: Issues and Answers for Schools,* 3rd ed. (2001); *Excellence in Library Services to Young Adults,* 3rd ed. (2000); *Delivering Web Reference Services to Young People* (1998). *Hit List for Children 2: Frequently Challenged Books* (2002); *Hit List for Young Adults 2: Frequently Challenged Books* (2002); *The Visible Librarian: Asserting Your Value with Marketing and Advocacy* (2003); *Information Power: Building Partnerships for Learning* (1998); *Information Powered Schools* (2001); and *Power Tools Recharged* (2004). Check the ALA Editions bookstore online for other available publications.

American Society for Information Science and Technology (ASIS&T), 1320 Fenwick Lane, Suite 510, Silver Spring, MD 20910. Telephone: 301-495-0900; Fax 301-495-0810; web site: http://www.asis.org/.

Established in 1937, the society acts as a clearinghouse for information on better theories and techniques as well as discussions about information systems and technologies that improve information access. There are approximately 4,000 members—individuals, students, and institutions. Members are generally information scientists, computer scientists, administrators, librarians, and others who are interested in the many phases of the information-transfer process, such as storage, retrieval, and use. Many members are actively engaged in significant stages of this process, such as classifying, indexing, retrieval, and system analysis. ASIS&T provides a forum for discussion and evaluation of the theory and practice that are involved in communications. It sponsors publications pertinent to its concerns, as well as an online jobline and it presents honors in the field. ASIS&T has several special-interest groups, such as Arts and Humanities, Digital Libraries, Management, Technology, Information & Society, which may be of interest to school library media specialists. Known before 1968 as the American Documentation Institute (ADI), the society is affiliated with ALA in that it works with information specialists and librarians to improve access to information. Both organizations have some of the same members. It holds an annual convention, generally in October. ASIS&T committees are:

Awards and Honors

Budget and Finance

Constitution and Bylaws

Information Science Education

Leadership Development

Membership

Nominations

Standards

Publications include *Information Architecture for the World Wide Web* (2002); *Models for Library Management, Decision-Making and Planning* (2001); *Beyond Our Control? Confronting the Limits of Our Legal System in the Age of Cyberspace* (2001); *Information Architecture, An Emerging 21st Century Profession* (2003); *Information Architecture, Blueprints for the Web* (2002) *Design Research: Methods and Perspectives* (2003); *Looking for Information: A Survey of Research on Information Seeking, Needs & Behavior* (2002); *Information Representation and Retrieval in the Digital Age* (2003); and *Information Architecture for Designers: Structuring Websites for Business Success* (2003).

Association for Educational Communications and Technology (AECT), 1800 N. Stonelake Drive, Suite 2, Bloomington, IN 47408. Telephone: 877-677-2328 or 812-335-7675; web site: http://www.aect.org/.

A professional association established in 1923, AECT deals with matters pertaining to improving instruction through educational technology. There are seven divisions, two councils, fifteen affiliated organizations, and seven chapters. The members are generally instructional technologists, school library media specialists or media specialists, religious educators, government media personnel, educational/training media producers, university professors and researchers, industrial/business training specialists, and school district or state department of education media program personnel. Some members are employed in museums, public libraries, hospitals, and other information agencies. AECT serves as a clearinghouse for the exchange and dissemination of ideas; it provides both national and international information for the improvement of instruction. It gathers information and prepares guidelines for standards and research, as well as summaries on topics of concern to the membership. The association maintains the Educational Communications and Technology Foundation (ECT), which gives financial aid to further the work of AECT. The international conventions are usually held in October. The AECT divisions are:

Management
Design & Development
Media & Technology (K–12)
Distance Learning
Performance
Teacher Education
Research and Theory

Publications include *Tech Trends* (with membership); *Educational Technology Research and Development,* and various other division publications. Some other nonperiodic publications are: *Distance Education: Definition and Glossary of Terms* (n.d.); *High Tech Law (In Plain English): An Entrepreneur's Guide; Handbook of Research for Educational Communications and Technology* (1996); and a *Code of Professional Ethics* (2001).

International Society for Technology in Education (ISTE), 480 Charnelton Street, Eugene, OR 97401-2626. Telephone: 800-336-5191; web site: http://www.iste.org/.

ISTE is a worldwide nonprofit professional organization that provides leadership and service in the use of technology for improvement of teaching and learning in K-12 education and teacher education. Members are provided information, networking opportunities, and guidance in integrating new technologies into schools. ISTE is the home of the National Educational Technology Standards (NETS), the Center for Applied Research in Educational Technology, and the National Educational Computing Conference (NECC). ISTE is a leader in conducting professional development workshops, forums and symposia, as well as doing research and disseminating findings about educational technology internationally. For more information, consult the ISTE web site, http://www.iste.org/about/.

Publications include one free periodical with membership, either *Learning & Leading with Technology* or *Journal of Research on Technology in Education.* ISTE offers a wide selection of books, including: *Technology, Innovation, an Educational Change—A Global Perspective* (2003); *Web Searching Strategies—An Introductory Curriculum for Students and Teachers* (2003); *Administrative Solutions for Handheld Technology in Schools* (2003); *101 Best Web Sites for Principals* (2003); *National Educational Technology Standards for Teachers—Resources for Assessment* (2003); *Pocket PC Computers—A Complete Resource for Classroom Teachers* (2004); *101 Best Web Sites for District Leaders* (2004); *We're Getting Wired, We're Getting Mobile, What's Next? Fresh Ideas for Educational Technology Planning* (2004); *Self-Assessment Activities for School Administrators* (2004).

Other Important Associations and Agencies

Consortium of College and University Media Centers (CCUMC), (formerly Consortium of University Film Centers [CUFC]), Instructional Technology Center, 1200 Communications Building, Iowa State University, Ames, IA 50011. Telephone: 515-294-1811; web site: http://www.indiana.edu/~ccumc/about.html.

CCUMC is a group of professional college and university personnel whose aim is to improve education and training through the effective use of media and instructional technology and to provide support for quality teaching in institutions of higher education. Founded in 1971 as the Consortium of University Film Centers (CUFC), it changed its name in 1988. Annual conferences are normally held in late October and the proceedings are published shortly thereafter. CCUMC provides a list of member institutions that have a video/film rental collection. CCUMC is responsible for publications such as a newsletter, *The Leader* and *College and University Media Review,* which are both a membership benefit.

Educational Products Information Exchange (Institute) (EPIE), 103 West Montauk Highway, Hampton Bays, NY 10046. Telephone: 631-728-1000. Or, PO Box 839, Water Mill, NY 11976. Telephone: 516-283-4922; web site: http://www.epie.org/.

A nonprofit institute, EPIE engages primarily in the evaluation of educational software information and the development for educational change. It also provides a source for teacher use, Learning Space, which allows teachers to store lesson plans and gives students the chance to be rewarded for evaluating web sites. They also provide a software review service, T.E.S.S. Services are made available to teachers, educators, and parents.

Educational Resources Information Center (ERIC), 2277 Research Boulevard, 6M, Rockville, MD 20850. Telephone: 800-538-3742; Fax 301-519-6760; web site: http://www.eric.ed.gov.

ERIC coordinates several clearinghouses, but those clearinghouses are not listed here. Overall, there are more than 1 million documents in ERIC, the world's largest education database, including journal articles, research reports, books, teaching guides, conference papers, and more. Documents are sold both as microfiche and paper copies. The ERIC database can be searched online. ERIC clearinghouses are now closed; however, a new government grant has been awarded for five years that will most likely support the clearinghouses. Because of the uncertainty of the situation about ERIC, the clearinghouses are not included in this chapter.

Support components of ERIC include the following:

- **ERIC Document Reproduction Service (EDRS).** DynEDRS, Inc., 7420 Fullerton Road, Suite 110, Springfield, VA 22153-2852. Telephone: 800-443-3742 or 703-440-1400; Fax: 703-440-1408; E-mail: service@edrs.com; web site: http://www.edrs.com.

- **ERIC Processing and Reference Facility.** Computer Sciences Corporation, 4483-A Forbes Boulevard Lanham, MD 20706. Telephone: 800-799-ERIC (3742) or 301-552-4200; Fax: 301-552-4700; E-mail: info@ericfac.piccard.csc.com; web site: http://www.ericfacility.org/.

  Publications include *ERIC Digests*, subscriptions to *Resources in Education (RIE)*, and the current index to *Journals in Education (CIJE)*. Greenwood Press monitors changes in *ERIC Thesaurus*. The Thesaurus can be searched online at http://www.ericfacility.net/extra/pub/thessearch.cfm. Significant changes are planned for ERIC which may change some current documents about ERIC mentioned here.

Library of Congress (LC), James Madison Building, 101 Independence Ave. S.E., Washington, DC 20540. Telephone: 202-707-5000; web site: http://www.loc.gov/.

Originally designated as the research arm of Congress, LC has been accepted popularly as the National Library of the United States. LC has numerous materials and services of interest to school library media specialists. The collections in LC contain more than 18 million books, 2.5 million recordings, 12 million photographs, 4.5 million maps and 54 million manuscripts. Some of the services offered are interlibrary loans for materials: traveling exhibits of prints and photographs; and MARC tapes for most media; folk-life materials and services; copyright for most media; national library service for the blind and physically handicapped, which provides materials and equipment for eligible persons; the Center for the Book (1977), which strives to stimulate appreciation for the printed word; the Geography and Map Division, which includes manuscript, topographical, and subject maps; photocopying and reproduction services; the National Referral Service, which refers people with questions to knowledgeable authorities, but does not provide technical or bibliographical information to any beyond its clientele (Congress); and the like.

Some LC publications are *Perspectives on American Book History: Artifacts and Commentary* (2002); *The Most Wonderful Books: Writers on Discovering the Pleasures of Reading* (1997); *Language of the Land: The Library of Congress Book of Literary Maps* (1999); *Library of Congress Geography and Maps: An Illustrated Guide* (2000); *A Handbook for the Study of Book History in the United States* (2000). Children's books can be found from the Library of Congress sales shop, such as: *New Big Book of U.S. Presidents* (2000); *Marshall, the Courthouse Mouse: A Tail of the U.S. Supreme Court* (2000); and *House Mouse, Senate Mouse* (1996).

National Audiovisual Center (NAC). U.S. Department of Commerce, Technology Administration, National Technology Information Service, 5285 Port Royal Road, Springfield, VA 22161. Telephone: 703-605-6000; web site: http://www.ntis.gov/products/types/audiovisual/index.asp.

NAC is a central clearinghouse for more than 9,000 AV materials produced by and for the federal government. Education materials subjects include history, health, agriculture and natural resources. It distributes CD-ROMs, videos, audiocassettes, and multimedia kits and provides access to audiovisual materials from several government agencies.

Publications available include *Statistical Abstract of the United States* (2002) in printed format or CD-ROM; *World Fact Book* (2003) in printed format or CD-ROM; *Occupational Outlook Handbook* on CD-ROM.

National Information Center for Educational Media (NICEM), P.O. Box 8640, Albuquerque, NM 87198. Telephone: 800-926-8328; web site: http://www.nicem.com/.

NICEM is a central facility that collects, catalogs, and disseminates information about nonprint material through audiovisual reference indexes. The center is well known for its indexes of AV material by format. *Film & Video Finder Online* is a large database of more than 440,000 items can be searched online. Additionally, NICEM maintains online a file of media producers and distributors. The NICEM Audiovisual Database is frequently used by media specialists as a cataloging tool because the records are available in MARC-tagged format. NICEM information is also made available through several partners, including SilverPlatter and the Library Corporation. Many NICEM products may be ordered from Plexus Publishing, Inc., 143 Old Marlton Pike, Medford, NJ 08055; Telephone: 609-654-6500, Fax: 609-654-4309; E-mail: info@plexuspublishing.com.

FEDERAL AND STATE AGENCIES AND PROGRAMS

Financial support of libraries by the federal government is a comparatively recent phenomenon. Although the Elementary and Secondary Act (ESEA) had its beginning in 1965 and renewed through block grants for several years, it was launched in 2002 as the No Child Left Behind Act (2001) designed to improve academic achievement of the disadvantaged and minority child in poverty schools. Funding for school libraries comes under the Reading First allocation for improving literacy through school libraries. Information about Improving Literacy Through School Libraries (LSL) grants can be found at the U.S. Department of Education web site: http://www.ed.gov/offices/OESE/LSL/. State education agencies administer the ESEA (No Child Left Behind) funds based on districts with twenty percent or higher family poverty. According to the Office of Elementary and Secondary Education of the U.S. Department of Education (2003) web site:

The Improving Literacy through School Libraries (LSL) program promotes comprehensive local strategies to improve student reading achievement by improving school library services and resources. The LSL program is one component of the Department's commitment to dramatically improve student achievement by focusing available resources, including those of school library media centers, on reading achievement.

School library media centers can contribute to improved student achievement by providing up-to-date instructional materials aligned to the curriculum and instructional practices, collaborating with and supporting teachers, administrators, and parents, and extending their hours of operation beyond the school day. (p. 1)

For more information about other possible sources of federal funding, contact the state education department.

A new organization, the Institute of Education Sciences, was formed under the Education Sciences Reform Act (2002). As a result of this act, the Office of Educational Research and Improvement in the U.S. Department of Education, which formerly was responsible for education research and statistics became extinct. In its place, the Institute took on a research arm by adding the National Center for Education Research (NCER), the National Center for Education Statistics (NCES), and the National Center for Education Evaluation and Regional Assistance as major research centers within the organizational structure of the Institute.

The National Center for Education Research (NCER) provides support for research that solves significant problems in education in this country. Research initiatives normally focus on quality education for all children, academic achievement improvement, closing the gap between low and high student achievement, and increasing access opportunities for postsecondary education. Information about the center is provided at the Institute's funding page: http://www.ed.gov/offices/IES/funding.html.

The National Center for Education Statistics (NCES) collects, analyzes and reports educational statistics for all levels of education, including preschool, elementary, secondary, postsecondary and adult, based on progress in education and its conditions. Other nations are also included in its work. NCES seeks to supply relevant data useful to practitioners, policy makers in the schools, researchers, and to the general public. Information about the center can be found at their web site: http://nces.ed.gov/.

The National Center for Education Evaluation and Regional Assistance (NCEE) conducts evaluations of federal program's impact on education, synthesizes and disseminates evaluation and research information, and provides technical assistance as a means to improve student achievement in the areas of reading, mathematics and science. A comprehensive reference service is provided which locates relevant education materials as a service to the public. Information about the center can be found at their web site: http://www.ed.gov/offices/IES/NCEE/.

There are three other offices in the Department of Education that administer legislation affecting school library media centers. The Office of Special Education and Rehabilitation Services (OSERS) provides services to people with disabilities of all ages. Support is provided to parents and individuals, school districts and states in the following areas: special education, vocational rehabilitation and research. As part of the No Child Left Behind agenda and New Freedom initiative, OSERS works to ensure that handicapped individuals are not left behind in school, in employment or in life. Funds are provided to programs that offer information and technical assistance to parents of children with disabilities as well the learning community that serves them.

The Office of Bilingual Language Acquisition, Language Enhancement, and Academic Achievement for Limited English Proficient Students (OELA) assists state and local agencies to develop and strengthen programs that help children who have limited English proficiency and whose first language is not English. Contact at this web site: http://www.ed.gov/offices/OBEMLA/. The Office for Vocational and Adult Education (OVAE), through its many services, assists states in training youths and adults for work. Web site: http://www.ed.gov/about/offices/list/OVAE/index.html?src=mr.

Some other government-related agencies that are sources of information and/or funds related to libraries are: The Institute of Museum and Library Services, which supports all types of libraries, including school library media centers, by fostering leadership and a lifetime of learning; the National Commission on Libraries and Information Science (NCLIS, a planning agency), which advises the President and Congress on national library and information policies and plans; the National Endowment for the Arts, which provides recognition of artistic excellence to enhance the nation's culture; the National Endowment for the Humanities (Washington, DC), which promotes excellence in the humanities and conveys lessons of history to American citizens; and the National Science Foundation, which promotes the progress of science through funding research and education.

State Education Agencies

The role of state educational agencies in the development and administration of local and district school library media programs has become one of increasing importance. One of the main sources of service to school library media centers in many states is the state library agency or state library. All fifty states do not have state libraries, but they frequently have a division in the state education department that works closely with libraries, including school media centers. In those states that have state library agencies, there is no set standard that fits all in how the agencies work with school media centers. They serve a diverse audience, and emphasis on library services varies from state to state. Because of the diversity of these functions, it is important that media personnel either individually or through a district office, establish and maintain contact with the appropriate state school library media center agency and use their services (see Appendix I for a list of state consultants and addresses to facilitate initial contacts). It should also be noted that many of the agencies supply documents that can be helpful in such areas as selection of materials and development of the center's instructional program.

The book, *The Functions and Roles of State Library Agencies* (2000) compiled by Ethel E. Himmel and William J. Wilson (Chicago: American Library Association), is a good source for an overview of state library agencies. It discusses services offered to libraries, collections administered by the agencies, and their roles in the electronic age.

A look at funding allocated by state legislatures needs to a closely monitored by school library media specialists. Some state departments of education post funding information on their web sites. Keeping abreast of the political scene and funding issues is crucial.

School Library Media Centers and the Political Process

The library profession has often been accused of having more interest in communicating internally than with those who make the major decisions affecting its future. Being involved in the legislative process through lobbying or application of other forms of political pressure is crucial to the future of school media centers. All media specialists need to become politically involved in the political process to ensure the support of school media centers. Becoming involved in state and national legislative days is a good political beginning. To become involved in legislative days, one must also become active in state and national organizations that keep track and lobby for legislation beneficial to school media centers. It is always a good idea to invite state legislators, board members, or local officials for a visit to the media center and to show them how students are learning. During their visit, it is a good time to express to them the research studies by Lance and others about the impact of school media centers on student achievement.

For the novice who is planning such an event, here are some pointers: Be sure to organize your activity well. Depending on the level of activity (local or statewide), this event might involve setting up a steering committee or forming a communications network to assist you in planning. Be sure to plan thoroughly by formally stating short- and long-range goals, devising a timetable, and preparing suitable data and supporting documents for presentation to the legislators or board members. Designing legislation workshops prior to the event can be of benefit if they cover topics such as an explanation of the legislative process, hints on how to establish a legislative network, and techniques on how to contact and communicate with key officials. Seek outside support and form alliances with other interested organizations such as local PTO groups, local or state educational organizations, and legislative groups like the League of Women Voters. Communicate your needs and position politely but effectively to the necessary individuals—politicians, legislators, and board members—who can act as change agents on your behalf. Before these encounters, whether by mail, telephone, or in person, prepare yourself to present your position succinctly, accurately, and in terms of how your suggestions will benefit students academically. Cover only one or two issues at a time, be concise, and suggest a specific course of action. In the case of legislators, send a personal letter after the visit expressing appreciation for the visit and a reminder of the legislation needing support. Do not ignore other forms of communication, such as letters to the editor, press releases, news conferences, interviews, handouts, buttons, community bulletin boards, and speaking engagements. The growing success rate of librarians in influencing the political process promises to be a challenge worth taking.

SCHOOL LIBRARY MEDIA CENTERS AND THE PUBLIC LIBRARY

Public libraries and school library media centers are a natural when it comes to collaboratively working together. They both have common interests in determining how they can better serve the needs of children and teens. Just like collaborative planning within the school, planning with the children and youth librarians in the public library is necessary to bring about needed services to the children and youth in schools. School media specialists need to visit their community public library and talk to their counterparts about how they can plan programs together, keep each other informed of student assignments, and promote each other within the community. A good beginning is to invite public librarians to talk with students about their services, and help students to get public library cards. Planning summer reading programs together will certainly be beneficial to students. A summer reading program for disadvantaged students would be an excellent place to begin. There are no limitations to what can be accomplished when media specialists and public librarians work together. It is a win-win situation that enhances student learning.

SCHOOL LIBRARY MEDIA CENTERS AND NETWORKING

School media centers are more adept in working cooperatively to share resources either in formal networks or informally. More states are developing formal library network systems to serve school media centers statewide. New York State is one of the earliest leaders in the nation to develop a formal network (BOCES) to serve the school media centers throughout the state. In 1984, the New York State Legislature authorized the development of school library systems based within the forty-one BOCES (Board of Cooperative Educational Services) and the five Big City School Districts. The systems are supported by state funds. Each system maintains an automated union catalog of resources in machine-readable catalog (MARC) format. Interlibrary loans among school libraries are an important part of the BOCES network.

A rather unique type of sharing of resources occurs in the Library Management Network based in Decatur, Alabama. One of the leaders in the network was Decatur High School, the first school media center in the State of Alabama to participate in a multi-type library network with public, academic, and special libraries in the early 1980s. The sharing of resources with community libraries is enhanced by all libraries working together. Students at Decatur High School search the online database to determine if materials are available at the public library and the community college library before going to request materials. Interlibrary loans among participating libraries reap major benefits for all involved.

Several states have developed networks to benefit school media centers. Some examples include: NCWiseOwl (North Carolina), INFOhio (Ohio), Texas Library Connect (TLC), and SUNLINK (Florida). For a more detailed description of these networks see Chapter 10.

Many school media centers are involved in more informal arrangements of borrowing materials from other schools in the district or in neighboring districts. Informal resource sharing is an effective way to build rapport with other school media specialists.

SCHOOL LIBRARY MEDIA SPECIALIST'S READING SHELF

At the end of each chapter in this book are suggestions for further reading, but each media specialist might wish to build a basic collection of books and materials to supplement this handbook. Several other works cover some of the same material. Two recommended titles are Blanche Woolls (2004), *School Library Media Manager,* 3rd ed. (Westport, CT: Libraries Unlimited) and Barbara L. Stein and Risa W. Brown (2002), *Running a School Library Media Center,* 2nd ed. (New York: Neal-Schuman). A practical, serviceable, basic work is Ann M. Wasman (1998), *New Steps to Service* (Chicago: American Library Association).

Any professional shelf should certainly contain the national guidelines, *Information Power: Building Partnerships for Learning* (Chicago: American Library Association/Association for Educational Communications and Technology, 1998). In developing the center's program, there are three books written by Patricia Potter Wilson and Roger Leslie that describe a variety of events designed to inspire students in elementary, middle school, and high school. The titles include: *Premier Events: Library Programs That Inspire Elementary School Patrons* (2001); *Center Stage: Library Programs That Inspire Middle School Patrons* (2001); *and Igniting the Spark: Library Programs That Inspire High School Patrons* (2001) (Westport, CT: Libraries Unlimited).

Two yearbooks cover various aspects of the world of libraries and media without too much overlapping: *The Bowker Annual of Library and Book Trade Almanac* (Medford, NJ: Information Today, Inc.) and *Educational Media and Technology Yearbook* (Westport, CT: Libraries Unlimited).

Two periodicals also cover news items and trends in the world of libraries and educational media: *American Libraries* and *Library Journal.* Periodicals geared specifically to school library media centers and work with children and young adults are *School Library Journal, Teacher Librarian, School Library Media Activities Monthly,* and *Library Media Connection.*

To this basic list of books and periodicals, each person will certainly add other titles that have proven helpful and are considered basic. Some candidates in the book category are:

Barron, Ann, et al. (2002). *Technologies for education* (4th ed.). Westport, CT: Libraries Unlimited.

Benson, Allen C. (2003). *Connecting kids and the web: A handbook for teaching Internet use and safety.* New York: Neal-Schuman.

Bilal, Dania. (2002). *Automating media centers and small libraries.* Westport, CT: Libraries Unlimited.

Bradburn, Frances Bryant. (1998). *Output measures for school library media programs.* New York: Neal-Schuman.

Braun, Linda. (2001). *Introducing the Internet to young learners.* New York: Neal-Schuman.

Church, Audrey. (2003). *Leverage your library program to raise test scores: A guide for library media specialists, principals, teachers and parents.* Worthington, OH: Linworth.

Coffman, Steve. (2003). *Going live: Starting and running a virtual reference service.* Chicago: American Library Association.

Craver, Kathleen W. (2002). *Creating cyber libraries: An instructional guide for school media specialists.* Westport, CT: Libraries Unlimited.

Crews, Kenneth D. (2000). *Copyright essentials for librarians and educators.* Chicago: American Library Association.

Dickinson, Gail. (2003). *Empty pockets and full plates: Effective budget administration for library media specialists.* Worthington, OH: Linworth.

Everhart, Nancy. (1998). *Evaluating the school library media center.* Westport, CT: Libraries Unlimited.

Flowers, Helen F. (1998). *Public relations for school library media programs.* New York: Neal-Schuman.

Johnson, Doug. (2003). *Learning right from wrong in the digital age: An ethics guide for parents, teachers, librarians, and others who care about computer-using young people.* Worthington, OH: Linworth.

Keeling, Joyce. (2002). *Lesson plans for the busy librarian: A standards-based approach for the elementary library media center.* Westport, CT: Libraries Unlimited.

Kravitz, Nancy. (2002). *Censorship and the school library media center.* Westport, CT: Libraries Unlimited.

Lance, Keith Curry & Loertscher, David. (2002). *Powering achievement: School library media programs make the difference: The evidence.* San Jose, CA: Hi Willow Research and Publishing.

Loertscher, David. (2000). *Taxonomies of the school library media program.* 2nd ed. San Jose, CA: Hi Willow Research & Publishing.

McCain, Mary Maud & Merrill, Martha. (2001). *Dictionary for school library media specialists: A practical and comprehensive guide.* Westport, CT: Libraries Unlimited.

Milam, Peggy. (2002). *InfoQuest: A new twist on information literacy.* Worthington, OH: Linworth.

Morrison, Gary, et al. (2004). *Designing effective instruction.* Hoboken, NJ: John Wiley & Sons.

Ohrich, Karen Browne. (2001). *Making flexible access and flexible scheduling work today*. Westport, CT: Libraries Unlimited.

Pappas, Marjorie L. & Tepe, Ann E. (2002). *Pathways to knowledge and inquiry learning*. Westport, CT: Libraries Unlimited.

Simpson, Carol. (2003). *Ethics in school librarianship: A reader*. Worthington, OH: Linworth.

Turner, Philip & Riedling, Ann Marlow. (2003). *Helping teacher's teach: A school library media specialist's role* (3rd ed.). Westport, CT: Libraries Unlimited.

Valenza, Joyce Kasman. (2002). *Power research tools: Learning activities and posters*. Chicago: American Library Association.

Valenza, Joyce Kasman. (2004). *Power tools recharged: 125+ essential forms and presentations for your school library information program*. Chicago: American Library Association.

Van Orden, Phyllis & Bishop, Kay. (2001). *The collection program in schools* (3rd ed.). Westport, CT: Libraries Unlimited.

Wilson, Patricia Potter & Lyders, Josette Ann. (2001). *Leadership for today's school library*. Westport, CT: Libraries Unlimited.

Yesner, Bernice L. & Jay, Hilda. (1998). *Operating and evaluating school library media programs*. New York: Neal-Schuman.

The practices that are discussed in this and the preceding chapters on managing a single school library media center point out the differences between the school library of the past and today's center. The conventional school library was adequate when information was transmitted in traditional ways. Now, however, the technology-rich environment makes it imperative that educators utilize new online sources of information and teach the information literacy skills necessary to understand and interpret them.

It is interesting to speculate on what the scope and contents of a handbook similar to this one will be in the future. Whatever the future may bring in education, it seems assured that school library media centers are destined to play an increasingly important role in the instructional process.

REFERENCES

American Association of School Librarians. (2003, September 3). *Issues and advocacy*. Retrieved May 10, 2004, from the ALA web site: http://www.ala.org/ala/issues/issuesadvocacy.htm

Himmel, Ethel E. & Wilson, William J. (Comps). (2000). *Functions and roles of state library agencies*. GraceAnne A. DeCandido (Ed.). Chicago: American Library Association.

U.S. Department of Education. (2003). *Improving literacy through school libraries.* Retrieved May 10, 2004, from: http://www.ed.gov/programs/sls/index.html

FURTHER READING

AASL Affiliate Assembly. *Directory of state and regional affiliated organizations.* Retrieved May 10, 2004, from the ALA web site: http://staging.ala.org/Content/NavigationMenu/AASL/About_AASL/Governance2/AASL_Affiliate_Assembly/Directory_of_AASL_State_and_Regional_Affiliated_Organizations.htm

Call your senator now! (2001, April). *School Library Journal, 47*(4), 22.

Colorado Department of Education. (2002, August 23). *Colorado students achieve power @ your library.* Retrieved April 13, 2004, from: http://www.cde.state.co.us/litstandards/qualschoollibs.htm

Baylis-Heerschop, Christen. (n.d.). *Federal aid to education.* Retrieved May 10, 2004, from: http://www.nd.edu/~rbarger/www7/fedaid.html

Callison, Daniel. (1997, Fall). Expanding collaboration for literacy promotion in school and public libraries. *Journal of Youth Services in Libraries, 11*(3), 37–48.

Fitzgibbons, Shirley A. (2000). *School and public library relationships: Essential ingredients implementing educational reform and improving student learning.* Retrieved April 13, 2004, from ALA web site: http://www.ala.org/Content/NavigationMenu/AASL/Publications_and_Journals/School_Library_Media_Research/Contents1/Volume_3_(2000)/relationships.htm

Iowa Educational Media Association. *Legislative issues.* Retrieved April 13, 2004, from: http://www.iema-ia.org/IEMA275.html

Jonassen, David H. (2004). *Learning to solve problems: An instructional design guide: A model for instructional design.* Indianapolis, IN: Jossey Bass Wiley.

Milbury, Peter. (2001). *Professional educational associations and organizations: Online resources for school librarians.* Retrieved April 13, 2004, from: http://www.school-libraries.org/resources/professional.html

Reiser, Robert & Dempsey, John. (2002). *Trends and issues in instructional design and technology.* Upper Saddle River, NJ: Prentice Hall.

Rogers, Patricia. (2003). *Designing instruction for technology enhanced learning.* Hershey, PA: Idea Group Publishing.

Schacter, John. (2003, June 1). Preventing summer reading loss during summer break. *The Achiever, 2*(10), 1–2. Retrieved May 10, 2004, from: http://www.nclb.gov/newletter

Vision of ideal cooperation between public and school libraries. (2003, August 13). Retrieved April 13, 2004, from Massachusetts Board of Library Commissioners web site: http://www.mlin.lib.ma.us/mblc/public_advisory/school_public/ps_vision.shtml

Walsh, Virginia. (1997). *Lobby for libraries: Putting marketing principles to work!* Retrieved April 13, 2004, from: http://alia.org.au/publishing/speeches/lobby. libraries.html

Woolls, Blanche. (2004). *School library media manager* (3rd ed.). Westport, CT: Libraries Unlimited.

Chapter 14

EVALUATION

According to the *Merriam Webster's Deluxe Dictionary* (1998), to evaluate is "to determine the significance, worth or condition of usually by careful appraisal and study." The evaluation of the school media program involves looking at all aspects of the functions of the school media center to determine the quality of each program component: the staff, the facilities, the collection and the services provided. Because educational quality is an ever-changing phenomenon, the evaluation of the school library media center must be continuous. It must be done with the mission statement, goals, and objectives of a particular school media center in mind.

The improvement of service is the major reason to evaluate the school library media center program. It is quality service that impacts the instructional program of the school. When teachers have a variety of resources at their fingertips and a school media specialist who is willing to collaborate with them, they can concentrate on a learning environment for students that is stimulating and rewarding. Service means providing the best materials, programs, and instruction to support the curriculum. Service means working with faculty to teach information literacy skills as an integral part of the content areas of the curriculum. Service means working with students to motivate them to be lifelong learners and to motivate them to read for enjoyment.

The school library media specialist has a wide-angle view of the instructional program from the viewpoint of the teacher and from the student's perspective. Because of this broad perspective, the school media specialist is in a unique position to evaluate quality service. Evaluation of the services to teachers should include how well the collection supports the curriculum, how the information literacy skills curriculum is integrated into subject content areas of the school, how bibliographies are provided for classrooms and individuals, how teaching is collaboratively planned with classroom teachers, and how well technology is integrated between the media center and classroom learning. In addition to instructional functions, service should also be evaluated for enrichment activities to teachers and students. For example, a professional collection is needed to enrich the teaching skills of the faculty and to keep them abreast of research in the field. Two ways of providing enrichment services to teachers is to route journal articles of interest to them, to provide them with personal reading materials and to offer professional development training for using the newest technologies and innovations. Going one step further, knowing the interests of the teacher is essential to providing good service. One benefit derived from providing reading materials to the faculty is that students who see adults reading want to emulate them and read more too. Enrichment services to students might be inviting an author to visit the school, or the school media specialist visiting classrooms for booktalks or storytelling, or teaching new technology skills.

Frequently, school library media specialists do not have evaluation instruments with which to begin the evaluation of their program. This chapter provides several evaluation instruments to be used in evaluating the program. (1) A self-evaluation instrument is provided for the school library media specialist to use to evaluate the program. (2) A self-evaluation form is provided for the media specialist to use to determine budget needs, to record staff and facilities needs, policies in place, public relations activities, and reports/records kept. (3) An evaluation form is provided for the principal to use in evaluating the school media specialist or the media specialist may use it as a self-evaluation instrument. (4) Another evaluation form is provided for the principal or media specialist to use as a self-evaluation instrument for the school library media program to determine if it's exemplary. (5) One evaluation form is designed specifically for the principal to use in evaluating the school library media specialist. (6) Two forms for evaluating the support staff are provided for the school media specialist to use. (7) Student questionnaires are provided for the school media specialist to use in soliciting evaluations from these school library media center users. (8) A teacher evaluation of the research services is also provided.

SCHOOL LIBRARY MEDIA SPECIALIST'S EVALUATION OF THE MEDIA PROGRAM

The first step in evaluating the services of the school library media center is for the school library media specialist to look at the program, reflect on its outcomes, and decide how to provide better service in the future. The school library media specialist who does a self-evaluation of the program and the services must take a long hard look at what is happening in the school media center and determine ways to make improvements. A form for self-evaluation is provided in Exhibit 14.1 that suggests the vital areas in the program that may be measured and that will give a quantitative and qualitative picture of the existing program. For example, ascertaining the numerical range of people served in each of the audiences will allow the school library media specialist to view the program realistically and consequently to reorder priorities and institute other services to give a better balance to the program in the individual school. Each school library media specialist may also wish to develop a special measure that relates more closely to the local school library media center. Evaluating a program for effectiveness and direction for future improvement is becoming increasingly important, as well as complex. Usually reflection of the successes and failures from the past year can give direction to improved services for the future. The process of program evaluation is continuous and includes the steps shown in the illustration. Exhibit 14.1 provides a self evaluation tool to evaluate services provided to the school, the students, the teachers and the administrators. Exhibit 14.2 allows the media specialist to evaluate support services, such as budget, staff, facilities information, equipment needs and policies of the center.

BUILDING LEVEL MEDIA PROGRAM EVALUATION

To evaluate the services of the school media center, the school library media specialists can compare the building level services, facilities, collection and so forth with quantitative and qualitative standards developed within the library profession or with standards developed within the state education departments. For qualitative standards, those identified in *Information Power* (AASL & AECT, 1998) are the present measures to use. Some state departments of education have developed standards for evaluating the school media collection, facilities, staff, and so forth. The evaluation instrument in Exhibit 14.3 can be used either by the school media

Exhibit 14.1.
School Library Media Specialist Self Evaluation: Services to School, Students, Teachers, & Administrators.

Mark the evaluation instrument below with the following: 1=Outstanding; 2=Competent; 3=Marginal; 4=Needs improvement				
Services to School	**1**	**2**	**3**	**4**
Media program that ensures effective use of ideas and information.				
Management of an effective media program.				
Evaluation of media program effectiveness as a means to improve services through reflective practice.				
Equitable access to new technologies and innovations.				
Instruction in new technologies and innovations.				
Equity and diversity in materials collection.				
Integrated media program with all aspects of school's instructional program.				
Advocacy of media program within school and community.				
Service to Students	**1**	**2**	**3**	**4**
Guidance in reading, viewing, & listening				
Regularly				
Infrequently				
Provide guidance in reading, viewing & listening before, during, and after school.				
Promote the joy of reading through programs such as booktalks, storytelling, and reader's theater.				
Demonstrate the effective use of media.				

Exhibit 14.1. (continued)

Teach media literacy.				
Reference and information services				
Assistance given to answer questions.				
Queries answered consistently.				
Assistance given in doing online bibliographic searches.				
Guidance in locating and evaluating information.				
Locate information outside the school.				
Participate in resource sharing with other libraries.				
Library media orientation				
Once a year				
Periodically				
Given to new students.				
Given to new teachers				
Information literacy instruction				
Regularly				
Infrequently				
Integrated with classroom instruction and not isolated.				
Collaboratively planned with teachers within subject content areas.				
Integrated use of media resources throughout the curriculum.				
Instruction on accessing information efficiently and effectively.				
Instruction in evaluating information critically and competently.				

Exhibit 14.1. (continued)

Demonstration of using information accurately and creatively.				
Independent learning				
Student need surveys to determine personal interests.				
Programs that develop an appreciation of literature and interpretations of information such as book talks and reader's theater.				
Research strategies that are innovative and exciting.				
New knowledge generated through video productions and the like.				
Social responsibility of information.				
Diverse points of view and multiple sources important to a democracy.				
Instruction on ethical use of information, intellectual freedom, and intellectual property rights of others as it relates to information technology.				
Group participation in finding and generating information.				
Local material production				
Taught as part of media program instruction.				
Supervised production of materials.				
Evaluation of media produced.				
Special programs				
Internet training				
Other technology training				

Exhibit 14.1. (continued)

	1	2	3	4
Booktalks				
Author visits				
Storytelling festival				
Services to Teachers	**1**	**2**	**3**	**4**
Media examination & selection				
Collaborative selection of media.				
Local production facilities training				
Taught as part of media program instruction.				
Supervised production of materials.				
Evaluation of media produced.				
Participation as a collaborative partner in teaching resource units.				
Collaboration in planning, implementing, and evaluating instruction.				
Integration of information literacy skills curriculum with classroom content through planning instruction, implementation of lessons, and evaluation of learning.				
Equitable access to new technologies and innovations.				
Integration of media resources as part of instruction.				
Learning styles inventory.				
Media center environment conducive to learning.				
Integration of reading promotion with total school program.				

Exhibit 14.1. (continued)

	1	2	3	4
Curriculum related media talks and celebrations.				
Bibliographies and resource lists.				
Media for teacher personal needs.				
Materials for university courses.				
Materials for pleasure reading.				
Materials for family reading.				
In-service instruction				
Orientation to media services for new teachers.				
Training in using new technologies and innovations.				
Training in using media center.				
Services to Administration	**1**	**2**	**3**	**4**
Serve as clearinghouse for information on professional courses, workshops, meetings & community resources.				
Resource lists provided for events of interest to school.				
New trends in education of interest to principal.				
Statistical information about education.				
Partner with principal for improving student achievement.				
Research studies provided about media centers and student achievement.				
Information about collaboration and its impact on student achievement.				
Reports about collaboration with teachers.				
Media for school programs.				

Exhibit 14.1. (continued)

Reports on school progress toward meeting resource goals.				
Annual report of media program.				
Media for personal needs.				
Materials for university courses.				
Materials for pleasure reading.				
Materials for family reading.				

specialist as a self-evaluation instrument or by the principal as an evaluation instrument to judge the quality of the school library media program. The Georgia State Department of Education (2003), uses an instrument for judging exemplary school library media programs, which is included in Exhibit 14.4.

Evaluation of School Media Specialist

Accountability in education is not a new phenomenon. Teachers are held accountable for their performance in the classroom. Most states have developed evaluations for teachers to determine their effectiveness. School library media specialists, in some states, have been evaluated using the same criteria used to judge teacher competence. However, teaching is only one of several functions of the school media specialist. To be evaluated on only one aspect of performance or to be judged by the same criteria as the classroom teacher seems unfair. The primary problem that principals have found in evaluating the school library media specialists is in the determination of the roles of the school media specialist. Principals are frequently asked to evaluate the school library media specialists with little prior knowledge of what their job entails. An instrument for evaluating school media specialists is provided in Exhibit 14.5.

STAFF EVALUATION

The quality of service available in the school library media center directly correlates to the adequacy of the school library media center staff.

Exhibit 14.2.
Support Services Self-Evaluation Form, Budget Information.

Materials			
Items	Quantity needed	Average cost per item	Total cost
Books			
Print			
Audio books			
E-books			
Periodicals			
Print			
Online newspaper & periodical subscription			
Reference materials			
Computer software			
VCR			
DVD			
Laser disks			
Audio cassettes			
Compact disks			
MP3			
CD-ROM products			
Transparencies			
Government documents			

Exhibit 14.2. (continued)

Materials			
Items	**Quantity needed**	**Average cost per item**	**Total cost**
Vertical file materials			
Slides and microslides			
Multimedia kits			
Art prints/flat pictures			
Games/Toys			
Maps & Globes			
Total materials			
Supplies			
Video rental			
Repairs			
Miscellaneous			
Total other expenses			

Equipment			
Item	**Quantity needed**	**Average cost per item**	**Total cost**
Cassette players recorders			
Cassette duplicators			
CD players			
Computers			
Desktop			

Exhibit 14.2. (continued)

Equipment			
Items	Quantity needed	Average cost per item	Total cost
Laptops			
Handheld (PDA)			
Copy stand			
Camera			
Digital			
Digital video			
35mm camera			
Instant print			
DVD player			
Fax machine			
Laminator			
Laser disc players			
LCD projectors			
Lettering machine			
Opaque projectors			
Overhead projectors			
PA system, portable			
Paper Cutter			
Photocopying machine			
Projection carts			
Scanner			
Screens			

Exhibit 14.2. (continued)

Equipment			
Items	Quantity needed	Average cost per item	Total cost
Portable			
Smartboards			
Slide projector			
Slide viewer, 35mm			
Splicer, cassette tape			
Splicer, VCR			
Telephone			
Tripods			
Video editing equipment			
VCR rewind machine			
Total equipment			

Staff Information				
Job Category	Number	Years in position	Years in district	Salaries
Professional				
Paraprofessional				
Non-professional				
Clerks				
Technicians				
Volunteers				
Student assistants				
Parents				

Exhibit 14.2. (continued)

Facilities Information		
Activities Areas	Size (Sq.ft.)	Location
Reading, viewing, listening		
Circulation		
Lounge area + current periodicals		
Picture file area		
Reference		
Vertical file area		
Workroom		
Conference rooms		
Offices		
Group instruction classrooms		
Production lab		
Computer lab		
Radio/TV Studio		
Equipment room		
Electronic control area		
Video viewing room		
Storage		
Print		
Nonprint		
Equipment		

Exhibit 14.2. (continued)

Facilities Information		
Activities Areas	**Size (Sq.ft.)**	**Location**
Periodicals		
Vertical file		
Picture file		
Environmental Elements		
Acoustics (curtains, carpet, & ceilings)		
Lighting control		
Electrical outlets		
Cables for TV, computers		
Circulation desk		
Temperature control		
Furniture (wood or metal)		
OPAC (online public access catalog)		
Study carrels (non-electronic)		
Study carrels (electronic)		
Vertical files		
Picture files		

Exhibit 14.2. (continued)

Policies
Public Relations:
Students_____ Teachers_____Administrators_____
Parents_____ Community_____ Public Library_____
Other Agencies_____
Hours Open:
Before school_____ After school_____
Evenings_____
Saturday_____ Summer_____
Communications
Internet_____ Provider_____
Telephone_____ Fax_____
E-Mail_____
Circulation
System used_____ Fines_____
Records generated_____
Records and Reports
Financial _____ Inventory_____
Policy & procedural manual_____

Exhibit 14.3.
Evaluation of the School Library Media Program.

School_____ Grade Levels _____

Number of Students_____ Number of faculty_____

Number of full-time library media specialists _____

Number of part-time library media specialists _____

Number of full-time paid library media center clerks_____

Number of part-time paid library media center clerks_____

Number of volunteers_____ Student assistants _____

THE LIBRARY MEDIA SPECIALIST

1=Definitely True, 2=Sometimes True, 3=Mostly Untrue,

4=Definitely Untrue, 5=Do Not Know

Indicators	1	2	3	4	5
Assists students in identifying and accessing information.					
Assists students in analyzing, interpreting, and evaluating information.					
Flexibly schedules all classes to allow for collaborative planning and delivery of instruction at the most appropriate time.					
Does not allow fines or loan restrictions to hinder student access to information.					
Informs school community of new materials, equipment, and services.					
Instructs students in locating and evaluating information in all formats.					
Instructs students in media production and communicating ideas.					
Instructs students in media literacy.					
Plans collaboratively with teachers so that instruction in information					

Exhibit 14.3. (continued)

1=Definitely True, 2=Sometimes True, 3=Mostly Untrue,

4=Definitely Untrue, 5=Do Not Know

Indicators	1	2	3	4	5
literacy and communication skills is integral to the curriculum rather than isolated.					
Provides teachers with in-service workshops, including introduction to new technology, use and production of media, and laws regarding copyright information.					
Models instructional techniques for faculty using a variety of media formats.					
Participates in school and district curriculum development and assessment.					
Plans with teachers about integrating information literacy skills and materials into the classroom curriculum.					

PERSONNEL

1=Definitely True, 2=Sometimes True, 3=Mostly Untrue,

4=Definitely Untrue, 5=Do Not Know

Indicators	1	2	3	4	5
Includes at least one full-time, certified media specialist.					
Includes one or more paid, full-time clerk or technician, for each library media professional.					
Is evaluated at the building level through instruments which address responsibilities of the media specialist.					
Is provided a district level media coordinator.					

Exhibit 14.3. (continued)

1=Definitely True, 2=Sometimes True, 3=Mostly Untrue,

4=Definitely Untrue, 5=Do Not Know

Indicators	1	2	3	4	5
Are innovatively arranged to encourage use of media, provide instruction, and to facilitate inquiry.					
Provide barrier-free learning environment for all users.					
Are flexibly arranged to accommodate changing needs created by newer technologies.					
Encourage easy access and frequent use.					
Are accessible before, during, and after school hours.					
Provide an aesthetically pleasing environment for all users.					
Provide independent study space.					
Accommodate both small and large group activities.					
Provide space for students to access print and electronic reference services.					
Provide lounge space for informal recreational reading.					
Have a telephone and fax allowing for access to other collections.					
Have Internet capabilities for several students at the same time.					
Provide security for materials and equipment.					

Exhibit 14.3. (continued)

THE LIBRARY MEDIA PROGRAM

1=Definitely True, 2=Sometimes True, 3=Mostly Untrue,

4=Definitely Untrue, 5=Do Not Know

Indicators	1	2	3	4	5
Is administered according to specifically defined mission/goals/objectives.					
Has mission/goals/objectives that are fully endorsed by the faculty, students, administration, and community.					
Is evaluated continually to assess effectiveness of services.					
Includes documenting progress toward goals and objectives through annual reports.					
Has a budgeting process cooperatively planned by library media specialist, principal, and district media director.					
Is funded adequately to provide necessary resources and personnel toward achievement of goals/objectives.					
Is effectively promoted in the school and community by library media specialist and staff.					
Is actively supported by the principal with teachers, students, and the community.					

COLLECTION (Resources and Equipment)

1=Definitely True, 2=Sometimes True, 3=Mostly Untrue,

4=Definitely Untrue, 5=Do Not Know

Indicators	1	2	3	4	5
Is selected collaboratively by media specialist, teachers, and students to support the curriculum.					
Includes materials in an assortment of formats.					
Includes a variety of materials to meet needs of all learners, including					

Exhibit 14.3. (continued)

1=Definitely True, 2=Sometimes True, 3=Mostly Untrue,

4=Definitely Untrue, 5=Do Not Know

Indicators	1	2	3	4	5
the handicapped, gifted, and linguistic minorities.					
Is enhanced by resources from outside the media center through interlibrary loan and the Internet.					
Uses a material selection policy approved by the school board.					
Reflects the collection development plan, including selection and replacement criteria as well as resource sharing options with other libraries.					
Is organized, classified, and cataloged using MARC format.					
Is acquired through an online jobber or directly from publishers.					
Is cataloged using an automated system.					
Is circulated using an automated system.					
Is circulated using procedures that ensure confidentiality of users.					
Is made easily accessible, including policies such as overnight circulation of magazines, reference, and nonprint materials.					
Is augmented by district or regional collection to support information needs.					
Is available for interlibrary loan and borrowing according to established policies.					

Exhibit 14.4.
Exemplary Media Program Self Evaluation Rubric.

Target Indicators And Categories	Levels of Proficiency		
Category 1 - Student Achievement and Instruction	**Basic**	**Proficient**	**Exemplary**
1. Information Literacy Standards, as defined in QCC Standards, are integrated into content instruction (*Information Power*; Principle 2; Pg. 58)	☐Information Literacy Skills curriculum is comprised of basic library media orientation skills and instruction on how to find information.	☐Information literacy skills are integrated into the curriculum through the collaborative efforts of the library media specialist and teachers.	☐The library media program fosters critical thinking skills and independent inquiry so students can learn to choose reliable information and become proactive and thoughtful users of information and resources.
2. Collaborative planning includes library media specialists and teachers to ensure use of library media center resources that support on-going classroom instruction and implementation of state curriculum (IFBD 160-4-4-.01)	☐Library media specialist participates in collaborative planning when initiated by the teacher.	☐Library media specialist encourages collaborative planning among teachers who are teaching units of similar content. The library media specialist is familiar with the *Georgia Learning Connections (GLC)* web site and encourages teachers to use the resources available on the GLC.	☐Library media specialist actively plans with and encourages every teacher to participate in the design of instruction. Learning strategies and activities for **all** students are designed with all teachers who are willing to plan collaboratively. All students with diverse learning styles, abilities, and needs are included in collaborative plans.
3. Professional library media staff are engaged in active teaching role/s. (*Information Power*; Principle 4, p. 58)	☐The library media specialist makes recommendations to students for class projects and pleasure reading. The library media specialist provides basic orientation and instruction on information location skills.	☐The library media specialist and teachers plan and teach collaboratively so that the library media program is an extension of classroom instruction.	☐The library media specialist uses a variety of teaching styles to meet diverse needs of students. Collaborative planning determines where and how student assessment takes place, and whether the teacher or the library media specialist does the assessment.
4. The library media center resources encourage and support reading, viewing, and listening. (*Information Power*; Principle 6, p. 58)	☐Bulletin boards and displays of books and reading materials reflect different aspects of the curriculum, holidays, and community interests to support recreational reading.	☐The library media center offers events and activities that appeal to a wide range of interests. Attendance statistics verify students' use.	☐The library media center is a critical element in the school's reading program. The library media program meets the needs of both the reading/language arts curriculum and recreational reading.

Exhibit 14.4. (continued)

Target Indicators And Categories	Levels of Proficiency		
Category 1 - Student Achievement and Instruction	**Basic**	**Proficient**	**Exemplary**
5. Services are provided to students who have diverse learning abilities, styles, and needs. *(Information Power;* Principle 7, p. 58)	☐ The library media center resources reflect diverse learning abilities, styles, and needs.	☐ The library media staff selects resources and informs teachers of these resources with recommendations to support students' diverse learning abilities and styles.	☐ The library media specialist and teachers collect and use student data to design activities that will lead to student achievement. The library media program supports instructional strategies and learning activities that meet individual needs.
6. Student achievement is routinely assessed. *(A Planning Guide for Information Power;* p. 36)	☐ The classroom teacher is responsible for assessing student achievement.	☐ Together the teacher and library media specialist develop a rubric(s) or another effective means for assessing student achievement.	☐ The teacher and library media specialist use a variety of collaboratively designed tools for assessing student achievement, e.g., rubrics, student self-evaluations, and student presentations to peers and/or adult professionals in a field of study.
Target Indicators And Categories	**Levels of Proficiency**		
Category 2 - Staffing	**Basic**	**Proficient**	**Exemplary**
7. If less than base size: A school system shall provide no less than half-time services of a library media specialist for each school less than base size and shall provide adult supervision in the library media center for the entire instructional day. (Base size defined by unweighted FTE: K-5, 450; 6-8, 624; 9-12, 970) (CGB, 160-5-1-.22)	☐ In compliance with state board rule.	☐ Full-time library media specialist is employed, but may be shared outside the library media center. Adult supervision may be parent/peer volunteers.	☐ Full-time library media specialist is employed and is not shared at any other time with other areas in the school nor does he/she provide services outside the library media cehter. Adult supervision by certified personnel is available for the entire day.

Exhibit 14.4. (continued)

Target Indicators And Categories	Levels of Proficiency		
Category 2 - Staffing	**Basic**	**Proficient**	**Exemplary**
8. If base size or larger: A school system shall employ a full-time library media specialist for each base size school or larger. (Base size defined by unweighted FTE: K-5, 450; 6-8, 624; 9-12, 970) (CGB, 160-5-1-.22)	☐ In compliance with state board rule, but the library media specialist may be required to perform other duties on a daily or frequent basis.	☐ Library media specialist is not required to perform other duties on a daily or frequent basis. A part-time library media paraprofessional is employed.	☐ The following criteria that exceed state rules are in place: Additional support personnel are employed in areas of the library media program. Library media staff is always available throughout the instructional day to assist teachers and students. Support staff is not shared in other areas of the school. A full-time paraprofessional person (clerk) is on staff in the library media center.

Target Indicators And Categories	Levels of Proficiency		
Category 3 - Facilities, Access, and Resources	**Basic**	**Proficient**	**Exemplary**
9. There shall be a plan for flexibly scheduled library media center access for students and teachers in groups or as individuals simultaneously throughout each instructional day. Accessibility shall refer to the facility, the staff, and the resources and shall be based on instructional need. (IFBD 160-4-4-.01)	☐ Flexible scheduling makes resources and assistance available at the time of learning need, but school schedules may override this preferable flexibility. Library media staff is available to teachers and students for most of the school day.	☐ Flexible scheduling and library media staff are available throughout the day to assist teachers and students regardless of ability or disability. The library media center is available either before or after school.	☐ Flexible scheduling is maintained allowing full participation of teachers and the library media specialist in collaborative planning and allowing students to come to the library media center at any time. The library media center is available both before and after school. Some evening hours may be scheduled for instructional needs of students and families.
10. School library media center square footage requirements based on FTE. *(Square Footage Requirements for Use in Developing the Local Facilities Plans)*	☐ Based on FTE, the library media center meets minimum square footage requirements.	☐ Based on FTE, the library media center exceeds minimum square footage requirements and is large enough to accommodate large and small groups and individuals working simultaneously. Shelving, storage areas, and electric wiring meet the needs of the collection.	☐ Based on FTE, the library media center exceeds minimum square footage requirements and is large enough to accommodate large and small groups and individuals working simultaneously. Shelving, storage areas, and electric wiring meet the needs of the collection. In addition, production and presentation space is available.

Exhibit 14.4. (continued)

Target Indicators And Categories	Levels of Proficiency		
Category 3 - Facilities, Access, and Resources	Basic	Proficient	Exemplary
11. Central electronic media distribution system for television and radio programs are available. (*Square Footage Requirements for Use in Developing the Local Facilities Plans*)	☐ School is not new; this requirement is in the facilities plan for future capital expenditures.	☐ By the end of 2003-2004 school year the electronic distribution system will be complete.	☐ Electronic distribution system meets state requirements.
12. Print and non-print resources and access to online information are basic to a library media program. A school network is effective for delivering media resources to the classroom and beyond. Multiple computers are available for student access to online resources that enhance instruction. (*FY02 Computers in the Classroom Technology Project - A Georgia Lottery Grant*)	☐ Print and non-print library media center resources are adequate to support the core curriculum. Two or three computers for student access to online resources are available in the library media center.	☐ Print and non-print resources, including subscription databases and other library media center resources are available online to multiple networked computers within the library media center only. A LAN (Local Area Network) is fully functional. Network services are delivered to all classrooms.	☐ Print and non-print resources, including subscription databases, access to the Internet, and other library media center resources are available on a LAN throughout the school. Some library media center resources are accessible via Internet access outside the school. Students use library media center technology independently for extended projects and information retrieval.
13. All library media resources are managed for maximum efficient use. The library media center has an electronic online public access catalog (OPAC). Funds for acquisition of computers are utilized to implement the goals/objectives set forth in the System Three-Year Technology Plan 1999 – 2002 or in the System Comprehensive School Improvement Plan. (*FY02 Computers in the Classroom Technology Project - A Georgia Lottery Grant*)	☐ Management and circulation workstations and at least one online catalog access (OPAC) exist in the library media center. MARC format is used.	☐ The OPAC is electronically networked to several computers within the library media center. New acquisitions are added based on reliable review sources, state and national award books, and curriculum needs. Weeding is an ongoing practice. A network distribution of resources beyond the library media center is not available.	☐ The OPAC is available on a LAN throughout the school. All resources are recorded in MARC format so that access is available on the LAN and weeding of out-of-date materials can be timely. The OPAC is up-to-date and reflects the library media center holdings. Some library media center resources are accessible via Internet access outside the school.

Exhibit 14.4. (continued)

Target Indicators And Categories	Levels of Proficiency		
Category 3 - Facilities, Access, and Resources	**Basic**	**Proficient**	**Exemplary**
14. One of the national educational technology goals states: "Effective and engaging software and on-line resources will be an integral part of every school's curriculum." The GALILEO on-line service provides Georgia students and teachers access to exceptional on-line resources at no cost to the local school district. Searches performed in GALILEO databases will exceed one million annually and the number of full-content items viewed will exceed one million annually. *State of Georgia Technology Plan 2003-2006.*	❑Number of GALILEO searches by students and staff will be the same as the previous year.	❑Number of GALILEO searches by students and staff will be more than the previous year. Instruction and promotion of GALILEO will be conducted in an organized manner.	❑Number of GALILEO searches by students and staff will be more than the previous year. Instruction and promotion of GALILEO will be conducted in an organized manner. Searches will be conducted in such a way that maximize efficiency and result in a high quality product for the student. Best Practices and Learning Models that encourage and endorse GALILEO will be produced, taught, and shared with students, teachers, administrators and other library media specialists throughout the state.
Target Indicators And Categories	**Levels of Proficiency**		
Category 4 - Administrative Support	**Basic**	**Proficient**	**Exemplary**
15. The local system superintendent shall appoint a system media contact person (SMCP) to serve as a liaison to the department. (IFBD, 160-4-4.-.01)	❑A system media contact person (SMCP) is appointed and communication from the SMCP is received and posted for all library media specialists and staff. The media coordinator or curriculum coordinator may serve as the SMCP to facilitate communication to and from DOE. The SMCP has Lotus Notes on his/her workstation.	❑The SMCP coordinates communication among all library media specialists in the district, and disseminates messages from DOE, GALILEO, and other entities. The SMCP has Lotus Notes on his/her workstation.	❑The SMCP has Lotus Notes on his/her workstation and maintains communication among library media specialists in the district. District level administrators facilitate the communication among the SMCP, library media specialists, and themselves. The SMCP understands the role of the library media specialist and encourages opportunities for library media specialists to meet regularly. The district encourages links on school and district web sites for library media center announcements and services.

Exhibit 14.4. (continued)

Target Indicators And Categories	Levels of Proficiency		
Category 4 - Administrative Support	Basic	Proficient	Exemplary
16. Administrative staff support at both the school and district levels is essential for the development of a strong library media program. *(Information Power;* Principle 4, p. 100)	☐ The school principal provides support to the library media program and makes time to meet with the library media specialist occasionally.	☐ The school principal and district administrators take an active role in encouraging teachers to integrate library media resources into the curriculum. School, department, and district level administrators meet regularly with the library media specialist.	☐ The school principal and district administrators take a leadership role in encouraging teachers to integrate library media resources into the curriculum, fostering a climate of collaboration and inquiry, encouraging the library media specialist to be knowledgeable about current educational trends, promoting occasional visits to exemplary programs, and providing budgetary support.
17. Each local board of education shall adopt a library media policy that provides for the establishment of a media committee at the system level and at each school. A media committee makes recommendations and decisions relating to planning, operation, evaluation, and improvement of the media program. This committee shall annually evaluate media services and develop a multi-year media plan for budget services and priorities. (IFBD, 160-4-4.-.01)	☐ System and local school library media committees support implementation of the library media program. A media advisory committee exists and meets once or twice a year. (This committee may be the same as the technology committee in some local schools.)	☐ A library media advisory committee exists and meets a minimum of twice a year. Planning and evaluation of the library program is executed regularly. (This committee may be the same as the technology committee in some schools.)	☐ A library media advisory committee is effective in the development of library media policy, e.g., budget development, acquisition of resources, and reconsideration of materials. This policy, which may be the media/technology plan in some schools, is the basis of operation for actions of the advisory committee, the library media staff, and administration. It is evaluated, reviewed, and updated annually.
18. Local Board approved library media policy is current. This policy requires development of procedures for the school system and for selecting materials locally, handling requests for reconsideration of materials, considering gifts of instructional resources, using non-school owned materials, and complying with the copyright law. (IFBD, 160-4-4.-.01)	☐ A library media policy and exists and is implemented inconsistently.	☐ A library media policy exists and is implemented consistently, and the library media specialist recommends periodic revisions.	☐ A library media policy sets out clear and comprehensive policies and is reviewed annually with guidance from the media advisory committee for update consideration and subsequent local board approval. It is used by the library media staff as a guiding document for the operation of the library media center.

Exhibit 14.4. (continued)

Target Indicators And Categories	Levels of Proficiency		
Category 4 - Administrative Support	**Basic**	**Proficient**	**Exemplary**
19. Each local school system shall spend 100 percent of the funds designated for library media center costs for such costs, and a minimum of 90 percent of such funds shall be spent at the school site in which such funds were earned. (O.C.G.A. 20-2-167)	☐ The library media program receives an allocation for expenditures every year. This amount meets the minimum expenditure tests.	☐ The library media program budget exceeds the minimum state allocation. Local funding supplements state allocation.	☐ The library media specialist, with guidance from the library media advisory committee, is a partner with school and district administrators in planning the media budget. Long-range strategic planning and supplemental funding plans are made cooperatively, and can include bond issues, grants, school fundraising, and business partnerships to supplement the budget.
Target Indicators And Categories	**Levels of Proficiency**		
Category 5 - Staff Development	**Basic**	**Proficient**	**Exemplary**
20. Staff development opportunities are available both for the library media staff to enhance their own professional knowledge and for the library media staff to provide information and technology literacy skills to other teachers and administrative staff. Professional resources and services for all faculty members are provided in the library media center for the "learning community". (*Information Power;* Principle 8, p. 100)	☐ Library media specialist participates in staff development options and provides informal staff development instruction during collaborative planning with teachers. Current professional resources are maintained in the library media center if the district does not provide a centralized professional resource center.	☐ Library media specialist seeks to enhance his/her professional skills, particularly technology skills, beyond those required for recertification or by the school district. Library media specialist provides occasional formal staff development instruction and informal instruction during collaborative planning with teachers. The school system makes staff development options available for library media support staff. The library media specialist is knowledgeable of the district professional development services.	☐ Library media specialist continually seeks to enhance his/her professional, particularly technology, skills. The library media specialist, when funding permits, also participates annually in state or national conferences. The library media specialist is included in planning the staff development program for the school staff and assists in teaching and organizing sessions. The library media specialist is recognized as a master teacher and provides staff development options beyond routine planning, e.g., providing a formal needs assessment to determine staff development needs of the faculty and designing formal courses to address those needs. The library media specialist draws on professional resources both at the local and district levels and online to provide individual assistance to teachers using technology and designing curriculum. The library media specialist may also offer assistance to the teacher in his/her graduate research and secure professional resources for them through interlibrary loan.

Printed with permission. Source: Georgia Department of Education. (2004). *Georgia DOE 2004 media program self-evaluation rubric.* Atlanta, GA: Author.

Exhibit 14.5.
Job Evaluation for School Library Media Specialist.

Name_____ School_____

Year_____

ADMINISTRATIVE

1=Outstanding, 2=Commendable 3=Competent, 4=Marginal,

5=Unsatisfactory

Indicators	1	2	3	4	5
Plans implementation of the school library media program.					
Specifies hours of service.					
Determines circulation policies and procedures.					
Flexibly schedules classes to use the resources of the media center and the expertise of the library media specialist at the time of need.					
Implements policies and procedures to manage the school library media program.					
Plans use of resources by students and teachers.					
Designs implementation of the information literacy skills curriculum.					
Defines collaboratively with faculty and administration the scope and sequence of the information literacy skills curriculum.					
Works collaboratively with faculty and administrators to integrate information literacy skills curriculum throughout the instructional program.					

Exhibit 14.5. (continued)

ADMINISTRATIVE

1=Outstanding, 2=Commendable 3=Competent, 4=Marginal,

5=Unsatisfactory

Indicators	1	2	3	4	5
Provides orientation program for faculty and students.					
Provides workshops and in-service programs for faculty.					
Evaluates the services, materials, and all aspects of the school library media program.					
Evaluates according to local needs of students, faculty and administration.					
Evaluates according to guidelines of state, regional, and national associations or accrediting agencies.					
Evaluates collaboratively with faculty and administration					
Develops and administers the budget.					
Approves orders and payments.					
Maintains expenditure records.					
Designs a public relations program.					
Prepares bulletin boards and displays					
Publishes newsletters, press releases, brochures and newspaper articles.					
Plans special events to publicize school library media activities.					
Designs a functional school library media center.					
Cooperates with outside agencies such as other school library media centers, local libraries and other library systems.					
Recruits, trains, and supervises support staff.					

Exhibit 14.5. (continued)

EDUCATIONAL

1=Outstanding, 2=Commendable 3=Competent, 4=Marginal,

5=Unsatisfactory

Indicators	1	2	3	4	5
Provides media services, Internet access, and resources to students and faculty.					
Selects and evaluates new materials and web sites.					
Evaluates the collection for worn and obsolete materials.					
Provides reference services, both print and online.					
Provides requested materials and equipment to students and teachers as needed.					
Prepares bibliographies as requested.					
Designs and implements programs to motivate reading, listening, viewing, and computing skills.					
Works collaboratively with teachers in designing and implementing instructional units.					
Supervises students collaboratively with teachers during instructional activities.					
Provides individual or group instruction in information literacy skills, Internet use, and media production in conjunction with classroom activities.					
Works collaboratively with Teachers in the design, implementation, and evaluation of instructional units.					
Plans strategies with teachers to develop students' critical thinking skills in organizing, evaluating and using information.					
Provides guidance and innovation in the use of new and emerging information technologies.					

Exhibit 14.5. (continued)

EDUCATIONAL

1=Outstanding, 2=Commendable 3=Competent, 4=Marginal,

5=Unsatisfactory

Indicators	1	2	3	4	5
Instructs students and faculty in utilizing new and emerging technologies to access information.					
Promotes understanding of copyright, confidentiality and other laws that promote access.					
Creates an inviting environment conducive to student learning.					
Teaches effective use of a variety of media formats.					
Teaches students to be responsible for the care of equipment, materials, and environment of the media center.					
Organizes the library media center facility to support a variety of learning activities.					
Builds an appropriate collection of materials for the instructional program based on student needs.					
Is familiar with content of all curriculum areas.					
Surveys students to determine interests and needed research materials.					
Surveys faculty to determine needed resources.					
Collaborates with teachers on determining resources for instructional units.					
Provides materials for the professional growth of the faculty.					
Promotes professional reading to the faculty.					
Scans professional journals and routes to faculty.					
Directs faculty to web sites pertaining to their area of expertise.					
Provides materials for the professional collection.					
Keeps abreast of educational trends and shares with faculty.					
Assumes a leadership role in departmental, faculty, curriculum and					

Exhibit 14.5. (continued)

EDUCATIONAL

1=Outstanding, 2=Commendable 3=Competent, 4=Marginal,

5=Unsatisfactory

Indicators	1	2	3	4	5
special committee meetings.					
Attends faculty, grade level, and department meetings.					
Serves on committees that directly affect the instructional program.					
Provides instruction in the use and production of media.					
Works collaboratively with faculty to encourage effective use of media services and resources.					

TECHNICAL

1=Outstanding, 2=Commendable 3=Competent, 4=Marginal,

5=Unsatisfactory

Indicators	1	2	3	4	5
Designs efficient procedures for acquiring, processing, classifying and cataloging materials and equipment.					
Reads reviews in professional journals as part of the selection process.					
Catalogs and classifies materials.					
Supervises ordering and processing of materials.					
Provides a collection that is current and accessible.					
Supervises withdrawal of worn, damaged, and obsolete materials.					
Establishes policies and procedures for equipment maintenance.					
Establishes circulation policies and procedures.					
Assembles and preserves essential records and statistics of library media center operations.					
Provides an inventory of materials and equipment regularly.					

Exhibit 14.5. (continued)

PROFESSIONAL

1=Outstanding, 2=Commendable 3=Competent, 4=Marginal,

5=Unsatisfactory

Indicators	1	2	3	4	5
Assumes an active role in professional organizations and their committees.					
Participates in local, state and national professional organizations through committee work, workshops and conferences.					
Professional growth and lifelong learning					
Continues to acquire knowledge through workshops and academic courses.					
Models a commitment to lifelong learning by continuing to improve knowledge and skills.					
Fosters an effective relationship with students, faculty, administration, media center staff and community.					

STAFF EVALUATION (continued)

An adequate size staff for the size of the school is essential for providing quality service. The staff must include a professionally trained school library media specialist and a support staff that is adequate to take care of clerical tasks. The support staff is crucial because it allows the school media specialist to spend quality time where it should be spent: with students and teachers providing professional leadership in the use of resources and actively involved in curriculum development of the school. Written job descriptions should be available for each school library media staff member. With a job description in place, the school media specialist can evaluate the performance of the staff members periodically. Two staff evaluation instruments are provided here: one for the clerical staff (Exhibit 14.6) and one for the technical staff (Exhibit 14.7). There are times when the school library media specialist is required to perform as a technology technician. Role clarification is sometimes vague and the media specialist normally picks up the slack in those cases.

Exhibit 14.6.
Job Evaluation for School Library Media Clerical Staff.

Name:_____School_____Year_____

0=Outstanding, 1=Commendable, 2=Competent, 3=Marginal,

4=Unsatisfactory

CLERICAL STAFF

Indicators	1	2	3	4	5
Fulfills common secretarial responsibilities.					
Types accurately with speed.					
Competent in word processing skills.					
Uses courtesy in answering the telephone.					
Keeps appointment log for school media specialist.					
Keeps office records organized.					
Competent in managing photocopying services.					
Promptly and efficiently handles mail.					
Organizes and maintains an efficient filing system.					
Assists in keeping track and organizing financial records.					
Compiles and organizes statistics.					
Monitors, gathers, compiles, and organizes circulation statistics for all media.					
Compiles and organizes statistical reports on use of equipment.					
Compiles and organizes statistical reports on use of the library.					
Compiles and organizes statistical reports on faculty use of media center.					
Compiles and organizes statistical reports on student use of media center.					
Assists in preparation of annual report.					
Places orders for materials and equipment and processes them upon their arrival in the media center.					
Efficient in preparing purchase orders.					

Exhibit 14.6. (continued)

0=Outstanding, 1=Commendable, 2=Competent, 3=Marginal,

4=Unsatisfactory

CLERICAL STAFF

Indicators	1	2	3	4	5
Compiles and organizes a materials consideration want list.					
Follows processing procedures authorized by school media specialist.					
Competent in preparing OPAC records.					
Maintains accession records for equipment.					
Maintains ordering records.					
Maintains an inventory of supplies and orders as necessary.					
Maintains a supply budget.					
Orders supplies as needed.					
Maintains inventory of supplies on hand.					
Prepares materials for circulation					
Affixes bar codes to materials and patron lists.					
Attaches security strips.					
Attaches plastic covers to Hardcover books and paperbacks.					
Attaches labels.					
Produces a patron name list for computer.					
Withdraws obsolete patron names from computer.					
Manages circulation desk.					
Shelves materials and equipment.					
Manages interlibrary loans.					
Compiles overdue notices.					
Assists with inventory.					
Works cooperatively with media center staff, faculty, students, administration, and parents.					
Works well with media center staff.					
Works well with teachers.					
Works well with students.					
Works well with administrators.					
Works well with parents.					
Willingness to provide all media center users with excellent service.					
Performs other media center duties as assigned by media specialist.					
Assists students and faculty with accessing and using materials and equipment.					

Exhibit 14.7.
Job Evaluation for School Library Media Technical
Staff.

Name_____ School _____

Year_____

0=Outstanding, 1=Commendable, 2=Competent, 3=Marginal,

4=Unsatisfactory

TECHNICAL

Indicators	1	2	3	4	5
Assists faculty and students to locate and use materials with the proper equipment.					
Provides answers to directional questions.					
Teaches proper use of software, equipment and new technology.					
Operates computers, audiovisual and production equipment.					
Maintains OPAC and network.					
Conducts preventive maintenance and minor repairs on equipment.					
Proficient in changing projection lamps.					
Cleans and lubricates equipment parts as a preventive maintenance measure.					
Inspects equipment for problems before sending to classrooms.					
Inspects equipment for needed repairs upon return to media center.					
Proficient in doing minor equipment repair and maintenance.					
Prepares bulletin boards and other displays.					
Maintains a bulletin board and display ideas file.					
Collects bulletin board and display materials.					
Maintains an inventory of bulletin board/display materials and supplies.					

Exhibit 14.7. (continued)

0=Outstanding, 1=Commendable, 2=Competent, 3=Marginal,

4=Unsatisfactory

TECHNICAL

Indicators	1	2	3	4	5
Rotates bulletin boards and displays every three weeks in school media center.					
Schedules use and delivery of computers, audiovisual materials, and equipment.					
Coordinates a daily audiovisual schedule for classroom use of materials and equipment.					
Coordinates a delivery and pickup schedule for audiovisual materials and equipment in classrooms.					
Orders and returns rental videos.					
Assists with preparation of bibliographies.					
Maintains audiovisual and vertical file collection.					
Orders replacement items for audiovisual materials.					
Reads and maintains audiovisual materials shelves and vertical file subject headings regularly.					
Withdraws audiovisual items as directed by school media specialist.					
Mends and repairs audiovisual materials as needed.					
Assists with inventory.					
Works cooperatively with media center staff, faculty, students, administration, and parents.					
Works well with media center staff.					
Works well with teachers.					
Works well with students.					
Works well with administration.					
Works well with parents.					
Willingness to provide all media center users with excellent service.					
Performs other media center duties as assigned by media specialist.					
Assists students and faculty with accessing and using materials and equipment.					

EVALUATION BY SCHOOL LIBRARY MEDIA CENTER USERS

The most effective way to determine if the services of the school library media center are appropriate is to ask the users of the services: the students and the faculty. From their input, a true picture evolves as to their perception of good service. The school media specialist and the principal may look at the program and the services from a totally different viewpoint from those of the users of the school library media program.

Student Evaluations

Service to students means taking an interest in them personally and professionally to help them to become proficient library users. It means that the school media specialist provides individual and group information literacy skills instruction collaboratively with the classroom teacher. It means that the school media specialist builds rapport with students that welcomes student input about the resources in the school media center and the services needed. It means that the school media specialist encourages students to go outside the school for their information needs when the need arises.

Two evaluation questionnaires are provided. Exhibit 14.8 is an elementary student evaluation questionnaire and Exhibit 14.9 is a questionnaire for the secondary school student.

Teacher Evaluations

When a teacher schedules the school library media center for research activities, it is appropriate to ask their evaluation of the collection and how well the research needs of their students are met. An evaluation of the collection from the teacher's perspective is valuable in determining weaknesses in the collection and to aid in the selection of specific topics within the content areas of the curriculum that need additional materials for research. The following evaluation form (Exhibit 14.10) is used when a teacher has made a research assignment and accompanied students to the school library media center in their search for research materials.

With the appearance of new technology in the library media center, there are many changes that occur which have an impact on the programs and services available to the students and staff. Evaluating the programs and services that have evolved because of technology is essential. Evalu-

Exhibit 14.8.
Student Evaluation of Elementary School Library Media Program.

Room_____ Date_____

Students should check box in column they think is appropriate.

Statement	Yes	No	Sometimes	Don't know
The media specialist helps me when I need it.				
The media specialist helps me with ideas about doing assignments.				
The media specialist or technician shows me how to use computers.				
The media specialist or technician shows me how to use audiovisual equipment, such as cassette players.				
The media center has interesting books to use for my assignments.				
The media center has interesting books I can read for fun.				
The rules in the media center are fair.				
The rules in the media center are enforced fairly by the media specialist.				
The media specialist taught me how to use the media center.				
I know how to use the media center computers.				
I would like to know more about the media center.				
I would like to know more about the computers in the media center.				
I know how to use the Internet.				
I would like to know more about using the Internet.				
I feel welcome in the media center.				
The media specialist does fun things that make me feel comfortable coming to the media center.				
When I come to the media center I like to:				
Listen to a story read aloud.				
Listen to a book on tape.				
Read magazines.				
Learn more about the media center.				
Use the computers.				

Exhibit 14.9.
Student Evaluation of Secondary School Library Media Program.

Please circle your grade: 9   10   11   12

Special ed. _____ Standard _____ Honors _____

1. How often do you visit the media center?

    a. Seldom _____

    b. Daily _____

    c. Monthly _____

    d. Never _____

2. How often do you use libraries other than ours?

    a. Seldom _____

    b. Frequently _____

    c. Never _____

3. If you use other libraries, which ones do you use?

    a. Public library _____

    b. College or university library _____

    c. Other school media center _____

    d. Other _____

4. What is your reason for using these libraries?

5. Please comment on how well we are doing in our media center in the following areas:

    a. Space (tables, chairs, lounging furniture, study

        carrels)

Exhibit 14.9. (continued)

    b. Assistance in answering questions

    c. Training you to use the center

    d. Accessible hours when center is open

    e. Friendly atmosphere

6. What subjects do you take that require little or no use of the media center to do assignments?

7. Number of books you have read this year other than textbooks?

8. How many books have you read for pleasure this year?

9. Materials for assignments are found:

    a. Always _____

    b. Sometimes _____

    c. Seldom_____

    d. Never_____

10. Books I read for pleasure are found:

    e. Always _____

    f. Sometimes _____

Exhibit 14.9. (continued)

g. Seldom_____

h. Never_____

11. What materials have you not found in our media center

that you need? Be very specific.

12. Please suggest ways you think the media center could

be improved on the back of this sheet.

13. Check the amount of use you make of the center for

each of the following purposes:

Purpose	Seldom go	Teacher takes or sends	Several times a week	Almost every day
Locate materials for assignments.				
Use the Internet for assignments.				
Find materials for pleasure reading.				
Do assignments in textbook.				
Meet friends.				
Socialize before school.				
Study before school.				
Socialize at lunch.				
Wait for event after school.				
Study after school.				
Socialize after school.				
Just to relax.				

Exhibit 14.10.
Teacher Evaluation of Research Materials.

Teacher_____

Date_____

Grade_____   Number of Students_____

Subject_____

Unit of Study_____

1. Approximate number of materials you found in the media
   center on the unit of study _____

2. Did the school library media center have adequate
   materials for the unit of study? Yes_____ No_____

3. What subjects within the unit of study would you like
   to find more information in the media center
   collection?

4. In what format would you like to see new materials?
   Books_____
   Online magazine databases_____
   Reference Books_____
   Audiovisual materials_____
   Internet web sites_____
   Please specify_____

5. Please list specific titles you would like to see
   added to the collection for this unit_____

Exhibit 14.10. (continued)

6. Did you class receive adequate assistance from the media staff for this assignment? Yes_____ No_____

7. Please specify the kind of assistance you would have found to be the most helpful.

8. Did you collaborate with the media specialist in planning the instructional unit or lesson?

9. If you collaborated with the media specialist in planning the instructional unit/lesson, what changes would you make for improvement?

10. What media center services below did your students use for their assignment?

Newspaper/ periodical database _____

Internet _____

Print magazines_____

Vertical file materials_____

Reference materials_____

Interlibrary loan_____

Info pass to college library_____

Other_____

ation serves as a means for the improvement of service that in turn has an impact on the quality of the instructional program in the school. It is the school media specialist's responsibility to see that the program is evaluated properly and that a plan for improvement is initiated and implemented. Once all of the evaluations of the program and the services are completed, the school media specialist should outline a plan of action that designates target dates to implement improvements for the program. Evaluation never stops—it is continuous. With an eye toward improving the school library media program, the school library media specialist can make changes full speed ahead to meet the challenges of the future.

REFERENCES

Merriam Webster's Deluxe Dictionary. (1998). Pleasantville, NY: Reader's Digest.

Georgia Department of Education. (2004). *Georgia DOE 2004 media program self-evaluation rubric.* Atlanta, GA: Author.

FURTHER READINGS

Alabama Department of Education. (2000). *Alabama professional education evaluation program: Self-assessment—electronic format, library media specialist system.* Retrieved April 14, 2004, from Alabama PEPE web site: http://www.alabamapepe.com/specialty/libselfasmnt.doc

American Library Association & American Association of School Librarians. (2003, March 5). *ALA/AASL Standards for initial programs for school library media specialist preparation.* Retrieved May 11, 2004, from the ALA web site: http://www.ala.org/Content/NavigationMenu/AASL/Education_and_Careers1/School_Library_Media_Education_Programs/ala-aasl_slms2003.pdf

Bradburn, Frances Bryant. (1998). *Output measures for school library media programs.* New York: Neal-Schuman.

Everhart, Nancy. (1998). *Evaluating the school library media center: Analysis techniques and research practices.* Westport, CT: Libraries Unlimited.

Everhart, Nancy. (2003, March). Evaluation of school library media centers: Demonstrating quality. *Library Media Connection, 21*(6), 14–21.

Haycock, Ken (Ed.). (1998). *Foundations for effective school library media programs.* Westport, CT: Libraries Unlimited.

Lance, Keith Curry. (2001, September). *Proof of the power: Quality library media programs affect student achievement.* Retrieved May 11, 2004, from: http://www.infotoday.com/MMSchools/sep01/lance.html

Loertscher, David V. (2000). *Taxonomies of the school library media program* (2nd ed.). San Jose, CA: Hi Willow Research & Publishing.

Maine Association of School Libraries. (1998). *SLMS evaluation kit.* Retrieved April 14, 2004, from the Maine Association of School Libraries web site: http://www.maslibraries.org/resources/slmseval/slmseval.html

Massachusetts School Library Media Association. (1997). *Standards for school library media centers in the commonwealth of Massachusetts.* Retrieved May 11, 2004, from the Massachusetts Department of Education web site: http://www.doe.mass.edu/mailings/1997/cm050797.pdf

Minnesota State Library Agency. (2000). *Minnesota standards for effective school library media programs.* Retrieved April 14, 2004, from the Minnesota State Library Agency web site: http://www.memoweb.org/links/standardsintro.pdf

Missouri State Department of Elementary and Secondary Education. (2000). *Guidelines for performance-based library media specialist evaluation.* Retrieved April 14, 2004, from the Missouri State Department of Elementary an Secondary Education web site: http://www.dese.state.mo.us/divteachqual/profdev/LMS.pdf

Nebraska Educational Media Association. (2000). *Guide for developing and evaluating school library media programs.* Westport, CT: Libraries Unlimited.

Rhode Island Educational Media Association. (2000). *School library and information literacy framework.* Retrieved April 14, 2004, from the Rhode Island Educational Media Association web site: http://www.ri.net/RIEMA/infolit.html

South Carolina Department of Education. (2003, August). *Achieving exemplary school libraries: Library media center program rubrics.* Retrieved April 14, 2004, from the South Carolina Department of Education web site: http://www.myscschools.com/offices/technology/ms/lms/Rubrics.pdf

Texas Education Agency. (n.d.). *Librarian professional development and appraisal system: Appraisal framework.* Retrieved April 14, 2004, from the Texas Education Agency: http://www.tea.state.tx.us/technology/libraries/lib_downloads/eval5.pdf

Texas State Library and Archives Commission. (2000). *School library programs: Standards and guidelines for Texas.* Retrieved April 14, 2004, from the Texas State Library web site: http://www.tsl.state.tx.us/ld/schoollibs/standards.html

Yesner, Bernice L. & Jay, Hilda. (1998). *Operating and evaluating school library media programs.* New York: Neal-Schuman.

Appendix I

DIRECTORY OF STATE SCHOOL LIBRARY MEDIA CENTER AGENCIES

Alabama
Alabama Public Library Service
6030 Monticello Drive
Montgomery, AL 36130
334-213-3900
1-800-723-8459 (within Alabama only)

Alaska
Sue Sherif
School Library/Youth Services Coordinator, Librarian III
Alaska State Library and Historical Collections
P.O. Box 110571
Juneau, AK 99811-0571
907-269-6569
sue_sherif@eed.state.ak.us

Arizona
Linda Edgington
Arizona Department of Education, Bin 48
1535 W. Jefferson
Phoenix, AZ 85007
602-542-5416
ledging@ade.az.gov

Arkansas
Margaret Crank
Library Media Services Specialist
Arkansas Department of Education
#4 Capitol Mall, Rm 103B
Little Rock, AR 72201
501-682-4396
mcrank@arkedu.k12.ar.us

California
Martha Rowland
Curriculum Frameworks and Instructional Resources
916-319-0451
mrowland@cde.ca.gov

Barbara Jeffus
Curriculum Frameworks and Instructional Resources
California Department of Education (CDE)
P.O. Box 944272
Sacramento, CA 94244-2720
916-319-0445
bjeffus@cde.ca.gov

Colorado
Nance Nassar
School Library Representative
Colorado State Library
201 E. Colfax Ave., Rm. 309
Denver, CO 80203
303-866-6772
nassar_n@cde.state.co.us

Connecticut
Betty Goyette, Consultant
Library Media/Instructional Television
Bureau of Curriculum and Instruction
Connecticut State Department of Education
165 Capitol Avenue
P.O. Box 2219
Hartford, CT 06145
Telephone: 860-713-6760

Delaware
Denise DiSabatino Allen
Education Associate
Library/Media/Technology
Delaware Department Of Education
302-739-4583
dallen@doe.k12.de.us

District of Columbia
Bester D. Bonner, PhD.
Director Library Media Services
District of Columbia Public Schools
Penn Center, 4th Floor
1709 3rd Street, NE
Washington, DC 20002
202-576-6317
Bester.bonner@k12.dc.us

Florida
Elizabeth Carrouth, Director
Instructional Materials, Library Media Services
532 Turlington Building
325 West Gaines Street
Tallahassee, Florida 32399-0400
850-487-8791
elizabeth.carrouth@fldoe.org

Georgia
Judy Serritella, Coordinator of Library Media Services
Educational Technology & Media
Georgia Department of Education
1952 Twin Towers East
Atlanta, GA 30334
404-657-9800
serritel@ix.netcom.com

Hawaii
Lucretia Leong
School Library Services
Hawaii Department of Education
475 22nd Avenue, Bldg. 302, Rm. 203
Honolulu, HI 96816
808-733-9150
luleong@k12.hi.us

Idaho
Valerie Fenske, Librarian
Curriculum/Technology
Idaho State Department of Education
650 West State Street
P.O. Box 83720
Boise, ID 83720-0037
208-334-2270
1-877-892-3937
Vfenske@sde.state.id.us

Illinois
Ms. Jamey Baiter
Principal Technology Consultant
eLearning Division
Illinois State Board of Education
100 N. 1st St. (E-439)
Springfield, IL 62777-0001
217-782-5439
jbaiter@isbe.net

Indiana
Judy R. Williams, Library Media Consultant
Indiana Department of Education
Room 229, State House
Indianapolis, IN 46204
317-232-9190
williams@doe.state.in.us

Iowa
John O'Connell
Bureau of Instructional Services
Department of Education
Grimes State Office Building
Des Moines, IA 50319-0146
515-242-6354
john.oconnell@ed.state.ia.us

Kansas
Jackie Lakin
Information Management Program Consultant
120 SE 10th Avenue
Topeka, KS 66612-1182
785-296-2144
JLakin@ksde.org

Kentucky
Jennifer Scarborough,
Interim Instructional Resources Consultant
Division of Extended Learning
500 Mero Street, 17th Floor
Frankfort, KY 40601
502-564-7056
jscarbor@kde.state.ky.us

Louisiana
(No contact in the State Education Department)
Phyllis Heroy, Chair, State Standards Committee
Director of Library Services & Instructional Technology
East Baton Rouge Parish School System
Christa McAuliffe Center
12000 Goodwood Blvd.
Baton Rouge, LA 70815
225-226-7610
pheroy@ebrschools.org

Maine
Sylvia Norton, Media Services Coordinator
State of Maine Department of Education
23 State Houston Station
Augusta, ME 04333-0023
207-287-5620
sylvia.norton@maine.gov

Maryland
Jayne E. Moore, Director
Instructional Technology & School Library Media
Maryland State Department of Education
200 West Baltimore Street
Baltimore, MD 21201
410-767-0382
jmoore@msde.state.md.us

Massachusetts
Barbara J. McLean, Library/Media Content Specialist
Massachusetts Department of Education
350 Main Street
Malden, MA 02148
781-338-3000
bmclean@doe.mass.edu

Michigan
Dr. William Anderson, Director
Department of History, Arts, and Libraries
702 W. Kalamazoo Street
P.O. Box 30738
Lansing, MI 48909-8238
517-373-2486
halexec@michigan.gov

Minnesota
Ken Hasledalen, CIO/Chief State Official for Libraries
Information Technologies/Library Development & Services
Minnesota Department of Children, Families & Learning
1500 Hwy 36 West
Roseville MN 55113
651-582-8808
ken.hasledalen@state.mn.us

Mississippi
April Roberson, M.S.
Library Media Specialist
Mississippi Department of Education
Suite 330—Central High School
P.O. Box 771
Jackson, MS 39205-0771
601-359-2586
aroberson@mde.k12.ms.us

Missouri
Lisa Walters
Library Media and Technology Consultant
Department of Elementary and Secondary Education (DESE)
P.O. Box 480
Jefferson City, MO 65102-0480
573-526-4900
lwalters@mail.dese.state.mo.us

Montana
Linda Vrooman-Peterson, Director of Accreditation
Montana Office of Public Instruction
1227 11th Ave, 2nd Floor
P.O. Box 202501
Helena, MT 59620-2501
406-444-5726
lvpeterson@state.mt.us

Nebraska
(No contact in the State Education Department)
Joie Taylor, Executive Secretary
Nebraska Educational Media Association
2301 31st Street
Columbus, NE 68601
rpasco@mail.unomaha.edu

Nevada
Bill Strader, Library/Learning Resources
Nevada Department of Education Technology and Innovative Programs
700 E. Fifth Street
Carson City, NV 89701
775-687-9245
strader@nsn.k12.nv.us

New Hampshire
Cathy Higgins
Educational Technology Consultant
Office of Educational Technology
New Hampshire Department of Education
101 Pleasant Street
Concord, NH 03301
603-271-2453
chiggins@ed.state.nh.us

New Jersey
Norma Blake
New Jersey State Library
P.O. Box 520
Trenton, NJ 08625-0520
609-292-6200
nblake@njstatelib.org

New Mexico
Sharon Dogruel
Program Manager/Libraries
Curriculum, Instruction, and Learning Technologies
New Mexico Public Education Department
Education Building
300 Don Gaspar
Santa Fe, NM 87501-2786
505-827-6572
sdogruel@sde.state.nm.us

New York
Frances Roscello
Associate
School Library Media Services
Office of NYC Schools and Community Services
NYS Education Department, Room 375 EBA
Albany, NY 12234
518-474-8485
froscell@mail.nysed.gov

North Carolina
John Brim, Section Chief for Educational Resources Evaluation Services
North Carolina Department of Public Instruction
301 N. Wilmington St.
Raleigh, NC 27601
919-807-3288
jbrim@dpi.state.nc.us

North Dakota
Doris Ott
North Dakota State Library
604 East Boulevard Dept. 250
Bismarck, ND 58505-0800
701-328-2492
dott@state.nd.us

Ohio
Carla Southers, Ohio Department of Education Library Liaison
Ohio Department of Education
25 South Front Street
Columbus, OH 43215-4183
1-877-644-6338
csouthers@ode.state.oh.us

Oklahoma
Jeanie Johnson, Director
Library Media/ITV
Oklahoma State Department of Education
2500 N. Lincoln, Suite 215
Oklahoma City, OK 73105-4599
405-521-2956
jeanie_johnson@sde.state.ok.us

Oregon
Carla Wade
Instructional Technology Specialist
Oregon Department of Education
255 Capitol St. NE
Salem, OR 97310
503-378-3600 x2283
carla.wade@state.or.us

Pennsylvania
John Emerick, Director
School Library Media Services Division
Pennsylvania Department of Education
333 Market St.
Harrisburg, PA 17126-0333
717-783-9542
jemerick@state.pa.us

Rhode Island
Benjamin Wakashige, Director
New Mexico State Library
1209 Camino Carlos Rey
Santa Fe, NM 87505
505-476-9762
ben@stlib.state.nm.us

South Carolina
Martha Alewine
Consultant for School Library Media Services
SC Department of Education
513-C Rutledge Building
1429 Senate St.
Columbia, SC 29201
803-734-6293
malewine@sde.state.sc.us

South Dakota
Pam Chamberlain, Children's Services Consultant or
Dana Ruby, Continuing Education Coordinator or
Dorothy M. Liegl, Deputy State Librarian
South Dakota State Library
800 Governors Drive
Pierre, SD 57501-2294
605-773-3131
Dorothy.Liegl@state.sd.us

Tennessee
Kimberly Buck, Education Consultant
5th Floor, Andrew Johnson Tower
710 James Robertson Parkway
Nashville, TN 37243-0379
615-253-2113
Kimberly.Buck@state.tn.us

Texas
Director of Library Services
1701 N. Congress Avenue
Austin, TX 78701-1494
512-936-2263
mlankfor@tea.state.tx.us

Utah
Georgia Loutensock, Library Media Specialist
Utah State Office of Education
250 E. 500 South
P.O. Box 144200
Salt Lake City, UT 84114-4200
801-538-7789
gloutens@usoe.k12.ut.us

Vermont
Leda Schubert
Vermont Department of Education
120 State St.
Montpelier, VT 05620
802-828-3842
lschubert@doe.state.vt.us

Virginia
Charlie Makela
Educational Technology Media and Research Services Specialist
Office of Educational Technology, Virginia Department of Education
P.O. Box 2120
Richmond VA 23218-2120
804-786-9412
cmakela@pen.k12.va.us

Washington
Gayle Pauley, Director of Title I, LAP & Title V
Washington State Board of Education
Office of the Superintendent of Public Instruction
P.O. Box 47286
Olympia, WA 98504
360-725-6100 or
360-725-6025
gpauley@ospi.wednet.edu

West Virginia
Brenda Williams
Executive Director
Office of Technology and Information Systems
West Virginia Department of Education
1900 Kanawha Blvd, East
Building 6, Room 346
Charleston, WV 25305
304-558-7880
brendaw@access.k12.wv.us

Wisconsin
Richard Grobschmidt,
Assistant State Superintendent
Division for Libraries, Technology, and Community Learning
125 S. Webster St.
P.O. Box 7841
Madison, WI 53707-7841
Richard.grobschmidt@dpi.state.wi.us

Wyoming
(No Contact in the State Department of Education.)
Mary Lou Bowles-Banks, Chair
Wyoming Library Association, School Library Media Personnel
c/o Laura Grott, Executive Secretary
P.O. Box 1387
Cheyenne, WY 82003-1387
1-800-441-4563
maryloub@rams.fremont2.k12.wy.us

Appendix II

DIRECTORY OF ASSOCIATIONS AND AGENCIES

Agency for Instructional Technology (AIT)
Box A, 1800 North Stonelake Drive
Bloomington, IN 47402
812-339-2203
800-457-4509

American Association for Gifted Children at Duke University
c/o Talent Identification Program
P.O. Box 90270
Durham, NC 27708-0270
919-684-3847

American Association for the Advancement of Science
1200 New York Avenue, NW
Washington, DC 20005
202-326-6400

American Association for Vocational Instructional Materials (AAVIM)
220 Smithonia Road
Winterville, GA 30683
800-228-4689 or
706-742-5355

American Association of Museums (AAM)
1575 Eye Street, NW, Suite 400
Washington, DC 20005
202-289-1818

American Association of School Administrators (AASA)
801 N. Quincy Street, Suite 700
Arlington, VA 22203
703-528-0700

American Council on Education
One Dupont Circle, NW, Suite 800
Washington, DC 20036
202-939-9300

American Film Institute (AFI)
John F. Kennedy Center for the Performing Arts
Washington, DC 20566
202-838-4000

American Film & Video Association (AFVA)
920 Barnsdale, Suite 152
LaGrange Park, IL 60525
708-482-4000

American Foundation for the Blind (AFB)
11 Penn Plaza, Suite 300
New York, NY 10001
212-502-7600

American Institute of Graphic Arts (AIGA)
164 Fifth Avenue
New York, NY 10010
212-807-1990

American Library Association (ALA)
50 E. Huron Street
Chicago, IL 60611
312-944-6780
800-545-2433

ALA Divisions (all located at ALA headquarters in Chicago):
American Association of School Librarians (AASL)
Association for Library Service to Children (ALSC)
Association of Specialized Cooperative Library Agencies (ASCLA)
Library Administration and Management Association (LAMA)
Library and Information Technology Association (LITA)
Reference and Adult Services Division (RASD)
Resources and Technical Services Division (RTSD)
Young Adult Services Division (YASD)

American Society for Information Science and Technology (ASIST)
1320 Fenwick Lane, Suite 510
Silver Spring, MD 20910
301-495-0900

American Toy Institute
1115 Broadway, Suite 400
New York, NY 10010
212-675-1141

Anti-Defamation League (ADL)
823 United Nations Plaza
New York, NY 10017
212-490-2525

Association for Childhood Education International (ACEI)
17904 Georgia Ave., Suite 215
Olney, MD 20832
301-570-2111
800-423-3563

Association for Educational Communication & Technology (AECT)
1800 N. Stonelake Drive, Suite 2
Bloomington, IN 47401
812-335-7675

Association for Information & Image Management
1100 Wayne Avenue, Suite 1100
Silver Spring, MD 20910
301-587-8202

Association for Supervision and Curriculum Development (ASCD)
1703 N. Beauregard Street
Alexandria, VA 22311
703-578-9600

Association of American Publishers
50 F Street NW, Suite 400
Washington, DC 20001
202-347-3375

Association of American University Presses (AAUP)
71 W. 23rd Street
New York, NY 10010
212-989-1010

Association of Independent Video & Filmmakers (AIVF) and the Foundation for Independent Video and Film (FIVE)
304 Hudson Street, 6th Floor
New York, NY 10013
212-807-1400

Bank Street College of Education
610 W. 112th Street
New York, NY 10025
212-875-4649

Bay Area Video Coalition (BAVC)
1717 Mariposa Street, 2nd Floor
San Francisco, CA 94107
415-861-3282

Canadian Education Association (CEA)
317 Adelaide Street West, Suite 300
Toronto, ON M5V 1P9 Canada
416-591-6300

Canadian Library Association
200 Elgin Street, Suite 602
Ottawa, ON K2P 1L5, Canada
613-232-9625

Catholic Library Association (CLA)
100 North Street, Suite 224
Pittsfield, MA 01201
413-443-2252

Child Welfare League of America
440 First Street NW, Suite 310
Washington, DC 20001
201-638-2952

Children's Book Council (CBC)
568 Broadway, Suite 404
New York, NY 10012
212-966-1900

Children's Film and Television Center of America
School of Cinema-TV, University of Southern California
850 W. 34th Street
Los Angeles, CA 90089
213-743-8358

Children's Television International, Inc.
P. O. Box 87723
San Diego, CA 92138

Church and Synagogue Library Association
Box 19357
Portland, OR 97280
503-244-6919

Consortium of College and University Media Centers (CCUMC)
IT Center
1200 Communications Building
Iowa State University
Ames, IA 50011
515-294-1811

Council for Basic Education
1319 F Street NW, Suite 900
Washington, DC 20004-1152
202-347-4171

Council for Exceptional Children (CEC)
1920 Association Drive
Reston, VA 20191
703-620-3660

Council of Chief State School Officers (CCSSO)
One Massachusetts Ave. NW, Suite 700
Washington, DC 20001
202-408-5505

Council on International Non-theatrical Events (CINE)
1112 16th Street, NW, Suite 510
Washington, DC 20036
202-785-1136

Council on Library and Information Resources
1755 Massachusetts Ave. NW, Suite 500
Washington, DC 20036
202-939-4750

CUE SOFTSWAP
Box 271704
Concord, CA 94527
415-685-7289

Educators Progress Center
55 Chapel Street
Newton, MA 02158
617-969-7100

Educators Progress Service
214 Center Street
Randolph, WI 53956
818-951-4469

EPIE Institute (Educational Products Information Exchange)
103 W. Montauk Way
Hampton Bays, NY 11046
631-728-9100

ERIC (Educational Resources Information Center)
2277 Research Blvd., 6M
Rockville, MD 20850
800-538-3742

Eastman Kodak Company
343 State Street
Rochester, NY 14650
585-724-4000

Educational Facilities Laboratories (EFL)
1090 Vermont Ave. NW, Suite 700
Washington, DC 20005
888-552-0624

Freedom of Information Center (FOI)
Box 858, 127 Neff Annex
University of Missouri
Columbia, MO 65211
573-882-4856

Freedom to Read Foundation (FTRF)
50 E. Huron St.
Chicago, IL 60611
312-280-4226

Great Plains National ITV Library (GPN)
Box 80699
Lincoln, NE 68501
402-472-2007
800-228-4630

Institute for Development of Educational Activities (IDEA)
259 Regency Ridge
Dayton, OH 45459
937-434-6969

Institute for Research on Teaching
College of Education
Michigan State University
134 Erickson Hall
East Lansing, MI 48824
517-432-2718

International Association of School Librarianship (IASL)
Box 34069, Dept. 300
Seattle, WA 98124
604-925-0266

Film/Video Arts, Inc.
817 Broadway, 2nd Floor
New York, NY 10003
212-673-9361

International Communications Industries Association (ICIA)
11242 Waples Mill Rd., Suite 200
Fairfax, VA 22030
703-273-7200

International Reading Association (IRA)
800 Barksdale Rd., Box 8139
Newark, DE 19714
302-731-1600

International Simulation and Gaming Association (ISAGA)
Department of Sociology
Rutgers—The State University
New Brunswick, NJ 08903
732-445-4035

Library of Congress
101 Independence Ave. SE
Washington, DC 20540
202-707-5000

Microform Review, Inc.
Meckler Corp.
11 Ferry Lane W.
Westport, CT 06880
203-226-6967

Minnesota Educational Computing Corporation (MECC)
6160 Summit Dr. N
Minneapolis MN 55430
612-569-1500

Modern Language Association of America (MLA)
26 Broadway, 3rd Floor
New York, NY 10004-1789
646-576-5000

National Association for the Education of Young Children (NAEYC)
1509 16th St.
Washington, DC 20036
202-232-8777

National Association of Biology Teachers
12030 Sunrise Valley Dr., Suite 110
Reston, VA 20191
703-264-9696 or
800-406-0775

National Association of Elementary School Principals (NAESP)
1615 Duke St.
Alexandria, VA 22314
703-684-3345

National Association of Secondary School Principals (NASSP)
1904 Association Dr.
Reston, VA 20191
703-860-0200

National Association of State Boards of Education (NASBE)
277 S. Washington St., Suite 100
Alexandria, VA 22314
703-684-4000

National Audiovisual Center (NAC)
U.S. Dept of Commerce
Technology Administration
National Technology Information Service
5285 Post Royal Road
Springfield, VA 22161
703-605-6000

National Center for Education Statistics (NCES)
Office of Educational Research and Improvement
U.S. Department of Education
1990 K Street NW
Washington, DC 20006
202-502-7300

National Clearinghouse for Bilingual Education (NCBE)
George Washington University
2121 K Street NW, Suite 260
Washington, DC 20037
202-467-0867

National Commission on Libraries and Information Science (NCLIS)
1110 Vermont Ave. NW, Suite 820
Washington, DC 20005
202-606-9200

National Council for the Social Studies (NCSS)
8555 11th St., Suite 500
Silver Spring, MD 20910
301-588-1800

National Council of Teachers of English (NCTE)
1111 Kenyon Rd.
Urbana, IL 61801
800-369-6283

National Council of Teachers of Mathematics (NCTM)
1906 Association Dr.
Reston, VA 20191
703-620-9840

National Education Association (NEA)
1201 16th St. NW
Washington, DC 20036
202-833-4000

National Film Information Service (NFIS)
333 S. LaCienega Blvd.
Beverly Hills, CA 90211
310-247-3000

National Information Center for Educational Media (NICEM)
Box 8640
Albuquerque, NM 87196
505-265-3591

National PTA
330 N. Wabash Ave., Suite 2100
Chicago, IL 60611
312-670-6782

National Radio Broadcasters Association (NRBA)
1771 N St. NW
Washington, DC 20036
202-429-5300

National School Supply and Equipment Association (NSSEA)
8300 Colesville Rd., Suite 250
Silver Spring, MD 20910
301-495-0240

National Science Foundation
4201 Wilson Blvd.
Arlington, VA 22230
703-306-1070

National Science Teachers Association (NSTA)
1840 Wilson Blvd
Arlington, VA 22201
703-243-7100

National Storytelling Association
101 Courthouse Square
Jonesborough, TN 37659
615-753-2171
800-525-4514

NETWORK (The)
136 Fenne Dr.
Rawley, MA 01969
978-948-7764

New York Library Association
250 Hudson
Albany, NY 12210
518-432-6952
800-252-6952

New York Public Library
Fifth Ave. & 42nd St.
New York, NY 10018
212-930-0800

OCLC, Inc. (Online Computer Library Center)
6565 Frantz Rd.
Dublin, OH 43017
614-764-6000

Online Audiovisual Catalogers, Inc. (OLAC)
Joyner Library
East Carolina University
Greenville, NC 27858
252-328-0293

Public Broadcasting Service (PBS)
1320 Braddock Pl.
Alexandria, VA 22314
703-739-5000

Puppeteers of America, Inc.
P. O. Box 29417
Parma, OH 44129
888-568-6235

Reading Is Fundamental, Inc.
1825 Connecticut Ave. NW, Suite 400
Washington, DC 20009
202-673-0020

Recording for the Blind
20 Roszel Rd.
Princeton, NJ 08540
609-452-0606

RICE (Resources in Computer Education)
MicroSIFT Project
Northwest Regional Educational Laboratory
101 S.W. Main St., Suite 500
Portland, OR 97204
503-275-9500

Society of Motion Picture and Television Engineers, Inc. (SMPTE)
595 W. Hartsdale Ave.
White Plains, NY 10607
914-761-1100

Superintendent of Documents
U.S. Government Printing Office
732 North Capitol St. NW
Washington, DC 20401
202-512-0000

Wisconsin Library Association
5250 E. Terrace Dr., Suite A
Madison, WI 53718
608-245-3640

World Pen Pals (WPP)
P. O. Box 337
Saugerties, NY 12477
845-246-7828

Appendix III

DIRECTORY OF SELECTED LIBRARY FURNITURE AND SUPPLY HOUSES

3M Library Systems
3M Center Bldg. 225-4N-14
St. Paul, MN 55112-2813
http://www.3m.com/library/

ABCO Office Furniture (Div. of Jami, Inc.)
P.O. Box 2790
Florence, AL 35630
1-800-336-0070

Acme Visible Filing Systems Ltd.
Unit 107
8173 128th Street
Surrey BC V3W 4G1
Canada
http://www.abcofurniture.com/abco.html

Adden Furniture, Inc.
26 Jackson Street
Lowell, MA 01852
800-625-3876
http://www.addenfurniture.com/

Adjustable Steel Products Company, Inc.
49 W. 27th Street
New York, NY 10001-6936
212-686-1030

All School Supplies.com
817 W. Colton Ave.
Redlands, CA 92374
866-330-7958
sonyavigil@hotmail.com
http://www.allschoolsupplies.com/bookstorage2.html

Anthro Corporation
10450 SW Manhassett Drive
Tualatin, OR 97062
1-800-325-3841
http://www.anthro.com/

The Arnold Group
200 Lexington Avenue, Suite 1413
New York, NY 10016
212-532-4144
nyshowroom@thearnoldgroup.com
http://www.thearnoldgroup.com/main/library.html

Bausman and Company
1520 South Bon View Avenue
Ontario, CA 91761
909-947-0139
http://www.bausman.net

BC Inventar
2216 Bissonnet Street
Houston, TX 77005
713-522-9715
http://www.bci-usa.com/

Berco
2210 Montrose Ave.
St. Louis, MO 63104
1-888-772-4788
http://www.bercoinc.com

Blanton & Moore Company
P.O. Box 70, Highway 21 South
Barium Springs, NC 28010-0070
704-528-4506
http://www.blantonandmoore.com

The Blockhouse Company
3285 Farmtrail Road
York, PA 17402-9602
1-800-346-1126
http://www.blockhouse.com/

Borroughs Division
Lear Siegler, Inc.
3002 North Burdick St.
Kalamazoo, MI 49007-1291
1-800-748-0227
http://www.borroughs.com

Bretford
11000 Seymour Avenue
Franklin Park, IL 60131
1-800-521-9614
http://www.bretford.com/

Brodart
Clinton County Industrial Park
100 North Road, P.O. Box 300
McElhattan, PA 17748
1-888-521-1884 ext. 360
http://www.shopbrodart.com/f/

Buckstaff
1127 S. Main Street
Oshkosh, WI 54901
1-800-755-5890

CI Designs
51 McGrath Hwy.
Somerville, MA 02143
617-776-7100

Cotterman Company
P.O. Box 168 / 130 Seltzer Road
Croswell, MI 48422-0168
1-800-552-3337
http://www.cotterman.com/

Current Designs Corporation
163 W 23rd Street
New York, NY 10011
212-463-0795

Demco, Inc.
4810 Forest Run Road, P.O. Box 7488
Madison,WI 53707
1-800-356-1200
http://www.demco.com

Elecompack Automated Storage & Retrieval Systems of America
225 West 34th Street
New York, NY 10122
212-760-1607
http://www.elecompack.com

Estey Company
Division of Tennsco Corp.
Box 606
Dickson, TN 37055
1-800-251-8184
http://www.tennsco.com

Euro Design Systems
820 East 47th Street, #B13
Tucson, AZ 85713-5073
520-770-1280

Executive Office Concepts
1705 Anderson Avenue
Compton, CA 90220
310-537-1657
http://www.eoccorp.com/

Herbert L. Farkas Co.
156 Algonquin Parkway
P.O. Box 160
Whippany, NJ 07981
973-428-1668
http://www.hlfarkas.com/library.htm

Fesny Facilities, Equipment and Service
Box 29
Liverpool, NY 13088
315-457-2828
http://www.fesny.com/libraryfurniture/

Fleetwood Group, Inc.
P.O. Box 1259
Holland, MI 49422-1259
1-800-257-6390
http://www.fleetwoodfurniture.com

For Kids Only
P.O. Box 111117
Tacoma, WA 98411-1117
1-800-979-8898
http://www.forkidzonly.com/libfurn.html

Fordham Equipment & Publishing Co.
3308 Edson Ave.
Bronx, NY 10469
1-800-249-5922
http://www.fordhamequip.com

Franklin Fixtures, Inc.
59 Commerce Park Road
Brewster, MA 02631
508-896-3713
http://www.franklinfixtures.com/

Gaylord
P.O. Box 4901
Syracuse, NY 13221-4901
1-800-448-6160
http://www.gaylord.com/

GF Furniture Systems
6655 Seville Dr.
Canfield, OH 44406
1-800-624-9751
http://www.gfoffice.com

Gressco Ltd.
328 Moravian Valley Road
P.O. Box 339
Waunakee, WI 53597-0339
608-849-6300
http://www.gresscoltd.com/

Group Four Furniture Inc.
33 Shepherd Road
Oakville, ON L6K 2G6 Canada
905-845-0211
http://members.aol.com/g4furn/recept2.htm

HAG, Inc.
108 Landmark Drive
Greensboro, NC 27409
1-800-334-4839
http://www.haginc.com

Gunlocke Company
One Gunlocke Drive
Wayland, NY 14572
1-800-828-6300
http://www.gunlocke.com/

Haworth
One Haworth Center
Holland, MI 49423
616-393-3000
http://www.haworth.com

W.C. Heller & Company
201 W. Wabash Avenue
Montipelier, OH 43543
419-485-3176
http://www.libsonline.com

Hertz Furniture Systems
95 McKee Dr.
Mahwah, NJ 07430
201-529-2100
http://www.hertzfurniture.com/

Highsmith Inc.
W 5527 State Road 106
P.O. Box 800
Fort Atkinson, WI 53538-0800
1-800-558-2110
www.highsmith.com

H.E. Hodge Company
240 Elm Street
Cumming, GA 30040
770-205-8312
http://www.hehodge.com/blantonandmoore.htm

Howe Furniture Corp.
9587 Dielman Industrial Drive
St. Louis, MO 63132-2214
1-800-888-4693
http://www.howefurniture.com

ICF Group
920 Broadway
New York, NY 10010
212-388-1000
http://www.icfsource.com/

International Library Furniture
525 S College
Keene, TX 76059
817-558-4800
http://www.internationallibrary.com/

Jasper Chair Company, Inc.
P.O. Box 311
Jasper, IN 47547-0311
812-482-5239
http://www.jasperchair.com/

Johnson Industries
1424 Davis Rd.
Elgin, IL 60123
708-695-1242
http://www.teamji.com/

Harry Joseph & Associates
110 W. 94th Street
New York, NY 10025
212-662-0620
http://www.hja.com/

JSI—Jasper Seating
932 Mill St.
Box 231
Jasper, IN 47546
1-800-622-5661
http://www.jasperseating.com/

Kardex
Box 171
Marietta, OH 45750
1-800-234-3654
http://www.kardex.com/

Knoll International
105 Wooster St.
New York, NY 10012
1-800-343-5665
http://www.knoll.com

Krueger International
1330 Bellevue Street
Green Bay, WI 54302
1-800-424-2432
http://www.ki-inc.com/

Labelon Corporation
10 Chapin Street
Canandaigua, NY 14424
1-800-428-5566
http://www.labelon.com/

Library Bureau
172 Industrial Road, P.O. Box 400
Fitchburg, MA 01420-0004
1-800-221-6638
http://www.librarybureau.com/

Library Display Design Systems
P.O. Box 8143
Berlin, CT 06037
203-828-6089
1-800-492-3434

Library Display Shelving Div./7 Mile Fishcamp Enterprises
173 West Ohio Ave.
Lake Helen, FL 32744
1-800-762-6209
malecki@librarydisplayshelving.com
http://librarydisplayshelving.com/

Library Interiors, Inc.
2801 Division St.
Metairie, LA 70002
1-800-982-9909
http://www.libraryinteriors.com

Library Store, Ltd.
7720 Wisconsin Avenue
Bethesda, MD 20814
1-800-858-8117
http://www.librarystoreltd.com/

FW Lombard Company
34 S. Pleasant Street
Ashburnham, MA 01430-0539
508-827-5333
http://www.fwlombard.com/products.php3?p=19

Lundia Storage Systems
600 Capitol Way
Jacksonville, IL 62650
217-243-8585
http://www.lundiausa.com/simple.htm

Luxor Corporation
2245 Delany Road
Waukegan, IL 60087
1-800-323-4656
http://www.luxorfurn.com/

Media Flex, Inc.
P.O. Box 1107
Champlain, NY 12919
518-298-2970
877-331-1022

MELOS, Inc.
7331 Dudie Road
Marshall, VA 20115
540-349-9571
http://www.melosinc.com/

Metropolitan Furniture Corp.
7220 Edgewater Drive
Oakland, CA 94621-3004
510-567-5200
http://www.metrofurniture.com/home.html

MJ Industries
Carleton Drive, P.O. Box 259
Georgetown, MA 01833
1-800-24SHELF
http://www.mjshelving.com/

Herman Miller, Inc. (and Meridian)
855 East Main Ave
P.O. Box 302
Zeeland, MI 49464-0302
1-888-443-4357
http://www.meridian-inc.com/

Nemschoff Chairs
2218 W. Water St.
Sheboygan, WI 53081
1-800-203-8916
http://www.nemschoff.com/

Nucraft Furniture
5151 W River Drive
Comstock Park, MI 49321
1-800-453-0100
http://www.nucraft.com/

Plymold Seating (Foldcraft Inc.)
615 Centennial Drive
Kenyon, MN 55946
1-800-759-6653
http://www.foldcraft.com/customer_service/how_to_buy/default.asp

PSC Lamps
45-13 North Ave.
Webster, NY 14580
1-800-772-5267
http://web.syr.edu/~lapawlew/ES/

Randal Displays, Inc.
507 N. Raddant Road
Batavia, IL 60510
630-761-0400
http://www.randaldisplays.com/

RHC's Spacemaster Systems
1400 N. 25th Ave.
Melrose Park, IL 60160-3083
708-345-2500
http://www.rhcspacemaster.com/companies/morg/morgan2_body.html

RPI Designs
7079 Peck Road
Marlette, MI 48453
517-635-7465
http://www.rpidesigns.com/

Russ Bassett
8189 Byron Road
Whittier, CA 97606-2615
1-800-539-2445
http://www.russbassett.com/

Safe Business Systems
30 Sovereign Court
St. Louis, MO 63011
1-800-605-8288
http://www.sbsfiling.com/sbsfiling/libraryfurniture.html

Sauder Manufacturing Company
930 W. Barre Road
Archbold, OH 43502
1-800-537-1530
http://www.saudercontract.com

Schooloutfitters.com
P.O. Box 141231
Cincinnati, OH, 45250-1231
1-800-260-2776
http://www.schooloutfitters.com/shop/libraryfurn.html

Smith System
P.O. Box 860415
Plano, TX 75086
1-800-328-1061
furniture@smithsystem.com
http://www.smithsystem.com/category.asp?ID=3

Spacesaver Corporation
1450 Janesville Avenue
Fort Atkinson, WI 53538-2798
1-800-492-3434
http://www.spacesaver.com/

TAB Products
935 Lakeview Parkway
Suite 195
Vernon Hills, IL 60061
847-968-5400
http://www.tab.com/

Tesco Industries, LP
1035 E. Hacienda
Bellville, TX 77418
1-800-699-5824
http://tesco-ind.com/

Texwood Furniture, Ltd.
1353 W. 2nd. Street
Taylor, TX 76574
1-888-878-0000
http://www.texwood.com/index.asp

Tuohy Furniture Corporation
42 Saint Albans Place
Chatfield, MN 55923-9798
507-867-4280
http://www.tuohyfurniture.com/

University Products, Inc.
517 Main St, P.O. Box 101
Holyoke, MA 01040
1-800-336-4847
http://www.universityproducts.com

Vecta Contract
1800 South Great Southwest Parkway
P.O. Box 534013
Grand Prairie, TX 75053
972-641-2860
http://www.vecta.com/

Vernon Library Supplies, Inc.
2851 Cole Court
Norcross, GA 30071
1-800-878-0253
http://www.vernlib.com/libfurn.asp

Wearing Williams Ltd.
725 Century Street
Winnipeg, MB R3H 0M2 Canada
800-954-5656
info@wearingwilliams.mb.ca
http://www.wearingwilliams.mb.ca/library.html

Wheelit, Inc.
P. O. Box 352800
Toledo, OH 43635-2800
1-800-523-7508
http://www.wheelitinc.com/

White Storage & Retrieval Systems, Inc.
30 Boright Avenue
Kenilworth, NJ 07033
908-272-8888
http://www.whitesrs.com

The Worden Company
199 East 17th Street
Holland, MI 49423
1-800-748-0561
http://www.wordencompany.com/about.html

Appendix IV

KEY DOCUMENTS

All of the following documents, except the AECT Code of Ethics, are printed with permission of the American Library Association.

Library Bill of Rights

The American Library Association affirms that all libraries are forums for information and ideas, and that the following basic policies should guide their services.

1. Books and other library resources should be provided for the interest, information, and enlightenment of all people of the community the library serves. Materials should not be excluded because of

the origin, background, or views of those contributing to their creation.

2. Libraries should provide materials and information presenting all points of view on current and historical issues. Materials should not be proscribed or removed because of partisan or doctrinal disapproval.

3. Libraries should challenge censorship in the fulfillment of their responsibility to provide information and enlightenment.

4. Libraries should cooperate with all persons and groups concerned with resisting abridgment of free expression and free access to ideas.

5. A person's right to use a library should not be denied or abridged because of origin, age, background, or views.

6. Libraries which make exhibit spaces and meeting rooms available to the public they serve should make such facilities available on an equitable basis, regardless of the beliefs or affiliations of individuals or groups requesting their use.

Printed with permission. Adopted June 18, 1948.
Amended February 2, 1961, and January 23, 1980,
inclusion of "age" reaffirmed January 23, 1996, by the ALA Council.

Access to Resources and Services in the School Library Media Program: An Interpretation of the Library Bill of Rights

The school library media program plays a unique role in promoting intellectual freedom. It serves as a point of voluntary access to information and ideas and as a learning laboratory for students as they acquire critical thinking and problem solving skills needed in a pluralistic society. Although the educational level and program of the school necessarily shapes the resources and services of a school library media program, the principles of the Library Bill of Rights apply equally to all libraries including school library media programs.

School library media professionals assume a leadership role in promoting the principles of intellectual freedom within the school by providing resources and services that create and sustain an atmosphere of free inquiry. School library media professionals work closely with teachers to integrate instructional activities in classroom units designed to equip students to locate, evaluate, and use a broad range of ideas effectively. Through resources, programming, and educational processes, students and teachers experience the free and robust debate characteristic of a democratic society.

School library media professionals cooperate with other individuals in building collections of resources appropriate to the developmental and maturity levels of students. These collections provide resources which support the curriculum and are consistent with the philosophy, goals, and objectives of the school district. Resources in school library media collections represent diverse points of view on current as well as historical issues.

While English is, by history and tradition, the customary language of the United States, the languages in use in any given community may vary. Schools serving communities in which other languages are used make efforts to accommodate the needs of students for whom English is a second language. To support these efforts, and to ensure equal access to resources and services, the school library media program provides resources which reflect the linguistic pluralism of the community.

Members of the school community involved in the collection development process employ educational criteria to select resources unfettered by their personal, political, social, or religious views. Students and educators served by the school library media program have access to resources and services free of constraints resulting from personal, partisan, or doctrinal disapproval. School library media professionals resist efforts by individuals or groups to define what is appropriate for all students or teachers to read, view, hear, or access via electronic means.

Major barriers between students and resources include but are not limited to: imposing age or grade level restrictions on the use of resources, limiting the use of interlibrary loan and access to electronic information, charging fees for information in specific formats, requiring permission from parents or teachers, establishing restricted shelves or closed collections, and labeling. Policies, procedures, and rules related to the use of resources and services support free and open access to information.

The school board adopts policies that guarantee students access to a broad range of ideas. These include policies on collection development and procedures for the review of resources about which concerns have been raised. Such policies, developed by persons in the school community, provide for a timely and fair hearing and assure that procedures are applied equitably to all expressions of concern.

School library media professionals implement district policies and procedures in the school.

Printed with permission. Adopted July 2, 1986;
amended January 10, 1990; July 12, 2000, by the ALA Council.

ALA Code of Ethics

As members of the American Library Association, we recognize the importance of codifying and making known to the profession and to the general public the ethical principles that guide the work of librarians, other professionals providing information services, library trustees, and library staffs.

Ethical dilemmas occur when values are in conflict. The American Library Association Code of Ethics states the values to which we are committed and embodies the ethical responsibilities of the profession in this changing information environment.

We significantly influence or control the selection, organization, preservation, and dissemination of information. In a political system grounded in an informed citizenry, we are members of a profession explicitly committed to intellectual freedom and the freedom of access to information. We have a special obligation to ensure the free flow of information and ideas to present and future generations.

The principles of this Code are expressed in broad statements to guide ethical decision making. These statements provide a framework; they cannot and do not dictate conduct to cover particular situations.

1. We provide the highest level of service to all library users through appropriate and usefully organized resources; equitable service policies; equitable access; and accurate, unbiased, and courteous responses to all requests.

2. We uphold the principles of intellectual freedom and resist all efforts to censor library resources.

3. We protect each library user's right to privacy and confidentiality with respect to information sought or received and resources consulted, borrowed, acquired, or transmitted.

4. We recognize and respect intellectual property rights.

5. We treat co-workers and other colleagues with respect, fairness and good faith, and advocate conditions of employment that safeguard the rights and welfare of all employees of our institutions.

6. We do not advance private interests at the expense of library users, colleagues, or our employing institutions.

7. We distinguish between our personal convictions and professional duties and do not allow our personal beliefs to interfere with fair representation of the aims of our institutions or the provision of access to their information resources.

8. We strive for excellence in the profession by maintaining and enhancing our own knowledge and skills, by encouraging the professional development of co-workers, and by fostering the aspirations of potential members of the profession.

Printed with permission. Adopted by the ALA Council June 28, 1995

AECT Code of Ethics

PREAMBLE

The Code of Ethics contained herein shall be considered to be principles of ethics. These principles are intended to aid members individually and collectively in maintaining a high level of professional conduct.

The Professional Ethics Committee will build documentation of opinion(interpretive briefs or ramifications of intent) relating to specific ethical statements enumerated herein.

Opinions may be generated in response to specific cases brought before the Professional Ethics Committee.

Amplification and/or clarification of the ethical principles may be generated by the Committee in response to a request submitted by a member.

SECTION 1—COMMITMENT TO THE INDIVIDUAL

In fulfilling obligations to the individual, the members:

1. Shall encourage independent action in an individual's pursuit of learning and shall provide open access to knowledge regardless of delivery medium or varying points of view of the knowledge.

2. Shall protect the individual rights of access to materials of varying points of view.

3. Shall guarantee to each individual the opportunity to participate in any appropriate program.

4. Shall conduct professional business so as to protect the privacy and maintain the personal integrity of the individual.

5. Shall follow sound professional procedures for evaluation and selection of materials, equipment, and furniture/carts used to create educational work areas.

6. Shall make reasonable efforts to protect the individual from conditions harmful to health and safety, including harmful conditions caused by technology itself.

7. Shall promote current and sound professional practices in the appropriate use of technology in education.

8. Shall in the design and selection of any educational program or media seek to avoid content that reinforces or promotes gender, ethnic, racial, or religious stereotypes. Shall seek to encourage the development of programs and media that emphasize the diversity of our society as a multi-cultural community.

9. Shall refrain from any behavior that would be judged to be discriminatory, harassing, insensitive, or offensive and, thus, is in conflict with valuing and promoting each individual's integrity, rights, and opportunity within a diverse profession and society.

SECTION 2—COMMITMENT TO SOCIETY

In fulfilling obligations to society, the member:

1. Shall honestly represent the institution or organization with which that person is affiliated, and shall take adequate precautions to distinguish between personal and institutional or organizational views.

2. Shall represent accurately and truthfully the facts concerning educational matters in direct and indirect public expressions.

3. Shall not use institutional or Associational privileges for private gain.

4. Shall accept no gratuities, gifts, or favors that might impair or appear to impair professional judgment, or offer any favor, service, or thing of value to obtain special advantage.

5. Shall engage in fair and equitable practices with those rendering service to the profession.

6. Shall promote positive and minimize negative environmental impacts of educational technologies.

SECTION 3—COMMITMENT TO THE PROFESSION

In fulfilling obligations to the profession, the member:

1. Shall accord just and equitable treatment to all members of the profession in terms of professional rights and responsibilities, including being actively committed to providing opportunities for culturally and intellectually diverse points of view in publications and conferences.

2. Shall not use coercive means or promise special treatment in order to influence professional decisions or colleagues.

3. Shall avoid commercial exploitation of that person's membership in the Association.

4. Shall strive continually to improve professional knowledge and skill and to make available to patrons and colleagues the benefit of that person's professional attainments.

5. Shall present honestly personal professional qualifications and the professional qualifications and evaluations of colleagues, including giving accurate credit to those whose work and ideas are associated with publishing in any form.

6. Shall conduct professional business through proper channels.

7. Shall delegate assigned tasks to qualified personnel. Qualified personnel are those who have appropriate training or credentials and/or who can demonstrate competency in performing the task.

8. Shall inform users of the stipulations and interpretations of the copyright law and other laws affecting the profession and encourage compliance.

9. Shall observe all laws relating to or affecting the profession; shall report, without hesitation, illegal or unethical conduct of fellow members of the profession to the AECT Professional Ethics Committee; shall participate in professional inquiry when requested by the Association.

10. Shall conduct research and practice using professionally accepted and institutional review board guidelines and procedures, especially as they apply to protecting human participants and other animals from harm. Humans and other animals shall not be used in any procedure that is physically invasive to them.

Used with permission of the Association for Educational Communications and Technology.

The Freedom to Read Statement

The freedom to read is essential to our democracy. It is continuously under attack. Private groups and public authorities in various parts of the country are working to remove or limit access to reading materials, to censor content in schools, to label "controversial" views, to distribute lists of "objectionable" books or authors, and to purge libraries. These actions apparently rise from a view that our national tradition of free expression is no longer valid; that censorship and suppression are needed to avoid the subversion of politics and the corruption of morals. We, as citizens devoted to reading and as librarians and publishers responsible for disseminating ideas, wish to assert the public interest in the preservation of the freedom to read.

Most attempts at suppression rest on a denial of the fundamental premise of democracy: that the ordinary citizen, by exercising critical judgment, will accept the good and reject the bad. The censors, public and private, assume that they should determine what is good and what is bad for their fellow citizens. We trust Americans to recognize propaganda and misinformation, and to make their own decisions about what they read and believe. We do not believe they need the help of censors to assist them in this task. We do not believe they are prepared to sacrifice their heritage of a free press in order to be "protected" against what others think may be bad for them. We believe they still favor free enterprise in ideas and expression.

These efforts at suppression are related to a larger pattern of pressures being brought against education, the press, art and images, films, broadcast media, and the Internet. The problem is not only one of actual censorship. The shadow of fear cast by these pressures leads, we suspect, to an even larger voluntary curtailment of expression by those who seek to avoid controversy.

Such pressure toward conformity is perhaps natural to a time of accelerated change. And yet suppression is never more dangerous than in such a time of social tension. Freedom has given the United States the elasticity to endure strain. Freedom keeps open the path of novel and creative solutions, and enables change to come by choice. Every silencing of a heresy, every enforcement of an orthodoxy, diminishes the toughness and resilience of our society and leaves it the less able to deal with controversy and difference.

Now as always in our history, reading is among our greatest free-
doms. The freedom to read and write is almost the only means for
making generally available ideas or manners of expression that can
initially command only a small audience. The written word is the
natural medium for the new idea and the untried voice from which
come the original contributions to social growth. It is essential to the
extended discussion that serious thought requires, and to the accu-
mulation of knowledge and ideas into organized collections.

We believe that free communication is essential to the preservation
of a free society and a creative culture. We believe that these pressures
toward conformity present the danger of limiting the range and variety of inquiry and expression on which our democracy and our culture depend. We believe that every American community must
jealously guard the freedom to publish and to circulate, in order to
preserve its own freedom to read. We believe that publishers and
librarians have a profound responsibility to give validity to that freedom to read by making it possible for the readers to choose freely
from a variety of offerings. The freedom to read is guaranteed by the
Constitution. Those with faith in free people will stand firm on these
constitutional guarantees of essential rights and will exercise the
responsibilities that accompany these rights.

We therefore affirm these propositions:

1. It is in the public interest for publishers and librarians to make
   available the widest diversity of views and expressions, including
   those that are unorthodox or unpopular with the majority. Creative
   thought is by definition new, and what is new is different. The
   bearer of every new thought is a rebel until that idea is refined and
   tested. Totalitarian systems attempt to maintain themselves in
   power by the ruthless suppression of any concept that challenges
   the established orthodoxy. The power of a democratic system to
   adapt to change is vastly strengthened by the freedom of its citizens to choose widely from among conflicting opinions offered
   freely to them. To stifle every nonconformist idea at birth would
   mark the end of the democratic process. Furthermore, only
   through the constant activity of weighing and selecting can the
   democratic mind attain the strength demanded by times like these.
   We need to know not only what we believe but why we believe it.

2. Publishers, librarians, and booksellers do not need to endorse every
   idea or presentation they make available. It would conflict with the
   public interest for them to establish their own political, moral, or

aesthetic views as a standard for determining what should be published or circulated.

Publishers and librarians serve the educational process by helping to make available knowledge and ideas required for the growth of the mind and the increase of learning. They do not foster education by imposing as mentors the patterns of their own thought. The people should have the freedom to read and consider a broader range of ideas than those that may be held by any single librarian or publisher or government or church. It is wrong that what one can read should be confined to what another thinks proper.

3. It is contrary to the public interest for publishers or librarians to bar access to writings on the basis of the personal history or political affiliations of the author.

No art or literature can flourish if it is to be measured by the political views or private lives of its creators. No society of free people can flourish that draws up lists of writers to whom it will not listen, whatever they may have to say.

4. There is no place in our society for efforts to coerce the taste of others, to confine adults to the reading matter deemed suitable for adolescents, or to inhibit the efforts of writers to achieve artistic expression.

To some, much of modern expression is shocking. But is not much of life itself shocking? We cut off literature at the source if we prevent writers from dealing with the stuff of life. Parents and teachers have a responsibility to prepare the young to meet the diversity of experiences in life to which they will be exposed, as they have a responsibility to help them learn to think critically for themselves. These are affirmative responsibilities, not to be discharged simply by preventing them from reading works for which they are not yet prepared. In these matters values differ, and values cannot be legislated; nor can machinery be devised that will suit the demands of one group without limiting the freedom of others.

5. It is not in the public interest to force a reader to accept with any expression the prejudgment of a label characterizing it or its author as subversive or dangerous.

The ideal of labeling presupposes the existence of individuals or groups with wisdom to determine by authority what is good or bad for the citizen. It presupposes that individuals must be directed in making up their minds about the ideas they examine. But Americans do not need others to do their thinking for them.

6. It is the responsibility of publishers and librarians, as guardians of the people's freedom to read, to contest encroachments upon that freedom by individuals or groups seeking to impose their own standards or tastes upon the community at large.

It is inevitable in the give and take of the democratic process that the political, the moral, or the aesthetic concepts of an individual or group will occasionally collide with those of another individual or group. In a free society individuals are free to determine for themselves what they wish to read, and each group is free to determine what it will recommend to its freely associated members. But no group has the right to take the law into its own hands, and to impose its own concept of politics or morality on other members of a democratic society. Freedom is no freedom if it is accorded only to the accepted and the inoffensive.

7. It is the responsibility of publishers and librarians to give full meaning to the freedom to read by providing books that enrich the quality and diversity of thought and expression. By the exercise of this affirmative responsibility, they can demonstrate that the answer to a "bad" book is a good one, the answer to a "bad" idea is a good one.

The freedom to read is of little consequence when the reader cannot obtain matter fit for that reader's purpose. What is needed is not only the absence of restraint, but the positive provision of opportunity for the people to read the best that has been thought and said. Books are the major channel by which the intellectual inheritance is handed down, and the principal means of its testing and growth. The defense of the freedom to read requires of all publishers and librarians the utmost of their faculties, and deserves of all citizens the fullest of their support.

We state these propositions neither lightly nor as easy generalizations. We here stake out a lofty claim for the value of the written word. We do so because we believe that it is possessed of enormous variety and usefulness, worthy of cherishing and keeping free. We realize that the application of these propositions may mean the dissemination of ideas and manners of expression that are repugnant to many persons. We do not state these propositions in the comfortable belief that what people read is unimportant. We believe rather that what people read is deeply important; that ideas can be dangerous, but that the suppression of ideas is fatal to a democratic society. Freedom itself is a dangerous way of life, but it is ours.

This statement was originally issued in May of 1953 by the Westchester Conference of the American Library Association and the American Book Publishers Council, which in 1970 consolidated with the American Educational Publishers Institute to become the Association of American Publishers.

Printed with permission. Adopted June 25, 1953; revised January 28, 1972, January 16, 1991, July 12, 2000, by the ALA Council and the AAP Freedom to Read Committee.

Freedom to View Statement

The FREEDOM TO VIEW, along with the freedom to speak, to hear, and to read, is protected by the First Amendment to the Constitution of the United States. In a free society, there is no place for censorship of any medium of expression. Therefore these principles are affirmed:

1. To provide the broadest access to film, video, and other audiovisual materials because they are a means for the communication of ideas. Liberty of circulation is essential to insure the constitutional guarantees of freedom of expression.

2. To protect the confidentiality of all individuals and institutions using film, video, and other audiovisual materials.

3. To provide film, video, and other audiovisual materials which represent a diversity of views and expression. Selection of a work does not constitute or imply agreement with or approval of the content.

4. To provide a diversity of viewpoints without the constraint of labeling or prejudging film, video, or other audiovisual materials on the basis of the moral, religious, or political beliefs of the producer or filmmaker or on the basis of controversial content.

5. To contest vigorously, by all lawful means, every encroachment upon the public's freedom to view.

Printed with permission. This statement was originally drafted by the Freedom to View Committee of the American Film and Video Association (formerly the Educational Film Library Association) and was adopted by the AFVA Board of Directors in February 1979. This statement was updated and approved by the AFVA Board of Directors in 1989. Endorsed by the ALA Council January 10, 1990

Position Statement on the Confidentiality of Library Records

The members of the American Library Association, recognizing the right to privacy of library users, believe that records held in libraries which connect specific individuals with specific resources, programs or services, are confidential and not to be used for purposes other than routine record keeping: i.e., to maintain access to resources, to assure that resources are available to users who need them, to arrange facilities, to provide resources for the comfort and safety of patrons, or to accomplish the purposes of the program or service. The library community recognizes that children and youth have the same rights to privacy as adults.

Libraries whose record keeping systems reveal the names of users would be in violation of the confidentiality of library record laws adopted in many states. School library media specialists are advised to seek the advice of counsel if in doubt about whether their record keeping systems violate the specific laws in their states. Efforts must be made within the reasonable constraints of budgets and school management procedures to eliminate such records as soon as reasonably possible.

With or without specific legislation, school library media specialists are urged to respect the rights of children and youth by adhering to the tenets expressed in the Confidentiality of Library Records Interpretation of the Library Bill of Rights and the ALA Code of Ethics.

Printed with permission. ALA Policy 52.4, 54.16

Position Statement on Flexible Scheduling

Schools must adopt the educational philosophy that the library media program is fully integrated into the educational program. This integration strengthens the teaching/learning process so that students can develop the vital skills necessary to locate, analyze, evaluate, interpret, and communicate information and ideas. When the library media program is fully integrated into the instructional program of the school, students, teachers, and library media specialists become partners in learning. The library program is an extension of the classroom. Information skills are taught and learned within the context of the classroom curriculum. The wide range of resources, technologies, and services needed to meet students learning and information needs are readily available in a cost-effective manner.

The integrated library media program philosophy requires that an open schedule must be maintained. Classes cannot be scheduled in the library media center to provide teacher release or preparation time. Students and teachers must be able to come to the center throughout the day to use information sources, to read for pleasure, and to meet and work with other students and teachers.

Planning between the library media specialist and the classroom teacher, which encourages both scheduled and informal visits, is the catalyst that makes this integrated library program work. The teacher brings to the planning process a knowledge of subject content and student needs. The library media specialist contributes a broad knowledge of resources and technology, an understanding of teaching methods, and a wide range of strategies that may be employed to help students learn information skills.

Cooperative planning by the teacher and library media specialist integrates information skills and materials into the classroom curriculum and results in the development of assignments that encourage open inquiry.

The responsibility for flexibly scheduled library media programs must be shared by the entire school community.

THE BOARD OF EDUCATION endorses the philosophy that the library program is an integral part of the district's educational program and ensures that flexible scheduling for library media centers is maintained in all buildings and at all levels.

THE DISTRICT ADMINISTRATION supports this philosophy and monitors staff assignments to ensure appropriate staffing levels so that all teachers, including the library media specialists, can fulfill their professional responsibilities.

THE PRINCIPAL creates the appropriate climate within the school by advocating the benefits of flexible scheduling to the faculty, by monitoring scheduling, by ensuring appropriate staffing levels, and by providing joint planning time for classroom teachers and library media specialists.

THE TEACHER uses resource-based instruction and views the library media program as a integral part of that instruction.

THE LIBRARY MEDIA SPECIALIST is knowledgeable about curriculum and classroom activities, and works cooperatively with the classroom teacher to integrate information skills into the curriculum.

Printed with permission. (6/91)

Statement on Labeling: An Interpretation of the Library Bill of Rights

Labeling is the practice of describing or designating materials by affixing a prejudicial label and/or segregating them by a prejudicial system. The American Library Association opposes these means of predisposing people's attitudes toward library materials for the following reasons:

1. Labeling is an attempt to prejudice attitudes and as such, it is a censor's tool.

2. Some find it easy and even proper, according to their ethics, to establish criteria for judging publications as objectionable. However, injustice and ignorance rather than justice and enlightenment result from such practices, and the American Library Association opposes the establishment of such criteria.

3. Libraries do not advocate the ideas found in their collections. The presence of books and other resources in a library does not indicate endorsement of their contents by the library.

A variety of private organizations promulgate rating systems and/or review materials as a means of advising either their members or the general public concerning their opinions of the contents and suitability or appropriate age for use of certain books, films, recordings, or other materials. For the library to adopt or enforce any of these private systems, to attach such ratings to library materials, to include them in bibliographic records, library catalogs, or other finding aids, or otherwise to endorse them would violate the Library Bill of Rights.

While some attempts have been made to adopt these systems into law, the constitutionality of such measures is extremely questionable. If such legislation is passed which applies within a library's jurisdiction, the library should seek competent legal advice concerning its applicability to library operations.

Publishers, industry groups, and distributors sometimes add ratings to material or include them as part of their packaging. Librarians should not endorse such practices. However, removing or obliterating such ratings—if placed there by or with permission of the copyright holder—could constitute expurgation, which is also unacceptable.

The American Library Association opposes efforts which aim at closing any path to knowledge. This statement, however, does not exclude the adoption of organizational schemes designed as directional aids or to facilitate access to materials.

Printed with permission. Adopted July 13, 1951. Amended June 25, 1971; July 1, 1981; June 26, 1990, by the ALA Council. Note: "Labeling," as it is referred to in this document, is the practice of describing or designating certain library materials, by affixing a prejudicial label to them or segregating them by a prejudicial system, so as to predispose readers against the materials.

Citizen's Request Form for Reevaluation of Media Center Materials

Initiated by _____

Telephone _____ Address_____

REPRESENTING

Self_____ Organization or group_____
                                    (name)

School _____

MATERIAL QUESTIONED

BOOK: author_____title_____

_____copyright date_____

AV MATERIAL: kind of media _____
                                    (film, filmstrip, record, etc.)

title _____

OTHER MATERIAL: identify_____

Please respond to the following questions. If sufficient space is not provided, please use additional sheet of paper.

1. Have you seen or read this material in its entirety?

_____

2. To what do you object? Please cite specific passages, pages, etc.

_____

3. What do you believe is the main idea of this material?

_____

4. What do you feel might result from use of this material?

_____

5. What reviews of this material have you read?

_____

6. For what other age group might this be suitable?

_____

7. What action do you recommend that the school take on this material?

_____

8. In its place, what material do you recommend that would provide adequate information on the subject?

_____

Date _____ Signature _____

INDEX

About the Author

BETTY J. MORRIS teaches media specialists in the Media and Instructional Technology Department of the College of Education at the State University of West Georgia. Her experience includes working as a media specialist, as a faculty member teaching media specialists at Long Island University, as a Library Power Director in Florida, and as an acquisitions editor for two publishing companies.